Better Homes and Gardens®

BIG BOOK OF HOME HOW-TO

JG PRESS

Library of Congress Cataloging-in-Publication Data is available upon request.

ISBN 978-1-572-15703-3 (cloth) – 978-1-572-15723-1 (pbk.)

Printed in China

10   9   8   7   6   5   4   3   2   1

Note to the Readers:
Due to differing conditions, tools, and individual skills, the publisher assumes no responsibility for any damages, injuries suffered, or losses incurred as a result of following the information published in this book. Before beginning any project, review the instructions carefully, and if any doubts or questions remain, consult local experts or authorities. Because codes and regulations vary greatly, you always should check with authorities to ensure that your project complies with all applicable local codes and regulations. Always read and observe all of the safety precautions provided by manufacturers of any tools, equipment, or supplies, and follow all accepted safety procedures.

TABLE OF CONTENTS

YOU AND YOUR HOME

WORKING UP TO CODE

Most likely, a local building department in your city or county has the authority to determine how all new building must be done in your locale. (Some rural areas have no building department.) A building department has exhaustive and detailed lists of regulations (codes) covering new home construction and remodeling projects, including wiring, plumbing, roofing, structural framing, and the installation of permanent appliances (like air-conditioners).

Though it may seem a hassle, your building department is there for your protection. The regulations are not arbitrary, but are based on decades of building experience. A project that is built up to code will likely be safe and durable; a project built without benefit of codes may be both dangerous and flimsy. When it comes time to sell your home, you could be in legal trouble if it is found that significant work was done without being inspected.

The consequences of ignoring these regulations can be harsh. You may be required to have the work professionally checked, or you may be ordered to tear out the work and start again. Also, insurance companies may balk at paying a claim for damage done to your house if you have not followed regulations.

As a general rule, the building department and its codes come into play whenever a new permanent structure is built, or when new electrical, plumbing, or gas service is installed.

So for instance, you probably do not need a permit in order to replace an existing toilet, sink, tub, or light fixture. However, if you run new electrical cable or new pipes in order to install fixtures where there were none before,

then you need a permit. A sand-laid patio (rather than one that involves a concrete slab), a simple storage shed with no wiring or plumbing, or a small deck that is not attached to the house may be exempt from inspections. However, always check with the building department to be sure.

Most codes are based on national standards but may be modified to suit local conditions. For example, construction techniques required for earthquake-prone areas are different than those for other areas, and construction in areas that are consistently wet may require weather-resistant materials in outdoor applications. Whenever you're undertaking home improvements, make sure you know what local building codes apply to your project. In addition,

be aware that codes may vary significantly from town to town—even within the same county.

Working with a building department involves several steps. First, go to your local building department and ask for general guidelines for the project you are proposing. They may have copies of regulations for common projects, or they may direct you to reference works.

Second, make a detailed, neat drawing of the project, including a materials list, and show it to an inspector in the office. The inspector may ask for changes and clarifications.

Finally, once your plans are approved, one or more inspections will be scheduled—typically, one inspection for the rough installation, and one for the finished project.

EXPERTS' INSIGHT

WORKING WITH AN INSPECTOR

Some inspectors are more friendly than others, but they are all there for your protection. Treat the inspector with respect, and you will likely have a mutually beneficial relationship.

■ Go to your inspector with a plan to be approved or amended; don't expect the building department to plan the job for you.

■ To avoid wasting the inspector's time, find out as much information as possible about your project before you talk to the inspector. Consult the building department's literature, national codes, or how-to books.

■ Draw plans that are close to professional quality. Everything

should be to scale and should be drawn clearly. You may need to make both a top view drawing and one or more other drawings.

■ Never argue with an inspector. Always be courteous. Follow instructions. Assume the inspector knows more than you do. Inspectors are wary of homeowners, because many take on projects beyond their abilities. Show the inspector you are serious about doing things the right way.

■ Be sure you clearly understand when you need to have inspections. Do not cover up any work that needs to be inspected.

■ If you are hiring a contractor, it is usually best to have the contractor, not you, deal directly with the inspector.

DO IT YOURSELF OR HIRE A PRO?

This book is designed for avid do-it-yourselfers. If you are the kind of homeowner who wants to help only with planning a project and doing the finishing touches after the majority of the work is done, see the tips below. Read the step-by-step instructions for projects in this book and then decide whether you want to tackle the job.

In an all-too-common scenario, a homeowner gets excited about an ambitious project and tears into walls or floors. Once the demolition is finished and some initial work is done, however, it becomes difficult to keep up the energy level. After a long day of work, the TV and the armchair are much more appealing than the tool belt. So the house remains an unfinished mess for weeks or months longer than was originally planned. Home life can become very difficult; many marriages founder under the stress of remodeling projects.

Remodeling always takes longer and is more difficult than new construction, because you run into so many obstacles. This is especially true if your home is an older one with plaster walls.

To gauge whether you are really ready to take on a large project, first try some modest repairs or installations. Once you (and your spouse) are convinced that you have the needed skills and can complete projects in a timely manner, it may be time to attempt a more serious job.

Professionals often charge what look to be fearsome rates. However, before you decide to save money by doing it yourself, consider all the factors: A pro can probably do things much more quickly than you. If you can make extra money by working overtime or taking on extra work in your field, chances are it will be easier to do so and hand over the remodeling project to a pro.

Some contractors are willing to lower their prices if the homeowner agrees to perform certain tasks. This sort of "sweat equity" arrangement can be beneficial, but only if the terms are clearly spelled out. The contract should state precisely what you will do, and when you will do it. Ideally, there should be a clear division between the contractor's work and yours. For instance, you might agree to install moldings and paint the walls, or to install the flooring.

FINDING AND HIRING A CONTRACTOR

To achieve a happy relationship and professional results, follow these steps to find and hire a pro:
■ Get the names of several contractors by asking friends for recommendations. Take a look at examples of their work to see if it meets your expectations.
■ Get rough estimates from all contractors who interest you. It will help you narrow the field of candidates and judge how candid they are about money matters.
■ For a major job, get at least three bids. Give a contractor about three weeks to produce the bid. Read the bids closely; they should detail the materials that will be used. If one contractor is much lower than the others, check to make sure he or she is truly capable and experienced.
■ When accepting bids, find out how long the contractor has been in business—the longer the better.

Ask who finances the contractor's company (usually it's a bank). Ask the bank about the contractor's general solvency. You don't want a contractor to go bankrupt in the middle of your project.
■ Determine whether the contractor carries insurance. Every contractor's insurance should cover property damage, liability, and workers' compensation. If the contractor is not covered, you could be liable for hefty fees in case of an accident.

Writing the Contract

Once you've chosen a bid, negotiate a contract. It should have these important elements:
■ Itemize in detail all work to be done. Specify the type and brand of materials and finishes to be used. Include a specific timetable. You may want to work in a penalty for late completion, or a reward for early completion.
■ A fixed-price contract should specify the total cost of the job. A cost-plus contract should specify the cost of materials and labor. Payments should be dependent on work completed.
■ Include a right of rescission, permitting you to rescind, or back out of, a contract within 72 hours of signing it.
■ A certificate of insurance guarantees that the contractor is covered. Include in the contract a warranty ensuring that the labor and materials are free from defects for at least a year.
■ An arbitration clause delineates the method for resolving disputes.
■ A release of liens clause ensures that you won't be responsible for liens filed against the contractor by suppliers or subcontractors.

STAYING SANE WHILE REMODELING

Whether you are doing it yourself or hiring a pro, a remodeling project can be stressful. Your normal routines are interrupted, you're engulfed by noise and dust, and your home is in turmoil. Kitchen remodels are the most stressful. Suddenly, the source of meals, snacks, and beverages is out of commission or barely accessible.

Careful planning and a few simple steps can minimize your family's emotional and physical discomfort. Here are some tips:

■ Do what you can to move the job along quickly. Even if it means paying a little more, you may save money in the long run because, in the case of a kitchen remodel, you will eat out less often. For a do-it-yourself project, consider hiring a pro to complete a specific aspect, such as running plumbing lines or roughing in the wiring. Often, hiring a laborer can also speed things up. If you are hiring a contractor, build incentives for timely completion into the contract.

■ Cultivate realistic expectations about how long the project will take—usually, longer than you think. If the estimate is two weeks, prepare yourself emotionally for three or four weeks.

■ For a kitchen remodel, take the time to set up a fairly pleasant temporary kitchen in another room that will be fairly quiet and free of dust. A pleasant "camping out" ambience can actually make for relatively fun and memorable family times.

■ Some or all family members may be able to actually leave the house for a couple of weeks, either for a vacation or to visit relatives.

Be aware, however, that most remodels involve many small decisions that are best considered when you are on the site.

■ Take extraordinary steps to minimize dust; see page 9.

■ Require that floors be swept and vacuumed and tools put neatly away at the end of every work day.

■ Go ahead and entertain informally. Under the circumstances, guests will not expect neatness, so having dinner guests can actually be easier than when the house is in good shape and you have to clean up. Guests often find a remodel project interesting. Outdoor entertaining is often the easiest.

■ If you have small children, demand that the area be kept clear of all sharp or otherwise dangerous objects.

WORKING WITH A CONTRACTOR

Once you've hired a contractor and written a clear contract, prepare for an unusual relationship. You'll be living in close quarters with one or more strangers. Together, you'll be completing complex projects involving your living space. To keep things on an even keel and achieve the best results, follow these tips:

■ Communication is the key. Start with a contract that spells out precisely the work to be done (see page 7). Don't be surprised, however, if some aspects of the job turn out differently than you expected—that's normal for a remodeling project. If you are displeased with the way things are turning out, tell the contractor as soon as possible. The longer you wait, the more difficult—and expensive—corrections will be.

■ Whenever there is a change in plans, put the new expectations in writing. A "change work" agreement should be just as precise and detailed as the original contract.

■ Keep close tabs on escalating costs created by mid-project changes. If, for example, unexpected structural or plumbing problems are discovered when walls are opened, it will cost extra to fix them. In order to keep within budget, you may need to settle for some less expensive installations.

■ Coordinate your schedules so you and your contractor are together long enough to communicate daily, but avoid getting in each others' hair. Perhaps the contractor could arrive about a half hour before you leave for work in the morning, or maybe you could make a point of returning from work before the contractor leaves. That way, you can quickly assess the work done and discuss any decisions that must be made.

If you do not go to work, arrange to be out of the house or in another part of the house for most of the day.

■ Be empathetic. Statistically, most contractors fail simply because it is a very difficult business. For instance, a mistake may be the contractor's fault, or it may instead be the fault of a supplier or subcontractor.

■ On the other hand, be firm and stand up for your rights. Don't let the contractor bully you into changes you do not want. If you feel you are being taken advantage of, don't hesitate to say so. If the problem persists, call in another contractor for arbitration.

MINIMIZING THE MESS OF HOME IMPROVEMENT

Though the final results of an upgrade will be beautiful, no doubt you will make a mess along the way. Out-of-control debris, clutter, and dust can make home life miserable. Follow these tips to minimize the anguish.

■ Contain the job. Having part of your home look like a construction site is usually bearable. If the mess migrates to the rest of the home, things get pretty depressing. Clearly mark off where the work zone ends and living quarters begin. That way, the mess becomes a place you visit, rather than the place where you live.

■ Take extraordinary measures to protect valuable wood or carpeted floors. Usually, one layer of protection is not enough. For a painting project, tape down plastic or protective paper, then lay a thick can-

vas drop cloth over that. If the top layer is plastic, you are liable to step in wet paint and then track it around. For a major renovation, carefully fit pieces of plywood or thick cardboard to the floor, followed by a drop cloth. Or purchase interlocking foam floor protectors made for the purpose.

■ Keep the dust from traveling. Construction typically produces a fine dust that will seep into every corner of your house if it gets a chance. (This is particularly true when cutting into a plaster wall or sanding drywall joint compound.) It's not enough to close a door. Seal off the construction site with plastic taped to the doorway. Place a fan or two in a window to blow dust out of the house.

■ Do as much work as possible outdoors or in the garage. Even if

it means taking extra steps before cutting boards, you will save hassle in the long run if you keep the dust out of your house.

■ Sweep and vacuum every day. At the end of a workday, cleaning up may be the last thing you want to do, but it's worth the effort to make the site well swept and organized for the next day. Make it a regular routine to spend the last 15 minutes of each day cleaning up. You'll find the site easier to live with and much more pleasant to return to in the morning.

■ Use the right cleaning tools. A wet/dry vacuum cleaner with a fine filter is ideal for eliminating dust. Or scatter sweeping compound to minimize flying dust while sweeping. Have several scrubbing devices on hand for cleaning buckets and tools.

WORKING SAFE AND SMART

Home improvement projects can be dangerous. Many tasks call for sharp tools or power tools that can cause injuries. Follow these safety rules:

■ Before using a power tool, read its instruction manual and follow the manufacturer's safety cautions. Tighten any adjustments and check that the guard is working before you operate a tool.

■ Keep power tools dry, and plug them into grounded electrical outlets. Take care not to cut the power cord.

■ Keep fingers well away from a power blade. Clamp small pieces of wood before cutting them, rather than holding them.

■ Wear work gloves when handling rough materials, but take them off and firmly roll up your sleeves if operating a power tool.

■ Wear eye and ear protection when cutting with a power tool.

■ Unplug a power saw before changing the blade.

■ Properly support a board to be cut so you will avoid kickback (see page 233).

■ When working on wiring, shut off the power to the circuit first. When working with plumbing, shut off the water first.

■ When working on a ladder, don't lean out to either side. Keep your body weight between the sides of the ladder. It may take longer to get off the ladder and move it to reach farther, but it is well worth your time. Falls are one of the most common causes of injuries in the home.

Avoid Physical Strain

You are probably not accustomed to physical construction work, so it is quite possible for you to strain

muscles or joints while engaging in remodeling work. Often, you feel fine while doing the work but wake up the next day in pain. Don't take chances. Follow these guidelines to avoid injury:

■ Don't overexert yourself when lifting heavy objects, or when repeatedly lifting lighter loads. Get a helper to do some of the work, and take plenty of breaks.

■ Working in an awkward position can put a strain on your back and other areas of your body. Take the time to move or to arrange things so that you are as comfortable as possible.

■ Lift with your legs, not your back. When picking up a heavy object, keep your back as upright and straight as possible. Bend your knees to reach the object.

GETTING TO KNOW YOUR HOME

An educated homeowner is prepared for emergencies and is able to handle repairs and upgrades with confidence. This book will help you understand your home's structural, electrical, plumbing, and heating/cooling systems. If you feel ignorant about important aspects of your home, hire a contractor or a professional house inspector to explain things.

Here's a basic list of things a homeowner should understand and be able to do:

■ Find and understand your electrical service panel. If your service is less than 100 amps, consult with an electrician to see if you need larger service. The panel should be easy for an adult to access, yet out of reach for small children. Know which breaker or fuse controls which parts of your electrical system, and understand how to flip a breaker or change a fuse when a circuit blows.

■ Know what sort of electrical cable runs through your walls, and be sure that the cables are kept safe from harm, especially when driving fasteners into walls.

■ In case of a plumbing crisis, know how to shut off water to individual fixtures and (more importantly) how to shut off water to the entire house (see page 120). Often there are two shutoffs—one in the crawlspace or basement or just outside the house, and one underground near the street.

■ Learn the basics of your plumbing system: what material the pipes are made of, where the vent pipes go, and where the main drain goes. If you have a septic system, locate it and contact a service company to make sure it is in good working order.

■ Understand your home's framing. If any floors sag, check to see whether they can be buttressed. If termites are a problem in your area, have your home inspected for them regularly.

■ Inspect your siding, roofing, and gutter system yearly for signs of damage. Often a timely repair will save money in the long run.

■ To be comfortable, a home must be well sealed with caulk and weatherstripping, and it must be properly ventilated. See pages 414–432 for tips and information.

■ Understand your HVAC system—what type it is, as well as how the pipes or vents are routed. Some systems require annual maintenance, which you neglect at your peril. It may be possible to improve your system's efficiency with a few simple steps. Solutions are found on pages 433–456.

IDENTIFYING A BEARING WALL

Every wall fits one of two structural categories—bearing walls, which support a load above, and nonbearing walls, which support only themselves. If you remove or make a big opening in a bearing wall, you could literally bring down the house.

To determine whether a wall is bearing or not, do some sleuthing in the basement or attic— wherever there are exposed joists or rafters. If the joists run parallel to the wall in question, you can be sure it's not a bearing wall.

However, if they are perpendicular to the wall—as shown below right—you can reasonably expect that the wall is bearing a load.

If you cannot see the joists, use a stud finder to locate them and determine the direction they run. Or use the techniques shown on page 12.

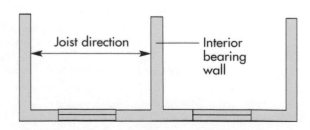

ASSESSING BASEMENTS AND FOUNDATIONS

The foundation of your house has several tough assignments. First, it supports the weight of the entire house. It also acts as a retaining wall and must be firm enough to hold back the earth—and moisture—around its perimeter. Finally, it may shelter a basement.

Basement/foundation walls begin with a concrete footing designed to stably distribute a load of thousands of pounds per square foot. The footing also supports the thinner slab used for most basement floors. Footings may or may not be protected from moisture by drain tiles laid in sand or gravel to remove water.

The walls may be made of concrete block, poured concrete, brick, stone, or even treated wood. Regardless of the material, the walls' exterior should be covered with a layer of waterproofing before the soil is replaced.

Basements suffer from a special ill that doesn't afflict other spaces in your home—moisture. Differences between the temperature below ground and that of the air upstairs or outside often create a slight mustiness, especially in muggy summer weather. This is normal.

However, if floors or walls in your basement chronically sweat—or worse, if puddles collect on the floor—the problem should be dealt with. To solve basement moisture problems or leaks, see pages 523–524.

On top, the walls support a wood sill plate upon which joists are laid for the subfloor and finish floor. (See pages 314 and 402–403 for more about sill plates and floors.)

Siding — Finish floor — Building paper — Subfloor — Floor joist — Band joist — Sill plate — Water-proofing — Drain tile — Footing — Expansion joint — Sand fill — Vapor barrier

EXPERTS' INSIGHT

CRAWLSPACES

If your house has a crawlspace underneath, the house either rests atop short supporting walls or is held up by a series of concrete or masonry piers.

Local climate and soil conditions determine how a crawlspace should be constructed. In some areas, it should be sealed off tightly, with only a few vents. In other areas, larger openings are needed. See pages 426–427 for ways to insulate a crawlspace.

Before crawling under your home, make sure it's safe. In some areas, poisonous insects and other critters pose a danger.

If your floor sags, resupporting it may involve jacking the floor up and installing a new post. Or, you may need to pour a new pier or part of a foundation wall.

Crawlspaces provide ample opportunities for wood-eating bugs. Have yours inspected regularly by an exterminator.

Understanding Interior Wall Surfaces

Most homes built after World War II have walls made of drywall, also known as Sheetrock® or wallboard. Most residential drywall is ½ inch thick. Installed on studs that are spaced 16 inches apart, this provides a fairly durable wall—one that will last for many decades, as long as it is not abused. However, slamming doorknobs or roughhousing adolescents can easily punch a hole through drywall. Fortunately, repairs are fairly easy, though time-consuming (see pages 560–563).

Drywall is only gypsum covered on each side with paper, so it's not very strong. If you need to hang anything heavy on a wall, it is important to find a stud and fasten the nail or screw to the stud.

Plaster walls.
Most plaster walls begin with the same framing that's used for drywall construction. To hold and strengthen the plaster, the studs must be covered with lath, usually made of narrow strips of wood, but more recent applications may use a heavy metal mesh instead. The lath then is covered by three successive layers of plaster. The scratch coat of plaster, the first to go down, grips the lath. The brown coat smooths out the surface. Finally, the finish coat is applied to produce a texture ranging from rough to glassy smooth. If your home has solid masonry walls, the plaster might be applied directly to the masonry.

Finding Studs

Studs are usually—but not always—spaced at regular intervals. After you've found one, you can often plot others by measuring.

Begin your search near the wall's center, not at the ends, where spacing might be irregular. Also, ignore the studs on either side of a door or window opening.

Electronic stud finders offer the easiest way to find studs and joists. However, they usually do not work in a plaster wall, because of the wood lath.

Once you've found one stud, measure 16 inches—the most common spacing—in one direction or the other. If you cannot find a second stud, try 24 inches, a spacing used in some newer houses.

Sound it out.
Often you can "sound out" a wall by rapping along it with your knuckles. A solid thunk indicates a stud. If rapping doesn't tell you anything, look for nails in the baseboard. They're usually driven into the studs.

Probe with a wire.
You can also drill a small, angled hole and probe with a straightened wire coat hanger to find the stud. Or, take the face plate off an electrical receptacle to check: Wall boxes usually are nailed to the side of a stud.

Hanging Light Objects

Choose hanging hardware that is appropriate for the object to be hung. It should be strong enough, but there's no need to go overboard, for instance using beefy screws to hang a small picture. Often, an appliance or fixture will come with its own hanging hardware. If you have lath-and-plaster walls, a screw driven into the lath will hold much better than a screw driven into drywall, though not as well as a screw driven into a stud. Make sure you hit a lath, not a space between.

YOU'LL NEED...

TIME: 10 to 20 minutes, depending on the material.

SKILLS: Basic skills.

TOOLS: Tape measure, drill and drill bits (perhaps a masonry bit), hammer, screwdriver or adjustable wrench.

Picture hooks.
Ordinary nailed picture hooks hold items up to about 10 pounds. These have the advantage of poking only tiny holes in the wall. Hooks that are attached to adhesive cloth can be used only on very lightweight objects.

Plastic anchors.
Plastic anchors grip by expanding as you drive screws into them. Drill the right-sized hole, and tap the anchor into the hole until it is flush with the wall surface. Then drive the screw.

Hollow-wall anchors and toggle bolts.
Hollow wall anchors open behind the wall surface for an installation that cannot pull loose. Toggle bolts screw into wings that pop open inside the wall. Assemble with the hanging hardware before inserting.

Attaching to two or more studs.
Bridging studs with a 1×4 or a strip of plywood adds strength and freedom from stud spacings. Nail or screw the hanger to the bridging.

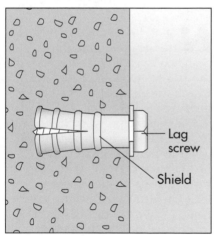

Lag screws and shields.
For hanging heavy items, buy lag screws with masonry shields. Drill the right-sized hole, then tap in the shield. When you drive the lag screw, the shield expands to grip the wall. For medium-weight items, use masonry screws, which are typically blue or green; these need no anchor. Drill the right-sized hole, then drive the screw.

SAFETY IN THE HOME

Keeping a home safe is often a simple matter of common sense and attentiveness—having fire extinguishers readily available and keeping harmful chemicals out of reach of children, for instance. However, many dangers are less obvious—like carbon monoxide gas (see page 16) and radon (page 17). The next six pages will acquaint you with some types of household hazards and their safeguards. In addition, here are some commonsense safety tips:

■ With your family, develop, discuss, and practice an emergency evacuation plan in case of fire. Make sure everyone has at least two routes for exiting the house, in case one route is blocked.

■ Install smoke alarms throughout the home, and install at least one fire extinguisher, preferably in the kitchen.

■ If you use a wood-burning stove or any other type of supplemental heat (especially kerosene or electric), take special precautions, because these units are notorious for starting fires.

■ Do not overload an electrical outlet. A cheap multiplug adapter, with four or five cords plugged into it, is a hazard. Instead, install a new outlet or purchase a power strip with its own breaker designed to handle a number of plugs.

■ Replace or repair any frayed or damaged wires. Don't use a thin household-type extension cord for a heavy appliance. If the cord gets warm when in use, it is unsafe.

■ If a circuit often overloads so you need to flip the breaker or change the fuse, call an electrician to fix the problem.

■ Don't use a lightbulb of a higher wattage than is recommended for the light fixture or lamp. If you do, it will overheat. In a closet or utility space, make sure you don't have a bare lightbulb within a foot of clothing or other flammable objects.

■ Have your furnace or boiler checked yearly, both to ensure that it is burning safely and to make sure it does not produce carbon monoxide. Place carbon monoxide detectors in at least two places in your home.

■ Be aware of dangers specific to your locale and your type of home construction. For example, an older home may have asbestos pipe insulation, or paint that contains lead. Radon is a problem in some areas, and some fairly new homes may be in danger of developing mold or mildew.

CHOOSING AND USING FIRE EXTINGUISHERS

Not all fire extinguishers are the same. Choose one designed to extinguish the type of fire you are most likely to have. Check the extinguisher's label for information.

For example, class A fire extinguishers contain pressurized water to put out simple fires involving wood and cloth. Class B extinguishers contain sodium bicarbonate or foam to suffocate flames. They can handle fires that involve flammable substances such as grease, oil, gasoline, and solvents. Class C extinguishers contain dry chemicals so that they can put out electrical fires. (Class A units would only spread such a fire.)

For general protection, purchase an "ABC" unit, which can handle most any type of fire. For a kitchen, you may choose a "BC"

extinguisher, since most fires there are electrical or involve burning grease. Sometimes the label rates how well an extinguisher can put out fires of each type.

Spend a little more for an extinguisher that has a high "UL" number, which indicates how much extinguishing agent it contains. The higher the number, the longer the unit will last and the larger the unit will be. Make sure the extinguisher is small enough so that all family members can use it.

Check your fire extinguishers regularly to make sure they are still at full pressure. A quick glance at the gauge will suffice; if you mount the extinguisher so that the gauge is visible, checking it will be simple.

Most household extinguishers are disposable; throw yours out if

you use it even for a very short burst, because it likely will not work the next time. A more expensive rechargeable model must be serviced by an authorized dealer between uses.

Read the label ahead of time to learn how to use the extinguisher; when a fire occurs, you will not have time. In most cases, there is a safety pin that must be pulled before you can squeeze the trigger.

Hold the extinguisher 5 or 6 feet away from the fire. Any closer could cause the fire to disperse, and any farther away might not be effective. Aim the spray at the base—the source— of the fire; hitting the flames in the middle will do little good. Use a sweeping motion when spraying to cover the area thoroughly. You can either use short bursts or a long spray.

INSTALLING SMOKE DETECTORS

There are two basic types of smoke detectors—photoelectric and ionization units. Photoelectric units include a beam of light and a photoelectric cell. When smoke enters the unit, it scatters the light, causing part of it to contact the photoelectric cell and trigger the alarm. Photoelectric smoke detectors react more readily to slow, smoldering fires than to fast, flaming blazes.

An ionization unit ionizes the air inside the detector and gives it an electrical charge. Smoke particles cut down current flow, which sounds a warning. Ionization detectors respond more quickly than photoelectric units to fast, flaming fires.

Combination units are also available that provide the benefits of both types. These are more expensive, however.

Each type has its advantages and drawbacks. While battery-operated photoelectric models are available, many models depend on house current, which means you lose protection during a power outage or electrical fire, and you must locate them near an electric outlet. Ionization units run on house current, batteries, or both. Besides reacting more slowly to smoldering fires, they're also more susceptible to false alarms, especially from a steamy shower or from someone smoking nearby.

Consider installing at least one of each—an ionization detector in your bedroom hallway plus a photoelectric unit in the living area. A deluxe system might also include a series of heat sensors wired in tandem with smoke detectors so that all the alarms will sound if any one senses heat or smoke. These require extensive wiring.

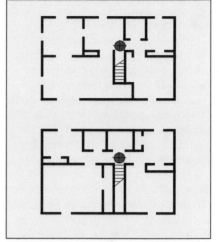

Where to place them.
Smoke detectors take only a few minutes to mount. Knowing where to place them, however, helps you decide how many you need.

Attach each unit to a ceiling, or high on a wall about 8 to 10 inches below ceiling level. Ideally, you should have at least one detector on each floor in hallways leading to bedrooms and at the top of stairwells. Analyze your home's air currents and avoid dead corners where there is poor air circulation. Also, keep detectors away from smoky kitchen, furnace, garage, or fireplace areas.

In a single-floor home with bedrooms clustered together, you can install one unit in a hallway between the bedroom and living areas. If your sleeping areas are spread out or are on different levels, you should use at least two detectors. Mount one at the top of the stairway.

Basements and garages.
Protect your basement and utility areas as well. Because smoke and heat always rise, install at the top of the basement stairway, if possible.

How smoke travels.
Once smoke reaches the ceiling, it spreads out horizontally. This makes the center of a room the optimum location for a smoke detector.

MAKING A HOME SAFE FOR CHILDREN

Small children love to experiment and explore, climbing into new places and tasting anything in reach. A child who is only crawling today may be standing up and reaching tomorrow, so parents need to plan ahead. Fortunately, a host of new products on the market make it easier than ever to shield children from danger. Here are some steps you can take:

■ A bathtub has hard and slippery surfaces. Cover the spout with an inflatable or foam spout cover. If the handles can be reached by a child, turn them off firmly; a child who turns on the hot water could be scalded. Apply slip-resistant strips to the bottom of the tub or buy a nonslip tub mat. Consider installing a grab bar or two. Keep all electrical appliances well away from the tub.

And, of course, never leave a young child unattended in the tub.
■ Turn the home's hot-water temperature down so it is just warm enough for a shower, and not so hot as to scald a child.
■ Many products commonly found in a bathroom, such as aftershave and perfume, can be harmful if swallowed or if they get in a child's eyes. Keep them out of reach.
■ At a certain stage, a child finds stairways irresistible. Use gates to keep the stairs out of bounds. Purchase only new gates, which meet modern safety standards.
■ Electrical cords are a potential hazard, especially if a child handles the plug with wet fingers. A child also might pull down a toaster or other appliance by the cord. Position furniture such that the child cannot reach plugs.

■ Cover unused electrical outlets with special plastic safety plugs or covers.
■ If you have heating units that get very hot—a wood-burning stove, a kerosene unit, electrical baseboard heaters, or even steam radiators—take special precautions to keep the child away.
■ If you are cooking while the child is in the kitchen, use the back burners whenever possible. Turn pan handles toward the back, and move hot pots out of a child's reach.
■ If a stove knob is left uncovered, a child can easily turn on a stove burner. Special covers are available to protect the knobs.
■ While the child is in the putting-everything-in-the-mouth stage, move all knickknacks up and out of reach.

CARBON MONOXIDE PROTECTION

Because it is invisible and odorless, carbon monoxide (CO) can be detected only with a carbon monoxide detector.

Symptoms of overexposure to carbon monoxide include headaches, nausea, dizziness, fatigue, and blurred vision. In a home where CO levels are slightly high, family members may experience some of these symptoms at a low level for years and not know the cause.

Carbon monoxide commonly enters a home because a furnace or water heater is improperly vented. Have your gas company come to your home to give a free inspection. Vent pipes might be clogged, inadequately joined, or installed in the wrong configuration. In any of these cases, repairs are simple. An inspection by a heating

professional can also reveal any CO problems.

Venting configurations can be complicated, especially if two appliances—most commonly a furnace and a water heater— are in the same room. Have a pro check the venting carefully.

Be sure to follow correct maintenance procedures for your furnace. A forced-air system is the most likely to cause problems. Make sure filters are changed regularly and that air can flow freely through the vents.

Any appliance that uses flammable fuels can be the source of CO poisoning.

A fireplace may also be the culprit. If the chimney does not draw well, or if the chimney bricks are not well mortared, CO from burning wood can leak into living areas—even if you do not smell

smoke. This often occurs on upper floors, so install a CO detector there as well.

Many homeowners neglect to install carbon monoxide detectors, but these are an essential line of defense. Place one detector near but not in the room that contains the water heater and heating unit. Place another in the main floor's living room. If you use your garage as a work space, place one there as well. You may want to place CO detectors next to your smoke detectors.

If your home tests for high levels of CO, open windows to provide some ventilation. If that does not solve the problem, evacuate the house. In either case, call in a heating contractor to make repairs.

TESTING FOR RADON

Like carbon monoxide, radon is a colorless and odorless gas, so it can affect your family's health in subtle or dramatic ways with no warning.

Usually, there are no immediate, apparent symptoms of radon poisoning. However, breathing radon for extended periods increases the risk of cancer.

Radon is a naturally occurring result of the decay of radium, an element that can be found in most any locale. According to some estimates, 1 in 15 houses in the United States is affected by radon poisoning.

Though it is present most everywhere, radon is more of a problem in some locales than in others. Before buying a home, check with an inspector to see whether radon is a danger in that neighborhood. Some communities require a radon test before selling a home.

To test for radon, you may choose to hire a company that specializes in testing for radon and other airborne dangers. Before hiring the company, check with your building department and the Better Business Bureau to make sure it is on the level: Radon detection and protection is fertile ground for unscrupulous contractors.

Alternatively, purchase a radon testing kit. Typically, a kit consists of a canister filled with charcoal. Leave the canister open for a few days in the house, then send it to a testing agency.

Radon typically seeps up through the ground and into a home via small openings in a basement or crawlspace. If a home is otherwise well sealed, radon will remain in the air. A well-ventilated home is somewhat less likely to be affected, but the real solution is to stop the radon from entering the home.

Sealing out radon is largely a low-tech affair. Check your basement or crawlspace, as well as lower parts of your first-floor siding or masonry, for any points of access. Use latex/silicone caulk to seal small gaps, such as around pipes and cables that enter from the outside. Stuff larger gaps with insulation or foam sealant.

If your basement walls are often moist, they could also be allowing radon into the home. Paint them with waterproofing basement paint. If you have a sump pump, install a tight-fitting lid. Then take steps to increase your home's ventilation.

TESTING FOR LEAD

Children are particularly susceptible to lead poisoning. Once it enters the human body, lead is very slow to leave, so prolonged exposure to even very low levels has an accumulative effect. Lead poisoning typically affects the brain. Symptoms may include nausea, headache, fatigue, short attention span, and clumsiness.

Prior to the 1970s, many homes were finished with paint that contained high levels of lead. As long as it remains on the wall, lead paint is not a problem. However, paint chips or dust, caused by flaking walls or two surfaces rubbing together (as with a sash window), are exceedingly poisonous if swallowed by a child.

A hardware store may carry a lead testing kit, which unfortunately is not guaranteed to be accurate. To be sure, hire a company to collect chips and send them to a lab for testing.

If you have lead paint in sound condition, the solution may be simply to paint over it. Scraping or sanding will create dangerous dust and chips. If the paint is peeling or otherwise unsound, contact a company that specializes in lead abatement.

A few older homes have lead pipes. A lead pipe is gray, and you can easily gouge it with a sharp object. In some older cities, the main supply pipe, which runs from the street to the house, is lead. Copper pipe installed before the 1970s may have joints held together with soldering that contains lead.

Some cities treat these problems by adding a trace element of phosphate to the water. This coats the lead pipes or joints so that virtually no lead leaches into drinking water. To be safe, however, contact your building department to see about having your water tested.

To further ensure that there's no lead in your drinking and cooking water, allow water to run for a minute or so before using it; water that has sat in pipes all night is more likely to pick up lead. Cook with cold water rather than hot water, which is also more likely to be contaminated.

Until the 1970s, automobiles ran on gasoline that contained lead. Consequently, soil near a busy street may be contaminated. Simply keeping a house and clothing clean can go a long way toward eliminating the possibility of lead poisoning.

ASSESSING POTENTIAL ASBESTOS HAZARDS

Until the 1970s, it was common to wrap pipes with insulation made of asbestos. Asbestos was also used as wall insulation, as a siding material, and as an ingredient of many floor tiles and sheet goods. Even the "cottage cheese" texture on some ceilings may contain asbestos.

Asbestos is an ideal material for many purposes because it is virtually impossible to burn. However, we now know that tiny particles of asbestos, when inhaled, can cause cancer of the lung or stomach. In many cases, symptoms are not apparent until 10 years or more after exposure. It's well worth your efforts to have your home inspected for asbestos and to require an inspection if buying a home.

When the dangers of asbestos first became apparent, companies and individuals spent thousands of dollars removing it. This proved a difficult process because even microscopic particles must be captured during removal.

Today, many experts say that covering, rather than removing, is the best solution. They've concluded that the very act of removing asbestos poses far more dangers than does undisturbed existing asbestos. Asbestos in good condition poses little danger, and asbestos that is adequately covered poses virtually no danger.

If your heat or water pipes are wrapped in old, cloth-covered insulation, it may be asbestos. If the material is brown, it's probably a type of cardboard. However, if it is light gray or white, chances are it is asbestos. Soak a small section thoroughly with water and, wearing long sleeves and gloves and a dust mask, cut out a small section. Place it in a plastic bag and take it to your building department to see if it is asbestos.

Loose-fill insulation in an older attic also may contain asbestos. Wet and collect a sample and have it tested. Older asphalt or vinyl tiles and sheet goods may contain asbestos. Wear a respirator when removing these products.

Local codes may require that asbestos be removed rather than encapsulated. You will have to hire an abatement company certified to do such work.

Otherwise, you may be able to deal with the problem yourself; consult with your building department first. Perhaps you will be allowed to wrap asbestos pipe insulation with plastic and tape approved for such use. You also may be permitted to seal over asbestos insulation with plastic, and then cover the plastic with plywood.

GUARDING AGAINST FORMALDEHYDE AND MOLD

Many modern composite building materials, including plywood, particleboard, oriented-strand board (OSB), and medium-density fiberboard (MDF), are made using resins that contain formaldehyde. These products are used to make cabinets, to cover subfloors and exterior walls and roofs, and to serve many other common purposes in home construction. Urea-formaldehyde foam insulation (UFFI) is no longer made, but was used to build many homes. Cloth that is used for draperies, carpet, and furniture also may contain formaldehyde.

So for most of us, formaldehyde is a fact of life; there's no way to completely eliminate it from the air. However, newer or recently remodeled homes generally have more formaldehyde; levels tend to degrade significantly as the years go by.

About 10 percent of the population is sensitive to formaldehyde exposure. For this group, formaldehyde can produce symptoms such as runny nose, difficulty breathing, coughing, headache, skin rash, and dizziness.

An environmental testing company can test your home for formaldehyde. Ask your building department for recommendations.

If you do have high levels of formaldehyde, it may not be a problem unless a family member is sensitive to it. To relieve symptoms of such sensitivity, improve ventilation in the home, and use a dehumidifier or air conditioner to keep the home drier.

Lately, there have been reports of homes with severe cases of mold. This typically propagates inside walls, ceilings, and floors, and becomes visible only when the problem is out of control.

These problems typically occur in newer homes that are tightly caulked and weatherstripped, but that lack adequate ventilation due to poor construction methods. Homes built correctly according to code will not have these problems.

Be aware that this super-mold problem, though very real, is quite rare. If you find mold or mildew on a wall or ceiling, simply wash it with a bleach solution. Then correct whatever is causing the area to remain moist for long periods.

DEALING WITH HAZARDOUS MATERIALS

We deal with some type of hazardous wastes almost daily. The chart below lists common waste products and how to dispose of them safely and responsibly.

Some items need special attention. For example, rags soaked in a flammable substance such as mineral spirits can burst into flames spontaneously if they're left in a bundle. That's why it's important to spread them out outdoors until all the solvent has evaporated.

Some of the substances cited below are best treated by rinsing with water until they are heavily diluted. Once diluted, flush them through a lower-floor toilet, which empties out quickly into the main drain. Pour, flush, wait for the tank to fill, and flush again.

For more difficult disposal problems, consult with your building department. In some locales, a special disposal truck visits your home for hazardous material pickup several times a year. Or there may be an annual hazardous waste dropoff day, or a designated site where you can deliver the materials anytime.

DISPOSING OF HAZARDOUS WASTES

Waste	OK in Trash	Dilute and Flush	Evaporate and Place in Trash	Recycle or Return	Special Disposal Problem
Aerosol cans, empty	I				
Automobile items					
Antifreeze			I		
Battery				I	
Diesel Fuel					I
Gasoline					I
Motor oil				I	
Tires					I
Cleaners and solvents					
Brush cleaner					I
Degreaser solvent					I
Drain cleaner		I			
Dry-cleaning fluid			I		
Mildew remover	I				
Oven cleaner		I			
Paints and finishes					
Latex paint			I		
Oil-based paint					I
Mineral spirits			I		
Paint stripper		I			
Paint thinner			I		
Rust remover		I			
Wood preservative					I
Pesticides					
Insecticide					I
Pet pest collar					I
Rat poison					I
Weed killer					I

CREATING UTILITY STORAGE

Time spent organizing your tools and lumber will pay off handsomely in the long run. Work can be positively fun when the things you need are in easy reach. A home center will carry a variety of utility storage units, which may cost little more than buying materials to make them yourself.

If you have the space, create a dedicated workroom, complete with workbench, shop tools, and organized storage. Plan the layout carefully. If, for instance, you want to run full sheets of plywood through a table saw, you will need more than 8 feet of space in front of and behind the saw. If space is limited, it may help to have movable rather than stationary shop tools.

An unfinished garage ceiling is ideal for storing things that you do not need to reach often, such as seasonal gear. Adding cross ties and nailing up plywood opens an entire level of new space.

Molding
1×4s or smaller
Lumber
Large sheet goods (more than 4' long)
About 4' 4"
6' to 8'
Small sheet goods (4' or shorter)

Lumber storage.
A storage setup with shelves up high keeps scrap lumber and sheet goods handy without taking up too much space or looking cluttered. Make plenty of shelves; if you end up stacking the lumber in more than a few layers, it will be difficult to get the bottom pieces out.

Plan the arrangement so it is easy to move pieces in and out. That means you will need ample room to the right or left of the sheet goods. Elevate the sheet goods on boards laid on the floor; if plywood or particleboard gets wet even once, it can be ruined. Place the larger sheets to the rear so you can see the smaller sheets.

Small-tool storage.
Locking cabinets are best for storing expensive tools, chemicals, paint, and other items that might attract children. For easy access, attach a sheet of pegboard to the studs, and use special hangers for the tools. For portable storage, use a large toolbox or a bucket with a pocketed fabric apron.

Large-tool storage.
Shovels, rakes, and other large tools are best protected from damage if they are hung, rather than simply propped in a corner. Inexpensive storage is easy to create with nails and scrap lumber. Or purchase special hangers designed for large tools.

WIRING BASICS

HOW CIRCUITS WORK

Electricity is the flow of electrons through a conductor. In home electrical systems, wires, consisting of highly conductive copper wrapped in insulation for safety, are the conductors—the assigned pathway through which the electricity travels. A host of other items—a fork, a screwdriver, you—also can serve as conductors, sometimes with disastrous results. It's the goal of a safe electrical system to prevent this from happening.

Electricity always flows in a loop, known as a circuit. When a circuit is interrupted at any point, the electricity shuts off. As soon as the circuit is reconnected, the flow begins again.

Electricity is generated by your local electric company. Overhead and underground wires bring power from the utility company lines to a home's service head, also called a weatherhead because it can withstand wind, heat, and ice. Although the utility company sends high-voltage electricity along some of its power lines, by the time it reaches your house, it is 120 volts per wire.

The electricity passes through an electric meter, which measures how much enters the house. It proceeds to a service panel (also called the breaker box or fuse box), which distributes electricity throughout the house along individual circuits. Each circuit flows out of the service panel, through a number of fixtures and receptacles, and back to the service panel. (For more on service panels, see pages 24–25.)

To make a circuit, electricity is carried out of the service panel on "hot" wires that usually have black insulation, although they sometimes may be red, and is returned to the panel on neutral wires that have white insulation.

The service panel contains

Following the flow

The flow of electricity in typical household circuits starts with the two 120-volt lines and single neutral line that enter the top of the service panel. Both 120-volt lines are used to make the 240-volt circuit, though only one neutral

circuit breakers or fuses—both are safety devices that shut off the power in case of a short circuit or other fault in the circuit (see pages 24–25, 63–64).

Each circuit has a number of outlets that lead to smaller circuits through which the electricity flows. These outlets might include receptacles, fixtures, and switches. For example, a wall switch interrupts (off) or completes (on) the circuit to one or more light fixtures. A heavy-use appliance—such as a dishwasher, garbage disposal, or microwave oven—may need a circuit to itself.

Most circuits carry current of 120 volts which will give most people quite a jolt but will not seriously harm them if they should accidentally come into contact

line is needed for the electricity to complete its loop. The 120-volt circuit has one hot wire (black) and one neutral wire (white), plus a copper ground wire (green). In case of a short, the ground wire carries the current safely into the ground.

with it. Most homes also have one or two 240-volt lines, which double the power by using two hot wires with one neutral wire. Because of the higher power, take special care when dealing with these.

Every electrical system must be grounded for safety. Grounding allows excess current to travel harmlessly into the earth in case of overload or a short circuit. Usually this is done by connecting a wire to a cold water pipe, to a grounding rod sunk deep into the ground, or sometimes to both.

Circuits in your home may be grounded with a grounding wire that is bare copper or green, or they may be grounded by means of the metal receptacle boxes and the metal sheathing that contains the wires (see pages 36–39).

light fixture

wall switch

service head, or
weatherhead

service wires

receptacles

electric
meter

grounding rod

Air-conditioning unit
requires 240 volts.

SERVICE PANELS

*E*lectrical projects always begin at the service panel, which is either a breaker box or a fuse box. When a short or an overload shuts down power to a circuit, this is where you go to restore the flow. It's also where you cut off power to a circuit before starting a project.

Power arrives from the meter through two main power wires, each of which carry 120 volts of electricity into the house. Usually these are black and/or red. In addition there is a white main neutral wire that carries electricity back to the utility. The main hot wires are connected to a main power shutoff. When you turn this off, you don't de-energize the hot wires, but you cut power to everything else in the box.

Breaker boxes

Emerging from a breaker box's main shutoff are two hot bus bars. The 120-volt breakers are each attached to one of these bars. (This means that if one of the main hot wires gets damaged outside your house, you will lose power to about half of the circuits in your house.) Each 240-volt breaker gets twice the power by being attached to both bus bars. When a circuit is overloaded or a short occurs, its breaker trips and shuts off power before the wires heat up and become a danger.

The main neutral wire is connected to the neutral bus bar. This bar is connected to a system ground wire, which leads to a grounding rod (see art on page 22). White wires for every circuit, and possibly bare or green ground wires, also connect to the neutral bus bar. As a result, each 120-volt circuit has a black or colored wire leading from a circuit breaker, a white wire leading to the neutral bus bar, and possibly a bare copper or green-covered ground wire also connected to the neutral bar. Each 240-volt circuit has two

wires leading to a circuit breaker. In addition, the 240-volt circuit has a neutral and, possibly, a ground wire connected to the neutral bus bar. Systems with conduit or armored cable do not need separate ground wires—the conduit or metal sheathing act as ground conductors (see page 80).

For how to troubleshoot the several types of circuit breakers and how to check for the cause of shorts, see page 63.

Labels in illustration: main power wires; main power shutoff; hot bus bars; 240-volt breaker; 120-volt breaker; main neutral wire; neutral bus bar; system ground wire

Breaker labels: MAIN ON ON 100 OFF OFF; RANGE 30; DRYER 30; BEDLTS 15; BASMT 20; KIT 20; KIT 20; BEDRM 20; GAR 20; LNLTS 15; WASH 20

CAUTION!

LEAVE INCOMING WIRES FOR THE UTILITY COMPANY
If you suspect that the wires entering your house may be damaged in any way, do not attempt to work on them yourself. Have the utility company inspect them. Usually it will inspect and repair them for free.

Fuse boxes

If you have an older home that has not been rewired in the last 25 or 30 years, chances are that its electrical heart is a fuse box rather than a breaker box.

Fuse boxes are wired and work the same way as breaker boxes (see page 24), but instead of tripping as a breaker does, a fuse "blows" when there's too much current in its circuit. When this happens, you must eliminate the short or the overload, remove the blown fuse, and screw in or plug in a new one.

Power comes into a fuse box through two main power wires. (In a house with no 240-volt equipment, there may be only one of these.) Current flows through a main disconnect, in this case a pullout block that holds a pair of cartridge fuses.

Next in line are a series of plug fuses that protect the black hot wires of the individual circuits, often called branch circuits. Unscrewing a fuse disconnects its circuit. A neutral bus bar receives the main neutral wire and a neutral wire for each of the branch circuits. A system ground wire leads from the neutral bus bar to a grounding rod outside the house.

For tips on troubleshooting a fuse box, see page 64.

main neutral wire

main power wires

neutral bus bar

plug fuse

system ground wire

pullout block

cartridge fuses

Typical plug fuse
A plug fuse is threaded and screws into the fuse box. Handle only the rim. Do not touch the threads while removing or replacing the fuse. For information on identifying and replacing a blown fuse, see page 64.

Handling pullout blocks
Larger 240-volt circuits, as well as main shutoff fuses, often are protected by pullout blocks that contain cartridge fuses. If you need to pull out a cartridge fuse that is not in a pullout block, do not use your fingers. Get a fuse puller (see pages 31 and 64).

GROUNDING AND POLARIZATION

Older homes often have receptacles and fixtures that are ungrounded, and many local codes do not require that they be rewired so they're grounded. Still, grounding is worth adding to your system because it adds protection against electrical shock. Grounding provides a third path for electricity to travel along, so if there is a leak of any sort, it will flow into the earth rather than into the body of a person who touches a defective fixture, appliance, or tool.

An electrical system is grounded with a grounding rod driven at least 8 feet into the ground outside the house or by connecting to a cold water pipe. Each individual branch circuit must be grounded as well, either with a separate wire that leads to the neutral bar of the service panel or with metal sheathing that runs without a break from each outlet to the panel. (In theory, electrical outlets can be grounded individually, but this is impractical.)

Some locations in your house—especially where the outlet and/or appliances may become wet—require ground-fault circuit-interrupter (GFCI) receptacles (see pages 98–99). Older, ungrounded circuits usually are protected by polarization, which is less effective than grounding but better than nothing. Grounded and polarized receptacles work only if they are wired correctly. See pages 58–59 to test for this.

require ground-fault circuit-interrupter (GFCI) receptacles (see pages 98–99).

A polarized receptacle
A polarized outlet has one slot that is longer than the other. This is to ensure that the plug is inserted so that its hot current flows through black or red wires, and neutral current flows through white wires. Although not as safe as a grounded system, polarization is the next best thing.

The grounded box safely carries away the electricity from the loose wire.

A grounded receptacle
The grounding circuit must follow an unbroken path to the earth. A third, rounded prong on a modern plug fits into the round slot in the receptacle. This slot connects to a wire—or to metal conduit or sheathing—that leads without interruption to the neutral bus bar of the breaker box. The system ground wire then leads from the bus bar to the earth. Instead of a grounding rod, a cold water pipe often is used for grounding because it is connected to water supply pipes that go deep under the ground.

> ## CAUTION!
> DON'T ALTER PRONGS ON PLUGS
> *Never clip or file down the prongs on a grounded or polarized plug. Go to the heart of the problem: Test and upgrade your circuit and receptacle.*

LIMITATIONS OF OLDER SYSTEMS

An older home may have electrical service that is inadequate or even unsafe. It can be confusing, as well. If you are unsure about your home's wiring, have a professional check it out.

Some older systems have only two wires—one hot (rather than two) and a neutral—entering the house. This means you will not be able to have any 240-volt circuits for large appliances.

Modern electrical service provides at least 100 amps of power, which is enough to power a medium-size house with an average number of appliances. A house built in the 1950s or before may only have 30-amp service (the circuit box will have only two fuses) or 60-amp service (four fuses). With so few circuits, the number of fixtures and appliances you can run will be limited.

Limited service
This 60-amp service panel has four 15-amp fuses and a switch lever for shutting off all power. If you have this or a 30-amp (two-fuse) box, it's a good idea to have a professional upgrade you to a 100-amp service panel with breakers.

Knob-and-tube wiring
This type of wiring was common in houses built before World War II. The individual wires are wrapped in a rubberized cloth and have no additional protection. There is no ground wire. These wires should be replaced with modern cable, particularly in areas where they are exposed, such as attics and basements.

Sources of shorts and faults
Loose taped wires, old wire damaged because it's exposed, and multiple wires slipping off a single terminal screw may seem like minor problems, but are not. Drastic consequences, such as fire and electrocution, are the reasons codes are strict about good wiring practices. See pages 45–47 for the correct way to connect wires.

Ungrounded, unpolarized circuits
If your outlets have two slots that are the same size, then they are neither polarized nor grounded (see page 26). This leaves you with no protection against shocks from defective fixtures or appliances using that outlet. At the very least you need to install polarized outlets.

HOUSEHOLD CIRCUITS

The electrical service in your house is divided into branch circuits, each of which supplies power to a defined area of your home. It is important to make sure that no branch circuit is carrying too great a load, or you will be constantly resetting breakers or replacing fuses. Some appliances need to have a circuit for themselves. An electric stove or dryer will have its own 240-volt circuit; other heavy-use appliances may require their own 120-volt circuits. More often a circuit supplies a number of outlets using a range of power.

To find out if a circuit is overloaded, add up the total power drawn by the circuit as outlined below. Check the breaker or fuse to see how many amps the circuit can deliver. If your total use exceeds the amperage the circuit can supply, change your usage. The solution may be as simple as plugging an appliance into a different receptacle—or you may have to add another circuit to your electrical system (see pages 68–71).

Typical circuit plan

A well-planned electrical system will have branch circuits that serve easily defined areas or purposes. Unfortunately, many homes— especially if they have been remodeled by do-it-yourselfers— have circuits that roam all over the house. Note that some appliances, such as the microwave oven, dishwasher, and disposal, need their own circuits. The electric stove needs its own 240-volt circuit. Otherwise, circuits are roughly organized by the rooms they serve and by their anticipated demand.

MEASUREMENTS

To figure your circuit loads, total the watts being used. Check the specification label on each appliance. Also note the wattage of the lightbulbs in fixtures on the circuit. Divide the total by 120 (the number of volts). The resulting number will tell you how many amperes ("amps") the circuit draws when all appliances and lights are on and whether or not you are placing too great a demand on it. Here are some typical watt and amperage figures for common household appliances.

refrigerator: 500 watts/ 4.2 amps

toaster: 1,050 watts/ 8.75 amps

gas dryer: 720 watts/ 6 amps

microwave oven: 800 watts/ 6.7 amps

washer: 600 watts/ 5 amps

7,500-BTU air-conditioner: 1,000 watts/ 8.3 amps

circular saw: 1,200 watts/ 10 amps

Mapping Your Circuits

When you look inside the door of your service panel, do you see a detailed description of what each branch circuit controls? If not, make a chart yourself. You'll be glad you mapped the circuits the next time you have to turn off a circuit for repairs or improvements.

Begin by making a map of each floor in the house. Take care to include all receptacles, switches, appliances, and fixtures. Be aware that 240-volt receptacles will have their own circuits. With a large house, you may have to make more than one drawing per floor.

Mapping is best done with a helper to flip switches and test outlets while you stay at the box and write down findings. If you must work alone, plug in a radio turned to peak volume to find the general area covered by the circuit. The radio will go silent when you switch off the current. Test outlets to find the extent of the circuit.

1. Test each outlet.
Mark each circuit breaker or fuse with a number. Turn on all the appliances and lights on one floor. Plug a lamp into every receptacle and turn on. Turn off one circuit and have your helper write the circuit number next to each outlet that went dead.

2. Make a record.
Continue the test with every circuit for every floor. Transfer the findings onto a sheet of paper you will affix to the inside of the circuit box door.

The NEC

Electrical codes are based on the National Electrical Code (NEC), which is published by a non-profit organization and is upgraded periodically. The NEC takes up a huge book that covers every conceivable electrical situation. It provides the model on which virtually all local codes are based.

Some communities simply adopt the code as their own; others modify it. Any time you want to make a change in your electrical service, check the NEC and local codes before you begin.

LOAD WORKSHEET		
circuit #5		
voltage 120		
circuit breaker amperage 20		
(20x.80=16 amps)		
CUSTOMER WATTS ÷ VOLTAGE	=	AMPERAGE
coffee pot 650 ÷ 120	=	5.42
fluorescent work lites		
ballast amperage	=	.66
toaster 1050 ÷ 120	=	8.75
total exist. load		14.80
new exhaust fan		
100 ÷ 120	=	.83
new total load		15.63

3. Make a circuit load sheet.
To really get a fix on how your house uses electricity, combine the information you have just gathered with the power-use information printed on appliances. Write up a load sheet, as shown. It will help you assess capacity for future additions to your electrical system.

Caution!

Handle Your Service Panel with Respect
Take special care when working around a service panel. Remove cover plates only when you absolutely have to and replace them as soon as you can. Keep the door shut whenever you are not inspecting the panel. Lock it, if you think your kids may get at it. Remember that even if you have shut off the main power breaker or switch, there is still power entering the box.

ESSENTIAL TOOLS

You don't need to purchase an arsenal of specialized tools to do the electrical projects in this book. For most repairs, a minor outlay will be enough to equip you adequately.

Needle-nose and **lineman's pliers** are musts. You need the first to bend wires into the loops required for many electrical connections. Lineman's pliers make it possible to neatly twist wires together. Both also are used

to cut wires. **Side-cutting pliers** make it easy to snip wires in tight places and are ideal for cutting sheathing off cable.

To strip wires use an **adjustable wire stripper** or a **combination tool** (which also crimps and cuts wire). If you're working with nonmetallic cable, use a **cable ripper** to remove the sheathing easily without nicking the wires. A simple **neon tester** will tell you if an outlet or fixture is live. A

beaded chain simplifies fishing thin, low-voltage wires or phone wires through walls.

General carpentry tools that come in handy when doing electrical work include an **electric drill** with a **spade bit** to make holes for cable to pass through; a **utility knife, screwdrivers,** a **keyhole saw** for cutting drywall, a **level,** a **hacksaw** for cutting conduit and metal-sheathed cable, and a **tape measure.**

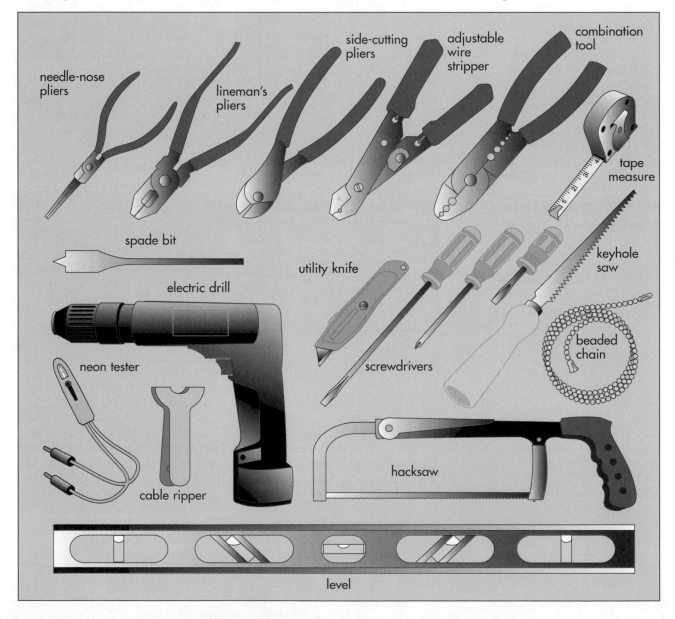

SPECIALIZED TOOLS

As you take on more complicated electrical projects, you will find that other tools are invaluable. Some of these tools are essential to such projects; others simply help you do a better, faster job.

If you need to drill holes deeper than the length of your spade bit, get a **bit extension.** A **soldering gun** with a spool of **lead-free, rosin-core solder** will be necessary if local codes require soldering.

Always use a **fuse puller** to remove a cartridge-type fuse; don't pull it by hand. A **BX cutter** (this tool can be rented) makes easy and safe work of cutting metal-sheathed cable. A **tubing cutter** quickly makes clean cuts in conduit. When working with conduit, use a **conduit bender** to shape the material without crimping it and **tongue-and-groove pliers** for tightening connectors. For running cable through finished walls and ceilings or wire through conduit, a **fish tape** makes the job easier.

A **continuity tester** has a small bulb and battery for testing fuses, switches, and sockets with the power off. A **voltmeter** works with the power on or off and indicates the amount of voltage at an outlet. A **receptacle analyzer** runs a number of tests, telling you if your receptacle has a good connection and if it is properly grounded and polarized.

tongue-and-groove pliers

soldering gun

fuse puller

lead-free, rosin-core solder

voltmeter

bit extension

BX cutter

receptacle analyzer

tubing cutter

fish tape

conduit bender

continuity tester

CHOOSING SWITCHES

Manufacturers offer a sometimes bewildering array of switches. To begin with you have a choice of colors—brown, ivory, and white are the most readily available. But the differences extend far beyond appearance.

For most of your needs you'll probably choose a **single-pole toggle,** which is available for a low price. "Toggle" simply refers to a switch that flips up and down.

Three-way and **four-way** switches are needed if you want to control a light from two or more separate switches. To learn about wiring them, see pages 102–106.

If you want to add a switch without putting in a larger box, a **double** switch may be the solution. It takes up the same amount of space as a single switch.

A **rocker** switch functions the same way as a standard toggle switch but is slightly easier to use.

A **dimmer** switch allows you to adjust lighting levels to suit your needs. A sliding dimmer brightens the light as you slide it upward. The rotary type comes in two versions. One version turns lights on or off with a push; the light level is altered by turning the knob. The other type dims the light as the knob is rotated counterclockwise until it turns off.

EXPERTS' INSIGHT

LOOK FOR THE UL SYMBOL

The UL symbol means that electrical materials have been checked for any defects by Underwriters Laboratories, an independent testing organization. Local codes may prohibit using items not UL-listed.

single-pole toggle   three-way   four-way

double   rocker

sliding dimmer   rotary dimmer

SELECTING SPECIALTY SWITCHES

O f the many available switches built to suit special needs, the ones on this page are some of the most common. Take a trip to a home center or a lighting store and you may find the switch that does exactly what you want. To find out how to install these switches, see page 94.

If you have power tools or other devices that you don't want children to play with, consider installing a **tamperproof** switch. It can be operated only with a key and wired to control the receptacle to which such items are connected.

For security in your backyard, or to have a light automatically greet you as you approach your house, choose a **motion-sensor security** switch. Its wide-angle infrared beam detects motion and turns a light on automatically. With most units, you can choose how long the light will stay on.

A **pilot-light** switch has a little bulb that glows when power is flowing through the switch. Use it when a fixture or appliance is out of sight. Closet lights, attic exhaust fans, basement lights, and garage lights often are controlled by pilot-light switches.

If you need to squeeze both a switch and an outlet into a single box, use a **switch/receptacle.** Also use this switch to easily add a receptacle to a room. This switch can be wired so the receptacle is live all the time or wired so the switch controls the receptacle.

A **programmable** switch comes with digital controls and can be programmed to turn lights on and off up to four times a day. This type of switch is useful for security and deterring burglars when you are away from home.

A **time-delay** switch has a dial that can be set to leave a fixture running for up to 60 minutes. Use one for a vent fan, space heater, heat lamp, or garage light.

tamperproof

motion-sensor security

pilot-light

switch/ receptacle

programmable

time-delay

CHOOSING RECEPTACLES

A standard duplex receptacle has two outlets for receiving plugs. Each outlet has a long (neutral) slot, a shorter (hot) slot, and a half-round grounding hole. This ensures that the plug will be polarized and grounded (see page 26). Receptacles are rated for maximum amps. A **20-amp grounded receptacle** has a T-shaped neutral slot; use it only on 20-amp circuits. For most purposes, a **15-amp grounded receptacle** is sufficient. When replacing a receptacle in an ungrounded outlet box, use a **15-amp ungrounded receptacle**, intended only for use in older homes without ground wires in the circuits. Use a three-pronged plug adapter on an ungrounded receptacle only if the wall-plate screw is grounded (see page 59 to test this). The switch in a combination **switch/receptacle** can be hooked up to control the receptacle it's paired with.

A **20-amp single grounded receptacle** makes it nearly impossible to overload a critical circuit. For outdoors, in basements, or within 6 feet of a water fixture, install **ground-fault circuit-interrupter (GFCI)** receptacles (see pages 98–99). Select a **240-volt receptacle** based on the appliance amperage rating. Plugs required for appliances of 15, 20, 30, and 50 amps will have different prong configurations.

> ## CAUTION!
> **REPLACE, DON'T CHANGE**
> *Replace a receptacle with one that is just like the old one. Change types only if you are certain that the wiring is suitable. Do not replace an ungrounded outlet with a grounded one unless you know the box is grounded.*

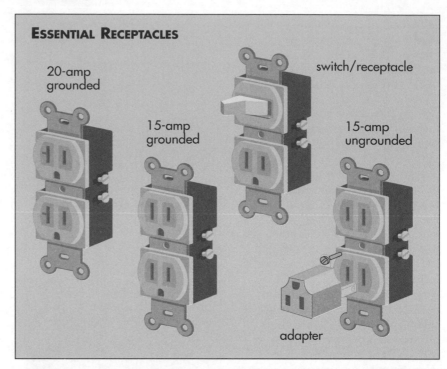

ESSENTIAL RECEPTACLES

20-amp grounded

15-amp grounded

switch/receptacle

15-amp ungrounded

adapter

SPECIALIZED RECEPTACLES

20-amp single grounded

50-amp 120/240-volt wall-mounted

GFCI receptacle

30-amp 120/240-volt floor-mounted

CHOOSING WIRE AND CABLE

Wire, cord, and cable (generically referred to as "conductors") are the pathways along which electricity travels. Wire is a solid strand of metal encased in insulation. Cord is a group of small strands encased in insulation. Cable is made of two or more wires wrapped in protective sheathing of metal or plastic.

Most local codes allow you to use nonmetallic sheathed cable (NM cable) inside walls, floors, and other places where it can't be damaged and won't get wet. Information printed on the sheathing tells you what is inside. The top example at right has two 14-gauge wires plus a bare ground wire, and is thus referred to as "14-2 G" cable ("G" for ground). Cable marked "14-3 G" has three wires plus a ground wire. Flexible armored cable (BX) contains wires wrapped in a flexible metal sheathing. It can be used for short runs in exposed areas such as attics or basements. BX needs no separate ground wire because the metal sheathing itself conducts the ground. Underground feed (UF) cable is watertight with the sheathing molded around the wire. Many municipalities permit this for underground lines.

Different gauge wires carry different amounts of electricity— 14-gauge carries a maximum of 15 amps, 12-gauge carries up to 20 amps, and 10-gauge wire up to 30 amps. Doorbells and other low-voltage circuits typically use 18-gauge wire. Unsheathed wires are pulled through flexible or rigid conduit. Flexible metal conduit, or Greenfield, looks like armored cable but doesn't contain wires. It is cut to length, wires are pulled through it, and the completed pieces installed (see pages 80–81). With conduit, you pull wires through it after it's installed (see pages 82–85).

Cable seen on end in clamp.

2-wire NM cable
14-2 G

3-wire NM cable
14-3 G

BX cable

Bushing protects wires from metal sheathing.

3-wire BX cable

UF cable
UF TYPE

10-gauge wire

12-gauge wire

14-gauge wire

18-gauge wire

WHAT THE COLORS MEAN

Color	Function
white	neutral, carrying power back to the service panel
black	hot, carrying power from the service panel
red and other colors	also hot, color-coded to help identify which circuit they are on
white with black tape	a white wire that is being used as a hot wire
bare or green	a ground wire

CHOOSING BOXES

An electrical box has one primary function—to house electrical connections. Those connections might be to a switch, a receptacle, the leads of a light fixture, or other sets of wires.

Electrical codes require that all wire connections or cable splices be inside an approved metal or plastic box. You cannot bury a box inside a wall; they all must be accessible. This protects your home from the danger of fire and makes it easier to inspect and upgrade your wiring in the future.

Codes govern how many connections you're allowed to make within a box, depending on its size. If you must make more connections, you have to use a larger box (see chart at right).

There are boxes to suit most any depth of wall or ceiling, boxes to support heavy fixtures such as ceiling fans, and boxes for remodeling work and new construction. If, for instance, you'll be pulling cables through a finished wall, you can choose from a number of retrofit boxes that can be mounted with a minimum of damage to the wall.

Boxes for switches and receptacles serve as the workhorses in any electrical installation. Some of the metal ones can be "ganged" into double, triple, or larger multiples by removing one side and linking them together. Switch/receptacle boxes made of plastic are accepted by most codes, but they can't be ganged. If you are using conduit, Greenfield, or BX, you must use metal boxes to ground the system.

Utility boxes are surface-mounted in basements and garages to hold switches or receptacles. Boxes for fixtures or junctions may support lighting fixtures or split circuits into separate branches.

MEASUREMENTS
CHOOSING THE CORRECT BOX SIZE

Type of Box	Size in Inches (Height × Width × Depth)	Maximum Number of Wires Allowed in a Box		
		14-gauge	12-gauge	10-gauge
switch/ receptacle	3×2×1½	3	3	3
	3×2×2	5	4	4
	3×2×2¼	5	4	4
	3×2×2½	6	5	5
	3×2×2¾	7	6	5
	3×2×3½	9	8	7
utility	4×2⅛×1½	5	4	4
	4×2⅛×1⅞	6	5	5
	4×2⅛×2⅛	7	6	5
fixture/ junction	4×1¼ round or octagonal	6	5	5
	4×1½ round or octagonal	7	6	6
	4×2⅛ round or octagonal	10	9	8
	4×1¼ square	9	8	7
	4×1½ square	10	9	8
	4×2⅛ square	15	13	12
	4¹¹⁄₁₆×1½ square	14	13	11
	4¹¹⁄₁₆×2⅛ square	21	18	16

EXPERTS' INSIGHT

BOX CAPACITY

Overcrowd a box and you risk damaging wire connectors, piercing insulation, and cracking a switch or receptacle, any of which could cause a short. That is why codes spell out how many wires you can install in a box.

The chart above gives standard requirements. Other items may add to the total number of wires a box can hold. As you count wires, keep in mind these rules:

■ Don't count fixture leads (the wires that are connected to the fixture).

■ Count a wire that enters and leaves without a splice as one.

■ Count each cable clamp, stud, or hickey inside the box as one wire.

■ Count each receptacle or switch as one.

■ Count grounding wires entering a box as one, but do not count grounding wires that begin and end in the box.

NEW INSTALLATION SWITCH/RECEPTACLE BOXES

These boxes are designed for quick installation when the framing is exposed. They all have built-in gauges to make it easy for you to install them flush with the surface of the finished wall.

4×4 box with nailing spurs.

Metal box with nailing bracket. Side removes so additional box can be added on.

2×4 box with front-nailing bracket.

Side "W" bracket holds box away from the stud.

2×4 plastic box with front nailing bracket.

2×4 plastic box with 16d nails.

4×4 plastic box with nails angled for easy fastening.

RETROFIT SWITCH/RECEPTACLE BOXES

When installing new electrical service where the walls are finished, use boxes designed to minimize damage to the wall. If the special clips do not work, you may be able to attach the boxes to framing pieces with screws driven through holes inside the boxes.

Metal "wings" slip behind wall; flaps fold over the box.

Tightening the screw pulls the pointed flanges forward.

Screw-in clamps move forward to hold box in place.

2×4 plastic box with plastic "ears" that swing out and forward as screws are tightened.

4×4 plastic box with plastic "ears."

NEW INSTALLATION FIXTURE/JUNCTION BOXES

"New installation" wiring refers to work done on a freshly framed wall. With no drywall or plaster in the way, it is easy to install ceiling fixture boxes that are solid enough to hold a heavy chandelier or a fan. Remember that all junction boxes must remain accessible—never cover them with drywall.

Telescoping brackets allow you to position these boxes anywhere between joists.

Metal octagonal box requires framing behind it if it is to support a heavy fixture.

Round plastic fixture box has a bracket with sharp points so you can quickly tap it in place, then secure it with screws.

Octagonal junction box with side bracket is nailed to framing.

RETROFIT FIXTURE/JUNCTION BOXES

The retrofitting of adding new wiring to old walls is challenging. Often it's not easy to secure a fixture box when there's drywall or plaster in the way. For heavy ceiling fixtures, use a brace bar that can be slipped into the hole and expanded from joist to joist (see page 103).

A shallow box like this is sometimes needed in older homes with plaster walls.

"Wings" come forward as you tighten their screws, clasping the box to the plaster or drywall.

Most retrofitting starts with standard junction boxes located in accessible areas.

EXPERTS' INSIGHT

USE NEW INSTALLATION BOXES IN UNFINISHED SPACES

Most homes have areas where the walls or ceilings are unfinished, such as basements, attics, and garages. Whenever you are adding improvements to these areas, or adding junction boxes that will serve existing circuits, use new installation boxes. Because the boxes may get bumped, use metal boxes with metal cover plates even if you are using nonmetallic sheathed cable.

SPECIALIZED BOXES

Wiring can be full of surprises. If you run into an unusual situation, chances are there is a specialized box that can help. Here are just a few of the many boxes designed to cope with tight spaces, new framing materials, and changes in wall-surface depth.

Weatherproof die-cast aluminum box can be surface-mounted for outdoor fixtures.

Metal studs are increasingly popular for house construction. Box mounts on either side of a metal stud.

Box mounts on the flat side of a metal stud.

depth-adjustment screw

A screw on the wall clip lets you adjust the depth of box to cope with the addition of tile or paneling.

1 1/4-inch-thick box fits shallow wall cavities.

Ceiling box slips onto a joist and is strong enough to support a ceiling fan.

BOX ACCESSORIES

Box accessories are myriad. Some, such as "mudrings," should be installed before the wall surface is applied. Others cap off boxes for special needs.

Extender ring brings a fixture box out 1/2 inch—especially useful when drywall is added over plaster.

Weatherproof cover plate for an exterior GFCI receptacle.

Knockout filler plugs a knockout hole that is not being used.

Blank plate, one- and two-device "mudrings" for placing receptacles in large boxes.

Blank plate covers an round (shown) or octagonal junction box.

Weathertight housings for an outdoor box: blank, 1-fixture, 2-fixture.

Box extender slides inside the box.

INSTALLING BOXES IN UNFINISHED SPACE

To wire a room with unfinished walls, such as a basement remodeling or a room addition, you'll need boxes fastened to the framing. When attaching the boxes, be sure they protrude from the framing the same thickness as your drywall or paneling—usually ½ inch. Run cable from box to box and to the service panel.

After you've roughed in the wiring, but before you install the switches and receptacles, put up the drywall on the walls and ceiling. Finish and prime the surfaces, and install the devices in the boxes.

YOU'LL NEED...

TIME: About 3 hours for installing 10 boxes.

SKILLS: Basic carpentry skills.

TOOLS: Tape measure, hammer or drill with screwdriver bit.

Nonmetallic handy box
Many boxes have a series of gauging notches on their sides. Determine the thickness of the drywall and/or paneling you will be installing, and align the box to the appropriate notch as you attach it. A nail-up box like this one is the easiest to install.

Gangable boxes
These have detachable sides, so you can attach them together to form double- or triple-size boxes. To attach such boxes without special mounting hardware, simply drive screws or nails through the holes and into the framing.

MEASUREMENTS

PLACING BOXES

In a typical room, place switch boxes 48–50 inches above the floor and receptacles 12–16 inches above floor level. Check with local codes to see how many receptacles you will need. In most cases they must be placed so that no point along any wall is more than 6 feet from a receptacle. This means that you'll have to install at least one receptacle every 12 feet along the wall. For kitchens and bathrooms, special requirements apply.

L-bracket box
Some L-bracket boxes adjust to suit the thickness of your wall material. Others accommodate only one thickness. Hold the box in position against the framing, and drive two nails or screws through the holes in the bracket.

Utility box
Use a utility box and conduit or armored cable in an area where you don't need a finished appearance. If you're attaching boxes to masonry, use anchors or masonry screws.

Fixture and junction boxes are easy to install in unfinished space. Install boxes so they will be flush with the finished surface of the ceiling or wall. Do not place any electrical box where it will be covered by drywall or paneling.

If there is a joist at the spot where you want the box, use a box with a **hanger bracket** or an **L-bracket.** This page shows various types available—some designed for installing from below, some for installing from above. These fasten to the joist with screws or nails. When attaching, allow for the thickness of the ceiling material.

If you need to install a fixture box between joists, use a box with a **bar hanger.** Attach the ends of the brackets to the joists, and slide the box into the desired position.

Junction boxes protect wire connections or cable splices. Some junction boxes come with brackets. Others just nail or screw to a joist, stud, or rafter.

Regardless of the type of box you're installing, always secure it with two fasteners. If the box will be supporting a ceiling fan or other heavy fixture, make sure it's anchored securely enough to carry the weight. If a box has been correctly mounted but still doesn't feel firm enough, add a framing piece and secure it to that as well.

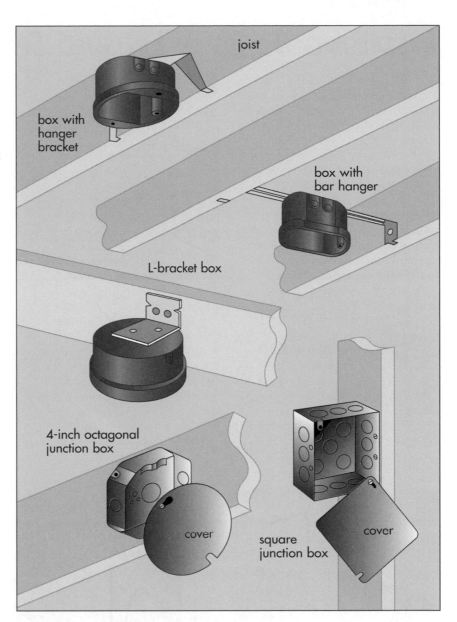

joist

box with hanger bracket

box with bar hanger

L-bracket box

4-inch octagonal junction box

cover

square junction box

cover

OVERHEAD LIGHT PLACEMENT

■ One pleasing way to light a room is with recessed can lights (see pages 90–91) or small fixtures. To plan for a group of symmetrically placed lights, make a map of your ceiling and experiment by drawing circles, each of which represents the area lit up by a recessed fixture.

■ When you experiment with your design, try to arrange the lights so they are half as far from the walls as they are from each other. A pleasingly symmetrical pattern usually results. Start by arranging lights 6 feet apart and 3 feet from walls. Position them at least 4 feet apart. Add to your plan any suspended or track lighting you need for task illumination or to accent an attractive area of the room.

■ Don't expect to achieve an arrangement that's perfectly symmetrical; few ceilings will allow for that. Also keep in mind that with recessed lighting, you may not be able to put all the lights exactly where you want them because there will be joists in the way (see page 90). In most cases, a less-than-perfect arrangement will not be noticeable.

INSTALLING BOXES IN FINISHED SPACE

Installing electrical work is a greater challenge when the walls and ceilings are finished. Often patching and painting can take far more time than the electrical work itself! Plan the placement so you avoid making unnecessary holes.

Wherever possible, avoid making contact with the framing. Using special boxes designed for installation in finished space, you often can simply make a hole the size of the box and secure the box to the wall or ceiling surface.

Before you begin, plan how you're going to get cable to the new location (see pages 72–73).

YOU'LL NEED...

TIME: About 30 minutes a box, not including running new wire.
SKILLS: Simple skills are required.
TOOLS: Keyhole saw, screwdriver, needle-nose pliers, utility knife, and neon tester.

1. Determine box location.
Drill a small hole in the wall. Insert a bent wire and rotate it. If you hit something, you've probably found a stud. Try 6 inches to one side. If you strike wood again, you may have hit a fire block. Drill another hole 3 inches higher or lower. Keep trying until you can rotate the bent wire freely.

2. Trace around box.
Some boxes come with a template that can be held against the surface and traced around. Otherwise, use the box itself and center it on the hole you could rotate the wire in. Make sure the template or box is plumb before you mark the outline.

3. Cut the opening.
Carefully cut around the traced outline. If the surface is drywall, use a utility knife. If you are cutting into plaster walls, use a keyhole saw. If the plaster is crumbly, mask the outline with tape. For a wood-surfaced wall, drill a ¼-inch access hole in each corner and use a saber saw. Run cable (see pages 72–75).

4. Fasten with side clamps...
Side-clamp boxes grip the wall from behind when you tighten the screws. Pull 8 inches of cable through the box and insert the box. Hold the box plumb as you tighten the clamps. Alternate from side to side as you work so the box seats evenly. Avoid overtightening the clamps.

wing bracket screw

wing bracket

...or tighten wing bracket screws.
Loosen the screw centered in the receptacle box until the wing bracket is at maximum extension from the back. Hold the wings against the body of the box and push the box into the hole. Tighten the screw until the box is held firmly in place.

box attached to framing

nails

With access from above

A ceiling box must support a fixture, so it must be securely attached to the framing. If you are fortunate enough to have

attic space above, the job can be done without damaging your ceiling. Mark the location of each box on the ceiling, and drive nails as reference points.

Cut the hole for the box. If there is a nearby joist, attach an L-bracket box directly to it. If not, either use a bar hanger or frame in a 2×4 support.

With no access from above

If you cannot work from above, use one of these methods. For light fixtures that weigh less than 5 pounds, use an old-work bracket. Cut the hole the size of the box, slip the bracket in, telescope it to fit between two joists, and attach the box to it.

For heavier fixtures, such as chandeliers and ceiling fans, make an opening in the ceiling and install hanging hardware. With a drywall ceiling, cut out a large rectangle and install a bar hanger. With plaster, chip out a path and use an offset bar hanger.

Repair the ceiling.

After checking the electrical installation, patch the ceiling. With drywall, you may be able to use the same piece you cut out. Nail the panel to the joists, and tape the seam with joint compound. For a plaster ceiling, fill with patching compound.

STRIPPING WIRE

Before making electrical connections, you'll need to remove some of the sheathing that encases the three or four wires of the cable and strip some of the insulation that coats the individual wires. Stripping techniques are simple, but exercise care when removing sheathing in order to avoid damaging any of the underlying insulation. Also be careful to strip the insulation without nicking the copper wire—this would weaken it.

Strip wires before inserting them into the box. That way, if you make a mistake, you can cut off the damaged portion and try again.

YOU'LL NEED...
TIME: About 5 minutes or less.
SKILLS: Simple stripping.
TOOLS: Cable ripper, utility knife, side cutters and combination tool or adjustable wire stripper.

cable ripper

Cut exactly down the middle.

1. Slit the sheathing.
The easiest way to remove plastic sheathing from nonmetallic sheathed cable is to use an inexpensive cable ripper. Slip 6 to 8 inches of cable into the ripper's jaws, squeeze, and pull. This slits open the sheathing without damaging the insulation of internal wires. The same job can be done with a knife, but you must be careful: Run the blade right down the middle so it doesn't strip insulation from the wires.

sheathing

insulated wire

2. Peel back the sheathing.
Pull back the sheathing you have just slit, as well as the paper wrapping or strips of thin plastic, if any. You'll find two or three separately insulated wires, as well as a bare ground wire.

side cutters

3. Cut away the sheathing.
Cut off the sheathing and paper. Remove the slit sheathing with a pair of side cutters. Or use a utility knife, taking care to point the blade away from the wires.

CAUTION!
This job is simple but it must be done with great care or you could end up with dangerous electrical shorts. If you think you may have accidentally damaged some insulation, cut the cable back to a place behind the potentially dangerous spot and start again. Another possible problem: If you cut into the copper wire while stripping the insulation, you can weaken the wire so that it is liable to break while you are making a connection later.

combination tool

adjustable wire stripper

4. Strip the wire.

To strip insulation from wires, use a combination tool, which has separate holes for the different sizes of wires. Locate the wire in the correct hole, clamp down, give it a twist, and pull the tool away from you. With an adjustable stripper, set it for the wire size, twist, then pull the tool away from you. Stripping also can be done with a utility knife, but be careful not to dig into the copper wire.

Place the wire on a scrap piece of wood, hold the blade at a slight angle, and strip the insulation by slicing off thin strips until you reach wire.

JOINING WIRES

lineman's pliers

stranded wire

Joining solid wires

Join solid wires by using a pair of lineman's pliers. Cross the two wires, grab both wires with the pliers, and twist clockwise. Both wires should twist—do not just twist one wire around the other. Twist for several revolutions, but don't twist so tightly that the wires are in danger of breaking. Screw a wire connector onto the two wires (see page 46).

1. Joining stranded to solid wires

Often a stranded wire (made of many thin wires) has to be spliced to a solid wire, as when hooking up a light fixture or dimmer switch. Because the stranded wire is more flexible, the two won't twist together. Wrap the stranded wire around the solid wire.

2. Fold the solid wire over.

Bend the solid wire so it clamps down on the stranded wire. Screw a wire connector onto the two wires (see page 46), and wrap the connection with electrician's tape.

WORKING WITH WIRE

The final—and most gratifying—phase of an electrical installation comes when you tie all those wires together and attach them to the switches, light fixtures, and receptacles. Don't take shortcuts with wire connections and splices. Cap splices with wire connectors rather than only tape, and wrap tape around each connector. Make pigtails (see page 47) wherever they are needed instead of trying to connect two or more wires to a terminal. Finally, don't overcrowd a box with too many wires (for limits, see chart on page 36).

HOW MANY WIRES IN A CONNECTOR?

Wire connector	12-gauge wires	14-gauge wires
red	2–4	2–5
yellow	2–3	2–4
orange	2	2–4

Using wire connectors

To complete a splice of two or more wires, use wire connectors. These come in a variety of sizes. Select the size you need depending on how many wires you will connect as well as the thickness of the wires (see chart, left). Wire connectors firm up the splice and protect bare wires better than tape. First twist the wires firmly together. Do not depend on the connector to do the joining. Twist the wire connector on, turning it by hand until it tightens firmly. As a final precaution, wrap the connector clockwise with electrical tape, overlapping the wires.

1. To connect a wire to a terminal, form a loop.
Strip just enough wire to wrap around the terminal—about ¾ inch. Then form it into a loop using needle-nose or lineman's pliers. It takes practice to make loops that lie flat and are neither too big nor too small.

Loop must go this way.

2. Fasten to the terminal.
Hook the wire clockwise around the terminal so that tightening the screw will close the loop. With receptacles, the black wires go to the brass side, white to silver. Tighten firmly, but avoid overtightening, which can damage the device. If you do crack a device in any way, throw it out.

3. Solder a splice.
A few codes require that splices be soldered. More often, soldering house wiring is prohibited. If you need to solder a splice, start by twisting the wires together. Heat the wires with a soldering iron, then touch lead-free, rosin-core solder to the splice. The solder should melt into the splice.

CONNECTING WIRES

Add a pigtail where two or more wires attach to a terminal...
Never attach more than one wire to a terminal. Codes prohibit it, and it's unsafe because terminal screws are made to hold only one wire. An easier way to join many wires to a terminal is to cut a short piece of wire (about 4 inches), strip both ends, and splice it to the other wires as shown to form a pigtail.

...or make a soldered splice.
Twist wires together so that one extends 1 inch beyond the splice. Solder the twist and loop the extended wire. Tape the soldered splice before screwing the wire to the terminal.

CAUTION!
Make sure local codes permit soldering.

CAUTION!
Most receptacles and switches have connection holes in the back. To make a connection, strip the wire (a stripping gauge often is provided, showing you how much insulation to remove) and poke it into the correct hole. On a receptacle the holes are marked for white and black wires. However most professionals do not use these holes. Wires inserted this way are simply not as secure as those screwed to a terminal.

Grounding receptacles and switches
How you ground devices like receptacles and switches depends on the type of wiring you're using as well as the type of box. With flexible armored cable (BX), Greenfield, or rigid conduit, the metal of the wiring casing and the metal of the box substitutes for the grounding wire. Simply by attaching the device firmly to the box, you have grounded it. Some local codes require that you also attach a short grounding wire, as shown. If you're working with nonmetallic sheathed cable (Romex) and metal boxes, connect short grounding wires to the box and to the device. With nonmetallic boxes, the cable's grounding wire connects directly to the device.

REPLACING PLUGS AND CORDS

Faulty plugs pose the most common shock and fire hazards in the house. Plugs get stepped on, bumped against, and yanked out by their cords. It's a good idea to regularly inspect your plugs, especially if you have some old ones, for loose connections, damaged wire insulation, and prongs that have been bent so often they are in danger of breaking.

Fortunately, it is easy to replace faulty plugs to make your home significantly safer.

YOU'LL NEED...
TIME: About half an hour to replace a plug.
SKILLS: Stripping, tying, and wrapping wire.
TOOLS: Wire stripper, screwdriver, and needle-nose pliers.

round-cord plug

flat-cord plug

30-amp, 240-volt plug

quick-connect plug (see page 62)

standard grounded and polarized plug

zip cord
table lamps, radios

grounded strand (16-3)
light extension cords

20-amp, 120-volt (12-3)
microwave ovens

30-amp, 240-volt (10-3)
window air-conditioners

Types of plugs
Round-cord plugs often accommodate fairly thick wire and are used for moderately heavy appliances such as irons. Flat-cord plugs are suitable for lamps, radios, and other low-amperage devices. Newer lamp and extension cord plugs are polarized, with one blade wider than the other (see page 26).

Standard grounded plugs have a third, round prong for grounding; the two flat prongs are polarized.

Appliances that use 240 volts require heavy-duty three-pronged plugs of various configurations. The one shown here is for a 30-amp, 240-volt dryer.

Types of cords
For flexibility, cord wires are stranded, not solid. Zip cord, so called because the two wires can be easily zipped apart, is for light duty. Use cords with 16-gauge wire for appliances pulling 15 amps or less and 12-gauge wire for 20 amps or less. For 240-volt appliances, use wire that is 10-gauge or thicker.

1. To replace a round-cord plug, strip and insert the cord.
Snip off the old plug. Remove the cardboard cover from the new plug, and slide the snipped-off end of the cord through. Strip off 3 inches of outer insulation and about ½ inch of wire insulation.

½"

3"

Pull both ends tight.

2. Tie Underwriters knot.
This special knot will ensure that tugging the cord won't loosen any electrical connections. Make the knot close to the end of the stripped outer insulation.

clockwise hooks

3. Bend hooks.
Twist the wire strands tight. With a pair of needle-nose pliers, shape clockwise hooks to wrap around the screw shafts.

4. Connect the wires.
Hook the wires on the screw shafts (attach the black wire to the brass-colored screw), and tighten. Tuck in stray strands.

5. Replace the cover.
Check to be sure all wires and strands are neatly inside the plug. Slip on the cardboard cover.

SAFETY

DON'T CHANGE THE PLUG TO FIT THE RECEPTACLE

■ If your appliance or tool has a plug with a third, round prong, then it should only be plugged into 3-hole outlets that are properly grounded. If you remove the grounding prong, or if you use a plug adapter that is not connected to a ground, you will disable a feature designed to protect against electrical shock.

■ Some appliances and tools are "double insulated" and do not need the extra protection of a grounding prong. You can plug them into an ungrounded outlet and still be protected from shock.

cord clamp

1. To repair a 240-volt plug, slide the plug onto the cord.
A 240-volt plug has a steel clamp that grips the cord, so you don't have to tie an Underwriters knot. Slide the plug onto the cord and strip about ½ inch of insulation from the ends of the three wires. Twist the strands tight, and use needle-nose pliers to form hooks.

2. Attach the wires.
Attach the black and red wires to brass-colored terminals, and the green one to the silver-colored terminal. Tuck in any loose strands as you tighten the terminal screws. Tuck all the wires in place, tighten the cord clamp, and slip on the cardboard cover.

WIRING QUICK-CONNECT, FLAT-CORD PLUGS

Keep a few quick-connect plugs on hand and you'll never again be tempted to put off replacing a faulty or questionable plug. Installing one is only slightly more difficult and time-consuming than changing a lightbulb.

Replacing a standard flat-cord plug is more like doing actual electrical work, but it takes only a little more time.

YOU'LL NEED...

TIME: About 5 minutes to install a quick-connect; 15 minutes for a flat-cord plug.

SKILLS: No skill at all for the quick-connect plug; stripping wire and connecting to a screw for the flat-cord plug.

TOOLS: Knife or scissors for the quick-connect; wire strippers and screwdriver for the flat-cord.

1. To wire a quick-connect plug, open the lever.
Snip off the old plug. Lift the lever on top of the new plug and insert the zip cord into the hole.

2. Close the lever.
Closing the lever pierces and holds the wire. Push the lever firmly down and you're done.

½ inch

1. To replace a flat-cord plug, slip on a shell and twist the wires.
Snip the old plug off. Slip the new shell onto the cord. Peel apart the wires, and strip away about ½ inch of insulation. Twist the strands tight with your fingers and use needle-nose pliers to form hooks that will wrap most of the way around each screw.

2. Connect the wires.
Wrap the wires clockwise around the screw threads, and tighten the screws to secure the connection. Tuck in any loose strands.

shell

core

3. Snap the shell on.
Grasp the shell of the plug and push the core toward it until it snaps into place. Put your appliance back into service.

REPLACING LAMP SOCKETS

Most standing lamps consist of a body, a base where the cord enters, a harp to support the shade, and a socket that receives the cord at one end and the lightbulb at the other. The cord usually runs through a hollow threaded rod from the base to the socket.

When a lamp won't work and you know the bulb and plug are OK, check the cord for damage. If the insulation is worn and cracked, replace the entire cord (see page 52). If the cord is OK, the problem is most likely in the socket.

Most lamps have felt bases that must be removed before repairing the lamps. Remove the felt by paring it off with a utility knife. After the repair, reapply the felt with white glue.

YOU'LL NEED...

TIME: About an hour to replace a lamp socket.
SKILLS: Stripping wire, connecting wire to screws.
TOOLS: Utility knife, wire strippers, screwdriver, needle-nose pliers.

1. Disassemble the socket.
Unplug the cord and remove the harp, if it is in the way. Examine the socket shell and find the word "press." Push hard here and the unit will pull apart into the components shown. Remove the cord from the socket.

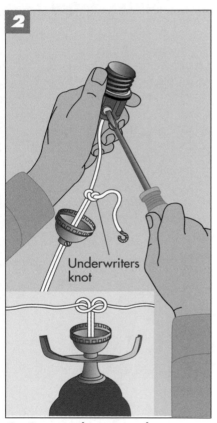

2. Connect the new socket.
Slip the new socket base onto the cord and tie an Underwriters knot (see page 49). Strip about ½ inch of insulation from the wires, twist the strands tight, and form them into hooks with a pair of needle-nose pliers. Wrap the wires clockwise around the shafts of the screws and tighten the screws. Reassemble the cardboard insulation and the outer shell. Attach the new socket to the lamp.

REWIRING LAMPS

Like plugs, lamp cords get stepped on and yanked. And if a lamp has a tendency to heat up, the cord's insulation can become cracked near the socket. Replace any cord with damaged insulation; it is dangerous.

Replacing a cord is not difficult. In fact, you may want to do it simply in order to have a cord that makes a lamp more attractive.

YOU'LL NEED...

TIME: About 45 minutes.
SKILLS: Stripping wire and connecting wire to screws.
TOOLS: Wire strippers, needle-nose pliers, and screwdriver.

CAUTION!
UNPLUG IT FIRST!
Never work on a lamp or appliance while it is plugged in. Always unplug it first.

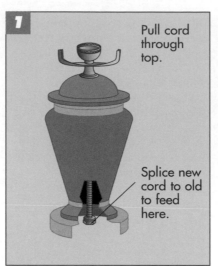

Pull cord through top.

Splice new cord to old to feed here.

1. Feed the new cord through.
Disconnect the old cord from the lamp socket, and snip off the plug. Tie the new cord to the old one with a piece of string or some tape. The trick is to make the connection thin enough so it slides through the center rod. Pull the new cord through as you withdraw the old one.

2½ inches

2. Secure the cord.
Snip off the old cord and discard it. Tie an Underwriters knot, as shown, leaving about 2½ inches of each wire to work with. Strip ½ inch of insulation from the end of each wire.

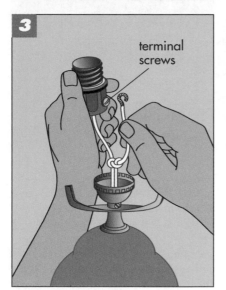

terminal screws

3. Attach the wires.
Twist the strands tight with your fingers. Use needle-nose pliers to form hooks and wrap them around the terminal screws. Tuck any loose strands in as you tighten the terminal screws.

harp

4. Reassemble the lamp.
Reassemble the socket and install the harp as shown. Attach a new plug (see pages 48–50). You're ready to put in a bulb, attach the shade, and plug in your lamp.

CAUTION!
REPLACE DAMAGED LAMP CORD—DON'T TAPE IT
■ It may not look dangerous, but nicked and cracked lamp wire insulation is the cause of many fires. Also you or your children could receive painful shocks if you touch a bare spot.
■ If you see a damaged spot and need to keep using the lamp, wrap electrician's tape around the damaged area. But be aware that this is a temporary solution. The tape can easily come unwrapped. And if one part of the cord is damaged, chances are other parts are as well. Replace the cord as soon as possible.

CHECKING INCANDESCENT FIXTURES

Though they vary widely in style, most incandescent fixtures have the same arrangement of components (see illustration, below right).

Mounting screws hold a canopy plate against the ceiling. The canopy has one or more sockets for bulbs. A translucent diffuser or globe cuts down on the glare of bare lightbulbs. In newer fixtures, a ring of fiber insulation provides added protection from heat damage to the wires and ceiling.

If a fixture shorts out, causing a circuit to blow and/or creating sparks, the problem is probably in the fixture. If it simply refuses to light, the wall switch may be faulty (see pages 56–57).

YOU'LL NEED...

TIME: To inspect a typical fixture, about ½ hour.
SKILLS: No special skills needed.
TOOLS: Screwdriver and steel wool.

CAUTION!

USE THE RIGHT BULBS
A label on the fixture will tell you the maximum bulb wattage allowed. Don't install higher-wattage bulbs or your fixture will overheat, burn up bulbs quickly, and become dangerous.

1. Inspect the socket.
Shut off the circuit that supplies power to the fixture. Inspect the socket. If it is cracked, or if its wires are scorched or melted, replace it or the entire fixture. If it's OK, remove the bulb and check the contact at the socket's base. If there's corrosion, scrape the contact with a flat screwdriver or steel wool, and pry up on it. Turn on circuit and retry.

2. Check the wiring.
If the problem remains, shut off the circuit again, loosen or remove the mounting screws, and drop the fixture from its outlet box. Check for loose connections and for nicked insulation. If you see drywall paper that is slightly

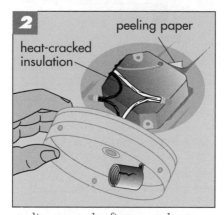

peeling near the fixture or heat-cracked wire insulation, your fixture is overheating. This means either that it is faulty or you need to reduce the wattage of the bulbs. Wrap any bare wires with electrical tape.

SAFETY

KEEP THE FIBER INSULATION
Although it makes installation a bit more difficult, don't remove the fiber insulation in the canopy plate. It provides extra protection against shorts.

TROUBLESHOOTING FLUORESCENT FIXTURES

The heart of a fluorescent fixture is its ballast, an electrical transformer that steps up voltage and sends it to a pair of lamp holders. The current passes through the lamp holders and excites a gas inside the fluorescent tube, causing its phosphorus-coated inner surface to glow with cool, diffused light.

Because they produce far less heat, fluorescent tubes last much longer than incandescent bulbs and consume considerably less electrical energy. However, problems with the fixtures sometimes arise. The ballasts burn out after years of steady use, and the lamp holders are easily cracked if they get bumped.

Older units have starters that must be replaced periodically.

YOU'LL NEED...
TIME: To inspect a fixture and replace a ballast (for example), about an hour.
SKILLS: No special skills needed.
TOOLS: Screwdriver.

lamp holder

tube

ballast

1. Wiggle the tube.
Fluorescent tubes rarely burn out abruptly; they flicker or dim. If a tube suddenly stops lighting, try wiggling and rotating its ends to make sure it's properly seated.

CAUTION!
Never get rid of burned out tubes by breaking them. They contain mercury. Dispose of them whole or request disposal guidelines.

normal graying

Black discoloration indicates a failing tube.

2. Replace a worn-out tube.
A working tube usually has a grayish tinge near its ends. If the tube is uniformly dim, it may simply need washing. To wash a tube, remove it from the fixture, wipe it with a damp cloth, and then replace the tube. If the tube ends turn dark gray or black, the tube is failing and needs to be replaced. Purchase a tube that is the same length and wattage as the old one.

Insert starter and turn clockwise.

3. Replace the starter.
Older, delayed-start fluorescent lights flicker momentarily as they light up. If the flickering continues for more than a few seconds, make sure the starter is seated properly. Push it in and turn clockwise. When the ends of a tube light up but its center does not, the starter is defective. Press in and turn counterclockwise to remove it. Insert a new starter and turn clockwise.

4

push-in release for removing wires

release opening

housing

See wiring diagram for color codes.

Remove screws holding ballast to housing.

4. Replace the ballast.

If the fixture hums or oozes a tarlike goop, the ballast needs replacing. (You may be better off replacing the entire unit. Compare prices.) **NOTE:** *Shut off the power.* To remove the ballast, release the wires at the sockets by pushing a screwdriver into the release openings. Unscrew the ballast and disconnect wires to power source. Reassemble with the new ballast.

5

5. Inspect the box.

If none of these steps locates the problem, you may not have power going into the fixture. Remove the fixture, and look for loose connections and broken or bare wires in the outlet box.

EXPERTS' INSIGHT

TROUBLESHOOTING CHART FOR FLUORESCENT FIXTURES

Symptom	Solution
Tube does not light	1. Rotate the tube to make sure it is properly seated.
	2. Replace any damaged lamp holders.
	3. Replace starter, if there is one.
	4. Check wall switch and outlet box to see that there is power to the fixture.
Tube flickers only lights partially	1. Rotate the tube to make sure it is properly seated.
	2. Replace any tubes that are discolored or have damaged pins.
	3. Replace the starter, if there is one.
Black substance or humming sound	1. Replace the ballast or the entire fixture.

TESTING AND REPLACING SWITCHES

After getting flipped thousands of times, a switch can wear out. Unless the problem is a loose wire connection, there is usually no way to repair a faulty switch; you'll need to replace it.

It is easy to test switches and easy to replace them. If you want to replace your old switch with something more sophisticated—for example, a dimmer—check out the switch options presented on pages 32–33.

YOU'LL NEED...

TIME: About 30 minutes to test and replace a switch.
SKILLS: Using testers (we'll show you how) and connecting wires to screw terminals.
TOOLS: Neon tester, continuity tester, and screwdriver.

CAUTION!

Hold only the metal flanges of the switch when pulling it out of a box. Be very careful not to touch the terminal screws or to allow the screws to touch the edge of the box.

TOOL TIP

SAFE USE OF A CONTINUITY TESTER

Never use a continuity tester on wires that might be live. Always shut off power and disconnect wires before testing. The continuity tester uses a battery that generates a small current to test for the flow of electricity from one point to another. It is not made to carry household current.

Use a neon tester...
NOTE: *Shut off power.* Remove the cover plate and the screws holding the switch. Pull the switch out from the box. Turn the switch to OFF and restore power to the circuit. Touch the probes of a neon tester to the switch's screw terminals. If the tester glows, the box has power. Turn the switch on. Touch the probes to the terminals again. If the tester glows this time, the switch is blown and must be replaced.

Test a three-way switch.
To check out a three-way switch, shut off the circuit and attach the clip to the common terminal (it's usually labeled on the switch body). Touch the probe to one of the other screw terminals and flip the switch. If it's OK, the tester will light when touching one of the two terminals. Flip the switch. The tester should light when the other terminal is touched.

...or use a continuity tester.
An easy way to test a switch is to use a continuity tester. Shut down the circuit leading to the switch and remove the switch from the box. Disconnect all wires. Attach the tester clip to one of the terminals and touch the probe to the other. If the switch is working, the tester will glow when the switch is on and not glow when the switch is off.

Test a switch/receptacle.
To test a device that has both a switch and a receptacle, attach the continuity tester clip to one of the top (switch) terminals and touch the probe to the top terminal on the other side. If the switch is working, the tester will glow when the switch is on, and not glow when it is off.

1. *To replace a switch, remove the old switch.*
NOTE: *Shut off power.* If a switch is damaged, remove the screws holding the switch to the box and gently pull out the device. Loosen the screw terminals and disconnect the wires.

2. *Attach wires to the new switch.*
Inspect the wires in the box and wrap any damaged insulation with electrical tape. Attach the wires to the terminals of the new switch and wrap electrical tape around the body of the switch so the terminals are covered.

3. *Reinstall the switch.*
Carefully tuck the wires and switch back into the box and connect the switch to the box by tightening the mounting screws. Don't force anything; switches crack easily.

Test a fixture-mounted switch.
Small switches that mount on fixtures work by pull chain, flipping up and down, or twisting. These switches are not long-lived, so if the light does not work and the bulb is not blown, there is a good chance that the problem is with the switch. To test, shut off power to the fixture (or unplug it).

Remove the connectors holding the switch's leads. Leave the bare wires twisted together, and arrange them so the connections are not in danger of touching each other or anything else. Restore power to the fixture and carefully touch a neon tester to the connections. If the switch is turned on and the tester lights, the switch is bad.

Replace a fixture-mounted switch.
NOTE: *Shut off power.* Remove the fixture and disconnect the wires. Release the pull-chain switch by loosening the terminal screws and two screws in the base of the socket. Install a replacement switch and remount the fixture.

Other porcelain fixtures have an integrated switch. In such cases, replace the entire fixture. Lamp pull chains cannot be repaired. Buy a new pull-chain socket and replace the old one (see page 51).

TESTING AND REPLACING RECEPTACLES

Receptacles can be damaged in ways that are not readily apparent. Small cracks can lead to a short. As receptacles grow old, they may hold plugs in place less firmly. The good news is that receptacles are inexpensive and easy to replace. Don't hesitate to replace one for any reason, such as because it is paint-glopped or the wrong color. However, if you want to replace your receptacle with one of a different type—for example, replace an ungrounded receptacle with a grounded one—read pages 26 and 34 first.

YOU'LL NEED...

TIME: About 5 minutes to test and 15 minutes to replace a receptacle.

SKILLS: Using a tester (we'll show you how) and connecting wires to terminals.

TOOLS: Neon tester, receptacle analyzer, and screwdriver.

---

1. To test for a faulty receptacle, see if receptacle is live.

With the power to the circuit on, insert one probe of a neon tester into each slot of the receptacle. Do not touch the metal probes; only touch the insulated wires of the tester. If the tester glows, the receptacle is working. Test both plugs of a duplex receptacle.

2. Test for power to the box.

If the receptacle is not live, check its power source. Shut off power to the outlet at the service panel, remove the cover plate, disconnect the screws holding the receptacle to the box, and pull the receptacle out. Restore power, and touch one probe of the neon tester to a brass screw terminal and the other to a silver-colored terminal. The tester light will glow if power is coming to the receptacle.

1. To replace a receptacle, remove the old receptacle.

NOTE: *Shut off power.* Note which wires are attached to which terminals. If necessary, make notations on pieces of tape and wrap them on the wires. Loosen the terminal screws and disconnect the wires.

2. Wire the new receptacle.

Inspect the wires in the box, and wrap electrical tape around any damaged insulation. Attach the wires to the receptacle, positioning each wire so it hooks clockwise on the terminal screw. Firmly tighten the terminal screws.

3. Wrap with tape and install.

Wrap the body of the receptacle with electrical tape, so that all the terminals are covered. Carefully tuck the wires and the receptacle into the box and connect the receptacle to the box by tightening the mounting screws. Don't force the receptacle into place—it may crack.

Test for grounding and polarization.
Do not turn off the power. Insert one prong of a neon tester into the short (hot) slot and the other into the grounding hole. If the tester glows, the receptacle is grounded and the slots are polarized. If the tester doesn't glow, put one probe in the grounding hole, the other in the long slot. If the tester glows, hot and neutral wires are reversed. If the tester doesn't glow in either place, the device isn't grounded.

Test a two-slot receptacle.
With the power on, insert one probe of a neon tester into the short (hot) slot, and touch the other probe to the cover plate screw (above). The screw head must be clean and paint-free. Or, remove the cover plate and insert one probe in the short slot and touch the other to the metal box (above right). If the neon tester glows, the box is grounded, and you can install a

grounded three-hole receptacle.
If the tester doesn't glow, insert one prong into the long (neutral) slot and touch the other to the cover-plate screw or the box. If the tester glows, the box is grounded, but the receptacle is not correctly polarized; the hot and neutral wires are reversed. If the tester doesn't glow in either position, the box is not grounded. Do not install a three-hole receptacle.

TOOL TIP

USING A RECEPTACLE ANALYZER

With this handy device, you can perform a series of tests almost instantly without having to dismantle anything.

Leave the power on, but unplug all equipment and flip all switches to off on the circuit of the receptacle you will be testing. Plug the analyzer in. A combination of glowing lights will tell you what is happening with your receptacle (far right).

ground not connected

neutral wire not connected

hot wire not connected

hot and ground wires switched

hot and neutral wires switched

receptacle wired correctly

TROUBLESHOOTING THERMOSTATS

A thermostat is a switch that senses temperature and turns your heater or air-conditioner on and off according to the control settings. Most homes have low-voltage units like the one described here. A transformer reduces power from 120 volts to around 24 volts and sends it to the thermostat. Some systems have two transformers: one for heating and one for air-conditioning.

Possible causes of thermostat problems include faulty wiring, a corroded thermostat, and a worn-out transformer.

YOU'LL NEED...

TIME: Most inspections and repairs can be done in an hour.
SKILLS: No special skills needed.
TOOLS: Voltmeter or multitester, continuity tester, screwdriver, artist's brush, and a short piece of wire.

Anatomy of a thermostat

A low-voltage system begins with a transformer that is either mounted to a panel on the furnace or connected to an electrical box. Anywhere from two to six thin wires (depending on how many items are being controlled) lead to the thermostat base where they are connected to terminals. The thermostat body contains the heat-sensing device and the control dial. Because the voltage is so low, it is not necessary to shut off power to the thermostat while working on it—unless you are working on the transformer.

1. Clean the thermostat.
Dust can cause a thermostat to malfunction. Remove the cover plate and brush the inner workings with an artist's brush. Pay special attention to dust and dirt on contacts.

2. Remove the body.
Unscrew the screws that hold the thermostat body to the base, and pull the body away. Check to see that the base is securely fastened to the wall. If it is loose, the thermostat could tilt, which would throw off the settings. Blow on the body to remove more dust, but do not handle the parts inside—they are sensitive.

3. Inspect connections to the base.
Look for loose, corroded, or broken wires coming into the base. If any are damaged, clip them, strip insulation from the ends, and reattach. Tighten all the terminal screws to make sure the connections are secure.

Set multitester to ACV 50.

4. Hot-wire the terminals.
Cut a short piece of wire and strip insulation from both ends. Use it to "jump" between terminals. Touch one end to the "R" terminal and one to "W," and the heater's burner should come on. Touch "Y" and "G," and the fan should come on. If they do not, the thermostat is faulty and should be replaced.

5. Test the transformer.
If the thermostat checks out, test the transformer. Touch one probe of a voltmeter or multitester to each of the low-voltage terminals on the transformer. Set dial to ACV 50. If the meter does not detect current, the transformer is defective and needs to be replaced.

6. Check power to transformer.
Before you go out and buy a new transformer, open up the transformer box and make sure that there is power leading to the transformer. Touch one probe of a neon tester to the hot wires and the other to the box (if grounded) or the neutral wires.

Installing a Programmable Thermostat

A programmable thermostat automatically changes the temperature in your home for sleeping and waking hours. It also can deliver different temperatures when you're away.

There are many options to choose from. Some control heat only and some also control air-conditioning. Some can be completely programmed in one sitting; others require a week-long run-through.

Write down the brand names and model numbers of your old thermostat and heating and air-conditioning units. Take this list when you shop for a thermostat to assure it will be compatible with your system. Here is a guide for installation, but follow the manufacturer's instructions that come with the unit.

Removal and installation
As you remove wires from the old thermostat, label them. Remove the old thermostat. Pull the wires through the new wall plate and mount the plate securely to the wall. Check that it is level. Push any excess wire

back into the wall and hook up the wires according to the manufacturer's instructions.

Attach the body to the cover plate. Set the clock and program the unit according to the manufacturer's instructions. Attach the cover.

ADDING SURGE PROTECTION

Occasionally your electrical service can experience sudden increases in power, known as surges. A surge almost certainly will not harm lights and appliances, but it could damage sensitive electronic equipment, such as a computer.

To protect a few pieces of equipment, purchase a surge protector that simply plugs into an outlet. Or you can replace an existing receptacle with a surge-protecting receptacle.

Install it as you would a normal receptacle, except that you will be connecting wires to wires rather than to screw terminals.

YOU'LL NEED...

TIME: About 15 minutes.
SKILLS: Joining wires.
TOOLS: Screwdriver, wire stripper, and lineman's pliers.

plug-in unit

surge-protecting receptacle

ADDING SURGE ARRESTERS TO CIRCUITS

To protect a circuit against surges, install this device in your service panel. At the service panel, shut off the main circuit breaker, and take off the panel cover. Remove the ½-inch knockout that is nearest to the circuit you want to protect. Insert the surge arrester through the knockout hole, and fix it in place by tightening the nut. Wire as shown, connecting the white wire to the neutral bus bar and the black wire(s) to breakers. Before connecting, cut wires as short as possible for maximum protection.

YOU'LL NEED...

TIME: About an hour.
SKILLS: Understanding of your service panel.
TOOLS: Screwdriver, tongue-and-groove pliers, and wire stripper.

neutral bus bar

neutral wire

2-pole breaker

nut

surge arrester

TROUBLESHOOTING CIRCUIT BREAKERS

*T*hink of a circuit breaker as a heat-sensing switch. As the illustrations at right show, when the toggle is on, current flows through a set of contacts attached to a spring and lever. The contacts are held together by tension in the bimetal strip through which the current flows.

If there is a short or an overload in the circuit, the bimetal strip heats up and bends. As it bends it releases a lever that opens the spring-loaded contact. The contact remains open until the toggle is manually reset by the homeowner.

ANATOMY OF A CIRCUIT BREAKER

toggle
lever
spring
bimetal strip
contacts
normal condition

Spring relaxes.
Contact is broken.
Bimetal strip bends due to heating.
tripped condition

YOU'LL NEED...

TIME: A few seconds to reset a breaker and about 10 minutes per device to inspect for shorts.
SKILLS: No special skills needed.
TOOLS: Screwdriver.

Identify a tripped breaker.

A tripped breaker will identify itself in any of the four ways shown at left. To find out whether the problem has corrected itself, reset the breaker. If the problem persists, the breaker will shut itself off again. Usually the problem is an overload, and you only need to unplug or turn off one of the circuit's big energy users. If the circuit breaker keeps tripping even though it isn't overloaded, suspect a short. A defective plug, cord, or socket may be the problem.

TRIPPED BREAKERS AND HOW TO RESET THEM

ON TRIP 15 OFF

tripped position: center to reset, flip off, then on

tripped position: off to reset, flip to on

ON 15 OFF

tripped position: red flag showing, switch in center to reset, flip off, then on

tripped position: off to reset, press in and release

wire pulled loose

Check connections in boxes.

Short circuits can occur in electrical boxes. Here, a wire has pulled loose from the switch and has shorted out against the box.

frayed insulation

Inspect wiring.

Frayed or nicked insulation will expose wire and could cause a short. Wrap damaged insulation with layers of electrical tape.

Watch for overheated fixtures.

High-wattage bulbs can melt insulation. Never use bulbs with higher wattage ratings than those for which the fixture is rated.

TROUBLESHOOTING FUSES

Fuses serve the same purpose as circuit breakers, but instead of tripping as a breaker does, a fuse contains a strip of metal that melts when too much current in the circuit produces heat. When this happens, you must eliminate the short or overload and replace the blown fuse.

YOU'LL NEED...

TIME: 10 minutes to inspect your fuses.
SKILLS: Using continuity tester.
TOOLS: Fuse puller and continuity tester.

Fuse options
A tamper-proof fuse is an important safety device that makes it impossible to install a fuse with a higher amperage rating than the circuit is designed for. It comes with a threaded adapter that fits permanently into the box. The adapter accepts only a fuse of the proper rating.

When an electric motor on a washing machine or refrigerator starts up, it causes a momentary overload that can blow fuses unnecessarily. A time-delay fuse avoids this problem by not blowing during the surge. Only a sustained overload will blow the fuse.

normal unblown fuse   shorted fuse   overloaded fuse

Understanding blown fuses
By examining a fuse you usually can tell what made it blow—an overload or a short. A short circuit usually explodes the strip, blackening the fuse window. An overload usually melts it, leaving the window clear.

Cartridge fuses
Fuses for 30- to 60-amp circuits typically are the ferrule-contact cartridge type. Knife-blade-contact fuses carry 70 amps or more. Handle both with extreme caution. Touching either with your bare hand could fatally shock you.

Removing cartridge fuses
For safety keep a plastic fuse puller with your spare fuses and use it as shown. Note, too, that the ends of a cartridge fuse get hot, so don't touch them immediately after you've pulled the fuse.

Testing cartridge fuses
To see if a cartridge fuse has blown, check it with a continuity tester. Clamp or hold the clip on one end and touch the probe to the other. The bulb will light if it is not blown.

ADVANCED WIRING

PLANNING PATHS FOR NEW CIRCUITS

Electric cable often does not run in a straight line. Instead, it zigzags from one outlet to another in a circuit. Sharp turns and long trips do not bother electricity. You can snake cable up and down walls, along or across joists, and around obstructions without impeding the flow of electrons.

In the home shown here, two general-purpose 120-volt circuits go from the service panel through the bottom plate of the stud wall and travel around perimeter walls to receptacle outlets. Two others go up into the ceiling for lighting and a 240-volt circuit follows along a floor joist to serve an electric stove receptacle.

Saving money by planning

Even though electricity isn't affected by bends and detours, cable is priced by the foot, and costs for extra feet can add up fast—in labor as well as materials. So to be economical, keep your runs as short and direct as possible.

In new work, that's not too difficult. In this illustration of a well-planned new home, most of the cables travel directly to their destinations. The plan saved money by installing the dryer outlet near the service panel, minimizing the amount of heavier, more costly cable needed for its 240-volt circuit.

The plan also saved the electrician time because there was no need for many bends in the conduit to carry the wire through exposed locations. For example, the cable for the 240-volt receptacle for the electric stove takes as direct a path as possible along the basement sill plate.

Drawing up your plan

In planning an electrical layout, especially if you'll be running more than one circuit, draw a floor plan of your home to scale, then mark the routes cable will travel. See page 40 for an example of circuits planned for one of the more complex areas of a home— the kitchen and family room.

To estimate how much cable you'll need, measure the distances involved, and add 10 percent for bends, unexpected detours, and waste. Be sure to add in another 6 to 8 inches to make connections each time cable enters or leaves a junction or outlet box.

Working in finished spaces

If you plan to fish through finished walls or ceilings, be prepared to use more cable than you would have to if the framing were exposed.

You'll also have some detective work ahead of you. Because cutting holes in walls and patching afterward takes so much time and effort, saving cable is a low priority when wiring in finished space. Search out the path that involves the least damage to your walls and the greatest ease in running the cable.

Your first task is to determine exactly what's in the space through which you want to run cable. If it's an exterior wall, for instance, there will probably be insulation, which makes fishing more difficult.

In addition, many older homes have fire blocking spanning the studs about halfway up the wall. If faced with these barriers, you will have to notch the wall surface at those points. See pages 42–43 and 72–75 for tips on running cable in finished spaces.

switch

outdoor receptacle

240-volt circuit
for electric stove

general-purpose
circuits

service
panel

junction
box

bottom
plate

branch
circuit

240-volt
circuit for
electric
dryer

PLANNING MAJOR CIRCUITS

Adding a new circuit to your home's service panel is an advanced project for which you may want to call in a professional —especially if your service panel is already crowded. Begin by seeing if you can add to an existing circuit. Failing that, make sure the service can be expanded. Look for an amperage rating on the main fuse, main circuit breaker, or disconnect switch. Older 60-amp service can't be easily upgraded; call in an electrician. Newer 100-amp service may have enough reserve to handle a new circuit or two, and 150- or 200-amp service usually has plenty of capacity.

YOU'LL NEED...

TIME: After running the cable to the service panel, 3 hours.
SKILLS: Understanding of electrical principles and general electrical skills.
TOOLS: Voltmeter and basic electrician's tools.

2. Estimate capacity needed.
If you can't add to an existing circuit, check the chart at right for the capacity your new circuit is likely to require. Rooms like living rooms and bedrooms that have about 10 light or receptacle outlets require only 15-amp capacity. Ideally, you should have one general-purpose circuit for every 500 square feet of living space. Some local codes require that lighting and receptacles be on separate general-purpose circuits.

The kitchen is appliance-intensive and needs at least two 20-amp circuits. A bathroom gets by on one 15-amp circuit protected by a ground-fault circuit interrupter. Circuits for the garage, laundry room, and workshop need 15- to 20-amp capacity.

general-purpose: 15-amp circuit

small appliances: 20-amp circuit

heavy-duty: single use, 20- to 50-amp circuit

1. Try adding to a circuit.
Different circuits have different capacities. If your need for extra capacity is modest, a few extra receptacles for a bedroom, for example, see if you can add to a general-purpose or small appliance circuit. (Never add on to a heavy-duty, single-use circuit.) Figure the total circuit load by totaling the demand of the appliances and fixtures (see page 28). Then check the chart at right to see if the demand is within safe capacity. The safe capacity of a circuit, as prescribed by the National Electric Code, is 20 percent less than maximum capacity.

CIRCUIT CAPACITY

Circuit rating	Maximum capacity	Safe capacity
15 amps	1,800 watts	1,440 watts
20 amps	2,400 watts	1,920 watts
25 amps	3,000 watts	2,400 watts
30 amps	3,600 watts	2,880 watts

CIRCUIT NEED SELECTOR

Location	Circuits
living and dining rooms, bedrooms, hallways, finished basements	A 15-amp general-purpose circuit for each 500 square feet. Separate circuits for lights and receptacles may be required by code. For a room air-conditioner, install a small appliance circuit.
kitchen	At least two 20-amp small-appliance circuits and a 15-amp lighting circuit. An electric range needs a 240-volt circuit. A microwave oven may need its own circuit.
bathroom	A 15-amp general-purpose circuit with GFCI protection.
garage	A 15- or 20-amp general-purpose circuit (depending on tools and machinery, if any), with GFCI protection.
laundry	A 20-amp small appliance circuit for the washer and a gas dryer. An electric dryer needs a 240-volt circuit.
workshop	A 20-amp GFCI circuit. For larger shops run two 20-amp circuits or a separate circuit for lighting.
outdoors	One 20-amp GFCI circuit.

3. Check the total service capacity.
Now that you know what additional circuit capacity you'll need, can your service capacity handle it? If you add up the amperage ratings for all the circuit breakers or fuses, plus the circuits you want to add, you may discover that the total equals or even exceeds the amperage rating of your service panel. Does that mean you can't add new circuits?

Not likely. Few if any of the circuits ever work at full amperage capacity. And some of your electrical fixtures and appliances never run at the same time—a furnace blower and an air-conditioner, for example. That's why codes allow you to de-rate your service capacity. De-rating is a standardized reduction used when computing service capacity. The chart shows a de-rating calculation for a 2,000-square-foot

3	DE-RATING SERVICE CAPACITY		
Formula		**Compute**	
Add			
general-purpose circuits (square footage x 3 watts)	6,000 W	The first 10,000 watts at 100 percent	10,000 W
small-appliance circuits (number x 1,500 watts)	7,500 W	the remaining 13,500 watts at 40 percent	+ 5,400 W
heavy-duty circuits (total of appliance name-plate ratings in watts)	10,000 W	De-rated total:	15,400 W
		Divide	
		The total de-rated wattage by voltage (240)	÷ 240 V
Total:	23,500 W	De-rated amperage	64.2 A

house with 100-amp service, five small-appliance circuits, and two heavy-duty circuits.

In assigning wattage values, don't count each general-purpose circuit. Instead, use 3 watts per square foot of house area. Small-appliance circuits rate at 1,500 watts each. Use the full wattage rating for heavy-duty circuits.

If two items never run simultaneously, ignore the one that draws less. Rate only the first 10,000 watts of the total at full value, then calculate 40 percent of the remainder. Divide the total by 240 volts. The answer, 64.2 amps, shows that the system could accommodate more circuits.

tandem devices, or "skinnies"

circuit breaker

unused terminal and socket

fuse

Unbroken knockout indicates space for new breakers.

4. Check for room in the box.
Once you've decided the type and capacity of your new circuit, see if you have room for it in your service panel. If your panel has circuit breakers, you might find a blank space or two. (Unbroken knockouts on the panel indicate space for a breaker underneath.) If not, you may be able to double up two circuits by replacing an existing breaker with a tandem device, also called a skinny. In a fuse box you might find an unused terminal and socket that could be used. More likely, you'll have to add a secondary fuse box called a subpanel (see page 71).

ADDING MAJOR CIRCUITS

1. To install new circuits, shut off power to the box.

Before working on the box itself, work backward from the new electrical installation. Mount boxes, connect them with cable, and run wiring back to the service panel (see pages 38–47 and 72–85) in what the pros call a "home run." Next comes the serious business of adding and tying into a new circuit. First, look for your home's main disconnect switch. You may have a switch outside the house near the meter (as shown) or inside near the service panel. If you have such a remote disconnect, flip the switch or pull the fuse. Then open the service panel and test it.

If your main disconnect is part of the service panel, seek advice from an electrician, an electrical inspector, or your utility company. To make sure there is no power coming into the service panel, you may have to ask the utility company to have the meter pulled and reconnected later.

EXPERTS' INSIGHT

Outdoor Shutoff Switches

■ If your indoor service panel is located more than 5 feet from the meter, an outdoor shutoff switch is required.

■ If you have an outdoor shutoff switch, it's a good idea to keep it secured with a padlock. Otherwise, anyone passing through your backyard can easily turn off the power to your entire house.

CAUTION!

Remember that the main breaker or main fuse in a service panel does not de-energize the main power cables coming into the box. If you cannot shut off power to the service panel, work carefully or call the power company to disconnect your service temporarily.

2. Test to make sure power is off.

Check that power is off, that main breakers are off or the main fuses are removed. Stand on a board, rubber mat, or other insulator. Being careful not to touch electrical or plumbing fittings, remove the cover plate. Test the terminals of the main power lines with the probes of a voltmeter. If you've got a reading, there is power to that point.

Meter shows no power to breaker panel.

Meter shows no power to fuse panel.

3. Hook up the new breakers.

Punch out the center from a convenient knockout on the circuit panel box. If needed, pry out one or more of the knockout's concentric rings to make a hole the size of the cable connector you'll be using.

Strip the cable sheathing, allowing for enough wire to reach the neutral bus bar as well as the blank space where you'll install the new breaker. Connect the cable to the box. Inside the service panel, run the white and ground wires (bare copper or green) to the neutral bus bar. (No ground wire is used if you are using conduit or BX.) For a 120-volt circuit, attach the black or red wire to the terminal of a single-pole breaker. To finish the job, simply clip the breaker onto one of the hot bus bars.

Some 240-volt appliances, such as water heaters, do not require a third neutral wire. For this type, connect two hot wires to a two-pole breaker (twice as wide as a single-pole breaker), and attach the ground wire to the neutral bar.

Most 240-volt circuits run a white neutral wire and are sometimes called 120/240-volt circuits. Connect the two hot wires to the two-pole breaker and the white wire to the neutral bar. GFCI breakers install somewhat differently (see pages 98–99).

4. Add a subpanel.

If you have a crowded fuse box or are adding several circuits far from the main service panel, connect them to a remote subpanel. Then make just one home run back to the main panel.

You will need a new panel with breakers or fuses, as well as three-wire cable with wire sized to handle the total amperage that the entire subpanel will draw. Connect the cable at the main service panel with terminal lugs.

RUNNING CABLE IN FINISHED SPACE

Do some detective work before running cable through finished walls and ceilings. As far as possible, determine what's in the wall or ceiling cavity. Look for access from an unfinished attic floor or basement ceiling. Check to see if there is insulation or blocking in the way. Determine whether or not there is a way to run cable parallel to the joists and studs. **TIP:** *Make as few holes as possible; often the most time-consuming part of running cable is patching walls and ceilings.* Use patching plaster, drywall tape, and compound to patch any holes.

YOU'LL NEED...

TIME: About 3 hours.
SKILLS: Drilling and patching.
TOOLS: Power drill, ¾- and 1-inch bits, fish tape, keyhole saw, utility knife, chisel, hammer, and standard carpentry tools.

1. Drill top or bottom plates...
If there is access from above or below, drill into the top or bottom plates of the wall frame. For a double plate or awkward angle, use a bit extension. After drilling the hole, feed the cable to the box opening. If you hit blocking (horizontal pieces between the studs), see Step 4.

...or cut an opening.
When there is no room for drilling through the plates from above or below, bore from the side instead. At the top of the wall, cut an opening to expose the single or double plate. At the bottom, there will only be a single plate; remove the baseboard, and make the cutout ¾ inch above the floor.

2. Drill the hole.
Using a bit extension, bore into the bottom of the plate, angling toward the center.

CAUTION!

Bore slowly to avoid burning out the drill. Watch out for nails. Wear goggles when working with power tools.

3. Push the cable through.
Push the cable up or down to the box opening. Then loop it through the plate. Pulling cable through walls is a two-person job. One person tugs—not too hard or the sheathing might tear—from the attic or basement. The other coils cable and feeds it through the opening, taking care to avoid kinks and knots.

4. Notch the blocking.
To locate fire blocking, slip a tape measure through the hole and push it until it strikes the blocking. Measure to that point and make an opening that straddles the blocking. Chisel a notch that is large enough to accommodate the cable easily. After you've run the cable, but before you patch the hole, install a nail plate (see page 76).

Short runs of cable

Often it is easiest to fish cable from a nearby outlet. Before tapping into an outlet, make sure you won't be overloading the circuit (see pages 66-69). **NOTE:** *Shut off the power, remove the cover plate, and see if the receptacle has a set of unused terminals. If it doesn't, add pigtails (see page 47) before reconnecting.*

YOU'LL NEED...

TIME: About 2 hours, not including wall patching.
SKILLS: Pulling wire and patching drywall or plaster.
TOOLS: Fish tape, keyhole saw, standard carpentry tools.

1. Open the box.
Disconnect the receptacle. Check for a cable clamp or other device that will attach the new cable to the box. If necessary, remove a knockout with a hammer and screwdriver and install a clamp.

2. Cut the new opening.
Use a box as a template to mark the new outlet opening, and cut it open with a utility knife or keyhole saw. If possible, locate the new box in the same wall cavity as the source box.

3. Connect fish tapes.
Thread one fish tape (or bent coat hanger) through the knockout hole, and another through the new opening. Wiggle one or both until they hook.

4. Pull tape and connect to cable.
Pull the tape from the existing box through the new opening. Strip some sheathing from the cable, hook the wires on the fish tape end, and wrap with tape.

5. Pull the cable through.
Finally, pull the cable through the new opening and into the old box. Connect the cable to the old box (see page 79) and install the new box (see page 42).

CUT NOTCHES

To run cable past studs, cut openings that span each of the studs. Save the cutouts. Chisel a notch in the stud. Install a nail plate to protect the cable (see page 76) and patch the wall.

RUNNING CABLE ALONG BASEBOARDS

1. Remove trim, notch for access.
After cutting the hole for your new outlet, remove trim. Avoid damaging the wall or cracking the trim. Pop nails loose one at a time, levering the wood away from the wall with a pry bar. Once the board is free, make a notch in the wall below the outlet that will be the power source. If possible, cut the notch so the baseboard covers it when you replace the baseboard.

YOU'LL NEED...

TIME: 2 hours.
SKILLS: Cutting holes, fishing cable, and simple carpentry.
TOOLS: Utility knife, keyhole saw, chisel, and common carpentry tools.

EXPERTS' INSIGHT

Use armored flexible cable
Use only armored flexible cable (BX) for this operation—never nonmetallic sheathed cable, which can be easily pierced with a nail. Plan the location of the cable and the location of the nails so there is no danger of hitting the cable with a nail. Be especially careful when renailing baseboard, casing, and trim.

2. Feed the cable along the floor.
If your home has drywall, you may find a gap at the wall's base that's large enough to accommodate the cable. If there's no gap, cut a channel in the drywall for it. Feed the cable through a knockout hole in the source box, and pull it out of the wall below. As you run the cable along the floor, be sure that it is set back from the wall surface.

3. Bring cable to the new outlet.
If the new opening is low enough, simply push the cable up through the wall to the opening. To pull the cable up to a higher opening, use a fish tape (see page 73).

4. Go around a door.
Carefully remove the casing from one side of the door jamb. Push the cable into the space between the jamb and the wall material, notching where necessary. When replacing the casing, be careful not to pierce the cable with the casing's nails.

RUNNING CABLE FOR CEILING FIXTURES

*T*o run cable for a switch-controlled ceiling fixture, first determine the location and direction of the wall studs and ceiling joists. If possible, run wires parallel with framing members to save time-consuming work patching and painting. When cutting notches in drywall, make clean cuts and save the cutout pieces, if possible. Later, glue them back in place with construction adhesive, and finish with drywall tape and compound. Notches in plaster will require more work to repair. Fill the void with nonshrinking patching plaster.

YOU'LL NEED...

TIME: With a helper, 3 hours.
SKILLS: Cutting clean holes in walls, and fishing cable.
TOOLS: Utility knife, keyhole saw, chisel, and fish tape.

1. Cut the holes.
Decide where to locate the fixture. If a framing member is in the way, move the location of the switch or fixture a few inches. If you have to run cable across framing members, make notches at each joist or stud (see page 73). Next, cut the holes for the switch and the fixture (see pages 42–43).

2. Cut an opening at the ceiling.
Where the wall and the ceiling meet, make a 1-inch-wide opening. Extend the opening at least 1 inch below the wall plate, and 2 inches at the ceiling. Chisel a channel into the framing deep enough to accommodate the cable.

3. Fish to the fixture.
Slowly feed fish tape into the ceiling opening. If the tape meets resistance and coils up, pull back a few feet, shake the tape, and try again. Shaking also makes the tape rattle in the wall—a sure way to locate the tape. For longer runs, use two tapes, feeding in one from either end and snagging them together (see page 73).

4. Run cable to the switch.
Typically the wall cavity will be clear enough to push the cable down through the wall to the switch opening. Or work a fish tape up, and pull the cable to the switch box opening. Staple the cable into the notches before patching the wall and ceiling.

RUNNING CABLE IN UNFINISHED SPACE

*I*f you're working on a new addition, or if you've gutted a room and removed the old walls, running cable will be much easier. Begin by installing the electrical boxes. Place all the receptacles and switches at uniform height (12 to 18 inches from the floor for receptacles, 48 inches for switches). Make sure the boxes protrude forward from the face of the studs so your drywall will be flush with the front of them. Once the boxes are in place, bore holes in the middle of framing members.

center of the stud

YOU'LL NEED...
TIME: 1 hour to install two boxes and run 10 feet of cable.
SKILLS: Drilling holes and fastening boxes in place.
TOOLS: Drill with spade bit, hammer, and chisel.

1. Bore the holes to run cable.
With an electric drill and a sharp ¾-inch spade bit, you can bore holes for a run of cable quickly. Have extra bits on hand for large jobs. Align the holes with each other by eye or use a chalk line to mark a guide. Bore as near the center of each stud as possible to maintain the strength of the framing and lessen the chance of drywall or trim nails piercing the cable. See Step 4 if the corners are solid wood.

6–8" loop of cable

Bend cable to work it around the corner.

Drill all holes at the same level and near the center of the stud.

2. Run the cable.
Run the cable fairly tightly so that it does not hang between studs. At the corners you may need to bend the cable sharply to keep it at least 1¼ inches from the outer face of the framing. At each box leave a loop of 6 to 8 inches of cable, but do not kink it. This loop gives a margin of error if the wire is damaged when stripped, and makes future repairs and improvements easier.

nail plate

TYPE NM   600 V

3. Add cable protectors.
If some of the holes end up less than 1¼ inches from the face of a framing member, install a nail plate. Inexpensive and easy to install, it shields live electrical wires from being pierced by nails or screws. Simply tap the nail plate into place with a hammer.

4. Cut notches at corners.

If the corner is solid wood, cut a notch to run cable around corners. Use a hand saw or a reciprocating saw to make two cuts in each stud, wide enough and deep enough for the cable to fit easily. Chisel out the wood between the two cuts. At inside corners, leave plenty of room—the cable cannot make sharp 90-degree turns. After running the cable, protect it by covering each notch with a nail plate.

5. Tighten and attach the cable.

Pull the cable fairly taut as you install it. At each box, leave a 6- to 8-inch loop and attach the cable with an insulated staple.

6. Drill plates for vertical runs.

Drill holes in top and bottom wall plates with a ¾-inch spade bit. Drill the holes near the center of the plates. If necessary, use a drill extension to bore through 2×4 plates. To avoid burning up the bit, stop periodically to let it cool. Drill at high speed and push gently.

7. Run and secure the cable.

On vertical runs, secure the cable with insulated staples every 4 feet or so, wherever you change direction, and 8 to 12 inches from each box. Avoid sharp bends in the cable.

RUNNING CABLE IN ATTICS AND FLOORS

How cable is run in an attic depends on how accessible and usable the attic is. Some local codes allow cable to be surface-mounted in seldom-used spaces. Cable can be attached to the top of the joists with insulated staples. Then 1×2 guard strips are nailed on either side. These strips will protect the cable from damage if anyone steps or sets a heavy object there.

1×2 guard strips

Running cable through holes

If your attic is readily accessible, bore holes through the joists, at least 1½ inches below the top of the joists (see near right). For best protection, and to add a utilitarian floor, install plywood over joists. If the attic has flooring, remove some of it to install the cable or take an alternate route along framing members. In a basement, run cable through holes in the joists (see far right).

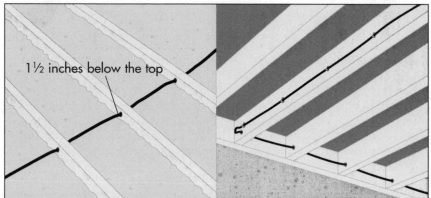

1½ inches below the top

strapping

240-volt receptacle

conduit

breaker box

Strapping thicker cable

Because the heavy cable (8-gauge or larger) used for 240-volt appliance circuits is too stiff to thread easily through holes in joists, some towns allow wiring to be strapped to the underside of joists and along joist plates. Check your local code; conduit may be required for all exposed runs.

CONNECTING CABLE TO BOXES

This page shows the most common systems for connecting nonmetallic cable to boxes. Other connectors are needed for metallic sheathed cable, Greenfield, and conduit (see pages 81 and 84). Leave ½ inch or more of sheathing inside the outlet box.

▶ **Nonmetallic box with clamp**
Some nonmetallic boxes come with internal clamps. However, clamping may not be necessary. Some local codes require only that the cable be secured within 8 inches of the box.

nonmetallic box with internal clamp

nail for fastening box to stud

No clamp may be needed if codes allow a staple to secure the cable.

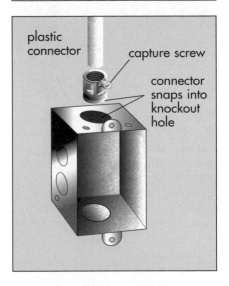

internal saddle clamp

holds 1 or 2 cables

◀ **Metal box with saddle clamp**
Some metal boxes come with internal saddle clamps. By tightening the saddle-clamp screw, one or two cables can be secured quickly.

▶ **Metal box with clamp connectors**
Remove a knockout hole in the box, insert a clamp connector into the hole, and secure it with a locknut. Slide the cable through the clamp connector and into the box. Tighten the saddle onto the cable. In some situations it is easier to clamp the connector to the cable first, then slide it into the box and screw on the locknut.

clamp connector

saddle

knockout hole

locknut

◀ **Plastic connector**
A plastic connector works like a clamp connector, but it is quicker and easier to use. Snap it into the knockout hole, insert 6 to 8 inches of cable, and tighten the capture screw. Other types grab the cable when you pry up on a wedge or squeeze the unit with pliers.

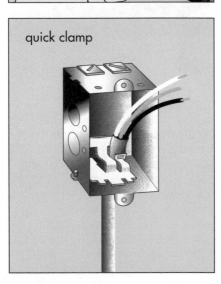

quick clamp

▶ **Quick clamp**
Some boxes come with internal quick clamps. Pry up a spring-metal tab and slip the cable through. The clamp springs back by itself to hold the cable securely.

plastic connector

capture screw

connector snaps into knockout hole

WORKING WITH BX, GREENFIELD

Flexible armored cable, or BX, is composed of a bendable metal sheathing containing insulated and ground wires. Greenfield, or flexible conduit, is a hollow, flexible metal sheath. Like conduit, it is a tube through which wires are pulled. Check local codes regarding use of these materials—restrictions vary. (See page 35 for the different types of wire and cable available.)

> **CAUTION!**
> *Whenever you work with these materials, you end up with cut ends that are sharp. If wires are allowed to rub against them, insulation could be stripped, resulting in an electrical short. Follow the procedures here carefully to protect wires at all times.*

1. Cut notch in the sheathing.
To get through the metal covering, hold a hacksaw at a right angle to the spirals and cut partway through the armor. With BX, be especially careful not to nick the insulation on the wires inside. For a safe and easy way to cut cable, use a BX cutter (see inset above).

2. Complete the cut.
Twist the armor and it will snap free. The paper-wrapped wires (and aluminum bonding strip, if there is one) can be snipped with ordinary wire cutters. To expose the wires for connecting to boxes and fixtures, cut off the armor at a second point about a foot away.

3. Thread through holes in framing members.
Run armored cable and flexible conduit through holes bored in the middle of framing members. Where necessary, use notches. BX and Greenfield are heavier and stiffer than nonmetallic cable, so it will take more room every time you want to change direction.

4. Protect the cable.
Even armored sheathing can be pierced with a nail, so anywhere that the cable is within 1¼ inches of the framing surface, protect it with a nail plate designed for the purpose. For short runs (see inset), flexible armored cable may be left exposed—check your local codes.

5. Secure the cable.
Support metal-clad cable with specially designed straps or staples every 4 feet or so and within 12 inches of boxes. If you're fishing through existing walls or ceilings, secure the run as best you can.

CONNECTING BX, GREENFIELD

1. To connect cable to boxes, choose the connectors.
In most cases, use a simple straight connector that holds the cable in place either by clamping it or with a setscrew. In some tight situations, you may need to use a

45-degree or 90-degree connector. To install a connector, choose the side of the box you wish to access, and remove the knockout. Cut the cable to length and trim off the armored sheathing (see page 80).

2. Install a bushing.
Pull the brown paper surrounding the wires in BX back about an inch inside the armor. This leaves room to slip in a bushing. If your cable has a bonding strip, fold it back as shown.

3. Attach the connector.
Slip on a connector, making sure the bushing is in place. Tighten the clamp or setscrew. Armored cable and conduit are self-grounding so you don't need a grounding wire. Some codes require that the bonding strip be attached to the tightening screw.

4. Insert the connector.
Slip the wires and connector into a knockout hole, slip on a locknut, and tighten with your fingers. As with all wiring, connections should be made only in boxes.

5. Tighten the locknut.
Tighten the locknut with a hammer and screwdriver. Finally, tug on the cable to make sure everything is securely fastened.

CUTTING AND ASSEMBLING CONDUIT

Codes sometimes require conduit, especially for exposed areas. Conduit has definite advantages: It protects the wires well, and the electrical system can be upgraded later simply by pulling new wires through the conduit. Conduit is the most difficult way to install wiring because it's hard to bend. But it is still within the reach for do-it-yourselfers. For small jobs, use elbows and connectors at each turn to avoid bending conduit.

Codes allow many wires to be pulled through conduit. But the more wires you pull, the more crowded the conduit, so buy larger conduit than is required by code—say, ¾-inch instead of ½-inch.

YOU'LL NEED...

TIME: About 2 hours for a run with three bends and two boxes.
SKILLS: Careful measuring, clean cutting, and screwing pieces together.
TOOLS: Tubing cutter or hacksaw, pliers, and screwdriver.

tubing cutter

Cleat helps keep conduit from rolling.

1. Measure and cut.
Measure the distance for the run—don't forget to subtract for the connector or elbow you will be using. Cut with a tubing cutter by clamping it to the conduit and rotating it a few times. Tighten and rotate until the cut is made. Or cut with a hacksaw. Hold conduit against a cleat or use a miter box to keep it from rolling as you saw.

reamer (part of tubing cutter)

file

2. Ream the ends.
Sharp edges can chew up wiring insulation in a hurry. Remove all burrs and rough spots from the inside of the conduit, using the reamer that's attached to the tubing cutter or a file. File rough spots on the outside as well, so the conduit can slip easily into a connector.

junction box

3. Install a junction box.
Where you have more than four turns to negotiate, install a junction box. When it's time to pull the wires, it will let you start another run. More boxes and few bends ease wire-pulling.

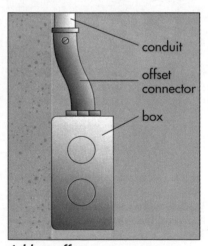

conduit

offset connector

box

Add an offset.
Use an offset connector to keep the conduit flush against the wall when it's attached to a box. The conduit can be bent to form an offset (see page 83), but adding an offset connector is easier.

pulling elbow

4. Install pulling elbows.
A pulling elbow makes negotiating corners easier. Remove the cover to pull the wires through. Don't make any connections inside a pulling elbow; wires must pass through without a break.

Bending Conduit

For larger jobs, it is expensive and time-consuming to use connectors at each corner. Instead, bend the conduit. Bending isn't difficult, but getting the bend in just the right location is tricky and requires some practice.

Runs begin and end at places where you can get at wires to pull them. Codes generally forbid a total of more than 360 degrees of bends in a run. Add up the degrees of the bends you'll be making in a single run before you start bending to ensure the total is less than 360 degrees.

YOU'LL NEED...

TIME: About 30 minutes to measure, bend a piece, and connect it on either end.
SKILLS: This is a specialized skill that requires practice.
TOOLS: Conduit bender, tape measure, and black marking pen.

1. Measure for a corner.
To get conduit around a corner, first measure from the box to the top of the bend (distance A). Then subtract the bend distance and mark the conduit. (The bend distance for ½-inch conduit is 5 inches. For ¾- and 1-inch conduit, allow 6 and 8 inches, respectively.) Slip the conduit bender onto the tubing and align it as shown. After making the bend, trim section B by holding the bent conduit in place for measuring, and cutting the end so it just reaches the box.

2. Make the bend.
With one foot on the rear of the bender, pull slowly and steadily on the handle. Be careful. Tugging too sharply will crimp the tubing and you'll have to start over again with another piece. (Codes forbid installing crimped conduit.) Making crimp-free bends takes practice, so don't be surprised if your first efforts fail.

3. To form an offset, start with a 15-degree bend...
When mounting conduit on a flat surface, you'll need to form an offset at each box. Offsets must be aligned with other bends in the tubing. A stripe painted along the length of the conduit helps you do this. First make a 15-degree bend.

...then bend in the other direction.
Roll the conduit over, move the bender a few inches farther from the end, and pull until the section beyond the first bend is parallel to the floor.

CONNECTING CONDUIT

1. Use couplings to join sections.
To join sections end to end, use either setscrew or compression couplings, securely fitted.

> ### CAUTION!
> *Make all connections mechanically strong. Pulling wires through conduit can put a strain on connections. Grounding depends on secure metal-to-metal connections.*

2. Anchor the conduit.
Anchor conduit runs with at least one strap every 8 feet and a strap within 3 feet of every box. For masonry walls, use screws and plastic anchors. When attaching to framing, simply drive barbed straps into the wood.

To mount conduit inside walls, bore holes in the studs (see pages 72–78), or notch the framing and secure it with straps or metal plates every 8 feet.

3. Connect to boxes.
The various types of box connectors differ mainly in the way they attach to conduit. Compression connectors grab the conduit as you tighten the nut with a wrench. To install a setscrew connector, slip it on and tighten the screw. Both types are available in 90-degree versions.

All these connectors attach to the box with the same threaded stud and locknut arrangement used with cable connectors (see page 79). Insert the stud into a knockout hole, turn the locknut finger tight, then tap the nut with a hammer and screwdriver to tighten it. A two-piece connector comes in handy when space is tight inside a box. Instead of a locknut, it has a compression fitting. As you tighten the nut, the fitting squeezes the conduit.

PULLING WIRE THROUGH CONDUIT

Now comes the moment when you realize why codes are so specific about bends, crimps, and burrs in conduit. Pulling wire can be surprisingly hard work. If you suspect that the wire is scraping against something that might damage the insulation, stop work, locate the trouble spot (you can find it easily by using the wire as a measuring device), and remove it. Purchase pulling grease, and lubricate the wires with it if you need to make a long pull.

YOU'LL NEED...

TIME: About an hour to pull cable through 60 feet of conduit.
SKILLS: Patience and some pulling muscle.
TOOLS: Fish tape, pulling grease, and electrical tape.

1. Push through short runs.
For short runs with only a couple of bends, you can probably just push the wires from one box to the other. Feed the wires carefully to protect the insulation.

electrical tape
bend a hook
fish tape
wrap neatly

2. Attach a fish tape.
If you can't push the wires, you'll need a fish tape and an assistant. Snake the fish tape through the conduit, hook the wires to the fish tape and secure with electrician's tape. Wrap the connection neatly so it can slide through the conduit.

3. Pull the wires through.
As one worker feeds the wire in and makes sure there are no kinks, the other pulls. Pull the wires with steady pressure—avoid tugging. As the wires work past bends, expect

to employ more muscle. If you have lots of wires or a long pull, lubricate the wires with pulling grease. Where possible, use gravity to aid the process. Feed the wires from above and pull from below.

Make all connections inside boxes.

4. Leave plenty of wire.
Leave 6 to 8 inches of wire at each box. Never splice wire inside conduit—all wires must run continuously from box to box.

HANGING CEILING FIXTURES

Dramatically change the appearance of a room by adding or replacing a ceiling light. Although the choices are many, from simple ceiling fixtures to elaborate chandeliers, all are installed in essentially the same way: Power is drawn from a ceiling-mounted box designed to support a particular fixture. If you are replacing a ceiling fixture, take the time to inspect the wires and the area around the outlet box for heat damage (see page 53).

YOU'LL NEED...
TIME: An hour to mount a simple fixture; more time is needed for elaborate units.
SKILLS: Basic carpentry and wiring skills
TOOLS: Screwdriver and pliers.

1. Remove a flush-mounted fixture.
NOTE: *Shut off the power.* Remove the globe or diffuser and the bulb(s). Remove the screws or the cap nut holding the canopy in place and drop the fixture down. Disconnect the black and white wires. Check wires for cracks in the insulation (see page 53). To replace wire, see pages 72–78.

2. Install a hanging fixture.
This hanging fixture attaches with a pair of studs screwed to the box. Connect the black and white wires and the ground wire, coil them up into the box, and push the canopy into place so the studs poke through. If the unit does not easily push up flush to the ceiling, drop it down and rearrange the wires. Secure the canopy by twisting cap nuts onto the studs.

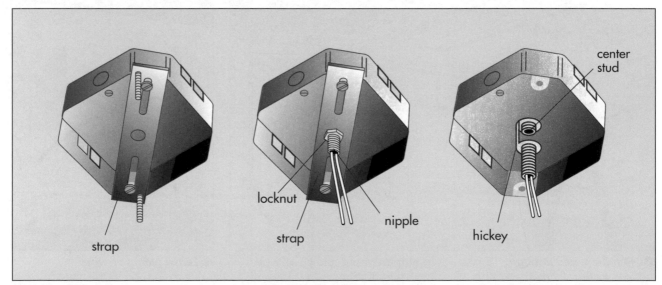

Mounting systems
If the holes in the canopy don't match those in the box, choose from the three mounting systems shown above. Adapt the box for fixtures with side mounting bolts by fastening a **strap** to the box. Some straps have several screw-in holes to choose from. For center-mounted fixtures, screw a **nipple** into the center hole of a strap and secure it in place with a locknut. If the box has a center stud, attaching a **hickey** is another way to adapt the box.

INSTALLING TRACK LIGHTING

Track lighting gives you a great deal of flexibility. After it is installed, you easily can change the number of lights, their positions, or the direction they point—even the type of light.

The initial hookup is much like other ceiling fixtures (see page 86). But installing the tracks involves measuring your ceiling and establishing lines for correct placement so the track is pleasingly aligned with your room. Have two ladders and one helper on hand for marking placement. (If you do not have an existing box to tie into, see pages 72–78.)

YOU'LL NEED...

TIME: If you are working from an existing ceiling box, 4–6 hours for a 12-foot system.

SKILLS: Connecting wires in a box, and careful measuring of and attaching to a ceiling.

TOOLS: Tape measure, Phillips screwdriver, and drill with screwdriver bit.

ceiling fixture box

canopy

live connector

track

connector unit

connector unit cover

How track lighting goes together. Instructions for your unit will tell you specifically how to make connections, but most track lights go together in the following way. A connector unit connects to the ceiling electrical box and transfers power to the tracks. Inside the tracks are two metal strips that run along its length. They are electrified by wires from the box. The lights themselves have two contacts at their base. When the contacts meet the electrified strips, the light comes on. A cover caps off the connector unit.

canopy

connector unit

1. Install the connector unit.
NOTE: *Shut off the power.* Attach the black, white, and ground wires from ceiling fixture box to the connector unit terminals. Hook wires clockwise on the screw shafts before tightening. Fasten the connector unit to the canopy.

Measure from the wall that is visually most important.

2. Lay out and install tracks.
To establish a line that the track will follow, measure off a wall at several points, and strike a line between them. Connect the track to the connector plate. Screw the track into ceiling joists or use toggle bolts.

canopy

connector unit cover

3. Install lights and attach cover.
Restore power to the circuit. Install lights according to instructions—in most cases, you twist them in place. Attach the canopy and any connector covers by snapping into place.

INSTALLING CEILING FANS

Whether it's keeping warm air down for heat in the winter, or circulating cool air in the summer, a ceiling fan can cut energy costs and help keep your home more comfortable all year long. Installing a ceiling fan is an ideal one-day project for homeowners with little or no wiring experience. Most fans have pull switches that turn the unit off and on and that control fan speed. You can also install wall switches to control the fan (see pages 100–106).

Turn off the electricity. When unpacking your fan, lay fan blades on a flat surface to check that they are not warped. If one is warped, ask your retailer to replace the entire set. Then check the blade irons. They are typically set at a 12-degree angle, though on small fans they can be pitched as high as 25 degrees. Set them on top of each other. If one doesn't match the others, have your retailer replace it.

YOU'LL NEED...

TIME: About 4 to 6 hours if you need to run new wiring.
SKILLS: Simple carpentry and wiring skills.
TOOLS: Screwdriver, utility knife, keyhole saw, wrench, socket driver, and needle-nose pliers.

1. Select a brace bar.
If you don't have access from above, you'll need a ceiling fan support, known as a brace bar, which can be inserted from the room below. Typically, it consists of an adjustable bar installed between two joists.

HOW TO CHOOSE A BRACE BAR AND CEILING BOX

You'll find many types of brace bars and ceiling boxes to choose from at your local hardware store or home center. Be sure both can support the size of fan you are installing.

You may not need a brace bar if you have access from above. You can add in framing and attach the ceiling box directly to it using general-purpose screws. Never install a fan support bracket or fixture box that is held up only by the ceiling material.

Ceiling boxes may be reinforced plastic or sturdy metal designed to support fans. If you are putting in a fan where there was once just a light fixture, you may need to replace the ceiling box, install a brace bar to support the added weight, or do both.

2. Test the assembly.
Do a dry run of assembling the brace bar, ceiling box, and box bracket. Be sure you fully understand how the brace bar is fastened in place and how the box is attached. Follow the instructions that come with it. Once installed, these items are hard to remove.

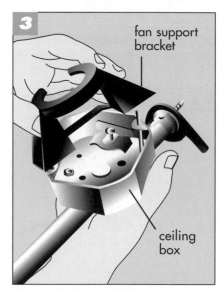

3. Test-fit the bracket.
Check that the fan support bracket fits and can be attached easily once the box is in place. Push out a ceiling box knockout (a tab covering a hole in the back or one of the sides), and install a cable clamp. Disassemble the brace bar, ceiling box, and box bracket.

4. Position brace bar.

Between joists, cut a hole in the ceiling about 5 inches in diameter (see page 43 for tips on locating it). Most brace bars have a screwlike fastener at each end that fixes the bar in place. Slip the bar through the hole and position it perpendicular to the joists.

5. Fasten the bar.

Turn the outermost piece of the brace bar until it locks into the nub. Continue turning until the first foot is fastened. Next turn the innermost bar to fasten the other foot.

6. Attach the box.

Pull wires into the receptacle box. Loosely fasten one side of box bracket and position the bracket on the brace bar. Feed the second bracket bolt through the box and fasten nuts on both of the bolts using a socket driver or pliers.

7. Wire the fan.

Attach the fan support bracket and the down pipe. Using wire connectors, connect the fan leads to the circuit wires. Be sure to attach white to white, black to black, and the ground wire to the green lead. Manufacturers usually provide instructions. Wire the fan following the instructions.

CHOOSE A CEILING FAN: CLEARANCES AND CAPACITIES

For safety, and to give the fan adequate space to effectively move air, use the clearances shown below. Select fan blades to suit the square footage of the room.

Fan Diameter (inches)	Room Area (square feet)
36	96
42	144
48	288
52	400

EXPERTS' INSIGHT

Balancing a wobbly fan

All may not be gentle breezes when you turn on your fan. Particularly at high speed, it may rock and roll. Don't panic. It might not be a manufacturer's defect or the result of shoddy installation. One of these two steps should fix the problem:

■ Check for any loose screws where the blades attach to the blade irons and the blade irons attach to motor.

■ Buy an inexpensive ceiling fan balancing kit and follow its simple procedures for checking the blades.

INSTALLING RECESSED CEILING LIGHTS

Recessed fixtures have much to recommend them: They are inexpensive, unobtrusive, and if you have no fixture box already in place, a recessed light is the easiest fixture to install because it comes with a box attached. Purchase a unit with a silver reflector for greater brightness or choose a black reflector for more subdued lighting. Make sure the fixture you buy will fit in your ceiling space. If your ceiling joists are smaller than 2×10, for instance, you will need a fixture with a side-mounted box.

YOU'LL NEED...
TIME: After running cable from the switch, about 1½ hours.
SKILLS: Cutting a clean hole in the ceiling and attaching wires.
TOOLS: Keyhole saw, screwdriver, and drill with screwdriver bit.

Anatomy of a recessed fixture
Designed for installation where there is no access from above (a common problem when adding recessed lighting in the first-floor ceiling of a two-story house), this unit sits atop drywall or plaster. The fixture can be installed from below. The mounting frame spreads out the weight of the unit.

CAUTION!
KEEP IT COOL
If you don't take precautions, a recessed light can build up a lot of heat, which can lead to prematurely burned-out bulbs, damage to your ceiling, melted wire insulation, or even fire. Allow the fixture room to breathe. Keep any ceiling insulation at least 3 inches away from it and don't place it in a cramped space. Use bulbs of the recommended type and wattage. You can increase the wattage if you use a floodlight bulb because it directs more heat away from the fixture than a regular bulb. Don't leave any flammable materials, such as scraps of insulation paper, anywhere near the fixture.

1. Cut a hole.
Determine the general location of the fixture and drill an exploratory hole. To make sure a joist is not in the way, use a bent wire, so when spun it will follow the circumference of the fixture. If the site is clear, mark and cut an opening with a keyhole saw.

2. Rough in the wiring.
NOTE: *Shut off the power.* For the rough wiring, simply run cable to the hole where the fixture will go. Leave a foot or so of extra cable sticking through the hole. See pages 100–106 for ways to wire a switched ceiling fixture.

3. Secure the mounting frame.

Slip the mounting frame up through the hole (it will just fit). Pull the cable down through the mounting frame. Place frame so the flange sits in the hole. Strip about 6 inches of sheathing from the cable and about ¾ inch of insulation from each wire (see pages 44–45).

4. Wire the fixture.

Remove the cover plate from the fixture's electrical box. Secure the cable to the box and connect the wires in the box. Follow the same procedures as if wiring a regular box—see pages 47 and 79. Push the wires into the box and replace the cover plate.

5. Install canister and trim.

Slide the canister up through the mounting plate until it is slightly recessed above the surface of the ceiling. Secure it to the mounting plate by tightening the screws provided. Attach the reflector. Screw in a lightbulb, and attach the trim.

Another configuration

There are several types of recessed lights, all with their own ways of connecting to the ceiling. Here is one that works well if you have access to the space above your ceiling. Once the fixture is positioned over the hole, sliding brackets attached to the canister extend out to reach joists on either side. When these brackets are secured to the joists, the unit is more firmly attached than most recessed fixtures. As with all recessed fixtures, it comes with its own electrical box.

Installing this type

Pound a nail up through the ceiling at the point where you want the light. Go into the space above, find the nail, cut back the insulation, and cut a hole. Install the reflector in the canister. Set the canister in the hole, slide out the brackets, and attach to the joists with nails or general-purpose screws. Wire the box, screw in a bulb, and attach trim.

ADDING WALL SCONCES

Wall sconces are ideal for hallways, stairways, and any room that needs indirect accent lighting. Installing a wall sconce is similar to adding a new light fixture. The only difference is location and the type of fixture box used. As with ceiling lights, you can control as many lights as you want with one switch, or control one or more of them from two different locations by using three-way switches. See pages 102–106 for the various options.

It's ideal if you can secure the fixture box to a framing member as well as the drywall or plaster. Use one of the standard retrofit boxes shown on page 37.

YOU'LL NEED...

TIME: About a full day to install a new switch and two sconces, not including any wall patching.
SKILLS: Basic electrical skills, plus cutting and patching walls.
TOOLS: Keyhole saw, screwdriver, lineman's pliers, drill, and fish tape.

Place sconces the same distance up from the floor.

power source

1. Cut holes and run cable.
NOTE: *Shut off the power.* Find a junction box or a receptacle with power you can use. Cut a vertical hole for the switch box and horizontal holes for the sconce boxes (see page 42). Run cable from the power source to the switch and from the switch to the openings cut in the wall for the sconces (see pages 70–71).

neutral wire

hot wire

ground wire

2. Wire the sconces.
Fasten cable to the boxes, allowing an extra 8 inches of cable to protrude at each box. Attach the boxes to the walls. Strip the sheathing and the wire insulation, and make the connections (see pages 44–45). Note that wires travel both into and out of the first sconce fixture box. Wire the switch (see page 100).

EXPERTS' INSIGHT

THE USES OF SCONCE LIGHTING

■ Wall sconces provide a splash of indirect light that creates the illusion that a room is larger than it is. For this reason, and because they are commonly placed slightly higher than eye level, keep the bulb wattage low.
■ In most cases wall sconces work best in conjunction with other lights rather than as the primary light source for a room. They work well for ambient light

but are insufficient for specific tasks, such as reading.
■ Install sconces 72 to 78 inches high. Any lower and you will bump into them; any higher and they will seem designed to light the ceiling rather than the room.
■ Typically it makes the most sense to add wall sconces to one wall where accent or indirect lighting is called for. A few sconces go a long way, so keep them spaced more than 6 feet from each other.

3. Install the sconces.
Tuck the wires into the box, screw a mounting strap to the box, and attach the sconce to the mounting strap. Secure the switch and its cover plate, and test.

INSTALLING UNDER-CABINET LIGHTING

A kitchen is a brighter, more pleasant place to work when its countertops are illuminated by under-cabinet fixtures. Under-cabinet lighting provides a sparkling decorative effect and gives you excellent task lighting.

A 120-volt system requires hours of fishing and installing fixture boxes in one of the most crowded and complicated areas of the house. An attractive alternative is the low-voltage system shown here. Low-voltage halogen lights operated with a remote-controlled, surface-mounted switch can be installed in a day and look as good as a more permanent system.

YOU'LL NEED...

TIME: About a day to install a switch and 10 lights.
SKILLS: Stripping and connecting wires and simple carpentry skills.
TOOLS: Screwdriver, drill, lineman's pliers, and keyhole saw.

transformer · power block · 120-volt receptacle · receiver module for remote switch · light fixture base with trim ring and lens · light fixture base

1. Install lights and transformer.
Determine a location for each light fixture where it won't shine in your eyes as you work. Halogen lights get hot; they can be safely attached to wooden cabinets but should be kept away from plastic and paper goods. Remove the trim ring and lens from each fixture base and attach them with screws to the underside of the cabinets. (Be sure the screws are the right length so they do not poke up into your cabinet.) Align fixtures so the bulbs aim in the same direction. Drill small holes to allow the wires to pass into your cabinet, and plug their ends into the power block located inside the cabinet. Coil excess wire inside the cabinet. Connect the power block to the transformer. Drill a hole and run a wire from the transformer to a 120-volt receptacle.

fixture base · bulb · reflector ring · lens cover

2. Assemble the lights.
Once the fixture bases are installed, snap the lens cover onto the reflector ring. Some under-cabinet lighting kits come with a warning label to attach inside the cabinet door to caution users about the heat of the units.

switch housing · cover plate

3. Install the switch.
The switch operates by battery power, so it can be installed anywhere in the kitchen and requires no wiring. Attach the switch housing by screwing it to the wall—use plastic anchors if you can't find a stud. Screw the cover plate to the switch housing.

EXPERTS' INSIGHT

FLUORESCENT UNDER-CABINET LIGHTING

The low-voltage halogen lighting shown here is a convenient improvement when cabinets are already installed. If you are in the process of installing cabinets, consider installing thin (1- to 1½-inch thick) fluorescent lights under the cabinets. To install fluorescent lights, run standard electrical cable behind the walls. Run wires behind the cabinets if possible so you won't have to patch the walls. Or use raceway wiring attached to the underside of the cabinets (see pages 96–97).

INSTALLING SPECIAL SWITCHES

One of the easiest ways to enhance your home's electrical system is to install special switches. Wiring them is rarely much more difficult than installing a standard switch.

Choose from a wide variety of options. The single-pole dimmer (shown at right), for instance, is touch-sensitive, like a modern elevator button. Touching its flush plate turns lights on and off. Holding a finger on it adjusts the light level. Even that minimal effort isn't necessary with the motion-sensitive switch. It turns on a light fixture whenever someone enters a room then stays on for a prescribed amount of time.

Be aware that some switches have limitations. For example, an ordinary dimmer can only handle up to 600 watts, so it may not be able to operate a chandelier. For higher-wattage fixtures, buy special dimmers able to handle 800, 1,000, or 1,500 watts. (For more information on these and other switches, see pages 32–33.)

If you have ground wires, they all should be connected together in the box, no matter what kind of switch you are installing.
NOTE: *Shut off the power before installing the switch.*

Single-pole dimmer
Most dimmers have a set of leads, or short wires, instead of screw terminals. Hook up a single-pole dimmer as shown.

Most dimmers are deeper than conventional switches, so you may have to rearrange wires in the box before you can fit one in. Don't force dimmers, because they crack easily. If there are too many wires, order a thin-profile unit.

Three-way dimmer
Three-way dimmers have three hot leads. Before you remove the old switch, determine which is the common terminal—it will be printed on the switch body, and/or the screw will be darker-colored than the others. Hook the common wire to the new switch's common lead, and connect the other wires. (For more on three-way switches, see pages 103–105.)

Pilot-light switch
This switch has a bulb that glows when its fixture is on. Connect the black feed wire to the brass terminal on the side that does not have a connecting tab. Pigtail two white wires, and connect them to the silver terminal. Connect the black wire that leads to the fixture to the terminal on the side with the connecting tab.

Motion-sensor switch
An infrared beam detects movement and turns on a light fixture. A time-delay feature lets you choose how long the light remains on. Connect the neutral wires to each other, not to the switch. Connect the black feed wire to one lead. To the other lead, attach the black wire that runs to the fixture.

Time-delay switch

With this type of switch, you turn a spring-driven dial to set the switch so it will turn off a fixture after a delay ranging from 1 to 60 minutes. Connect the black leads to the black wires in the box, and connect the white wires together, not to the switch.

Fluorescent dimmer

Fluorescent dimmer switches connect in the same way as incandescent dimmers (see page 94), but you must equip each lamp with a special ballast. Remove the fixture. Mark the wires with pieces of tape so you'll know where to refasten them. Remove the lamp holders and disconnect their wires by poking into the terminals with a nail or thin screwdriver. Remove the old ballast and install a new dimming ballast. Reconnect the lamp holders. Reinstall the fluorescent fixture. If more than one fluorescent light is connected to a dimmer switch, all the bulbs must be the same size and share the same ballast (for replacing a ballast, see page 55).

Double switch

This unit has two switches that fit into a single-switch space. Attach the feed wire to a terminal on the side with the connecting tab. (This tab enables the wire to supply power to both switches.) Connect the two wires that lead to the two fixtures to the terminals on the other side, and connect the white wires together, not to the switch.

Cord dimmer

You can purchase in-line cord dimmers for lamps that do not have switches. Some, such as this one, automatically pierce the insulation when you put the unit together. Others require stripping the wires before assembling.

Money $ Saver

These switches not only give you greater control over your lighting but can save money as well. A dimmer switch enables you to operate a bulb at less than its full intensity so you save energy and prolong the life of the bulb. Time-delay and pilot-light switches keep you from burning lights unnecessarily. Programmable switches (see page 33) save money and provide security while you are on vacation. You can program them to turn lights on and off in a pattern that makes it appear you are at home.

ADDING SURFACE-MOUNTED WIRING

If you do not want to cut into your walls, fish wires, and patch and paint afterward, consider surface-mounted wiring, often called "raceway" wiring. Surface-mounted components are available in metal or plastic and are comparatively easy to install. The system's main drawback is the way it looks. But for informal settings—a basement or a work room, for instance—it is a convenient alternative.

NOTE: *Shut off the power before tying into existing receptacles.*

YOU'LL NEED...

TIME: For a system like the one shown, about 4 hours.
SKILLS: Connecting wires and measuring and cutting the components.
TOOLS: Hacksaw, miter box, and basic electrician's tools.

Plan the job.
Check your local codes. They probably limit raceway wiring to dry locations where the walls are not subject to damage (as they are, for example, in a garage). Map where you want the pieces to go and measure carefully for all the runs. Take your plan to your electrical supplier and have a salesperson help you choose the parts you need.

Baseboard channel
Decorative and functional plastic baseboard channel can be added onto existing baseboard or even substituted for it. This type of channel is designed to simultaneously carry household wiring, coaxial cable, and telephone and computer lines. Extension boxes with receptacles, phone jacks, and coaxial hookups can be added along its length.

How the pieces go together
A raceway system begins by tapping into an existing circuit at a receptacle by using a "starter box." This extends the existing outlet so it can match up with the wall-mounted channel. Twist-away holes allow you to exit the box with raceway channel from any direction. Additional receptacles—as well as switches and light fixtures—mount directly on the wall. Begin by selecting a receptacle on a circuit that has enough capacity for additional outlets (see pages 68–69).

1. Start at the box.
NOTE: *Shut off the power.* Remove the receptacle and install the starter box, onto which the receptacle will be reinstalled as shown. Map out the system from this starting point.

2. Cut and assemble components.
When you measure the channel sections for cutting, take into account every elbow, T, and other connector. Cut the channels with a hacksaw and a miter box. Use extension connectors to tie the ends of channels together, and T and elbow connectors at corners. Measure carefully from the floor and use a level to make sure the receptacles are at the same height.

3. Attach components securely.
The channels will be bumped by furniture and normal household traffic, so take care to attach them securely. Attach channel back by locating studs and drilling screws into them where possible. Use plastic anchors for places where you can't reach studs.

4. Run the wires.
Run the wiring and hold it in place every foot or so with specially designed clips. Be sure to leave 6–8 inches of wire at each outlet so you will have room to strip and make connections.

5. Make the connections.
Connect all fixtures and receptacles (see pages 46–47). Connect to the existing receptacle, turn the power back on, and test the new fixtures and receptacles (see page 58). Install the snap-on covers for the channels, fittings, and boxes.

CHOOSING GFCI RECEPTACLES AND BREAKERS

Fuses and circuit breakers protect the wiring in your home. A ground-fault circuit interrupter (GFCI) protects people who might otherwise get a dangerous shock.

A GFCI has a microprocessor that senses tiny leakages of current and shuts off the power instantly. In most circumstances, leakage of current isn't a big problem. In properly grounded systems most of it is carried back to the service panel. What remains would scarcely give you a tickle. But if you are well grounded—standing on a wet lawn or touching a plumbing component, for example—that tiny bit of current would pass through your body on its way to the earth. As little as $\frac{1}{5}$ of an amp, just enough to light a 25-watt bulb, can be dangerous.

A GFCI is wired into both wires of a circuit so it can continuously monitor the hot and neutral current levels and compare them. These should always be equal. If the microprocessor senses a difference of just $\frac{1}{200}$ of an amp, it instantly trips the circuit. Power is

plug-in GFCI   GFCI receptacle   GFCI breaker

interrupted in $\frac{1}{40}$ of a second or less, cutting off the power before you're seriously hurt. Any ground fault is a potential hazard. If a tool or appliance is faulty, it can give you a serious shock even if its grounding wire is in good condition. So GFCI protection is a good idea anywhere you might be in contact with any dampness while using electricity.

There are three types of GFCIs: plug-ins, receptacles, and breakers. To use a portable plug-in unit, simply insert its blades into a

receptacle and plug the appliance into it. A GFCI receptacle replaces a conventional receptacle and, properly placed, can protect other receptacles on the same circuit. Install a GFCI breaker into a service panel to protect a circuit.

YOU'LL NEED...

TIME: To install either a receptacle or a breaker, 1 to 2 hours.
SKILLS: Connecting wires.
TOOLS: Screwdriver, wire stripper, and lineman's pliers.

Electrical codes require GFCI receptacles in the places where you're likely to ground an

electrical appliance. In a kitchen, GFCIs often are required for all receptacles within 6 feet of a

sink. All bathroom receptacles, as well as all outdoor receptacles, must be GFCI-protected.

INSTALLING *GFCI* DEVICES

ground

load lines

power source, NM cable

Wire a GFCI receptacle.
Attach a GFCI receptacle as shown above, connecting multiple wires with pigtails. Incoming power goes to the line leads or terminals. Load lines carry it to other receptacles on the circuit. If you install a GFCI in the first receptacle of a circuit, the entire circuit will be protected. If you are installing a GFCI at the end of a line, cap off the load leads with wire connectors or buy a version that protects only one receptacle.

SAFETY

box extender

A GFCI receptacle is bulkier than a standard receptacle, so things can get tight in the box. If gently pushing wires around doesn't seat the GFCI properly, don't try forcing it in. Force can break, and wire connections can come loose. Install a box extender to store the wires safely.

1

circuit to be protected

GFCI breaker

setscrew terminals

Clip attaches to hot bus bar.

pigtail

neutral bus bar

1. To install a GFCI breaker, connect hot and neutral wires.
You can clip a GFCI breaker into a service panel as you would an ordinary breaker (see page 71), but you must wire it differently. **NOTE:** *Shut off the power.* Shut off the main breaker and be careful not to touch the hot wires coming into the box (see pages 70–71). Select the circuit you wish to protect, unclip the old breaker from the hot bus bar, and slip it out of the service panel. Disconnect the hot and neutral wires from the old breaker. Attach both wires to the setscrew terminals of the new GFCI breaker as shown. Strip half an inch of insulation from the pigtail.

2

PUSH TO TEST

new GFCI

GFCI clips onto hot bus bar.

2. Ground and install the breaker.
Loosen a terminal on the neutral bus bar, and connect the white pigtail by inserting the wire and tightening the screw. Clipping the GFCI breaker into place attaches it to the hot bus bar. Turn the power back on, set the breaker, and push the test button. The breaker should trip.

WIRING CEILING FIXTURES WITH SWITCHES

Depending on which way is easier to run cable, you can wire a ceiling fixture with the power coming into the fixture box (as on this page), or with power coming into the switch (as on page 101).

Here, as with the configurations on the following six pages, the type of fixture doesn't matter. Whether it is a flush-mounted light, track lighting, a chandelier, or a ceiling fan, the rough wiring to the fixture is the same.

YOU'LL NEED...

TIME: Not including running the cable and installing boxes, about an hour making connections.
SKILLS: Basic electrical skills.
TOOLS: Lineman's pliers, screwdriver, wire stripper, cable ripper, and side-cutting pliers or combination tool.

power source

junction box

direction of power

ground wire

fixture box   switch box

1. Begin making connections.
NOTE: *Shut off power.* Install fixture and switch box, if they do not already exist (see pages 72–73 and 86). Find a junction box that

has power from a circuit you can use. Run two-wire cable from the junction box to the fixture box, and from the fixture box to the switch. Connect the ground wires

as shown. Connect all the black wires as shown. Note how the black wire picks up power at the junction box and carries it to the fixture box, then on to the switch.

junction box

switch box

black tape

fixture box

black tape

2. Complete the connections.
Mark the white wire running from the switch box to the fixture box with black tape on both ends.

Attach one end to the switch. At the fixture box, connect the black-taped white wire to the black fixture wire, and the untaped

white wire to the white fixture wire. At the junction box, connect all white wires together. (For how to connect wires, see page 46.)

WIRING TWO CEILING FIXTURES

*I*n this wiring configuration, power comes to the switch first, then goes to one or more fixtures by extending the run from one to the next. If you have multiple fixtures on a single line, make sure the wattage or amperage total of fixtures on the line doesn't exceed the maximum indicated on the body of the switch or what's available on that fuse or breaker (see page 69).

YOU'LL NEED...

TIME: Not including running the cable and installing boxes, about 1½ hours to plan and complete the connections.
SKILLS: Basic electrical skills.
TOOLS: Lineman's pliers, needle-nose pliers, wire stripper, cable ripper, screwdriver, and side-cutting pliers or combination tool.

power source

2-wire cable

direction of power

2-wire cable

2-wire cable

1. Begin making connections.
NOTE: *Shut off power.* Install fixture boxes and a switch box, if they do not already exist (see pages 72–73 and 86). Find a junction box that has power from a circuit you can use. Run two-wire cable from the junction box to the fixture box (see pages 42–43 for instructions on running cable), and from the fixture box to the next fixture box. Connect the ground wires as shown (see page 46). At the switch box, hook both black wires to the terminals. The current in the black wires passes through the switch, which can allow it to flow (on) or stop (off).

2. Complete the connections.
At the switch box, connect the two white wires together. At the first fixture box, connect all three black wires together, and connect all three white wires together. At the second fixture box, connect the black wires together, and connect the white wires together.

Note that you also can control two or more fixtures with the power coming to the fixture, but it's more complicated. Route the power as on page 120, and connect the second fixture's black wire to the black-taped white wire in the first fixture box. (For how to connect wires, see page 46.)

WIRING FIXTURES WITH SEPARATE SWITCHES

If you are installing ceiling fixtures and a switch box, with a little more work you can provide individual switches for the fixtures. Use a two-gang box for the switches and run three-wire cable between the fixtures and to the switch. Power comes to the fixtures by means of two-wire cable. Electricians are fond of three-wire cable because in many instances it allows you to run one cable instead of two.

YOU'LL NEED...

TIME: Not including running the cable and installing boxes, about 1½ hours to make connections.
SKILLS: Basic electrical skills.
TOOLS: Lineman's pliers, cable ripper, screwdriver, wire stripper, needle-nose pliers, and side-cutting pliers or combination tool.

to junction box

1. Begin making connections.
NOTE: *Shut off power.* Install fixture boxes and a switch box, if they do not already exist (see pages 72–73 and 100). Run two-wire cable from a junction box to the first fixture box. Run three-wire cable from the first to the second fixture box, and from there to the switch box. Connect all ground wires as shown, using green connectors. Bring power to the switches by connecting the black wires in all three boxes as shown. In the switch box, cut pigtails (the two short pieces of wire) and connect them to the switches.

2. Complete the connections.
At the switch box, connect the red wire to a switch and the white wire to the other switch. Wrap black tape on the white wire, both at the switch box and at the second fixture box, to show that it is hot. At the second fixture box, connect the two red wires together. At both fixture boxes, connect the hot and neutral wires to the fixture wires, as shown. Or install this wiring configuration with power coming to the switch. Split the incoming black wire and run the outgoing red and black wires to the fixtures. The neutral white wire, shared by both switches, passes on through.

WIRING THREE-WAY SWITCHES

Three-way switches control power to a fixture from two points, allowing you to control a light from either side of a room. Three-way switches use a three-wire system composed of a power wire and two interconnecting wires called travelers. Unless you have metal conduit or armored cable, you also need a fourth grounding wire. Power comes in through one switch, travels to the fixture and to the second switch (see page 104 for the ABCs of three-way switching).

YOU'LL NEED...

TIME: Not including running the cable and installing boxes, about 1½ hours to make connections.
SKILLS: Basic electrical skills.
TOOLS: Lineman's pliers, wire stripper, cable ripper, needle-nose pliers, side-cutting pliers, and screwdriver.

1. Begin making connections.
NOTE: *Shut off power.* Install switch boxes and a fixture box (see pages 72–73 and 100). Run two-wire cable from a junction box to the first switch box. Run three-wire cable from the first switch box to the fixture box, and from the fixture box to the second switch box. Connect all ground wires as shown (for how to connect wires, see page 46). At the first switch box, connect the hot wire to the common terminal on the switch (it is labeled and/or is darker than the other two). Attach traveler wires to the other two terminals.

At the second switch box, attach the red and white wires to the noncommon terminals of the switch. Wrap a piece of black tape on the white wire, both here and at the fixture box. At the fixture box, connect the two red wires, and connect the marked white wire to the black wire that comes from the first switch.

2. Complete the connections.
At the second switch box, connect the black wire to the common terminal on the switch. This completes the hot portion of the circuit. At the first switch box, connect the two white wires. At the fixture box, connect the white and black wires to the fixture. Once completed, either switch will operate the light.

WIRING THREE-WAYS, POWER TO SWITCH

Page 103 shows how to wire three-way switches when the light is between two switches. Here you see the light beyond both switches. A dimmer is included in this example. (With most dimmers, you can use only one per circuit.)

For this configuration, you run three-wire cable only between the switches. Power comes into the first switch and out of the second on just two wires.

YOU'LL NEED...

TIME: Not including running the cable and installing boxes, about 1½ hours to make the connections.
SKILLS: Basic electrical skills.
TOOLS: Lineman's pliers, cable ripper, screwdriver, wire stripper, needle-nose pliers, and side-cutting pliers or combination tool.

power source

1

first switch box

2-wire cable from junction box

ground wire

common terminal

3-wire cable

second switch box

2-wire cable

ground wire

traveler wires

3-way dimmer

1. Begin making connections.
NOTE: *Shut off power.* Install switch boxes and a fixture box (see pages 72–73 and 100). Run two-wire cable from a junction box to the first switch box. Run three-wire cable from the first switch box to the second, and

two-wire cable from the second switch box to the fixture box (see page 103). Connect ground wires as shown. At the first switch box, connect the black (hot) wire of the power source to the switch's common terminal (see page 46). Connect traveler wires to the other

terminals. At the second switch box, connect the travelers. (Note: A three-way dimmer can burn out if hooked up incorrectly. Check by setting up the circuit with ordinary three-way switches and turning on the power. Then replace one switch with a dimmer.)

2

2-wire cable

3-wire cable

2-wire cable

2. Complete the connections.
At the second switch box, connect the black wire that goes to the fixture box with the dimmer's

common wire. Connect the two white wires.
At the first switch box, connect the white wires. At the fixture box,

connect black to black wires and white to white wires. Install the switches and switch plates and the light fixture.

WIRING THREE-WAYS, POWER TO FIXTURE

In this situation, power comes to the light fixture, then proceeds to the two switches. A two-wire cable runs to the fixture and to the the first switch box. A three-wire cable runs only from switch box to switch box.

YOU'LL NEED...

TIME: After running cable and installing boxes, 1½ hours
SKILLS: Basic electrical skills.
TOOLS: See page 104.

ABCs OF THREE-WAYS

Follow these principles when installing any three-way configuration: **A.** Always attach the incoming hot (black) wire to the common terminal of one switch. **B.** Use traveler wires to connect the other terminals to each other, never to the light. C. Connect the common terminal of the second switch only to the black fixture wire.

power source

second switch box

2-wire cable from junction box

traveler wires

black tape

2-wire cable

first switch box

black tape

3-wire cable

1. Begin making connections.
At the ceiling box, connect the black, hot wires. At the first switch box, connect the hot wire to the common terminal and the traveler wires to the other terminals. Wrap a piece of black tape on either end of the white wire to show that it is hot. At the second switch box, attach the traveler wires.

2-wire cable

3-wire cable

2-wire cable

black tape

black tape

2. Complete the connections.
At the second switch, connect the black wire to the common terminal. At the first switch box, connect the black and white wires, and wrap a piece of black tape at either end of the white wire to show that it is hot. At the fixture box, connect white to white wire and the black-taped white wire to the black wire of the fixture.

WIRING FOUR-WAY SWITCHES

To control a fixture from three or more different switches, use one or more four-way switches. You can install any number of them between a pair of three-way switches. In four-way situations, the first and last switches must always be three-ways.

In this illustration the power flows from junction box to switch to switch to switch to the fixture. It also could be routed as shown on pages 103–105.

YOU'LL NEED...

TIME: Not including running the cable and installing boxes, about 2 hours to make the connections for a fixture and three switches.
SKILLS: Basic electrical skills.
TOOLS: Lineman's pliers, cable ripper, wire stripper, screwdriver, needle-nose pliers, and side-cutting pliers or combination tool.

power source

1. Begin making connections.
NOTE: *Shut off power.* Install switch boxes and a fixture box. Run two-wire cable from a junction box to the first switch box. Run three-wire cable from the first switch box to the second and third ones, and two-wire cable from the third switch box to the fixture box. Connect all ground wires.

At the first switch box, connect the black wire from the power source to the switch's common terminal. Connect the traveler wires to the other terminals.

At the second and third switches, connect the traveler wires as shown. The four-way switch carries only traveler wires. (For how to connect wires, see page 46.)

2. Complete the connections.
At the third switch, connect the fixture box's black wire to the common terminal. Connect the white wires. Connect the white wires at the first and second switch boxes. Connect the fixture to the two wires at the fixture box and install the switches and switch plates. Once completed, you can turn the fixture on and off from any of the three switches.

ADDING RECEPTACLES

Once you find a usable power source, adding a receptacle is easy to figure out. Most of the work is cutting the wall, installing a box, fishing the cable, and patching the wall.

You can tap into an existing receptacle, as shown on this page, only if it is at the end of a wiring run. If it's in the middle of a run, all of its terminals will be occupied.

YOU'LL NEED...

TIME: Not including running the cable and installing boxes, about an hour to make connections.
SKILLS: Basic electrical skills.
TOOLS: Lineman's pliers, cable ripper, screwdriver, wire stripper, needle-nose pliers, and side-cutting pliers or combination tool.

1. Begin making connections. NOTE: *Shut off power.* Find a receptacle box where you can draw power without overcrowding the box or overloading the circuit. (You also can draw power from a junction box. Just connect to the hot and neutral wires instead of to the receptacle.) Install the new receptacle box. Run a two-wire cable from the existing box to the new box.

Remove the screws that secure the existing receptacle to the box, and pull it out so you can work on it. Connect the ground wires in both boxes as shown.

2. Complete the connections. At the existing box, connect the black wire to the hot receptacle terminal, which is brass-colored. Connect the white wire to the other terminal. At the new box, also connect the black wire to the hot terminal and the white wire to the other terminal. Wrap both receptacles with electrician's tape so that all the terminals are covered. Fasten both receptacles in place, turn on power and test your installation. Finally, attach the receptacle plates.

ADDING 240-VOLT RECEPTACLES

Some 240-volt equipment—central air-conditioning units and electric water heaters, for example—have no plugs and are wired directly into junction boxes because they do not need to be moved. Ranges, clothes dryers, and other appliances are connected by cords and plugs and require special receptacles.

The wiring requirements for 240-volt circuits are specific. For a 30-amp dryer, use a 30-amp breaker and 10-gauge wire. For a 50-amp range, use a 50-amp breaker and 6-gauge wire. Choose a receptacle designed to provide the correct amperage for your appliance and has holes to match the prongs on the plug.

YOU'LL NEED...

TIME: To install a 240-volt receptacle after the wiring is completed, about an hour.
SKILLS: Running cable and stripping and connecting wires.
TOOLS: Screwdriver, wire stripper, and lineman's pliers.

CAUTION!

DANGER! HIGH VOLTAGE! Wiring for 240-volt receptacles is no different from 120-volt lines except that the danger is much, much greater. Even if you are dry and are wearing rubber-soled shoes, a jolt of this current could do you serious physical harm and perhaps even kill you. Check and double-check that the power is off before installing a 240-volt receptacle. This is one job where you may want to call in an experienced electrician, just for safety's sake.

240-volt wiring
NOTE: *Shut off the power.* Wiring starts at a 240-volt breaker or fuse in the service panel and ends at a specially designed receptacle. A 240-volt circuit should supply only one appliance; no other receptacles can be attached to it. Connect 120-volt wires to a breaker and the neutral wire to the neutral bus (see pages 70–71)

Floor-mounted 240-volt receptacle
If no outlet box is available, you can install this unit on the floor. Position it so it won't get bumped when you move the appliance. Remove the cover and connect the neutral wire to the terminal marked "white," and the red and black wires to the other terminals. All receptacles shown on this page use the neutral wire as ground.

Wall-mounted 240-volt receptacle
Install a receptacle box and run 10-3 cable (for a 30-amp breaker) or 6-3 cable (for a 50-amp breaker) to it. (For information on running cable in finished spaces, see pages 72–73; for information on selecting cable, see page 35.) Strip the black, red, and white wires (see pages 44–45) to the length marked on the receptacle housing and attach.

Surface-mounted 240-volt receptacle for basement or garage
Install a box (see page 38) and run conduit (see pages 82–84) to the desired location. Fish red, black, and white 10- or 6-gauge wire (see page 85). Strip wires and insert them into the slots in the terminals as shown; tighten the screws.

SPLITTING, SWITCHING RECEPTACLES

*E*xamine a standard duplex receptacle, and you'll see that each set of terminals on either side is connected by a small metal tab—one silver-colored, one brass-colored (see Step 3 below). If you break the brass bridge, the upper and lower receptacles can be used independently, one controlled by a switch and one functioning like a standard receptacle. A split receptacle is handy when you want to turn a lamp on and off from a wall switch, for example, but still leave half of the receptacle for general use. Sometimes you may need a split receptacle when you want to supply the two outlets of a heavily used receptacle with two different circuits.

YOU'LL NEED...
TIME: With the cables and boxes in place, about an hour to make the connections.
SKILLS: Basic electrical skills.
TOOLS: Screwdriver, wire strippers, lineman's pliers, and needle-nose pliers.

1. Install cable and boxes.
NOTE: *Shut off the power.* Disconnect the receptacle and run two-wire cable to a switch box. Connect the ground wires.

2. Attach and connect black wires.
Route power to the switch by tying the two black wires together with a pigtail at the receptacle box. At the switch box, connect the black wire.

3. Continue wiring and split outlets.
Add black tape to both ends of the white wire that runs between the boxes to show that it's hot. Connect it to the switch and receptacle terminals. Connect the remaining black wire to the receptacle. Snap off the brass tab with needle-nose pliers to split the outlets. Leave the silver-colored metal tab in place.

4. Complete the wiring.
Connect the white and ground wires to the receptacle, screw the receptacle and switch to their boxes, turn on the power, and test. In this example, the upper outlet will be live only when the switch is on. The lower one remains on at all times.

ADDING OUTDOOR RECEPTACLES

The easiest way to bring power to the outside of your house is to install a receptacle directly opposite an existing interior receptacle. If you need to place the outdoor receptacle elsewhere, see page 97 for ideas on fishing the cable. Be sure that the interior receptacle box you choose has room for new wires. Check that you will not be overloading the circuit (see page 69). Codes usually require a GFCI receptacle with a weatherproof cover plate with a spring-loaded door.

YOU'LL NEED...

TIME: Barring unexpected obstacles, plan on 3 hours.
SKILLS: Basic electrical skills.
TOOLS: Drill with spade bit and perhaps a bit extension; screwdriver; lineman's pliers; and a jigsaw, saber saw, or keyhole saw. If you have a masonry exterior, a masonry bit, cold chisel, and hammer.

Drill at an angle to offset the boxes from each other.

1. Drill a hole to the outside.
NOTE: *Be sure to shut off the power.* Remove the face plate and the interior outlet. To accurately locate your new receptacle, punch out a knockout hole in the back of the box, and drill a hole through the house to the outside. To make sure you have room for a box on each side (the wall may not be thick enough), drill off to the side.

2. Cut the exterior opening.
Find the hole on the outside of your house, and draw an outline of the new box (see page 73). Drill a hole at each corner of the box, and cut out with a jigsaw. If you have a masonry exterior, drill a series of closely spaced holes with a masonry bit. Knock out the hole with a cold chisel and hammer.

3. Connect the cable.
Cut a piece of cable long enough to allow you working room. Connect it to the interior box—you will need a helper to reach through the exterior hole and hold the locknut in position while you tighten the locknut. Connect cable to the exterior box.

GFCI receptacle

4. Make the electrical connections.
With the box pushed into place, strip the sheathing and the ends of the wires and make connections on both ends of the cable (see pages 44–47). Be sure to connect to the "line" terminals on the GFCI receptacle and the load terminals on the existing interior receptacle.

weatherproof cover plate

foam gasket

5. Install the box and cover.
Attach the box firmly in place. With a masonry wall, insert screws into the back of the box and attach them to a framing member, or mortar the box in place. Fasten the GFCI receptacle to the box. Finally, attach the gasket and weatherproof cover plate.

INSTALLING OUTDOOR LIGHTING

*I*f you have eaves overhanging an exterior door, it makes sense to install a light there, where it will be better protected from weather than a wall-mounted unit would be. You're also likely to find it easy to run cable from an attic junction box to the eaves.

Consider installing a motion-detector floodlight. These are quite inexpensive, and if you wire it to be controlled with a regular wall switch, you can switch off the motion-sensing feature.

YOU'LL NEED...

TIME: With no unusual obstacles, plan on 4 hours.
SKILLS: Basic electrical skills, measuring and cutting eaves.
TOOLS: Screwdriver, lineman's pliers, drill, saber saw or keyhole saw, and fish tape.

Center the light above the door.

1. Cut a hole in the eaves.
NOTE: *Shut off the power.* Draw an outline of the new box—a retrofit box with wings for attaching to the eaves will probably work best. Drill starter holes, and cut the hole with a saber saw or a keyhole saw.

2. Run the cable, install the box.
Fish cable and make connections to an interior switch (see pages 47 and 85). Connect the cable to the new box, and firmly attach the box to the eaves.

3. Wire the floodlight.
Connect the wires to the floodlight using wire connectors (see page 46), and screw the light firmly to the box. If your unit has a motion detector, wait until nighttime and adjust the direction of the sensor so it turns on as people approach the door.

transformer

GFCI outdoor receptacle

Locate transformer 3' above ground.

INSTALL A LOW-VOLTAGE LIGHTING SYSTEM

For highlighting your landscaping, the easiest and least costly choice is low-voltage lighting. Kits containing 10 or more lights, a transformer, and lots of wire are inexpensive and readily available. Installation is simple: Assemble the lights, and attach the cable. The lights usually can be poked into the ground, and you don't need to dig a trench for the wiring—just cover it with a bit of mulch. Fasten the transformer to a wall at least 3 feet above the ground and plug it into an outdoor receptacle.

ADDING BATHROOM VENT FANS/LIGHTS

*I*f your bathroom does not have a window that opens, most codes require that you have a vent fan to remove moisture and odor. Adding a fan can make your bathroom more pleasant, protect your walls from mildew and moisture damage, and can lower air-conditioning costs. You can wire a bathroom fan so that it operates by itself, but some codes require the fan to switch on with the light.

YOU'LL NEED...

TIME: About one day.
SKILLS: Basic electrical skills and carpentry skills.
TOOLS: Screwdriver, lineman's pliers, drill, and saber saw.

flush with surface of ceiling

1. Install the fan unit.
NOTE: *Shut off the power.* Cut a ceiling opening between joists. From the attic, nail or screw the unit's mounting brackets securely to the framing. Make sure the fan assembly is level and flush with the surface of the ceiling below before fastening.

MEASUREMENTS

WILL IT REALLY VENT?

Many bathroom fans do little more than make noise because they lack the power to draw moisture through the ductwork to the outside. The larger the bathroom and the longer the duct, the more powerful the fan needs to be. When you shop for a vent fan, know the size of the bathroom and how long the ducting will be. If the salesperson cannot help you choose the right size fan, open a fan box and check the manufacturer's instructions.

2. Run the ductwork.
In some climates, and if your attic has adequate cross-ventilation, you may be able to get by without venting to the outside—check local codes. Otherwise, run flexible ducting to a soffit or to a roof-mounted outlet. To increase the efficiency of your fan, run the ducts as straight as possible.

3. Wire the switches.
For a combination fan and light, fish two-wire cable to the switches, then run three wires from the switches to the unit. For a fan-only installation, run two-wire cable to the unit (for instructions on running wire in finished and unfinished spaces, see pages 72–77). If the fan has a heater, you'll probably need to run a 15- or 20-amp circuit (see pages 68–71 for information about planning and adding circuits).

4. Wire the vent fan unit.
Inside the unit, connect the wires according to the manufacturer's directions. Typical connections are shown above. Install the working parts in the housing, and plug them into the appropriate receptacles. Turn on the power, and test the fan and light. Finally, fit the grille. Once a year, remove the grille and clean the fan blades and other parts inside the fan.

ADDING ATTIC FANS

On a hot summer day, attic temperatures can reach 150 degrees Fahrenheit. Turbine-type roof ventilators can help dissipate the heat but, because they depend on wind to supplement the upward draft of hot air, you're out of luck on a still day when the heat buildup may be most intense.

A thermostat-controlled attic fan mounted in the roof or a gable-end wall automatically turns the fan on to vent overheated attics.

YOU'LL NEED...

TIME: A full day, with a helper.
SKILLS: Basic electrical and carpentry skills.
TOOLS: Ladder to get to the roof, roof jacks to provide a safe standing place if the roof is steep, drill, saber saw or keyhole saw, utility knife, hammer, screwdriver, and lineman's pliers.

Money $ Saver

COMBINE WHOLE-HOUSE FANS AND ATTIC FANS

Depending on your climate and use pattern, it may make economic sense to combine a thermostat-controlled fan with a whole-house fan. Here's why:
■ Even after sundown, super-heated air continues to put a heavy strain on your home's air-conditioning system. Improving attic ventilation can cut cooling costs up to 30 percent.
■ A whole-house fan will pull a strong, steady draft up through the house—and push air out of the attic—on those days when you choose not to use the air-conditioning. It is not, however, efficient to use a whole-house fan while the air-conditioning is on.

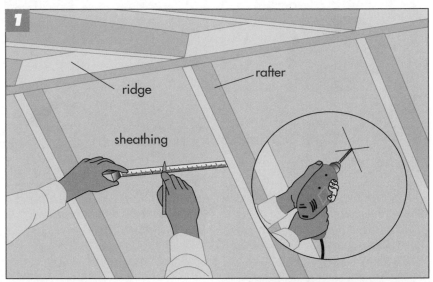

ridge
rafter
sheathing

1. Drill a locating hole.
Position your fan as close to the ridge as you can so as little hot air as possible will build up in the attic area above the fan. Choose a slope of the roof that's not visible from the street. Go into the attic and pick a pair of rafters close to the attic's center. Measure to a point midway between them. Drill up through the roof at this point. Leave the drill bit in place or push a piece of wire up through the hole as a marker.

MEASUREMENTS

HOW BIG A FAN DO YOU NEED?

To determine how powerful a unit to buy, multiply the square footage of your attic by 0.7. Add 15 percent if your roofing is dark-colored—it will absorb more heat from sunlight than a lighter, more reflective roofing color. The resulting number tells you the cubic feet per minute (CFM) that your fan should pull.

2. Cut the roofing.
Find the locating hole on the roof and set the fan in place on top of it. The flashing should tuck neatly under shingles above the fan housing. To minimize the number of shingles you will have to trim, adjust the unit up or down slightly. Trace the outline of the unit on the roofing.

Use the template that comes with the fan to mark for a circular cut on the shingles. Cut the shingles with a utility knife.

For a gable-end installation, cut through the siding only—not the sheathing—with a circular saw. If the wall has a window or louvers, adapt the opening to fit the fan.

3. Cut the sheathing.
A second template will guide you in marking a smaller circle inside the cutaway shingles. Use a saber saw or keyhole saw to cut through the roofing paper and sheathing. Remove any nails in the shingles that lie in the top two-thirds of the unit's outline you traced onto the roof. Now you're ready to slip the unit into place.

4. Install the exhaust vent.
Turn the fan over and coat the underside of its flashing with roofing cement. Slide it under the shingles above and on either side; the flashing should overlap the shingles below the housing. Center the fan over the hole. Pry up shingles covering the flashing and nail it in place. Drive the nails so they penetrate the sheathing, and cover them with roofing cement.

EXPERTS' INSIGHT

BUILDING A DEFENSE AGAINST HUMIDITY
If you live in an area known for high humidity, consider purchasing an attic fan that comes equipped with a humidistat in addition to a thermostat. A humidistat reads the humidity in the same way a thermostat reads the temperature, giving you another measurement for controlling the comfort level of your home.

On humid days an attic fan can make your home more comfortable by removing some of the moist air. Keeping attic moisture under control also helps keep your fiberglass insulation from compacting and losing its effectiveness.

5. Install the thermostat.
Back in the attic, screw the thermostat switch to a stud or rafter above the fan and out of the fan's airstream. Remove the box cover plate.

6. Make the wiring connections.
Run cable from a junction box to the thermostat. Install cable to an accessible switch that can be used to override the automatic control. Follow the fan manufacturer's instructions for wiring. If instructions weren't provided, make the connections as indicated above, using wire connectors.

7. Test and adjust.
Turn on the power and test your installation. An adjusting screw in the thermostat box lets you set the temperature that will activate the fan. The temperature setting will vary depending on your roof and the fan's capacity. Consult the manufacturer's instructions for the right temperature for your attic.

ADDING WHOLE-HOUSE FANS

Before you select a whole-house fan, plan the overall venting of your house. The fan should pull air through open windows and doors on the lower floors and out through vents in the attic, eaves, and gables. Without adequate openings below and above the fan, it will not be able to do its job. Leave at least 2 feet of clearance between the fan and any obstructions. If you stack your attic with boxes, the fan may not have room to breathe, which will make it noisy as well as inefficient. Installation is not as difficult as you may think: The fan sits on top of joists in the attic, so cutting and reframing aren't necessary.

YOU'LL NEED...

TIME: About a day, if fishing the cable is straightforward.
SKILLS: Basic electrical and carpentry skills.
TOOLS: Drill, saber saw, screwdriver, and lineman's pliers.

MEASUREMENTS

CHOOSING A FAN

■ Buy a fan that's rated to pull a minimum cubic feet per minute (CFM) equal to the square footage of your house multiplied by 3.

■ Do you really plan on venting the whole house? If you plan to open the windows of just a few rooms, use only their square footage to figure the needed CFM.

■ Often a hall is the best spot for a fan. Will it fit in yours? Fans designed to vent houses larger than 1,800 square feet (5,400 CFM) generally have louver panels of 38 inches or more—too wide for some hallways.

1. Establish a location.
Find a spot for the fan—the top-floor hallway ceiling is the usual place. Measure from a point common to the hall and the attic, choose a location for the fan, and clear away the insulation. Beside the joists, drill locator holes for cutting away the drywall or plaster. From below, cut a hole in the ceiling. Don't cut any joists.

2. Install the fan.
Set the fan on top of the joists, directly above the ceiling hole. Secure it by driving screws into the joists. Fasten it down tight so it cannot vibrate. Install the plastic baffles provided with the fan. They seal the cavities between the joists so the fan draws properly.

3. Install the louver panel.
From below tip the louver panel into place so it covers the entire hole. Attach it to the ceiling by driving screws up into the joists. The louver is lightly spring-loaded so it stays shut when the fan is not in use but opens when the fan is switched on.

4. Make the electrical connections.
Run power up into a switch then to the fan (see page 75). Consider installing a timer switch or a programmable switch (see page 95) so you can have the fan run during those times of the day when it is most needed.

REPLACING DOORBELLS

A doorbell system starts with a transformer that reduces current from 120 volts to somewhere between 6 and 30 volts. From the transformer, light-gauge wire connects the bell, chime, or buzzer with the back in a circuit that is usually open at the button. Pressing the button, which is a spring-loaded switch, closes the circuit and sends low-voltage power to activate the bell, chime, or buzzer.

If your bell does not work, find the cause by using the process of elimination described in the steps below. A voltmeter or multitester will make the job easier, but you also can do most tests with a short piece of bell wire or a screwdriver.

Unless you are working on the transformer, there's no need to shut off power while inspecting a bell. The voltage coming from the transformer is so low you will barely feel it.

YOU'LL NEED...
TIME: You may find and solve the problem in minutes, or it could take several hours.
SKILLS: Using continuity tester and ability to work methodically.
TOOLS: Voltmeter or multitester or short length of wire, and screwdriver.

1. Check wires to the button.
To check a doorbell system, remove the button, turn it over, and examine the connections. Attach a spring clip to the wires to make sure that they cannot accidentally slip back through the hole. Scrape away any corrosion on the terminals. If the wires are corroded, cut off bad, strip (see pages 44–45), and reconnect. Tighten the connections to the terminals. Wrap any faulty insulation with electrical tape.

single-button system

button

low-voltage transformer

chime

120 volts

two-button system

rear

front

1

Clip keeps wires from slipping into hole.

terminals

back of button

2. Test the button by jumping...
Weather and abuse make buttons the most vulnerable parts of a bell system. Test a button by jumping its terminals with a short piece of wire, as shown above. If the bell sounds, the button is faulty and should be replaced.

...or use a continuity tester.
You can also test the button by disconnecting the wires and touching both terminals with a continuity tester. If the tester glows when the button is pressed, the button is working. If the bell still doesn't sound, disconnect the button, twist its wires together, and test further.

3. Check wires to the transformer.
Find your transformer. It may be near your home's service panel or attached to a junction box in the vicinity of the door or the bell. Look for corrosion, wires that have come loose, or faulty insulation.

4. Test the transformer...
To check the transformer, disconnect both wires and touch each terminal with the probes of a voltmeter or multitester. Set the dial at ACV 50 or less. If the meter shows no current at all,

the transformer is the culprit and should be replaced. You also can jump the low-voltage terminals with a screwdriver to test the transformer. It is OK if you see a weak spark.

...and replace if necessary.
NOTE: *Shut off the power.* Remove the cover plate of the electrical box, remove the transformer, and disconnect the wires. Wire the new transformer just like the old one, and reassemble the bell.

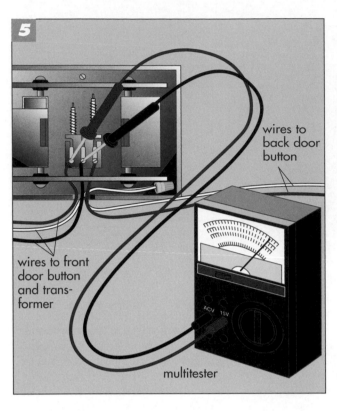

wires to back door button

wires to front door button and transformer

multitester

5. Inspect the bell.

If the button, the wires, and the transformer are not to blame, check the bell itself. Remove the cover. Look for loose or broken connections. Even if you don't have a second button, the chime will have terminals labeled front and rear. Touch the voltmeter or multitester probes to the front and trans (meaning "transformer") terminals. If the meter registers a reading, then power is going to the bell, but the bell is defective. If you have a rear button, test again, touching rear and trans.

If you don't have a voltmeter, test the bell by removing it and temporarily wiring it directly to the transformer. If it is working, it will ring.

EXPERTS' INSIGHT

IF EVERYTHING IS OK, IT'S THE WIRES

If the button, transformer, and bell check out, a wire likely has broken. Disconnect the wires going into the bell and test current flow with a voltmeter or multitester. Or touch the front and rear wires to the transformer wire and look for a spark.

REPLACING CHIME UNITS

When shopping for a doorbell, consider your wall: Will the new unit cover up the discolored area left by the old one, or will it require you to do some touch-up painting? Make sure the doorbell you choose has the same voltage rating as its

TIME-SAVER

INSTALL A REMOTE-CONTROLLED CHIME

Running new wires is a time-consuming job. If you have damaged wires, consider installing a remote-controlled bell. This type costs more than a regular unit, but saves you the trouble of running wires.

1. Label wires and remove chime.
Shut off power to the circuit if you like, but it shouldn't be necessary because the voltage is so low. The terminals are labeled, so label the wires the same as you disconnect them. These labels also will prevent the wires from accidentally slipping through the hole and into the wall. Unscrew the chime from the wall, and remove it.

2. Install the new chime.
Attach the new chime to the wall with mounting screws. Use plastic anchors if you cannot drive a screw into a stud. Connect the low-voltage wires to the terminals, and attach the cover.

PLUMBING BASICS

GETTING TO KNOW YOUR SYSTEM

With so many pipes and fittings running unseen inside walls and floors, a plumbing system can seem complicated and mysterious. But plumbing is actually a straightforward matter of distributing incoming water to where it's wanted and facilitating the outflow of waste. Here's an overview of how household plumbing works.

Supply, drain, and vent systems

The supply system brings water into your house, divides it into hot and cold water lines, and distributes it to various fixtures (sinks, toilets, showers, tubs) and appliances (washing machines, dishwashers, water heaters, heating system boilers).

The drain system carries water away from the fixtures and appliances and out of the house. The vent system supplies air to the drain pipes so waste flows out freely. Because drains and vents use the same types of pipes and are tied together, they often are referred to as the drain-waste-vent system, or DWV.

Locating the water meter and main shutoffs

The first step toward gaining mastery over your house's plumbing system is to locate the water meter and, more important, the main shutoff.

Look for the place where water first enters your house. Usually, you'll find a pipe an inch or so thick, called a water main, coming up through the floor in your basement or first floor. If you have metered water, the pipe will enter and exit a round gauge, the water meter. This has either a digital readout that looks like a car's odometer or a series of five or six dials. The meter tells how much water passes into the house. If you have a well, or if your bill does not change no matter how much water you use, you don't have a meter.

Near the place where the water main enters your house, look for one or two valves that you can turn on and off by hand. This is the main shutoff for the house.

You may have an additional shutoff outside the house, buried in a cavity sometimes called a "buffalo box." To find it, look for a round metal cover in the ground near the street or the edge of your property. It may be overgrown with grass. Pry it up and look inside with a flashlight. There may be a valve that you can turn by hand, or you may need a special long-handled "key." Older homes in warm weather locations sometimes have an exposed valve just outside the house.

If you have an older home, don't depend entirely on the inside shutoff; it can break, leak, or stop shutting off completely. If you'll have to shut down the system often during a project, learn where your outside shutoff is and use it to shut off the water.

> ## CAUTION!
> ### ALWAYS BE PREPARED TO SHUT OFF THE WATER
> In case of a burst pipe or other emergency, be ready to shut off the main water supply quickly. Let members of your family know where the main shutoff is. Clear away boxes and furniture so it is easy to get at. If it takes a special tool to shut off your water, keep it handy.

> ## WHERE YOUR RESPONSIBILITY ENDS
> The water meter is the continental divide when it comes to assigning responsibility for plumbing repairs. Most often, the water meter and pipes leading away from the house are the responsibility of the water company. Anything on the house side of the meter is your responsibility. However, if you will be adding new fixtures (not just replacing old ones), you may be required to have a larger water main coming into the house. If so, you'll have to pay for it. Check when you get your permit.

> ## THE NEW AND THE OLD
> In the old days, plumbers installed cast-iron drain lines. They had to pack each joint with tarred oakum, then pour in molten lead—a practice dating from the time of the Romans. For supply lines and smaller drain lines, they used galvanized pipe, which is strong but can rust and corrode over time.
>
> Plastic drain lines and copper supply lines are superior to the old materials. They last much longer and are easier to work with. However, it took many years for different localities' codes to make the switch to modern materials. In some places, for instance, cast-iron was required by code well into the 1980s. Even to this day, some municipalities require that supply lines be made with galvanized pipe.
>
> If you have old pipe, there's no need to rip it out. Many products are available that make it easy to connect the new to the old. These products often use gaskets that can remain leakproof for many decades.

SUPPLY SYSTEM

Water enters your house through a pipe that connects either to a municipal water line or a private well. If your bill changes according to how much water you use, your water flows through a water meter. Near the meter you will find one or two main shutoffs.

From there water travels to the water heater. Water from a private well goes to a pressure tank before going to the heater.

From the water heater, a pair of water lines—one hot and one cold—branch out through the house to serve the various fixtures (toilets, tubs, sinks, showers) and water-using appliances (dishwashers, washing machines, heating system boilers).

These supply lines are always under pressure; if they are opened or a break occurs, water will shoot out and not stop until it is shut off in some way. That is why modern homes have stop (or shutoff) valves for every fixture and appliance. If your home is not equipped with them, plan to install them. They'll make maintenance and repairs more convenient and will more than pay for themselves should you face a serious break.

Older homes have plumbing systems that use galvanized pipe, which will corrode over time, leading to low pressure and leaks. Newer homes use copper and plastic supply lines, which last much longer.

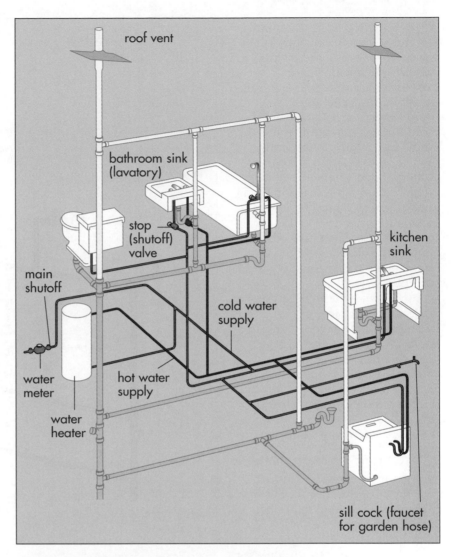

roof vent

bathroom sink (lavatory)

stop (shutoff) valve

main shutoff

cold water supply

kitchen sink

water meter

hot water supply

water heater

sill cock (faucet for garden hose)

SUPPLY SYSTEM PROBLEM SOLVER

For answers to these problems and questions   **see pages**

DRAIN SYSTEM

Drain pipes use gravity to rid the house of liquid and solid waste. This system also guards against foul-smelling and potentially harmful gases entering the house from the municipal drain system or the septic field.

All fixtures except the toilet empty into a trap (toilets have built-in traps). A trap is a curved section of drain pipe that holds enough standing water to make an airtight seal that prevents sewer gases from backing up and leaking into the home. Each time a fixture is used, the old water in the trap is forced down the line and replaced with new water.

After leaving the trap, drain water moves in pipes sloped at no less than ¼ inch per foot toward a waste stack (also called a soil pipe), a large, vertical pipe that carries water below the floor. There it takes a bend and proceeds out to a municipal sewer line or a private septic system. A clean-out is a place where you can insert an auger to clear the line. Traps serve the same function.

Drain pipes come in 1¼-inch pipe for a bathroom sink, 1½-inch for kitchen sinks and bathtubs, and 3- or 4-inch for toilets. The stack is usually a 4-inch pipe. Older homes use cast-iron pipe for the stacks and galvanized pipe for the other drain lines. New homes use plastic, and occasionally copper, for stacks and drains.

roof vent

toilet with internal trap

trap

trap

trap

clean-out

floor drain

waste stack or soil pipe

flexible drain line for washing machine

DRAIN SYSTEM PROBLEM SOLVER

For answers to these problems and questions   **see pages**

VENT SYSTEM

*T*o flow freely, drain pipes need air. Without air, water will glug down a drain like soda pop from a bottle. A plumbing vent plays the same role as that little second opening in a gasoline can. With the stopper closed, gas pours out slowly. But once the stopper is opened, the air entering the can equalizes the pressure and allows the liquid to flow freely.

Also the air supplied by a vent prevents siphoning action, which might otherwise pull water up out of traps and toilets and allow sewage gases to escape into the house. Instead vents carry the gases through your roof. Sewer gas, composed largely of methane, is not only smelly, it is harmful and dangerous. Install a top quality venting system, even if it means a lot of work.

A main vent is an extension of the waste stack and reaches upward through the roof. Branch vents tie into the main vent. Each and every plumbing fixture and appliance must be vented properly, either by tying into a main vent or by having a vent of its own that extends through the roof.

When installing a new fixture in a new location (not just replacing an existing fixture), venting is often the most difficult problem to overcome. Local codes require that venting adhere to specific dimension requirements. Research these requirements before you begin planning. Vent pipes are made of the same materials as drain pipes, although sometimes they are of smaller dimensions.

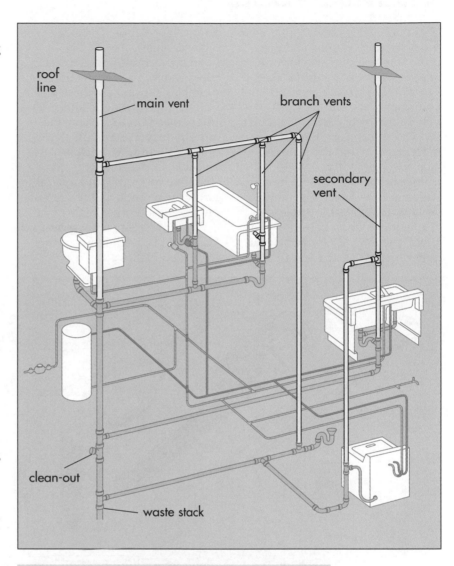

roof line
main vent
branch vents
secondary vent
clean-out
waste stack

VENT SYSTEM PROBLEM SOLVER

For answers to these problems and questions   **see pages**

fittings for vents .162–163
types of pipe used for venting 160–161

ESSENTIAL TOOLS

Plumbing does not require a lot of expensive tools, and even those that you may use for only one job are well worth the cost. The money you save by doing your own work will pay for them many times over. Using the tools shown on this page, you can tackle most plumbing projects.

To clear drain lines, get a **plunger.** The type shown here, with the extra flange extending downward, is ideal for toilets and also works well on bathtubs and sinks. Use a hand-cranked **drain auger** to clear away clogs that

won't plunge away. For toilets, use a **closet auger**.

To disassemble and connect pipes and to make many other plumbing repairs, purchase a pair of high-quality **tongue-and-groove pliers** that adjust to grab almost any size pipe. A standard **adjustable pipe wrench** is essential for working with threaded iron pipe. An **adjustable Crescent wrench** will fit the nuts on faucets and other fixtures.

To cut pipe, use a **hacksaw.** Hacksaw blades dull quickly so have extra blades on hand.

For running new pipes through walls, you will need a **drill** with plenty of **spade bits**. To cut away drywall or plaster to make room for the plumbing, use a **keyhole saw.** A **flashlight** comes in handy when you need to peer into wall cavities and under sinks.

For delicate chores such as removing faucet O-rings and clips, have a pair of **needle-nose pliers** on hand. And have a ready supply of general-purpose tools, including **screwdrivers**, a **putty knife**, a **utility knife**, and a **tape measure**.

adjustable pipe wrench

needle-nose pliers

adjustable Crescent wrench

keyhole saw

tongue-and-groove pliers

drill

spade bit

tape measure

utility knife

screwdrivers

hacksaw

putty knife

drain auger

closet auger

flashlight

plunger

SPECIALIZED TOOLS

Some tools are designed for specialized plumbing tasks. Choose the ones that will help you work with your materials and fixtures.

If you will be soldering copper pipe, you must have a **propane torch.** If you have a lot to do, pay the extra money for a self-igniting model. Otherwise, get an inexpensive **spark lighter.**

To bend flexible copper tubing without kinking it, use a **tubing bender.** A two-part **flaring tool** is necessary if you want to make flare joints in copper tubing. If you plan on cutting copper pipe or tubing, buy a **tubing cutter.** It makes easier and cleaner cuts than a **hacksaw** and will not squeeze tubing out of shape. For cutting plastic supply pipes, a **plastic tubing cutter** makes the job easier. To set the proper incline for drain pipes, you'll need a **level.**

When working on faucets and sinks, you will sometimes need a **basin wrench** to get at nuts you cannot reach with pliers. If you have a damaged faucet seat that needs replacing, don't take a chance with a screwdriver—use a **seat wrench.** For those big nuts that hold on the basket strainers of kitchen sinks, you may need a **spud wrench.**

When plunging and augering don't clear out a clog, a **blow bag** will often do the trick: hook up a garden hose to it, insert it into the drain pipe, and turn on the water.

For large-scale demolition, notching studs and joists, and quickly cutting galvanized pipe, a **reciprocating saw** makes the job much easier. If you need to chip away tiles to get at plumbing, use a **cold chisel.**

propane torch

spark lighter

cold chisel

seat wrench

plastic tubing cutter

spud wrench

flaring tool

basin wrench

tubing cutter

blow bag

tubing bender

reciprocating saw

level

PREVENTING FREEZE-UPS

Ice-cold tap water may taste refreshing, but it also can be a chilling sign that your plumbing is in trouble. Burst pipes from freezing are difficult and expensive to fix, so take precautions if there is reason to believe that your system will not survive the coldest days of the year. New homes with pipes placed near an exterior wall can be as prone to having frozen pipes as poorly insulated older homes. Often the best solution is insulating the wall or ceiling that contains the pipes. This helps keep your home warm and protects your pipes. This page shows some additional ways to prevent plumbing freeze-ups.

> ### YOU'LL NEED...
> **TIME:** About three hours to prepare the average home.
> **SKILLS:** Beginner carpentry and plumbing skills.
> **TOOLS:** Knife and flashlight.

1. Insulate the pipes.
Insulation goes a long way toward preventing freeze-ups, as long as every square inch of pipe—including connections—is protected. Pipe jacketing comes in standard lengths that can be cut with a knife and secured with electrical tape. Ordinary insulation, cut in strips and bundled around pipes, works equally well for less cost but more labor. In an extremely cold wall or floor, pack the entire cavity with insulation. Also consider insulating long hot water runs, especially those that pass through unheated spaces. The added insulation will conserve water-heating energy.

2. Wrap pipes with heat tape.
Electric heat tape draws only modest amounts of current, so it is safe and inexpensive to use. Wrap tape around the pipe, and plug the tape into a receptacle. A thermostat turns the tape on and off as needed. However tape will not work during a power outage—the very time when the protection may be most needed.

3. Protect the sill cock.
Before winter, remove and drain garden hoses to prevent them from splitting. Shut off the water leading to the sill cock, allow it to drain, and leave it open. If there is no indoor shutoff, install one (see page 178), or install a freeze-proof sill cock—an improvement that may be required by local codes.

4. Precautions for very cold days
As a preventive measure on extremely cold days, turn on the faucets that have vulnerable parts and let water trickle continuously. If there is a cabinet underneath, open its doors to let room heat warm the pipes. Use a small lamp to warm pipes that run through cold areas.

WINTERIZING A HOUSE

If you're leaving a house or cabin for an extended period of time during the winter, you don't have to leave the heat on in order to avoid plumbing disasters. You can save money by turning off your utilities and winterizing, which involves shutting off the water supply and draining the whole plumbing system. If you have a private water system, the process is slightly more involved—you'll also have to drain the holding tank and any water-treating apparatus. The result will be peace of mind that the plumbing system is safely dormant, without the expense of keeping the home fires burning.

YOU'LL NEED...

TIME: About four hours to winterize a modest house.
SKILLS: Disconnecting pipes.
TOOLS: Pipe wrench, Crescent wrench, and bucket.

1. Drain the system.
Have the water department shut off the water valve outside your home, or do it yourself. Then open every faucet in the house, starting at the top of the system. Shut down and drain the water heater (see page 184). Detach drain hoses on dish and clothes washers.

2. Open valves and unions.
Look to see if you have a drainable valve or two—often they are near the water meter. Open the drain cock on each. Drain supply lines completely. If you find a low-lying pipe that doesn't have a faucet or drain cock, open a union where two pipes join (see page 172).

3. Replace water with antifreeze.
Flush toilets, then pour a gallon of antifreeze solution (non-toxic antifreeze mixed with water, according to directions on the container) into the bowl. This will start a mild flushing action. Some of it will remain in the

toilet's trap. Pour antifreeze solution into all fixtures with a trap—sinks, showers, bathtubs, and the washing-machine standpipe. If your house has a main house trap, fill the elbow portion with full-strength antifreeze.

HOME AGAIN

After returning to your winterized house, follow these steps, in order:

■ Turn all faucets off, including the sill cock. Remove any aerators on the faucets, and clean if necessary.

■ Reconnect all disconnected pipes, and close down all drainable valves.

■ Turn on the main water-supply valve.

■ Turn all the faucets on slowly, beginning at the sill cock. The water will "spit" out for a while, then assume a normal flow.

■ Replace the aerators.

FIXING LEAKS AND FROZEN PIPES

Water escaping from a pipe can wreak havoc in your house. Even a tiny leak that is left to drip day and night will soon rot away everything in its vicinity. A pipe that freezes and bursts can produce a major flood.

As soon as you spot a leak, shut off the water to take pressure off the line. Then locate exactly where the problem is. If the pipe is not visible, this may be difficult: Water can run quite a ways along the outside of the pipe, a floor joist, or a subfloor before becoming visible. Eventually, any leaking pipe must be replaced (see pages 160–176). Here are emergency measures to temporarily stop the flow.

YOU'LL NEED...

TIME: An hour or so to clamp or apply epoxy to a leak.
SKILLS: No special skills needed.
TOOLS: Screwdriver and putty knife.

Wrap with tape.
For a pinhole leak, dry off the pipe, and wrap it tightly with several layers of duct tape. Wrap it about 6 inches on either side of the hole. This is extremely temporary, but the tape should hold while you make a trip to the hardware store for a pipe clamp and rubber gasket.

hose clamp

Apply a clamp.
An automotive hose clamp with a piece of rubber—both available at any hardware store—makes a somewhat better leak-stopper. Again, it works only for pinhole leaks. Wrap the rubber around the pipe, and tighten up the clamp. Be sure that the clamp itself is placed directly over the hole.

rubber gasket

1. To install a pipe clamp, position the gasket.
The best temporary solution to a leaking pipe is a pipe clamp specially made for this purpose. It will seal small gashes, cracks, and pinhole leaks. It also is semipermanent—expect it to last several years. Position the rubber gasket so the hole is centered under it.

clamp
nut

2. Tighten the clamp.
Assemble the clamp pieces around the gasket and tighten. Take care that the gasket does not move as you work. Tighten all four nuts evenly, working from nut to nut until all are tight.

EXPERTS' INSIGHT

IT MAY NOT BE A LEAK...
If a pipe shows drips all along its length, it may be condensing water from humid air rather than leaking. Wrap it with insulation to stop the condensation (see page 126).

...OR IT MAY BE MORE
An isolated leak may be a sign that pipes are aging. The galvanized pipe common to older homes tends to rust from the inside out. Once a leak appears, expect others to follow. If the pipes in your house have begun to deteriorate, buy a supply of pipe clamps to fit your lines.

Apply plumber's epoxy at fittings.
If the leak is coming from a fitting, don't try to clamp it. Your best bet is plumber's epoxy. Unless the leak is a real gusher, don't shut off the water. The epoxy comes in two parts. Cut a piece of each and knead them together until the color is uniform. Pack the epoxy into the connection by pushing it in with your thumb or a putty knife. Pack it until the leak stops.

Seal a leaking clean-out.
Drain lines are less leak-prone than supply lines. Once in a while, however, a clean-out plug may seep waste water. Warn everyone in the household not to use any fixtures. Remove the plug (it may screw out or pull out). Reseal screw-in plugs by applying Teflon tape to the male threads. If it has an O-ring, replace it.

Tighten joints in cast-iron pipe.
If you have a leak at the joint of cast-iron pipes, it is usually easy to deal with. For the hub-and-spigot type shown here, use a hammer and chisel to tamp down the soft lead that fills the joint. Don't whack the pipe hard—you could crack it. If you have the no-hub system, tightening the clamp will likely stop the leak.

To thaw exposed frozen pipes, heat with a blow dryer...
Open the faucet the pipe supplies so any steam can escape. If it is exposed, apply heat directly with a hair dryer or a heat gun turned to its lowest setting. Move the dryer or gun back and forth—don't hold it in one spot.

...or pour hot water.
Another solution for an exposed frozen pipe is to wrap a cloth around it, then pour boiling water over the cloth. Allow the water to cool, pour again, and repeat until the pipe is thawed. Be sure a faucet is open while you do this so steam can escape.

Thaw concealed pipes.
If the pipes are concealed, thawing will take more time. Open a faucet. Beam a heat lamp or electric space heater at the wall containing the pipe. Monitor closely to make sure the heat doesn't damage the wall surface.

IDENTIFYING STEM FAUCETS

When a faucet develops a leak—most often, a drip from the spout or a leak around the base—the problem is usually easy to fix. Very likely, you'll be able to purchase a repair kit for your type of faucet. Repair techniques vary from faucet to faucet, but in most cases you can easily do it yourself. When buying replacement parts, take the old unit to the store. If the faucet cannot be repaired, it is not difficult to replace it with a new

one (see pages 180–191).

The first step is to identify the type of faucet you have. The anatomy drawings here and on pages 134, 136, 138, and 140 show you the various types.

The most common type is the seat-and-washer faucet, often called a compression faucet. All stem faucets have separate hot and cold controls. In its off position, the stem compresses a flexible washer on the stem into a beveled seat located in the faucet base,

stopping the flow of water. As the washer wears, you have to apply more and more pressure to turn off the unit. That's when dripping usually begins.

Two newer versions are types of washerless stem faucets—cartridge and diaphragm. The cartridge type rotates rather than raising and lowering to control flow. It uses a rubber seal and O-rings. The diaphragm type uses a durable diaphragm instead of the seat washer.

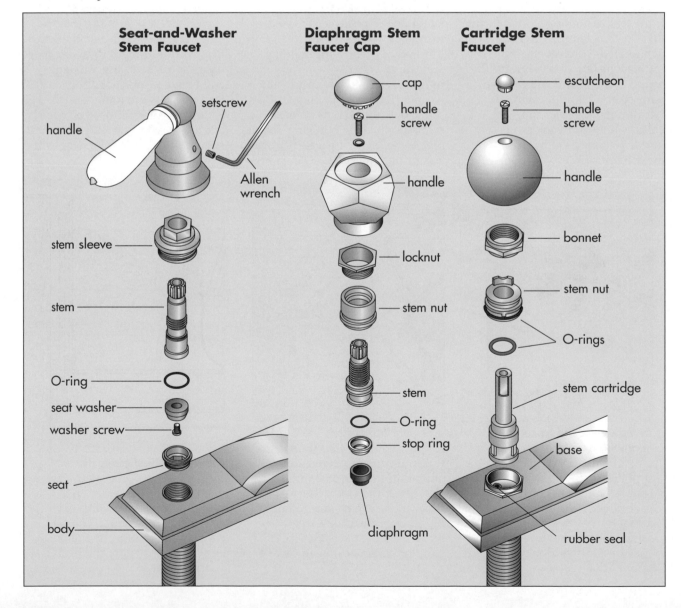

Seat-and-Washer Stem Faucet

- handle
- setscrew
- Allen wrench
- stem sleeve
- stem
- O-ring
- seat washer
- washer screw
- seat
- body

Diaphragm Stem Faucet Cap

- cap
- handle screw
- handle
- locknut
- stem nut
- stem
- O-ring
- stop ring
- diaphragm

Cartridge Stem Faucet

- escutcheon
- handle screw
- handle
- bonnet
- stem nut
- O-rings
- stem cartridge
- base
- rubber seal

PULLING OUT HANDLES AND STEMS

The first step in replacing the inner workings of a stem faucet is to pull out the handles and stems and take them to the store so you can buy proper replacement parts. If you can identify the faucet by brand name, it will be easier to find the right part. Often no brand name is visible, so you'll have to take out the stem and compare it with the drawings on pages 130, 134, 136, 138, and 140.

Note: *When working on faucets, shut off the water.*

YOU'LL NEED...

TIME: About 15 minutes, unless the parts are stuck.
SKILLS: No special skills needed.
TOOLS: Screwdriver, tongue-and-groove pliers, and possibly a handle puller.

1. Remove escutcheon and screw.
If your handle is round, it is probably connected to the stem with a screw from the top. You may have to pry off an escutcheon (usually marked "H" or "C") to get to it. Some handles are attached with setscrews—see the handle on the seat-and-washer stem faucet on page 130. Remove the setscrew with an Allen wrench and pull the handle off.

2. Pull out handle and stem.
Usually, the handle will come out if you pull it up firmly or pry it up with a screwdriver. Take care not to mar the finish on the handle. If it is really stuck, use a handle puller that grips the handle from underneath and draws the handle off the stem. Once the handle is off, unscrew the stem with pliers.

REPLACING SEAT WASHERS

Perhaps the most common plumbing repair of all is replacing a seat washer. If yours is a seat-and-washer stem faucet, the washer often becomes worn. Most commonly, there is a depression running in a ring around the washer, or the washer has begun to crumble from old age.

If a washer wears out quickly, the seat is damaged and nicks the washer every time you shut the water off, making the faucet drip (see page 141 to replace a seat).

YOU'LL NEED...

TIME: About 30 minutes, plus a trip to your supplier if you don't have the right washer.
SKILLS: No special skills needed.
TOOLS: Screwdriver.

1. Remove the old washer.
Examine your washer. If it is damaged in any way, remove the washer screw and pull the old washer off. Clean away any debris or deposits from the bottom of the stem. Take your stem and old washer to your supplier if you are not sure how to select a new washer that will fit.

2. Insert a new washer.
Find a washer the exact same size and shape as the old one. If the old washer has been squashed out of shape, this may be difficult to determine, so double-check by slipping the new washer onto the bottom of the stem. It should fit snugly. Replace and tighten the screw, and reinstall the stem.

REPAIRING DIAPHRAGM AND CARTRIDGE STEMS

Diaphragm and cartridge stem faucets are just as easy to repair as seat-and-washer stem faucets. Often the most difficult part of the job is finding the right parts. There are hundreds of O-ring sizes. The safest way to choose is to remove the stem, take it to your supplier, and show it to a salesperson. That way, the O-rings fit the stem exactly. **NOTE:** *Be sure to shut off the water before removing stems.*

YOU'LL NEED...

TIME: Just a few minutes, once you've got the right parts, the faucet handle is removed, and the stem unscrewed.
SKILLS: No special skills needed.
TOOLS: Small screwdriver or a sharp-pointed tool.

Replace a diaphragm.
Sometimes called a top hat stem, a diaphragm stem has a diaphragm that functions much like a seat washer. To replace it, simply pull off the worn diaphragm, and snap a new one on.

Replace O-ring, seal, and spring.
For a cartridge stem, fix leaks by replacing the seal and O-ring. Remove the rubber seal from the base of the faucet with the sharpened end of a pencil; a small spring will come out as well. Remove the O-ring by hand, or carefully pry it off with a sharp tool. Lubricate the new parts lightly with heatproof grease after you install them.

REPAIRING LEAKS FROM HANDLES

If the faucet leaks around the handle, you'll need to remove the stem to get at the source of the problem. Older faucets have packing wound around the top of the stem to keep water from seeping out the top. Don't be put off by this old-fashioned material; it is easy to replace, and new packing will last for years. Newer stems have O-rings. Once you have the stem out, inspect the rest of the faucet and replace any parts that look as if they're starting to wear out. **NOTE:** *Be sure to shut off the water.*

YOU'LL NEED...

TIME: Fifteen minutes to repack a spindle and replace an O-ring.
SKILLS: No special skills needed.
TOOLS: None.

Wrap on new packing string.
If your faucet has packing wound around the spindle just under the packing nut (see page 179), remove all of it and clean the spindle. Use either Teflon tape or strand packing, and wind it fairly tight. Leave just enough room so the packing nut can be screwed on when the stem is replaced.

Replace the O-ring.
Newer stems have an O-ring instead of packing. Simply remove the old O-ring, and replace it with one that fits exactly. Lightly lubricate the O-ring with heatproof grease after you install it and before you reinstall the stem.

REPLACING AND GRINDING SEATS

When the spout of a stem faucet (either a seat-and-washer or a diaphragm type) leaks, be sure to inspect the seat as well as the washer or diaphragm. If the seat is pitted or scored, it is scraping the washer or diaphragm every time you turn the faucet off. It will quickly damage a seat washer, and your faucet will leak again even after you've fixed it.

If the seat is damaged, it is best to replace it. Sometimes, however, it is hard to extract the old one. In those cases, try grinding it smooth with a special tool.

YOU'LL NEED...

TIME: About 20 minutes to replace or grind a seat, once you have the part or tool.
SKILLS: No special skills needed, but you must work carefully.
TOOLS: Flashlight and seat wrench or seat cutter.

seat washer

seat

Inspect the seat.
Remove the stem (see page 130), and inspect the washer or diaphragm. If it looks cut up, the likely cause is a damaged seat. Whether the washer or diaphragm looks damaged or not, examine the seat, first by looking at it with a flashlight, then by feeling with your finger. If it appears or feels less than smooth, your washer or diaphragm will have a hard time sealing water off when you crank down on the handle. The seat needs to be replaced or ground smooth with a seat grinder.

seat wrench

Replace a damaged seat.
Though it is sometimes possible to remove a seat with a screwdriver, this is risky—you may damage the seat so that it cannot be removed. Purchase a seat wrench, which is designed to remove seats of various sizes. Insert it into the seat, push down firmly, and turn counterclockwise. Install the new seat with the same tool.

stem nut

cutter head

1. Use a seat grinder for a seat that cannot be removed.
Purchase a seat grinder. Slip the stem nut over the shaft of the seat grinder—it helps stabilize the grinder. Select a cutter head that fits easily inside the body and is as wide as the seat.

stem nut

2. Rotate the grinder.
Screw the stem nut into the faucet body to hold the shaft securely without wobbling. Push down gently, and turn the handle clockwise three full rotations. Remove the grinder and inspect the seat with a flashlight. If it is not smooth, try again.

REPAIRING CARTRIDGE FAUCETS

Most washerless faucets use a combination of seals and O-rings to control and direct water. A cartridge faucet (manufactured by Kohler, Moen, Price-Pfister, and others) uses a series of strategically placed O-rings and/or seals.

In the type shown, the cartridge O-rings fit snugly against the inside of the faucet body. One O-ring forms a seal between the hot and cold supply lines. The others protect against leaks from the spout and from under the handle. On swivel-spout models, another ring protects against leaks from under the spout. Raising the handle lifts the stem so it slides upward inside the cartridge. Holes in the stem align with the openings in the cartridge in various combinations.

Other types have fewer O-rings and use other types of seals. Repair kits are available for each manufacturer and model.

When this type of faucet leaks, you can replace either the O-rings or the cartridge itself if it has corroded. Because the design is simple, repairs usually don't take long. In fact, disassembly is usually the bulk of the work, and your only problem may be finding the retainer clip that holds the cartridge in the faucet.

YOU'LL NEED...

TIME: About an hour, once you have the replacement parts.
SKILLS: No special skills needed.
TOOLS: Screwdriver, needle-nose pliers, and tongue-and-groove pliers.

handle cover

handle setscrew

handle lever

handle body

retainer nut

retainer clip

cross section of faucet

cartridge O-ring

cartridge

spout assembly

escutcheon

1. Remove the handle housing.
NOTE: *Shut off the water and drain the line.* Cartridge faucets vary in design from model to model, but you disassemble most of them as follows: Pry off the decorative cover that conceals the handle screw. Be careful not to crack the cover in doing so; most are made of plastic. You may need to remove an external retaining clip to get the cover off.

2. Remove handle assembly.
Cover the drain with a rag to avoid losing any small parts. Beneath the handle housing is a setscrew that holds the handle in place. Remove the handle screw, and lift off the handle body and lever. If there is no retainer nut (next step), lift out the spout.

3. Remove retainer nut and spout.
Swivel-spout models will have a retainer nut. Unscrew it, then lift off the spout.

You'll need to disassemble some models differently. Pry off the cap on top of the faucet, remove the screw, and remove the handle by tilting it back and pulling up. Then remove the plastic threaded retaining ring.

4. Pull out the retainer clip.
Depending on the model you have, you may need to lift off a cylindrical sleeve to get at the cartridge. You should now be able to see the retainer clip, a metal piece that holds the cartridge in place. Use needle-nose pliers to remove the clip from its slot. Be careful not to misplace it.

5. Remove the cartridge.
With tongue-and-groove pliers, lift the cartridge from the faucet body. Take note of the position of the cartridge ears, and be sure that when you put the cartridge back in, its ears are facing in the same direction. Otherwise, hot and cold will be reversed. If you are replacing O-rings, give them a light coating of heatproof lubricant. When reassembling the faucet, tighten firmly, but don't crank down hard—there are many plastic parts that can crack.

EXPERTS' INSIGHT

BUY QUALITY REPLACEMENT PARTS
Your local hardware store or building supply center may have replacement parts that are inexpensive but a bit flimsy. As long as you are investing a fair amount of your time in making the repair, pay the relatively small extra cost to install long-lasting parts. It usually is best to buy replacement parts made by the faucet manufacturer, rather than by a general supplier that only makes replacement parts.

If you cannot find the manufacturer's name on the faucet, remove the parts and take them to your supplier to ensure the right match.

REPAIRING ROTATING BALL FAUCETS

Inside a rotating ball faucet a slotted ball sits atop a pair of spring-loaded seals. When the handle is lowered to the "off" position, this ball, held tight against the seals by the faucet's cap, closes off the water supply. This type of faucet is often called a Delta faucet, after its primary manufacturer.

As the handle is raised, the ball rotates in such a way that the openings align with the supply line ports. This allows water to pass through the ball and out the spout. Moving the handle to the left allows more hot water to flow out; moving it to the right adds cold water.

Most leaks can be fixed by replacing the ball and gaskets in the faucet (see page 137). In addition, seals and springs can give out and need replacement.

These faucets also can spring leaks from around the handle and, with swivel-spout models, from under the base of the spout. Handle leaks indicate that the adjusting ring has loosened or the seal above the ball is worn.

Leaks from under the spout result from O-ring failure. Inspect the rings encircling the body and—on units with diverter valves for a sprayer—the valve O-ring. Replace the O-rings if they look worn.

CAUTION!
To avoid damage to flooring and walls, turn off supply lines or the main water valve.

YOU'LL NEED...
TIME: About two hours to rebuild and reassemble a faucet.
SKILLS: Patience and an eye for detail.
TOOLS: Allen wrench, adjustable pliers, wrench that comes with the rebuild kit, and awl or other sharp-pointed tool.

1. Remove handle and cap.
Shut off the water supply and drain the lines by lifting straight up on the handle. Using an Allen wrench, loosen the setscrew that holds the handle in place (see inset above). Loosen the adjusting ring using the wrench that comes packed with your purchased repair kit.

2. Disassemble cam, ball, spout.
Unscrew the cap with cloth- or tape-covered adjustable pliers. Lift out the cam assembly, the ball, and, in the case of a swivel-spout faucet, the spout. The spout fits tightly against the O-rings of the body, so it may prove stubborn. Be careful not to scratch the spout as you remove it.

3. Remove seals and springs.
To remove worn seals and springs from the body, insert a pencil into each seal to pull it out. Check for blockage at the supply inlet ports and scrape away any buildup. Then insert new springs and seals.

4. Replace O-rings.
If the faucet has a swivel spout, remove the O-rings by prying them away from the body using an awl or other sharp-pointed tool. Roll the new ones down over the body until they rest in the appropriate grooves. Replace the diverter O-ring in the same way. Lightly coat the O-rings and the inside of the spout with heatproof grease.

5. Reassemble.
Be sure to align the slot in the side of the ball with the pin inside the body. Also, the key on the cam assembly fits into a corresponding notch in the body. Hand-tighten the cap and tighten the adjusting ring for a good seal between the ball and the cam. If the faucet leaks, tighten further.

EXPERTS' INSIGHT

Select quality parts
Repair kits of lesser or greater quality are available for this type of faucet. Some include plastic balls; others include longer-lasting metal parts. If your hardware store only has the cheaper kit, try a plumbing supply store for a kit with longer-lasting, though more expensive, parts.

Consider a complete rebuild
When a faucet is old enough to have one part wear out, other parts will soon wear out as well. As long as you are fixing one part of the faucet, do a complete rebuild.

REPAIRING CERAMIC DISK FAUCETS

When you raise the faucet lever of a disk faucet, the upper disk in the cartridge slides across the lower disk, allowing water to enter the mixing chamber. The higher you raise the lever, the more water enters through the inlet ports of the faucet body. Moving the lever from side to side determines whether hot or cold water or a mixture of the two comes out of the spout.

The disk assembly itself, generally made of a long-lasting ceramic material, rarely needs replacing. However, the inlet ports can become clogged with mineral deposits. If this happens, simply disassemble the faucet and scrape away the crusty buildup.

If the faucet leaks at the base of the lever, one or more of the inlet seals on the cartridge may need replacing. See page 139 for how to replace the seals and the cartridge. While the faucet is dismantled, replace all of the seals. If one is worn, the others don't have long to live. Before you go to your supplier, get the brand name of your faucet from the faucet body—or take the disk assembly along. You probably can buy a repair kit with the parts you need.

YOU'LL NEED...

TIME: About an hour for repairs.
SKILLS: No special skills needed.
TOOLS: Small screwdriver and tongue-and-groove pliers.

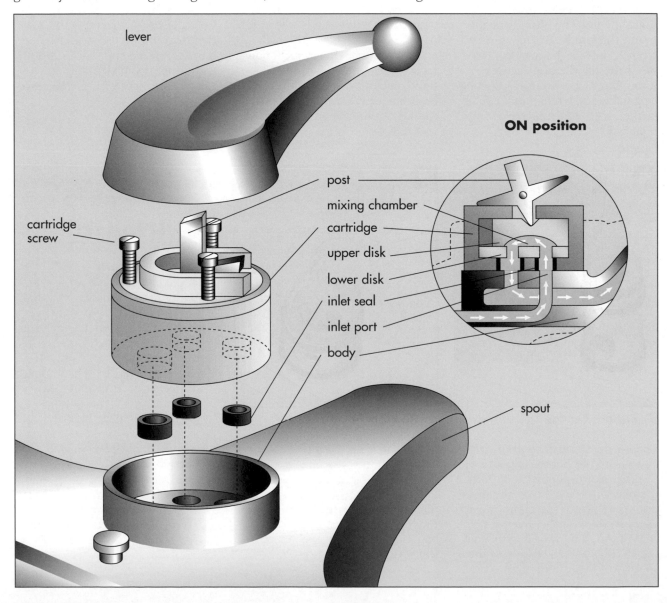

lever

ON position

post
mixing chamber
cartridge
upper disk
lower disk
inlet seal
inlet port
body

cartridge screw

spout

1. Remove the lever and cap.
Note: *Shut off the water.*
Under the lever you'll see a setscrew that holds the lever to the lever post. Use an appropriately sized screwdriver to unscrew the setscrew—don't try to unscrew it with a knife or you may damage it. Loosen the screw until you can raise the lever off the post. You may have to gently pry it off with a large screwdriver.

Lift off or unscrew the decorative cap that covers the cartridge. Then loosen the screws holding the cartridge to the faucet body and lift out the cartridge.

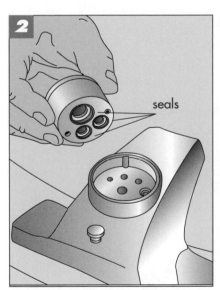

2. Remove the seals.
On the underside of the cartridge you'll find a set of seals. Pull them out with your fingers or carefully use a sharp-pointed tool, being careful not to scratch the cartridge.

3. Clean the openings.
Check the openings for sediment buildup and clean it. Use a nonmetallic scrubber or a sponge.

4. Replace the seals; reassemble.
Put the seals back or install replacement seals. Reassemble the faucet. Turn the water back on and test. If the faucet continues to leak after you have cleaned the cartridge and replaced the seals, install a new cartridge.

REPAIRING GASKETED CARTRIDGE FAUCETS

Gasketed cartridge faucets use a gasket with a group of openings at the bottom of the faucet cartridge to mix hot and cold water and direct water to the spout. Newer models have ceramic cartridges; older ones have plastic.

YOU'LL NEED...

TIME: About an hour, plus shopping time.
SKILLS: Basic plumbing skills.
TOOLS: Screwdriver, and tongue-and-groove pliers.

Note: *Shut off the water before disassembling.*
If you're trying to fix a leak from the body of the faucet, first try tightening the cap by hand—do not crank down on it with a wrench. If that doesn't work, disassemble the faucet and replace the two O-rings. Coat them lightly with heatproof grease.

To disassemble, pry off the escutcheon and remove the lever screw. Lift off the lever and unscrew the cap and the retainer nut. The other parts will pull out.

If you're trying to fix a drip from the spout, the cartridge probably needs to be replaced. Check the retainer nut as well. If its threads are stripped, replace it.

These parts are specific to the faucet manufacturer, so take the old parts with you when you go to the store to make sure you buy the right replacement parts.

If the faucet operates stiffly, debris may have built up in the cartridge. In most cases, it will be more trouble to clean the cartridge than it is to buy a new one and replace it.

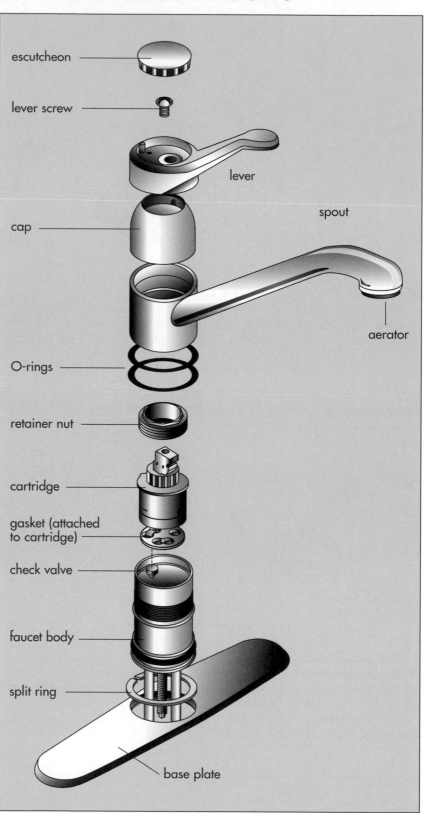

SEALING LEAKY BASE PLATES

If you find water in the cabinet below the sink, it could be from three places—the supply lines, the drain, or water leaking into the cabinet from under the faucet base plate. The problem may be solved by simply tightening the supply lines (see page 143). If the leak comes from the drain, see page 153. If neither of those is the cause, you may have a leaky base plate that allows splashed water to seep through mounting holes. Follow the steps on this page to solve this last problem.

You'll Need...

TIME: Two hours to remove, seal, and replace the faucet.
SKILLS: Basic plumbing skills.
TOOLS: Putty knife, and tongue-and-groove pliers or basin wrench.

1. Tighten the mounting nuts.
It may be that your faucet is not held tight against the sink. Get under your sink in as comfortable a position as possible and tighten the mounting nuts. If you can't turn them with pliers, use a basin wrench (see page 161). If this does not solve the problem, try Step 2.

2. Loosen, stuff with putty.
First try to fix the leak without removing the faucet. Loosen the mounting nuts enough to raise the faucet base about a half inch above the sink. Scrape out any hardened gunk. Holding the base plate just above the sink, stuff plumber's putty under it evenly. Retighten the mounting nuts. If it continues to leak, proceed to Step 3.

3. Remove the faucet and scrape.
NOTE: *Shut off the water and drain the line.* To entirely reseat the base plate, remove the faucet. Disconnect the supply lines, remove the mounting nuts, and pull the faucet out. Scrape any old putty away and clean the area thoroughly. Take care not to scratch the sink.

gasket

4. Replace the gasket...
If the faucet has a gasket, throw it out, and replace it with a new one. If you have trouble finding a replacement, a new gasket can be made by purchasing a piece of rubber of a similar thickness. You can use the old gasket as a pattern and cut out a new one.

putty

...or apply new putty.
Many plumbers believe putty lasts longer than gaskets, so even if your faucet has a gasket, you may want to discard it and apply putty instead. Roll a rope of putty, about ¼ inch in diameter, and apply it to the sink or to the underside of the faucet. Reinstall the faucet, and check for leaks.

FIXING SPRAYERS, DIVERTERS, AND AERATORS

*S*ink sprayers can be obstructed at the connections, gaskets, and the nozzle. If your faucet has low water pressure, check the aerator. Aerators may develop leaks if their seals are worn, or they can get clogged up. See below to unclog. If water doesn't come out of the sprayer, the problem is most likely a faulty diverter valve: You can replace either the rubber seal or the diverter. Remove the diverter and take it to your supplier to be sure you get the correct replacement.

Diverters vary in shape and location, but all work in much the same way. When water isn't flowing toward the spray outlet, the valve remains open and directs the water flow toward the spout. When you press the sprayer lever, the flow of water shifts toward the sprayer head.

YOU'LL NEED...

TIME: One to two hours.
SKILLS: Basic plumbing skills and attention to detail.
TOOLS: Tongue-and-groove pliers, old toothbrush, and awl or nail.

From diverter to sprayer

In a typical one-handle faucet, remove the spout to find the diverter; it's usually located in front.

If you get low or no water pressure from the sprayer, first check the hose for kinks. A slow stream of water coupled with some water coming from the spout may signal a stuck valve or a worn washer or O-ring. Replace the rubber parts or the diverter valve. Or the sprayer screen may be clogged (see below).

Troubleshoot the sprayer.

Minerals may be restricting the flow of water through the sprayer. Clean the spray disk with an awl or a nail as shown. Replace any worn parts and tighten all the connections.

Clean the aerator.

To clean out the aerator, unscrew it from the faucet spout and disassemble it. Brush all the parts clean and soak the pieces in vinegar overnight. If it is heavily clogged, just buy a new one.

STOPPING LEAKS IN FLEXIBLE SUPPLY LINES

*T*here are three basic types of flexible supply lines. Plain or chrome-plated copper tubing uses ferrules and nuts for connections. Flexible plastic lines use knobby ends that take the place of ferrules. Flexible supply lines—either plastic or stainless-steel-braided—use nuts preattached at each end. The last type is the easiest to use. Be sure you buy lines that are long enough.

YOU'LL NEED...

TIME: An hour for most repairs and replacements.
SKILLS: Tightening and loosening nuts in tight places.
TOOLS: Basin wrench or tongue-and-groove pliers and adjustable wrenches.

1. Tighten the nuts.
Often fixing a leak is simple—just tighten the nut at the point where you see a leak. Take care not to crank down too hard; you can crack the nut or strip the threads.

Use only adjustable wrenches, not pipe wrenches. If the leak persists, loosen the nuts and recoat the threads or ferrules with Teflon tape or pipe joint compound as shown in Step 2.

nut

ferrule

2. Coat the ferrule...
Note: *Be sure to shut off the water, and drain the line.*
If you have a tubing-and-ferrule arrangement, remove the nut and pull the line at least partway out. Take care not to kink it. Coat the ferrule with joint compound or wrap it with Teflon tape. Hook it back up, tighten, and test.

...or the threads.
If you have a plastic or braided flexible line, shut off the water, unscrew the nut, and apply joint compound or Teflon tape to the male threads of the shutoff valve or the faucet. Reconnect, tighten, and test.

3. Install a new line.
If these measures do not solve your problem quickly, don't keep fussing with the old line. Shut off the water and remove the old supply line. Buy a new flexible line, apply Teflon tape or joint compound to the male threads, and screw the new flexible line on. Tighten both ends and test.

REPAIRING TOILETS

Because it gets used so often, your toilet has a good chance of eventually needing repair. Although some people find the prospect of working on a toilet distasteful, as long as you flush it once or twice before beginning, you will be dealing with clean water only. (If it won't flush, see page 156.) You may find some rust and sediment in the tank.

The inner parts of a toilet are fairly simple. When someone flips the flush handle, a chain reaction of events starts. The handle lifts the trip lever, which in turn pulls a chain that lifts the tank flapper off the flush valve. (In older units, a lift rod raises a tank ball.) As water rushes down through the opening into the bowl, the reservoir of water and the waste in the bowl yield to gravity and pass through the toilet's trap, down through the closet bend, and out a drain line.

Inside the tank, the float (or in older systems the float ball) descends along with the outrushing water until, at a predetermined level, the shutoff rod is attached to trips the ballcock, which is a water supply valve. At the same time, the tank flapper settles back into the flush valve, stopping water from leaving the tank. The ballcock opens to shoot a new supply of water into the tank through a refill tube and into the bowl through the overflow tube. When the float rises to its filled position, the ballcock shuts the water off.

A wax ring seals the toilet bowl to a flange on the closet bend and keeps water from leaking out onto the floor. A spud gasket seals the tank to the bowl.

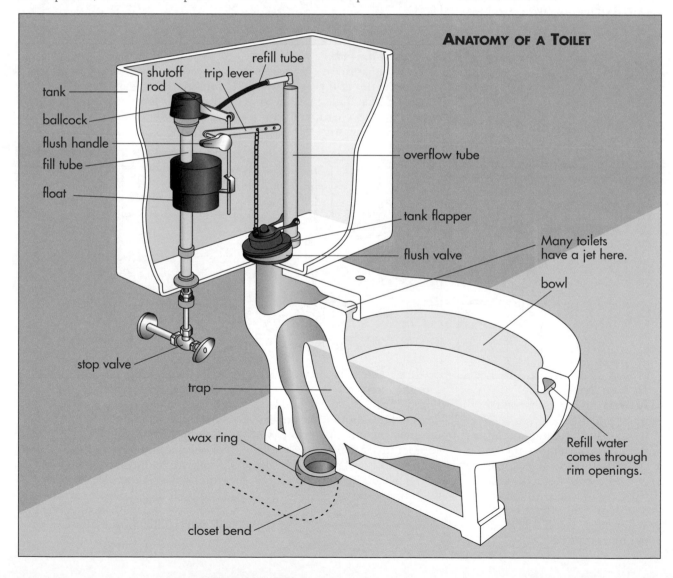

ANATOMY OF A TOILET

tank

ballcock

flush handle

fill tube

float

shutoff rod

trip lever

refill tube

overflow tube

tank flapper

flush valve

Many toilets have a jet here.

bowl

Refill water comes through rim openings.

stop valve

trap

wax ring

closet bend

TOILET REPAIR CHART

Symptom	Cause	Repair
Water continuously trickles or runs into tank and/or bowl (tank run-on).	Water level is too high.	Adjust trip lever chain, adjust water level in tank, or replace leaky float (see below).
	Flapper or tank ball isn't sealing properly.	Clean the flush valve under the flapper, or replace worn flapper.
	Ballcock is faulty.	Repair or replace ballcock.
Bowl overflows when flushed. Toilet flushes incompletely.	Trap or drain is partially clogged.	Run a toilet auger through the toilet (see page 156), or clear drain (see page 157).
	Trap or bowl is clogged.	
Tank leaks.	Water is spraying up against the lid.	Anchor the refill tube so it sprays into the overflow tube.
	Gasket between tank and bowl is faulty.	Replace the spud gasket.
	Tank is cracked.	Replace the tank.
Bowl leaks. Leak appears as a wet spot on the floor.	Wax ring is not sealing.	Pull up the toilet and replace the wax ring (see page 147).
	Bowl is cracked.	Replace the bowl.
Tank "sweats"—drops of water appear on the outside.	Condensation occurs due to difference in temperature between air and tank water.	Buy an insulation kit and install in the inside of the tank.

FIXING TANK RUN-ON

Most of a toilet's mechanical action goes on inside the flush tank, and that's where most common toilet problems develop. If water continually trickles or flows into the tank and/or bowl, start with the simplest diagnosis: The float may be rising too high, causing water to trickle down the overflow tube. If fixing that doesn't solve the problem, see if the chain is tangled or has fallen off. Check flapper and ballcock (see page 144).

YOU'LL NEED...

TIME: Five minutes to adjust the float, a half hour to adjust and clean the flush valve; one hour to replace a ballcock.
SKILLS: General mechanical aptitude.
TOOLS: Screwdriver and tongue-and-groove pliers.

Adjust the float ball.
Remove the tank lid, and look to see if the water level is too high—it should not be above the overflow tube. If it is, the water will shut off when you pull up on the float ball. Bend the rod slightly downward so the float ball sits a bit lower. With a float like the one shown on page 144, adjust the clip.

Check the float for damage.
A cracked float takes on water. When this happens, the ball won't rise enough to trip the ballcock. To check out this possibility, agitate the ball. A faulty ball will make a swishing sound. Unscrew a faulty float ball, and replace it with a new one.

Fix a leaky flush valve seat.

If water continually trickles into the bowl, and perhaps even causes the toilet to weakly flush occasionally, the problem is probably in the flush valve. It has two parts: a flapper or a tank ball, and the flush valve seat into which the flapper or ball drops to seal the bottom of the tank while it fills. Often the seat simply needs cleaning.

NOTE: *Shut off the water to the tank, and flush the toilet to get the water out.* Check the tank ball or flapper. If it has gunk on it, wipe it clean and smooth it using an abrasive pad. Once it's cleaned, feel the valve seat to see if it is pitted or corroded if it's metal. Flexible seats can be pried out and replaced. If you have a damaged metal seat, replace the entire flush valve.

Repair a diaphragm ballcock.

NOTE: *Shut off the water and flush the toilet.* Remove the four screws on top of the ballcock, and lift off the bonnet. Clean out any deposits. Replace any worn parts, including the plunger. If a number of parts look worn, replace the entire ballcock.

Repair a plunger ballcock.

NOTE: *Shut off the water and flush the toilet.* This is the oldest type of ballcock, and there are a number of parts that can go bad. You may need to replace it with either a diaphragm or float-cup ballcock. But first try cleaning and replacing the washers.

Remove the thumbscrews holding the float rod mechanism

in place, then lift it out and set it aside. Remove the plunger by pulling up on it. Typically you'll find a seat washer as well as a couple of other washers. (In very old models, you may even find leather washers.) Remove and replace all of the washers, reassemble the mechanism, and turn the water back on.

Repair a float-cup ballcock.

NOTE: *Shut off the water and flush the toilet.* This is the newest and the simplest design, and it rarely acts up. Pry off the cap, then remove the bonnet by lifting the shutoff lever on the float rod mechanism, pushing the mechanism down, and twisting counterclockwise firmly. Clean out any gunk, and replace the seal if it looks worn.

Fixing Leaky Tanks and Bowls

Puddling of water on the floor near the toilet can be fixed in several ways. On a hot, humid day, condensation dripping from the cool outside of the tank or bowl could be substantial enough to make a puddle. You can simply live with it or install rigid-foam tank insulation.

A chronic leak probably means a faulty water supply connection, spud gasket, or wax ring. Often you simply need to tighten the hold-down bolts to solve the problem. A crack in a tank can sometimes be patched from the inside with silicone sealant. A cracked bowl should be replaced.

YOU'LL NEED...

TIME: About two hours to replace a spud gasket or a wax ring.
SKILLS: No special skills, but be careful not to crack the toilet.
TOOLS: Wrenches, screwdriver, and putty knife.

A leak at the water supply line
If the leak comes from where the water supply enters the tank, first tighten the locknut. If that doesn't work, shut off the water, flush the toilet, and sponge out the water that remains in the tank. Disconnect the water supply line, remove the locknut, and replace the old beveled gasket and rubber washer with new ones.

A leak between the tank and bowl
Extended use can cause the tank hold-down bolts to loosen enough to produce a leak at the spud gasket. Use a screwdriver and a wrench to tighten the bolts to squeeze the tank against the spud gasket. If the leak persists, shut off the water, flush, and sponge out any water. Detach the supply line, remove the hold-down bolts, lift out the tank, and replace the spud gasket (see page 182). Reassemble.

Older-style connections
With some old toilets, the tank connects to the bowl with a fitting. If leaks develop at either end of the fitting, tightening the nuts may stop the leak. If not, take the toilet apart and replace any worn parts from a plumbing supply source.

A leak at the base of the bowl
If the bowl is cracked, you'll have to replace it. If the bowl is sound, try gently tightening the hold-down nuts (see page 182). If that doesn't stop the leak, replace the wax ring. Begin by shutting off the water, flushing the toilet, and sponging out any remaining water.

Disconnect the water supply line, and remove the nuts on the hold-down bolts. Lift out the toilet. Scrape away the old wax ring and any old putty on the bottom of the bowl. Press a new wax ring in place according to the manufacturer's directions. Reinstall the toilet (see page 182).

REPAIRING TUB AND SHOWER CONTROLS

Tub and shower controls work much the same way as sink faucets, so repairing them involves many of the same operations, except you are working horizontally rather than vertically. Also tub and shower controls are a bit more complicated because in addition to mixing hot and cold water, they must divert water either to the tub spout or to the showerhead. The drawings on these pages show the inner workings of common types.

Sometimes the parts are hard to get at. You may have to chip away at tiles in order to get your tools to the shower control parts.

If a shower control body is damaged and needs to be replaced, look at the other side of the wall to see if you have an access panel. If so you may be able to work from behind and minimize damage to your shower wall. Usually replacing a shower control body means tearing up a shower wall and retiling.

Note: *Be sure to shut off the supply stop valves, built-in shutoff valves, or the main water valve before making these repairs.*

Two-handle control

The handles on these usually contain stems with washers. Each washer presses against a seat in order to shut the water off (see pages 131–140). To stop a drip, shut off the water, and remove the stem—you may have to use a special stem wrench or a deep socket, or chip away at the tiles to get at the packing nut. Replace the washer and the seat, if necessary, just as you would on a sink faucet (see page 142). If the diverter valve on the spout is not working properly, replace the spout.

Three-handle control

This type is much like a two-handle control but it has a central handle that controls a diverter valve. The valve directs water either up or down—out the showerhead or out the spout. If the diverter valve sticks or if it does not completely divert water to either the showerhead or to the spout, shut off the water and remove the valve just as you would a regular stem (see page 142). Take it apart, clean it, and replace any washers or O-rings. Or, replace the whole stem with a new one.

One-handle ball control

This type has seals and springs like ball-type sink faucets, so repairs are similar to those shown on pages 136–137. As the handle is raised, the ball rotates in such a way that its openings begin to align with the supply line ports, allowing water to pass through the ball and out the spout.

Impeded flow is usually the result of clogged orifices or worn seals. Shut the water off and remove the ball—a few ball controls have setscrews that you may have to remove to do this. Clean out the orifices, replace any worn rubber parts, and lubricate the new seals with heatproof grease.

While you have the faucet apart, check the ball for wear and corrosion; if you find either, replace the ball.

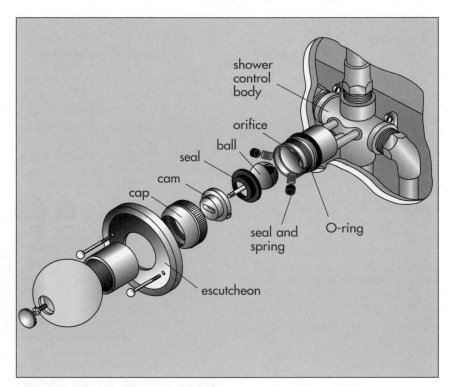

One-handle cartridge control

There are other configurations of one-handled cartridge controls besides the one shown here, so you may have to search out the location of your parts, such as the retaining clip. Parts are usually made of plastic; be careful not to crack them.

To repair a leak or limited flow, remove the handle, unscrew the retainer nut, and pull out the cartridge. Clean away any deposits and replace worn rubber or plastic parts. Lubricate all rubber parts with heatproof grease. Or simply replace the cartridge itself. When you remove the cartridge, be sure to note its original position and insert the new one the same way. If you don't, your hot and cold water will be reversed.

See pages 134–135 for more on repairing cartridge faucets.

OPENING CLOGGED DRAINS

Sooner or later every homeowner encounters a clogged drain. If you hire a professional to clear it out, you will usually get a better price if you call someone who specializes in clearing drains rather than a general plumber. But it will still cost you plenty; a professional's time costs the same whether the job requires something highly specialized or something you could have done yourself.

Most clogs are not due to faulty plumbing but to the slow buildup of solids that sink drains aren't intended to cope with. Only toilets are plumbed to handle solid waste; sinks, tubs, and showers have drains designed to carry away water only. Hair, grease, soap, food scraps, and gunk will clog up a drain. With a few basic tools, you can clear most clogs and get the system flowing again.

ANATOMY OF A SINK

lift rod

pop-up assembly

pivot rod

blockage

Water in trap blocks sewer gas.

trap

blockage

drainpipe

blockage

Where clogs happen
The slow buildup of soapy slime inside a drainpipe, a point of resistance such as a drain assembly, or a sharp bend in the drain can cause a clog. If a fixture is often clogged, install a strainer to keep solids from going down the drain. It will be well worth cleaning the strainer occasionally.

TOOLS TO USE

POWER AUGERS
■ For extra augering power, rent or buy a power auger or an augering attachment for a drill. The drill attachment is less expensive but not as sturdy as a power auger.
■ A high-quality tool will have a second cable that runs through the middle of the wound-wire augering cable. This keeps the auger cable from kinking, and it allows you to retrieve the auger cable if it should break. If your auger does not have this second cable and it breaks—a real possibility, especially if you are doing heavy-duty augering—you'll have a length of auger cable stuck in your pipe.

EXPERTS' INSIGHT

USING DRAIN CLEANERS
■ If your drain is completely stopped up and water is not moving through it at all, do not use a drain cleaner. It will not help the problem, and some types will actually harden if they cannot get through, making the clog worse. Drain cleaner can damage pipes, and it might splash you when you plunge or auger the drain.
■ If your drain is sluggish, use only nonacid drain cleaners (sodium hydroxide and copper sulfide are safe). Pour them in when the drain is sluggish, not when it is completely stopped. Regular use of a drain cleaner can keep the pipes clear of hair, soap, grease, and so on.
■ To maintain a smooth-flowing drain, every week or so run very hot water into the drain for a minute or two. This will clear away small amounts of grease and soap and keep them from building up.

USING SIMPLE UNCLOGGING METHODS

When a sink clogs up, first figure out where the blockage might be. It could be anywhere along the three main sections of a household drain system: in the fixture drain, in the drain stack that serves multiple fixtures, or in the main sewer line that carries waste out of the house (see page 121). Usually the problem will be close to a fixture because the drain pipe and trap near a fixture are narrower than the stack and main sewer lines they tie into. To verify that the clog is near the fixture, check other drains in your home. If more than one won't clear, something is stuck in a drain stack. If no drains work, the problem is farther down the line, probably in the main sewer line.

YOU'LL NEED...
TIME: An hour or two to perform the operations shown.
SKILLS: No special skills needed.
TOOLS: Screwdriver, auger, and plunger.

EXPERTS' INSIGHT

PLUNGING SINKS WITH MORE THAN ONE DRAIN
■ When plunging a double sink, it's best to have a helper block up one of the drain holes by pressing a wet rag firmly into it, while you plunge the other drain hole.
■ A dishwasher drains through a hose into the disposal or the sink plumbing (see page 204). Before plunging, use a C-clamp and two wood blocks to seal the drain hose and keep water from backing into the dishwasher.

1. Clean the strainer.
Clearing a sink may involve nothing more than removing the strainer or stopper from the drain opening. Push the stopper up and pull away any soap, hair, food matter, or other debris that may clog the opening or be dangling down into the drain.

2. Detach the pop-up assembly.
The strainers in kitchen sinks and many bathroom sinks simply lift out. Others require a slight turn before they will come out. With some, you must pull out the pivot rod before the stopper will come out. If you want to auger the sink, you will have to remove the pivot rod (see below).

rags stuffed in overflow outlet

blockage

3. Plunge a sink.
A plunger uses water pressure to blast out obstructions and suction to bring stuff up. The plunger's rubber cup must seal tightly around the drain opening. Water in the sink helps create a seal; rubbing petroleum jelly on the plunger rim also helps. Stuff a rag into any openings, such as an overflow outlet. Push and pull rapidly with the plunger.

crank auger

blockage

4. Auger a sink.
If plunging doesn't work, fit an auger down the drain. Cranking the auger handle rotates a stiff spring that bores through a stubborn blockage. Augering may push blockage through, or it may snag something so you can pull it up and out. If none of these techniques works, see page 154.

DISMANTLING FIXTURE TRAPS

When plunging doesn't clear a clog, or if you've dropped something valuable into a drain, your next step is to dismantle the trap. Before dismantling the trap, see if it has a nutlike clean-out fitting at its lowest point. If so, open it, and fit the auger into the hole. If there is no clean-out, don't be discouraged. Dismantling a trap is not all that difficult or time-consuming. Usually, the worst part of the job is getting a wrench into position if the trap is in an awkward place.

YOU'LL NEED...

TIME: About an hour to dismantle and reassemble a trap.
SKILLS: Beginner plumbing skills.
TOOLS: Tongue-and-groove pliers, Teflon tape or pipe joint compound, some extra washers, and a dishpan or bucket.

1. Open and drain the trap.
Turn off the faucet firmly. As an extra precaution, turn off the supply valves. Position a bucket to catch the water that will spill out when you remove the trap. Loosen the slip nuts that secure the trap. Protect the nuts from scratches by wrapping electrical tape around the jaws of your wrench or pliers. After a half-turn or so, the nuts can be unscrewed by hand.

2. Disassemble the trap.
The joints of the trap have a nut and a flexible washer. Keep track of these by pushing them up the tailpiece and elbow. Dump out the water that sits in the trap.

3. Clean out the trap.
Remove any gunk that has collected. Clean the inside of the trap with a small wire brush, or run a piece of cloth through it. Replace any washers that show signs of wear and slide the trap back into position.

4. Reassemble.
Wrap the male threads with Teflon tape or brush on joint compound. Position trap, slide washers into place, and hand-tighten the slip nuts. Use an adjustable wrench for final tightening. Test for leaks by filling the bowl then removing the plug. Tighten slip nut if necessary.

REPLACING SINK STRAINERS

A slight leak under the sink at the tailpiece is likely the result of a poor seal between the strainer body and the sink. To check for this, plug the sink, fill the bowl, and look for drips. If water drips from where the strainer body joins the sink, disassemble the strainer and apply new putty. Leaks may also occur where the tailpiece joins the strainer body. If so, tighten the slip nut. If that does not solve the problem, replace the washer.

YOU'LL NEED...

TIME: About two hours to disassemble and reassemble a strainer.
SKILLS: Intermediate plumbing techniques.
TOOLS: Adjustable wrench (and possibly a spud wrench), putty knife, plumber's putty, and pipe joint compound or Teflon tape. You may need replacement parts.

Sink strainer parts
Waste that would clog the drain is captured by the sink strainer. Its wide bowl is held snug against the sink bottom by the locknut. Putty and a rubber gasket sandwich the sink for a tight seal. The next important joint is where the strainer body meets the tailpiece. Here the seal is made watertight with a washer and a slip nut.

1. Remove the tailpiece.
Loosen the slip nut beneath the strainer body and the slip nut above the trap bend using an adjustable wrench. Finish unscrewing it by hand and remove the tailpiece.

2. Remove the locknut.
Removing the locknut can be difficult, especially if it is hard to get to. Consider purchasing a spud wrench, which is specially designed to fit on locknuts. Otherwise, place a screwdriver against a rib and tap gently with a hammer to loosen the nut.

3. Remove old putty.
Use a putty knife to scrape the old putty from the drain opening. Clean the opening thoroughly with a scouring pad soaked with paint thinner. If you will be reusing the strainer, clean off the flange of the strainer as well.

4. Apply putty and reinstall.
Make a rope of putty, and place it on the lip of the drain opening. Press the strainer into the opening. From under the sink, slip on the rubber gasket and the friction ring; screw on the locknut. Tighten the locknut until the strainer nests completely into the sink. Reinstall the tailpiece.

AUGERING TECHNIQUES

1. Set up a drop cloth and pan.
Be prepared for a mess. Place a drop cloth and a dishpan below the drain opening. Wearing gloves, remove the trap and elbow (see page 152) as well as the pipe leading to the wall. Loosen the setscrew of the auger, and push the auger cable in until you feel it meet resistance.

2. Set the screw and crank.
Give yourself 6 to 8 inches of cable to work with, and tighten the setscrew. Crank the auger handle clockwise, and push in until the auger moves forward. Once it is past an obstruction, like a bend in the pipe, you may be able to push the cable in without cranking.

3. Push and pull.
Augers can pass through soft obstructions such as soap clogs. Use a push-and-pull motion to ream out such clogs. If the auger comes to a place where it will not crank easily, pull it out; often the blockage will come out with it. Sometimes you can use the auger to clear the line by pushing the blockage through to a larger pipe.

UNCLOGGING SHOWERS

If a shower stall drains sluggishly, try filling the base with an inch of water and plunging. If the clogged shower drain does not respond to plunging, remove the strainer and attempt to clear the blockage with the two methods shown here. Begin by prying up the strainer with a screwdriver. (Some strainers may have a center screw. Remove it, then pry up.)

YOU'LL NEED...
TIME: Allow yourself two hours to try both methods.
SKILLS: Beginner plumbing skills.
TOOLS: Auger, garden hose attached to a spout, and rags.

1. Run an auger.
Push an auger down the drain and through the trap. Push and pull to remove a soap clog. If the auger hits a blockage, pull out the auger. The blockage may come with it. If it doesn't, push the auger to try to force the clog into a larger pipe.

2. Push in a hose.
If all else fails, try forcing out the blockage with a hose. Stick it in as far as it will easily go and pack rags tightly around the hose at the drain opening. Hold everything in place and have a helper turn the water fully on and off a few times.

UNCLOGGING TUBS

1. Plunge.
Try plunging first. If your tub has a pop-up stopper, remove it before plunging. Wiggle it to free the linkage assembly—the mechanism that connects the trap lever with the stopper mechanism. Before plunging, plug the overflow and run an inch or so of water in the tub to help the plunger seal.

2. Auger through the strainer.
If plunging doesn't work, thread in an auger. The tub will have a stopper or a trip-lever assembly like the one above. Pry up or unscrew the strainer to insert the auger. This method will reach only to the tee fitting. If the clog is farther down, you'll have to go through the overflow tube.

3. Auger through the overflow.
Remove the pop-up or trip-lever assembly by unscrewing the overflow plate and pulling out the parts (see page 206). Feed the auger down through the overflow tube and into the trap and beyond. If the auger goes in a long way and the stoppage remains, find a clean-out point on the main drain and auger there.

CLEANING DRUM TRAPS

1. Open the drum trap.
Many older bathrooms have a removable metal cap on the floor, usually near the tub. This covers a drum trap. Before opening it, bail out the tub and remove standing water with rags or a large sponge.

2. Auger through the drum trap.
Removing the cap may be difficult. If a wrench does not do the trick, use a hammer and cold chisel or screwdriver. Damage the trap cap if necessary (it can be replaced easily), but don't hurt the threads on the trap. Open the trap slowly, watching for water to well up around the threads. If the trap is full, work the auger away from the tub toward the main drain. If the trap is only partially full (as shown), the obstruction is between the tub and the trap, so auger back and forth. Drum traps are no longer to code and should be replaced with a P-trap as shown on page 154.

UNCLOGGING TOILETS

When a toilet clogs, do not continue to flush it. Additional flushing will not push objects through and may flood the bathroom floor. Instead bail out the toilet until the bowl is about half full. More water than this can lead to a sloshy mess while plunging, but too little water will prevent the plunger from making a tight seal around the bowl's outlet. Add water to the toilet if necessary. Most toilet clogs occur because the toilet trap is blocked. If plunging and using a toilet auger do not clear things up, the waste-vent stack may be blocked.

CAUTION!
Never attempt to unclog a toilet with a chemical drain cleaner. Chances are, it won't do the job, and you'll be forced to plunge or auger through a strong solution that could burn your skin or eyes.

EXPERTS' INSIGHT

How to stop a toilet overflow
If the toilet begins to overflow, act fast. Remove everything atop the tank, and take off the lid. Pull the float up, and push down on the flapper at the tank bottom. The flush will stop.

toilet trap

1. Plunge.
An ordinary plunger can clear a toilet, but the molded-cup type shown here generates stronger suction. Work up and down vigorously for about a dozen strokes, then quickly yank away the plunger.

If the water disappears with a glug, it's likely the plunging has succeeded. But don't flush yet. First pour in more water, until the bowl empties several times. If plunging doesn't work, the toilet will have to be augered.

Plastic cover protects toilet.

spring

2. Use a closet auger.
A closet auger makes short work of most toilet stoppages. This specialized tool has a long handle with a plastic cover at the bend to protect your toilet from scratches. To operate the auger, pull the spring all the way up into the handle so the spring barely protrudes from the plastic protective cover. Insert the bit into the bowl outlet and crank. If you meet resistance, pull back slightly, wiggle the handle, and try again. A closet auger can grab and pull many blockages, but not solid objects such as toys. If you hear something other than the auger rattling around, remove the toilet to get at the item (see page 182).

CLEARING MAIN DRAINS AND SEWER LINES

If more than one of your fixtures is sluggish or clogged, or if plunging and augering fail to solve the problem, you may have a clogged drain or sewer line. Look for clean-outs, places where you can remove a large nut and slip in an auger.

Start with the highest clean-out you can find that is below the clogged fixture. If augering it does not work, continue working downward. Sometimes it proves best to go up on the roof and run an auger down through the vent stack. This job often warrants calling in a plumber or a drain-cleaning service, especially if the line is clogged with tree roots.

> ### CAUTION!
> Before removing any clean-out plug from a main drain line, have buckets on hand to catch the wastewater.

Auger a main drain.
Look for a clean-out near the bottom of your home's waste stack. Loosen the plug of the clean-out. If water flows out, the blockage is below. (If no water flows out, the blockage is holding the water above, so replace the

clean-out plug and auger from a higher point.) Insert the auger into the opening and run it back and forth several times (see page 154). Another solution is to use a blow bag. Once the blow bag is in place, run the water in the hose full force on and off several times.

Auger a house trap.
If neither procedure works, move farther down the line. Some houses have a house trap near where the drain line leaves the house. Open one of the two plugs and thread in an auger. The blockage may be in the trap itself.

Clear a sewer line.
If the blockage still does not go away, the outdoor sewer line may be blocked. Often fine tree roots work their way into the line, creating a tough blockage that can only be removed with a heavy auger with a cutting bit.

First try feeding in a garden hose to push and flush out the obstruction. If that doesn't work, call in a professional or rent a heavy-duty power auger. Running one of these is a two-person job. Get a demonstration from the rental center on its use.

CLEANING SHOWERHEADS

If your showerhead sprays unevenly, take it apart and clean it or replace it. If it leaks at the arm, or if it doesn't stay in position, tighten the retainer or collar nut. If that doesn't work, replace the O-ring—or replace the showerhead.

If you want to replace your showerhead, take the old one with you to your supplier to make sure you get one that will fit your pipe. You'll find a wide range of styles and features.

YOU'LL NEED...

TIME: About an hour for removal and scrubbing; overnight soaking for a thorough cleaning.
SKILLS: Basic plumbing skills.
TOOLS: Wrench, screwdriver, sharp-pointed tool or thin wire, and old toothbrush.

Two basic types

Newer showerheads simply screw onto the shower arm, the chromed pipe that extends from the wall. Older models require a shower arm with a ball-shaped end that acts as a swivel (see inset). In most cases you can switch to a newer style by replacing the shower arm. If you wish to replace the shower arm, remove it from the drop ell. Wrap Teflon tape around the male threads of the new shower arm before screwing it into place.

Removing a showerhead

This is a simple matter of unscrewing the nut at the shower arm. Take care not to mar the finish of the shower head or arm: Use a wrench rather than pliers. For an added precaution, cushion your wrench with a rag as you work.

Clean the holes.

Shower heads often spray unevenly because the tiny holes have gotten clogged with mineral deposits. Use an old toothbrush to clean the head. Then run a sharp blast of water backward through the showerhead.

Dismantle and clean.

For a thorough cleaning, take the head apart, use a pin to poke out any mineral buildup or debris, and brush away all deposits. Then soak the parts in vinegar overnight to dissolve remaining mineral deposits. Reassemble and reinstall the showerhead.

ADVANCED PLUMBING

CHOOSING PIPE

The first step in choosing pipe is to find out which type of pipe you have in your home. It's often easiest to use the same type when adding on, but it's not mandatory. To change type, you must purchase special adapter fittings to switch from one material to another in the middle of a pipe run.

For supply lines—the pipes that carry pressurized water to your fixtures—the usual choices are copper and plastic. However if your home is old enough to have galvanized pipe and you need to install only a short run of pipe, it makes sense to continue with galvanized. In many localities, plastic supply pipe is not allowed. Keep in mind that you must learn how to solder (see pages 166–167) before you can install copper pipe.

When making final connections to a fixture or a faucet, usually it is easiest to install a flexible supply line. Use copper or plastic flexible tubing. Be careful to avoid kinks.

Plastic pipe—either PVC or ABS—is now used almost exclusively for drains. If you have old cast-iron, galvanized, or copper drain pipes, make the transition to plastic. It is much easier to install and less expensive.

Before you buy any pipe, check with the local building department to make sure you're using material approved for use in your area.

flexible copper

rigid copper

galvanized steel

black steel

rigid plastic supply

flexible plastic

plastic drain

cast-iron

EXPERTS' INSIGHT

GAS LINES

■ Gas lines are almost always made of black steel pipe. It has the same texture as galvanized pipe but not the shiny silver color. Black steel pipe is installed in the same way as galvanized pipe (see pages 172–173). Check for leaks by turning the gas on, pouring soapy water on all the joints, and looking for tiny bubbles.

■ Do not use copper pipe for long gas lines. A chemical reaction causes the inside of the pipe to flake, which can plug orifices and damage appliances. Contrary to some opinions, you can use galvanized pipe for gas, but it's more expensive.

MEASUREMENTS

THE MOST COMMON SIZES

Here are the pipe sizes commonly used in residential plumbing in North America. (To determine the size of your pipe, see page 164.)

■ Main water-supply line entering a house: ¾–1 inch.

■ Water-supply lines after the water heater usually are ½ inch, sometimes ¾ inch.

■ Gas lines are most often ¾ inch and sometimes are ½ inch.

■ Main drain pipes, called stacks, are 3 or 4 inches.

■ Kitchen, tub, and shower drains are almost always 1½ inches.

■ Bathroom sink drains are almost always 1¼ inches.

Material	Type	Uses	Features and Joining Techniques
Copper	Rigid	Hot and cold supply lines; rarely for DWV (drain-waste-vent) lines	Sold in 10' and 20' lengths. The most widely used pipe for supply lines. Lightweight and durable, though a bit expensive. Once the soldering technique is learned, you can cut it on the spot and put it together quickly. Type M is the thinnest, and is a good choice for home projects. Types L and K are used mainly in commercial projects.
	Flexible	Hot and cold supply lines, for short final runs to fixtures	Comes in easily bent 60' and 100' coils or by the foot. Can be soldered like rigid copper, but usually is connected with compression fittings.
Threaded Steel	Galvanized	Supply and occasionally DWV	Because it's cumbersome to work with and tends to build up lime deposits that constrict water flow, it is not used widely anymore. It takes expensive equipment to cut and thread it, so you must buy pre-cut pieces from your supplier. If you have a good selection of shorter pieces on hand, you can cut down on trips to the supplier.
	Black	Gas lines	Rusts readily, so it must not be used for water supply.
Plastic	ABS	DWV only	Black in color, in 10' or 20' lengths. Lightweight and easy to work with, you can cut it with an ordinary saw and cement it together with a special glue. Check local codes before using.
	PVC	Cold water supply and DWV	Cream-colored, blue-gray, or white, in 10' or 20' lengths. This has the same properties as ABS except that you must apply primer before cementing it. Do not mix PVC with ABS or interchange their cements.
	CPVC	Hot and cold supply lines	White, gray, or cream-colored, available in 10' lengths. Has the same properties as ABS and PVC.
	Flexible PB (polybutylene)	Hot and cold supply lines, usually for short runs	White or cream-colored, sold in 25' or 100' coils or by the foot. Flexible. Expensive and not widely used, it is joined with special fittings.
	Flexible PE (polyethylene)	Supply lines	Black-colored, sold in 25' or 100' coils or by the foot. Same properties as PB. Used for sprinkler systems.
Cast-Iron	Hub-and-Spigot	DWV	Cast-iron is extremely heavy and difficult to work with, so don't try to install any new pipes of this material. Hub-and-spigot is joined with oakum and molten lead.
	No-Hub	DWV	Joins with gaskets and clamps, but still is hard to work with. Make the transition to plastic.

CHOOSING THE RIGHT FITTING

*T*he parts bins at a plumbing supplier contain hundreds of fittings that let you connect any pipe material in just about any way. To get the best pipe for your needs, familiarize yourself with the terms on this page. Items in bold are illustrated.

Supply fittings connect the pipes that bring water to fixtures and faucets. When changing direction in a supply run, use an **elbow (ell)**. The most common ones make 45- or 90-degree turns and have female threads on each end. A **street ell** has male and female connections to allow for insertion into another fitting. A reducing ell joins one size pipe to another. Use a **drop ell** to anchor the pipes to framing where they will protrude into a room.

Use **tees** wherever two runs intersect. A **reducing tee** lets you join pipes of different diameters; for example, adding a ½-inch branch to a ¾-inch main supply.

A **coupling** connects pipes end to end. **Reducing couplings** let you step down from one pipe diameter to a smaller one. Slip couplings function the same way as unions, joining sections of copper or plastic line. Use a **cap** to seal off a line.

A plastic-to-copper **transition fitting** is one of many transition fittings that connect one pipe material to another. (Do not make the transition from steel to copper without a special dielectric fitting, or the joint will corrode.)

In any run of threaded pipe, you'll need a **union** somewhere. This fitting compensates for the frustrating fact that you can't simultaneously turn a pipe into fittings at either end.

Nipples—lengths of pipe less than 12 inches long—are sold in standard sizes because short pieces are difficult to cut and thread.

Examine drainage fittings, and you'll see how they're designed to keep waste water flowing downhill. Sometimes called **sanitary fittings**, they have gentle curves rather than sharp angles, so waste will not get hung up.

Choose ¼ **bends** to make 90-degree turns, and ⅛ **bends** for 45 degrees. Also available are ⅕ bends for 72-degree turns, and ⅙ bends for 60 degrees. All types of bends also come in more gradual curves, known as **long-turn bends**, which make for a smoother flow.

Sanitary branches such as the **tee** and **cross** shown here, come in a variety of configurations that suit situations where two or more lines converge. These can be tricky to order, so make a sketch of your proposed drain lines, identifying all pipe sizes, and take it to your supplier when you order.

Toilet hookups require a **closet bend,** which connects to the main drain, and a **closet flange,** which fits onto the bend. The flange is anchored to the floor and anchors the toilet bowl. To connect a sink trap to the drainpipe, use a **trap adapter.** To make the transition from cast-iron drain to plastic drain, use a **no-hub adapter.**

EXPERTS' INSIGHT

ORDERING OR FINDING FITTINGS

When ordering materials, organize your description of a fitting in this way: first the size, then the material, and finally the type of fitting. You might, for example, ask or look for a ½-inch galvanized, 90-degree ell. With reducing fittings, the larger size comes first, then the smaller.

Copper Supply: 90-degree elbow

Galvanized Supply: street ell

Plastic Supply: 90-degree ell

Plastic Drain: ¼ (90-degree) long-turn bend

45-degree elbow

tee

coupling

reducing coupling

drop ell

cap

reducing tee

nipple

union

cap

coupling

⅛ (45-degree) bend

drop ell plastic-to-copper transition

tee

reducing coupling

trap adapter for transition from galvanized steel to plastic

plastic-to-copper transition fitting

sanitary tee

sanitary cross

closet flange

trap adapter

plastic-to-cast-iron no-hub adapter

closet bend

MEASURING PIPES AND FITTINGS

*B*eginning plumbers often spend more time running back and forth to their supplier than they spend doing the actual work because it takes practice and experience to be able to figure out everything you need ahead of time. The first step in becoming an efficient plumber is to learn to correctly identify the pipes and fittings a job requires.

Plumbing dimensions aren't always what they appear to be. A plastic pipe with a ⅞-inch outside diameter, for instance, is actually called a ½-inch pipe because it has a ½-inch inside diameter and pipes are usually sized according

To find out a pipe's size, measure the inside...
If you have a pipe with an exposed end, simply measure the pipe's inside diameter and round off to the nearest ⅛ inch. Some manufacturers indicate the size on the fittings.

...or figure from the outside.
You also can determine pipe size by measuring its outside circumference. Wrap a string around the pipe, straighten it out, and measure it. Use the chart below to find the nominal size you'll need to order.

MEASUREMENTS: PIPE DIMENSIONS

Material	Inside Diameter (ID) Nominal Size	Approximate Outside Diameter (OD)	Approximate Circumference	Approximate Socket Depth
Copper	¼"	⅜"	1⅛"	⁵⁄₁₆"
	⅜"	½"	1½"	⅜"
	½"	⅝"	2"	½"
	¾"	⅞"	2¾"	¾"
	1"	1⅛"	3½"	¹⁵⁄₁₆"
	1¼"	1⅜"	4⁵⁄₁₆"	1"
	1½"	1⅝"	5⅛"	1⅛"
Threaded	⅜"	⅝"	2"	⅜"
	½"	¾"	2⅜"	½"
	¾"	1"	3⅛"	⁹⁄₁₆"
	1"	1¼"	4"	¹¹⁄₁₆"
	1¼"	1½"	4¾"	¹¹⁄₁₆"
	1½"	1¾"	5½"	¹¹⁄₁₆"
	2"	2¼"	7"	¾"
Plastic	½"	⅞"	2¾"	½"
	¾"	1⅛"	3½"	⅝"
	1"	1⅜"	4⁵⁄₁₆"	¾"
	1¼"	1⅝"	5⅛"	¹¹⁄₁₆"
	1½"	1⅞"	6"	¹¹⁄₁₆"
	2"	2⅜"	7½"	¾"
	3"	3⅜"	10½"	1½"
	4"	4⅜"	14"	1¾"
Cast-Iron	2"	2¼"	7"	2½"
	3"	3¼"	10⅛"	2¾"
	4"	4¼"	13⅜"	3"

to their inside diameter (ID). (See chart on page 182.) This dimension is also referred to as the nominal size, the size you ask for at a plumbing supplier.

If you are at all unsure about getting the right material, make things perfectly clear by specifying ID for most pipes. In a minority of cases—flexible copper lines, for example—pipe is ordered by using the outside diameter (OD).

If you can measure the inside dimension, you're home free. However often you won't have a way of measuring the inside of the pipe. Holding a ruler against a pipe will give you only a rough idea of the outside diameter. Instead, use a string or a set of calipers for a more exact measurement. Once you find the outside dimension, use the chart, opposite, to find the nominal size.

Fittings can be just as confusing. Their inside diameters must be large enough to fit over the pipe's outside diameter. A half-inch plastic elbow, for example, has an outside diameter of about 1¼ inches.

As a rule of thumb, the OD of copper is ⅛ inch greater than its ID, the nominal size. For plastic pipe, measure the OD and subtract ⅜ inch. For threaded and cast-iron, subtract ¼ inch.

Another mathematical pitfall for a beginning plumber is measuring the length of a pipe running from one fitting to the next. Pipes must fully extend into fixture and fitting sockets (see illustration, right), or the joint could leak. Socket depths vary from one pipe size and material to another, so you must account for the depth of each fitting's socket in the total length of pipe needed between fittings.

The only times you don't have to take socket depth into account are when you are using no-hub cast-iron pipes (see pages 160–161) or slip couplings with copper or plastic pipe.

socket depth

face-to-face distance

FULLY JOINED PIPE

socket depth

copper

ID equals OD less ⅛"

plastic

ID equals OD less ⅜"

threaded

ID equals OD less ¼"

Add the socket depths.

To figure the length of a pipe, first measure from face to face, as shown above. Next check the chart on page 182 for the socket depth of the material you're working with. Because pipes have fittings on both ends, multiply by 2, and add the face-to-face length.

Measure copper or plastic in place.

When working with copper or plastic—materials you can cut on the job—often the most accurate way of measuring is to insert the pipe into one fitting and mark the other end, rather than using a tape measure.

EXPERTS' INSIGHT

Don't leave the household high and dry while you drive back and forth to the plumbing supplier. When buying fittings, invest in a handful of caps (see page 163) in different sizes. That way, if you've misread a dimension—as even experienced plumbers do occasionally—you can cap off the line and turn the water on.

WORKING WITH RIGID COPPER PIPE

To solder rigid copper plumbing lines, you must learn a skill that is unlike other household repair skills. At first it may seem frustratingly slow. But once you get the knack, soldering will go faster than screwing together threaded pipe.

Sometimes soldering is called "sweating." Soldering works by using capillary action to flow molten solder into the fitting. Just as an ink blotter soaks up ink, a joint absorbs molten solder, making a watertight bond as strong as the pipe itself.

YOU'LL NEED...

TIME: With practice, an hour to connect five joints.
SKILLS: Soldering is a specialized skill that takes time to learn.
MATERIALS: Pipe and lead-free solder.
TOOLS: Tubing cutter or hacksaw, emery cloth, wire brush, flux brush, propane torch, and tongue-and-groove pliers.

EXPERTS' INSIGHT

ELIMINATING MOISTURE

If you are adding on to existing plumbing, there may be a little water inside the pipes. This must be dried up if you are to solder a tight joint.
■ Stuff in a piece of white bread (not the crust) just upstream of the connection. It will absorb the water and dissolve when the water is turned on.
■ Buy specially made waxy capsules that plug the line while you work. Later apply heat where the capsule lodged to melt the capsule away.

1. Cut the pipe.
Use a hacksaw or a tubing cutter (it makes cleaner cuts). Clamp the cutter onto the tubing, rotate a few revolutions, tighten, and rotate some more. Make hacksaw cuts in a miter box. Don't nick the metal—this could cause the connection to leak.

2. Remove burrs.
Remove any burrs on the inside of the pipe by inserting the reaming blade of the tubing cutter and twisting. If you don't have a tubing cutter, use a metal file.

3. Polish the pipe and fitting.
Polish the outside of the pipe and the inside of the fitting with emery cloth or steel wool. This removes grease, dirt, and oxidation that could impede the flow of solder. Stop polishing when the metal is shiny. Avoid touching polished surfaces—oil from your fingers could interfere with the solder flow and cause a leak.

4. Dry-fit the pieces.
Dry-fit a number of pipe pieces and fittings to make sure they are the right length. If you have difficulty pushing pieces together, the pipe may have been squeezed out of shape during cutting. Cut a new piece. Once you are satisfied, take them apart and set them on a clean surface.

5. Apply flux.

Brush on a light, even coating of flux (also called soldering paste) to both surfaces. Flux retards oxidation when the copper is heated. As solder flows into the joint, the flux burns away. Use rosin- (not acid-) type flux for plumbing work.

6. Protect flammable surfaces.

If you're working near framing, paper-sheathed insulation, or other flammable materials, shield them from the propane torch flame with an old cookie sheet or a piece of sheet metal.

7. Form the solder.

Bend the solder so it's easy to work with but long enough to keep your fingers away from the flame. Unwind about 10 inches of solder, straighten it, and bend 2 inches at a 60-degree angle. Light the torch. Adjust the flame until the inner (blue) cone is about 2 inches long.

8. Assemble the connection.

Heat the middle of the fitting—not the joint—with the inner cone of the flame. Touch the solder to the joint. If it is hot enough, capillary action will pull solder into the joint. Remove the flame when solder drips from the pipe.

> **CAUTION!**
> *Any gaps will leak. Be sure the joint has an even bead around its circumference to prevent leaks.*

9. Wipe away excess.

For a neat, professional look, lightly brush the joint with a damp rag. Take care not to burn your fingers.

Most pros lay out an entire run of copper, first cutting and dry-fitting all of its components. After dry-fitting, they go back to clean, flux, and solder each joint.

10. Check for leaks.

Test the system by turning the water on. If you have a leak, there is no easy solution—it cannot be fixed while water is present. Shut off the water, drain the line, disassemble the joint (see page 168), and discard the old fitting. Dry the inside of the pipes. Polish the pipe end and the inside of the new fitting, apply flux, reassemble, and solder again.

11. Install pipe hangers.
Copper supply lines need support at least every 6 feet. The plastic type of hanger pictured here is easy to install, helps quiet noisy pipes, and is slightly flexible so it doesn't damage the pipes.

brass valve

1. To install a brass valve, remove any heat-sensitive parts.
A valve stem has rubber or plastic parts that will melt during soldering. Remove the stem with a wrench. Polish the pipe end and the inside of the fitting as you would with a copper joint.

2. Solder the joint.
Fit the pieces together. (If the valve has an arrow, be sure it is pointing in the direction of water flow). Heat the body of the valve, moving the flame back and forth to heat both sides evenly. Brass requires more heating than copper. Apply solder as you would with a copper fitting (see page 167).

1. To take apart soldered joints, heat the fitting.
NOTE: *Shut off the water.* Drain the line by opening faucets above and below the run. Light a propane torch, set it so the inner (blue) cone of the flame is about 2 inches long, and heat the fitting. Point the flame at both sides of the fitting, but not directly at the soldered joint.

2. Pull the pieces apart.
While the pipe is hot, grasp the fitting and pipe with pliers, and pull the joint apart.

> ### CAUTION!
> *Once the fitting is heated, you have only a few seconds to take the joint apart. Prepare a safe place to set the torch and have two pairs of pliers within easy reach. Work carefully— the pipes are very hot.*

3. Polish the pipe ends.
To remove old solder, heat the pipe end with the torch and quickly wipe with a dry rag. Do this carefully—the pipe is very hot. Allow the pipe to cool and polish the end with emery cloth. Never reuse an old copper fitting—a watertight seal can only be made with a new fitting.

WORKING WITH FLEXIBLE COPPER TUBING

Flexible copper tubing is pliable enough to make all but the sharpest turns. This means you don't have to install a fitting every time you make a turn as you would with rigid pipe. In almost every case, you should connect flexible tubing to compression and flare fittings (see pages 170–171) rather than soldering them.

Do not use copper tubing for a gas line. Natural gas will cause the inside of the copper tube to flake, which can damage appliances.

YOU'LL NEED...
TIME: To bend and cut tubing for a short run, about 15 minutes.
SKILLS: Patience and care to keep from kinking tubing.
TOOLS: Tubing cutter and coil-spring tubing bender.

1. Uncoil the tubing.
Because flexible copper tubing is soft, always handle it gently. Uncoil tubing by straightening it out every few inches as you go. If the tubing comes in a box, grip the box and carefully pull the tubing upward.

tubing cutter

retracted reaming blade

2. Cut the tubing.
Cut flexible tubing with a tubing cutter or a hacksaw. Remove any burrs on the inside of the tubing by inserting the reaming blade of the tubing cutter and twisting (see page 166). Or use a metal file.

kinked tubing

coil-spring tubing bender

3. Bend the tubing.
Bend the flexible tubing in gradual, sweeping arcs or it will surprise you by suddenly kinking and you'll have to throw the piece away. Kinks seriously impede water flow and are almost impossible to reshape.

If you need to make a fairly tight turn, use a coil-spring tubing bender like the one shown here. Slide the bender to the point you need a tight bend and, with it in place, bend the tubing. With one of these tools, it is nearly impossible to kink the tubing.

4. Polish the end.
Rub the end of the tubing lightly with emery cloth to remove dirt and grease. With compression or flare fittings, you don't need to polish as much as for a soldered joint. Join tubing by using compression fittings (see page 170) or flare fittings (see page 171), or by soldering (see pages 166–167).

USING COMPRESSION FITTINGS

Use compression fittings in places where you may need to take the run apart someday or where it is difficult to solder. One common location is on supply lines for a sink, which have compression fittings at both the stop valve and the faucet inlet. Flexible supply lines are an even easier way to make this connection (see page 169).

Compression fittings usually are used with flexible copper tubing, but may also be used with type-M rigid copper (see page 166). These fittings are not as strong as soldered joints so they should not be hidden inside walls.

YOU'LL NEED...

TIME: About 15 minutes to make a simple connection.
SKILLS: No special skills needed.
TOOLS: Two Crescent wrenches.

1. To make a compression joint, position the parts.
Bend the tubing into position (see page 169), and slip on the nut and the ferrule. The ferrule will not go on if the tubing end is bent or out of round. You may have to sand the tubing with emery cloth to get the ferrule to slide on. Smear pipe joint compound on the ferrule and the male threads of the fitting.

2. Tighten the nut.
Tighten the compression nut with a wrench, forcing the ferrule down into the tubing to secure and seal the connection. If the joint leaks when the water is turned on, tighten the nut a quarter turn at a time until the leak stops. Don't overtighten the joint—too much pressure can crush the tubing or crack the nut.

1. To join a compression union, position the parts.
Bend the tubing pieces into position (see page 169) and slip a nut and a ferrule onto each piece of tubing. Smear pipe joint compound on the ferrules and on the male threads of the union. Slide the pieces together, and hand-tighten the nuts.

2. Tighten each side.
Place one wrench on the union. Use another wrench to tighten each side. Once snug, tighten about a half turn more. Turn on the water; if there is a leak, gently tighten more.

How it works
The compression nut forms a seal by squeezing the ferrule against the copper pipe. Because copper is a soft metal, the seal can be extremely tight. Still, use pipe joint compound to make sure the seal is watertight. Anchor or support the tubing within 2 feet of either side of the fitting.

USING FLARE FITTINGS

*F*lare fittings, like compression fittings, are useful in places where it's difficult to solder a joint. Do not hide flare fittings inside a wall. You can use flare fittings only with flexible copper tubing; they cannot be used on rigid pipe. Unlike compression fittings, this type of fitting requires a flaring tool. The two-piece tool reshapes the end of the copper tubing, "flaring" it to fit into a special flare fitting. If possible, make the flared connection first, then cut the tubing to length because sometimes tubing splits while being flared.

YOU'LL NEED...

TIME: About half an hour to join two pieces together in a union.
SKILLS: Use of the flaring tool is not difficult.
TOOLS: Flaring tool and adjustable wrenches.

1. Flare the tubing ends.
Make sure the tubing is cut square across. Also remember to slip the flaring nut on before you flare the end of the tubing.

Choose the hole in the flaring block that matches the outside diameter of the tubing. Clamp the tool onto the tubing. Align the compression cone on the tubing's end and tighten the screw. As you turn the handle, the cone flares the tubing's end. Inspect your work carefully after removing the tubing from the flaring block. If the end has split, cut off the flared portion and repeat the process.

2. Assemble the pieces.
Seat the flare union against one of the flared ends of the tubing, slide the nut down, and hand-tighten. Do the same on the other side. No pipe joint compound is necessary.

3. Tighten and test.
Place one wrench on the union and one on a nut. Don't over-tighten a flared joint. Once snug, give a half turn on each nut. Turn the water on and test. If the joint leaks, tighten it carefully until the leak stops. If tightening won't stop the leak, dismantle the joint and examine it to see if the tubing was cut squarely. Make sure that the nut was not cross-threaded on the fitting. Anchor or support the tubing within 2 feet of either side of the flare fitting.

REMOVING OLD THREADED PIPE

After your first experience with threaded pipe, you'll appreciate why this material is all but extinct in new installations. Cutting, threading, and assembling steel pipe requires muscle. Sometimes when you're trying to take old pipe apart, you'll swear it is welded together.

If your home was built before World War II, its supply pipes are likely to be threaded steel. This doesn't mean you have to use the same pipe for improvements or repairs. Special fittings let you break into a line and add copper or plastic (see pages 162–163).

Black threaded pipe, which lacks the shiny gray color of galvanized, is meant for gas only and is still commonly used. Do not use black pipe for water lines.

1. Start at a union.
NOTE: *Shut off water, and drain the pipes.* Examine the way your pipes and fittings thread together and you'll see you can't simply begin unscrewing them anywhere. Somewhere in every pipe run is a union that allows you to unlock and dismantle the piping. To crack open a union, determine which of the smaller union nuts the ring nut is threaded onto. Use a wrench on the union nut to hold it stable. Put another wrench on the ring nut to turn it counterclockwise. Once it's unthreaded, you have the break you need and can start unscrewing pipes from fittings.

YOU'LL NEED...

TIME: To take apart four or five sections of pipe with fittings, about an hour.
SKILLS: Use of a pipe wrench and sometimes brute strength.
TOOLS: Two pipe wrenches, hacksaw, and maybe a propane torch.

EXPERTS' INSIGHT

SWITCHING MATERIALS

If you have good water pressure and can find no serious rust, there is no need to replace your threaded steel pipe with copper or plastic. But if water pressure is low, aerators fill up with rust, and leaks develop, it is time for a change. Replace the worst-looking pipes first. Don't cut holes into walls and get involved in a major refit unless it is absolutely necessary.

2. When necessary, cut the pipe. If there is no union handy, cut a pipe with a hacksaw or a reciprocating saw fitted with a metal-cutting blade. When you reassemble this run you'll have to install a union using prethreaded nipples on either side of the union.

3. If the pipe won't budge Stubborn joints may respond to penetrating oil, or try heating the fitting with a propane torch. Then use a larger pipe wrench, or slip a piece of 1¼-inch or 1½-inch pipe onto the handle of your wrench to increase its leverage.

INSTALLING THREADED PIPE

If you choose to work with threaded pipe, one difficulty is ending the run at the right place. Because the ends of the pipe are threaded, you can't just cut a piece to fit, as with copper or plastic. Purchase long pieces that take up most of the runs and have on hand plenty of couplings and a selection of nipples—or short lengths of pipe that are threaded on each end. You will then have a number of options to choose from to end the run in the right spot.

You'll Need...

TIME: In an hour you can assemble about four pipe lengths with fittings.
SKILLS: Pipe measuring and use of pipe wrench.
TOOLS: Tape measure and two pipe wrenches.

EXPERTS' INSIGHT

BOOSTING PRESSURE

■ Poor water pressure in an old house may be due to galvanized pipes that are clogged with rust. If the problem is limited to one fixture, try replacing a few of the pipes leading up to it. If the problem is throughout your house, call in a professional.

■ There are companies that specialize in unclogging galvanized pipe. They use a process that causes rust and corrosion to fall away from the inside of the pipe. The process can take months, will clog faucets, and may require repairing leaks found as gunk plugging holes is removed. In the end, however, water will flow through your pipes as if they were new.

Assembling the parts
This typical installation combines standard-length pipes with joints and nipples to end up exactly at the right location. (For background on measuring pipe accurately, see pages 164–165.) Many plumbing suppliers have ready-cut galvanized pipe in standard sizes—12 inches, 48 inches, and so on—for less cost and delay than having pieces custom-cut. Try to use these pieces; if you make a mistake in measuring, you may not be allowed to return a custom-cut piece.

Joining the pieces
Before you thread a pipe and fitting together, seal the pipe threads using pipe joint compound or Teflon tape. Assemble the pipes and fittings one at a time, tightening each as you go. If your assembly requires a union, work from each end toward the union. The union is installed last. Support runs of threaded pipe at least every 6 feet.

WORKING WITH RIGID PLASTIC PIPE

Plastic plumbing is popular with do-it-yourselfers because it is inexpensive and easy to work with. Plastic pipe cuts with an ordinary hacksaw and goes together without special tools or techniques. You simply clean the burrs from the cut, prime, and then glue the parts together.

Installing plastic pipe requires attention to detail, planning ahead, and doing things in the right order. If you make a mistake, the parts cannot be disassembled. You'll have to cut out the faulty section, throw it out, and start again.

There are various types of plastic, so check local codes to make sure you are using the right type for your purpose. In most localities, either ABS or PVC are acceptable (sometimes even required) for drain lines. Many localities do not accept plastic pipe for supply lines; others specify CPVC. See pages 160–161 for types of plastic pipe. Do not mix ABS with PVC. Each expands at a different rate, and each uses a differently formulated cement. Plastic pipe is not as stiff as metal. Be sure to support horizontal runs every 4 to 5 feet.

YOU'LL NEED...

TIME: With practice you can cut and install about five fittings and five pieces of pipe in an hour.
SKILLS: Measuring, cutting, and assembling components in a logical manner.
TOOLS: Plastic pipe saw or hacksaw, miter box, tape measure, utility knife, pencil, emery cloth, and plastic tubing cutter for supply lines.

1. Measure and cut.
When measuring pipe for cutting, take the socket depth of the fitting into account (see page 165). Cut with any fine-tooth saw, using a miter box. Avoid diagonal cuts because they reduce the bonding area at the deepest part of the fitting's socket—the most critical part of the joint.

2. Remove burrs from the cut end.
After you've made the cut, use a knife or file to remove any burrs from the inside and outside of the cut end. Burrs can scrape away cement when the pipe is pushed into the fitting, seriously weakening the bond and resulting in leaks.

3. Test the fitting.
Dry-fit the connection. You should be able to push it in at least one-third of the way. If the pipe bottoms out and feels loose, try another fitting. Unlike copper components, plastic systems are designed with tapered walls on the inside of the socket so that the pipe makes contact well before the pipe reaches the socket shoulder.

4. Mark for alignment.
When gluing the pieces together, you will have less than a minute to correctly position the pipe and fitting before the glue sets. Draw an alignment mark across the pipe and fitting of each joint. When you fit the pieces together, the mark will indicate exactly how to position the pipe and fitting.

5. Clean and prime.

Wipe the inside of the fitting and the outside of the pipe end with a clean cloth. If you are working with PVC or CPVC (but not ABS), coat the outside of the pipe end with a special primer. Many inspectors require purple-colored primer so they can easily see that joints have been primed.

6. Apply cement to pipe.

Use the cement designed for the material you're working with. Immediately after you've primed, swab a smooth coating of cement onto the pipe end.

7. Prime and cement fitting.

Repeat the process on the inside of the fitting socket. Apply cement liberally, but don't let it puddle inside the fitting. Reapply a coating of cement to the pipe end.

EXPERTS' INSIGHT

DRY-FIT 3 OR 4 PIECES AHEAD

Whenever possible, cut and dry-fit three or four pieces before priming and gluing. That way, you can get things lined up ahead of time and avoid going back and forth between cans of primer and cement.

However, don't dry-fit more than four pieces, and don't dry-fit an entire section that must come out to an exact length. Plastic is not like copper pipe, which will solder together exactly the way it dry-fit. Once the cement is applied, plastic pipes may slide farther in than they did during the dry run, which can throw your measurements off as much as ¼ inch per fitting.

8. Twist and hold.

Forcefully push the two together to ensure the pipe moves fully into the socket. Twist a quarter turn as you push to help spread the cement evenly. Complete the twist until your alignment marks come together. Hold the pipe and fitting together for about 20 seconds while they fuse into a single piece. Wipe away excess cement.

Cut off any incorrect joints.

If you misalign a connection, saw it off, making sure to cut squarely. Install a new fitting with a spacer and slip coupling as shown. Cemented joints are strong enough to handle after 15 minutes, but don't run water in the line for about two hours.

WORKING WITH FLEXIBLE PLASTIC TUBING

Flexible plastic tubing comes in long coils that you can snake through tight spots without using fittings. It kinks if bent too far, but doesn't kink as readily as flexible copper tubing. Codes in your area may disallow it entirely. If they do allow it, they will specify which type can be used in specific situations. PB (polybutylene) flexible plastic tubing can be used for hot and cold lines. Less expensive PE (polyethylene) tubing is affected by heat and therefore can only be used to carry cold water. Many communities allow PE use underground for wells and sprinkler systems.

Both types of plastic are easy to work with: Cut the tubing with a knife and join sections with clamps or compression fittings. Connect flexible plastic to other pipe materials with transition fittings that allow expansion and contraction. Support tubing every 32 inches and clamp it loosely. PE and PB can be punctured, so don't use either for exposed runs.

YOU'LL NEED...

TIME: About two hours to connect three lengths.
SKILLS: No special skills needed.
TOOLS: Utility knife, pliers, and screwdriver.

TOOLS TO USE

PLASTIC TUBING CUTTER
If you have a lot of tubing to cut (as you will if you are installing a sprinkler system), buy a plastic tubing cutter. With this tool, you can snip the tubing easily.

Connect PE flexible tubing with inserts and clamps.
Use insert fittings to connect PE tubing. Slip hose clamps over the ends of the tubing, push the tubing onto the insert, and tighten the clamp. Check that the serrations of the fittings are fully inserted in the tubing. The hose clamp should be positioned squarely on the serrations.

Soften PE with hot water.
Sometimes it takes a lot of muscle to push PE tubing over an insert fitting. Soak the tubing in hot water or pour hot water over the tubing to soften it so it slips on easily. Use the same technique to dismantle a stubborn connection.

For PB flexible tubing, use compression fittings.
Attach PB to a metal shutoff valve with a compression nut and ferrule. A brass insert keeps the tubing from collapsing as the nut is tightened. Two sections of tubing can be joined by a flexible tubing union; tighten only by hand. Tees, ells, and other supply fittings fit every configuration.

Use flexible plastic supplies.
PB makes an excellent choice for stop-to-fixture hookups, allowing you a margin of error during installation. Avoid bending it excessively or it may kink. Don't overtighten the nuts.

QUIETING NOISY PIPES

Sudden changes in water pressure can vibrate pipes, causing noise when the pipes hit the house's framing. This page tells you what causes the noise and what you can do about it.

First identify the type of noise and its cause. Water hammer is the most common pipe noise. It results from a sudden stop in the flow of water, as when you turn off a faucet. The abrupt halting of water flow creates a shock wave in the pipes, causing them to vibrate and hit against framing members.

A ticking noise can be traced to a hot water pipe that was cool, then suddenly is heated by water running through it. Pipe insulation dampens the noise. Chattering or moaning sounds may be caused by water pressure that is too high. If this is a persistent problem, call a professional to check the pressure.

YOU'LL NEED...

TIME: Several hours to install an air chamber or cushion pipes.
SKILLS: Connecting pipes.
TOOLS: Knife and hammer for pipe insulation; and basic plumbing tools for adding an air chamber.

EXPERTS' INSIGHT

DON'T BLAME PIPES

■ A machine-gun rattle, that annoying sound sometimes heard when you barely open a faucet, usually is caused by a defective seat washer.

■ Do pipes pound only when the dishwasher is running? An aging pump valve creates the same effect as a defective seat washer. Replace the pump.

foam pipe insulation

foam pipe insulation

Cushion hammering pipes.
Have a helper do whatever it is that causes the noise while you search for the location of the noise. Once you find it, check to see if one of the pipes has been knocking up against or rubbing a joist. Cushion the pipe at the trouble spot with pieces of foam pipe insulation or use sound-insulating pipe hangers.

air chamber near a faucet

anatomy of an air chamber

cap

¾" pipe

¾"-to-½" reducer coupling

½" pipe

tee

system air chamber

Install an air chamber.
To eliminate pipe noises, install air chambers at accessible points in your supply lines. These provide a pocket of air for water to bump against. Cut the pipe, install a tee (see pages 162–163), and solder the chamber in place. For galvanized pipe, cut the pipe and with nipples and a union, install a tee to which the chamber can be attached (see pages 162–163).

INSTALLING STOP VALVES

Any time a water line bursts, a faucet needs repair, or a toilet needs replacing, you'll be grateful to have a stop valve in the right place. Without one of these handy devices, you may have to shut off the water to the entire house simply to change a faucet washer. If you have an older home that lacks stop valves under sinks and toilets, plan to install them.

No matter what the material or size of your pipes, there's a stop valve made to order. With copper lines, use brass valves. Galvanized and plastic pipes take steel and plastic stop valves respectively. You can also use a transition fitting (see page 181) to change material just prior to the stop. If the valve will be in view, choose a chrome finish.

To make the connection from a stop valve to a sink or toilet, you can use flexible copper or plastic line. Or throw away the nut and ferrule that come with the valve and use the handy plastic or braided-metal flexible supply lines that simply screw on.

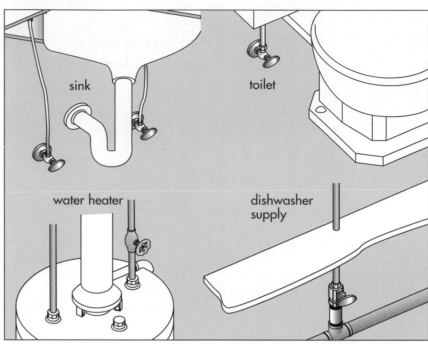

Where stop valves are needed
To determine your stop valve needs, simply take a look at your home's plumbing fixtures. Sinks, tubs, showers, and clothes washers should have one on both the hot and cold lines. Toilets and water heaters require one only on the cold water line, and dishwashers need one only on the hot line. The water meter should have a valve just inside the house from it.

MEASUREMENTS

MATCH THE VALVE WITH THE FLEXIBLE LINE
Stop valves for sinks and toilets come with either ½- or ⅜-inch outlets. Make sure your flexible line is the same size.

1. Cut pipe or tubing.
In the example shown, the existing plumbing consists of galvanized pipe and flexible copper tubing. To make room for the stop valve, cut enough tubing off to make room for the valve. Leave enough supply to fit the compression fitting and allow for tightening the stop valve on the steel pipe.

2. Install the valve.
One end of the stop valve is sized to fit regular pipe, and the other receives a compression-fitted flexible line. Wrap the galvanized pipe clockwise with Teflon tape and install the stop valve. Slip the copper line into the other end, and tighten the compression fitting, holding the stop valve in place with a second wrench.

TROUBLESHOOTING MAIN LINE VALVES

*I*n an older home, the shutoff valves for your main line may be worn and rusted. If you have a shutoff up-line from the valve, you can easily shut off the water and replace the valve. But often there is none, so you may have to live with a less-than-perfect valve rather than paying the water company to shut off your water while you change valves.

If the shutoff valve handle breaks off in such a way that you cannot simply replace it, use pliers or a pipe wrench for those few times when you need to use the valve. However to make sure all household members can turn off the water in case of an emergency, replace the valve.

Another common problem is a slight leak from the packing nut when the valve is opened or closed. When this happens, try tightening the nut gently. Don't apply too much force when tightening or the valve may crack. If you still have a slow drip, place a bucket under it and watch for a day or two; sometimes the leak will stop on its own.

If you still have a leak, you will need to repack the valve. Shut the valve by turning it clockwise until it tightens. Unscrew the screw at the top and remove the handle. Loosen and remove the packing nut. Apply strand packing or a packing washer, and reinstall the packing nut.

You can purchase valves that screw onto galvanized pipe or brass adapters, or solder-on types for copper lines.

YOU'LL NEED...
TIME: About an hour.
SKILLS: No special skills needed.
TOOLS: Screwdriver, Crescent wrench, tongue-and-groove pliers, and pipe wrench.

Gate valve
This style of valve, commonly found in older houses, is not as reliable as a globe or ball valve, so replace it if you have the opportunity. A wedge-shaped brass "gate" screws up and down to control water flow. If it does not fully stop water flow, it cannot be repaired. Repair a leak around the handle by replacing the packing washer or strand packing.

EXPERTS' INSIGHT

AVOID CLOGGING FAUCETS
Over the years, old pipes build up rust, lime, and sediment deposits. Whenever you shut off water and turn it back on in a house with old galvanized pipe, you will cause these deposits to loosen and flow through the pipes. After turning off the main valve, take the time to remove aerators from the faucets and let the water run for a couple of minutes to flush out the gunk.

Globe valve
This works in much the same way as stem faucets (see page 130). It is more reliable and more easily repaired than a gate valve. If it does not fully stop water, and if you can shut off the flow prior to the valve, replace the stem washer. Repair a leak around the handle by replacing the packing washer.

Ball valve
These cost more than the other valves but are more reliable and are easy to shut off quickly. The lever rotates a ball-like gate pierced by an opening. The gate pivots to control the flow of water.

REPLACING FAUCETS

*E*ven though thousands of styles of faucets have been made and continue to be made, there are few variations in basic design. Bathroom faucets have pop-up drain assemblies, and kitchen faucets may have sprayers.

Also there are two possibilities for supply connections: Your faucet may have flexible copper supply inlets in the center of the unit, as shown at right, or its inlets may be located under the hot and cold handles, as seen in Step 2 on page 181.

YOU'LL NEED...

TIME: Several hours to remove an old faucet and install a new one.
SKILLS: No special skills needed, but it may be hard work getting the old faucet out.
TOOLS: Tongue-and-groove pliers, basin wrench, and screwdriver.

EXPERTS' INSIGHT

MAKING IT EASY

■ The hardest part of the job will be getting at the faucet from underneath. Remove any cabinet doors that may be in the way, hook up a work light, and make your work area as comfortable as possible.

■ If you are installing a sink at the same time as the faucet, attach the faucet to the sink before you install the sink.

■ Often even penetrating oil won't loosen old locknuts. You may have to knock the nut loose with a hammer and screwdriver.

mounting nut

spray outlet

basin wrench

flexible copper inlets

compression fittings

supply lines

1. Remove the old fixture.
Note: *Shut off the water.* (This illustration shows a faucet with flexible copper inlets.) Before you worm your way into the space below the sink, gather the tools you'll need, as well as some penetrating oil in case the mounting nuts are stuck. It helps to have someone around who can hand you tools as you work.

If your faucet has a sprayer, remove the nuts securing the hose to the faucet body and the spray head to the sink. Unhook the supply lines and move them out of the way. Use the basin wrench to loosen and remove the mounting nuts holding the faucet body to the sink.

Lift the faucet out from above. Scrape the sink top clean of old putty and mineral deposits.

2. Attach the faucet to the sink.

(Here we show a faucet with inlets located under the handles.) Install a gasket or a rope of plumber's putty to the faucet or to the sink (see page 141). Set the faucet in place, making sure it is parallel to the backsplash. Crawl under the sink and have a helper hold the faucet in position while you work. Screw a washer and mounting nut onto each inlet and tighten with a basin wrench.

For faucets with sprayers, secure the hose guide to the sink with a washer and mounting nut. Thread the spray hose down through the hole in the guide. Apply pipe joint compound or Teflon tape to the threaded nipple at the end of the hose and secure it to the spray outlet of the faucet.

3. Connect the supply lines.

Brush the inlet threads with pipe joint compound or wrap them with Teflon tape. Twist the supply line nut onto the inlet and tighten first by hand, then with a basin wrench. Connect the other end of the supply line to the shutoff valve in the same way.

4. Connect and adjust the pop-up drain assembly.

For a bathroom faucet, insert the ball rod into the opening in the drain body and secure it with the nut provided. Slip the rod through the clevis strap and secure it with the spring clip. Lower the pop-up rod down through the hole near the rear of the faucet spout and through the holes at the upper end of the clevis strap. Lightly tighten the thumbscrew and adjust the rod so the stopper seals when the rod is pulled up. When the stopper opens and closes easily, tighten the thumbscrew further to secure the rod.

Connecting to flexible inlets

Some faucets use flexible copper inlets for the water supply. Connect supply lines to these lines in the same way as you would regular inlets, but take special care not to twist the copper tubes. If they become kinked, the faucet will be ruined. Use one wrench to hold, another to turn, as shown.

REPLACING TOILETS

Replacing a toilet is surprisingly easy. Problems arise only if the closet flange isn't at the floor surface (see below) or if the floor isn't level (shim the toilet after you set it on the hold-down bolts).

Toilets are ceramic, so work carefully. It is possible to crack a toilet if you bang it or screw down a nut too hard. Most toilets sold today have their drains centered 12 inches from the back wall. Measure yours from the wall to the hold-down bolt. If yours is centered 10 inches from the wall, either buy a 10-inch toilet or install a special offset closet flange. If you need to run supply and drain lines for a new installation.

YOU'LL NEED...

TIME: Three hours to remove an old toilet and install a new one.
SKILLS: No special skills needed—just work carefully.
TOOLS: Wrenches, screwdriver, hacksaw, tongue-and-groove pliers, and putty knife.

EXPERTS' INSIGHT

IF THE FLANGE IS LOW

If your bathroom has a new layer of flooring, the closet flange often will end up below the floor surface. In that case, a regular wax ring may not be thick enough to seal the toilet bowl to the flange. You can extend the ring upward with a special flange extender (see page 183) or double the wax ring. Place a wax ring without a plastic flange on the toilet, then place a flanged ring on top of it.

1. Remove the old toilet.
Note: *Shut off the water.*
Flush the toilet and remove remaining water with a sponge. Disconnect the water supply line and unscrew the hold-down nuts. Often these are rusted tight. If penetrating oil does not loosen them, cut the nuts with a hacksaw. Lift the toilet out.

2. Prepare the new toilet bowl.
Carefully remove the new toilet bowl from its container and turn it upside down on a cushioned surface, such as a throw rug or folded drop cloth. Run a rope of plumber's putty around the perimeter of the bowl's base and fit a wax ring (sold separately) over the outlet opening.

3. Install the bowl.
Return the bowl to its upright position and gently set it in place atop the closet flange. Make sure the hold-down bolts align with the holes in the base. Press down on the bowl with both hands and align it. Slip a metal washer and a nut over each bolt and tighten slowly. Don't overtighten or you could crack the bowl. Set caps on.

4. You're ready for the tank.
First lay the spud gasket, beveled side down, over the bowl inlet opening. This forms the seal between the tank and the bowl. Or slip the spud gasket onto the threaded tailpiece located at the bottom of the tank if you have older-style connectors.

tank hold-down bolt

rubber washer

5. Install the tank.

Gently lower the tank onto the bowl, aligning the tank holes with those toward the rear of the bowl. Secure the tank to the bowl with the hold-down bolts, washers, and nuts provided with the toilet. Be sure that the rubber washer goes inside the tank under the bolt.

bolt for toilet seat

shutoff valve

6. Attach water supply.

Complete the installation by hooking up the water supply line. The easiest way is to use a flexible plastic or chrome-braided supply line. Or use chrome-finished flexible copper tubing and compression fittings (see page 170).

Money $ Saver

WATER-SAVING TOILETS

In most localities, toilets that use only 1.6 gallons of water are required for new installations. These save money by reducing water consumption, but they do not flush strongly. They differ from older models by having a smaller tank or a mechanism that restricts the amount of water in the tank.

Don't buy a new toilet simply to save money in water use. Reduce an old toilet's consumption by setting a brick into the tank or by bending the float ball's rod so the ball sits lower in the tank. Most people don't mind the reduced flushing power of new models. If it is a problem for you, get a pressure-assisted toilet.

extender ring

flexible gasket

new tile

1. Install a closet flange extender.

If your floor surface is more than half an inch above the closet flange (as will happen when you install new tile), you must extend the flange so it's flush with the floor. A closet flange extender with flexible gaskets and a plastic extender ring make up the difference. First clean off old wax, insert new bolts, and slip on a flexible gasket and the extender ring.

flexible gasket

2. Make a waxless seal.

The closet flange extender should now fit flush with the surface of your new flooring. (If it does not, add an additional extender ring.) Add the second flexible gasket. This gasket takes the place of the wax ring. Most kits also include handy plastic shims for leveling the toilet once it is placed on the hold-down bolts. See page 182 for completing the bowl installation.

toilet seat bolt

nut

Install a toilet seat.

To remove an old toilet seat, lower the seat and cover and pry up the little lids that cover the toilet seat bolts. Hold each nut from below, unscrew each bolt, and lift out the seat.

Clean out the area around the bolt holes and install the new seat by aligning the seat with the holes and installing the bolts. Screw nuts onto the bolts and tighten the bolts just enough to firmly hold the seat.

MAINTAINING AND FIXING WATER HEATERS

Water heaters are little more than giant insulated water bottles with heaters. As hot water is used, cold water enters through a dip tube. This lowers the water temperature inside the tank, causing a thermostat to call for heat. In gas units, burners beneath the water tank kick in and continue heating the water until the desired temperature is reached. Heating elements perform the same function in electric water heaters. Most water heater problems are the result of sediment buildup or rust. You can help prevent this by opening the drain valve every few months and flushing out a few gallons of water. This purges rust and mineral buildup from the heater.

YOU'LL NEED...

TIME: Allow two hours for inspection and minor repairs.
SKILLS: No special skills needed.
TOOLS: Crescent wrench and tongue-and-groove pliers.

MEASUREMENTS

VITAL NUMBERS

The nameplate on the outside of your water heater gives the unit's vital statistics. Look for:
■ **Tank Capacity:** The more gallons it holds, the less chance you'll run out of hot water during a shower. A 40-gallon tank suits most households.
■ **R-Value:** The better insulated the unit is, the more efficient it will be. If yours has an R-value of less than 7, wrap the tank with insulation.
■ **Installation Clearances:** This tells you how much room you must leave between the unit and any combustible materials.

gas water heater
- cold water inlet
- flue
- dip tube
- flue
- gas control
- burner
- pilot
- thermocouple
- hot water outlet
- temperature-and-pressure-relief valve
- outer shell
- tank
- insulation
- drain valve

electric water heater
- cold water inlet
- temperature-and-pressure-relief valve
- anode rod (attracts materials that otherwise would corrode the tank)
- upper heating element
- dip tube
- lower heating element
- drain valve
- electrical supply
- hot water outlet
- tank
- upper thermostat
- insulation
- access cover
- lower thermostat

WATER HEATER REPAIR CHART

Symptom	Cause	Repair
No hot water.	No power to the heater (electric). Pilot light out (gas).	Check circuit breaker or fuse (electric). Relight pilot; replace thermocouple if pilot does not stay lit.
Water not hot enough.	Upper element burned out (electric).	Replace upper element.
Not enough hot water—hot water runs out quickly.	Thermostat set too low. Hot water must travel a long way to get to faucets. Sediment buildup in tank. Lower element burned out (electric). Burner blocked by dirt (gas). Leaking faucets. Tank not large enough for demand.	Turn thermostat up. Insulate hot water pipes (see page 126). Drain and refill tank. Replace lower element. Clean burner, or call gas company. Repair faucets. Replace with a larger tank.
Tank makes noise.	Sediment in tank.	Drain and refill tank.
Leak from temperature-and-pressure-relief valve.	Thermostat set too high. Defective temperature-and-pressure-relief valve.	Lower thermostat setting. Replace valve.
Leak around tank base.	Tank corrosion has created a leak.	Replace water heater.

Replace a leaking drain valve.
If your water heater's drain valve leaks, shut off the cold water stop valve, shut off the gas or the electrical current, and drain the water heater. Unscrew the faulty valve. Apply Teflon tape or pipe joint compound to the male threads of a new valve, and install. Fill tank, and restore power or gas.

Test a relief valve.
Either on top or high on the side of the water heater, you'll find a relief valve that opens if the temperature or pressure in the tank gets too high (thus, it is called a "T-and-P-relief valve"). Test it once a year by pulling on the handle; water should rush out of the pipe it is attached to.

Replace a faulty relief valve.
If no water comes out, replace the valve. Shut off the cold water, turn off power or gas to the unit, and drain some of the water. Remove the attached drainpipe and the valve. Apply Teflon tape or pipe joint compound to the male threads when you install the new valve.

REPAIRING ELECTRIC WATER HEATERS

*I*f you are not getting enough hot water, make sure the thermostat is set correctly. Also drain the heater if you suspect it is filled with sediment. If you have no hot water, check for power to the unit. If none of these measures solves the problem, you need to replace the thermostats and heating elements. To determine which thermostat and element to replace, see Experts' Insight below.

YOU'LL NEED...
TIME: About two hours.
SKILLS: Making electrical connections.
TOOLS: Screwdriver, tongue-and-groove pliers, neon circuit tester.

CAUTION!
DANGER! HIGH VOLTAGE! Electric water heaters use 240-volt current, twice the voltage in other receptacles. Be sure to remove the fuse or shut off the breaker at the service panel. Test wires for electricity before disassembling anything.

EXPERTS' INSIGHT

WHICH TO REPLACE?
Electric water heaters have two thermostats and heating elements (see page 184). To find out which pair is defective, turn on a hot water faucet. If the water gets warm but not hot, the upper thermostat and element are the culprits and should be replaced. If the water is hot for awhile then goes cold, replace the lower element and thermostat.

1. Remove the thermostat.
Note: *Shut off the power, shut off the water to the heater, and drain the heater.* Remove the cover plate and use a neon circuit tester to make sure the power is off. Drain the water heater (see page 188). Push aside insulation, label and disconnect the wires, and remove the thermostat.

2. Remove the element.
Use tongue-and-groove pliers to unscrew the element, then pull it out. Remove the gasket if there is one. Take the old element and thermostat with you to your supplier to make sure you get the correct replacement.

3. Replace the element.
If the replacement element has a gasket, coat both sides of the gasket with pipe joint compound and then slide the gasket onto the new element. Slide the element in and screw it in place. Tighten with tongue-and-groove pliers.

4. Install, set the thermostat.
Slide the new thermostat into place and reconnect the wires, using your labels as guides. Snap in the plastic guard. Use a screwdriver to set the thermostat. Press the red reset button on the thermostat. Make sure the drain valve is closed and turn on the shutoff valve to fill the tank. When water flows to your hot water faucets, turn off the faucets and restore electrical power.

REPAIRING GAS WATER HEATERS

If you suddenly lose hot water, or if your unit is not heating water efficiently, remove the access panel at the bottom of your water heater and check the pilot light. If it's not burning, relight it according to directions printed on the unit. If it won't relight, you need a new thermocouple. If you have yellow rather than blue flame, you need to replace the thermocouple and/or clean the burner. If you smell smoke or fumes, check your flue immediately.

YOU'LL NEED...

TIME: An hour or two for any of the operations on this page.
SKILLS: Handling compression fittings on gas tubes.
TOOLS: Wrench or pliers, thin wire, small wire brush, and vacuum cleaner.

EXPERTS' INSIGHT

REGULAR MAINTENANCE FOR YOUR GAS WATER HEATER

■ To avoid the dangerous buildup of fumes from a faulty flue, check your flue at least once a year. Be sure it is efficiently pulling fumes out of your house (see Step 4). To dismantle the flue to check for debris, see page 188.
■ Once a year, or at least whenever you replace the thermocouple, clean the burner, even if it shows no symptoms of being clogged. A clean burner will burn more efficiently and help your water heater last longer.

1. Remove the burner unit.
Note: *Shut off the gas.* If you need to replace a thermocouple or clean the burner, first remove the burner unit. Disconnect the pilot light tube, the burner gas tube, and the thermocouple line. Pull down on the tubes, and carefully pull the entire burner unit out.

2. Clean the burner and tube.
Turn the burner counterclockwise to unscrew it from the tube. With a thin piece of wire, clean out the small orifice at the point where the tube enters the burner. Also use wire to clean the small orifice in the pilot light tube. Use a vacuum cleaner to suck out any rust and debris from the burner jets and inside the burner area of the unit.

3. Replace a thermocouple.
If your pilot light won't light or is not staying lit, pull the old thermocouple from its bracket. Take it to your supplier to get one exactly like it. Push the new one into place until it clicks tight. The tip of the thermocouple should be right next to the end of the pilot gas tube so the pilot flame will touch it.

4. Maintain the flue.
A rusted, clogged, or loose-fitting flue will cause harmful fumes to enter your home. To check if the flue is drawing, light a piece of paper and blow it out. While it is smoking, hold it near the opening at the bottom of the flue. If the smoke is not sucked out, your flue needs cleaning. Also check for leaks by holding a candle near flue openings. If the flame is drawn, tighten the joint.

REPLACING GAS WATER HEATERS

*T*hough water heaters sometimes last 25 years or more, they usually give out sooner—the victims of rust and sediment. When yours fails, there's no need to call in a plumber. Though it may seem like a complicated job, installing a gas water heater involves only two or three pipe hookups, and an electric heater requires connecting some wires. Removing the old unit is often the most difficult part of the job.

First make sure your old water heater can't be fixed. If the tank itself leaks—not the pipes—the lining has rusted and the heater must be replaced. If your heater is not producing enough hot water, it may simply be suffering from a buildup of rust and sediment, which insulates the water from the burner and forces it to work more often to satisfy demand. Drain the heater. You may be able to flush out enough sediment to make it efficient. If it still produces too little hot water, replace it.

EXPERTS' INSIGHT

CHOOSING THE RIGHT WATER HEATER

■ Check the nameplate on the old unit and note its capacity. You'll be safe purchasing a new one of the same size, unless you have recently installed or plan to buy an appliance that consumes a lot of hot water, such as a dishwasher. Usually, a 30- to 50-gallon unit will have enough capacity for an average home.

■ Units designed to heat water quickly, called fast recovery units, are more expensive to buy and operate, but they handle peak demand times better. Standard units don't heat as fast but are more economical to run.

■ If you have hard water, consider a unit with an extra anode rod for collecting mineral deposits (see drawing on page 184).

YOU'LL NEED...

TIME: Allow a day to remove the old heater and install the new.
SKILLS: Basic plumbing skills.
TOOLS: Wrenches for loosening unions or flexible fittings, garden hose, level, appliance dolly, and screwdriver.

CAUTION!

PRECAUTIONS WITH GAS
If you do not have a gas shutoff near the water heater, shut off the gas to your house by turning the valve on the gas meter with a large wrench. Relight all the pilot lights in your house after you turn the gas back on. Consider adding a shutoff.

1. Drain the tank.
NOTE: *Shut off the main water valve to your house and shut off the gas at the heater.* Drain the water lines in your home by opening hot and cold taps in an upstairs faucet. Also open both taps positioned closest to the system's lowest point. Attach a garden hose to the water heater drain valve, open the valve, and drain the tank.

2. Dismantle the flue.
Remove the sheet-metal screws and dismantle enough ductwork to give yourself room to work. Keep track of which piece of ductwork goes where and be careful not to bend it.

3. Disconnect the gas line.
Many localities require that gas line be rigid pipe all the way to the water heater; others allow you to use a flexible gas line. Take apart a gas line union (as shown), or disconnect the flexible line.

4. Disconnect the water lines.

Mark hot and cold water lines so you won't hook up the new heater backward. If you have galvanized pipe, open unions near the unit. If you have rigid copper, cut the pipe with a hacksaw or tubing cutter just below the shutoff valves. Make the cuts straight so you can tap into the lines easily with new soldered pipe or flexible water lines when you install the new heater. If you have flexible lines, disconnect them. Move the old unit out with an appliance dolly.

> **CAUTION!**
> It MAY BE HEAVY!
> If sediment buildup clogged your old heater, it will be extremely heavy. Have a helper and a good appliance dolly, and take care not to strain your back.

5. Set the new unit in place.

Move the new water heater into place. Position it to make your gas connection as easy as possible. Check for plumb and level, shimming if necessary. If the unit is in an area prone to dampness, purchase a traylike base to protect it.

If you need to, shim at base to plumb.

stop valve

rigid copper

union

heat-saver nipples

ball valve

6. Connect the water lines.

Find out code requirements for the water lines. If they're permitted, flexible copper water connectors are usually the easiest way to go. Otherwise solder rigid copper or install galvanized pipe with a union. To save energy, install heat-saver nipples at each inlet. These temperature-sensitive in-line valves hold back water until it's needed. Follow directions, installing the cold water nipple with the arrow pointing down, the hot water nipple with the arrow pointing up.

7. Install T & P relief valve.

You may have to purchase a temperature-and-pressure-relief valve separately. Be sure it matches the working-pressure rating of the tank as given on the nameplate. Wrap the threads with Teflon tape and screw the valve in—either on top or near the top on the side.

T & P relief valve

outlet pipe

8. Hook up the gas.

Connect a gas (black pipe) nipple to the burner control of the water heater and connect the nipple to the gas line. Be sure to install a drip leg to collect sediment and moisture from the gas line.

9. Install the flue.

If your old flue worked well and your new water heater is the same height as the old one, you can reuse the old flue. Make sure it isn't blocked. Clean out any dust, rust, or sediment from the flue. If you replace or add to the vent, use galvanized pipe fittings that are designed for venting gas. When running a horizontal section, maintain at least a ¼-inch-per-foot rise. Insert male ends of the vent into female ends away from the water heater so the fumes will not have a chance to escape. Fasten each joint of the vent with two sheet-metal screws.

10. Check for gas leaks.

Open the gas stop valve. Test for leaks by brushing soapy water on all the connections. Watch for bubbles. If you see any, tighten the connection. If they persist, shut off the gas, disassemble, carefully clean the threads, and check again.

11. Turn on the water.

Open the water supply valve. Open the nearest hot faucet about halfway and allow the system to "bleed." First air will come out, then the spattering of water mixed with air. When the water flows freely, close the faucet.

12. Light the pilot.

Open the access panel at the bottom of the tank and light the pilot according to the directions printed on the water heater. Adjust the temperature setting.

REPLACING ELECTRIC WATER HEATERS

Installing an electric water heater is similar to installing a gas unit. The differences are that you make electrical rather than gas connections, and there is no flue on an electric water heater.

YOU'LL NEED...

TIME About a day.
SKILLS: Making electrical and plumbing connections.
TOOLS: Wrenches for unions or flexible fittings, garden hose for draining, level, appliance dolly, screwdriver, and neon tester.

CAUTION!
*DANGER! HIGH VOLTAGE!
Working with 240-volt circuits is a serious matter. Remove the fuse or turn off the circuit breaker, and then check to make sure the power is off.*

1. Remove the panel and test.
NOTE: *Shut off the power and water.* Remove the access panel for the thermostat (usually behind the lower panel), push aside any insulation, and lift or remove the plastic guard. Test for current with a neon tester to make sure you have turned off the circuit.

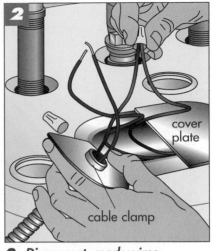

2. Disconnect, mark wires.
Remove the electrical cover plate at the side or the top of the unit. Disconnect the wires and mark them with pieces of tape so you'll know exactly where to attach them on the new unit. Loosen the screw on the cable clamp and carefully pull the cable out.

Complete steps 1, 4, and 5 on pages 188–189.

3. Connect water pipes.
Install water lines (see page 189). Supply lines can be galvanized steel pipe (see page 173), rigid copper (see pages 166–167), or flexible water connectors (see page 188–189). Install a ball valve on the supply line (see page 178). Install a relief valve, and attach an outlet pipe (see page 189).

4. Make the electrical connections.
Connect the black and white wires with wire connectors, and attach the ground wire to the ground screw. Tighten the screw on the clamp to hold the cable in place, gently push the wires inside, and replace the cover plate.

5. Set the thermostat.
Set the water heater to the temperature you want. Press the reset button, and replace the plastic guard, insulation, and access panels. Turn the water on as shown in Step 11 on page 190.

INSTALLING RIMMED SINKS

Setting a new sink in place is one of the truly satisfying plumbing tasks. It signals completion of a fairly easy job that gets noticed by your family.

When shopping for a new deck-mounted fixture, you'll find plenty of options—stainless steel, cast-iron, plastic composite, vitreous china, and more. Nowadays most sinks—for the kitchen and bathroom—are self-rimming, which means you just put some putty on the rim and clamp the sink down on the countertop.

To remove an old sink, first turn off the supply stops or shut off the water to your house and drain the lines. Disconnect the supply lines and the trap joining the sink to the drainpipe. Remove any mounting clips from underneath, and pry the sink up. Add stop valve (see page 178).

YOU'LL NEED...

TIME: Half a day to cut a hole in the vanity top, install the sink, and hook up faucet and drain.
SKILLS: Basic plumbing and carpentry skills.
TOOLS: Sabersaw and extra blades, screwdriver, and tongue-and-groove pliers.

1. To install a bathroom sink, first cut an opening.
If you need to cut a hole for the sink, trace the template provided with the sink. Drill an entry hole and cut with a sabersaw and fine-toothed blade.

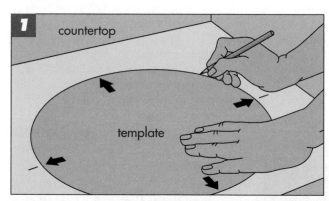

3. Set the sink.
Apply a thick bead of silicone adhesive around the underside of the fixture's flange, about ¼ inch from the edge. Turn the sink right side up and lower it carefully into the opening. Press down on the sink; some of the caulk will ooze out. Wipe away the excess with a damp cloth. After the silicone adhesive has set (about two hours), apply latex caulk around the sink.

2. Attach faucet and drain.
Before lowering the sink into the opening, hook up the faucet (see pages 180–181) and drain assembly (see page 206). With bathroom sinks, the drain assembly consists of a basin outlet flange, a drain body, a gasket, a locknut, and a tailpiece that slides into the P-trap. (Installing these after you install the sink is not only difficult, but you also run a greater risk of damaging the parts.) Lay a bead of plumber's putty around the basin outlet, insert the flange, and screw together the other parts of the drain assembly.

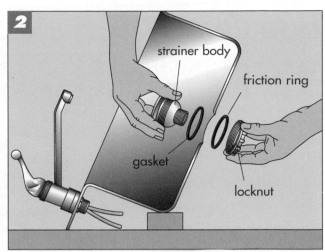

1. *For a stainless-steel sink, mark and cut opening.*
Turn your sink upside down on the countertop. Make sure it is in the correct position, safely set back from the cabinet beneath. Trace the outline of the sink, then draw a line that is an inch or so to the inside of that outline. Erase the first line to make sure you do not cut it. Test to make sure the sink fits. Cut the opening using a circular saw with a fine-toothed blade for the straight cuts and a sabersaw for curves. Take your time to avoid splintering the laminate.

2. *Attach the faucet and strainers.*
Attach a basket strainer to each bowl. Lay a bead of putty around the outlet, set the gasket in place, and lower the strainer body into the hole. With your other hand, from underneath, slip the friction ring in place, and screw on the locknut. Tighten, and clean away the putty that oozes out. You also can attach the tailpiece and trap assembly at this point. To install the faucet, see page 181.

3. *Set and secure the sink.*
To set the sink, place a rope of plumber's putty all around the rim so it will seal everywhere. Turn the sink right side up and lower it into the opening. Secure the sink to the countertop with sink clips every 6 to 8 inches. Working from underneath the sink, tighten the clips with a screwdriver. Remove excess putty with a putty knife and a rag dipped in paint thinner.

Install a cast-iron sink.
To set a cast-iron kitchen sink, use the same technique as for the rimmed sink (see page 192). Run a bead of silicone sealant under the rim, turn the sink right side up, set it in place, and wipe away the excess sealant. Run caulk along the edge, and smooth it with a wet finger.

INSTALLING WALL-HUNG SINKS

Wall-hung bathroom sinks are not as popular as they once were but remain useful where space is limited or a retro style is called for. Installing the bracket support is the most time-consuming part of this job.

YOU'LL NEED...

TIME: A half day to add framing and install a new sink.
SKILLS: Basic plumbing and carpentry skills.
TOOLS: Keyhole saw, hammer, level, screwdriver, and tongue-and-groove pliers or pipe wrench.

CAUTION!

WATCH YOUR WEIGHT!
Bracket-supported sinks stand up well to normal everyday use, but warn members of the household not to sit on them. They could crack or pull away from the wall.

Notch studs and anchor a piece of 2×10.

1. Rough-in, provide bracing.
Note: *Be sure to shut off the water and drain the line.* To remove an old fixture, disconnect the drain and supply lines and look underneath to see if it is held in by bolts. If so, loosen or cut the bolts. Pull straight up on the sink to dislodge it.

For a new installation, run new supply lines, and provide solid framing for the hanger bracket.

level
mounting bracket

2. Finish wall, anchor bracket.
Install the drywall. You may even want to tape and paint it—it will be easier to do now than after the sink is in place. Secure the hanger bracket to the 2×10 blocking. Use plenty of screws and make sure the bracket is level. If they are not already in place, equip each supply line with a stop valve (see page 178).

3. Set sink in place.
Turn the sink on its side, and install the faucet and the drain assembly (see pages 180–18

4. Attach legs.
If your sink comes with support legs, insert them into the holes in the bottom of the sink, plumb them, and adjust them so they firmly support the sink. To do this, twist the top portion of each leg. Check to see that the sink is level.

5. Hook up supplies, drain.
Connect the flexible supply lines to the stop valves. Connect the trap to the sink drain and to the drainpipe. Restore water pressure and check supply lines for leaks. To test the drain for leaks, pull the stopper lever up, fill the bowl, and open the stopper.

INSTALLING PEDESTAL SINKS

Pedestal sinks are popular because of their sleek good looks. They hide the plumbing without a cabinet. However installation is more difficult than for a regular wall-hung sink or a vanity. You have to get all the plumbing to fit inside the pedestal, and you must attach the sink at the right height so the pedestal fits just beneath it. Watch out for less expensive units that have narrower than usual pedestals.

YOU'LL NEED...

TIME: A day to move the plumbing and install the sink.
SKILLS: Basic plumbing and carpentry skills.
TOOLS: Keyhole saw, hammer or drill, screwdriver, and tongue-and-groove pliers.

1. Install plumbing, framing.
Note: *Shut off the water.* Open the wall, and install a 2×10 (see page 194). Measure the width of the pedestal and install the drain and supply lines so they will fit inside it. Finish the walls and install stop valves (see page 178). Position the sink and pedestal against the wall to mark the bracket's location. Attach the bracket to the wall.

2. Assemble, install the sink.
Carefully set the sink into the bracket and fasten with the nuts and bolts or toggle bolts provided. Slide the pedestal in and caulk around the bottom with bathtub caulk. Restore water pressure and check for leaks.

ADDING VANITIES

Vanities are popular because they add much-needed storage space. They're easier to install than a wall-hung or pedestal unit because the sink sits on the vanity rather than hanging from the wall. As a result, measurements and cuts don't have to be as exact. If your vanity has a back panel, you don't have to finish the wall around the plumbing—the vanity covers it. Install a stop valve if one is not already there (see page 178).
Note: *Be sure to shut off the water*

YOU'LL NEED...

TIME: A day to add the vanity and install the basic plumbing.
SKILLS: Basic plumbing and carpentry skills.
TOOLS: Sabersaw, screwdriver, channel-type pliers, caulk gun.

1. Install plumbing, cabinet.
Install the supply lines and drain line (see page 206). Be sure they will be covered by the cabinet and won't interfere with the sink. If the cabinet has a back, measure carefully, and cut out holes. Slide the cabinet into position and level it from side to side and front to back with shims. Anchor it to the wall by driving screws through the cabinet frame and into studs.

2. Hook up the sink top.
Turn the sink top on its side, and install the faucet, the flexible supply lines, and the drain assembly (see pages 180–181, 206). Run a bead of silicone caulk under the sink to anchor it to the cabinet. Set it on top of the cabinet, and make the final connections. Restore water pressure, and check for leaks.

INSTALLING PREFAB UNITS

Purchase the unit before you build the framing. Consult the manufacturer's instructions closely regarding the exact dimensions needed. You may need to leave one wall of framing open until the unit is in place.

Install the drain in the center of the stall, following manufacturer's instructions. Frame for the unit, providing a nailing surface where needed. Check framing for plumb.

YOU'LL NEED...

TIME: Several days in most situations.
SKILLS: Good plumbing, carpentry, and wall-preparation and finishing skills.
TOOLS: A complete set of plumbing and carpentry tools (a reciprocating saw often comes in handy).

1. Anchor plumbing.
Anchor supply lines, the faucet, and the shower arm to framing—don't rely on the unit's walls for support.

To reduce noise, install insulation between the studs. Slice the insulation's foil or paper face so moisture will not get trapped between the insulation and the walls of the prefab shower.

2. Attach unit, finish walls.
Drill holes in the unit's walls for the faucet and shower arm. Slide the parts into place and attach to the framing. Install the finish plumbing pieces: drain piece, shower handle, escutcheon, and showerhead. Caulk the seams and check for leaks. Finish the walls and install a shower door or

PREPARING FOR TILE

Install the drain and the shower base. Check for leaks by pouring water down the drain. Install any necessary new framing. Be sure to leave an opening that's the right size for your shower door. Purchase the door kit in advance so you can check the finished opening dimensions. Make sure new and old walls are plumb or you'll end up with crooked grout lines. Install the shower supply lines, faucet, and shower arm before preparing the walls for tile.

YOU'LL NEED...

TIME: Two days, once the plumbing is in place.
SKILLS: Carpentry and tiling.
TOOLS: Knife, drill, taping knife, notched trowel, and grout float.

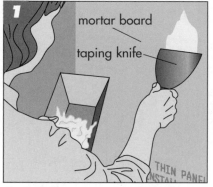

1. Install, tape cement board.
Check for plumb and any waviness in the walls. Shim the walls as required. Use cement board for the most stable and long-lasting subsurface. Cut this material with a utility knife in the same way as drywall, and attach it with galvanized screws. Cover the screws or nails and the corner joints with wallboard compound using a taping knife.

2. Install tile.
Plan your tile job carefully. Use field tiles for most of the walls, but at all exposed edges, use caps. These have one finished edge. Special corner pieces have two finished edges. Apply the adhesive with a notched trowel, set the tiles, and let them dry for 24 hours. Apply grout with a grout float, wipe away excess, and clean it several times. Apply bathroom caulk to all inside corners.

INSTALLING HAND SHOWERS

A hand shower attached to an existing shower is a luxurious addition to a shower/tub area. A hand shower attached to a tub faucet can be an economical alternative to a complete shower installation, giving you a shower without the trouble of cutting open walls and installing new plumbing. Whichever type of unit you choose, a variety of showerheads are available, ranging from the simple to the exotic. Installing them is quick and easy: a straightforward bathroom upgrade well within the skill level of any do-it-yourselfer.

YOU'LL NEED...

TIME: An hour or two for either installation.
SKILLS: No special skills needed.
TOOLS: Screwdriver, tongue-and-groove pliers, drill with masonry bit, hammer, and awl.

At an existing shower
Remove the showerhead. Protect chrome parts from scratches by taping the jaws of the pliers. Clean the threads. If your shower arm does not have male threads, replace it with one that does. Wrap the threads with Teflon tape, and screw on the hand shower with pliers. The hand shower connector may have a diverter (which allows you to choose either the fixed or the hand-held head), a hanger bracket (the new head fits on it), or a direct hose hookup (the hose attaches to the shower arm). For the last, install a shower hanger (see below).

A tub-only unit
Remove the old spout by inserting the handle of a hammer into the spout opening and turning counterclockwise. Clean the pipe threads to which the spout was attached. You may need to remove the existing nipple and install one that is longer or shorter. Apply Teflon tape and screw on the new spout with diverter valve. Attach the hose to the shower-hose fitting.

Mount the shower hanger.
Be sure the wall is absolutely clean and dry before starting. Some hangers can be mounted by simply peeling the paper off the backs and sticking them in place. For a more permanent attachment, hold the hanger in position and mark for the screw holes. With a hammer and a

sharp-pointed awl or nail, tap a little nick in the tile—gently, so you don't crack the tile. This will keep your masonry bit from slipping on the ceramic glaze as you start the hole. Drill the holes, push plastic anchors in place, and secure the hanger with screws.

INSTALLING WATER FILTRATION SYSTEMS

*I*f you receive municipal water, information concerning water quality should be available at city hall. However if you have a well, you are on your own. Your local department of health can recommend a company to test your water to see if you need a filter. A test for bacteria is relatively inexpensive, but a full test that includes a search for pesticides, organic matter, and other potential problems can be costly. Local officials should be able to tell you if other people in your area have had similar tests done and what, if any, contaminants were found.

If the taste of your drinking water is your major concern, try a faucet filter before you get involved with a more expensive installation. If you have mineral-laden hard water that makes it difficult to wash clothes and leaves ugly deposits on fixtures, install a water softener.

WATER FILTRATION OPTIONS

Sediment	This option uses a filter to screen out particles that can clog your aerators and may make your water look cloudy. Usually a sediment filter is used in conjunction with an activated-charcoal filter.
Activated-Charcoal	This filter will remove organic chemicals and pesticides. If your water is heavily chlorinated, it will remove much of the chlorine, improving the taste of your water. If taste is your major concern, install a small unit at the kitchen spout. A unit serving the whole house will need to have the charcoal filter replaced fairly frequently.
Reverse Osmosis	This is the most extreme measure, and it is capable of removing bacteria and harmful chemicals. It is expensive and bulky, requiring at least one holding tank. This system can be combined with an activated-charcoal system installed near the kitchen sink.
Water Softener	Also called an ion-exchange unit, this system will greatly reduce minerals such as calcium and iron. Have a water softener company install one for you—the piping is specialized and complicated.

INSTALLING WHOLE-HOUSE FILTERS

*T*his typical whole-house system combines a sediment filter with an activated-charcoal unit. The plumbing is not complicated, but you will have to shut off water to the whole house before beginning. Also, you may have to reroute or raise pipes in order to gain enough room to install the two units.

YOU'LL NEED...
TIME: Half a day.
SKILLS: Good plumbing skills.
TOOLS: Wrenches and pliers, and propane torch if you need to solder copper pipe.

NOTE: *Shut off the water and drain the line.* At a convenient point near the outlet side of the water meter (or just inside the house, if you have no meter), break into the line by opening a union or cutting the pipe. Install a shutoff valve if you don't have one (see page 178).

Remove 4 feet of pipe and work toward the meter. If you wish, add a stop valve to cut off backflow when changing filters. Then install the charcoal filter, a nipple, and finally the sediment filter. Make the last joint with a union or sleeve coupling.

INSTALLING UNDER-SINK FILTRATION UNITS

A whole-house filtration system will supply you with filtered water in every tap and likely prolong the life of your water-using appliances. Because it is difficult to install and requires regular filter changes, however, it is not installed by many homeowners. They reason that most of their water does not need to be treated because it is used for bathing, flushing away waste, and washing clothes. They choose to filter the water that counts most, their drinking and cooking water.

You can install a unit that gives you filtered water every time you turn on the cold water at your kitchen sink, or you can install a separate faucet with the filter. The first type saves you the trouble of drilling a hole and installing a separate faucet. The separate faucet will mean that you will change filter cartridges less often.

Some systems include an activated-charcoal filter. This two-canister system takes a little more time to install but adds another stage of filtration.

Before you purchase a unit, measure your space under the sink and make sure the new unit will fit. There are various types, but the connectors for all of them are fairly simple, ranging from standard compression fittings to simple connectors designed for a quick hookup to flexible supply lines. In most cases, you need only to shut off the cold water supply, cut into a flexible supply, and install the system.

YOU'LL NEED...

TIME: Usually a half hour.
SKILLS: Basic plumbing skills.
TOOLS: Tubing cutter, flashlight, and screwdriver.

1. Filtering the cold water tap.
Anchor the filter in a location where you can get at it to replace its filter cartridges. Allow for enough clearance underneath to unscrew the canister when replacing cartridges. Use the screws provided to fasten it to the cabinet back or wall. If you do not have a flexible cold water supply line, install one (see page 176). Cut into the cold water supply using a tubing cutter or plastic tubing cutter.

2. Hook up the filter.
Note which filter inlet is marked for the incoming supply, and connect that flexible tube to the section of supply line nearest the shutoff valve. For the connectors shown, you simply push the tubing in and they're joined. Connect the tube carrying filtered water to the section of flexible supply line for the faucet. Follow the manufacturer's directions for lubricating the canister seal and breaking in the system.

PLUMBING ICEMAKERS

If your refrigerator has an icemaker, supplying it with cold water is not difficult. The main problem will be to choose a path for the ¼-inch outside dimension flexible copper tubing. The cold water line under your kitchen sink may be the nearest source, but you may not be able to run the line so it isn't visible. If you have a basement, it's often easier to run the supply line through the floor to the pipes below.

YOU'LL NEED...

TIME: Several hours for an average installation.
SKILLS: Drilling holes and running flexible copper tubing without kinking it.
TOOLS: Drill, tongue-and-groove pliers or wrench, and screwdriver.

EXPERTS' INSIGHT

ICEMAKER TIPS

■ Some localities may not allow saddle valves. If so, or if you are concerned that your water may clog up the tiny opening in a saddle valve, break into your line and install a standard tee fitting, nipple, shutoff valve, and an adapter fitting.
■ If you don't like the taste of your water, purify the ice cubes the same way you purify your drinking water: Install a carbon filter prior to the icemaker line (see pages 198 and 199).
■ Even if you have flushed the line (Step 3), throw out the first two batches of ice to make sure the line is completely clean.

1. Install a saddle valve.
NOTE: *Shut off the water and drain the line.* There are two types of saddle valves. One uses a spike to puncture the water supply pipe. You clamp it in place and twist the valve handle until it punctures the pipe. The other requires that you drill a hole in the line, twist the valve into the hole, and clamp the unit firmly on the pipe.

3. Connect to the saddle valve.
Taking care not to kink the tubing, bend it so you can stick it straight into the valve. Slip on a nut and ferrule, slide the tubing in, and tighten the nut. It is a good idea to flush the line before you start making ice. Place the other end of the tubing in a large bucket, and have a helper briefly turn the water back on to clear any sediment.

2. Run the flexible tubing.
Starting at the floor behind your refrigerator, drill a hole for the flexible copper line. Place it so the refrigerator will not bump into the line. Straighten the tubing carefully to avoid kinking it and push it through the hole toward the saddle valve. Leave an ample amount of tubing in a springlike coil so you can pull the refrigerator away from the wall without kinking the tubing.

4. Connect to the refrigerator.
Position the refrigerator as if you were about to do that semiannual under-the-fridge floor cleaning. Carefully uncoil the tubing and attach it to the icemaker connection as you did at the saddle valve. Turn on the valve at the refrigerator and turn the water back on. If you used a drill-type saddle valve, open the saddle valve and turn on the icemaker.

INSTALLING GARBAGE DISPOSALS

A garbage disposal is a useful upgrade to your kitchen that is not too difficult to install. The hardest part is working under your sink, so work on plenty of towels to make it as comfortable as possible. If you're installing a new sink, attach the disposal to the sink first, then set the sink in place. Begin by removing the trap from one of the sink strainers.

YOU'LL NEED...

TIME: Several hours, not including installing an electrical receptacle and switch.
SKILLS: Basic electrical and plumbing connections.
TOOLS: Hammer, spud wrench, screwdriver, tongue-and-groove pliers, putty knife, and wire stripper.

1. Supply electricity.
If there isn't one already, install an electrical box under the sink near the disposal. Install a GFCI receptacle and plug the disposal in. Or hard-wire the disposal (see Step 6 on page 202). Unless you are using a self-switching disposal, install a switch as well.

TIME SAVER

SELF-SWITCHING DISPOSAL
Most disposals will require a switched receptacle, leaving the homeowner with the difficult job of finding a good location for the switch. A wall switch usually means fishing an electrical line up the wall above the countertop. Another option is a switch on the face of the lower cabinets, but that puts it within the reach of children.

To avoid these problems, spend the extra money for a self-switching garbage disposal. Just plug it into a regular always hot receptacle. It turns on when food is pushed into it.

2. Remove the basket strainer.
Disconnect the trap assembly from the basket strainer and the drainpipe. Remove the locknut holding the strainer in place using a spud wrench or a hammer and screwdriver as shown. Lift out the strainer, and clean away old putty from around the sink opening using a putty knife, paint thinner, and an abrasive pad.

3. Install the mounting assembly.
You'll usually need to take apart the mounting assembly. To do this, remove the snap ring, mounting rings, and gasket from the flange.

Lay a rope of putty around the sink opening and seat the flange in the opening. Have a helper hold the flange in place as you work from underneath. Slip the gasket, mounting rings, and snap ring up onto the flange. The snap ring will keep the mounting assembly in place temporarily.

Tighten the mounting assembly against the sink by turning the screws counterclockwise, as shown. Tighten each screw a little at a time to assure a tight seal.

4. Connect the electrical cord.

Remove the electrical cover plate on the disposal. Strip sheathing and wire insulation from an approved appliance cord (see pages 182–183) and insert it into the opening. Tighten the clamp while holding the cord in place. Make the electrical connections in the disposal, ease the wires into place, and reinstall the cover plate.

5. Attach the disposal.

Secure the drain elbow to the disposal. If you'll drain a dishwasher through the unit, remove the knockout inside the nipple. To mount the disposal, lift it into place, and rotate it until it engages and tightens. (This may take some muscle.) Once the connection is made, rotate the disposal to the best position for attaching the drain lines.

6. Make the electrical connection.

If you installed an electrical receptacle, simply insert the disposal's plug. For a hard-wired installation, *first shut off power.* Then connect the source black wire to the switch black wire, the white switch wire to the black wire leading to the disposal, the white disposal wire to the white power source wire, and all the ground wires together.

7. Connect the drain.

Fit a slip nut and a rubber washer onto the drain elbow, and fasten the trap to the elbow and the drainpipe. You may need to cut the elbow to make the connection. For double sinks connect the elbow to the second bowl drain. If you will be draining a dishwasher through the disposal, connect the dishwasher drain hose to the drain nipple of the disposal. Use an automotive clamp to attach the hose, tightening it in place with a screwdriver or ratchet and socket. Test for leaks by running water down through the disposal. Turn the electrical power back on. With standing water in the bowl, turn the disposal on, and make sure it is securely attached.

EXPERTS' INSIGHT

TIPS ON INSTALLING THE DRAINPIPES

■ On a double-bowl sink, it is possible to remove the drain elbow of the disposal and run pipe straight across to the trap of the other bowl. But the best way is to install a separate trap for the disposal so each bowl has its own trap.

■ If the original drain traps are in good condition, reuse them. In most cases if you buy one extension piece you will have enough material to complete the piping. If your old trap looks at all worn, save yourself a repair job later by replacing it while you have everything apart.

MAINTAINING GARBAGE DISPOSALS

*T*o avoid maintenance problems, be sure you have cold water running before you turn on your disposal. Gradually feed in food waste. Do not stick a spatula or any silverware down past the splash guard. With the cold water continuing to flow, run the disposal for a few seconds after the food has been ground. If you hear a clanking sound, or if the disposal stops, remove the object that has caused the problem by following the steps shown here.

Remove stuck objects.
If a fork, bottle cap, or any other solid object drops down through the splash guard, it can cause the disposal to jam. If this happens, turn off the power (if it has not already shut itself off). Remove the splash guard and peer down the disposal with a flashlight. If you can't free the object, rotate the grinder with a broom handle.

Use a special turning tool.
Your disposal may come with an Allen wrench that fits into a hole at the bottom of the disposal. If not, you can purchase a tool like the one shown. In either case, use the tool to turn the disposal back and forth. Once it's free, remove any obstructions, replace the splash guard, turn on the cold water, and test the disposal.

YOU'LL NEED...

TIME: Less than an hour to deal with most problems.
SKILLS: No special skills needed, unless you need to auger.
TOOLS: Allen wrench or disposal turning tool, flashlight, auger, and broom handle.

Reset an overloaded disposal.
If your disposal motor shuts off during operation, its overload protector has sensed overheating and has broken the electrical connection. Wait a few minutes for the unit to cool, then push the red reset button on the bottom of the disposal. If that doesn't work, check to see that you have power to the unit by inspecting the cord and the fuse or circuit breaker.

Disassemble and auger the drain.
Because a disposal gobbles up huge amounts of food waste, it's to be expected that occasionally the drain line will clog. If this happens, disassemble and remove the P-trap (make sure you have a bucket handy to catch the water that will spill), and clean out the trap (see page 170). If the trap itself is clear, thread a drain auger into the drainpipe (see page 172).

CAUTION
DON'T USE CHEMICALS
Do not attempt to clear a blocked drain line with chemicals of any type—not even "safe" chemicals. If the solution does not work, you'll be in danger of getting spattered with the stuff when you work to clear the line.

REPLACING AND INSTALLING DISHWASHERS

Replacing a dishwasher is fairly simple. Most units fit neatly into a 24-inch-wide undercounter cavity, and all are prewired and ready for simple supply, drainage, and electrical hookups. Installing a new dishwasher, however, is a much larger job: You must make room for it and bring in electrical, supply, and drain lines. To avoid straining the discharge pump, position the dishwasher as near to the sink as possible.

YOU'LL NEED...

TIME: About two hours to replace a dishwasher; a full day or more to put in a new one.
SKILLS: Simple electrical and plumbing skills for replacing; carpentry and basic plumbing and electrical skills for a new installation.
TOOLS: Drill, electrical tools, carpentry tools, screwdriver, and tongue-and-groove pliers.

electrical cable

1. Prepare the opening.
NOTE: *Shut off the water and shut off the electrical power.*
If you are replacing an existing dishwasher, remove its lower panel and disconnect the supply line, the drain hose, and the electrical line. Remove any screws attaching it to the countertop, and carefully pull the unit out.

For a new installation, remove a 24-inch-wide base cabinet, or tailor a space to fit the dishwasher. Bore a hole large enough to allow for the supply and drain lines near the lower back of the side panel of the adjoining cabinet. The dishwasher will need its own 15- or 20-amp circuit. Run a circuit from the service panel (you may want to hire a licensed electrician to install this).

approximate location of the dishwasher supply fitting

flexible copper line

shutoff valve

tee

2. Run the supply line.
Cut into the hot water supply line, and insert a standard tee fitting, a nipple, and a shutoff valve. Run flexible copper tubing into the cavity, leaving enough line to reach the dishwasher supply fitting. (See pages 166–167 and 172–175 for information on working with various types of pipes.)

dishwasher tailpiece

dishwater waste fitting

dishwasher drain nipple on garbage disposal

3. Provide a drain fitting.
Your dishwasher can drain either into the sink drain or into a garbage disposal if you have one.

For sink drainage, install a dishwasher tailpiece. Loosen the slip nuts and remove the tailpiece, insert the dishwasher tailpiece into the trap, and cut the old tailpiece to fit above it. Connect all the pieces, and tighten the slip nuts.

To drain a dishwasher into a garbage disposal, use a screwdriver and hammer to remove the metal knockout inside the dishwasher drain nipple located near the top of the disposal. The knockout, when freed, may fall into the grinding chamber of the disposal, so be sure to take it out.

4. Attach the drain line.
Thread the drain line through the hole in the cabinet, and slip it onto the dishwasher tailpiece or drain nipple—you may have to push hard. Secure it with an automotive hose clamp.

To ensure proper operation of the appliance, the drain line must make a loop as shown at top right, so that at some point it is raised near the height of the countertop. Support the drain line securely—it will vibrate during use—by wrapping a couple of lengths of wire around it and fastening them to screws driven into the underside of the countertop. Take care that the screws do not poke through the countertop.

Some local codes require an air gap (see inset) at the top of the loop. You can place this in a knockout hole in the sink or drill a hole for it in the countertop. Run one line from the drain nipple to the air gap, another from the air gap to the dishwasher drain outlet.

5. Make the hookups.
Position the ends of the three lines approximately at the locations where they will be connected to the dishwasher. Remove the bottom cover plate from the dishwasher, and slide the unit carefully into place, watching to make sure no lines are damaged. Make sure the dishwasher is all the way in position.

Make the connections as shown in the detail drawings. Tighten the compression nut and drain line clamp firmly, and make secure electrical connections.

Adjust the dishwasher by turning the leveling screws on the legs; then check with a level. Anchor the dishwasher to the underside of the countertop with screws. Turn on the water and the electrical power. Before reattaching access panels, run the washer, watching carefully for leaks.

If the water in your bathroom sink or tub gradually leaks out when you've stopped the drain, or if it doesn't drain out as quickly as you would like, you may need to adjust your drain assembly.

Before dismantling the assembly, pull up the strainer or stopper, and remove any hair or other debris hanging from it. Next thoroughly clean away soap or other gunk that may be keeping the strainer or stopper from

YOU'LL NEED...

TIME: An hour for most adjustments.
SKILLS: Basic plumbing skills.
TOOLS: Screwdriver and pliers.

Pop-up drains

If you've cleaned out the strainer and stopper and the problem persists, check the stopper seal. If it's damaged, replace any rubber parts or replace the stopper itself. Look for signs of wear on the flange the stopper seats into.

On a bathroom sink, examine the pivot rod. When the stopper is closed, it should slant slightly up from the pivot to the clevis. If it doesn't, loosen the setscrew, raise or lower the clevis on the lift rod, and retighten the screw.

If the stopper doesn't operate as easily now as you would like,

squeeze the spring clip, pull the pivot rod out of the clevis, and reinsert it into the next higher or lower hole. If water drips from the pivot, try tightening its cap. If the pivot still drips, you may need to replace the seal inside.

To adjust a tub pop-up, unscrew the overflow plate, withdraw the entire assembly, and loosen the adjusting nuts. If the stopper doesn't seat tightly, move the middle link higher on the striker rod. If the tub is slow to drain, lower the link.

Trip-lever drain

A trip lever lifts and lowers a seal plug at the base of the overflow tube. When the seal plug drops into its seat, water from the tub drain can't get past. But because the plug is hollow, water can still flow through the overflow tube through the overflow passage in the seal plug.

Dismantle and adjust a trip lever as you would a tub pop-up unit. Also check the seal on the bottom of the plug and replace it if it appears to be worn.

CARPENTRY BASICS

SELECTING HAND TOOLS

Often, the right hand tool makes your job easier and yields better results. Hand tools are relatively inexpensive so it's easy to gather quite a collection. To avoid becoming a tool junkie who fills the basement with tools that will never be used, assemble a basic tool kit and add to your collection only when the job at hand requires a new tool.

Typically, the top-of-the-line contractor-type tool model will be of higher quality than an average homeowner needs, but inexpensive tools will not perform well. Your best choice is a mid-priced model. If you need a tool to complete an unusual task and probably won't need it very often, go with the cheaper version.

Few tools see more action than the flexible **tape measure.** Buy a 25-foot one with a 1-inch-wide blade; this will extend farther and last longer than a ¾-inch one. Some carpenters prefer a folding ruler for smaller jobs. Purchase one with a metal pull-out extension for making precise inside-to-inside measurements (see page 225).

A **framing square** (also called a carpenter's square) is used to check corners for square and to mark for rafters and stringers. More often, you'll need a smaller square. A triangular **speed square** is easy to use, allows you to quickly figure 45-degree-angle cuts, and holds its shape after getting banged around. It slips into your back pocket and is handy for quickly marking cut lines on planks and framing material. A **combination square** is helpful for scribing lines (see page 228). A **T-bevel** can be set to duplicate an angle.

Plumb and level large and small projects with a **carpenter's level.** A 2- or 4-foot model works well for most projects. A **plumb bob** establishes true vertical lines. Snap long, straight lines with a **chalk line.** A chalk line also can double as a plumb bob.

Although you will do most of your cutting with power tools, a **handsaw** still comes in handy. You may want to choose a smaller saw that fits into a tool box. For accurate miter cuts, use a **backsaw** and **miter box.** Use a **drywall saw** to cut curves in drywall. To make rough curved cuts in wood, choose a **keyhole saw.** Cut intricate and precise curves in thin materials with a **coping saw.**

Wood chisels enable you to shape mortises and make rough notches in places where a saw will not reach. Choose chisels with metal-capped handles. Have a **utility knife** close at hand for razor-sharp cuts. Most people prefer one with a retractable blade. To shave wood along the length of a board, use a **plane** for the smoothest cut. For final shaping, use a **rasp** or a **wood file.**

Buy a **hammer** that is comfortable and solidly built. The most popular model weighs 16 ounces and has curved claws. You'll find a baffling array of specialty hammers, including framing and wallboard hammers. Stick to the basic curved-claw hammer. To sink the heads of finishing nails below the surface of the work, use a **nail set.**

Have plenty of **screwdrivers** on hand; get various sizes of both Phillips-tipped and slot-tipped types, or buy a combination screwdriver that has four tips in one tool. Make pilot holes for small screws with an **awl.**

To fasten nuts, bolts, and lag screws, use an **adjustable wrench.** For holding pieces of wood firmly, have **C-clamps** of various sizes handy. A pair of **locking pliers** helps to hold fasteners or pieces of wood tight while you work.

carpenter's level

plumb bob

chalk line

awl

25-foot, 1-inch-wide tape measure

framing square

combination square

speed square

T-bevel

drywall saw

handsaw

backsaw

keyhole saw

miter box

coping saw

C-clamp

hammer

screwdrivers

adjustable wrench

nail set

utility knife

wood chisel

plane

Phillips-tipped

slot-tipped

locking pliers

rasp

wood file

Tongue-and-groove pliers are one of the most useful tools you can buy so it makes sense to pay extra for a high-quality pair. They grab most anything firmly and work well for pulling nails. **Lineman's pliers** enable you to grab things tightly from the front rather than the side of the tool and also will cut nails or screws. **Side-cutting pliers** enable you to cut nails nearly flush to the surface. They also are useful for grabbing the pointed ends of finishing nails to pull them out of the back of molding without marring the face.

A **flat pry bar** is indispensable. With it, you can pry apart fastened lumber pieces with minimal damage to the wood. It also is handy for levering heavy objects into place; for example, reattaching a door on its hinges.

A **cat's paw** (also called a nail puller) makes it easy to pull nails, although it will damage the wood (see page 254). It's indispensable if you are planning any demolition.

For patching damaged walls and for taping drywall, have a variety of sizes of **taping knives** to apply wallboard compound (see pages 297–298). If you have 6-, 8-, and 12-inch blades you will be prepared to tape or patch most any surface. If you have a lot of drywall to cut, you'll thank yourself for buying a **drywall square.** You'll find it is also very useful for marking cut lines on pieces of plywood.

Sanding large wall and ceiling areas is much easier if you have a **pole sander.** Buy a smaller sanding block for detail work (see pages 265–266).

Use a **caulking gun** to fill cracks with caulk or to apply construction adhesive. Purchase a **staple gun** to attach sheets of plastic or felt or to install fiberglass insulation batts.

A **forming tool** is easier to use than a plane for working wood, but it will not cut as straight or as smooth. It is more versatile, however, and comes in handy for fine-tuning anything from foam board to wallboard.

When you need to stabilize something that is too thick to handle with a C-clamp, use a quick-fitting **adjustable clamp.** To clamp a straightedge in place or hold thin materials that might be marred by a C-clamp (see page 209) or adjustable clamp, use a **squeeze clamp** (see page 256 for other specialized clamps).

flat pry bar

caulking gun

cat's paw

drywall square

pole sander

side-cutting pliers

lineman's pliers

tongue-and-groove pliers

drywall taping knives

forming tool

adjustable clamp

squeeze clamp

staple gun

SELECTING BASIC POWER TOOLS

A circular saw, a power drill, and a sabersaw are musts for your basic tool kit. With the two saws you can make straight and curved cuts quickly in almost any material. The drill lets you make holes of almost any size and drive screws quickly and easily. With these three tools, you can handle most any household carpentry job.

A **circular saw** crosscuts, angle-cuts, rips (cuts lengthwise), and even bevels lumber easily and cleanly. Don't worry if the saw has a plastic housing; many plastics are very strong. Do take a look at the metal baseplate. A baseplate made of thin, stamped metal can warp; look for a thicker base made of extruded or cast metal. A saw that takes 7¼-inch blades is the usual choice. It lets you cut to a depth of about 2½ inches at 90 degrees and to cut through a piece of 2× lumber even when the blade is set at 45 degrees.

Horsepower is not important when choosing a circular saw. Instead, look at the amperage and the type of bearings. A low-cost saw pulls only 9 or 10 amps and runs on rollers or sleeve bearings. This means less power, a shorter life because it heats up easily, and less precise cuts because the blade wobbles somewhat. Better saws are rated at 12 or 13 amps and run on ball bearings. This combination of extra power and smoother operation makes for long life and more precise cutting. Worm-drive saws, which are the most powerful saws and have the longest-lasting bearings, are heavy and hard to use. As is often the case, a mid-priced saw is your best choice.

Be sure to get a variable-speed, reversible **power drill.** Unless you will be doing heavy-duty work, you don't need one with a ½-inch chuck; a ⅜-inch one is fine. Buy a drill that pulls at least 3.5 amps. A keyless chuck makes changing bits quick and easy, but some people prefer a keyed chuck for a tighter grip on the bit.

A **cordless drill** frees you to work without the mess of electrical cords. Buy one that uses at least 9.6 volts, preferably more. If possible, get an extra battery pack so you won't have to wait for a battery to charge.

When buying a **sabersaw,** examine the baseplate and the mechanism for adjusting it. On cheaper saws, these are flimsy and eventually wobble, making it difficult to keep the blade aligned vertically. Variable speed is a useful option. A saw pulling 3 amps or more handles most difficult jobs.

power drill

sabersaw

circular saw

cordless drill

SELECTING SPECIALIZED POWER TOOLS

The more carpentry jobs you take on, the more power tools you will need or want to own. Many of these are high-priced items, so do some careful research before making a purchase. If the tool is one you will turn to often, pay extra money to get a good-quality one that will last. If you will use it only rarely, settle for a lesser-quality tool.

To determine the quality of a tool, check the amperage rather than the horsepower. Compare models and avoid buying the one with the lowest amperage rating. A plastic housing is not necessarily a sign of poor quality. But do check any mechanisms and metal

attachments to see if they're solid. A tool with ball bearings runs smoother and lasts longer than one with other types of bearings.

For quick sanding of large areas, nothing beats a **belt sander.** Make sure it uses belts that are easily available—3×24 inches is the most common size. A good belt sander is fairly heavy and has a large dust collector. You can switch from rough to fine sanding belts; however, because a belt sander is difficult to handle for fine work, you probably will want to use another method for the final sanding—either a hand-sanding block or a smaller mechanized sander, such as a **random-orbit**

sander. It works by moving rapidly in small circles. Some people prefer the finish of an older-style vibrating sander, which simply moves back and forth. Some units switch from random-orbit to vibrating action.

With a **router,** you can mill lumber to a wide variety of shapes (see page 248). If you choose a solid model with plenty of power and a base that won't warp with age, you can produce pieces that are just as straight and smooth as millwork from a factory.

If you plan a project that calls for joining two pieces of lumber side by side, a **biscuit joiner** produces professional-looking

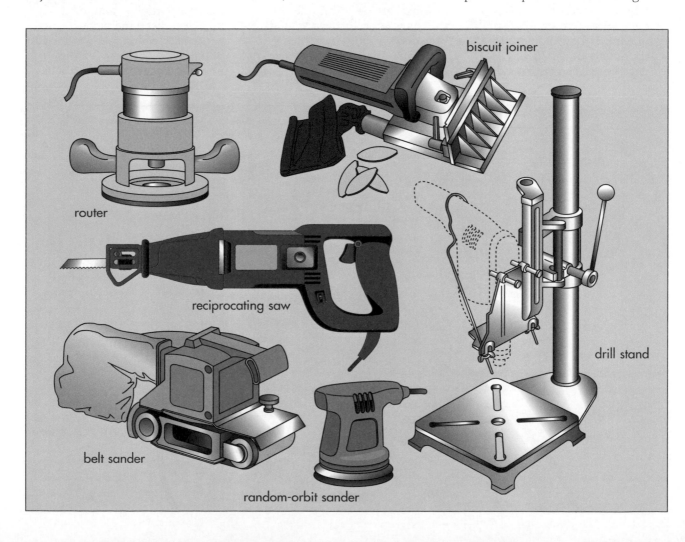

biscuit joiner

router

reciprocating saw

drill stand

belt sander

random-orbit sander

results with ease (see page 262).

Need to drill holes that are precisely vertical? You can purchase a drill press or a **drill stand** that uses a regular power drill. A stand is less expensive than a drill press, but does take more time to set up and use.

For demolition work, nothing beats a **reciprocating saw.** It can make cuts in places where no other saw will reach. If you need to remove portions of walls or floors, this tool can save you a lot of time and frustration.

If you have to cut a lot of molding or exterior siding, consider a **power miter saw.** This tool (also called a chopsaw or cutoff saw) is simply a circular saw mounted on a pivot assembly. It makes quick, precise crosscuts and miter cuts. Make sure you get a saw large enough to cut all the way through the stock you want to cut; a 10-inch blade handles most projects. Unless you will be doing complicated framing, there is no need to buy a model that makes compound miter cuts.

Use a **bench grinder** to sharpen tools and shape wood and metal

objects. Clamp it to your work bench, and it will be ready to use at a moment's notice.

With a good **tablesaw** you can make perfectly straight, long cuts. Use it for dado cuts as well. It also works for crosscuts and miter cuts (see page 246), but not as easily as a power miter saw. Choose a model that has a solid table that will not wiggle as you work on it, a fence that stays firmly in place, and a powerful motor. Keep in mind that you will need a good deal of room in your shop if you are going to use a tablesaw to cut sheets of plywood or long pieces of lumber.

A **radial-arm saw** is a general-purpose power saw. It makes long cuts like a tablesaw and crosscuts and miter cuts like a power miter saw. But like many multipurpose tools, it takes more time to do the job with it than with more specialized tools. Homeowners with limited space and funds, however, find this tool works quite well for a variety of cutting jobs; others prefer to buy the more specialized tools.

SAFETY

TOOL SAFETY TIPS

Safety is the result of following guidelines and exercising common sense. When working with a powerful electric tool, just one moment's lapse of concentration can lead to disaster. To minimize risks with power tools, keep the following guidelines in mind:

■ Use tools only for the jobs they were designed to do. If a tool came with an instruction manual, take the time to read it to find out what the tool will do and what it will not do.

■ Check on the condition of a tool before using it. A dull cutting edge or a loose-fitting hammer head, for example, spells trouble. Also inspect the cord of a power tool to make sure it's not damaged.

■ Don't work with tools if you're tired or in a hurry.

■ Don't work with tools if you have been drinking alcoholic beverages recently.

■ Wear goggles whenever the operation you are performing could result in eye injury.

■ The safety mechanisms on power tools are there for your protection. Do not tamper with or remove them from the tool.

■ Do not wear loose-fitting clothes or dangling jewelry while you are using tools.

■ Keep people, especially children, at a safe distance while you're using any tool. Before you let children use a tool, instruct them on how to operate it and don't let children operate a tool unsupervised.

■ Before servicing or adjusting a power tool, unplug it and allow moving parts to come to a standstill.

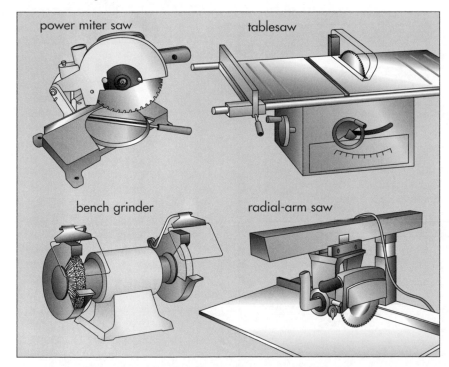

power miter saw

tablesaw

bench grinder

radial-arm saw

SELECTING AND BUYING LUMBER

As you learn carpentry techniques, it's important to become familiar with the characteristics and uses of various types of lumber and how to choose the wood that will work best for a particular project.

There are two basic types of lumber—softwoods, typically made from coniferous trees, and hardwoods, made from deciduous trees. Wood is graded according to how many knots it has and the quality of its surface (see the chart below for the most common grades). Some lumberyards have their own grading systems, but they usually simply rename these standard grades.

No matter what species of lumber you buy, be on the lookout for the types of wood problems shown at *right*. A board that is heavily **twisted, bowed, cupped,** or **crooked** usually is not usable, although some bows will lie down as you nail them in place. **Knots** are only a cosmetic problem unless they are loose and likely to pop out. **Checking,** which is a rift in the surface, also is only cosmetic. **Splits** cannot be repaired and will widen in time. Cut them off.

The nominal dimensions of wood are used when ordering lumber. Keep in mind that the actual dimensions of the lumber will be less (see the chart on page 215). Large quantities of lumber are sometimes figured by the board foot. A board foot is the wood equivalent of a piece 12 nominal inches square and 1 inch thick (see chart at *bottom*). Most lumberyards will not require you to figure board feet.

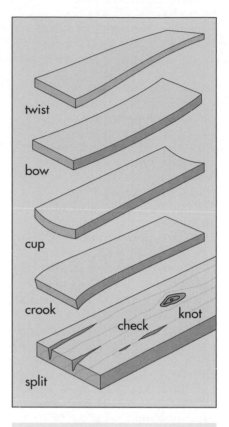

twist
bow
cup
crook
check
knot
split

Some Common Grades of Wood	
Grades	**Characteristics**
Clear	Has no knots.
Select or select structural	Very high-quality wood. Broken down into Nos. 1–3 or grades A–D; the lower grades will have more knots.
No. 2 common	Has tight knots, no major blemishes; good for shelving.
No. 3 common	Some knots may be loose, often blemished or damaged.
Construction or standard	Good strength; used for general framing.
Utility	Economy grade used for rough framing.

To determine board feet, multiply nominal width by nominal thickness in inches. Then multiply by the actual length in feet and divide by 12.

1"×12"×1'
1 board foot

1×3
(1"×3"×4')÷12=1 board foot

2×6
(2"×6"×6')÷12=6 board feet

LUMBER SELECTOR

Type		Description and Uses	Nominal Sizes	Actual Sizes
Furring		Rough wood of small dimensions. For furring drywall and paneling, interior and exterior trim, shimming, stakes, crates, light-duty frames, latticework, and edging.	1×2 1×3	$\frac{3}{4}$×1$\frac{1}{2}$ $\frac{3}{4}$×2$\frac{1}{2}$
Finish lumber		Smooth-finished lumber. For paneling, trim, shelving, light framing, structural finishing, forming, siding, decking, casing, valances, cabinets, built-ins, and furniture.	1×4 1×6 1×8 1×10 1×12	$\frac{3}{4}$×3$\frac{1}{2}$ $\frac{3}{4}$×5$\frac{1}{2}$ $\frac{3}{4}$×7$\frac{1}{4}$ $\frac{3}{4}$×9$\frac{1}{4}$ $\frac{3}{4}$×11$\frac{1}{4}$
Tongue-and-groove		Tongues and grooves fit into each other for a tight fit. For decorative interior wall treatments, exterior siding, flooring, and subflooring.	1×4 1×6 1×8	Actual sizes vary from mill to mill
Shiplap		One edge fits on top of the other. For decorative wall treatments, siding, decking, exterior sheathing, subflooring, and roof sheathing.	1×4 1×6 1×8	$\frac{3}{4}$×3$\frac{1}{8}$ $\frac{3}{4}$×5$\frac{1}{8}$ $\frac{3}{4}$×6$\frac{7}{8}$
Dimensional lumber		Studs are usually 2×4, sometimes 2×6. "Planks" are 6 or more inches wide. For structural framing (wall studs, ceiling and floor joists, rafters, headers, top and bottom plates), structural finishing, forming, exterior decking and fencing, and stair components (stringers, steps).	2×2 2×3 2×4 2×6 2×8 2×10 2×12 4×4 4×6 6×6	1$\frac{1}{2}$×1$\frac{1}{2}$ 1$\frac{1}{2}$×2$\frac{1}{2}$ 1$\frac{1}{2}$×3$\frac{1}{2}$ 1$\frac{1}{2}$×5$\frac{1}{2}$ 1$\frac{1}{2}$×7$\frac{1}{4}$ 1$\frac{1}{2}$×9$\frac{1}{4}$ 1$\frac{1}{2}$×11$\frac{1}{4}$ 3$\frac{1}{2}$×3$\frac{1}{2}$ 3$\frac{1}{2}$×5$\frac{1}{2}$ 5$\frac{1}{2}$×5$\frac{1}{2}$
Glue-laminate		Layers of dimensional lumber laid flat on top of each other and laminated into one solid piece. Used for rafters, joists, and beams. Can be stained for exposed beams.	4×10 4×12 6×10 6×12	3$\frac{1}{2}$×9 3$\frac{1}{2}$×12 5$\frac{1}{2}$×9 5$\frac{1}{2}$×12
Micro-laminate		Veneers glued together with crossing grains like plywood, only thicker. For rafters, joists, and beams.	4×12	3$\frac{1}{2}$×11$\frac{3}{8}$

SELECTING SOFTWOODS

Unless you're installing major structural components, such as floor or ceiling joists, that will bear significant weight, you can't make a serious mistake when buying softwoods. In most cases, you simply want to buy the wood that looks best or is the least-expensive alternative.

Softwood usually is less expensive than hardwood (see page 217) because it comes from trees that grow faster. In general, the disadvantage of softwood is evident in its name; it actually is soft. If you use softwood for furniture and other objects that will get handled and bumped against, plan on applying a hard finish or paint. Even then, it will not be as durable as hardwood.

Most retail suppliers stock only a few species of softwood. The chart below summarizes the chief characteristics of each. In most cases, you won't be choosing between species, but between grades of lumber. Which grade you choose depends on the nature of your project.

Softwood grading is tricky because several grading systems exist. Most often, however, you'll find two general classifications: select and common.

Use select lumber, which comes in several subgrades, for trim or cabinetry where finished appearance counts. For all other projects, common lumber will do nicely. Common lumber is graded as No. 1, No. 2, and No. 3.

With some suppliers, you can dispense with the grades and talk about more straightforward categories, such as "clear" (without knots) and "tight-knot" (having only small knots without cracks).

Of course, the better the grade—that is, the fewer the defects—the more you pay for the product. Often, however, a better grade is only slightly more expensive. Once you gain some experience, if you sort through the lumber rack carefully, you often can find pieces that are out of their class—for instance, a piece of No. 2 common that actually could have been classified as select.

SOFTWOOD SELECTOR

Species	Characteristics	Common Uses
Cedar, cypress	Similar to redwood—only the darker wood is rot-resistant. Weak, brittle; resists warping; pleasant aroma; easy to cut.	Siding, paneling, rough trim, roof shingles and shakes, decks.
Fir, larch	Heavy, very strong, hard; holds nails well; good resistance to warping and shrinkage; somewhat difficult to cut.	Framing studs, joists, posts, and beams; flooring; subflooring.
"Hem/fir"	A general classification that takes in a variety of species. Lightweight, soft, fairly strong; warps easily; may shrink; easy to cut.	Framing, exterior fascia, flooring, subflooring, trim.
Pine	From eastern, northern, and western trees. Very light, soft, fairly weak; good resistance to warping, but with a tendency to shrink; easy to cut.	Paneling, trim (molding), flooring, cabinets.
Redwood	Durable and resistant to rot and insects if you get the darker-colored heartwood. Light, soft, not as strong as fir or Southern pine; tendency to split; easy to cut.	Exterior posts and beams, siding, paneling, decks, fences.
Southern pine	Very hard, stiff, excellent strength; holds nails well; has a tendency to crack, splinter, warp; cuts with average ease.	Framing, subflooring.
Spruce	Lightweight, soft, fairly strong; resistant to splitting and warping; easy to work.	Framing, flooring, subflooring, trim (molding).
Treated lumber	Several species can be treated—most often, fir, "hem/fir," and Southern pine are used. Green or brown color will fade in time, leaving the wood a dirty gray; extremely resistant to rot and insects.	Bottom framing plates that rest on concrete; other framing that might come into contact with water, decks, fences.

SELECTING HARDWOODS

You can buy various types of plastic-laminated products made to look like hardwood, but there is no substitute for the real thing. Hardwood flooring and trim give a home an elegance unmatched by any other product. For furniture and cabinetry, nothing quite measures up in appearance and durability.

Unfortunately, hardwood trees grow slowly, so prices tend to be higher than for softwood. But prices fluctuate widely from year to year, and often the difference is surprisingly small. Oak flooring, for example, is sometimes cheaper than softwood flooring.

The more expensive hardwoods are milled to make use of virtually every splinter of wood. Instead of the standard sizes, some hardwoods are sold in pieces of varying lengths and widths. Sometimes the boards are smooth-surfaced only on two sides (S2S), leaving the edges rough. Hardwoods may be priced by the board foot (see page 214).

Hardwood grading differs from that of softwoods. It is based primarily on the amount of clear surface area on the board. The best grade is FAS (firsts and seconds), which is the most knot-free. Select boards have defects on one side only: No. 1 Common has tiny, tight knots; No. 2 Common has larger knots.

Most lumberyards and home centers can't afford to maintain an extensive inventory of hardwood lumber and generally stock only a limited assortment of a few species. For the best selection, find a store that specializes in hardwoods. They stock or can order a wide selection of species.

(see page 214)

EXPERTS' INSIGHT

HARDWOOD FROM MANAGED FORESTS

Concerned that your lumber may come from irreplaceable forests? The Forest Certification Resource Center lists suppliers of wood products derived from sustainable forests. You can search the FCRC's on-line data on contact it on the Internet at: http://www.certifiedwood.org/

HARDWOOD SELECTOR

Species	Characteristics	Common Uses
Birch	Hard, strong; fine-grained; resists shrinking and warping. Similar in color to maple—sometimes used as a cheaper replacement. Finishes fairly well; hard to cut.	Paintable cabinets, paneling, furniture.
Mahogany	Durable; fine-grained; resistant to shrinking, warping, and swelling. Finishes well; easy to cut. (Not to be confused with lauan mahogany, a much cheaper material that is used for veneers and plywoods.)	Fine furniture, cabinets, millwork, veneers.
Maple	Extremely hard, strong; pieces with bird's-eye or wavy grains are highly prized. Color ranges from reddish to nearly white in color. Finishes well; difficult to cut.	Flooring (basketball and bowling alley floors are made of maple), butcher blocks, veneers, millwork, and molding.
Poplar	Lightweight, soft for a hardwood; fine-grained. White to yellow-brown in color. Paints well; easy to cut.	Paintable furniture, cabinets, trim, places where a less-expensive hardwood will do.
Red oak	Hard, strong, rigid; pronounced open grain; resists warping, but may shrink if not well dried. Reddish color. Finishes well; moderately hard to cut.	Flooring, furniture, cabinets, molding, stair rails.
Walnut	Hard, heavy, extra strong; fairly pronounced, straight grain; resists warping and shrinking. Light to dark brown in color. Finishes well; cuts fairly easily.	Fine furniture and cabinets, millwork, paneling, inlays, veneers.
White oak	Hard, strong; open-grained, but not as pronounced as red oak; resists shrinking and warping. Golden color. Finishes well; moderately hard to cut.	Better than red oak for flooring—less variation in color. Millwork, molding, furniture, cabinets, stair rails, balusters.

SELECTING SHEET GOODS

Sheet goods are easy to work with and an inexpensive way to neatly cover large surface areas. For many applications, they provide the strength and appearance you need at a fraction of the cost of dimensional lumber.

Plywood is made by laminating thin layers (or plies) of wood to each other using water-resistant glue. The plies are sandwiched with the grain of each successive ply running at 90 degrees to the grain of the previous layer. This gives plywood its tremendous strength, as you will find if you try to break a piece in two. The front and back surface plies may be made of softwood, usually fir, or hardwood. A plywood face surface rated "A" is smooth and free of defects; "B," "C," and "D" faces are progressively rougher. Both faces need not be graded the same, for example, "A-C." T–111 plywood siding is made with exterior adhesive and a rough veneer.

Wood particles, sawdust, and glue are compressed and bonded together by heat to form **particleboard** and **hardboard.** This process produces a material that is hard, but easy to break. Hardboard comes in tempered (very hard) and untempered (softer) composition and is available in a variety of textures. Particleboard also comes in a variety of densities. Particleboard laminated with a plastic surface is handy for cabinet construction. **Waferboard** is made by a similar process, but with scraps of thin wood rather than sawdust, making it similar to plywood.

Drywall, sometimes called wallboard, is made of gypsum powder sandwiched between layers of heavy paper. **Cement board** is made with crushed rock and a nylon mesh.

SHEET GOODS SELECTOR

Material	Grades and Common Types	Thickness (in inches)	Common Panel Sizes (in feet)	Typical Uses
Plywood sheathing	C-D, C-D Exterior	$\frac{3}{8}$, $\frac{1}{2}$, $\frac{5}{8}$, $\frac{3}{4}$	4×8	Sheathing, subflooring, underlayment, structural supports. Tongue-and-groove and shiplap versions are available.
Finish plywood	A-B, A-C, B-C	$\frac{1}{4}$, $\frac{3}{8}$, $\frac{1}{2}$, $\frac{5}{8}$, $\frac{3}{4}$	4×8, 2×4	Cabinets, cabinet doors, shelves, soffits.
Hardwood plywood	A-A (or A-2), G1S (good one side); hardwood side sometimes labeled N	$\frac{1}{4}$, $\frac{3}{4}$	4×8, 2×4	Cabinets, cabinet doors, shelves, wall panels.
Lauan subflooring	Only one type	$\frac{1}{4}$	4×8, 2×4	Underlayment for vinyl tiles or sheet goods, backing for cabinets.
T-111 siding	Rough, with grooves variously spaced	$\frac{3}{8}$, $\frac{1}{2}$, $\frac{5}{8}$	4×8, 4×9	Exterior siding.
Waferboard	Only one type	$\frac{1}{4}$, $\frac{7}{16}$, $\frac{1}{2}$, $\frac{3}{4}$	4×8	Roof sheathing, underlayment.
Particleboard	Density of material varies	$\frac{1}{4}$, $\frac{3}{8}$, $\frac{1}{2}$, $\frac{5}{8}$, $\frac{3}{4}$	4×8, 2×4	Underlayment, core material for laminated furniture and countertops.
Hardboard	Standard, tempered, perforated	$\frac{1}{8}$, $\frac{1}{4}$	4×8, 2×4	Underlayment, drawer bottoms and partitions, cabinet backs, perforated tool organizers.
Drywall	Standard, greenboard (water-resistant)	$\frac{3}{8}$, $\frac{1}{2}$, $\frac{5}{8}$	4×8, 4×10, 4×12	Interior walls.
Cement board	Only one type	$\frac{5}{16}$, $\frac{1}{2}$	32"×60"	Backing for wall tiles, underlayment for ceramic floors.

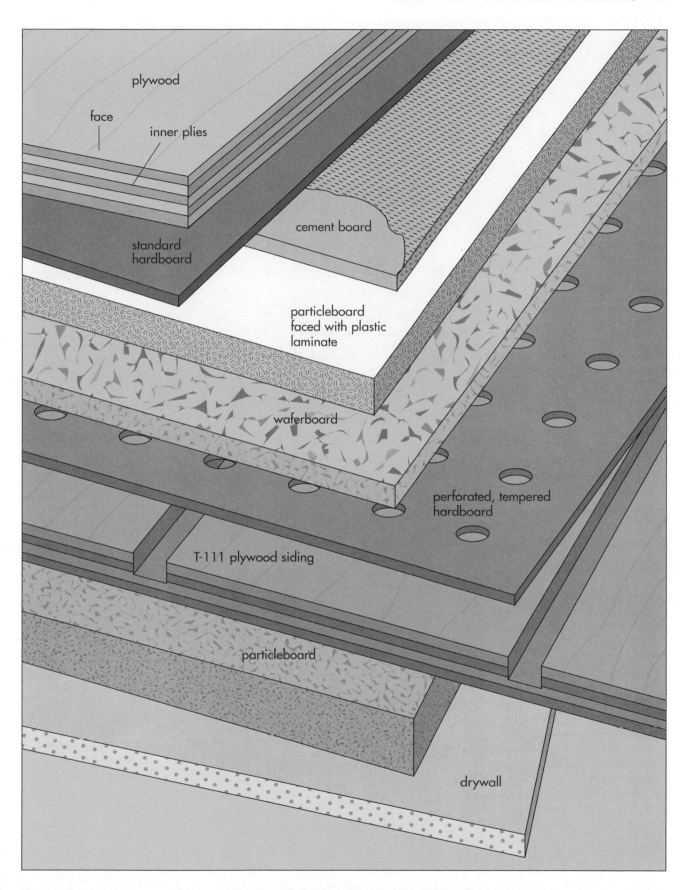

plywood

face

inner plies

standard
hardboard

cement board

particleboard
faced with plastic
laminate

waferboard

perforated, tempered
hardboard

T-111 plywood siding

particleboard

drywall

SELECTING AND ORDERING MOLDING

All rooms use at least some molding, usually along the base of walls and around windows and doors. In those places, molding covers up gaps. Other molding protects corners from dents or protects walls from damage by chair backs. In other places, such as around mantels, along the ceiling, and where paint and wall coverings meet in the middle of a wall, molding serves a decorative function. The molding you choose goes a long way toward defining the look of a room, whether it's minimalist or lushly decorative.

Molding is available in random lengths from 6 to 16 feet. Most is made of softwood, usually pine. Some popular types are available in hardwood, usually oak. These are a little more expensive.

The cost of molding does add up, so make a list of each piece you need, rounding the length up to the nearest foot, then add 5 percent to allow for trimming and fitting. See pages 269–272 for molding installation tips.

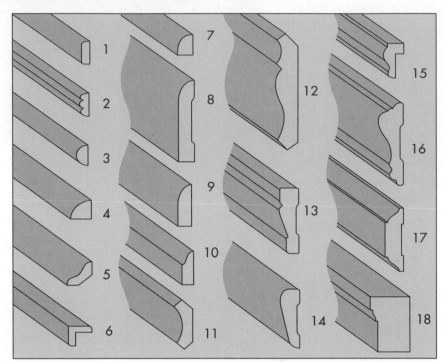

Money $ Saver

ALTERNATIVE MATERIALS

■ Finger-jointed molding is made of short pieces joined end to end. It costs less than regular molding, but you may need to sand the joints smooth.
■ Plastic molding is inexpensive, but has wood-grain finishes that may not suit your style. (Some can be painted.)
■ If you plan to paint molding rather than stain it, you may be able to save time and money with a preprimed molding.
■ Paper-covered hardboard molding also costs less, but can be difficult to cut neatly and the paper may tear later.

MOLDING SELECTOR

Common Types	Typical Uses
Screen bead; regular (1) and fluted (2)	Both cover seams where screening fastens to frames; finish edges of shelves.
Half round (3)	Serves as screen bead, shelf edging, and lattice.
Quarter round (4)	Serves as base shoe and inside corner guard.
Inside corner (5) and outside corner (6)	Both conceal seams and protect areas where walls meet at corners.
Base shoe (7) and baseboard (8)	Both trim and protect walls at their base.
Stop; ranch (9) and colonial (10)	Both attach to door jambs to limit door swing; hold inside sash of windows in place.
Cove (11) and crown (12)	Both trim and conceal joint between walls and ceilings.
Casing; colonial (13) and ranch (14)	Both trim around interior windows and doors.
Plycap (15)	Conceals plywood edge; tops off wainscoting.
Chair rail (16)	Protects walls from chair backs; hides seams where wall materials meet.
Batten (17)	Conceals vertical and horizontal panel seams.
Brick mold (18)	Used with all types of exterior cladding (not just brick) to trim around doors and windows.

SELECTING NAILS

Many types and sizes of nails are available, each one engineered for a specific use. The differences may seem small, but they can have a significant effect on the soundness and appearance of your job. Here's a guide to choosing among the standard types of nails:

Use **common** nails and **box** nails for framing jobs. Box nails are a bit thinner for lighter work. **Cement-coated** nails drive in more easily and hold more firmly. Use **roofing** nails for roof shingles and wherever a wide head is needed to hold material that might tear if a smaller head is used. Choose hot-dipped over electroplated **galvanized** nails; they'll last much longer.

Casing and **finishing** nails handle medium- and heavy-duty finishing work. For very fine work, use **wire brads. Ring-shank** and **spiral** nails grab wood more tightly than conventional nails. Specially hardened **masonry** nails penetrate mortar joints, brick, and even concrete. **Corrugated fasteners** are used mainly for strengthening wood joints; they do not hold well by themselves.

You can save money by buying nails in bulk, rather than in the box. However, it is handy to have boxes marked with the nail size.

MEASUREMENTS

PENNIES AND INCHES
In Great Britain in the 1400s, you could buy 100 medium-size nails for 8 pennies. It didn't take long for inflation to destroy that designation, but we use the term penny to this day to size nails. The abbreviation "d" for penny is derived from *denarius,* a small, silver Roman coin used in Britain that, from early times, equated with a penny.

Inch equivalent of nails sizes:

3d=1¼"	10d=3"
4d=1½"	12d=3¼"
6d=2"	16d=3½"
7d=2¼"	20d=4"
8d=2½"	

THE NAIL FOR THE JOB
Use nails three times as long as the thickness of the material you are fastening. For instance, to attach a 1×4 (¾ inch thick), a 6-penny nail (2 inches long) will be a bit short. An 8-penny nail (2½ inches long, a little more than three times the thickness of the 1×4) will do better. Make sure the nail will not poke through the material to which you are fastening.

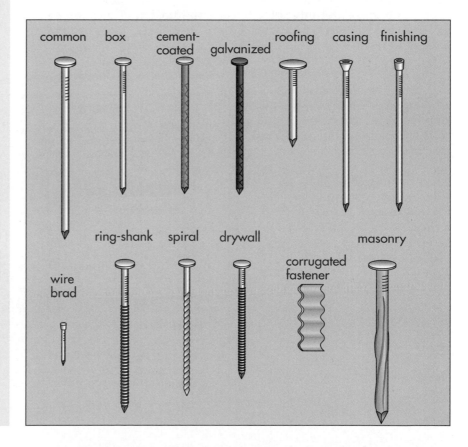

common box cement-coated galvanized roofing casing finishing

wire brad ring-shank spiral drywall corrugated fastener masonry

SELECTING SCREWS AND BOLTS

For the few seconds they take to drive in, nails do a remarkable holding job. Yet for the little extra time it takes to drive in a screw, you get a tighter-holding fastener, a neater appearance, and another plus—ease of disassembly. In fact, drywall screws teamed with cordless electric drills have created a mini-revolution in fasteners, including everything from deck screws to general-purpose wood screws.

The most common slot configurations for screws are the **slotted head** and the **Phillips head**, which has an X-shaped slot. **Square-drive** screws are more rare, but are growing in popularity.

There are three head shapes from which to choose. A **flathead** screw can be driven flush with or slightly below the surface of the wood. Use **ovalhead** screws with trim washers for a finished appearance. Install **roundhead** screws when you want the screw head to show.

General-purpose or **drywall** screws offer an inexpensive and easy way to fasten items together. You can buy them by the pound, and they drive easily using a drill with a screwdriver bit. **Trim head** screws use a smaller Phillips or square-drive bit. They hold better than finishing nails, but the countersink hole will be larger.

Use **masonry** screws (often referred to by the brand name Tap-Con) to fasten material to masonry or concrete surfaces. Simply drill the correct-size hole in the masonry surface and drive in the screw. Drive a **hanger** screw into a ceiling joist and fasten the object to be hung using the nut and thread on its lower half.

Use **lag** screws for heavy-duty fastening. Drill a pilot hole and drive in the screw with a wrench.

As with nails, screws should be three times as long as the thickness of the board being fastened. When buying screws, specify the gauge (diameter) you want. The thicker the gauge, the greater its holding power. Make sure you have the correct-size drill bit if drilling pilot holes (see the box at right). For more on driving in screws, see pages 245–246.

Machine bolts have a head that can be turned with a wrench. **Carriage bolts** have round heads for a finished appearance. When buying bolts, be sure to get the correct gauge and length; it must be longer than the materials you are fastening, so you can add the nut and washers. (For more on fastening with bolts, see page 253.) Thin metal can be joined with self-tapping **sheet-metal screws**.

ADHESIVES

Many carpentry jobs call for adhesives, either as the primary or secondary fastener. Purchase a supply of wood glue for general-purpose work, construction adhesive in tubes, two-part epoxy glue for extra-strong holding, panel adhesive for installing drywall or paneling, and perhaps a hot-glue gun with glue sticks.

EXPERTS' INSIGHT

DRILLING PILOT HOLES

To see if a drill bit is the correct size to make your pilot hole, grip both bit and screw together with your fingers. The bit should be slightly thinner than the width of the screw threads.

The thickness of a pilot hole can vary depending on the wood. With softwoods, you can use a smaller hole than you would with hardwoods. Always drill a test hole and make sure the screw will hold tight before you proceed to drill a number of holes in the finished material.

wood screw — flathead, ovalhead, roundhead

lag screw

hanger screw

machine bolt

carriage bolt

slotted head

Phillips head

sheet-metal screw

lock washer

flat washer

trim washer

deck screw

drywall screw

trim head screw

masonry (Tap-Con) screw

SELECTING HARDWARE

The items shown on these two pages represent just a few of the options available in specialized hardware. At your hardware store or home center, you'll find a product designed for almost every conceivable carpentry need.

When you want to strengthen a weak wood joint, reach for a metal plate or brace, as shown *below left*. **Mending plates** reinforce end-to-end joints; **T-plates** handle end-to-edge joints. **Flat corner irons** strengthen corner joints by attaching to the face of the material; **angle brackets** do the same thing, but attach to the inside or outside edges.

Shelf standards, as shown *below right*, come in a variety of configurations and finishes suitable for utility or more decorative uses. Most standards can be installed on the wall or into supports behind the shelves. Some standards can be installed on either side of the shelves. **Adjustable standards and brackets** come in a variety of colors, sizes, and finishes. Use **utility brackets** for nonadjustable shelving in places where appearance is not important. **Closet rod brackets** let you attach a shelf and a closet rod to the same piece of hardware.

There is a large choice of door and cabinet hardware, as shown on *page 224*. Most full-size doors hang on the classic **butt hinge**, *opposite*. **Piano hinges** mount flush on cabinets and chests, combining great strength with a slim, finished look. **Strap hinges** and **T-hinges** often are used on gates and trunk lids.

There are four basic types of cabinet hinges. **Decorative hinges** work only for doors that are flush with the frame. Use **front- or side-mount offset hinges** for doors that are either flush with the frame or that have lips that overlay the frame. If a door completely overlays the frame, use a **pivot hinge** or a self-closing **European-style hidden hinge**. To open your cabinet doors, fit them with **knobs** or **pulls**, available in many sizes and styles. **Friction, roller, bullet,** or **magnetic catches** keep cabinet doors closed. (If you are using self-closing hinges, these catches aren't necessary.)

For smooth-operating drawers, choose side-mounted **drawer slides** like the one shown on *page 224*. For extra household security, add a **chain lock** to your door.

Select appropriate joint and reinforcing hardware.
For a quick and fairly permanent joint or repair, use inexpensive plates like these. For best results, clamp the material together before attaching the plates. Drill pilot holes as centered as possible; otherwise, screws may pull the joint apart as they are driven in.

Choose from many types of shelf brackets.
If you've ever tried to make a shelf bracket out of lumber, you'll know how much time and effort is saved by these handy pieces of hardware. For more on installing shelf hardware and shelf construction, see pages 301–308.

piano hinge

butt hinge

T-hinge

strap hinge

decorative hinge

front-mount offset hinge

pivot hinge

side-mount offset hinge

magnetic catch

European-style hidden hinge

chain lock

knob

friction catch

drawer slide

roller catch

bullet catch

pull

MEASURING AND MARKING

Accurate measuring and marking are the bases of successful carpentry. A mistake in measuring often means wasted time and material. Though it may seem simple, good measuring technique does not come naturally. It takes practice.

Don't rush your measuring. Take your time and double-check your work. Adopt the carpenters' maxim, "Measure twice, cut once."

No matter what measuring device you use, get comfortable with it and learn how to read it accurately. Many a board has met its ruin because someone couldn't distinguish a ¼-inch mark from a ⅛-inch mark. Once you've made a measurement, don't trust your memory. Jot down the figure on a piece of paper or a wood scrap.

Marking, not reading, the measurement is the difficulty. Make a clear mark (see page 226) using a sharp No. 2 pencil, the thin edge of a sharpened carpenter's pencil, a knife, or a scratch awl (especially if working with sheet metal).

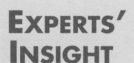

Make a clear mark (see page 226)

EXPERTS' INSIGHT

COMPARE MEASURING DEVICES

Odd as it may seem, different measuring tapes or rulers can differ slightly—differences that will show up when dealing with long spans of lumber. This can lead to frustration if you are calling out measurements for someone else to cut. Before you accuse your partner of sloppy cutting, compare measuring devices to be sure they're calibrated the same.

For the first few inches, most tapes show ¹⁄₃₂-inch marks.

Hook slides to compensate for its thickness.

Measure with a steel tape.
A steel tape is the most popular measuring device because it does most jobs with ease. Note that the hook at the end of the tape slides back and forth slightly to compensate for its own thickness. This means that whether you hook the tape on a board end for an outside measurement or push it against a surface for an inside measurement, the result will be accurate. For the first few inches of most tapes, each inch is divided into ¹⁄₃₂-inch increments to facilitate extra-fine measurements.

slide-out metal piece

folding ruler

Take an inside measurement.
Where outside measurement is difficult (here the drywall is in the way of measuring between the outside edges of the 2×4s) make an inside-to-inside measurement. A folding ruler with a slide-out metal piece works best. Extend it, measure, and hold the slide with your thumb until the measurement is transferred. You can use a tape measure for such measurements, but it is difficult to be accurate because you have to add an amount to compensate for the length of the tape body.

Make a V mark, not a line.

Marking with a simple line often leads to inaccuracies. By the time you're ready to saw, it's easy to forget which end of the line marks the spot—or where to cut on a thick line from a blunt pencil. For greater accuracy, mark your measurements with a V so you know precisely where to strike the cut line. To ensure pinpoint accuracy, place the point of your pencil at the V, slide the square to it, then make your line.

If you need to extend cut lines across several boards, use a framing square. For longer lines, use a drywall square.

Mark a V.

Slide the square to the mark.

Mark for rip cuts.

Need to mark a cutoff line along the length of a board or a piece of plywood? If the line is parallel to the edge of the board and accuracy isn't critical, use your tape measure as a scribing device. Hold your tape so that a pencil laid against its end will make the correct line. Hold the tape and pencil firmly and pull evenly toward you, letting the tape body or your thumbnail slide along the board edge. For sheet goods, first mark the cutoff line at both ends, then snap a chalk line between the two marks, or clamp a straightedge in place and draw a mark.

tape measure

Use side of finger as guide.

Pull straight up and let go.

Allow for the saw kerf.

When you cut material, the saw blade reduces some of it to sawdust. So, when measuring, you must allow for the narrow opening left in the blade's wake—called the kerf. Usually, a kerf is about 1/8 inch wide. If you're making just one cut, account for the kerf by marking the waste side of the cutoff line with an X. There's no confusion then as to the side of the line on which to cut.

If you are cutting multiple pieces out of the same piece of lumber, make double marks to allow for the kerf. Otherwise, you will cut each piece too short.

cut line

scrap

Mark a double line to allow for saw kerf.

HOLDING AND MEASURING IN PLACE

The most accurate and mistake-proof way of measuring is not to use a measuring device at all. Simply hold a piece where it needs to fit and mark it. You can do this for a simple cutoff. At other times, such as when you need to cut a board in two directions, use a combination of techniques: Hold and mark, then measure. Often this method isn't feasible, especially where access is limited or when the lumber being cut is too bulky to be held in place. But take advantage of this foolproof approach when you can.

YOU'LL NEED

TIME: Less than a minute for most measurements.
SKILLS: A steady hand and a good eye for accurate marking.
TOOLS: Pencil, speed square.

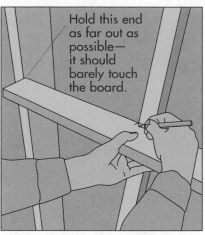

Hold this end as far out as possible—it should barely touch the board.

Hold and mark for a cutoff.
When you need to cut a board to length, begin by checking one end of the board for square. Press the square-cut end against one side of the opening, and mark the other end for cutting. To avoid distorting the measurement, don't push the square-cut end into the space any more than needed.

EXPERTS' INSIGHT

NO-MISTAKE MEASURING

Carpenters make measuring mistakes every day, so don't be surprised when you do also. Here are some common mistakes and how to avoid them:

■ **Sawing on the wrong side of the line.** If you cut on the good rather than the scrap side of the line, the board will be ⅛ inch short. Always draw an X on the scrap side (see page 226).
■ **Misreading upside-down numbers.** Is it a "6" or a "9"? Make sure you know.
■ **Simply forgetting.** Write down all measurements immediately, so you won't forget.

windowsill / Measure for depth of cut. / length of notch / Hold board in position.

1. To mark for a cutout, first measure the depth of the cut.
When you need to cut a board in two or three directions to make it fit around something, begin by holding the board in place. Make a small mark showing where the cutout is to be cut to length. Then measure how deep the cutout must be by measuring the distance between the leading edge of the board and the place where it must end up once it's cut.

depth mark / length mark / area to be cut out / depth mark

2. Transfer measurement mark.
Use a square to extend the length mark. With a tape measure, transfer the depth measurement to two places on the board—at the length mark and at the end of the cutout. Use a square to draw a line from the length mark to the depth mark. With a straightedge, mark a line between the two depth marks.

16" mark at middle of stud location

Lay out a plate for a stud wall.
When building a wall, the studs (upright 2×4s) must be 16 inches on center; that is, you want 48- or 96-inch drywall or paneling sheets to end in the middle of a stud. To make marks for studs, mark every 16 inches, minus ¾ inch (15¼ inches, 31¼ inches, and so on). Measure over 1½ inches and make another mark. Draw lines at your marks and an X between to show stud location (see page 226).

SQUARING, PLUMBING, AND LEVELING

Most carpentry projects—from making simple shelves to building walls—require that you square the work. Check for square at every stage of your work: corners, uprights, and board ends.

Making sure that work is plumb and level is equally important. Walls, cabinets, doors—nearly every permanent installation—must be plumb (perpendicular to the earth) and level (parallel to the earth). Don't assume existing walls or floors are square, level, or plumb. Most often they are not because of imperfect construction or settling that has taken place over the years. Techniques shown in this section will help you keep your carpentry projects straight and true.

TOOLS TO USE

THE MULTIPURPOSE SPEED SQUARE

Almost every carpenter's belt contains a hammer, utility knife, pencil, and the ever-handy speed square. With a speed square, you can quickly mark 45- and 90-degree angles simply by holding the square with its body firmly against a factory edge. Other angles are marked on the body of the square and can be used with a fair degree of accuracy. In addition, the speed square is handy as a guide for cutting square corners (see page 209).

Check board ends for square.
All your careful measuring will be wasted if you start with a piece of lumber that is not square—one edge will be longer than the other. Check the board end by holding a combination square with the body or handle firmly against a factory edge. If the end isn't square, mark a square line and trim the board.

Use a combination square.
With this tool you can easily check for either 45- or 90-degree angles. Also, by sliding the blade, you can check depths. This tool can go out of square if it is dropped, so check it once in a while against a square factory edge (such as the corner of a sheet of plywood).

outside measure

blade

inside measure

90°

tongue

Use a framing square.
For larger jobs, use a framing square. Lay the square up against two members where they meet. If the tongue and the blade of the square rest neatly against the members, the sides are perpendicular. Or, place the square on the outside. Again, if the square touches the members at all points, the unit is square. When using a framing square for measuring, be sure to read the correct scale—inside or outside.

TOOLS TO USE

DRYWALL SQUARE

This tool, sometimes called a T-square, helps you cut drywall much faster than other tools. It is well worth its price if you need to cut a lot of drywall. It also is useful for measuring and marking other sheet goods, particularly plywood and particleboard. Because the blade is a full 4 feet long, you need make only one mark rather than two when marking for a cutoff, and you don't have to align straightedges or mess with chalk lines. A drywall square can get out of square if you're not careful with it. Take care to rest it in places where it won't get banged around. Periodically test it for square by holding it against two factory edges of a sheet of drywall or plywood.

Use the 3-4-5 method.

For large projects, test if a corner is square by using geometry. You don't need to remember the Pythagorean theorem. Just remember "3-4-5." On one side, mark a point 3 feet from the corner. On the other side, mark a point 4 feet from the corner. If the distance between the two marks is exactly 5 feet, it is square. For extra large projects, use multiples such as 6-8-10 or 9-12-15.

As a double check, measure the length of the diagonals. If the project is square, the distance between two opposite corners (marked A in the drawing *above*) will equal the distance between the other two corners (B).

Check for plumb.

To see if a piece is perfectly vertical—plumb—hold a level against one face of the vertical surface and look at the air bubble in the level's lower glass vial. If it rests between the two guide marks, the piece is plumb.

First mark and fasten here.

Then level cleat and fasten here.

Check for level.

In most cases, you can simply set your carpenter's level atop the piece to see if it's level. Raise or lower the piece until the bubble rests between the marks. Mark the position of the piece and remove the level (you don't want to risk knocking it to the floor). Add a fastener to the cleat near the level mark, level the cleat, and finish fastening.

To test for level over long distances, use a board ...

If you need to see if an entire floor is level, select a long, straight board. (Sight down its length to see that it's not bowed.) Place a carpenter's level in the center of the board and raise one end or the other until the bubble is centered between the two lines. Slide the board around until you are sure you have found the high point of the floor. Level the board from this high point and measure the distance from the floor to the bottom of the raised end of the board to see how far out of level the floor is.

or use a water level.

This tool enables you to quickly check for level in awkward situations or over long distances. Basically a long hose and two transparent tubes filled with water, this tool works on the principle that water seeks its own level. Mark at water level.

Use small levels in tight spots.

In places where you can't fit in a carpenter's level, use the level that comes on some combination squares or a torpedo level (a short version of a carpenter's level). Or, if you know that an adjoining member or wall is plumb, measure to see that the piece is square to it.

Plumb a cabinet.

When installing cabinets, make sure they are plumb in both directions or the doors will shut or open by themselves. With the cabinet fastened to the wall loosely, hold a level against a vertical framing piece. Tap in shims until the bubble indicates that the cabinet is plumb.

USING SPECIAL MARKING TECHNIQUES

A flexible steel tape measure, a square, and a level usually will equip you to mark your lumber for cutting. But sometimes you'll come across a situation where you'll have to mark around the irregular contours of molding, brick, or stone; mark curved shapes; or mark for angles other than 45 degrees and 90 degrees. These aren't challenges to be left only to master carpenters. The simple techniques in this section are for marking unusual shapes.

EXPERTS' INSIGHT

MAKING AND USING TEMPLATES

■ For material in which you are making multiple or complicated cuts, make a template or pattern before you make the cut. Often, the piece of lumber or sheet goods you are replacing can serve as the template. Carefully remove the old piece, take out any nails or screws that are in it, place it over the new lumber, and trace its outline.

■ At other times, you may need to make a template. Cut a piece of stiff cardboard with a knife or make a pattern out of a piece of scrap wood. Experiment until the template fits exactly, but don't experiment on your final, expensive materials.

■ Whenever you use a template, be sure that it does not slide around as you make your marks—you may need to clamp or tack it in place. Watch your pencil line carefully to see that it is tight against the template at all points.

Scribe the bottom of a door.
If the bottom of a door is sticking, close it as far as possible. Set a compass to the correct height above the floor—usually the thickness of the threshold plus ⅛ inch for clearance. Hold the compass point on the floor and the pencil end of the compass on the door. Move the compass along the floor, scribing a parallel cutoff line on the door.

Mark for irregular cuts.
For a complicated contour cut, use a compass that can be tightened firmly so it won't collapse or expand as you trace the contour. Place the new material next to the object it will fit around. Set the compass to the greatest width to be cut off. Take care to hold the two compass points on the same plane (in this case, parallel to the floor) as you make the mark.

Use a T-bevel for odd angles.
If you want to duplicate an angle that is neither 45 nor 90 degrees, use a sliding T-bevel. Loosen the wing nut so the blade can be moved without difficulty. Hold the handle against one edge and move the blade until it rests firmly against the other edge. Tighten the wing nut firmly. The tool holds the angle you need, allowing you to transfer it to the wood you are cutting. When making an inside measurement, as shown *above,* extend the blade fully to ensure an accurate reading.

Draw circles with a compass.

To mark small circles—for boards that will be cut to accept pipes, lighting fixtures, etc.—a simple compass will do the job. Mark a spot at the center of the hole and set the compass width to one-half the diameter of the hole. For accuracy, be sure the compass is tightly clamped in position and hold it as perpendicular to the surface as possible.

Step off with dividers.

If you need to mark a series of equidistant points along a straight line, use dividers. Steel pins at the base of each leg grip the surface of the material you're measuring for good control. Use a swiveling motion as you step from one leg to the other leg.

Find a center point with a compass.

If you need to find the exact center point of a board, doing it with math can be confusing—what's half of $9\frac{3}{8}$ inches, for instance? To quickly find the center point, open your compass to a bit more than half the board's width and make two arcing marks as shown. The line between the points where the curved lines intersect is the center of the board.

Make a tool for larger circles.

A compass works well for small circles, but if you have to cut out for a sink or another large, round object, you will have to use a little ingenuity. Make your own compass out of a pencil, brad, and string. Be sure to hold the pencil vertical as you draw.

For greater accuracy, make a notch at one end of a small piece of wood. Nail the wood piece in place with a brad at the center of the circle. The notch holds the pencil in place for a smooth, accurate line.

Sometimes, you may be able to find a round household object, such as a can, a bucket, or a wastebasket, that is close enough to the correct size. Place it on the work and trace around it.

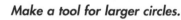

CUTTING WITH A CIRCULAR SAW

Chances are you will do most of your cutting with a circular saw. Whether cross-cutting 1-inch stock, ripping plywood, or cutting bricks with a masonry blade, you'll do the job better if you follow a few basic rules when using this versatile tool.

Whenever you cut, allow the saw to reach full operating speed, then slowly push the blade into the wood. Some carpenters look at the blade as they cut; others rely on the gunsight notch. Choose the method that suits you best. Avoid making slight turns as you cut. Instead, find the right path, and push the saw through the material smoothly. It will take some practice before you can do this consistently. This is a powerful tool with sharp teeth, so take care. It demands your respect.

gunsight notch

Support the material properly.
Well-supported work results in clean, safe cuts. If the scrap piece is short, support the board on the nonscrap side. If the scrap is long, it could bind the blade or splinter as it falls away at the end of the cut. To achieve a neat cut and avoid saw kickback, support the lumber in four places. Even with such precautions, you may want to make two cuts: one to cut the work roughly to size, the other for the finish cut.

TOOLS TO USE

CHOOSING A CIRCULAR SAW AND BLADES

■ Choose a circular saw that is comfortable. It should have some heft, but should not be so heavy that it is difficult to maneuver. You should be able to see the blade and gunsight notch easily. Check for ease of depth and angle adjustments. (For more tips, see page 211.)

■ If you buy only one blade for a circular saw, choose a carbide-tipped combination blade that has at least 24 teeth. It works well for rough work and makes cuts clean enough for most finish work. For fine work, buy a plywood blade or a hollow-ground planer blade. For extensive remodeling jobs, get a second carbide-tipped blade that you can use when you may need to cut through nails or other rough materials.

CAUTION!
AVOIDING AND PREPARING FOR KICKBACK

It happens to even the most experienced carpenter: A blade binds, causing a circular saw to jump backward. Kickback can mar the lumber you are working on, and it is dangerous. Unsupported work often is the culprit. But also watch for these situations:

■ A dull blade will bind and cause the saw to kick. Change your blade if you have to push hard to make it cut.

■ Bending or twisting lumber will grab a blade. Sheets of plywood are particularly prone to this. Make sure it is evenly supported, like the 1× above.

■ Kickback also can occur when you back up while cutting or when you try to make a turn. If your cut is going off line, stop the saw, back up, and start again.

■ Occasionally, certain types of wood grain will grab the blade and cause a kickback. There's nothing you can do about this except be prepared.

■ Don't wear long sleeves and don't position your face near the circular saw.

falling scrap

dull blade

bending plywood

EXPERTS' INSIGHT

SET THE BLADE DEPTH CORRECTLY

Before you make any cut, check to see that the blade is set to about ¼ inch deeper than the thickness of the wood. (Be sure to unplug the saw before you do this.) This may seem like a lot of bother, especially if you are constantly switching between 1× and 2× lumber, but here's why it is worth the trouble:

■ A saw blade that extends only slightly below the material will produce a much cleaner cut than a blade that extends way below the material.

■ The deeper the blade is set, the more prone it will be to binding and kickback, jeopardizing the work and your safety.

Unplug the saw.

Square the blade.
To square a blade, hold a speed square against the blade and adjust it. (Be sure to position the square between the teeth.) To test if your blade is square to the baseplate, crosscut a piece of 2× lumber. Flip the piece over and press cut edge against cut edge. If you see a gap at the top or the bottom, the blade is not square.

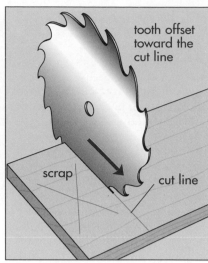

tooth offset toward the cut line

scrap   cut line

Align the blade with the cut line.
Once you have drawn an accurate cutoff line and have properly supported the board, position the saw blade to the scrap side of the line. The teeth on most circular saw blades are offset in an alternating pattern, half to the left and half to the right. When clamping a guide, align a tooth that points toward the cutoff line.

speed square

Use a square as a guide.
With practice, you will learn to cut accurately without using a guide. But for cuts that have to be precise, use a guide. For 90-degree cuts, a speed square works well because it's easy to hold stable. Align the blade, then slide the square into position against the saw's baseplate. Grab the board along with the square, so the square won't slip out of position.

T-bevel

distance between blade and edge of baseplate

Use other guides for angle cuts.
With care, you can improvise a saw guide that will be as accurate as a miter box. Set a T-bevel to the desired angle (see page 231) and transfer the angle to the board.

Select a straight piece of 1× and clamp it along the cutting line as a saw guide. To offset the guide correctly, measure the distance between the blade and the edge of the saw's baseplate and clamp the

guide that distance from the cut line. It may take some experimenting before you get this correct. Be sure to align the blade to the correct side of the line.

You can use the same principle for long rip cuts. Clamp a straightedge—the factory edge of a 1× or a drywall square—onto the material, setting it back from the cut line to allow for the width of the saw's baseplate.

Support sheet goods.
Cut sheet goods with a carbide-tipped combination blade or a plywood-cutting blade for a smoother cut. It is important to support the sheet properly, or the blade will bind. You can do this by setting four 2× support pieces on the floor, a table, or a pair of sawhorses. Arrange two support pieces on either side of the cut line so that when the cut is complete, both pieces of the sheet are stable.

Use a guide.
Use a guide to make a straight, long cut. Get a straightedge that is as long as the material you are cutting—a straight 1×4 or the factory edge of a piece of plywood. Measure the distance from the edge of the saw's baseplate to the blade and clamp the guide that distance away from the cut line. Set the saw in place and check alignment with the cut line. Clamp the opposite end of the guide the same distance from the edge.

Make a plunge cut.
Use a plunge cut, also called a pocket cut, to make a hole or slit in the middle of a board or sheet. Set the blade to the correct depth. Retract the safety guard and tilt the saw forward, setting the front of the baseplate on your work. Start the saw and lower it slowly into the cut line until the base rests on the stock. Complete the cut.
Note: *Because you will be exposing the blade, any twist could result in a dangerous kickback. Be careful.*

USING A MITER BOX

A miter joint is made when two pieces of wood are angle-cut or bevel-cut at the same angle then joined to form a corner. Most often, two pieces that have been cut at 45 degrees are joined to make a 90-degree corner. Miter cuts must be precise. If they are off even one degree, the corner will be noticeably out of true.

The most inexpensive way to make angle or bevel cuts in narrow stock is to use a miter box—essentially a jig for holding the saw at the proper angle to the work. If you have a lot of joinery to cut, consider buying a power miter saw (see page 213).

Before placing the piece in the miter box, support it on a scrap of 1×4 or some other suitable material. This allows you to saw completely through the work

without marring the bottom of the miter box. Place the member against the far side of the miter box, positioned as it will be when in use, and make the cut with a backsaw. Hold the work firmly against the back of the box with your free hand.

If there's any trick to using a miter box, it's not in the cutting technique, but in correctly measuring and marking for the cut. Whenever possible, make your miter cut first, then cut the other end of the piece to the proper length with a straight cut.

CUTTING WITH A HANDSAW

Although you will probably do most of your cutting with power tools, there are times when a handsaw is more convenient. Learn the proper technique, and hand-cutting may turn out to be easier than you expected.

Make a crosscut with a handsaw.
To make a crosscut with a handsaw in narrow goods, set the blade's heel end (nearest the handle) at a 45-degree angle to the work. Set the teeth on the scrap side of the cut line. To make sure the blade doesn't wander, use your thumbnail as a guide. Pull the saw back toward you several times to start the cut. Don't force the blade; use the weight of the saw to start the cut while you guide it. Saw with a rocking motion, using a steeper angle at the beginning of the downstroke and a flatter angle at its completion. Again, don't force it; let the saw do the work.

Begin at a steep angle...

and end at a flatter angle.

Use thumbnail as a guide.

Finish the cut cleanly.
When you near the end of the cut, support the scrap end of the piece of wood. Grasp it firmly with your free hand, exerting a slight upward pressure to keep it from binding. This also will keep the piece from snapping and splintering on the last stroke.

Make a cutout.
To notch the corner of a board, position the blade of the saw so it is perpendicular to the work as you near the end of each cut. In that way, the bottom of the board is cut the same distance as the top. Often it is helpful to reverse the position of the saw, as shown *above*.

MAKING INSIDE AND CONTOUR CUTS

Often you need to make a cut in the center of a piece of lumber or sheet goods or make a curved or irregularly shaped cut. These cuts require two basic steps. First you need to drill or plunge-cut an access hole in the material. Then you need to use a narrow-bladed tool that can handle curved cuts to follow the contours.

To begin an inside cut, you can use a circular saw to make a plunge cut (see page 235). You will need a sabersaw or handsaw to finish the job. If you find it difficult to make a precise plunge cut, use a drill and sabersaw—especially when the finished work will be highly visible.

Note: *Do not attempt to make a curved cut with a circular saw. Such a practice not only can damage your saw and saw blades, but it also can be dangerous.*

Make an inside cut.
How you start an inside cut depends on the material you're cutting. With lumber and sheet goods, the safest way is to drill a starter hole at each corner of the cutout, as close as possible to the cut lines. Insert the blade of a sabersaw or keyhole saw into one of the holes and complete the cut.

If you are experienced with a sabersaw, make a plunge cut. Tip the saw forward on its baseplate, as shown. Start the saw and slowly lower the blade into the wood along the cut line. A sabersaw blade tends to dance before cutting into the surface, which can badly mar your work. You may want to practice on a scrap of wood first.

Cut holes in drywall.
For a clean cut, score the paper face of the drywall with a knife before sawing it. Poke the tip of a drywall saw (a type of keyhole saw) into the drywall at a cut line. Either push or punch the saw handle with the heel of your hand.

3. Return to make this cut.

2. Make curved cut from first line to second line.

1. Cut to intersection here, then back up.

Cut corners without a pilot hole.
You can maneuver a sabersaw around fairly tight corners, but don't try to make 90-degree turns. Use a three-step procedure to cut such corners. On your first approach to a corner, cut just up to the intersecting line. Carefully

back the saw up about 2 inches and cut a gentle curve over to the next cut line. Continue in this direction, supporting the scrap material as you cut, until the scrap piece is free. Then go back and finish trimming the corners with short, straight cuts.

Cut curves with a sabersaw.

For most contour cuts, use a sabersaw. Once you get the knack of using this tool, you can cut curves that are as smooth as any line you can draw. Be sure the piece you are going to cut is stable; clamp it if necessary. Check that nothing is blocking the path of the blade underneath the piece you are cutting.

Turn the saw on, then begin the cut. Guide the saw slowly, without forcing the blade. One sharp turn can break a blade. If the saw begins to bog down or overheat, you're cutting too fast. If you wander from the line, don't try to make a correction with a sharp turn. Instead, back up and start again. Support the scrap material as you reach the end of each cut to prevent it from breaking off.

Use a coping saw for fine work.

For intricate cutting or scrollwork, use a coping saw. This hand tool allows you to set the blade in any direction in relation to its frame. To begin a cut from the inside of a board, remove the blade from the saw frame and reinstall it through a starter hole. For delicate cuts, install the blade with the teeth angled toward the handle so the saw cuts on the backstroke.

Use coping cuts for moldings.

When you're working with moldings, it's difficult to get perfectly matched mitered joints for inside corners, especially because the corners of walls often are not square. That's why professionals usually cope inside corner joints.

Start by cutting the first piece of molding at a 90-degree angle so it butts against the adjacent wall. To cope the overlapping piece, make an inside 45-degree miter cut, as shown. Use a coping saw to cut away the excess wood along the molding profile. Back-cut slightly (cut a little more off the back of the piece than the front) to ensure a neat fit. Whenever possible, make the cut on the coped end first, hold the piece in place, then mark for the cut on the other end.

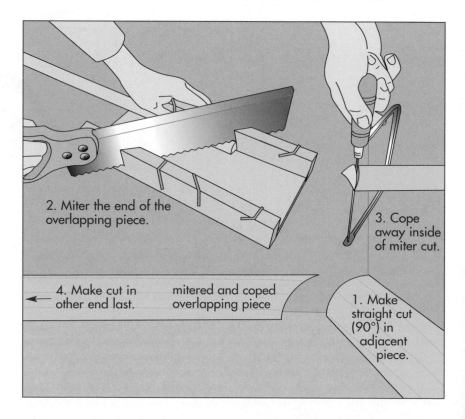

2. Miter the end of the overlapping piece.

3. Cope away inside of miter cut.

4. Make cut in other end last.

mitered and coped overlapping piece

1. Make straight cut (90°) in adjacent piece.

USING CHISELS

Although you may not use a chisel every day, it pays to keep a couple of them on hand. Nothing can replace a chisel for making mortises, dadoes, or notches. An old one often comes in handy for demolition jobs.

Whenever you pick up a chisel, keep both hands behind the cutting face of the blade. As you work, point the chisel away from your body. Because it takes two hands to operate a chisel, always clamp or anchor the material you're working on. Save yourself wasted effort and ruined materials by keeping your chisels sharp. A properly sharpened chisel should slice through paper easily.

TOOLS TO USE

SHARPENING NICKED OR BADLY WORN TOOLS

To sharpen a badly nicked or worn chisel, a single-cut file or a bench grinder works better than a whetstone.

■ To sharpen a chisel with a file, clamp the chisel tightly in a vise with the cutting edge pointing up. Remove nicks by filing nearly perpendicular to the chisel edge. Then hold the file at the same angle as the chisel bevel and file diagonally across the bevel. Work slowly and evenly to obtain a sharp edge. Remove burrs on the flat side with an oiled whetstone.

■ To remove nicks from a chisel's blade with a bench grinder, hold the chisel nearly perpendicular to the wheel and grind until the nicks disappear. Regrind the bevel, using the guide on the grinder to hold the chisel at the bevel angle. Go slowly: Never let the cutting edge blacken or get red hot.

1. To sharpen with a whetstone, grind the cutting edge.
A dull chisel edge will look flat and reflect light. It also may have nicks in it. Drip a pool of oil on a whetstone. Brace the whetstone firmly on a flat surface. Hold the chisel bevel-face-down, at an angle slightly steeper than the bevel, so you are not grinding the entire beveled face. Grind by pressing gently and moving back and forth.

2. Smooth the flat side.
Turn the chisel over and lay its flat side on the whetstone. Add more oil if the stone is dry or if a thick paste has built up. Hone the flat side by pressing gently, moving the chisel with a circular motion. You don't want to grind a new cutting edge on this side; only remove the burrs created after grinding the beveled face.

Notch a piece of framing.
Set your circular saw blade to the desired depth of the notch and make cuts at the top and bottom of the notch. If the notch is wide, make one or more cuts in the center of the notch as well. Position the chisel with the bevel outward. Begin cutting at a slight outward angle that gets flatter as you proceed.

Make a deep mortise cut.
It is difficult to chisel deeply into a narrow board without splintering it. Begin by drilling a series of adjacent holes within the scored outline of the mortise. If possible, use a drill bit that is the same diameter as the width of the mortise. Finish the cut with a chisel, holding the beveled face toward the inside of the mortise as you gently tap.

1. Mark to mortise for a hinge.
Do not attempt to mark a mortise for a hinge with a measuring device. Use the actual hinge as a template. Position it correctly on the edge of the door and mark its perimeter with a sharp pencil. Mark for the thickness of the mortise also.

2. Score the lines.
To prevent the wood grain from splintering at the edges of chisel cuts, score the lines you have just marked by gently cutting with a sharp knife. Once the score lines have been established, go over them again with the knife until you have cut to the depth of the mortise. A butt marker also can be used to score lines.

3. Chisel out the mortise.
Hold the chisel with the beveled face down at the angle shown. Whenever possible, cut in the direction in which the wood grain runs to the edge of the board. Otherwise, the chisel will follow the grain deeper down into the board than you intended. Drive the chisel to the depth of the mortise, making several slices across its width.

1. To make dado notches, first lay out the lines.
When laying out dado cuts across the width of a board, take extra care to draw lines that are straight and square and that mark the exact thickness of the boards that will be set into them. Use a framing or a smaller square to mark both the top and bottom of the cut.

2. Cut lines with a circular saw.
Adjust your circular saw blade to the correct depth—usually one-third of the thickness of the board. Use a speed square (see page 228) or a clamp-on guide to ensure that you stay on the outline marks. After cutting the two outside lines for wide dadoes, make a series of passes through the center of each notch.

3. Chisel out the waste.
Using a chisel the same width or narrower than your dado notches, tap out the remaining slivers of wood. Start from one edge and work toward the middle, then work from the other side. Smooth the bottom of the notch by scraping it with your chisel, flat side down.

DRILLING

Some carpenters still haul out a brace and expandable auger bit when they can't find a spade bit of the right size. But now the electric drill usually is the tool of choice. Not only can you drill a hole of about any size with a variable-speed power drill, but you also can use a drill to drive screws into wood or metal, buff and grind, and even mix paint or mortar.

Some carpenters keep two drills on hand—one for drilling pilot holes, the other for driving screws. That way, they don't waste time changing bits. A power drill with a keyless chuck speeds up a bit change, although you may find bits slip during heavy-duty tasks.

For perfectly perpendicular holes, you'll need a drill press. But if you learn the techniques here and on the next three pages, you can bore holes that are straight enough for household carpentry.

EXPERTS' INSIGHT

CHOOSING A DRILL

■ Avoid buying a cheap drill with a ¼-inch chuck. It will not have the power you need and will soon burn out. One tipoff to a better-quality tool is the cord. Look for a long cord that flexes more like rubber than plastic.

■ A hammer drill, or a drill with a hammer option, bangs away at the material as it drills. It's useful when boring holes in concrete.

■ A cordless drill can make your work go more easily, but only if it is powerful enough to do most things that a corded drill can do.

■ Some drills are designed specifically for driving in drywall screws. These set the head of the screw at the required depth—deep enough to make an indentation, but not so deep that it damages the drywall.

■ Specialized tasks often require a high-speed drill (one with high revolutions per minute). For example, self-tapping steel stud screws (see page 289) require a drill rated to at least 2,500 rpm.

■ For heavy-duty work, choose a drill with a ½-inch chuck. This will run at fewer revolutions per minute, but will be more powerful than a standard ⅜-inch drill.

For additional information on choosing a drill, see page 211.

solid-center auger bit
masonry bit
countersink bit
twist bit
spade bit
star drill
screwdriver bit
awl
brad-point bit
holesaw
combination bit
expandable auger bit

Choose the correct bit.
Shown at *left* are some of the more common drill bits. **Auger** bits, either solid-center or expandable, are designed to be used with a hand brace, as is a **screwdriver** bit. For holes ½ inch or smaller in diameter, use **twist** bits. A **brad-point** bit makes a cleaner hole than a twist bit. For holes from ½ to 1¼ inches in diameter, use a **spade** bit. For making holes in masonry or concrete, use a carbide-tipped **masonry** bit or a **star drill,** which you drive with a hammer. A **countersink** bit bores a shallow hole so you can set screw heads flush with or below the surface. A **combination** bit drills both a pilot hole and a countersink hole in one step. Use a simple **awl** to prepare the way for a small screw. For holes larger than 1¼ inches, and/or for drilling precise holes through tough materials, use a **holesaw.**

Start upright, then move to the desired angle.

Make a starter hole.

Drill bits tend to skate away when you begin boring holes, so make a shallow starter hole with an awl or a center punch. In softwoods, a gentle tap on an awl with the palm of your hand will do the job. With hardwoods or metal, you may need to tap the center punch or awl with a hammer.

Improvise a guide.

Usually, you'll want to drill holes perpendicular to the board. Check the bit for square as it enters the material by clamping a piece of square-cut scrap lumber in place, as shown. With some drills, you can hold a square on the material and against the body of the drill.

Sometimes you'll want your bit to enter the material at an angle.

Fashion a guide by cutting the edge of a piece of scrap lumber to the desired angle of your hole. Clamp the guide so it aligns the tip of the bit exactly on your center mark. Begin the hole by drilling perpendicular to the surface. Once you have gone deep enough to keep the bit from skating away, shift the drill to the correct angle.

Mark with tape at desired depth.

Mark the bit for depth.

When you want to drill one or more holes to a certain depth, wrap masking or electrical tape around your drill bit so the bottom edge of the tape contacts the surface of the material at the desired depth. Drill with gentle pressure. Back the bit out as soon as the tape touches the surface of the material.

starter bit   holesaw

Use a holesaw.

When drilling large-diameter holes with a holesaw, make a starter hole on your center mark to guide the starter bit. To ensure that the other side of the material doesn't splinter when the bit penetrates it, clamp a piece of scrap stock against the other side. Or, drill just far enough so the starter bit pokes through, then drill from the other side.

CAUTION!
AVOID DAMAGING YOUR DRILL BITS AND DRILL

Drilling is a simple procedure, but it's easy to dull or break a drill bit. Be careful not to overheat the bit; an overheated bit will become dull quickly. If you see smoke, stop drilling immediately. Pause once in a while and test the bit for heat by quickly tapping it with your finger. If you own a homeowner-type drill rather than a professional model, it is not designed for constant use. If you feel the body of the drill heating up, stop and give it a rest, or you could burn it out. Hold the drill firmly upright as you work. If you tip the tool while drilling, there's a good chance the bit will break.

Drill until point of spade bit barely pierces material.

Drill from the other side to complete the hole.

Back up to pull wood particles out.

Clean particles from the flute.

Avoid splinters with a spade bit.
When using a spade bit, drill through the material until the tip of the bit begins to poke out the back side of the material. Carefully reverse the bit out of the hole. Complete the hole by drilling from the other side, using the pilot hole you've just made.

Keep particles from clogging hole.
When you drill deep holes into thick material, wood particles build up in the hole, clogging the bit and causing it to bind. Don't force the bit in farther than it wants to go or you will burn it out. Instead, feed the bit into the wood slowly and back out of the hole frequently with the drill

motor still running. This will pull trapped wood particles to the surface. If you're working with sappy or wet wood, shavings may clog the flute of the bit. If this happens, stop the drill, and use the tip of a nail to scrape out the shavings. If the bit jams, reverse the drill rotation. Pull the bit straight up and out.

1. Drill pilot hole.

2. Enlarge for screw.

3. Countersink for screw head.

4. Insert the screw.

For flush screw heads, drill to this point.

For countersunk screw heads, drill to this point.

For the best fit, drill three holes...
When you use wood screws to fasten two pieces of material together, take the time to provide clearance for the screw to ensure easy driving and to avoid splits. Using a bit that is slightly smaller than the screw, drill through the top and bottom piece. Then select a bit that is as thick as the screw shank and drill through the top board. The screw should slide easily through this top hole and grip tightly as it passes into the smaller hole. Use a countersink bit to bore a space for the screw head. When you drive the screw, it will fit without cracking the wood.

or use a combination bit.
If you're driving a lot of screws, buy a combination countersink-counterbore bit, which drills three holes in one action. Be sure to get the correct bits for the screws you will be driving. If you want the screw head to be flush with the surface, drill until the spot marked on the bit is even with the surface. To counterbore the screw head, drill deeper.

EXPERTS' INSIGHT

DRILLING THROUGH METAL

If you need to make a hole in metal, it is best to use a high-quality titanium bit. But if you work carefully, you can drill through metal with any sharp twist bit. The trick is to keep the bit and the metal lubricated with light oil at all times. If the bit is dry for even a couple of seconds while drilling, it can burn out and become dull.

Before you start, drip motor oil onto the bit and the spot to be drilled. Add oil as you work. Take your time, stopping often to make sure the bit is oiled and not overheating.

If you need to drill a hole larger than ¼ inch in diameter, drill a smaller hole first, then use a bigger bit.

Drill into masonry and concrete.
Use a masonry bit when drilling into brick or concrete surfaces. Usually, brick is easy to drill into and concrete is more difficult. Check the bit often to make sure it's not overheating. If you see smoke, stop immediately.

Here is a trick that works surprisingly well: Spray the bit and the hole with window cleaner as you work. Not only does this keep the bit cool, but the foaming action of the cleaner brings debris up and out of the hole.

Occasionally when drilling into concrete, you will run into an especially hard spot (usually a rock embedded in the concrete). Take the bit out, insert a masonry nail or thin cold chisel, and bang with a hammer to crack the rock and give your bit a place to grab. If you have a lot of masonry drilling to do, buy a hammer drill, which bangs away as you drill.

Drill through ceramic tile.
Wall tiles are usually soft, but floor tiles can be very tough. Nick the surface of the tile just enough so the bit will not wander as you drill. Keep the bit and the hole lubricated with a few drops of oil. Use a masonry bit or a special tile bit like the one shown *above*.

Use a brace and expandable bit.
A brace is an old-fashioned tool that works faster than you may expect. To drill large diameter holes, bore until the lead screw of the bit pokes through the material. Then drill through from the other side. To get more pressure on the brace, hold its head against your body and lean into the work.

Bore and plug for a finished look.
For a handcrafted appearance, drill pilot holes, then drill a wooden plug using a plug-cutting bit. Drive the screw in, squirt a little white glue into the hole, and tap in the plug. Allow the plug to stick out slightly. After the glue has dried, chisel and sand the plug flush with the surface.

USING A TABLESAW

When shopping for a tablesaw, use a straightedge to check the table; it should be a perfectly flat plane. If the table has extensions, make sure they are flat as well. A small, lightweight tablesaw is handy if you need to move it around often. However, the smaller table area makes it more difficult to use, and you will have a hard time making accurate cuts on large pieces of material.

The fence of a tablesaw should move smoothly along its guide rails and lock firmly and exactly parallel to the blade.

If possible, turn the saw on and watch the blade. There should be no hint of a wobble. A belt-driven tablesaw works more smoothly and lasts longer than one with direct drive.

EXPERTS' INSIGHT

TABLESAW, RADIAL-ARM SAW, OR POWER MITER SAW?

■ A tablesaw and a power miter saw make an ideal combination. With a tablesaw, you can make straight, long cuts with ease. A tablesaw also is superior for cutting dadoes. With a power miter saw, you can crosscut long narrow pieces easily—a task that can be tricky with a tablesaw.

■ A radial-arm saw does the jobs of a tablesaw and power miter saw, but not quite as well. It crosscuts with less precision than the miter saw. Cutting angles other than 90 degrees may be a problem. Making long rip cuts in sheets of plywood also is difficult.

CAUTION!

SAFETY MEASURES FOR A TABLESAW

Because a tablesaw runs so smoothly and seems so stable, it's easy to lose safety-consciousness while working with one. A tablesaw is a tool worthy of respect. Many professionals have had parts of fingers cut off by a tablesaw blade.

Always keep your fingers well away from the blade. Never wear long sleeves or loose clothing. Never reach across the saw blade while it is running. Keep push sticks and an anti-kickback featherboard handy and develop the habit of using them (see page 246). Turn the saw off when you need to free a piece of wood that has become stuck.

Make a rip cut.
Check that the fence is perfectly parallel to the blade by measuring the space between the blade and the fence at the front and the rear of the blade. Set the blade depth so it is ¼ inch above the top of the board. Start the motor and allow it to reach full speed. Hold the lumber against the fence so the wood glides smoothly and is flush against it at all points as you push it forward. Never allow your fingers to come within 6 inches of the blade; use a push stick when you come to the end of the cut (see page 246).

Make a crosscut.
Make sure the miter gauge is exactly perpendicular to the blade; slip it into its channel and square it using the edge of the table as a guide. Set the blade depth ¼ inch above the board and start the motor. Hold the board firmly against the miter guide and slide it toward the blade. Hold the board only at the miter gauge. If you hold the wood on both sides of the cut, the blade may bind, causing a dangerous kickback. Keep your fingers well away from the blade.

Make a bevel rip cut.

To set the bevel, use the saw gauge or mark the bevel angle on the butt end of the board and tilt the blade until it aligns with the mark. Hold the board against the blade at the correct location, slide the fence against the board, and lock the fence in position. Follow the same procedures as for a rip cut (see page 245).

Always set the height correctly.

Before every cut, adjust the blade depth so it is about ¼ inch above the top of the board you are cutting. This makes a cleaner cut and helps avoid binding and a dangerous kickback. If you are cutting a sheet of plywood that is warped, you may need to raise the blade higher, so it cuts through the sheet completely at all points. Always unplug the tablesaw before making blade adjustments.

Use push sticks and featherboard.

To make an anti-kickback featherboard, cut one end of a 16-inch-long 1×6 at 60 degrees, then cut 8-inch-long slots ¼ inch apart on the angled end. When clamped as shown *above,* it ensures a straight cut and prevents kickback in case the blade binds. Make push sticks out of 1× lumber or ½-inch plywood and use them whenever you need to hold the board within 6 inches of the blade.

Cut dadoes, rabbets, and tenons.

With a dado blade, you can make a variety of groove sizes. With a regular dado blade, sandwich a combination of chippers between the two outside cutter blades to get your desired width. To set the blade to the desired depth, mark the depth on the board and hold it next to the blade as you adjust it. Adjustable dado blades dial to the desired width.

If you need to make a groove wider than the dado blade, make repeated passes, moving the board a little less than the width of the blade for each pass.

On a tablesaw, you will not be able to see the cut as you make it, so test your settings on a scrap piece to make sure the dado is the correct width and depth. Then make the real cut.

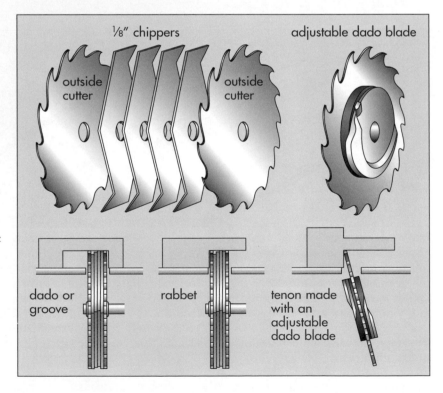

USING A RADIAL-ARM OR POWER MITER SAW

A radial-arm saw works best for crosscutting wood, but you can use it for ripping as well as long as you take it slowly and use precautions (see below right). With attachments available on some models, you can use a radial-arm saw as a router or a sander.

A radial-arm saw table is made of particleboard or plywood rather than metal because the saw blade must cut into the table slightly to cut boards completely. When the tabletop becomes shredded after years of use, you should replace it. The fence, usually a piece of 1×2, needs to be replaced more often.

A power miter saw is designed for two purposes only: miter-cutting and crosscutting small-width boards (usually 1×6 or smaller). Highly portable, a power miter saw sets up easily on a couple of sawhorses. It's ideal for cutting molding on the spot.

Make a miter cut or crosscut.
Test your saw for accuracy by cutting scraps at 45 and 90 degrees and adjust the fence or the saw if necessary. To make the cut, hold the board firmly against the fence. Make sure the board is fully supported and lies flat on the table. Pull the saw toward you, cutting the board so the saw kerf is on the scrap side of the line.

Cut a dado or rabbet.
To cut a notch for a dado or rabbet, raise the blade to the desired height; test the cut depth on a scrap. Check that the board lies flat; any warp will distort the cut. Cut on each side of the notch, then make a series of cuts in the interior. Clean out the notch with a chisel. If you have a lot of notching to do, use dado blades.

Make a rip cut or beveled rip cut.
Turn the saw so the blade rotates up against the board, the opposite of a crosscut or dado cut. Start the saw with the blade slightly raised above the tabletop, then lower it to the cut line. To avoid kickback, hold the board firmly as you feed it into the blade. Pull the board through the blade to finish the cut.

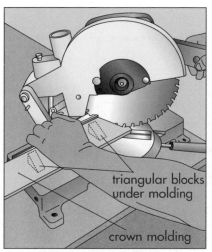

Cut molding with a chopsaw.
Hold the piece firmly against the fence, start the saw, and lower the blade to make the cut. In many cases, the cut will not begin at the edge of a board, but in the middle; make your marks accordingly. When cutting crown molding, hold wood at the correct angle with triangular blocks.

CAUTION!
DEVELOP SAFETY HABITS
Radial-arm or power miter saws can be extremely dangerous. Not only can you cut yourself with the blades, but a radial-arm saw almost certainly will kick a board back at bullet-like speed if you are not careful. Develop these safety habits:

■ *Never remove the saw guard. Take the time to adjust the guard for maximum safety before making each cut.*

■ *When ripping boards with a radial-arm saw, use a push stick and featherboard like those for a tablesaw (see page 246). Also, stand to the side of the board, so if it does shoot back, it won't hit you.*

■ *Keep work well supported so the blade will not bind.*

USING A ROUTER

With the versatility and power of a router, you can custom-design and mill lumber to your own specifications. In addition to choosing among a wide variety of bits (shown *below*), you can set your bit to the depth of cut that suits you. Often, it's possible to save money by milling your own lumber rather than buying expensive moldings. For rounding off edges, a router produces a far more professional-looking finish than does a rasp or sander.

> ## CAUTION!
> ### BITS ARE SHARP!
> *Most of the time, you will not even see your router bit as you work. Don't let that lull you into complacency: A router's sharp bit, rotating at tremendous speeds, can do a lot of damage in a millisecond. Keep your hands well away from the work.*

Use a guide.
You can make accurate cuts using a router guide. Sometimes a simple straightedge will suffice; just hold the baseplate tight against it as you cut. A template guide like the one shown allows you to follow a precut template. You may want to purchase a router table, which holds the router in an upside-down position; you can adjust and operate it much as you would a tablesaw.

Move router counterclockwise for best cut.

Use specialty guides.
A variety of guides is available for special purposes. To cut smooth circles or curves, use a trammel-point guide like the one shown. A router bit spins clockwise, so you will get the best results if you move the router counterclockwise. You also can buy guides for cutting dovetail joints or hinge mortises.

flush trim | rabbet | straight cut | dado | core box
chamfer | corner round | plunge cut | V-groove | dovetail

Choose among many bits.
Piloted bits, such as the **flush trim, rabbet, chamfer,** and **corner round**, are self-guiding; you don't need to use a guide or template when cutting with them. Use these bits to shape edges of boards or to final-cut laminates

after they have been applied. Bits with ball-bearing guides usually work more smoothly.

The other bits shown require a guide or a steady hand. You can use two or more bits in succession to make intricate shapes.

EXPERTS' INSIGHT

CHOOSING A ROUTER

■ As a general rule, the more power a router has, the cleaner and faster it will cut. Get one that is at least 1 horsepower. A variable-speed router has some advantages because some bits are designed to be used at lower speeds than others.

■ Buy a model that can be attached to a table easily or that has a variety of guides you can assemble quickly. You don't want to spend half your work time setting up the router.

■ Be sure you can change bits quickly and adjust the router depth easily.

NAILING

*T*he quickest way to make a job look shoddy and amateurish is to make a nailing mistake that mars the wood. All your careful measuring and cutting will be for naught if the wood ends up with "smiles" and "frowns" made by a hammer that missed the nail, or if you bend a nail while driving it.

Professional carpenters make nailing look easy—and for good reason. When properly done, pounding a nail home is not a struggle, but is done with smooth, fluid motions. You may never be as fast at nailing as professionals because they get plenty of practice, but you can learn to drive in nails accurately without damaging the material or yourself.

Set the nail.
Practice on scrap pieces before you pound nails into finished work. To ensure that the hammer strikes the nail and not your fingers and that the nail will be driven into the board squarely, grasp the nail near its head and the hammer near the end of the handle. Lightly tap the nail until it stands by itself.

If you must drive a nail near the end of a board, drill a pilot hole or turn the nail upside down and blunt its point with a hammer. Either technique will reduce the risk of splitting the wood.

Use proper nailing techniques.
Once the nail is set in place, remove your hand from it. Keep your eye on the nail as you swing the hammer, letting the weight of the hammer head do the driving.

Beginners tend to hold a hammer stiffly and keep their shoulders stiff, swinging from the elbow. This leads to a tired, sore arm and to mistakes. Loosen up. Your whole arm should move as you swing from the shoulder. Keep your wrist loose so the hammer can give a final "snap" at the end of each blow. The entire motion should be relaxed and smooth.

With the last hammer blow, push the head of the nail flush or nearly flush with the surface of the wood. The convex shape of the hammer face allows you to do this without marring the surface.

EXPERTS' INSIGHT

GETTING THE HOLDING POWER YOU NEED

■ How well a nail will hold in wood depends on how much of its surface contacts the wood. The longer and thicker the nail, the better it will hold.

■ When possible, use the Rule of Three: A nail should be three times as long as the thickness of the board being fastened. Two-thirds of the nail then will be in the second board to which you are fastening the first one. If the nail must penetrate through dead space or drywall, increase the nail length by that distance.

■ A thick nail holds better, but not if it splits the wood. In that case, most of its holding power is lost. Special nails, such as ring-shank and cement-coated nails, hold better than standard nails. A headed nail holds better than a finish nail.

Countersink finishing nails.

In most cases, it's best to drive the heads of finishing or casing nails below the surface. You can fill the hole with wood putty later. This actually doesn't take all that long and leads to a much better-looking finish than nails driven flush. Hold a nail set against the nailhead and tap it in.

Stagger nails to avoid splits.

When driving several nails along the length of a board, stagger them so you don't split the board. The idea is to avoid pounding neighboring nails through the same grain line; two nails will stress the grain twice as much as one nail. If the work will be visible, stagger the nails in a regular pattern.

Drill pilot holes.

When you nail within 2 inches of the end of a board or into hardwood, drill pilot holes to avoid splitting the wood. Pilot holes should be slightly smaller than the diameter of the nail. When attaching a base shoe, drive nails into pilot holes so they miss the flooring, which needs room to expand and contract with changes in temperature and humidity.

EXPERTS' INSIGHT

USING MASONRY NAILS

■ Masonry nails offer a quick way to attach materials to concrete, brick, and masonry block. With flat-style masonry nails, be sure to turn the nail in the direction of the grain so it's less likely to split the wood.

■ You can use a standard hammer, but the job is easier with a heavy mallet. Hold the board in place, and drive the masonry nail through it. Once the nail hits the masonry surface, strike it with hard strokes. With subsequent nails, check to see if you have dislodged any nails; you may have to put in more.

Skew nails for a stronger hold.

In situations where you cannot use as long a nail as you would like, drive nails in at an angle. Drive in one nail at about a 60-degree angle in one direction, then drive in another one in the opposite direction. The skewed nails will work together, making it difficult for the board to pull loose. Set the nailheads into the surface for a finished appearance.

Clinch nails for the best hold.

If looks are not important, but strength is, use nails about 1 inch longer than the thickness of the pieces you're fastening. Drive in the nails, then turn the boards over and bend the exposed portion of the nails so they are nearly flush with the surface and parallel to the wood grain. The resulting joint will be extremely difficult to pull apart.

FASTENING WITH SCREWS

It's not hard to see why screws fasten so well. The threads grip wood fibers in a way that a smooth nail cannot. When the screw is driven home, the threads exert tremendous pressure against the screw head to hold the fastener firmly in place. With the right tools (see box below), driving screws can be almost as quick as nailing. If you make a mistake, it's easy to remove a screw without damaging your work. Screws must be driven with care, however. If you do not start out straight, there is no way to correct the mistake as you continue driving the screw. Without a pilot hole, the screw may split the wood and the screw will not hold securely. If the pilot hole is too large, again, the screw will not grip well.

Make a starter hole with an awl.
Small screws seldom require pilot holes (see the box, below right). However, they do need a starter hole. Poke a hole with a scratch awl. Give it a few twists, back it out, and you're ready to drive in the screw.

Drive with a hand screwdriver.
Start screws by holding the screwdriver handle with one hand and the screwdriver blade with the other. Don't hold the screw. If the screw is spinning around and not going into the wood, put two hands on the handle to apply more pressure.

TOOLS TO USE

Power-driven screws hold tightly, go in quickly, and are removed easily. Here are some tools that make working with them even more convenient.
■ A variable-speed, reversible drill starts the screws slowly and removes them if necessary.
■ With a magnetic sleeve, screws stick to the bit, making it easy to drive them in hard-to-reach places. Changing bit tips is easy; simply press them into the sleeve.
■ Have on hand a collection of drill bit tips, particularly #1 and #2 Phillips bits and some slotted bits, as well.
■ Consider buying square-headed screws and bits. These bits fit into and grab the screw slot better than Phillips-head and slotted screws.

slotted screw bit

Power-drive slotted screws.
Even a few screws can take a long time to drive by hand, so consider using a drill with a screwdriver bit. When driving slotted screws, take care that the bit does not wander partway out of the slot, or you could damage the surface into which you are screwing. Don't drive screws too quickly, or the bit may slip out of the slot. Maintain firm, even pressure as you work.

EXPERTS' INSIGHT

WHEN DO YOU NEED A PILOT HOLE?

If there is a danger of cracking the wood, you should always drill a pilot hole, no matter how small the screw. For instance, if the wood is brittle or if you will be driving a screw near the end of a board, almost any screw can split the wood. But if you are drilling into a sound board at a spot 2 inches or more from its end, it usually will be safe to drive in a No. 6 or thinner screw without a pilot hole. If you are drilling into plywood or framing lumber, you should be able to drive No. 8 screws without pilot holes. For advice on selecting the correct-size bit, see page 241.

Use Phillips-head drywall screws.

You can buy drywall screws by the pound at bargain prices and drive them into most materials in which you would use nails. If you use a magnetic sleeve, place the screw on the bit first, then set the tip of the screw in place on the material. If you need to hold the screw to keep it from wandering, hold the head only, not the sharp threads.

Attach items to walls with special wall fasteners.

If you need to attach something to a wall, the ideal way is to drive a screw into a stud. But often that's not possible. The screws and bolts shown *above* are designed to hold items firmly in drywall or plaster walls. To use **expanding anchors** and **plastic anchors**, drill holes and tap the unit into the wall; the

anchor will spread and grip as you tighten the screw. Use **self-drilling anchors** only in drywall. You don't need to drill a hole; just screw them in and insert a screw. To use a **toggle bolt**, drill a hole large enough for the folded-back toggles to fit through. Push the toggles through the hole, and turn the bolt until the toggles snug up to the back side of the wall.

Screw into end grain.

When a fastener is driven into the end grain of a board, it will not hold as well as it does across the grain because it runs parallel to the grain rather than at an angle to it. Use a longer screw than you usually would. Where holding power is critical, drill a hole and install a dowel, as shown, into which you can drive the screw.

Deal with hard-to-drive screws.

If the going gets tough, the screw may stop turning. Exert pressure on the screwdriver with the palm of one hand and turn it with the other. If you still can't drive it, remove the screw and drill a slightly larger pilot hole. Another solution is to lubricate the threads with candle wax and try again.

EXPERTS' INSIGHT

FASTENING TO METAL WITH SCREWS

■ For fastening thin sheet metal or soft metal, such as brass, you can use one of several types of self-tapping sheet-metal screws (see page 222). Simply drive the screw in; it makes its own path with a metal-cutting point.

■ For heavier metals, drill a pilot hole using the techniques for drilling through metal (see page 244). Then install a sheet-metal screw.

■ For metal $\frac{1}{8}$ inch or thicker and where you want an extra-strong joint, buy a drill-and-tap kit. With this, you can make a machine-threaded hole that will accept a machine bolt.

FASTENING WITH BOLTS

Nails and screws depend on friction between the fastener and the wood to do their job. When you tighten a nut on a bolt, however, you're actually clamping adjoining members together, producing the sturdiest of all joints. All types of bolts require a hole bored through both pieces being joined together. Here's information about installing machine and carriage bolts. For help with toggle bolts and other anchors, see page 287.

CAUTION!
Overtightening bolts can strip threads and damage wood, reducing the holding power of the bolt. Tighten the nut and bolt firmly against the wood, give them another half turn, then stop.

Fasten with machine bolts.
Machine bolts have hexagonal heads and threads running partway or all the way along the shank. When fastening two pieces of wood together, slip a flat washer onto the bolt and slide the bolt through the holes in both pieces of material. Add another flat washer, then a lock washer. Screw the nut on and tighten it. The flat washer keeps the nut and the bolt head from biting into the wood. The lock washer prevents the nut from coming loose. Use two wrenches to draw the nut down onto the bolt: one to steady the nut, the other to turn the bolt head.

Tighten a countersunk bolt head.
To install a machine bolt in a hard-to-get-at place or when you have to countersink the bolt head, use a socket wrench with a socket extension to reach into the recess. Hold the nut with another wrench.

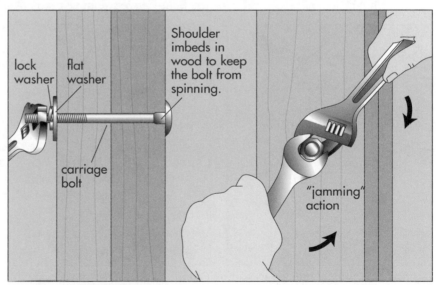

Install a carriage bolt.
A carriage bolt has a plain, round head. Insert it into the hole and tap the head flush with the surface. Slip a flat washer, a lock washer, and a nut onto the bolt. Tighten the nut. The square or hexagonal shoulder under the bolt head keeps the bolt from spinning as the nut is tightened. No washer is needed under the head.

The lock washer should keep the bolt from working loose. As added protection, you can thread another nut onto the bolt, snug it against the first, then "jam" the two together by turning them in opposite directions.

REMOVING NAILS AND SCREWS

Mistakes are a part of every carpenter's day. In fact, knowing how to undo mistakes is one of the hallmarks of an experienced carpenter, and that necessitates a good knowledge of how to remove nails and screws. Whether you're correcting mistakes, disassembling an old structure, or recycling used lumber, you'll find it's worth it to learn how to remove old fasteners quickly and neatly.

Removing screws often is just a matter of reversing your drill and screwing the old fastener out. However, you may be faced with a stripped head or an extra-tight screw (see page 255).

Most commonly, you'll be faced with removing nails. Don't just start whacking away in frustration, or you'll damage the wood. Use these methods and accept that nail removal is a normal part of a carpenter's job.

Pry with a flat bar.
If the head of the nail has not been set into the wood, it may be possible to shoehorn a flat bar under it and pry the nail up. Tap the notch of the chisel-like head of the bar under the nailhead and pull back on the bar. Because of its smooth, flat body, a pry bar makes only a slight indentation in the board as you remove the nail.

Use a wood block.
There are two good reasons for using a wood block when removing a nail. First, the raised height gives your hammer extra leverage, making it much easier to pull the nail out. Second, the block protects your work. Without it, the head of the hammer would dig in and make an unsightly indentation.

Pound so claws grab nailhead.

Lever nail out of wood.

Dig nails out with a cat's paw.
A cat's paw removes nails that are embedded deeply in lumber. Its drawback is that it also must bite deeply into the wood to grip the nailhead. Place the clawed tip behind the nailhead at a 45-degree angle. Pound the claws under the nailhead, pry the nail partway out, then use a hammer and block.

Tap out to release nails.

Tap in to expose nailheads.

Pound out board to loosen nails.
If you have access to the back side of the joined material, strike the joint from behind, then hammer the members back together from the front. This usually pops the nailheads out far enough for you to get hold of them with your hammer claw.

tight-work hacksaw

Cut the nails.
Where access is tight, sometimes you can disjoin two members by sawing through the nails. If you have a reciprocating saw with a metal-cutting blade, this will be easy. Otherwise, use a tight-work hacksaw. After you break the joint, use a nail set to force the heads out, then remove the nails.

Punch through and pry.

To avoid splitting molding, punch the finishing nails that hold it in place through the molding with a nail set. Try not to make the hole larger; use a small-diameter nail set. Pound the head of the finishing nail deeply into the molding. You'll feel the board come loose. Once the nails are punched through, pry off the molding with a putty knife or chisel, taking care not to mar the wood.

Clean out a painted screw head.

When removing old screws that have been painted, take the time to clean the paint out of the slots. If you don't clean the head, you may strip the screw head, making it even more difficult to remove. Place a screwdriver as shown *above,* and tap with a hammer.

EXPERTS' INSIGHT

REMOVING OLD SCREWS

Here are some tips for removing stubborn old screws:

■ For a slotted screw that has been stripped so much that a screwdriver can't get a good hold, deepen the slot by cutting into it with a hacksaw.

■ Extremely tight screws often can be loosened with heat. Hold the tip of a soldering gun against the screw head for a minute or two, then try it.

■ For stripped Phillips-head screws, it sometimes helps to drill a small hole in the center of the head to give the screwdriver more to grab onto.

■ For an extremely stubborn screw, buy a screw and bolt extracting tool. Drill a small hole in the screw head, insert the tool, turn it with a wrench, and twist the screw out.

Add force to a screwdriver.

If you need greater turning power, use a screwdriver with a square shank in conjunction with an adjustable wrench. Adjust the wrench so it fits tightly on the screwdriver. Press down on the handle of the screwdriver with the palm of your hand as you turn with the wrench.

Cut a stubborn nut.

Rusty or damaged bolt threads make it hard to remove a nut. You can solve the problem quickly with a hacksaw. Align the saw blade so it rubs against the threads and cut down through the nut. You will cut off about one-third of the nut. Once you have done this, it will be easy to knock the nut loose or unscrew it.

GLUING AND CLAMPING

A joint will be stronger if you use glue in addition to nails or screws. For some projects that do not require great strength, glue alone will be enough.

Use contact cement to attach wood veneers or plastic laminates to wood surfaces. Apply the cement to both surfaces and let them dry. Align the parts precisely before you join them—the first bond is permanent (see page 258). Use paneling adhesives to attach sheet goods to walls. For interior projects, use carpenter's glue with aliphatic resin. This is superior to standard white glue because it sets up faster, resists heat and moisture better, and is stronger. For the glue to work, however, the pieces must be clamped together firmly until the glue sets.

Use speedy squeeze clamps.
For light work, these are the easiest clamps to use. Apply glue to both pieces and place them together in correct alignment. Squeeze the clamp handles to spread the jaws. When you release the handles, the springs will clamp the work together. You may want to have several sizes of these inexpensive clamps on hand.

Use the right clamp for the job.
C-clamps are inexpensive and work well when the pieces are not too wide. Use blocks of wood to keep the clamps from marring the boards. For miter joints, use **miter clamps** that hold the boards at a

90-degree angle. For large projects, use **pipe clamps**. You should alternate them to prevent buckling. A **strap clamp** works well for cabinetry projects. It will clamp several joints at once and will not mar the wood.

Use handscrew clamps for angles.
These clamps work well for cabinetmaking and other woodworking projects. Because their jaws are made of wood, you don't have to worry about marring your project. Adjust the clamp to almost any size or angle by simply turning the two handscrews.

CAULKING AND APPLYING MASTIC

It takes practice before you can lay down a clean-looking bead of caulk. Practice on scrap materials or start in an inconspicuous area before you caulk an area that is highly visible.

Choose among a wide variety of adhesives that are designed for particular jobs (see the chart, *below right*). When working with adhesives, be careful to apply the material smoothly and evenly, so the piece will adhere uniformly. Avoid applying too much adhesive; cleaning up messes can take longer than the actual job.

YOU'LL NEED

TIME: About 20 minutes to caulk around a bathtub or countertop; 10 to 30 minutes to adhere laminate or paneling.
SKILLS: Smooth, steady control.
TOOLS: Utility knife, caulking gun, notched trowel.

Apply a bead of caulk.
Make sure the joint to be caulked is free of dirt and grease and there are no gaps wider than your bead of caulk. Snip the nozzle of the caulk tube at about a 45-degree angle. The closer to the tip you cut, the smaller the bead will be. You may need to puncture the inside seal with a long nail. Squeeze the handle until caulk starts coming out; move smoothly to apply an even bead.

Attach paneling with adhesive.
To attach paneling to walls, apply a bead of adhesive on either the wall or the back of the panel. Use a notched trowel or make a squiggle pattern using a caulking gun. Press the panel against the wall, then pull it out slightly. Wait for a few minutes for the adhesive to get tacky (the manufacturer's instructions will tell you how long), then press the materials together again.

Apply with a notched trowel.
For a smooth, even application, use a notched trowel to apply adhesives. Check the adhesive container for the type and size of notches the trowel should have. Apply the adhesive with the trowel held nearly parallel to the surface to make sure it sticks. Tilt the trowel up at about a 45-degree angle and press firmly as you spread the adhesive.

SELECTING ADHESIVES

Adhesive Type	Primary Use	Holding Power	Moisture-Resistance	Set/Cure Time	Type of Applicator
Contact cement	Applying wood veneer and plastic laminate.	Excellent	Excellent	Must dry first/ 1–2 days	Brush, notched trowel, or paint roller
Epoxy adhesive	Bonding almost any materials. Must mix the parts.	Excellent	Excellent	30 minutes/ 1–10 hours	Throwaway brush or flat stick
Panel adhesive	Attaching drywall or paneling to walls.	Good	Good	1 hour/ 24 hours	Caulk tube or notched trowel
Carpenter's glue	Bonding wood together for small projects.	Good	Fair	30 minutes/ 24 hours	Squeeze-type container
Cyanoacrylate (superglue)	Bonding small items of most any material.	Good	Fair	1–2 minutes/ 24 hours	Squeeze tube

APPLYING LAMINATE

Plastic laminate comes in a variety of colors, patterns, and textures. With practice and the right tools, you can lay down laminate as well, if not as quickly, as a professional.

Be sure that the surface to which you are attaching the laminate is straight, smooth, and supported so it will not flex. New particleboard works best, although laminate also can be applied to plywood and old laminate.

YOU'LL NEED

TIME: About half a day to cover a couple of straightforward countertops.
SKILLS: Accurate measuring and cutting, smooth application of cement, use of a router.
TOOLS: Circular saw or carbide-tipped knife; brush, paint roller, or notched trowel; roller; router, file, or sanding block.

Support piece to avoid cracks.

1. Cut the laminate.
Cut the laminate so it is about ½ inch larger than the surface in both directions; you'll trim it exactly after it is installed. Cut it with a circular saw or score its face with a carbide-tipped knife. Cut with the face up if you are using a tablesaw or with the face down if you are using a circular saw.

particleboard

contact cement

2. Apply the adhesive.
Choose professional-grade contact cement, which costs a bit more than the homeowner-type cement. Spread it evenly on the back of the laminate and the base surface, using a brush, paint roller, or a notched trowel. Allow both surfaces to dry completely before adhering.

3. Attach the laminate.
Cover the surface with brown wrapping paper and position the laminate on top. When the laminate is exactly where you want it, carefully pull out the paper. Roll the entire surface with a rolling pin, starting in the middle and working outward.

4. Attach edging, and trim.
Attach the edging pieces so they butt tightly against the underside of the top laminate piece. To finish the project, trim the overhanging edges of laminate with a router, file, or sanding block. Take care not to crack the laminate or lift it up as you work.

TOOLS TO USE

■ For the best results, use a router with a special laminate edging bit. This will give you smooth, professional-looking edges that you can't get with a sanding block, rasp, or file. Experiment with the router on scrap pieces to get the depth of the bit set right; if it is too deep, you will cut away too much and ruin the project.
■ For small jobs or for areas where the router can't reach, use a sanding block or a rasp. Work slowly. If you sand away too much laminate, there is no way to fix it.

MAKING SIMPLE, STRONG JOINTS

Strong, good-looking wood joints are essential to all carpentry and woodworking projects. Here are some of the simplest and strongest joinery methods. Each of these joints can be made with hand tools, but if you have shop tools, such as a tablesaw or power miter saw, the job will go faster and the joint will be tighter. None of them requires cabinetmaking expertise.

You'll need to hone your measuring, cutting, and fastening skills to make neat, sturdy joints. See pages 225–242 for a review of the basic techniques.

All of the joints shown on this page are **butt joints**—two square-cut pieces joined together by positioning the end of one member against the face or edge of another member. A butt joint can be fastened with nails or screws only. It will be stronger, however, if reinforced with corner braces, T-plates, angle brackets, dowels, a plywood gusset, or a wood block.

YOU'LL NEED

TIME About 10 to 20 minutes per joint, depending on complexity.
SKILLS: Ability to make square cuts, drill, use fasteners.
TOOLS: Square, ruler, pencil, saw, drill, drill bits, hammer, nail set, screwdriver.

Butt joints

angle brackets

T-plate

wood block

corner braces

plywood overlap

corrugated fastener with dowels

flat corner iron

dowels

plywood gusset

Lap joints are stronger than butt joints and often look better, as well. To make an **overlap joint**, simply lay one of the members on top of the other and nail or screw it in place. For a **full-lap joint**, cut a notch into one member that is as deep as the second piece is thick. Clamp and glue the two pieces together, adding fasteners if you prefer. The **half-lap joint** is the strongest joint (see page 261).

Dado joints are attractive and strong, but are difficult to make.

A **stopped dado** has the strength of a dado and hides the joinery (see page 261).

For a finished-looking corner, make a **miter joint**. Cut the pieces at the same angle (usually 45 degrees), then glue the joint and drive in finishing nails.

A **biscuit joint** also is strong and has the advantage of being completely hidden, To make it, however, requires a biscuit joiner power tool (see page 262).

YOU'LL NEED

TIME About 10 to 30 minutes per joint, depending on complexity.
SKILLS: Ability to make square cuts, drill, use fasteners, and make neat notches.
TOOLS: Square, ruler, pencil, saw, drill and bits, hammer, nail set, screwdriver. The biscuit joint requires a biscuit joiner tool.

Lap joints

Dado joints

overlap

Miter joint

dado

full-lap

Biscuit joint

half-lap

stopped dado

MAKING A HALF-LAP OR DADO JOINT

Shelves and other wooden structures made with half-lap or dado joints are clearly a cut above those made with butt or even miter joints. Half-laps and dadoes are the stuff of cabinetry rather than carpentry. However, these strong joints don't require a talent for fine woodworking skills, just some skill with basic marking, cutting, and chiseling. Both joints require precise notches. Use sharp saw blades and chisels. To hone your notching skills, practice on a scrap piece of lumber.

YOU'LL NEED

TIME: Allow about 1 hour to make two joints.
SKILLS: Precise marking, cutting, and chiseling skills.
TOOLS: Circular, table, or radial-arm saw; square; chisel.

1. Mark for a half-lap joint ...
Overlap the pieces where you want the half-lap joint. You may want to use clamps. Mark for the notches by running a sharp pencil or a knife along the edge of the board. Mark for the notch on the second board using the same method. Or, wait until the first notch has been cut so you can set it over the second board before making your marks.

or for a dado.
Hold one piece up against the piece that will be notched. Mark along both sides with a sharp pencil or a knife. Or, mark a perpendicular line and use a scrap piece as a spacer to mark the second line. If you are sure of your skills, you can use a ruler or tape measure to mark for both sides of the notch.

2. Cut a series of kerfs ...
For a half-lap joint, set your saw blade so it cuts exactly halfway through the board. For a dado joint, set the blade to cut one-third of the way through. Keeping the blade on the inside of the notch at all times, make the two outside cuts, then make a series of cuts about ⅜ inch apart in the area between.

or cut out a notch.
If your cut falls at the end of the board (whether for a half-lap or a dado joint), you simply can cut out a notch. Set your power saw to cut a kerf where the notch will end. Taking care to keep the blade square on both sides, use a backsaw to cut into the end of the board until the blade reaches the first kerf.

3. Clean out and join.
Using a chisel with its beveled surface down, clean remaining wood out of the notch. Make sure the visible edges are straight and there are no bumps in the middle of the notch. Dry-fit the pieces to make sure they are tight. Apply carpenter's glue, clamp, and fasten with nails or screws.

FASTENING WITH DOWELS

A dowel joint is not impressive-looking like a half-lap or dado joint, but it is strong. Making a dowel joint requires no special tools, but there are two difficulties: You must hold the boards square as you work and you must hold the drill as straight as possible to keep from poking a hole through the edge or side of a board. Work on a flat surface to keep the face of the boards even. If possible, clamp the boards together before adding the dowels.

YOU'LL NEED

TIME: 1 hour to make two dowel joints.
SKILLS: Good drilling skills.
TOOLS: Drill with an extra-long bit, backsaw, hammer.

1. Temporarily join and drill.
Position the boards the way you want them and join them temporarily with fasteners or clamps. If you use fasteners, make sure they will not be in the way of the dowels. Square up the corner and drill holes for the dowels.

2. Drive the dowels and trim off.
Squirt carpenter's glue into the drill holes and insert the dowels. Tap them all the way in and clean away excess glue. Cut off the dowels as flush to the board as possible without scratching the edge. Sand the remainder smooth.

FASTENING WITH A BISCUIT JOINER

With this tool, you can create neat, sturdy joints with ease. Biscuit fasteners are oval-shaped pieces of plywood that fit invisibly into incisions inside the joint. You can use a biscuit joiner to fasten two boards on edge, join ¾-inch or thicker edging to plywood, or make butt or miter joints. Be sure you hold the tool with its base perfectly flat against the board as you make the cuts. If you will be using more than three or four biscuits on a joint, work fast and have a helper on hand.

YOU'LL NEED

TIME: About 30 minutes to make two joints with eight biscuits.
SKILLS: Use of power tools, ability to align the tool and hold it flat.
TOOLS: Biscuit joiner, hammer, clamps, square.

1. Mark and cut.
Position the boards as you want them joined. For every place you want to install a biscuit, mark a line running from one board to the other (see inset). Set the tool to the correct depth for the size biscuit you're using. Hold the tool flat against the board as you make each incision.

2. Glue, join, and clamp.
After dry-fitting the boards with the biscuits in place, squirt a little carpenter's glue into each incision. Set the biscuits into the incisions and tap the second board into place, sliding the biscuits into their respective slots. Check that the joint is tight and clamp. Wipe away excess glue and allow to dry.

SHAPING AND PLANING

Beveling edges and corners, planing down doors, trueing edges and ends of lumber—most carpentry projects include at least one of these shaping tasks. Three types of tools work best for shaping wood surfaces: planes, surface-forming tools, and rasps or wood files. With practice and a clean, sharp tool, shaping can be a pleasure rather than a chore.

However, even the sharpest shaping tools are no match for a board that's badly twisted, bowed, cupped, or warped (see page 214). Always inspect your material for flaws and select only the stock suitable for the job. Don't assume you can shape it up later.

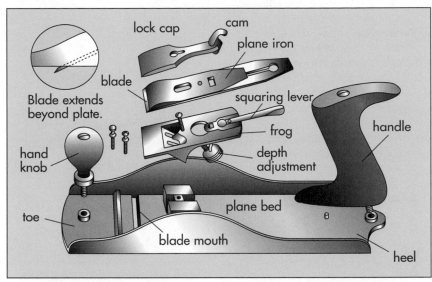

Blade extends beyond plate.

lock cap · cam · plane iron · blade · squaring lever · frog · depth adjustment · handle · hand knob · toe · blade mouth · plane bed · plane bed · heel

EXPERTS' INSIGHT

SCRIBING A TRUE LINE

■ To straighten out a piece of lumber or a door, you must first draw the line indicating where the piece should end. This is called a true line. A true line is usually straight, but not always. For instance, a door often must be planed to fit an opening that is not straight. To make a true line, scribe it by holding the piece up against the place into which it must fit. Run your pencil along the opening as you mark the piece for planing.

■ When scribing a line, check the angle at which you are holding the pencil and the thickness of the pencil line. Hold the pencil at the same angle at all points along your scribe line or you will cut off too little or too much wood. Decide if you want to cut off all of the pencil mark or just up to the mark.

Keep planes in working order.

Various types and sizes of planes are available. Most carpenters use a smoothing plane (shown *above*) or a small block plane (see page 264). To help keep the blade from dulling, lay it on its side when not in use. Retract the blade into the body when storing it. If any parts become rusty, clean them with a little oil and fine steel wool. Adjust the blade so it cuts thin shavings easily; you should not have to fight against the wood.

Use a block of wood to support plane when shaving a narrow edge.

Follow general planing rules.
Follow these tips when using a plane or surface-former:
■ It takes both hands to operate the tool, so clamp your work.
■ Plane with the grain.
■ If you get anything but a continuous, even shaving, the blade is dull or adjusted too thick, or you're planing against the grain.
■ To avoid nicking corners, apply pressure to the knob of the tool at the beginning of your cut and to its heel at the end of the cut.
■ When planing a narrow edge, grip a square-cornered block of wood against the bottom of the plane as you work.

CAUTION!

BEVEL OR SCORE FIRST TO AVOID SPLINTERING

When you shave the end of a door or a sheet of plywood, there's a good chance you will chip the veneer sheet when you cut across its grain, seriously marring its appearance. To avoid what might be an expensive mistake, take the following precautions.

■ *Bevel the veneer first. Turn the plane or shaping tool and cut a bevel downward toward the bottom of your work.*

■ *Use a knife and a straight-edge to score the veneer about ⅛ inch above the scribe line. After shaving the piece, use a sanding block to make an attractive bevel from the bottom of the piece to the scored line.*

Angle tool for rough cutting.

Work straight on for smooth cutting.

Shape with surface-forming tools.
Surface-forming tools, also known as sure-form tools, come in a variety of sizes and shapes. The one shown, *above*, works much like a plane. You cannot adjust the depth of the cut and it will not produce as smooth a cut as a

plane, but it is easy to use.

You can regulate the cut by the way you position the tool against the material. For rough-cutting, hold the tool at a 45-degree angle to the work as you push it. For a smoother result, hold the tool parallel to the board's edge.

block plane

Bevel to avoid splintering.

Shape end grain with a block.
As long as you're shaping wood parallel to the grain, planing will go smoothly. But when you need to shape the end grain, you will be working at a 90-degree angle to the grain. A small block plane works best on end grain. Bevel the

Plane end grain toward center.

end grain

corners first, with the bottom of the bevel at the final cut line. For narrow stock, just plane in one direction. For wider material, shave from each end of the board toward the center. Finish the job by shaving off the hump that remains in the middle.

TOOLS TO USE

POWER PLANER AND BELT SANDER

■ If you have a lot of planing to do, buy a power planer. The depth is easy to adjust, and as long as you hold the base flat against the surface, you will get a smooth cut with little effort. Be sure to use carbide-tipped blades, or you will have to change them often.

■ If you can work carefully, a belt sander shaves material, especially softwoods, with relative ease. Start with a coarse sandpaper. Hold the sanding belt flat to the surface; you'll make gouges if you tip the tool. Once you have taken off almost as much material as you need to, switch to a smoother paper.

SANDING

Once you've taken the time to cut and assemble your project, don't skimp when it comes to the final steps. Do a thorough job of sanding, so the wood will be well prepared for its final finish. Don't expect stain, varnish, or paint to smooth out the surface for you. They will only follow the contours of the wood, and often will accentuate, rather than hide, imperfections. Unless you are using a belt sander with a rough abrasive, don't expect sanding to remove more than ⅛ inch of material; shape or plane instead (see pages 263–264).

CAUTION!
Particularly when sanding with power tools, wear a face mask. To avoid difficult cleanup later, seal the room.

Use a belt sander for rough work.
Use this tool only on rough surfaces and only if you are sure of yourself; it is easy to make gouges if you tip the tool or if you rest it in one spot too long. Always run the sander with the grain, never against it. Don't apply pressure as you work; just let the weight of the sander do the work.

Use a detail sander in tight spots.
For awkward areas, a detail sander can spare you hours of finger-throbbing work. Sanding pads are self-adhesive; just lift one off and put the next one on. Proceed carefully. A detail sander works with an oscillating action. Because it concentrates on such a small area, it takes off material quickly.

Hand-sand with a block.
Except in hard-to-reach areas, never use abrasive sheets alone—always use some sort of sanding block, either store-bought or improvised. Sanding with a block is less tiring and produces more uniform results.

Tear abrasive sheets to size, rather than cutting them, or you will dull your knife blade quickly.

Check that the bottom of your block is clean and smooth. Any debris can tear the paper and mar your work.

Sand only in the direction of the wood grain. Sanding across the grain or in a circular motion can leave hard-to-remove lines. Don't exert a lot of pressure. If you're using the right grade of paper, light strokes are all you'll need.

EXPERTS' INSIGHT

SAND THREE TIMES

■ Take the time and trouble to sand three times, using progressively finer sandpaper. The wood surface may feel smooth after your first and second sandings, but it will get smoother as you move on to finer-grit sandpapers. A common progression is to start with 80-grit paper, then proceed to 120-, 180-, and possibly even 240-grit abrasives. Clean dust from the wood between sandings.

■ If you can't sand out a stain or discoloration, apply a small amount of laundry bleach to the stain. Try several applications until you get the right color. Dry before sanding it again.

Use ingenuity for tight spots.
When smoothing wood in tight quarters or in unusual situations, special tools can help. Consider buying or renting a detail sander (see page 265) or a contour sanding attachment for your drill.

Often, however, you can get the job done with a sheet of abrasive and a little ingenuity, as these three examples show.

To sand two surfaces where they meet at an inside corner, wrap a creased sheet of abrasive around a sharp-cornered block. To smooth inside edges of bored holes and small cutouts, wrap abrasive around your finger or a small round object. For sanding outside curves, wrap a sheet of abrasive around a dowel.

Sand a small piece.
When you need to smooth the surface of a small item, sand it on a full sheet of abrasive held flat with your free hand. This keeps the surface of the piece even and flat. If the abrasive fills with dust, wipe it with a clean cloth or give it a few slaps against your bench.

Round off edges.
Because wood edges are susceptible to nicks and splinters, it is a good idea to blunt them with a light sanding. Hold the sanding block at an angle; use gentle pressure combined with a rocking motion. A molded rubber sanding block like the one shown, *above,* is ideal for this purpose because its base gives slightly.

Protect edges with tape.
Sometimes you'll want to sand one surface without scratching an adjoining surface. To do this, protect the surface you don't want sanded with masking tape. Affix the tape carefully, making sure it is stuck down tightly at all points. Watch closely as you sand and immediately replace any tape that gets ripped or damaged.

FILLING AND FINISHING

Paint, stain, or clear finishes rarely cover up imperfections in wood. Often, they make things look worse rather than better. It pays to prepare your wood carefully before you add a finish.

Fill in holes with wood filler and sand the surface smooth. If you're applying a clear finish, limit your use of putty to small spots; even putty that is made to accept stain never quite looks like real wood. Even if you're going to paint the surface, cover exposed plywood edges. They soak up paint like a sponge and will look rough no matter how many coats of paint you apply to them.

Once the wood surface is prepared, match your paint or clear finish to the intended use of your project. See chart on page 268

Cover plywood edges.
To conceal a plywood edge, cut a thin piece of molding to fit, apply carpenter's glue to the edge, and fasten the molding with brads (small finishing nails). You also can cover an edge with wood veneer tape. Buy tape that is wider than the thickness of the material and matches its surface. Cut the tape with scissors, leaving at least ¼ inch extra on all edges. Position iron-on tape carefully, so it covers the edge along the entire length. Apply even, steady pressure with a household iron set on high. Use contact cement to apply non-iron-on veneer. Trim the edges with a sharp knife, then sand the corners lightly.

Fill in nail and screw holes.
For small holes, use a dough-type wood filler. Apply filler either before or after staining; experiment to find out which looks best. Begin by tamping a small amount of the filler into the hole with your thumb. Smooth it with a putty knife. Wipe away the excess with a rag dampened with water or mineral spirits, depending on the type of putty (check manufacturer's directions).

Fill in large areas.
If you're going to paint the entire surface of a project, water-mix putty excels at filling shallow depressions over a large surface area. The putty sets up quickly, so don't mix more than you can use in 10 minutes. To fill cracks around a knot, mix the putty to a pastelike consistency and force it into all the cracks with a putty knife. Feather out the patch to the surrounding wood. To fill edges of plywood or the end grain of boards, mix the putty to a thinner consistency. Sand and apply a second coat if necessary. For deep holes, you may have to apply two layers to allow for any shrinkage of the putty.

SELECTING CLEAR FINISHES

Type	Characteristics	Application and Drying Time
Natural-resin varnish	Resists scratches, scuffs. Spar varnish good outdoors.	Use varnish brush or cheesecloth pad. Dries in 24–36 hours. In humid weather, allow 36 hours.
Polyurethane varnish	Mar-resistant, durable, remains clear.	Use natural-bristle brush, roller, or spray. Let dry 1–2 hours; 12 hours between coats.
Two-part epoxy varnish	High resistance to scuffs and mars. Ideal for floors.	Use brush. Check directions if coating wood filler. First coat dries in 3 hours; second in 5–8 hours.
Shellac	Easily damaged by water. Clear or pigmented.	Use small brush with chiseled tip. Thin with alcohol or recommended solvent. Dries in about 2 hours.
Lacquer	Fast-drying. Ideal for furniture.	Best sprayed in many thin coats. Let last coat dry 48–60 hours, then rub with fine steel wool or hard wax.
Resin oil	Soaks into and hardens grain. Resists scratches.	Usually hand-rubbed in 2–3 coats. Needs 8–12 hours to dry.

Apply penetrating stain.
Apply stain with a brush and wait for a few minutes. The heavier the application and the longer you wait, the deeper the color. Wipe with a clean rag, taking care to make the color even throughout the piece. To make it darker, apply a second coat. If it is too dark, rub with a cloth moistened with the recommended thinner.

Begin with strokes across the grain.

Finish with long strokes with the grain.

Paint correctly for a smooth look.
Painting with a brush may seem like a simple task, but here are a few tips to keep in mind. Begin applying paint to wood surfaces with short strokes across the wood grain, laying down paint in both directions. Don't bear down too hard on the bristles.

Finish painting with longer, sweeping strokes in one direction only—this time with the wood grain. Use just the tips of the bristles to smooth out the paint.

INSTALLING MOLDING

Installing molding to finish off a project can be the most gratifying part of the job. Although it's easier than you might expect, installing molding takes some practice. Start installing molding in an area of the room where it will be the least visible. You'll soon surprise yourself with your speed and neat joinery. The most common mistake is to cut a miter in the wrong direction. Whenever possible, mark pieces clearly, not only for length, but also for the direction of cut.

YOU'LL NEED

TIME: About 10 minutes per piece of molding.
SKILLS: Precise measuring and cutting, figuring out the direction of cuts, nailing.
TOOLS: Tape measure, miter box and backsaw or power miter saw, coping saw, hammer, nail set.

EXPERTS' INSIGHT

BUYING MOLDING

Molding can be expensive, so determine exactly how many pieces of each size you need. On a piece of paper, make columns for each size—8 feet, 10 feet, 12 feet, etc. As you measure for individual pieces, tally how many you need under each column. If you have an old house, you may need moldings that are not made any longer. A lumberyard with a mill or a millwork company can make replicas. If the price is too high or you need only a small piece of molding, you can make a reasonable facsimile using a router, tablesaw, radial-arm saw, and belt sander.

mitered casing   butted casing   blocked casing

chair rail

baseboard with shoe   3-piece base   wainscoting

jamb

1/4" reveal on edge

1. Measure and mark precisely.
Whenever possible, hold a piece of molding in place and mark it with a knife, rather than using a tape measure. For window and door casings, take into account the 1/4-inch reveal on the edge of the jamb. As a guide, use a compass set to 1/4 inch to mark the reveal on the jamb.

2. Cut the miter.
Sight down the blade of the saw and slide the molding until the saw will cut just to the scrap side of your mark. Hold the molding against the back of the miter box, as shown *above*. Grasp it tightly so it will not slide as you cut it. As an alternative, use a power miter saw or radial-arm saw (see page 247).

INSTALLING BASE MOLDING

Install door and window casing and other vertical molding before you install molding at the bottom of your walls. Choose from ranch or colonial base molding or use a three-piece base for a traditional look (see page 269). It is best to add a quarter round or base shoe as well. These types bend easily with variations in the flooring and buffer scuffs from vacuum cleaners.

You may be tempted simply to miter-cut pieces for inside corners. This often leads to unsightly gaps and misaligned joints because the corners are almost never true 90-degree angles. Instead, cut the first piece to length with a regular 90-degree cut and cope-cut the second piece (see page 238).

butt splice

45° scarf joint splice for a more finished look

inside coped corner

Install the corner piece first, then the baseboards.

two 45° cuts for outside corner

ACHIEVING THAT PROFESSIONAL LOOK

■ Avoid splits. Thin stock, such as often is used for base-board molding, is prone to splitting and cracking. Don't take chances. Wherever you will be driving a nail within 3 inches of the edge of a piece, drill a pilot hole. You may be able to simply attach a short piece of molding with con-struction adhesive.

■ Don't overnail. The most common mistake amateurs make when installing moldings is to put in too many nails. Drive in only as many as you need to hold the piece firmly flush against the wall.

■ Stain first, but paint second. If you will be staining molding, do it before you install it. If you will be painting, install the molding first, then paint.

Mark outside corners.
As with all molding, for greater accuracy, hold and mark the pieces in place wherever possible. For an outside corner, butt one end of the molding in place, allowing the other to extend past the corner. Make the mark exactly even with the corner.

Bow slightly for a tight fit.

Install an inside-to-inside piece.
Mark and cut the piece about $1/16$ inch longer than the space. If you are butting against a piece of casing, make sure the casing is well-secured so it does not move when you press against it. Install the baseboard by bending it into position. This will give you a tight fit on both sides.

INSTALLING CROWN MOLDING

Transform a boxy room with the elegant and softening beauty of crown molding. With more and more molding profiles available, you have plenty of options for adding an attractive finishing touch to your home.

Although installing crown molding takes patience and a few tricks of the trade, homeowners who are comfortable with basic carpentry tools and who have coped molding miters before should have few problems. Careful fitting and refitting are crucial to obtaining a close fit between sections of molding.

When working over your head, a solid working platform makes all the difference. Don't try to do the careful fitting and nailing that crown molding requires while working from a stepladder. Make the job easier on yourself by finding a plank and two sturdy sawhorses to make a platform to stand on while installing the molding. In addition, enlist a coworker to hold the lengths of molding while you measure, position, and fasten them.

Before beginning this challenging project, review marking and measuring techniques (pages 225–226), how to use a miter box (page 235), and nailing techniques (pages 249–250).

YOU'LL NEED
TIME: About 4 hours for a 12×12-foot room
SKILLS: Precise measuring, use of miter box or power miter saw, driving nails.
TOOLS: Deep miter box with backsaw or power miter box, drill, hammer, nail set.

CAUTION!
WHICH SIDE IS UP?
Remember to think upside down as you make miter cuts. Double-check which edge of the crown molding goes up — the difference is subtle.

Money $ Saver

PRACTICE MAKES PERFECT
To avoid expensive mistakes with crown molding, you should hone your mitering and coping skills before you plunge into the job. Ask your local home center or lumber dealer for a 2- or 3-foot scrap of molding similar to the type you plan to use. Practice the steps shown on these pages.

It is particularly important to gain some familiarity with the way molding is cut and coped. The more proficient you are at making overlapping joints, the less likely you are to make costly errors.

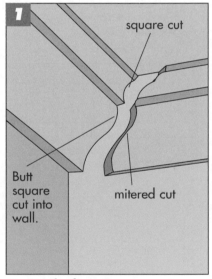

1. Cut the first piece square.
To achieve a mitered look with corners that are seldom perfectly square, run the first piece of crown molding tightly into the corner. Cope-cut the second piece in the shape of the profile of the molding, so it can butt neatly against the face of the first piece.

2. Make a miter cut.
Use a deep miter box and a fine-toothed backsaw to make a cut that reveals the profile of the molding. Position the molding so that it is upside down in the miter box. The face of the molding that goes against the ceiling will be on the bottom of the miter box. Remember, for inside corners, the bottom of the crown molding will be the longest edge.

Carve away
excess along
coped cut.

coping saw

3. Cope the profile.

If the mitered cut is correct, you'll be able to see the profile of the molding. Cut away the excess wood along the back side of the molding with a coping saw. Err on the side of removing too much rather than too little; only the outermost edge of the coped molding will be seen.

4. Fine-tune your cut.

Use a utility knife to remove any excess material you missed with the coping saw. Be careful that you do not cut into the exposed face of the molding. Hold the piece in place to test the fit. Take it down and do more carving if necessary.

5. Plan each joint.

Map out the job so that one end of each piece of crown molding always will be cut straight and one end will be mitered and coped. Use butt joints for long runs. Save the most visible parts of the job for last, when you've honed your coping skills.

ceiling joists

drywall nail

framing

drywall

drywall screw

2×2 nailer

6d finishing nail

6. Nail in place ...

If the molding runs perpendicular to the ceiling joists, determine the location of the joists. Drill pilot holes to keep the molding from splitting. As you attach the molding, tack it in place with a few nails. Take a good look at the positioning before completing the nailing.

or add a nailer.

To provide a solid nailing area where the joists run parallel to the crown molding, cut a beveled face on a 2×2, as shown. Cut the 2×2 to length and screw it to the wall so it's in the corner of the ceiling and the wall. The 2×2 provides a surface, at the proper angle, to which you can nail the molding.

TOOLS TO USE

BE SHARP

The right tools—kept clean and sharp—help make a precise job, such as installing crown molding, easier. Here are some tips:

■ Drop off your saw for professional sharpening well before you begin the job. A sharpened saw provides better control and a cleaner cut, and it makes the job go more pleasantly.

■ Buy new coping-saw blades. They break easily, so have half a dozen on hand.

■ Have plenty of clamps to hold the molding while you cut it. The less you rely on your own holding power, the easier and more accurately you'll be able to make the saw cuts.

Chapter 7

INDOOR CARPENTRY PROJECTS

For more ideas and projects involving drywall and surface finishing, see Chapter 14, beginning on page 533.

PLANNING FOR NEW CABINETS

Preparation for installing kitchen cabinets usually is more involved than actually hanging them.

Once you've removed the old cabinets and appliances, install and check plumbing lines, both drain and supply. Run the gas line if needed for a gas cooktop, oven, or range.

Rough in the electrical outlets, switches, and cables for dishwashers. If you will be installing undercabinet lights that are not low-voltage (see page 93), have standard electrical cable sticking out of the walls at points just below the bottom of the wall cabinets. Cut out a vent hole for a range hood.

Smooth and prime all wall and ceiling surfaces, especially those that will show after the cabinets are in place. In most cases, it makes sense to install the flooring before installing the cabinets. Piecing around them is difficult and time-consuming. While you may waste material under the cabinets, a smooth finished floor to work on makes the job easier. If you are using expensive flooring, however, you may want to leave the area under the cabinets uncovered. Overlap the footprint of your base cabinets with the flooring. Add pieces of flooring at all four corners to level each cabinet.

Carefully mark the location of each cabinet on the walls. Allow for small spacers at the corners so you will not have to cram things in too tightly. Mark the location of all the wall studs.

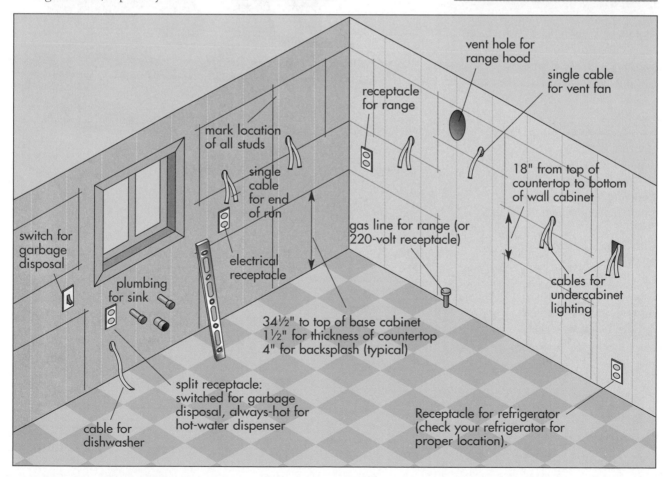

- vent hole for range hood
- single cable for vent fan
- receptacle for range
- mark location of all studs
- single cable for end of run
- 18" from top of countertop to bottom of wall cabinet
- switch for garbage disposal
- electrical receptacle
- gas line for range (or 220-volt receptacle)
- cables for undercabinet lighting
- plumbing for sink
- 34½" to top of base cabinet
  1½" for thickness of countertop
  4" for backsplash (typical)
- split receptacle: switched for garbage disposal, always-hot for hot-water dispenser
- cable for dishwasher
- Receptacle for refrigerator (check your refrigerator for proper location).

INSTALLING WALL CABINETS

*T*ake the cabinets out of their boxes and inspect them carefully; you won't be able to return them once you have driven screws into them. If you are installing undercabinet lighting, you may need to drill holes in the back lower lip of the cabinets for the electrical cable to slip through.

If your walls are not plumb or square, you may end up with a cabinet that doesn't fit. Check in advance and reposition your layout accordingly.

Always work with a helper, and have a stable stepladder on hand. If any of the cabinets are heavy, remove the doors to reduce the weight and lessen the chance of damaging the cabinets.

YOU'LL NEED

TIME: Several hours for six or seven cabinets.
SKILLS: Leveling, driving screws.
TOOLS: Level, drill with screwdriver bit, clamps.

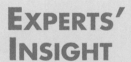

EXPERTS' INSIGHT

FASTEN WALL CABINETS TO WALL STUDS

If you've carried a stack of 10 or 12 dishes, you know how heavy they are. Cabinets holding dishes or canned goods bear a surprisingly heavy load. Because wall cabinets do not rest on anything, the screws attaching them to the wall carry all the weight. Make sure you drive screws into wall studs. If you are attaching to a masonry wall, use metal masonry shields.

1. Attach a temporary ledger.
Anchor a straight piece of 2×4 lumber to the wall so you can rest the cabinets on it as you work. Level it and attach it with just a few screws or nails, so you won't create a big wall-patching job when you remove it.

2. Fasten the cabinets.
While a helper holds the cabinet, check for plumb in both directions. Use shims, as shown, if necessary. Once the cabinet is positioned, drive 2½- or 3-inch screws through the cabinet frames and into wall studs. If your cabinet has a lip on top, drive the screws in there so they will not show. Use trim washers for a more finished look on the inside of the cabinet.

3. Install spacers.
Where the last cabinet meets up against a side wall, hold the cabinet in place and measure for a spacer. Cut it and attach as shown, using clamps to hold it firmly while you drill pilot holes and drive screws from the cabinet into the spacer.

4. Install spacer for inside corner.
If you simply attach two cabinets at an inside corner, usually at least one door will not open fully. Before installing them, attach a spacer to one of the cabinets (see Step 3) and then attach the other cabinet to the spacer. Drill pilot holes and drive in screws.

SETTING BASE CABINETS

Take the time to make sure all the cabinets are level from the beginning. If you give in to the temptation to cheat a little, you will run into frustrating problems, both in installing the other cabinets and in putting on the countertop.

If a baseboard or other piece of molding gets in the way, it is almost always best to take it off the wall and cut it, rather than cutting the cabinet to fit around the trim.

YOU'LL NEED

TIME: Most of a day for an average-size kitchen.
SKILLS: Leveling, driving screws, clamping, cutting.
TOOLS: Drill, level, hammer, chisel, pry bar.

Level in both directions.

Test the floor for its high point.

Add shim to level.

1. Level and plumb the first unit.
Find the highest point on your floor and start there because you can shim up but not down. Set the first cabinet in place and check it for level in both directions. As a further check, make sure the stiles or door faces are plumb. Use shims at the floor to level and solidly support the cabinets. If your wall is out of plumb or wavy, you may need to shim the back of the cabinet as well—make sure when you drive the screws in (see next step) you don't pull the cabinet out of level.

shim

cabinet frame

2. Attach to the walls.
Drive in screws through the back of the cabinet and into the wall studs. When possible, screw through solid framing pieces. After driving in the screws, check to see that the cabinet is still sitting flat on the floor. If not, back out the screws and adjust the shims before driving the screws back in. Check again for level and plumb.

Edges flush here,

and here.

Chisel off protruding shims.

3. Join cabinets together.
After installing the first cabinet, use clamps to hold the next one in alignment as you screw them together. Make sure that their surfaces are flush with each other—not just the face frames, but the top edges as well.

Also make sure the screws are the right length, so they will not poke through the stiles. To keep the surface of the stiles smooth, drill pilot and countersink holes, then drive in the screws.

In most cases, you can use a hammer and chisel to nip off shims that stick out. With layers of shim, use a handsaw.

4. Install a corner cabinet...

You may buy a complete corner cabinet with sides or a less-expensive knockdown unit like the one shown above. For this type of corner cabinet, install the base first, then set the two adjoining cabinets in place next to it. Insert the door frame and join it to the adjoining cabinets. Install 1×2 cleats on the walls to support the countertop.

or join two base cabinets.

This method provides you with less usable space, but it may save money. Be sure to install at least one spacer so both doors swing freely. Clamp, drill pilot and countersink holes, and drive in screws.

5. Install a cabinet island.

When there is no wall to attach a cabinet to, as in the case of an island or peninsula, provide strong framing on the floor. Lay the cabinet on its side and measure its inside dimensions. Measure and install 2×4 cleats on the floor carefully so the cabinet slips over the cleats tightly. For exposed areas use finishing nails; otherwise drill pilot holes and use screws.

6. Install the last filler piece.

When you come to an inside wall, measure the distance between the cabinet and the wall at both the top and bottom. Rip a filler piece to fit snugly and position it flush with the cabinet face. Drill pilot and countersink holes and drive in screws. Unless the filler piece is more than 4 inches wide, you do not need to attach it to the wall.

7. Install panels.

If your design calls for an exposed edge that is not the side of a cabinet, as is the case when a dishwasher is at the end of a run, purchase an end panel made for the purpose of completing the run. Use clips at the floor, countertop, and wall so the panel can be removed to service the dishwasher.

EXPERTS' INSIGHT

INSTALLATION TIPS

Even durable cabinets made to hold up to decades of normal use can be scratched or dinged easily by carpentry tools. Take special care not to damage cabinets as you work on them. Cover installed cabinets with heavy drop cloths or cardboard from their shipping boxes and keep sharp tools well away from door and drawer faces.

If your floor is out of level or wavy, avoid unsightly gaps at the bottom of your cabinets by installing vinyl cove base. Or remove the kickboard, take out the nails, and reinstall it tight against the floor.

BUILDING AN ISLAND OR PENINSULA

*I*f you purchase custom cabinets, you can design an island or peninsula to suit your needs exactly. If your budget is limited, you can combine standard-sized base cabinets to make your own unit. In both cases, you need to make or have a countertop specialist make a countertop. This simple island, made of two base cabinets, side panels, and a veneered plywood back panel, is simple to construct. The countertop is something most do-it-yourselfers can build. The most difficult part of the project is the installation of electrical cables, gas pipe, plumbing supply and drains, and the vent duct.

machine bolt, nut, and washers

back panel

corner molding

side panels installed with adhesive

toekick

YOU'LL NEED

TIME: About half a day to build the island.
SKILLS: Basic carpentry, wiring, plumbing.
TOOLS: Screwdriver, drill, adjustable wrench, circular saw, block plane, sandpaper.

Combining stock cabinets

When using stock base cabinets, you will have access to the shelves from one side only. If you want the countertop to be at a good height for people sitting on stools, trim the cabinets down by cutting off the toekick. To anchor the island to the floor, see page 277.

Join the cabinets together by clamping, drilling pilot holes, and installing bolts. As an alternative, drive general-purpose screws through the frames, being careful not to pierce the other side. Install panels on the sides using construction adhesive. Cover the back with a single panel.

Finish the corners with corner molding. If building a peninsula, vary the design so it butts against your base cabinets.

Adding a countertop

Plan an island countertop carefully: If it is to be an eating counter, make it wide enough to accommodate seating but not so wide as to hinder traffic flow. Round off exposed corners, to avoid painful encounters.

Countertops usually are made of chipboard, which means they cannot handle much weight if they are not supported from underneath. Make a cantilevered countertop stronger by using plywood attached to a 1×2 frame to thicken the edge. Add bracket supports if you wish to extend the top to make a stool-height informal eating area. Install wood base shoe or vinyl cove base at the bottom. Attach the island to the floor as shown on page 277.

¾" plywood for countertop of base cabinet

1×2 countertop frame edge

support bracket

base shoe or vinyl cove base

ADDING A STAINLESS-STEEL BACKSPLASH

Here's an unusual touch for a household kitchen—a stainless-steel backsplash. It looks stylish and provides a commercial-grade, easy-to-maintain surface between your countertop and the wall cabinets.

The first step is to find a source of the material. If your home center or hardware store can't help you, check in the Yellow Pages under stainless steel or sheet metal. Find a shop that can provide pieces of stainless steel to the exact length you want. Often, stainless steel has to be ordered from a specialty supplier, so schedule accordingly.

Check your measurements or provide a template to be sure you get the correct sizes of pieces. Although it is extremely hard, stainless steel can be damaged during installation. As you work, support the material so it doesn't crimp or get scratched because stainless steel is expensive.

TOOLS TO USE

IF YOU MUST CUT STAINLESS STEEL

You can make rough cuts around outlets because the edges will be covered up. But it's hard to make a straight, smooth cut in this amazingly hard material. Use a drill to start the hole, then cut the opening with a sabersaw with a metal-cutting blade designed for cutting stainless steel.

Check angle between walls and cabinet for square.

Mark location of every other stud.

Mark location of every other stud.

base cabinet

1. Lay out the job.
If possible, do this job before installing the countertop or the wall cabinets. Check the walls for square and measure the lengths you need. Corners are the critical areas; any variation along the length of the piece will be covered by the wall cabinet above and the countertop below. If your walls are plumb, you may be able to get away without the corner trim pieces shown in Step 3. If the walls are out of plumb, you may be able to compensate by cutting a slot in the corner and sliding a bit of one piece of steel into it.

Score.

Drill.

Add trim washer.

2. Attach with screws, washers.
Set the metal in place and make sure the pieces line up. Drill holes and drive stainless-steel screws, fitted with trim washers, into studs. Because the material is rigid and will be anchored by the cabinets as well, two screws driven in every other stud are adequate.

Corner piece behind panels

3. Use corner molding pieces.
If you have trouble getting the corners to match up, use a piece of corner molding, attaching it to the wall with clear silicone sealant and butting each panel against it. If one wall is wavy, you can, with patience, scribe and curve-cut one

CHOOSING COUNTERTOPS

Next to cabinets, countertops do the most to set the style of your kitchen. In addition, they are working surfaces that need to be made of a material you are comfortable with. A number of options are available, all of which do the job well. They range from inexpensive post-form laminates you can buy at a home center (only a few colors will be available) to high-priced granite and solid-surface materials.

Wood, such as maple butcher block, is also an option. But such countertops require careful maintenance: Keep them well waxed or give them regular applications of mineral oil. Otherwise, the countertop will discolor and possibly start coming apart at the seams.

Solid-surface
These are durable and can accommodate a seamless sink. They come in a variety of colors and patterns, many of which rival stone. Their cost rivals stone as well; consider this material among the most expensive countertop options. This is not a do-it-yourself material; solid-surface countertops must be fabricated and installed by specialists.

Laminate
Color-core laminates withstand scratches better than laminates on which the color is applied only on the surface. You can buy a ready-made post-form, with either a rolled front edge and a built-in backsplash or a square-edged top. With patience, you can laminate a square-edge top yourself, but the cost of materials may be nearly as much as a factory-made top.

Granite
This beautiful natural product provides decades of use if installed properly. You must hire a contractor to measure and install it for you; they know how to handle this heavy material and have equipment for buffing all the surfaces to a shine. Marble is not recommended as countertop material because it stains easily.

Tile
There are many colors and sizes of tile from which to choose. Be sure the edging and backsplash pieces come in the colors you want. Avoid wall tiles. They are not made to take impact and chip easily. Some people find the grout joints hard to clean; others dislike an uneven surface. But well-installed tile is durable and stylish.

EXPERTS' INSIGHT

HOW MUCH COUNTERTOP SPACE?

■ Dedicated cooks will tell you there's no such thing as too much countertop space. Countertops that provide ample room for day-to-day food preparation may seem cramped during holidays or when you throw a party. In general, if you can add countertop area to your kitchen, you will be making an improvement that you will be grateful for in the long run.

■ If your kitchen is smaller than 150 square feet, you should have at least 11 running feet of countertop. For larger kitchens, plan for 16 or more running feet of countertop.

INSTALLING A LAMINATE COUNTERTOP

You can make your own laminate countertop. Unless you are a skilled do-it-yourselfer, however, it may not be worth the time and effort. If your countertop configuration is fairly typical, you can save money by purchasing post-form countertops from your home center. Made with precut corners, these countertops can be trimmed to fit most base cabinets.

But if you don't like the colors available at your home center or if you have an unusual situation, such as a wide counter for an island or a narrow counter for a tight spot, you will need to have a countertop made for you. You may have a wider selection of color and pattern if you choose a square-edge top rather than a post-form (see page 280).

YOU'LL NEED

TIME: Half a day to install several tops carefully.
SKILLS: General carpentry, working carefully to avoid damaging the tops as you work.
TOOLS: Level, carpenter's square, drill, circular saw, compass, belt sander, laundry iron.

CAUTION!

*BE SURE THE TOP
HUGS YOUR WALLS
If you have a wavy wall or if
your walls are more than
3/8 inch out of square, a ready-
made top may not fit snugly
against your walls. Take
measures to straighten out
your walls or hire a
professional countertop maker
to come in and take precise
measurements so a custom
countertop can be made
to fit your space.*

1. Check walls, cabinets for level and square.
Make sure cabinets are level all around so the top will be able to sit flat on them. If necessary, install cleats on walls, as shown, or end panels (see page 277) to support the top firmly. Check walls to ensure they are square with each other and free of major bulges by laying a straightedge down the full length of each. Most post-forms have a "scribe," a lip of laminate that can be trimmed (see below) to compensate for variations of up to 3/8 inch. A square-edged top with a separate backsplash will let you compensate for up to 3/4 inch.

2. Cut a top to length.
If you purchase a factory-made top that you must cut yourself, do this with great care. Use a fine-cutting blade and cut it with the face side down to avoid nicks. Check that the blade on your circular saw is square to the base and use a clamp-on guide to make sure your cut is straight. Be sure to support the waste side so it does not fall off before you finish the cut—an easy way to chip laminate.

3. Scribe a backsplash line.
The countertop might not fit tight against the wall, either because the walls are out of square or the wall is wavy. If such is the case, push the countertop against the wall, making sure it is aligned correctly with the base cabinets. Use a compass to scribe a line as wide as the largest gap between the countertop and the wall.

4. Belt-sand to the scribe mark.

Don't attempt to cut to the scribe mark with a sabersaw or circular saw—you'll almost certainly end up chipping the countertop. Use a belt sander with a fairly coarse 36-grit sanding belt. Pressing lightly, slowly sand away material up to the scribed mark.

5. Make a splice.

If you need to splice pieces at a corner or in the middle of a run, have a professional make the cuts and rout the grooves for the clamps. Apply waterproof glue to the edges of the pieces, line up the pieces, and start to tighten the clamps. Check the countertop as you work to make sure it doesn't slide out of alignment.

6. Attach the top to the cabinets.

Screws should extend as far into the countertop as possible without poking through it. Drill pilot holes every 2 to 3 feet along the front and rear of the top and drive in screws upward to hold the counter firmly. Screw into structurally sound sections of the cabinet framing. Make sure the countertop does not move as you work.

7. Attach end caps.

Buy a precut end cap to cover the end of a post form. If it has heat-activated glue, hold it in place so it overhangs the countertop edge. (You'll remove the excess later.) Slowly run a hot laundry iron along the end cap, being careful not to burn the laminate, until the glue adheres. File, sand, or rout away the excess material.

Install a square-edged countertop.

If you buy a square-edged countertop and your walls are not square, this type of edging covers up the gap. Set the top so it overhangs the cabinets evenly. Cut the backsplash pieces to fit and set them in place. Mark their position on the countertop, then pull the top away from the wall. Run a bead of bathtub caulk along the bottom of the edging, set the edging in place, and fasten it with screws from underneath. Attach the top from underneath as shown in Step 6. If your wall bows, fasten the top in place, then glue the edging pieces to the wall with construction adhesive. Brace them with pieces of 1× or heavy objects so the edging conforms to the wall.

ADDING A GARDEN WINDOW

A garden window not only lets in light and makes a room seem more spacious, it gives you a place to nurture flowers or herbs right in your kitchen.

Some units have side windows that open casement-style with a crank; the other glass pieces are fixed in place. Prices vary widely, depending on whether you prefer a vinyl, metal, or wood unit. Some manufacturers offer off-the-shelf units made to standard window dimensions; others produce made-to-measure units only.

YOU'LL NEED

TIME: 1 day to remove a window and add a garden window.
SKILLS: Demolition, measuring, cutting, sealing.
TOOLS: Hammer, flat pry bar, reciprocating saw or metal-cutting keyhole saw, drill, caulking gun, level.

MEASUREMENTS

DETERMINING THE ROUGH OPENING

Garden windows often are not in stock, so you'll need accurate measurements of the rough opening (without removing the old window) to place an order. Here are some hints:

■ If you have old double-hung sash windows with ropes (or chains) attached to weights in the side cavities, measure from jamb to jamb (the surfaces that the sides of the sash slide against) and add 5 inches.

■ For newer-style windows, measure the casing (the molding that is on the wall) from outside edge to outside edge, and subtract 3 inches.

1. Remove the old window.
Use a hammer and flat pry bar to pull off the molding, both inside and outside. On the sides and at the top, you will be able to look through your wall. You'll see a series of nails holding the window in place. Cut the nails with a reciprocating saw or metal-cutting keyhole saw, or chop them in two by chiseling through them with the pry bar and hammer. Remove the window.

2. Measure, fill in.
The directions accompanying your window will tell you what the size of the rough opening should be. Cut away framing pieces only if you know how to reframe the opening in keeping with local codes. Make the opening smaller by filling in the space with 1× or 2× spacers. Allow about ½ inch of wiggle room on all sides of the garden window—you can shim the difference later.

3. Install the window.
Tip the garden window into place, making sure the front edge is flush with the wall surface so the molding will sit flat. Level and plumb, then firmly anchor it to the framing with shims and screws. On the outside, apply generous beads of exterior caulk before covering over the seam with molding. If your new window is a good deal smaller than the old one, you may need to use extra-wide molding (see inset). This is a simpler solution than filling in exterior siding or masonry.

Building a Wall

Behind most finished residential walls lies a rather simple construction. Vertical members, called studs, butt at the top and bottom against horizontal members, called plates. Although it looks straightforward, building a wall takes thoughtful planning. When you cover the framing with sheets of drywall or paneling, the seams between sheets must fall in the center of studs. There must be a nailing surface for the sheets at all the corners (see page 287). And, all framing members must be aligned along a flat plane.

If the floor and ceiling are nearly level, it's rather easy to preassemble a stud wall on the floor and then raise it into position. If the floor and ceiling are uneven, or if you're building the wall in tight quarters, it's best to build the wall in place, custom-cutting each stud to fit and toenailing it to the top and bottom plates (see page 286).

Whichever approach you choose, make sure you have a way to attach your wall to the ceiling. If the wall runs perpendicular to the ceiling joists, simply fasten the wall's top plate with two 16-penny nails at every joist. If it runs parallel to the joists, you will have to install cross braces, so you can nail the top plate into solid material (see page 287).

You'll Need

Time: About 2 hours to build a simple 10-foot wall; longer if you need to build it in place or in awkward situations.
Skills: Cutting, measuring, fastening with nails.
Tools: Tape measure, chalk line, pencil, framing square, saw, speed or combination square, level, hammer.

Use a framing square to establish a perpendicular line.

Pull the line taut and snap it.

chalk line

1. Mark the wall location.
Begin by deciding exactly where the wall will go. Use a framing square and a chalk line to mark its location on the floor. For long walls, check for square using the 3-4-5 method (see page 229).

Using a level and a straight 2×4 that is as high as your ceiling, mark the wall location on the ceiling, joists, or cross bracing. These marks will help you position the wall before you plumb it. Make sure there is adequate framing in the ceiling to which you can nail the top plate.

31¼"

15¼"

48"

center of studs

32"   16"

2. Cut and mark the plates.
Using your floor layout as a guide, mark and cut 2×4s for the top and bottom plates (usually the same length). Place them on edge beside each other and mark for the studs. The first stud will be at the end of the wall. The remaining studs should be 16 (or 24) inches on center, meaning that from the edge of the wall to the center of each stud will be a multiple of 16 (or 24). Make a mark every 16 inches; then with a combination or speed square draw lines ¾ inch on each side of your first marks. Draw an X in the middle of the marks to show where to nail the studs.

BUILDING A WALL

3. Provide nailers, cut studs.
If your new wall runs parallel to the ceiling joists, cut pieces of 2× material to fit tightly between the ceiling joists and install them every 2 feet or so. Measure for your studs (see page 284) and cut them to length.

4. Assemble the wall.
Working on a flat surface, lay the studs on edge between the top and bottom plates. It helps to have something solid, such as a wall, to hold the framing against while you assemble and nail the wall.

For speed, nail one plate at a time to the studs. Drive two 16-penny nails through the plate and into the ends of each stud. Because hammer blows tend to knock studs out of alignment, continually double-check your work while nailing. Keep the edges of the studs flush with the plate edges. If any of the studs are twisted or bowed, replace them.

5. Raise the frame.
Framework can be cumbersome, so have a helper on hand. Position the bottom plate about where it needs to go and tip the wall into position. If the wall fits so tightly against the ceiling that you have to hammer it into place, protect the framing with a scrap of 2×4 as you pound. Tap both ends of the frame until it is roughly plumb in both directions.

6. Snug the frame with shims.
If the wall is a bit short in places, drive shims between the bottom plate and the floor or between the top plate and the ceiling joists. Have your helper steady the framework while you drive the pieces in place. Drive shims in from both sides, thin edge to thin edge, to keep the plate from tilting.

7. Fasten frame to wall and floor.
Once the frame is snug, recheck that the wall is plumb in both directions. Check both ends of the wall and every other stud. Fasten the top plate to the ceiling by driving in a 16-penny nail through the plate and into each joist. Fasten the bottom plate to the floor. Use 16-penny nails if the floor is wood; use masonry nails or a power hammer if the floor is concrete.

MEASUREMENTS

GETTING THE STUD LENGTH CORRECT

Few things are more frustrating than building a stud wall only to find that your measurements were off and the wall is ¼ inch too tall. When that happens, the only thing you can do is take the wall down, pull off one plate, remove the nails, cut all the studs, and nail it back together again.

To measure for stud length, nail together two scraps of 2×4 to represent the top and bottom plates. Set this double 2×4 on the floor, measure up to the joist, and subtract ¼ inch for shimming. Take measurements every few feet.

1. Install top and bottom plates.
If building a wall on the floor and raising it into position are not practical in your situation, begin by cutting the top and bottom plates, and marking them for studs (see page 284). Transfer the marks to the faces of the plates, making sure the marks are clear so you can see them easily to align the studs while toenailing.

Nail the top plate to the joists. Use a level and a straight board to mark the location of the bottom plate or use a chalk line case as a plumb bob. Mark the floor in two places and make an X to indicate on which side of the mark the plate should be positioned.

Use masonry nails or a power hammer to fasten the bottom plate to the floor.

16d nails

2. Cut and install the studs.

With top and bottom plates installed, measure the required length of each stud individually. Add $1/16$ inch for a snug fit and cut. Tap each stud into place. If you really have to whack it to get it into place, it is too long. Don't risk splitting the stud; take it down and trim it a little.

4. Frame at corners.

When framing corners, make sure there is a nailing surface for every piece of drywall or paneling that will be installed. This means adding nonstructural nailers.

In Situation 1, *right,* the extra stud is turned sideways to offer a nailing surface and strengthen the corner. Drive 16-penny nails first through end stud #1 and into the extra stud, then through end stud #2 and into the extra stud and end stud #1.

In Situation 2, *right,* several foot-long 2×4 scraps (usually three in a standard 8-foot wall) serve as spacers between two full-length studs placed at the end of one wall. Tie the wall sections together with 16-penny nails.

Situation 3, *right,* shows two intersecting walls. Nail three studs together and to the plates, then attach to the adjoining wall.

3. Toenail the studs.

To secure the studs, drive 8-penny nails at an angle through the side of studs and into the plate; this is called toenailing. Tap the nail once or twice while holding it parallel to the floor or ceiling. When the nail tip bites into the wood, change the angle to 45 degrees. Drive four to six nails into each joint, two on each side, with an optional one at the front and back. The first nail may move the stud, but the second nail, driven from the other side, will move it back.

If you have difficulty toenailing, drill pilot holes for the nails, using a $3/32$-inch bit. Or, place a $14\frac{1}{2}$-inch board between studs to serve as a temporary nailing brace.

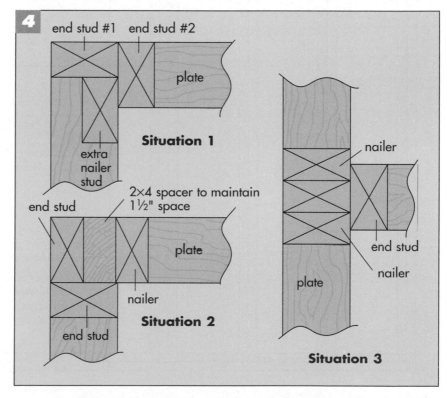

temporary nailing brace

Situation 1
end stud #1   end stud #2
plate
extra nailer stud

Situation 2
end stud
plate
2×4 spacer to maintain 1½" space
nailer
end stud

Situation 3
nailer
end stud
nailer
plate

ROUGHING-IN AN OPENING

*I*f you plan to install a door in your wall, find out the rough opening dimensions you'll need. For a prehung door, measure the outside dimensions of the jamb and add ½ inch for shimming. With a slab door (one that is not prehung), measure the width of the door, add 2½ inches for the side jambs and shims, and add 2 inches to the height for the head jamb, shims, and flooring. Standard door widths are 24, 26, 28, 30, 32, and 36 inches. Door heights usually are 80 inches.

Once you know the opening's size, build the wall as described on pages 284–286, with the addition of the framing members shown below. These framing members have special names and functions.

Jack studs are the vertical 2×4s on each side of the door opening. They are attached to a **king stud** or to another jack stud. This doubling of studs provides solid, unbending support for the door.

The **header** is made of two 2×6s with a ½-inch plywood spacer sandwiched in between. (The plywood is needed to make the header 3½ inches thick, the same thickness as the wall framing.) The header rests on top of the jack studs and spans the top of the opening, supporting overhead loads. For openings that are less than 3 feet wide, you can use 2×4s instead of 2×6s.

Cripples are the short 2×4s added between the header and the top plate. They maintain a 16-inch on-center stud spacing for nailing the drywall and help distribute the weight equally from above.

A window opening is much like a door opening. You install a sill (much like a header) at the bottom height of the window and add more cripples between it and the wall's bottom plate.

16"

cripples

header

king stud

width of door plus 2½"

jack studs

height of door plus 2" from floor

width of door plus 2½"

Cut at these points with a handsaw to remove this section of the plate.

Top horizontal piece is fastened to the verticals and to the joists.

bottom horizontal

cross pieces every 4'

2×4s or 2×2s

Frame around an I-beam.
Use 2×2s to frame around a narrow obstruction, such as a beam. Fasten the frame together with screws rather than nails because the structure will be wobbly as you work. Drill pilot holes whenever you drive a screw near the end of a board.

Make chalk lines on the joists, 1⅝ inches out from either side of the beam. On every other joist,

attach a vertical 2×2 to the joists, cutting them to extend 1¾ inches below the bottom of the beam. Fasten horizontal pieces to the bottom ends of the verticals, then fasten horizontal pieces at the top, driving screws into both the vertical supports and the joists. Finish the framing by installing short horizontal cross pieces about every 4 feet between the bottom horizontal frame members.

Frame around a pipe.
You can cover a soil stack or other tall, narrow obstruction with a frame. Mark lines on the floor and measure for top and bottom plates as you would a regular wall. Draw plumb lines on the walls to use as guides. Build three narrow walls of 2×4s or 2×2s; raise them into position; and fasten them to the floor, ceiling, wall, and each other.

WORKING WITH METAL STUDS

Metal framing costs a good deal less than wood 2×4s, and it is lighter. Metal is not susceptible to rot or insect damage, and the factory-made pieces are free from bows, twists, knots, and other imperfections that sometimes make wood hard to work with.

Working with metal studs takes some adjustments. You can't build walls on the floor then raise them up. Instead, you must install the top and floor runners, then insert the studs. Cut metal studs with tin snips or a circular saw and metal-cutting blade. Fasten the pieces together with self-tapping screws.

If you make a mistake, it usually is easier to move a metal stud than a wood one. Running electrical wiring and pipes for plumbing is easy because punchout holes are precut in the studs.

On the downside, once walls are built, you can't attach items to

metal stud walls as easily as you can with wood walls. You can fasten items to a metal stud with a screw, but not a nail. If you plan to hang cabinets or shelves on the wall, cross-brace the wall with C-runners. Door jambs and windows can be attached to steel framing, but it's easier to shim and attach the units if you use wood framing, fastened to the metal studs, around these openings.

You'll Need
Time: 1 to 2 hours to build a basic 12 foot wall.
Skills: Measuring and marking for walls, cutting with tin snips, fastening with a drill or screw gun.
Tools: Tape measure, level, tin snips or circular saw with metal-cutting blade, drill or screw gun, plumb bob.

Caution!
WATCH OUT FOR METAL
■ *The ends of metal studs, especially those that you cut, often are very sharp. When working with metal, wear gloves. If you're cutting with a circular saw and metal cutting blade, wear long sleeves that are not loose or floppy.*
■ *Cutting metal also can be dangerous because small pieces of metal fly through the air. Be sure to wear eye protection whenever you cut metal studs.*
■ *If you run electrical wiring through metal framing, use sections of plastic foam pipe insulation or specially made plastic grommets to protect wires from damage.*

1. Cut the studs.
Lay out framing as you would for a wood wall (see pages 284–287). Cut the runners to be used for top and bottom plates to length with tin snips. Or, use a metal-cutting blade on a circular saw. Using a circular saw is faster, but make sure no one is in the area as you cut, and wear protective eye wear and clothing as you work.

2. Attach the ceiling runner.
Position the ceiling runner and attach it to each joist with a drywall screw. If joists run parallel to the wall, install cross-bracing so there is something to which you can attach the runner. Position the floor runner directly below the ceiling runner, using a plumb bob. Attach it to the floor with screws or masonry nails.

3. Cut and insert the studs.
Cut the studs to length with tin snips. Insert them into the runners, starting at a slight angle and twisting them into place. For easier plumbing or electrical installation, make sure all the stud legs are pointed in the same direction and all the predrilled punchouts line up.

4. Attach studs to the runners.
Once studs are placed correctly, drive in $7/16$-inch pan- or wafer-headed screws through the runners and into the studs. Hold the stud flange firmly against the runner as you work. Drive in four screws, one on either side of each runner at the top and bottom.

5. Attach headers.
Where you need a door or window header, cut a stud piece 8 inches longer than the width of the opening. Cut the two sides of the stud 4 inches from each end so you can bend back a tab, as shown. Slip the tabs into place and attach with screws.

6. Install the drywall.
Inspect the framing to make sure you have a fastening surface for drywall at all points. Attach the drywall with drywall screws placed 8 to 12 inches apart. Install corner beads with screws or staples. Tape and finish the walls (see pages 297–298).

FURRING BASEMENT WALLS

When finishing basement walls, one option is to build regular stud walls (see pages 284–287), and fasten them to the concrete or masonry walls. A stud wall goes up quickly, gives you room to add plenty of insulation, and ensures that the new walls will be straight, even if the existing walls are not. The disadvantage is you lose some floor space because of the thickness of the walls.

If insulation is not a problem and your basement walls are fairly smooth and straight, you may want to save money in materials and preserve some square footage by building the walls with 1×2, 1×3, or 1×4 furring strips.

The layout is the same as for stud walls. The seams between drywall or paneling sheets must fall on a furring strip, and there must be a nailing surface in all corners and at ends of the sheets.

The construction method, however, is much different. Furring strips are shimmed where necessary, then fastened with glue and masonry nails or with a power hammer, which shoots nails with gunpowder charges (see the "Tools to Use" box, *opposite*).

> ### YOU'LL NEED
> **TIME:** A day for a 12×12 room.
> **SKILLS:** Laying out, measuring, cutting, and hammering.
> **TOOLS:** Hammer, baby sledge, caulking gun, circular saw, tape measure, level, chalk line.

1 Shim where necessary to plumb furring strips.

Fill in horizontals at top and bottom.

Cut out for conduit and pipes.

Install verticals first.

Add nailers around doorway.

Insulate between furring with rigid foam insulation.

Plumb all verticals.

16" on center

16" on center

Use 1×2s, 1×3s, or 1×4s as furring.

Keep base pieces ½" off floor.

1. Plan the furring layout.
Begin the job by marking the locations of the vertical furring strips. One easy way to do this is to position a sheet of your wall material in the corner of the room, plumb it, and strike a chalk line down its outside edge. Using this line as a guide and 16 inches as the center-to-center measurement, mark the locations of the other vertical strips along that wall.

Measure and cut each strip to fit between the floor and ceiling. Cut each piece ½ inch short, so that it will be fastened a bit above the floor as a safeguard against flooding and settling.

2. Apply adhesive.

With a caulking gun, squeeze a wavy ¼-inch bead of construction adhesive onto the furring strip. As you finish, turn the gun's handle to ease pressure on the adhesive, discontinuing the flow. Push the strip against the wall in its correct location, pressing firmly to help spread the adhesive.

3. Set adhesive.

Pull the strip off the wall and lean it against another wall to dry and let the adhesive begin to set up. After letting it set for the time specified by the manufacturer, press the strip back into place.

4. Plumb and shim as needed.

Check the strip for plumb. If a dip or bulge is noticeable to the eye, tuck pairs of shims behind the strip and wedge it into line. Double-check your work as the job progresses by holding a straightedge horizontally across four or five vertical pieces. Correct any gaps or bulges.

5. Drive in fasteners.

Hammer concrete nails through the strip and the shims and into the masonry wall. On a brick or block wall, it often is easiest to drive the nails into the mortar joints. Use a baby sledge if you have one. Driving nails into concrete walls is extremely difficult; consider a power hammer (see box at *right*).

6. Install the horizontal pieces.

After all the verticals are in place, aligned, and secured, begin work on the top and bottom horizontal pieces. Measure and cut them one at a time. Apply adhesive, shim if necessary, and install them as you did the verticals.

TOOLS TO USE

POWER HAMMER

Choose a power hammer that loads quickly. It usually makes sense to rent a better-quality power tool, rather than buying a cheap one. Experiment with several types of loads to find one powerful enough to drive in the nails completely, but not so powerful as to drive them through the furring strips. ***Note:*** *Follow the manufacturer's directions carefully. A power hammer is literally a firearm, and is dangerous if mishandled.*

QUART-SIZE CAULKING GUN

On large jobs, this tool will pay for itself because adhesive purchased in large tubes costs less per ounce. It also will save you time and create less mess because you'll need to change tubes 2½ times less often.

LAYING OUT AND CUTTING DRYWALL

Drywall is inexpensive, and hanging and finishing skills are within the reach of a homeowner. But hanging drywall is difficult work. The sheets are heavy and unwieldy because they are so large. Most rooms are out of square, so cutting is often difficult.

Finishing drywall to a perfectly smooth surface takes three applications of compound and sandings for professionals—four or five for beginners. Finishing success relies in part on careful hanging. So, this is one job you may want to get estimates for hanging and finishing and hire the job out to a professional.

Check framing to make sure you have adequate nailing surfaces (see page 285). Add members that are missing. If you are covering an existing wall, locate all the joists and studs and clearly mark their locations on the walls and ceilings. Draft a strong helper—hanging drywall alone is nearly impossible.

YOU'LL NEED

TIME: With a helper, a day to drywall a 12×12-foot room.
SKILLS: Measuring, physical strength, thoroughness.
TOOLS: Tape measure, drywall square, utility knife, drywall saw, chalk line.

TOOLS TO USE

DRYWALL SQUARE

Don't hesitate to spend the money for a drywall square (see page 208). It quickly pays for itself in time and labor savings. For crosscuts, you simply make one measurement, set the square in place, and run your knife along the square's blade for a square cut. It also simplifies rip cuts (see page 87).

Lay out the job.
Plan where each sheet will go. Begin by hanging sheets on the ceiling, then butt the wall pieces up against the ceiling. Remember that taping and finishing (see pages 297–298) the drywall takes more time than hanging it (see pages 295–296), so minimize seams wherever possible. Sometimes you can eliminate a butt seam, which is the hardest type of seam to tape, by using 10- or 12-foot sheets instead of standard 8-foot sheets. Installing these big sheets may seem like a lot of trouble, but it will save you time and effort in the long run.

Make a crosscut.
Store drywall sheets flat or on edge on pieces of 1× or 2× scrap lumber to hold the sheets off the floor. Before cutting a sheet, make sure the finished surface is facing you. Mark your cut line, stand the sheet on edge, and set your drywall square in place. Clasp the square firmly on top, and brace it at its base with your foot. With the edge of the knife blade against the square, cut downward most of the way, then finish by cutting up from the bottom. Snap the segment back away from your cut line. Finally slice through the backing paper with your knife.

Measure for the last piece.

To determine the correct cutoff length of a corner sheet, measure the distance from the last sheet to the corner at both the top and the bottom. If it is more than ¼ inch out of square, mark both ends of the cut, rather than making a square cut with a drywall square.

Make a rip cut.

If you need to make a parallel rip cut—one that is the same width all along its length—use your drywall square. Set the square on the edge of the sheet, and hold the knife against it at the measured distance. Slide the square along with the knife in

Slide the square and the knife together.

Use a chalk line for cuts not parallel to the edge of the sheet.

position, cutting as you go.

Often a rip cut will not be square; it will be shorter at one end than the other. In this case, make a mark at each end of the sheet and chalk a line between the marks. Cut freehand or use a straightedge as a guide if you need precision.

Make a rectangular cutout.

To make a cut for a receptacle box, measure the distance from the box edges to the edge of the last panel. Then measure the distance from the top and bottom of the electrical box to the floor (minus ½ inch) or from the piece above it. Transfer the measurements to the sheet and draw a rectangle. Score the surface with a utility knife, then cut it with a drywall saw.

Cut around pipes.

To cut a hole for a pipe, measure and mark the sheet for the center of the pipe. Drill a hole using a holesaw bit that is slightly larger than the pipe diameter. Or, you can draw a circle and cut it out with a drywall saw or a knife.

EXPERTS' INSIGHT

AVOID MOISTURE DAMAGE IN A BASEMENT

■ Wood framing can withstand occasional wetness as long as it is allowed to dry out. But drywall that gets wet once will lose its strength and crumble.

■ If you are drywalling a basement or another place that is subject to chronic dampness or occasional flooding, add nailers to the base of the framing and cut the drywall sheets so they are held off the floor 2 to 3 inches. When you install the baseboard molding, you will need to fur out the gap.

■ To raise drywall even higher, add a 1×6 baseboard directly to the framing and set the drywall on top of it. This will keep the drywall 5½ inches off the floor.

HANGING DRYWALL

Be prepared for strenuous labor when it comes time to hang drywall. The sheets are heavy, you'll be working in awkward positions, and you'll have to hold the sheets in place while you drive in nails or screws. It's tempting to rush the job, but you'll kick yourself later if you do sloppy work. Wide gaps between drywall sheets take a long time to tape, and nobody wants nails popping out later. Here's how to do the job correctly the first time.

Ceiling pattern
nails only

Wall patterns
nails only

nails and adhesive

12"

16"

7"

24"

7"

adhesive in middle

YOU'LL NEED

TIME: 20 minutes per sheet for walls, 30 minutes per ceiling sheet.
SKILLS: A strong back, fastening in difficult circumstances.
TOOLS: Tape measure, good ladders or scaffolding, hammer or drill with drywall-type screwdriver attachment, drywall taping blades.

Nail or screw according to code.
Local building codes specify how many nails or screws you should use to hang drywall and in what sort of pattern. Codes vary not only from region to region, but from room to room; for example, more fasteners may be required in bathrooms. Check with your building department.

Many professionals don't nail in pairs, but there is good reason to do so: If one nail pops through the paper, the other will hold.

For ceiling panels, the general practice is to pair nails at 12-inch intervals around the perimeter and 12 inches along each joist. Requirements are less stringent for walls. If you don't use adhesive, install two nails into the wall studs at 16-inch intervals and a single nail every 7 inches along edges. When using adhesive, install two nails at 24-inch intervals and one nail at 7 inches along the edge. Keep adhesive 6 inches away from top and bottom of sheet.

WRONG:
Nailhead protrudes.

CORRECT:
Nailhead set in dimple.

WRONG:
Paper broken.

Set nailheads correctly.
If you simply drive in a nail flush, you will not be able to cover over it with joint compound. If you drive the nail too deeply, you will break the paper on the drywall. When the paper is broken, the nail won't hold; it tears right through the gypsum inner core.

Try to drive the nail so the nailhead is set into a slightly dimpled surface. No portion of the nailhead should protrude above the surface of the drywall.

To test if your nails are driven deeply enough, run a taping blade along the surface of the wall. You should not feel any nailheads click against the blade as you pull it across. Pull out any nails that miss a joist or stud. Swat the hole with your hammer to dimple it.

Attach drywall with screws.
If you are using screws, the same principles apply as with nailing: The screw head must be set below the surface, but it must not break the paper. This is difficult to do with a simple screwdriver bit. Use a dimpler bit or a drywall screwdriver (see box on page 296). Always drive in screws perpendicular to the sheet or their heads will tear the paper.

Install the ceiling sheets.

Hang drywall on the ceiling before installing the wall sheets. Start in a corner and against one side of the room and work out from there, keeping the panels perpendicular to the joists. Take time before you start to locate joists and mark their locations on the sheet and the wall. Searching for joists while holding the sheet up with your head is no fun.

The quickest, but most difficult, way to install drywall on a ceiling is to set the panel in place and support it with your head, leaving your hands free to hold and drive nails or screws. Wearing a baseball cap greatly minimizes pulled hair and a sore head.

To make things easier, construct one or two 2×2 T-braces to use as props. Or, rent a drywall hoist. Either solution will make the process easier and result in a much neater job.

T-brace made of 2×2s

drywall hoist

TOOLS TO USE

DRYWALL HAMMER

There are hammers made especially for drywall installation. They are light, for easy handling; they have wide heads so it's easier to make a dimple without damaging the paper; and their heads are tilted a bit for access into corners. You may not use one very often, but it will make hanging and, subsequently, taping easier.

DRYWALL SCREWDRIVER OR DIMPLER BIT

A drywall screwdriver has an adjustable bit that, once set correctly, will drive the bit to the correct depth, then stop. A less expensive, and just as good, option is a dimpler bit that you can attach to a drill.

Install the wall sheets.

Once the ceiling panels are up, hang sheets on the walls. If you are installing sheets horizontally, begin with the upper sheets, butting them firmly against the ceiling drywall. Make sure all vertical seams hit studs. Butt the lower panels firmly against the upper panels, tapered edge to tapered edge. Raise up sheets tightly with a wedge or lever.

If you are installing sheets

Ceiling corner

Nail 7" from ceiling corner.

ceiling joist

Inside corner

Place first.

Place first.

Outside corner

vertically, check the tapered edges to make sure they fall midway across a stud. If they don't, either cut the drywall or attach pieces of lumber to the stud to give yourself a nailing surface for the next piece.

Overlap pieces at corners, as shown *above*. Finish the job by adding the filler pieces, measuring and cutting each piece to size. Make sure each piece has at least two nailing members to support it.

TAPING DRYWALL

Once you've gained some experience, three coats of drywall compound, with sandings, will produce smooth walls. But as a beginner, don't be surprised if it takes you four or five coats. Unless you have large holes that require patching plaster, use ready-mixed drywall joint compound. Dry-mix compounds provide more strength for trouble areas, but you'll need to work fast if you use them. To hide imperfections, apply texture to your walls with a rented texture gun and hopper.

YOU'LL NEED

TIME: For a typical bedroom, 5 hours for the first coat and 2 hours for subsequent coats, plus time for sanding and drying.
SKILLS: Patience and willingness to learn.
TOOLS: Utility knife; 6-, 10-, and 12-inch taping blades; corner taping tool; pole sander or hand sander; tin snips.

EXPERTS' INSIGHT

DRYWALL FINISHING TIPS

■ Use self-sticking mesh tape on the drywall wherever a tapered edge meets a tapered edge, as shown *above*. Use paper tape everywhere else. Mesh tape requires less joint compound, but does not work as well for inside corners.
■ Rusty, gunked-up tools ruin your work. Scrape, wash, and dry blades after every use.
■ When sanding, control the extremely fine dust by using a fan to pull the dust out a window. Seal doorways and wear a breathing mask.

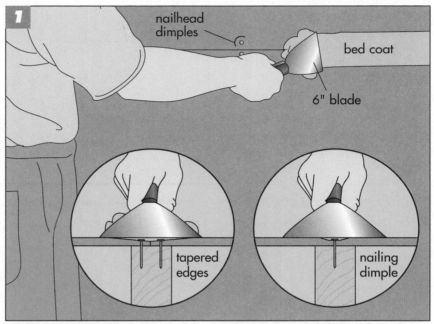

1. Apply a bed coat.
Conceal nailheads by putting compound on a 6-inch taping blade and passing over the spot twice. Make sure you leave compound only in the depression and none on the rest of the sheet. Do this with each coat until the dimple is filled in completely.

Joints are much more difficult— butt joints especially. If you are using self-sticking mesh tape, simply cut pieces to fit, press them into place, and begin applying joint compound. For paper tape, start by spreading a bed coat over the joint with a 6-inch taping blade. Apply just enough for the paper tape to adhere.

2. Embed the tape in compound.
(Skip this step if you are using mesh tape.) Immediately after applying the bed coat to a joint, center a length of paper tape over the joint and press the tape firmly against the filled joint by running your taping blade along it. If the tape begins to slide, hold it in place with your hand. If bubbles form under the tape, if there are places where the tape is not sticking to the bed coat, or if wrinkles appear, peel the tape back and apply more compound. Then press the tape back again.

3. *Apply compound over the tape.*

Load a 10-inch taping blade with compound and apply a smooth coat over the tape. Where two tapered joints meet, make sure the blade extends past both tapers. Fill in the tapers only, so you have a flat wall surface. For butt joints, feather out the compound 7 to 9 inches on each side; a small ridge in the middle can be sanded later. After the compound dries, scrape off ridges and bumps, and sand. Apply and sand successive coats until the surface is smooth.

4. *Coat outside corners.*

To protect and conceal the drywall edges that meet at an outside corner, cut a piece of metal corner bead using tin snips. Fit the strip over the corner and fasten it to the wall one side at a time. Drive in nails or screws at 10-inch intervals. Check to make sure the flange of the corner bead does not protrude above what will be the finished surface by running a taping blade along the length of the corner bead. Fasten down any areas of flange that protrude. Apply a coat of joint compound with a 6-inch blade angled away from the corner. Allow one side of the blade to ride on the bead, the other side on the wall. For subsequent coats, use 10- and 12-inch blades.

5. *Tape inside corners.*

Outside corners can be almost fun, but inside corners are more difficult. Apply a bed coat of compound to both sides with a 6-inch blade. Cut a piece of paper tape to the correct length, fold it, and place it in position by hand. Keep it straight to avoid wrinkles. Run a corner taping tool along its length to embed the tape in the compound. Lift and reapply compound wherever the tape has wrinkles, bubbles, or nonadhering spots. Once the tape is embedded, apply some compound to the walls and some to the corner tool. Stroke on a smooth coat. This will take several passes and some practice. You may find it easier to feather out the edges with an 8-inch blade.

INSTALLING PANELING

Sheet paneling needs a solid, plumb backing. Typically, this is a stud wall covered with ½-inch drywall. On the inside of exterior and below-grade walls, sandwich insulation and a vapor barrier between the studs and the drywall to protect panels from moisture.

As you estimate materials, keep in mind that panel seams must hit studs. Lay out the job to avoid thin strips of paneling. It's better to cut 14 inches off the first panel on a wall than end up with a piece 2 inches wide at the end of the wall. Stand the panels up for 48 hours in the room in which they'll be installed to condition them.

YOU'LL NEED

TIME: About a day to panel a medium-size room.
SKILLS: Measuring, scribing, cutting sheets, nailing.
TOOLS: Level, hammer, nail set, caulking gun.

EXPERTS' INSIGHT

CHOOSING PANELING

Sheet paneling is inexpensive and easy to install, but it is also thin and flexible. If your walls are at all wavy, the paneling will accentuate the curves rather than hide them.

If you have problem walls, consider tongue-and-groove planks. They are more expensive and take longer to install, but they'll straighten the walls. Planking requires furring strips and shims every 16 vertical inches for backing.

Be sure to inspect sheet paneling for variations in color, flaws, and splinters.

Cut this side so other side sits on a stud.

Run a marker along this edge.

1. Mark the seams.
Mark the location of the studs where the panel edges will meet. Cut the first sheet so its edge falls on the middle of a stud. Set the first piece in place without attaching it. Panels should have a ⅟₁₆-inch gap between them to allow for expansion and contraction. To disguise the gap, run a felt marker along the seam.

adhesive in caulking gun

2. Apply adhesive.
Using a caulking gun, apply a ½-inch bead of panel adhesive on the wall in a wavy pattern so there is no gap larger than 8 inches between adhesive beads. (A large caulking gun that holds quart tubes may be a worthwhile investment.) Press the panel back in place and elevate it above the floor about ½ inch.

Drive in nails only halfway.

3. Tack the sheet in place.
Align the panel so it is plumb and drive three or more finish or color-matched paneling nails halfway in along the top edge of the panel. With the panel dangling, compress the adhesive behind it by hammering on the surface with a block of wood wrapped in cloth.

4. Let adhesive set, attach panel.
Pull out the bottom of the panel and insert a spacer to keep it away from the wall while the adhesive sets up. After the time specified for the adhesive (typically, 3 minutes), press the panel against the wall and drive in nails every 8 inches along the edges and every 12 inches into intermediate studs.

5. Panel around an opening.

To panel around a door or window, measure over from the last panel installed. Measure up from the floor or down from the ceiling to find the height of the opening. Measure in the A, B, C, D sequence shown. If possible, lay out panels so their seams fall over the center of openings. Remember to allow a 1/16-inch gap between the panels.

6. Fit the last panel on a wall.

For the last piece, you'll need to precision-cut a panel to fit neatly against the inside edge of the wall. Most likely, the corner will not be plumb, so measure from the previous panel to the corner at several points along the panel edge and draw a line with a straightedge. Cut with a circular saw or a sabersaw if the curves are pronounced. When cutting with either of these tools, flip the panel over so the finish side is down.

7. Fine-tune the edge.

It may take several attempts before you get a piece to fit against an irregular corner. Be conservative in your cutting; you can always cut more, but you can't make the sheet bigger. Use a block plane or surface-forming tool to shave off small amounts of material. Hold the tool at an angle so the bulk of the material is cut from the back of the panel, leaving a thin, easily trimmed edge at the surface for final fitting.

8. Make cutouts.

To cut openings for electrical outlets, measure the distance between the last panel installed and the right and left edges of the outlet. Then measure the distance from the floor to the outlet top and bottom, subtracting the height the panel will be off the floor. Transfer your measurements to the paneling and cut out the hole with a keyhole saw.

9. Cut around complex obstructions.

To cut around such structures as a fireplace and mantel, measure the distance from the last installed sheet to the farthest point along the structure. Measure the height of the structure, allowing for the gap along the floor. Transfer your measurements to the paneling, connect the cut lines with a straightedge, and saw out the bulk of the waste area.

Temporarily nail up the sheet so it is plumb and alongside the structure at the proper elevation. Set a compass (see pages 231–232) to the width the sheet needs to move to meet the last one installed, and scribe the contours onto the sheet.

Make the cut using a sabersaw with a fine-tooth blade or a coping saw. Fit the panel and make fine adjustments with a utility knife. Secure the panel in place.

BUILDING A FIXED-SHELF UNIT

Whether you need a freestanding or wall-mounted shelf, a basic box with fixed shelves is sturdy and can be adapted to most any style. Freestanding units can be stacked and moved into new and different configurations; several wall-mounted units can be combined for ease of installation.

Beginner carpenters can make this unit. Butt-joining the outside corners produces a clean-looking joint with little trouble. If you have some carpentry experience, you may want the cleaner look of mitered joints. Try mitered joints only if you are sure of your ability to make perfectly straight miter cuts; gaps will ruin the project.

To support the shelves, simple butt joints can be strong and stable if fastened with screws. Or reinforce a butt joint by attaching a cleat under the shelf.

A dado joint is the strongest and virtually guarantees that the shelves and the outside pieces will not warp. When you get the hang of dadoes, cutting them is not time-consuming.

The shelves are simple and require precise cutting. Before starting, test your power saw with scrap pieces to make sure you can cut perfectly straight and square without raising splinters. Use a sharp blade. Often it is possible to stack pieces roughly cut to length and make the final cuts on several shelves at once.

The miter-jointed box shown in the steps on page 302 is the most difficult method.

YOU'LL NEED

TIME: Most of a day to build a fixed unit with several shelves and a back.
SKILLS: Accurate measuring and cutting, drilling and driving screws, cutting dadoes.
TOOLS: Power saw, drill, hammer, tape measure, chisel.

EXPERTS' INSIGHT

FINISHING OR PAINTING A SHELF UNIT

■ Painting a cabinet can be very time-consuming, especially if you need to brush on two coats. Painting boards before they are put together is much easier and faster. Give the boards a primer coat before assembly. (Many primers dry in an hour or less.) If you want two coats of paint over the primer, apply one coat before assembly.

■ If you need to paint a number of units, consider buying an inexpensive paint sprayer or renting an airless sprayer.

■ Staining assembled shelves is difficult; it's hard to get a consistent color in the corners. Stain the pieces, assemble them, and then apply a finish.

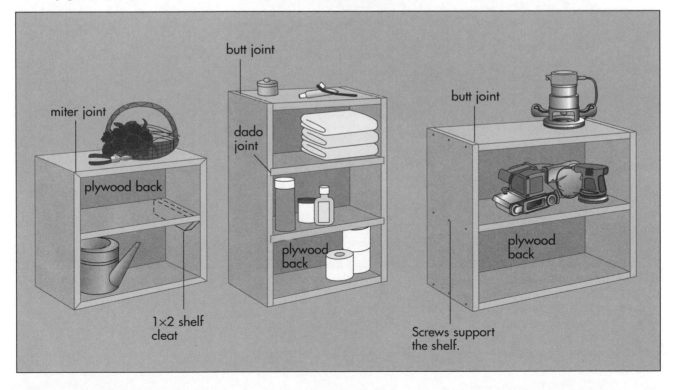

miter joint
butt joint
dado joint
butt joint
plywood back
plywood back
plywood back
1×2 shelf cleat
Screws support the shelf.

1. Cut outside pieces.

For precise miter cuts, rough cut the outside pieces slightly longer than needed, then cut the miters. Place the two verticals side by side, and clamp them firmly. Draw dado layout lines for each shelf, and use a scrap piece of shelf to make sure you have marked the width correctly. Cut the dadoes $5/16$ inch deep using a circular, radial-arm, or table saw (see pages 211–213). Clean out the dadoes by chiseling out the waste (see inset). Then use the chisel to smooth the bottom of the groove.

2. Assemble and measure.

Join the pieces to form a rectangle by drilling pilot holes and driving $2\frac{1}{4}$-inch finish screws. Check for square continually as you fasten. Measure from dado to dado for the lengths of the shelves before cutting the shelves to ensure the best fit.

3. Tap shelves into place.

Carefully slip a shelf into both dadoes. Tap it down using a scrap of wood to keep from marring the shelf edge. Avoid tapping one end down farther than the other; alternate between ends every inch or so or gently tap the middle of the shelf to work it into place. When the shelf edges are flush with the edges of the outside pieces, drill pilot holes and drive screws to reinforce and tighten the joints.

4. Add the back.

Cut a piece of $1/4$-inch plywood $1/4$ inch smaller than the shelf unit in both directions. Center it on the back so there is a $1/8$-inch reveal all around. Drive 4d box nails every 6 inches or so.

INSTALLING ADJUSTABLE SHELVES

Inside a frame, support adjustable shelves near each corner and in the middle of the span if needed. The most common method is to use metal support strips with clips, sometimes called pilasters. Attach them to the inside faces of the side pieces, or cut grooves and set them in. You can also opt for one of the pin methods shown on page 304.

The important thing is to get all four supports level with one another. Work systematically and double-check often—it's easy to misalign the supports.

YOU'LL NEED

TIME: An hour for support strips; several hours for other methods.
SKILLS: Measuring, drilling, attaching with screws.
TOOLS: Drill, hacksaw, tape measure, square, pegboard.

The total system.
Space clips as you would other supports. If the span between vertical outside pieces is too great, install a center stile with a support strip attached. The shelf must be wide enough to fit snugly between the stile and the rear support strip.

EXPERTS' INSIGHT

TALL UNITS NEED A FIXED SHELF

■ Place support strips on side pieces that are stable and strong; if they warp, the clips may no longer support the shelf. Support strips will add some rigidity, but not much.

■ If the vertical pieces are made of 1-by lumber and are longer than 4 feet, install one fixed shelf about halfway up to ensure that the sides do not bow outward. Attach the shelf with a butt joint or a dado joint (see page 261–262). Then install support strips or pins above and below the fixed shelf.

1. Mark for cutting strips.
Cut one piece to the desired height. It doesn't need to extend to the top of the unit, just a notch or two beyond the top shelf. Use the first piece to measure for the others. Line up the slots. To help position the clips later, line up the numbers as well.

about 1" out

2. Mark and cut dadoes.
Position each strip an inch or so from the edge of the unit, and trace lines. See pages 261 for instructions on cutting dadoes. (If you want to set the support strips into dadoes, remember to cut the dadoes before beginning to assemble the shelf unit.)

awl

3. Attach with screws.
Position the support strip and use an awl or sharp pencil to mark for the screws. Drill pilot holes with a drill bit and a depth guide so you won't drill through. A piece of tape wrapped around the drill bit will serve this purpose. Drive screws to attach it.

Pin options.
For an inconspicuous support system, drill holes at regular intervals and insert pins. Metal (or plastic) pins come in two types, a flat pin and a bracket pin. Or cut lengths of hardwood dowel to fit into the holes. When using pins, the shelves must fit tightly; if there is more than a ⅛-inch gap between a shelf and the vertical board, the pin could work itself loose and cause the shelf to fall.

MEASUREMENTS

TIPS FOR DRILLING A GRID OF PIN HOLES

■ If the shelf unit has one or more vertical dividers in the middle of the unit, avoid placing holes directly opposite each other on the divider, or else the holes will meet and poke all the way through. To prevent this, offset the vertical lines by ½ inch or so.

■ Save yourself time by drilling only as many holes as you really need. The grid need not extend the length of the vertical board. Start at the lowest possible position for the bottom shelf, and end at the highest possible position for the top shelf.

To space holes, use pegboard...
Cut a piece of perforated hardboard (pegboard) to fit into the space, and use it as a guide. Note which end goes up, so you always align it the same way.

... or use a square.
Draw vertical lines about an inch in from the front and rear edges of the unit. Measure with a framing square or tape measure, and mark evenly spaced horizontal lines at one of the vertical lines. Then use a square to copy the horizontal measurements onto the other vertical line. Use a drill bit depth guide so you don't drill through the standard.

INSTALLING RECESSED SHELVING

*R*ecessed shelves are real space savers, ideal for collectibles and knickknacks. Setting shelves inside a wall looks more difficult than it actually is; checking that the wall cavity is free of electrical and plumbing lines and cutting a clean opening are the most difficult steps. Otherwise you simply build a box shelf (see page 302) and insert it in the wall. The unit shown here spans across two studs. If a unit 14½ inches wide will suit your needs, you can build it without cutting a stud.

You'll Need

TIME: A full day.
SKILLS: Cutting walls, basic cabinetmaking.
TOOLS: Saber saw, reciprocating saw or keyhole saw, drill, hammer, tape measure, level.

1. Lay out and cut the wall.
Locate studs by rapping on the wall, drilling test holes, or using a stud sensor. Drill holes and insert an unbent coat hanger to explore behind the opening. Do not cut the wall if electrical or plumbing lines are between the studs.

Cut the drywall with a saber saw or keyhole saw. (If the wall is plaster, cutting will be difficult: Score lines deeply with a knife first to prevent cracking the surrounding area.) Cut alongside the studs for vertical lines; mark horizontal cut lines with a level.

CAUTION!

IS IT A LOAD-BEARING WALL?
Some interior walls are simply partitions between rooms. Others are "load-bearing," meaning that they support the roof or a wall on the floor above. Walls that run parallel to joists above are not usually load-bearing. Outside walls are load-bearing, and walls that run perpendicular to overhead joists may be load-bearing as well. Check by taking measurements to see whether a wall above is directly on top of the wall you want to cut into. Do not cut a stud of a load-bearing wall. Consult with a carpenter if you are not sure.

2. Cut the stud and install the sill.

Use a reciprocating saw to cut the center stud at the bottom and the top. Or cut as deeply as you can with a circular saw, then finish the cut with a handsaw. Be careful not to cut through the wall surface on the other side. Cut a 2×4 sill to the width of the opening, and attach it with screws. Make sure it is level.

3. Build the recessed unit.

Build a shelf unit like this butt-jointed frame with adjustable shelves resting on support pins (see pages 304). Rip-cut the boards to the depth of the opening, less ¼ inch for the back piece. Make the unit ½ inch smaller than the opening on all sides. Before assembling, drill holes for bracket pins.

4. Install shelf unit in the opening.

Set the unit in place. Check for level and plumb, and make sure the front edge is flush with the wall surface. Use shims if necessary. Drill pilot holes and drive 6d finish nails through the sides and bottom; drive one nail through the top into the cut stud.

5. Trim it out.

Install molding around the perimeter. Butt-jointed casing is the simplest, although you may prefer to miter the corners. Drill pilot holes to avoid cracking the wood, and drive 6d nails into studs and 4d nails into the shelf unit.

ADDING UNDER-STAIR SHELVES

The area under a basement stairway often goes to waste; stacking boxes there is awkward because the space is triangular. A shelf system provides a convenient place to store canned goods, bulk purchases, and sports equipment.

Because basement floors may become damp, the bottom shelf should be raised a bit by resting it on pressure-treated 2×4 sleepers, which will not rot even if they get soaked occasionally.

Rather than measuring each upright individually—a complicated process—the technique shown here allows you to quickly cut the outline of the triangle, then make shelves to fit.

You'll Need

TIME: Most of a day.
SKILLS: Careful measuring, making bevel cuts, fastening with screws.
TOOLS: Power saw, drill, level, framing square, chalk line.

Under-stair shelves.
Basic shelves like these can be quickly assembled with screws. Offset the shelves so they do not line up horizontally; that way, you will be able to drive screws straight through the uprights and into the shelves. For a more finished look and for greater strength, you can set the shelves in dadoes (see pages 234), cut into the uprights.

1. Mark and cut backing plywood.
Place a piece of ¼-inch plywood against the stairway, resting it on top of a piece of 2×4, positioned along the stairway where it will be at the back of the shelves. Be sure to check for plumb before measuring and marking. Mark each side, snap a chalk line, and cut. Do the same for the other backing pieces.

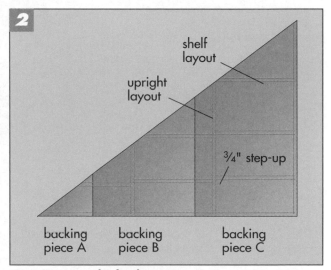

2. Lay out on the backing pieces.
Test to see that the backing pieces fit. Then lay them down and draw layout lines indicating shelves and uprights. Step up each shelf ¾ inch so you can fasten each from the side. Avoid making unusably small triangular shelves. The shelves will be wide; use ¾-inch plywood so they won't sag.

T-bevel

circular saw

pressure-treated 2×4

3. Bevel-cut the pieces.
The uprights should be bevel-cut at an angle, where they meet the stringer, and the shelves at another angle. Hold a T-bevel against the plywood backing pieces to find the correct angle, and transfer that angle to a circular saw, table saw, or radial arm saw. Cut the pieces to width. Measure the layout lines, and cut all shelves and uprights to length. Then cut the bevels.

4. Attach sleepers to the floor.
Cut two pieces of pressure-treated 2×4 to fit along the bottom of the shelf system. Attach them to a concrete floor with 2-inch masonry nails every foot or so.

2" general-purpose screw

beveled edge of upright

plywood backing

fastens to stringer

2" general-purpose screw

5. Assemble the shelf unit.
Place the shelves and uprights on the backing pieces to make sure they are correctly cut. Use a framing square to line up the shelves. Attach the components by driving 2-inch general-purpose screws every few inches at each joint. Check for square continually, and make sure none of the pieces extends beyond the plywood backing. Slide the assembled unit into place, and fasten the beveled shelf edges to the stringer.

EXPERTS' INSIGHT

BUILDING WIDE PLYWOOD SHELVES

■ Plywood can soak up a lot of paint, making for a costly and time-consuming job. Consider covering the shelf tops with shelf paper, and giving the other surfaces a quick coat of polyurethane. If you choose to paint, birch-veneer plywood soaks up less paint than pine.

■ Whenever cutting across the surface grain of plywood, first score the cut line with a utility knife to prevent splintering. You do not need to do this when cutting with the grain.

■ Give exposed plywood edges a quick sanding with a hand sander to remove burrs and to prevent splinters from developing.

INSTALLING CLOSET ORGANIZERS

A standard closet, with a single rod and shelf, wastes valuable space. Improve your usable storage by dividing it into sections tailored to suit your needs.

Divide hanging clothes into two or three groups according to height. Determine how much width each group requires; make sure the clothes will not be crammed together. Figure how much shelf space you need for sweaters, as well as rack space for shoes. You may want to purchase plastic storage boxes that fit on the shelves. Allow extra room throughout for future purchases.

Draw a diagram of your shelf system on graph paper, and make a materials list that includes ¾-inch plywood and edging for the shelves and upright supports. Use 1×2 for cleats and heel stops, 1¼-inch dowels for hanging rods, metal standards and clips to support the shelves, and hardware to hold rods.

Cut the uprights for the tower of shelves, and install metal standards for adjustable shelves (see page 303). Fasten the fixed shelves with glue and 8d finish nails. Position the shelf unit, check for square, and attach it to the wall with angle brackets and screws.

Cut the top shelf to fit between the side walls and the middle shelf to fit to the shelf tower. Attach 1×2 cleats to the wall, and attach the shelves to the cleats. Cut and install closet rods using special closet-rod hardware. Cut and attach shoe shelves at about a 30-degree angle, and nail 1×2s for heel stops.

cleat

1¼" closet rod

top shelf

1¼" closet rod

76–82"

miscellaneous storage

¾" plywood

middle shelf

adjustable shelf standards

1¼" closet rod

rod/shelf bracket

shoe shelf

heel stop

38–40"

space for suits, coats, and dresses

fixed shelf

space for shirts and blouses

space for pants and skirts

pull-out basket

shoe rack

space for pants and skirts

Wire closet organizers are easy to install, need no painting, and may actually be cheaper than the materials needed to build wood shelves. You may be able to buy a kit that fits your space with little cutting.

Take a drawing with exact dimensions to a home center and ask a salesperson to supply you with all the parts. You'll need shelves with hanger rods, wall-hanging clips, end clips, diagonal supports for shelves over 2 feet, and rubber caps to cover any exposed metal rod ends. You may also want a drawer unit.

Install the drawer tower first; then cut shelves to fit above and on both sides of it. Draw level lines on the walls, install the clips so they are level, and then snap the shelves into the clips.

Install wall-hanging clips at the rear wall. Some types have plastic anchors so you can screw them directly into drywall. Mount hardware to wall studs when possible. Install end wall clips at the side walls.

Cut the shelves with a hacksaw or a pair of bolt cutters. After snapping the shelves in place, install shelf supports.

MEASUREMENTS

COMMON CLOSET SIZES

A closet for hanging clothes is usually 24 inches deep. Make shelves 18 inches deep. Shirts, blouses, and skirts usually require 36 vertical inches. For men's and women's suits and slacks, allow 42 inches. Coats and dresses are usually 54 inches long. Robes and long dresses may require up to 68 inches.

ADDING A WINDOW SEAT

With open shelves on both sides, this seat makes a flat window feel like a bay window. A seat 20 inches deep affords ample room for lounging. Two large drawers underneath are handy for storing linens, and the shelves hold a small collection of books, making this a cozy reading nook.

Begin by removing base molding from the wall; cut and reinstall it on the uncovered wall sections after installing the unit. Mark studs so you can install brackets for holding the shelves and seat in place.

YOU'LL NEED

TIME: A day to build and paint.
SKILLS: Cutting dadoes and rabbets, squaring, attaching with nails and screws.
TOOLS: Power saw, saber saw, drill, hammer, square, level.

1. Build the box and face frame.

From ³⁄₄-inch plywood, cut two side pieces, a top piece, and a back piece to the dimensions shown. Working on a flat surface, fasten the back to the side pieces by driving 2-inch screws through the back and into the sides. Set the top piece in place and drive 2-inch screws through it and into the sides and back.

Cut 1×4 and 1×2 rails and stiles to the dimensions shown. Position the bottom rail so it runs past the box sides ¼ inch on each side, and so the center piece is in its exact middle. Attach by drilling pilot holes, applying wood glue, and driving 6d finishing nails. Attach the stiles and the top rail in the same way; the top rail will be 1½ inches above the plywood pieces. Cut a top piece to fit, and attach it with wood glue and 6d finish nails. Cut four strips for the glide bases, and attach them with 1¼-inch screws.

1

48"
¾" plywood top piece
19¼"

48"
48½" ¾" plywood back
16"

1×4
½ × 4" plywood
¾ × 4" plywood
10½"
¾" plywood side piece

1×2
1×4
18½"

1×2 backer
1×4

2 ¾" plywood top 11⅛" wide — ledger

1×6

adjustable standards

1×2

¾" ×9½" plywood

ledger

1×4

1×4 kick plate

¾" plywood, 11⅛" wide, double with 1×2s sandwiched between

2. Build the shelves.

Decide on the height and width of the shelf units; in a narrow room with a low ceiling, you can run them to the side walls and from floor to ceiling. Make each shelf standard of two pieces of ¾-inch plywood, 11⅛ inches wide, with two 1×2s sandwiched in between. If you choose to support the shelves with dowels or pins, bore holes now. (Metal standards can be installed later.) Build each shelf unit by first attaching one standard to the window seat using 3½-inch screws. Plumb it and attach it to the rear wall using angle brackets, then install the second standard. Install the kick plate and bottom shelf. Prefab the face frame, joining the pieces with glue and dowels. Install the face frame by drilling pilot holes and driving 1⅝-inch trimhead screws every 6 inches. Build the shelves using 9½-inch plywood with 1×2 edging.

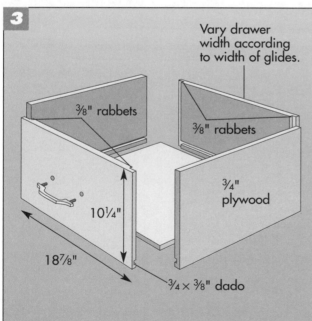

3

Vary drawer width according to width of glides.

⅜" rabbets

⅜" rabbets

¾" plywood

10¼"

18⅞"

¾ × ⅜" dado

3. Build the drawers.

Measure the openings in the base unit, and build drawers to fit. Use ¾-inch plywood for all the pieces. Check the drawer glides to see how much smaller than the opening the drawers should be. Install the drawer pull.

4

4. Install the drawers.

Attach drawer glides to the drawers and to the drawer unit, and slide in the drawers.

Give the entire unit two coats of enamel paint, or stain it and apply a polyurethane finish. Have a cushion (or cushions) made by an upholsterer.

FLOORING

For more tile flooring projects, see Chapter 12,
beginning on page 457.

SILENCING SQUEAKS

Most wood floors develop squeaks at some time or another. Temperature and humidity changes cause various floor parts to shrink and swell at different rates. The result: Squeaks develop where loose boards rub against each other or against loose nails.

Modern building codes determine how big the joists must be (typically 2×6 or 2×8), depending on the length they must span. Some older homes, however, were built without benefit of effective codes and may develop sags because the joists are undersized or too widely spaced.

In an older home, the subfloor may be made of 1× planks laid diagonally to the joists; tongue-and-groove softwood strips may be installed over the subfloor. In newer homes, the subflooring may be a single sheet of ¾-inch plywood, or there may be two layers of ⅝-inch plywood.

In other older arrangements, 1×3 "sleepers" are laid across the floor every 12 inches or so. The tongue-and-groove flooring rests on top of the sleepers.

If joists below the squeaks are concealed, repair from above, using the techniques on this page.

If the joists are exposed below, watch while someone walks on the noisy spot. If the subfloor moves, use shims or cleats to support it. Lack of movement may mean that the finished floor is loose and needs to be pulled down with screws. Strengthen any weak joists by installing bridging.

YOU'LL NEED...

TIME: 10 to 15 minutes per squeak.
SKILLS: Basic carpentry skills.
TOOLS: Drill, hammer, and nail set.

Anatomy of a floor.
Typically a subfloor rests on 2× joists stiffened by bridging or blocking. Underlayment may be used to add rigidity and smoothness for a finished surface, such as carpeting or tile. Tongue-and-groove flooring may rest on a plywood or plank subfloor or on underlayment.

1. To fix a squeak from above, drill pilot holes.
To quiet a loose board from above, nail it to the subfloor. To prevent the wood from splitting, drill pilot holes, angling them as shown.

2. Drive in flooring nails.
Drive ringshank nails or finish-head screws. If your flooring was installed with sleepers, there may be a space between the flooring and the subfloor. If so, you must use longer nails. Sink fastener heads below the surface, then fill with wood putty.

If the subfloor moves and you can work from below, insert a shim...
Use a tapered shim to tighten a loose subfloor board. Dip the tip of the shim in glue and tap it between the joist and subfloor until it's snug.

...or install cleats.
To tighten a series of boards, force a 2×4 up against the subfloor using a temporary prop. Nail or screw the 2×4 to the joist. Repeat on the other side.

Screw upward.
Pull loose finished boards tightly against the subflooring using 1¼-inch roundhead screws. Drill pilot holes (take care not to drill all the way through the flooring), and use washers so the screws won't pull through the subfloor.

Improve the bridging.
If the bridging isn't tight between joists, drive in new, larger nails or screws at an angle. If squeaks persist, add steel bridging. Push it tight up against the subfloor, then nail it to the bottom inside of the joists.

Lift a sagging floor.
If a floor has a major sag, you may have to add a supporting jack post under it. Break out a section of the basement floor, and pour a 24×24×8-inch concrete pad for the post to sit on. Let the concrete cure for a week. Place the jack post on the pad and set a 4×4 pressure-treated beam, long enough to span several joists, on top of the jack. Jack up the beam until it is snug against the joists, then raise it a quarter turn more. Wait a week and make another quarter turn, continuing this process until the sag is gone. Don't lift faster, or you may cause structural damage.

PATCHING WOOD FLOORS

Replacing a section of a finished floor that is interlocked with tongues and grooves requires patience and hard work. If several boards are damaged, take the time to weave in new boards, rather than cutting straight lines at each end; such a patch is unattractive.

Use the technique shown here for short sections of boards. If the floorboard is very long and most of the board is in good condition, cut out the damaged section of the flooring with a circular saw. Set the saw to a depth exactly equal to the thickness of the finished flooring. Cut as far as possible without piercing adjacent flooring; complete the cut by chiseling, then pry out the damaged section.

YOU'LL NEED...

TIME: About 45 to 60 minutes per area.
SKILLS: Basic carpentry skills.
TOOLS: Drill with spade bit, hammer, chisel, pry bar, nail set, and circular saw.

FINDING REPLACEMENT BOARDS

New tongue-and-groove flooring is expensive, and it may not match the old flooring in appearance. Also new flooring strips have to be sanded and stained to match the existing floor—a difficult job.

The solution is to find pieces from elsewhere in the house. Pry out boards from a closet, or from under carpeting. Get more than you need at present so you can have them on hand for later repairs. Fill the resulting voids with plywood.

1. Drill holes in the boards.
Using a spade or Forstner bit, bore holes across the width of the board at the ends and in the middle. Drill only through the flooring board; don't damage the subfloor.

2. Split the board with a chisel.
Use a wood chisel to split the board lengthwise between the drilled holes.

3. Pry out the damaged board.
Slip a flat pry bar into a split. Place a scrap of wood under the bar to protect the good flooring. Pry out the split pieces from the middle, then pry out the rest of the board. Also pry out any little slivers left under the tongue of the adjacent board.

4. Pull out old nails.
Using a claw hammer, pull out any old nails that remain in the subfloor. Use a scrap of wood to protect the flooring.

5. Cut new boards.
Use a miter box (see page 235) or a power miter saw (see page 247) to cut new pieces to length. If you are replacing more than one piece, see that adjacent joints are offset at least 2 inches. Cut pieces to fit well but not too tightly.

6. Modify the last board.
Prepare the replacement board (or the last board to be placed when repairing a section of flooring) by turning it over and chiseling away part of its groove (see inset). Note how the boards will interlock.

EXPERTS' INSIGHT

WHAT CAUSED THE DAMAGE?

If only a few boards are damaged due to heavy scratching, a simple repair will solve the problem. Other types of damage may be more serious.

If boards have tunnels running through them on the inside, termites or carpenter ants are the likely culprits. Call an exterminator.

If more than a few boards are cracked, the subflooring may be weak. See pages 314–315 for strengthening options.

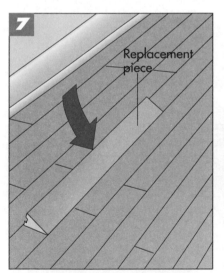

7. Install replacement board(s).
Test-fit the replacement piece. If you are replacing more than one board, slip the groove of each new piece into the tongue of the adjacent board and tap it in place. Bore pilot holes and angle-nail (see page 314) each piece through the tongue every 12 inches or so before installing the next piece.

8. Glue the board in place.
Apply flooring adhesive to the subfloor, tongue, and half-groove of the replacement piece (or the last piece when repairing a section), then tap it into place. Use a scrap of wood to protect the flooring surface as you tap.

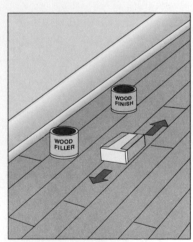

Removing scratches.
Remove surface cuts or scratches with steel wool and a solvent, such as mineral spirits. Rub with the grain, rinse, and refinish. For deeper cuts, sand with the grain and work in wood filler with a brush. Let the filler set overnight, sand with the grain, and refinish.

REFINISHING WOOD FLOORS

Refinishing a wood floor is a job that takes care and patience. You'll need to rent a random-orbital sander or upright drum sander and a disc-type edge sander. Ask the rental dealer to demonstrate the machines. A sander that uses 220 volts will work much better than a standard 120-volt machine; be sure you plug it into the correct receptacle.

Sanding a floor with a drum sander requires concentration and smooth movements. If you allow the sander to dig into the floor, it will create an unsightly dip. For floors without heavy finish buildup or deep scratches, an upright random-orbital sander (also called a jitterbug sander) is a better choice. It doesn't work as fast as a drum sander but is less likely to damage the floor.

If only the finish is damaged and you do not need to remove deep scratches, consider "screening" rather than sanding. Rent a janitor's buffing machine, and buy circular screens to fit. If a home center does not have this equipment, check with a flooring supply store.

Do this work on a day when you can open doors and windows to let out the dust. Wear a respirator to contend with fine dust, and seal off adjoining rooms with dampened sheets.

YOU'LL NEED...

TIME: 6 to 8 hours over 2 days for a 10×12-foot room. Allow an additional 2 to 4 days for applying the finish.
SKILLS: Basic carpentry skills.
TOOLS: Hammer, nail set, drum or random-orbital sander, disc-type edge sander, paint scraper or chisel, vacuum, tack cloth, putty knife, and paintbrush or wax applicator.

1. Remove the base shoe.
After you have removed the furnishings, pry off the baseboard shoe molding—the piece at the very bottom. If there is no shoe, remove the baseboard itself. If the pieces are in good shape, number them on the back so you can reinstall them. Otherwise plan to install new molding.

2. Set popped nails.
Any protruding metal will quickly rip up a sanding disc or belt. Use a nail set to drive any popped nails below the surface.

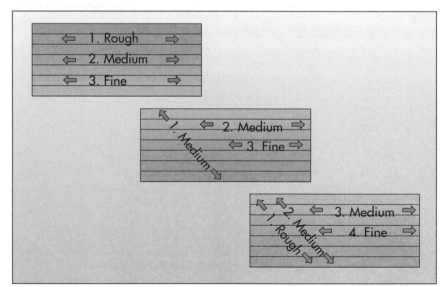

Drum-sanding techniques.
Different situations call for different sanding techniques. For most floors use three sandpaper grits—sanding *with* the grain. It may take several passes with each grit.

Getting nowhere sanding with the grain? Try one diagonal pass, but never sand directly across the grain. Finish up by sanding with the grain.

Badly cupped or warped old floors may require four cuts—two diagonal passes and two with the grain. Be sure to always overlap each pass.

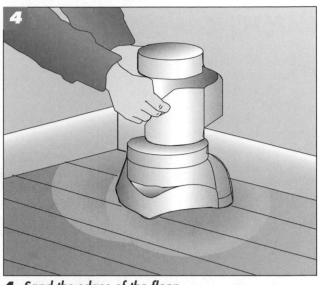

3. Sand the main floor.

Make the first cut with coarse-grit sandpaper. Use coarse grit until you reach bare wood and most of the scratches have disappeared. With a jitterbug sander (as shown above) you don't have to follow the grain of the wood. Use medium- and fine-grit sandpaper for the next two cuts. At each stage expect to use several sheets of sandpaper on each of the four oscillating heads.

4. Sand the edges of the floor.

Use an edge sander for hard-to-reach areas. Work slowly, and finish with a very fine sandpaper so the circular lines will not be visible. In corners that the sander cannot reach, use a sharp paint scraper or chisel, always working with the grain.

Tack cloth

WOOD FILLER

POLYURETHANE

5. Remove dust with a tack cloth.

After each sanding pass, vacuum the floor thoroughly. Use a tack cloth after the last vacuuming to pick up the remaining dust.

6. Apply a filler.

Fill in any holes and gaps between the boards using paste wood filler. Apply it first with a putty knife. Always work with the grain. When the filler begins to set, wipe across the grain with an old rag to remove excess. Let the filler dry overnight.

7. Finish with polyurethane.

Apply two to four coats of polyurethane finish with a brush or a wax applicator, sanding with fine sandpaper between coats. Use a tack cloth to pick up all the dust between coats. Do not apply wax over a polyurethane finish.

PATCHING RESILIENT TILE

Most resilient floor tiles will lift out easily once you apply some heat to soften the adhesive underneath.

If you cannot raise a corner, use a chisel, working out from the center to the edges. Once the tile is removed, scrape or sand all remnants of old adhesive off the floor so the new tile will lie flat.

If you cannot find an exact replacement tile, steal a tile from under the refrigerator or another inconspicuous spot, and replace it with a fairly close match.

Different types of tile require different adhesives. To avoid confusion, ask a tile salesperson to recommend a suitable product.

To make the new tile look less conspicuous, rub off the gloss with fine steel wool.

YOU'LL NEED...

TIME: About 15 to 20 minutes, depending on how hard it is to remove the old tile.
SKILLS: Basic skills.
TOOLS: Putty knife, straightedge, utility knife, sanding block, framing square, clothes iron, chisel, and adhesive applicator.

CAUTION!

ASBESTOS TILE
Some older tiles contain asbestos, which is toxic if inhaled. If you are not sure, call in a pro for evaluation. If you must remove asbestos tile yourself, wear a respirator-type dust mask. Keep the area damp while you pry the tile out so fibers cannot fly through the air. Better yet, hire an experienced pro.

1. Soften the tile with an iron.
Lay a towel on top and soften the tile with a medium-hot iron. Take care that the iron doesn't overlap onto adjacent tiles.

2. Pry out the tile.
While the tile is still hot, slip a putty knife under a corner and pry up. Make sure not to pry against the surrounding tiles.

3. Scrape away the adhesive.
Use a putty knife or a paint scraper to remove all of the adhesive. If it does not come up, try heating the area again. You may need to sand away the last remnants of adhesive. Take particular care to remove adhesive from the perimeter of the patch.

Trim line

4. Test the fit of the new tile.
Be sure the new tile will fit and lie flat. If the tile is slightly large and you have to force it in, use a sanding block or plane to shave one or two sides until it fits properly.

5. Cut the tile to fit.
If the new tile is too large, use a utility knife and a straightedge to cut it. Slice with several passes, then bend the scrap back to break it off. Smooth any rough edges with sandpaper wrapped around a scrap of wood.

6. Spread adhesive.
Apply adhesive with an applicator (as shown above), a notched trowel, or a brush (check the manufacturer's instructions). With some types, you must wait until the adhesive has dried to a tacky feel before setting the tile. With other types, the tile should be set while the adhesive is wet.

7. Soften the tile with an iron.
Use the iron to soften the new tile. Protect the tile's surface with a cloth.

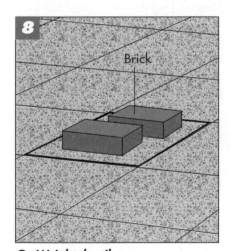

8. Weight the tile.
Set—do not slide—the new tile into position. Wipe away any squeezed-out adhesive using a cloth dampened with water or mineral spirits, depending on the type of adhesive. Weight the tile down for 24 hours before walking on it.

EXPERTS' INSIGHT

SOLVING OTHER TILE PROBLEMS

There are two basic types of resilient tile—commercial tile, which has flecks of color that run through the tile, and surface-printed tile, which has an embossed pattern.

■ **Tears:** Cheaper varieties of surface-printed tiles are easily torn. If this is a recurring problem, remove all the tiles and install tiles of a higher quality.

■ **Lifts:** Surface-printed tiles are often made to be self-sticking, but the self-sticking adhesive is not very strong. When installing a replacement tile, use tile mastic to enhance sticking power.

■ **Scratches:** Scratched commercial tile will often heal itself in time. If you fill a scratch with wax or acrylic finish, the damage will disappear eventually. (See also the Experts' Insight on page 323.)

■ **Burns:** Scouring—plus some careful scraping with a sharp knife—also will remove shallow burns.

■ **Stains:** You can often remove stains by rubbing them with a mild detergent solution. If that doesn't work, try a white appliance wax. As a last resort, scour stains with very fine steel wool and a household cleanser.

PATCHING SHEET FLOORING

Most sheet flooring is glued to the floor in a bed of adhesive. Some newer types of flooring, designed especially for do-it-yourself installation, require adhesive only at seams and edges.

If the entire floor has been laid in adhesive, you usually can work a putty knife underneath and peel up the damaged piece. You may need to apply heat with an iron (see page 320) to loosen it. To make the patch less conspicuous, take time to carefully match its pattern to the surrounding area. To patch the newer types of flooring, cut out the damaged section and cement a patch as you would the seam of a new floor.

Though it is often referred to as "linoleum," most sheet flooring today is made of vinyl with an embossed surface-printed pattern. This product can be durable but if it is deeply scratched or torn, it must be patched or replaced. (Genuine linoleum, which is making a comeback, has color that runs through its body. That means any scratches will conceal themselves.)

A "no-wax" finish will eventually wear away. Rejuvenate the floor using acrylic finish or a product made specifically for no-wax floors.

YOU'LL NEED...

TIME: 20 to 25 minutes, depending on the time needed to clean the underlayment.
SKILLS: Basic skills.
TOOLS: Utility knife, framing square, putty knife, and adhesive spreader.

1. Mark with a framing square.
Use a framing square to mark and cut around the damaged area. Cut with a utility knife.

Flooring scrap

2. Trace the cutout.
Lay the cutout on a piece of matching material so that the pattern lines up precisely. Use a pencil or felt-tipped pen to trace around it. Accuracy is essential for a good fit.

Framing square

3. Cut with a square.
Either leave the cutout in place and use it as a cutting guide or use a framing square to cut along the trace lines. Place a scrap of plywood under the patching material to prevent damaging the floor.

4. Scrape the underlayment.
Clean the underlayment, making absolutely sure to remove all of the adhesive. Then test-fit the patch. If it is too large, sand the edges.

5. *Apply adhesive to the new tile.*
If the area around the patch is not set in adhesive, lift up its edges and apply adhesive around the perimeter. Apply adhesive to the patch with a serrated spreader or a brush. Align one edge, matching the pattern, and lower the new section into place.

6. *Weight down the patch.*
Wipe off adhesive that has oozed out from the edges, then weight down the patch evenly for at least 24 hours.

TOOLS TO USE

FLOOR SCRAPERS

■ Vinyl sheet flooring shows even the tiniest imperfection in the underlayment. Use the right tools to make the underlayment perfectly smooth.

■ To remove adhesive or flooring from a large area, buy or rent a floor scraper, which can be operated while standing up. It has removable blades that scrape much more efficiently than a putty knife.

■ Once most of the adhesive has been removed, sand the area. Alternatively, wipe with a solvent-soaked rag to clean up and smooth the adhesive.

EXPERTS' INSIGHT

SOLVING OTHER SHEET FLOORING PROBLEMS

■ **Scratches:** Shallow scratches in wax or a no-wax finish may heal themselves. If you fill shallow scratches with floor wax or acrylic finish, they often seem to disappear. For deeper cuts compress the edges of the torn flooring by dragging a worn coin along—not across—them.

■ **Tears:** If the material has torn all the way through, lift the edges of the wound, scrape away any old adhesive, apply fresh adhesive, and stick the edges down again. For the repair to lie flat, you may need to sand one edge.

■ **Blisters:** If a blister develops in your flooring, flatten it by making a clean cut through its center. Alternating edges, press down on one edge of the cut, work adhesive underneath the other edge, and apply weight.

■ **Holes:** Filling small holes in vinyl flooring is a tougher assignment. The best and quickest way is to fill the void with a special seam-welding product offered by the manufacturer of the flooring. This product dissolves the vinyl, then sets up again to complete the repair.

■ **Patches:** Scrape flakes from a piece of scrap flooring and grind them into a powder. Mix the powder with clear lacquer or nail polish to make a putty-like paste. Work the paste into the hole, packing it well and mounding slightly to compensate for shrinkage. After the paste dries, sand the repair and wax according to the manufacturer's directions.

CLEANING CARPETS

Keeping carpets fresh requires commitment. Once a week—more often in high-traffic areas—use an upright or canister vacuum cleaner with a power (beater) nozzle. This keeps dirt from settling to the bottom and grinding at the fibers. Once a year, shampoo or steam-clean your carpets, depending on how deep the dirt is embedded.

Shampoo comes as either a concentrated liquid detergent you mix with water or an aerosol spray foam. Remember that shampoo is a surface cleaner only. Either remove all of the furniture at once or allow two days, doing half the carpet each day. Whip the detergent into a foam by vigorously scrubbing the carpet. Let the foam dry, then vacuum the dried detergent and loosened dirt. Do not soak the carpet—it might shrink, the colors might run, and mildew might grow.

Steam-cleaning machines actually spray a mix of hot water and detergent deep into the pile, then immediately vacuum up both the solution and dislodged dirt before the carpet becomes soaked. Steaming is much more effective than shampooing. Hardware stores, home centers, and carpet stores usually have steamers for rent. Or purchase an inexpensive steam cleaner.

Oriental and antique rugs require professional cleaning to make sure they don't run or shrink.

In day-to-day life, when a spill occurs, speedy cleanup is of the essence to avoid permanent staining. Remove as much of the spill as possible with a large spoon, a spatula, a putty knife, or a large knife.

Consult the table at right to select a cleaning agent. Apply the first cleaning agent listed for the type of stain. Do not pour the agent directly onto the spill area. Instead pour it onto a sponge and blot—don't rub—the stained area. Remove as much liquid as possible by pressing a paper towel into the stain.

Repeat the pour-into-sponge, blot, and dry sequence with the remaining cleaning agents listed in the table. After all the agents have been applied and removed, rinse the area with fresh water. Dry the area by stepping on a pile of paper towels stacked on the wet area.

If the stain type is not listed, try trichloroethane, a dry-cleaning solution available at many stores, followed by detergent.

CARPET STAIN FIRST AID

Spill	Treatment
Blood	Water, then detergent
Butter	Trichloroethane, then detergent
Chocolate	Detergent, then ammonia
Coffee or wine	Detergent, then vinegar
Crayon	Trichloroethane, then detergent
Egg or fruit juice	Detergent, then ammonia, then vinegar
Furniture polish, grease or oil	Trichloroethane, then detergent
Ice cream	Detergent, then ammonia, then vinegar
Ketchup	Detergent, then ammonia
Lipstick	Trichloroethane, then detergent, then ammonia, then vinegar
Mayonnaise	Trichloroethane, then detergent
Paint (oil)	Trichloroethane
Paint (latex)	Detergent
Shoe polish	Trichloroethane, then detergent, then ammonia, then vinegar
Tea	Detergent, then vinegar, then trichloroethane
Urine	Vinegar, then ammonia, then vinegar again, then detergent
Wax	Scrape, then apply trichloroethane

PATCHING DAMAGED CARPET

Wall-to-wall pile carpeting or machine-made area rugs can be repaired with relative ease. Handmade or Oriental rugs, however, require special care and should be taken to a professional.

To install new carpeting, see pages 335–340.

To install new carpeting, see pages 335–340.

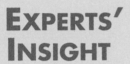

YOU'LL NEED...

TIME: 1 hour, plus 1 day for the adhesive to set.
SKILLS: No special skills needed.
TOOLS: Hammer, clean can lid, and utility knife.

EXPERTS' INSIGHT

OTHER CARPET REPAIRS

■ If carpeting is pulling up at the edges, press it back into place with a putty knife or tap it with a hammer. If that doesn't do the trick, you may need to stretch it or install a new tackless strip (see page 336).

■ To lift an indentation caused by a furniture leg, lay a damp towel over the area and press with a heated iron for a few seconds. Lift up the towel and rub the indentation with the edge of a coin. Repeat if necessary.

■ To repair a tear or slice, pull back the carpet to reveal the underside. Apply seam tape, and heat it. Or stitch the tear from below, using a heavy needle and carpet thread.

■ To patch a small hole, cut a replacement section of pile and attach it to the padding or flooring using superglue.

1. Tack a lid over the area.
Partially nail a clean can lid or other template over the damaged area. Leave the heads of the nails projecting.

2. Cut out the damaged area and make a patch.
Using the lid as a guide, cut through the carpet with a sharp utility knife. Repeat Steps 1 and 2 on a piece of scrap carpet to make a matching patch.

3. Apply tape and seam cement.
Vacuum up loose fibers. Slip double-sided tape halfway under the cutout edges of the old carpet. Apply a thin ribbon of seam cement to the edge of the carpet patch.

4. Weight the patch overnight.
Press the patch into place. Weight the patch overnight with a book or board and a heavy object.

FIXING STAIRS

The staircases in your home have many parts—all of them interlocked with sophisticated joinery that is usually concealed from view.

A pair of stringers (also called carriages) slopes from one level to the next. The stringers support a series of steps, called treads. A simple staircase—such as one that leads to a basement or deck—consists of little more than stringers and treads (see page 327).

The illustration at right shows both "open-" and "closed-stringer" staircases. An open stringer has notches cut out of it; treads rest on the notches. A closed stringer has a series of grooves into which treads and risers fit.

In most interior stairways, risers fill the vertical gaps between the treads. Risers give a more finished appearance, keep dirt and objects from falling to the floor below, and add strength.

Finally, a balustrade—which consists of a handrail, balusters, and a newel post—provides safety along at least one side. Because all the parts are subject to various stresses, they all must fit tightly.

On most interior stairways, the balusters fit into the treads with dado, dowel (see pages 261–262), or dovetail joints. Balusters come in many styles, ranging from simple to ornate. On less-formal and outdoor stairways, the balusters may be attached to a bottom rail, which runs parallel to the railing a few inches above the treads.

You can treat most of the ills that afflict staircases using the techniques shown on pages 327–329. If you want to build a basic, open-riser staircase.

Anatomy of a Staircase

Treads and risers.
Interior stairway construction typically uses hardwood pieces milled to exact specifications and assembled much like cabinetry. Treads and risers usually fit together with dado joints (above left). In some cases wood blocks provide additional support.

In another arrangement (above right), treads and risers fit into grooves cut in a closed stringer. Wood wedges are tapped in and glued snug to the treads and risers.

Balusters.
Balusters fit into grooves or holes in the underside of the handrail. At the stairway end, balusters often fit into holes in the stair treads. At the bottom of the stairway, a newel post is firmly anchored to the stair's framing.

If there is a wall on one side of the stairway, it may have a handrail, usually attached to special handrail supports that are anchored to studs in the wall.

Simple stairway.
A stairway for a porch or a basement may consist of stringers and treads. Usually a loose tread can be firmed up by drilling pilot holes and driving new screws. Even the simplest stairway should have a solid handrail.

TIGHTENING RAILS AND BALUSTERS

Wobbly handrails call for detective work. Is the handrail working loose from the balusters, or are the balusters parting company with the treads or bottom rail? If the handrail is pulling away from a newel post, use the technique at right.

A newel post handles a lot of stress. It is usually attached to the stringer, and may be attached to the house's framing as well. Unless you see an obvious solution to a wobbling newel post, call in a pro for help.

YOU'LL NEED...
TIME: About 15 minutes to firm up a baluster. **SKILLS:** Basic carpentry skills. **TOOLS:** Drill, screwdriver or screwdriver bit, hammer, and utility knife.

Screw and glue.
Drill a pilot hole at an angle through the baluster into the rail or tread. Countersink a trimhead screw in the hole. Alternatively, drill pilot holes through the railing and into the baluster. Work wood glue into the joint, and drive finishing nails or finishing screws.

Add blocking.
If the entire railing is loose, add blocking as shown. Use a T-bevel (see page 231) and a miter box (see page 235) or a power miter saw (see page 247) to cut angles for a snug fit. Drill pilot holes, apply wood glue, and drive finishing nails or trimhead screws.

SILENCING STAIR SQUEAKS FROM ABOVE

Most staircase squeaks result from a loose tread rubbing against the top or bottom of a riser or a stringer. To locate the problem, watch as someone rocks back and forth on each tread. If the tread moves, it's time to take corrective action.

You can stop a squeak by forcing the tread either down or up, and wedging it firmly in place.

A small problem can sometimes be solved using finishing nails. However, take care: If you drive a nail near the edge of a tread or riser, continued flexing of the riser could cause the wood to crack.

Work from below if you have access to the underside of the staircase. Otherwise you'll have to attack the situation from above. A few well-placed nails, screws, or hardwood wedges will usually solve the problem.

The directions on these pages enable you to repair several squeaky treads. If the stairway squeaks or groans at many points, however, the problem is likely structural. Go under the stairway and look for a cracked stringer, a closed stringer that is pulling away from the wall, or treads that are pulling away from a closed stringer. To correct a major problem, call in a pro.

YOU'LL NEED...
TIME: About 15 minutes per tread.
SKILLS: Basic carpentry skills.
TOOLS: Backsaw, coping saw, hammer, pry bar, drill, utility knife or chisel, screwdriver bit, and nail set.

Powdered graphite.
Lubricating squeaks with powdered graphite may quiet them, but only temporarily. Squirt graphite into suspect joints and wipe away any excess graphite.

Trimhead screw

Drive nails or screws.
If the front of a tread is loose and you don't mind the appearance of small holes in the tread, drill pilot holes at opposing angles. Drive in ring-shank flooring nails or trim-head wood screws. Countersink the fastener heads and fill with wood putty.

Wedge

Install glued wedges.
If the tread is loose at the back, coat hardwood wedges (not softwood shims) with glue, tap into place, and let dry. Cut off exposed wedge ends with a utility knife or a chisel.

Quarter round

Add quarter-round molding.
For uncarpeted stairs, you can tighten joints with molding. The larger the molding, the better—¾-inch quarter round works well. Apply glue, drill pilot holes, and drive finishing nails into both risers and treads. Use a nail set to sink the nail heads.

Silencing Stair Squeaks from Below

Usually repairs made from underneath the stairs will be stronger and more durable than repairs made from above. The problem is getting there. Stairs leading to a basement may be exposed on the underside. Most other interior stairs are not so easy to access.

You'll Need...

Time: 10 to 15 minutes.
Skills: Basic carpentry skills.
Tools: Drill, hammer, screwdriver, and utility knife.

Experts' Insight

Gaining Access

Removing one or more treads or risers may give you enough room to work. Because one stair part is often set into another part's groove, disassembly is often difficult. But as long as one side of the stairway is open, you should be able to take things apart. Often it helps to cut through nails or screws using a reciprocating saw. When you reassemble the stairs after the repair, the last tread will probably need to be fastened from above.

If the area under the stairway is covered with drywall and extensive repairs are needed, consider removing the drywall, even though replacing and finishing the drywall will be a substantial job.

Tighten with hardwood blocks.
Purchase a length of 2×2 oak, birch, or other hardwood, and cut it into pieces about 4 inches long. Drill four pilot holes, running in two directions (see inset).

Where a tread or riser needs support, apply wood glue to the wood block, press it firmly in place, and drive wood screws to fasten it. Make sure the screws are not long enough to poke through the surface of the tread.

Use angle brackets for a loose tread.
If the entire tread is loose, use two or three metal angle brackets to tighten it down to the riser. Small brackets act much like wood blocks; larger brackets support the entire tread.

Replace loose wedges.
If old wedges are loose, remove and replace them. If a wedge comes out easily and in one piece, apply wood glue and hammer it back tightly into place. If a wedge is stuck but not supporting the stairway, chisel it out and replace it with a new wedge.

INSTALLING LAMINATE FLOORING

Prefinished plank flooring is as easy to install as hardwood flooring and offers the same appearance. The "planks" consist of medium-density fiberboard (MDF) sandwiched between plastic laminate. The top laminate looks like random-grain wood, but its plastic composition makes it scratch- and stain-resistant.

Precision-milled tongue-and-groove edges make precise installation a snap. The whole assembly is glued together at the edges and floats on a thin, closed-cell polyethylene foam pad.

YOU'LL NEED...

TIME: 6 to 8 hours for a small room.
SKILLS: Basic carpentry skills.
TOOLS: Circular saw, hammer, pry bar, coping saw, and offset handsaw.

1. Lay polyethylene.
Make sure the subfloor is clean, dry, and level. If the subfloor is bare concrete or you suspect that it will become moist, spread a layer of 8-mil polyethylene, and temporarily hold it in place with weights.

2" minimum

2. Plan the last row.
Show the layout for the room to a flooring dealer and plan the installation so the width of the last row will be at least 2 inches. You may need to rip-cut the first row to achieve this. Also check that the wall where you begin is parallel to the wall where you will end; if not, rip-cut planks at an angle on the wall that will be least visible.

Straightedge

3. Unroll and nail down foam.
Unroll the first strip of foam in the direction the planks will run. Do not overlap the foam edges or adhere the foam to the floor. If you're not starting against a wall or if the wall is uneven, nail a straightedge to the floor to align the first row.

Tongue

4. Lay the first strip.
Lay the first strip with ¼-inch spacers between the grooved end and the wall; the tongue should face outward into the room. Fill end grooves with glue and tap the pieces together. Use a damp towel to wipe up any squeezed-out glue.

Pry bar

5. Fit planks with a pry bar.
Cut the last piece in the first row, leaving a ¼-inch space at the end. Use a pry bar to push the planks tightly together, then insert spacers and shims to keep them tight. Save the cutoff plank for use elsewhere.

6. Begin the second row.

Cut the first plank of the second row 12 inches shorter; cut the grooved end. Fill all the grooves with glue and tap the pieces tightly together. In some systems you will assemble five or six rows of planks, then use special straps and hardware to hold the pieces tightly together until the glue has dried.

7. Tape foam strips together.

After the first strip of padding is nearly covered, unroll the next strip, butt the edges (do not overlap), and tape them together. Continue gluing planks to the last row.

8. Undercut the door casings.

Undercut door casings with an offset handsaw. Use a piece of scrap flooring as a depth gauge. Hold the blade of the saw flat on top of the scrap as you cut.

9. Cut around pipes.

Cut planking with a coping saw to fit around pipes, making holes ¼ inch larger than the pipes. The planks should not touch the pipes at any point. See page 231 for hints on how to mark contours.

10. Cut the last plank.

Ripsaw the tongued edge of the last plank ¼ inch narrower than the remaining gap. Glue its groove and pry the piece into place. Use spacers and shims to fit the piece snug against its neighbor until the glue has set.

11. Nail shoe moldings to wall.

Once the glue has set, remove the spacers and nail the shoe molding to the wall. Drive nails into the wall, but not into the floor, so the floor can expand and contract with changes in humidity. Wash the floor with clean, warm water.

CHOOSING WOOD FLOORING

Wood flooring comes in strips or planks. Hardwood strip flooring, by far the most common, typically measures 2¼ inches wide and ¾ inch thick; some maple flooring is 1½ inches wide. Strips have tongues and grooves that fit together tightly.

Oak is the most common type of hardwood strip flooring. "Select," which has no knots and is consistent in color, is the most expensive grade. Less-expensive "No. 1 common" has small knots, and the pieces vary in color. Maple, cherry, rainforest woods (sometimes called "cherry"), and fir are also used for making tongue-and-groove flooring.

Nowadays tongue-and-groove strip flooring is usually laid on plywood that has been covered with roofing felt to minimize squeaks. Strips can be installed directly over existing strip flooring only if the new flooring does not run in the same direction as the old. The strips are installed using a special flooring nailer that ties them tightly together while anchoring them to the subfloor. Once installed the floor must be sanded with three passes using a special floor sander (see pages 318–319). Then the floor may or may not be stained. Finally two or three coats of finish—usually polyurethane—must be applied. The entire process takes a week or more, but produces a floor that is very smooth and durable. If the floor is badly scratched, it can be resanded and refinished as many as three times.

Another option is prefinished tongue-and-groove strip flooring, which is usually a plywood product with a top layer of finished hardwood. The flooring itself costs more, but this option saves in other materials costs, as well as labor, because it needs no sanding or finishing. However a prefinished floor is not completely smooth; there are slight level differences from one board to the next. Additionally, if scratched, the surface layer of veneer can be sanded only once.

Flooring grades vary depending on the kind of wood. Clear typically is the best, followed by select, No. 1 common, No. 2 common, and 1½-foot shorts, which are the remnants from the other grades.

Before you lay flooring, it is important to let the wood acclimate to the moisture conditions in your house. Have it delivered at least 72 hours in advance, and spread it out in the room where it is to be laid.

One hammer blow starts the nail, the second drives and sets it.

Pistol grip lets you move the machine with one hand, and swing the hammer with other.

Shoe aims nail at 50° angle.

Spring-loaded feeder supplies nails.

Using a power nailer.
Most wood flooring interlocks with tongues and grooves. Fasteners are driven at a 50-degree angle through the tongue.

A power nailer—available from flooring or rental stores—speeds the job and saves your back. It drives long staples, which are loaded in clips. Using a heavy hammer, you simply hit the piston drive mechanism to set each nail. The hammer usually has two heads—one for hitting the nailer, and one for tapping boards tightly against each other. Newer nailers are connected to an air compressor by a long hose.

EXPERTS' INSIGHT

SOFTWOOD FLOORING
Softwood plank flooring is wider than hardwood planks—3 to 8 inches versus 1½ to 2¼ inches—and often is installed in combinations of different widths. Pine and fir are the most common species used. Typically the planks do not have tongues and grooves. The resulting floor is not as smooth as a tongue-and-groove hardwood floor, but many people prefer its casual charm. Planks are face-nailed. Nail heads may be left exposed for a rustic look or covered with wood putty or wood plugs.

INSTALLING TONGUE-AND-GROOVE FLOORING

If you need to firm up a floor, install sheets of plywood. If the new flooring will be too high compared to nearby floors—most people find a height difference of ¾ inch to be a tripping hazard—you may need to remove old flooring before installing the new.

Sweep the floor well, set any popped nails, and remove the baseboard shoes or moldings. If the molding is in good shape, write numbers on the backs so you can remember where the pieces go. Otherwise plan on installing new moldings.

Level any bad dips by pulling up the old flooring, nailing shims to the joists, and renailing the old boards. Staple one or two layers of roofing felt (tar paper) onto the subfloor. This will help prevent squeaks.

Use spacers to create a ⅜-inch gap between the flooring and walls or baseboards. This is important; boards that are installed tight against the wall may buckle. Shoe molding will cover the gap when you're done.

YOU'LL NEED...

TIME: A day for a 12×14-foot room if the subfloor is prepared.
SKILLS: Intermediate carpentry skills.
TOOLS: Square, compass, string line, hammer, pry bar, drill and drill bits, power flooring nailer and mallet, power miter saw, saber saw, and nail set.

⅜" spacer

1. Nail the first board into place.
Place the grooved edge of the first board ⅜ inch from the wall. The power nailer will not be able to reach this close to the wall. Drill pilot holes and drive flooring nails at a 45-degree angle through the tongue every 12 inches.

Driving block

2. Tap the boards together.
To keep the courses parallel, tap the boards together before nailing. Use a wood scrap as a driving block to protect the flooring. Or use the neoprene head of the power nailer mallet. For a professional appearance, offset all neighboring joints by at least 2 inches.

Neoprene head

3. Use the power nailer.
Load the power flooring nailer with staples recommended for your type of floor. Experiment with depth settings; the staple heads should just barely sink below the wood surface. Fit the nailer to a tongue, make sure it rests flat, and hit it with the mallet.

4. Measure for cut pieces.
Measure before cutting the last piece in each course, and cut with a power miter saw or a circular saw. Don't cut off the edge with the tongue or the groove that you'll need. About every six courses, stretch a string line to check for straightness.

5. Scribe around irregularities.
Cut casings at the bottom, using a scrap of flooring as a guide (see page 331, Step 8). To fit around other irregularities, scribe with a compass (see page 231) and cut with a saber saw.

6. Secure the last rows.
You may need to ripsaw the last course. Protecting the wall with a wood scrap, push the last courses tight with a pry bar. Drill pilot holes and drive finishing nails through the face of the boards. Set the nails and fill with wood putty.

LAYING WOOD FLOORING OVER CONCRETE

Strip or plank flooring can't be attached directly to concrete. Seal the concrete against moisture with a layer or two of plastic sheeting, and then provide a wood surface to attach the flooring to. Laying strip or plank flooring over concrete requires a vapor barrier, sleepers, and a subfloor.

YOU'LL NEED...

TIME: 2 days to install a vapor barrier, sleepers, subfloor, and finished flooring for a 12×14-foot room.
SKILLS: Intermediate carpentry skills.
TOOLS: Hammer, nail set, pry bar, power flooring nailer, power miter saw, and saber saw.

Finished floor — Subfloor — Rigid foam insulation — Sleeper — Polyethylene vapor barrier

Build a subfloor over the concrete.
Lay a polyethylene vapor barrier over the concrete; consult with a carpenter or a building inspector to make sure the barrier will be effective in your conditions.

Install 2×4 sleepers, allowing 14½ inches of space between them. To attach the sleepers, drive masonry nails or screws every 16 inches (see pages 389–390). Lay rigid foam insulation over or between the sleepers. Then screw a ¾-inch plywood subfloor to the sleepers. Install the flooring as shown at on these pages.

CHOOSING AND BUYING CARPET

Carpeting offers more colors and textures than anything else you can put underfoot. Compare the fibers to determine the one that best fits your needs and ask your carpet dealer about the density of the fiber or pile. The more fibers per square inch, the longer the carpet life.

Most carpeting sold is tufted or "jute-backed," meaning the yarn is pulled through a woven backing and an additional backing is added for strength and stability.

Carpeting is sold by the square yard in widths of 9, 12, and 15 feet. To compute square yards, divide the square footage by 9. Take a drawing of your room to a carpet salesperson, who can figure the exact yardage requirements.

A good pad prolongs carpet life and insulates against noise and cold. Avoid felt in high-humidity areas and avoid rubber over radiant-heated floors.

Integral-pad carpeting is bonded to a cushioned backing. It's skid-proof, mildew-proof, and ravel-proof, which means you can lay it directly over a concrete basement floor. Installation is easy (see pages 339–340). Indoor/outdoor carpeting also can be laid without a pad.

Carpet-laying tools.
No matter what the job, things go more smoothly with the right tools. Carpet laying is no exception. You probably already have some of the basic tools: a utility knife, tape measure, hacksaw, straightedge, chalk line, pliers, and an awl.

With integral-pad carpeting (see page 339), you can get by without all the rented gear. But if you plan to stretch the carpeting, you'll need to rent several other items.

A **strip cutter** makes quick work of cutting tackless strip, which fits around the perimeter of a room. A **staple hammer** fastens padding to wood floors. (Use pad adhesive if the floor is concrete.) Join pieces of carpeting using seam tape and a **seaming iron**. A **knee kicker** and a **power stretcher** help you pull the carpeting taut. In addition a specialty carpet trimmer cuts neatly along walls.

COMPARING CARPET FIBERS

Fiber	Properties	Relative Cost
Wool	The traditional standard against which other fibers are compared; durable, resilient, and abrasion-resistant; needs mothproofing; fairly easy to clean.	Expensive
Acrylic	Closest to wool of all synthetic fibers; resists abrasion, mildew, insects, and crushing; wide choice of colors; some tendency to pill (form fuzz balls); sheds dirt.	Moderate
Nylon	The strongest synthetic fiber; very durable and resistant to abrasion, mildew, and moths; should be treated for static electricity; hides dirt.	Wide price range
Polyester	Bright, clear colors; cool to the touch; resists mildew and moisture; can be used anywhere; susceptible to oil-based stains; resists soiling	Moderate
Polypropylene olefin	A key fiber in most indoor/outdoor carpeting; extremely durable, moisture-resistant, and nonabsorbent; lower-priced versions tend to crush; the most stain-resistant of all carpets.	Wide price range

INSTALLING A TACKLESS STRIP AND PADDING

Before you start, unroll the carpet and padding in a separate room. Make sure you have the right amount of carpet, and see that it is free of defects.

Prepare the room by removing all the furniture and baseboard shoe moldings. Plane down the high spots in the floor and fill wide cracks or dips with floor-leveling compound. For badly worn floors, install underlayment (see page 342). Then install the tackless strip, carpet pad, and the carpet, using the techniques shown here and on page 337.

A tackless strip creates a framework over which carpeting is stretched and held tight. A standard tackless strip is designed to be installed onto hardwood or softwood; strips for concrete floors are also available.

When abutting a floor covering other than carpeting, nail a metal threshold strip with gripper pins to the floor. Where one carpet section adjoins another, do not use a tackless strip. Later you will seam the pieces together.

Lay the carpet padding within the framework and cut it to size with a utility knife. Make sure the side with the slick membrane faces up. Staple the padding in place, paying special attention to seam lines and edges. If the floor is concrete, roll back one section of padding at a time and spread pad adhesive. Lay the padding back in place.

1. Nail a strip to the floor.
Cut a strip to fit and place it ½ inch from the wall, with the pins facing the adjacent wall or opening. The strip has integrated nails; pound them into the floor.

Tackless strip

Cut line

Padding

2. Attach the padding.
Staple or nail padding to wood floors; glue it to concrete floors. Do not stretch the padding while you install it. Cut the padding precisely so that it just reaches the strip but does not overlap it.

Threshold hardware

3. Install a threshold.
When abutting a hard surface, such as tile or wood flooring, use a metal threshold. Hammer the lip flat, using a protective board.

Padding

4. Finish the edge.
Another way to finish an edge is to fold the carpeting under itself and tack along the edge. Be sure to stop the padding short if you will use this method.

YOU'LL NEED...

TIME: About 5 hours for a 12×15-foot room, if it doesn't have complex corners.
SKILLS: Intermediate skills.
TOOLS: Hammer, plane, putty knife, and carpeting tools (see page 335).

STRETCHING AND TRIMMING CARPETING

*L*aying carpeting can be done only with the correct stretching tools; otherwise the carpet will soon develop folds and waves. Rent or buy a knee kicker a a power stretcher (see page 335). A knee kicker is a short tool used near the wall. A power stretcher telescopes out to the length needed. It has teeth at one end and butts against a wall at the other end. To operate, bend it up in the middle, set the teeth, and position the other end against a wall. Then push down in the middle to stretch the carpeting. Rent a power stretcher that's long enough to reach most of the way across the the room.

If the layout requires a carpet seam, position it in a low-traffic or out-of-the-way area. Be sure to run the seam perpendicular to a window or other light source—it will be less visible there.

1. Stretch the carpeting.
Use the following sequence:
1. Use a knee kicker to stretch carpeting tight to the wall opposite the doorway.
2. Knee-kick the carpeting tight to the adjacent wall.
3. Power-stretch the carpeting into the adjacent corner.
4. Knee-kick to the adjacent wall.
5. Power-stretch the carpeting diagonally into the opposite corner. After each stretch or kick, push the carpeting down on the tackless strip with the heel of your hand to be sure it grabs.

2. Trim the carpet.
Start trimming anywhere and work your way around the edge of the room, using either a utility knife or a carpet trimmer. Leave ¼ inch of excess carpeting as you trim. Use a masonry chisel to tuck this edge between the tackless strip and the baseboard.

3. Replace the shoe molding.
Finish the job by replacing the shoe moldings. Old molding may look out of place next to new carpeting; if so, replace it with new molding. Nail the molding to the baseboard, not the floor.

Carpet seaming.
You once needed a heavy-duty needle, some thread, and lots of patience to join two pieces of carpeting. Now most pros bond a special heat-setting tape to the backing, as shown above. Make seams prior to stretching the carpet. Trim the carpet edges straight and butt them carefully.

Fold both edges back and lay the tape along the floor where the seam will fall. Move the heated iron slowly along the tape. As the adhesive melts, press the edges of the carpeting into it with your other hand. Weight down the seam for a few minutes after joining the carpeting.

CARPETING A STAIRWAY

*T*o carpet stairs, you can use a strip left over from carpeting an adjoining room or purchase a runner. If you opt to use a carpeting strip, use tackless stair strips to anchor it. Make sure the pile of the carpet runs down the stairs (that is, it feels smoother when you run your hand in the downstairs direction).

If you decide to use a runner, the best way to secure it is with rods. Stair rods are work to install, but add a decorative touch and are easy to maintain. To install rods, first lay padding in one strip from top to bottom and tack it temporarily at the top. Tack the runner face down to the bottom tread next to the second riser; then stretch the runner under the nosing at the top of the first riser and tack it in place. Then attach the rods as described at far right.

Secure carpet with tackless strips...
You can use special tackless strips to secure carpeting. Lay the pad first, then nail the strips on top of the padding. Cut the carpet several inches wider than needed, and lay it by pressing into the tackless strips as you go. Then trim the sides.

...or install stair rods.
Screw an eye or rod bracket to each side of the tread, ½ inch outside the carpet edge. Slip a rod over the carpeting and through the eye. Pull the carpeting taut. Proceed to the next step. At the top, nail carpet tacks to the end just under the nosing.

LAYING INTEGRAL-PAD CARPETING

Integral-pad (or cushion-backed) carpeting is bonded to its own cushioned backing, thus eliminating the need for a carpet pad. It's especially ideal for applying carpet directly over concrete. Cut-pile, berber, and other styles are available in a good selection of colors.

In small spaces, such as bathrooms and closets, you can cut the carpeting to fit and lay it without carpet tape. Edges have a tendency to curl in time, however, so it's best to anchor big pieces with double-sided tape.

Prepare the room as you would for any other type of carpeting (see page 336). The floor should be structurally sound. Clean the floor well so the tape can adhere.

Buy double-sided carpet tape, which is 2 inches wide. It has a protective paper that covers the top; remove the paper only when you are ready to attach the carpet. If the installation involves seams, buy 5-inch-wide carpet tape and a seam adhesive recommended for your type of carpeting.

YOU'LL NEED...

TIME: 2 to 3 hours for a 12×15-foot room.
SKILLS: Basic carpeting skills.
TOOLS: Tape measure, utility knife, seam roller or kitchen rolling pin, drill and drill bits, hammer, and nail set.

1. Test fit the carpeting.
Cut the carpeting several inches larger than the room and set it in place. Make sure piles fall in the same direction. Allow about 1 inch extra all around the perimeter of the room.

2. Mark for seam locations.
Join any seams by folding back one piece and drawing a line on the floor along the edge of the other piece.

3. Apply double-sided tape.
Center double-sided tape on the line and stick it to the floor. Check to see that the seam runs through the middle of the tape, then peel off the protective paper on top.

4. Apply seam adhesive.
Press one piece of carpeting into place, taking care not to create folds. Apply seam adhesive along its edge to cement the pieces together.

5. Roll a seam.
Use a rolling pin or seam roller to press the carpeting firmly against the tape. Brushing the pile will cause the seam to virtually disappear.

6. Make a tape border.
Without sliding the carpeting out of position, fold it back from two of the walls and apply a tape border. Smooth the tape before removing the paper.

7. Smooth the edges.
Roll the carpeting back so it retains its original position, then drop—don't slide—it onto the tape. Smooth the edges with your hands so the tape adhesive gets a good grip.

EXPERTS' INSIGHT

ADHESIVE INSTALLATION

Integral-pad carpeting can also be installed using a latex adhesive. This holds the carpet more firmly in place, thus reducing wear and helping the carpet last longer. (Of course adhered carpeting is much more difficult to remove.) To install, cut the carpet to fit and set it in place. Fold back half the carpet, and use a notched trowel to spread adhesive onto the floor. Unfold the carpet and press into place. Repeat for the other half of the floor.

8. Trim off excess.
Trim off excess carpeting with a utility knife or a carpet knife. Tamp the edges down by rubbing the carpet with the heel of your hand. The pile will hide minor irregularities.

9. Finish with base shoe molding.
Finish by installing or replacing the base shoe molding. Nail molding to the baseboard, not the floor. Drill pilot holes and drive in finishing nails. Set the heads of the finishing nails with a nail set.

CHOOSING AND BUYING RESILIENT FLOORING

Resilient flooring—softer underfoot than any other flooring except carpeting—is available in the form of tiles or sheet goods.

Resilient tiles have been a popular do-it-yourself item since World War II, although they have changed considerably in size (from 9 to 12 inches square), appearance (from dull, streaked greens and beiges to vivid colors and patterns), and composition (from asphalt and asbestos to varying blends of vinyl).

Sheet goods have been around awhile also. Because they come in rolls up to 12 feet wide, installing them is more difficult. Installation kits are available, but be aware that a cutting mistake can ruin an entire roll, not just a single tile.

Choosing the right resilient flooring depends to some extent on the type of use your new floor will get (see chart below).

Cushioned sheet flooring, usually with a pattern printed on the surface, is soft underfoot, has a minimum of dirt-catching seams, and does a decent job of sound-proofing. Some surface-printed tiles are similarly cushioned. "Commercial" tiles are less expensive, easier to install, and much more resistant to dents from items, such as chair legs. Also you should consider whether you want a smooth or a textured surface.

Before you buy, be sure you are clear about the installation directions. Most resilient flooring can be installed on any sound subsurface. Install over existing resilient flooring only if it is firmly stuck at all points.

Beware: Resilient flooring does not cover up imperfections in the subsurface; this is especially true of surface-printed tiles and sheets. If the existing floor cannot be sanded smooth, install subflooring and underlayment above it (see page 342).

Because most of today's tiles are 1-foot square, determining how many you will need requires only simple computations. Estimating the amount of sheet flooring needed is trickier, especially if there's a pattern involved and a seam is needed. It's best to make an accurate plan of the room on graph paper and then take it to a flooring dealer.

CAUTION!
Asbestos Tile
If you need to remove tiles to lay a new floor, be aware that many older tiles contain asbestos. Some states require a licensed asbestos remover to take them out. Ask your flooring dealer how to test old tiles for asbestos and whether you need to hire a licensed firm to remove them.

COMPARING RESILIENT FLOORINGS

Material	Properties	Relative Cost
Linoleum	True linoleum is making a comeback. This is a natural product with color that runs through its thickness. It hides scratches well.	Moderate
Cushioned sheet vinyl	Several grades are available—from moderately durable to very durable. Durability ranges from that of vinyl asbestos tile to about one-half as durable. Resistant to abrasion and discoloration. Vulnerable to burns. Usually contains a vinyl foam layer.	Wide price range
Commercial vinyl or rubber tile	Often used for grocery stores and other commercial spaces, these tiles have random flecks or dots of color that run through the body of the tile. Tiles of different colors can be mixed to form patterns and borders. Rubber tile is a little more expensive, with a similar appearance and even greater durability.	Inexpensive
Surface-printed vinyl tile	Basically the same composition and characteristics as sheet vinyl, but tiles are easier to install.	Wide price range

INSTALLING UNDERLAYMENT

The most common underlayment material is ¼ inch thick and is available in 4×4 sheets. A series of + marks stamped on the surface indicates where to drive nails or screws. Underlayment only smooths a floor. If the floor needs strengthening, see pages 314–315.

To secure the underlayment, you will need lots of ringshank flooring nails or screws. Drive one in every 4 inches around the perimeter and every 8 inches across the sheets into joists. Stagger the sheet joints.

YOU'LL NEED...

TIME: 2 to 3 hours for a simple 12×15-foot room.
SKILLS: Basic carpentry skills.
TOOLS: Tape measure, hammer, straightedge, circular saw, and straight trowel.

1. Create an underlayment layout.
Begin near the center of the room and arrange 4×4 panels so that four corners never meet at a point. As much as possible, avoid having to install a narrow strip at the perimeter.

2. Drive fasteners.
Drive nails or ringshank flooring nails through the subfloor. If the subfloor is only a single sheet of plywood, use screws rather than nails to anchor the underlayment surface securely.

3. Mark a sheet for cutting.
Along the edges of the room, slide a sheet of material against the wall, overlapping and squaring it with the previously nailed panel. With a scrap of underlayment or a straightedge as a guide, draw a line along the length of the edge piece. Cut the sheet along the line.

4. Secure the edge pieces.
Fasten the edge pieces into place. Don't worry if the fit isn't exact along the wall. The base shoe will cover a gap of at least ½ inch.

5. Fill and sand.
See that all fastener heads are dimpled slightly below the surface. Using a straight trowel, fill all fastener dimples and joints with flooring patch. Allow the patch to dry, then sand the floor smooth.

LAYING RESILIENT TILE

Because thin surface-printed tiles show even the tiniest imperfections in the subsurface, it is necessary to prepare a floor surface that is very smooth. Thicker surface-printed tiles and commercial tiles can bridge small gaps like fastener dimples, but will show any larger flaws.

Plan the layout first by making a scale drawing of the room, and then by setting out tiles in a dry run. Aim to eliminate any slivers at the perimeter, unless the area will be covered up by furniture.

Self-stick tiles can be installed without adhesive, but they may start to peel after a year or two. Spread adhesive on the floor to ensure a solid installation.

YOU'LL NEED...

TIME: 4 hours for a 12×15-foot room.
SKILLS: Basic skills.
TOOLS: Tape measure, framing square, chalk line, utility knife, and notched trowel.

TOOLS TO USE

CUTTING TOOLS

Cutting resilient tile is not difficult, but it can be time-consuming. To pick up the pace, have a collection of tools ready at hand. Set the tile to be cut on a small sheet of ply-wood, to prevent damage to the floor. For a square, use a full-sized tile marked with an **X** so you will be sure not to lay it on the floor. Replace knife blades as soon as they start to become dull. If you have plenty of cutting to do, rent a vinyl tile cutter, which makes a straight cut in a couple of seconds.

1. Snap layout lines.
Snap chalk lines between the midpoints of the walls. Adjust the lines, if necessary, so that the lines make a right angle.

2. Dry-lay rows of tiles.
Dry-lay tiles in an L-shape, starting from the center. Check the border tiles. If necessary shift the L half a tile over, and snap new chalk lines.

3. Apply mastic.
Use a small notched trowel or a paint roller to spread adhesive over as much of the floor as possible, as long as you can reach the layout lines without walking on adhesive. Allow the adhesive to dry until it is tacky.

4. Lay the tiles.
Apply tiles starting with the **L** corner and building a pyramid. Be certain to keep the tiles square with chalk lines. Don't slide tiles into position: Butt edges against adjacent tiles, fold down into place, and press firmly.

5. Mark for a straight cut.

At the baseboard, tiles need not be cut precisely because the base shoe will cover about ½ inch. To mark for a straight cut, lay a tile on top of the last full one in the row. Put another against the wall, and mark the overlap.

6. Mark for a corner cut.

Corners are not difficult to figure. Mark from one of the walls, just as you would for a border tile. Shift the tiles to the other wall (but don't turn them), and mark again. Mark an **X** on the section to be cut out.

7. Use a template.

For odd shapes, make a cardboard template first; cut with scissors, and transfer the pattern to the tile.

1. To lay a diagonal pattern, begin with chalk lines.

For a diagonal pattern, locate the center of the room and snap chalk lines at 45-degree angles to the wall.

2. Then dry-lay the tiles.

Dry-lay tiles along the lines and adjust for good border spacing. At the walls, you'll need to cut triangles. Cut a tile in half at a 45-degree angle and use it as a guide for the cuts.

3. Add a border if you like.

For an interesting look, border the diagonal field with a row of straight-laid tiles. Install the border first, then cut the diagonals carefully to butt against the border.

DOORS AND WINDOWS

UNDERSTANDING WINDOWS

*I*n addition to providing views of the outside world, windows control the flow of air throughout the interior spaces of your home. Some windows are not intended to be opened, but most windows include one or more movable sashes. Keeping them—and their related coverings—in good working order is the focus of the next 14 pages.

To learn how to replace windowpanes, windowsills, and storm/screen windows, see pages 372–377.

There is more to a window than meets the eye, especially with the older double-hung type shown at right. Concealed behind the side jambs of the frame are heavy sash weights. Connected with a rope-and-pulley system, the weights counterbalance the sashes— making them easier to open—and hold them in any vertical position you wish.

A series of stops fitted to the jambs provides channels in which the sashes slide. Check the top view (below right) and note that although the outside blind stop is more or less permanently affixed, the parting stop and inside stop can be pried loose if you want to remove the sashes.

In newer double-hung windows the weight-and-pulley mechanisms are replaced with a pair of spring lift devices (see page 349).

With both types of windows, the lower sash comes to rest behind a flat stool. Its outside counterpart, the sill, slopes so that water can run off. Trim—called *casing* at the sides and top and an *apron* below—covers gaps between the jambs and the wall material.

Casement window

Casement windows open and close like a door. In the version shown, muntins separate the panes. However with newer double-glazed casements the muntins—often referred to as grills—snap to the inside of the window to facilitate cleaning or are absent altogether.

Sliding window

As with double-hung sashes, sliding sashes (also called gliding sashes) open up only 50 percent of the total window area for ventilation. Some sliding windows have one fixed and one sliding sash, as shown. With others, both sashes slide along tracks. Sliding windows can be

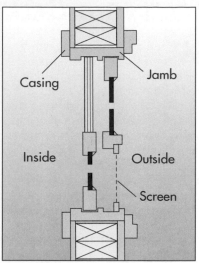

made with wood, metal, or vinyl. In most models, the movable sash slides in the bottom track; in some, it glides on an upper track. An older window's track may be a simple groove made of wood. Newer windows have metal or vinyl tracks, and the sash may have rollers for smooth operation.

Jalousie window

Turning the crank of a jalousie window pivots a series of glass slats. The frames consist of short metal channels at both ends of the slats. The glass-to-glass joints tend to leak air, so jalousies usually are used only in breezeways, porches, and other unheated zones.

Awning window

An awning window works in the same fashion as a casement window, but the sash tilts outward from the bottom. Some awnings slide downward as they tilt, so that you can open them to a nearly horizontal position

for maximum cooling airflow.

An awning window opens with a side-mounted or two-armed mechanism, operated by a crank, sometimes called a roto-handle. Hinges usually can be disengaged so you can easily remove the sash.

FREEING A BALKY SASH

When a double-hung window binds or refuses to open, don't try to force it. Take a look around the sash, both inside and out. Chances are you will find that paint has sealed the sash shut or that a stop molding has warped. The steps shown here will enable you to gently pry and free the sash, preventing damage. If the top sash is painted shut, you may choose to leave it that way, unless you need to move it for cleaning.

YOU'LL NEED...

TIME: 30 minutes or more, depending on the cause.
SKILLS: Basic skills.
TOOLS: Sash knife or utility knife, flat pry bar, and hammer.

1. Break the paint seal.
To break a paint seal, use a sash knife, which is specially designed for this purpose. Or run a sharp utility knife several times between the sash and stop. Be sure to cut through the paint at every point.

2. Pry the window open.
Pry from the outside edges with a pry bar and a protective block of wood. Take your time, using gentle to moderate pressure at several points. Alternating sides, work inward from the edges until the sash pops free.

3. Spread the stops.
If a sash is binding between its stops, try separating the stops slightly by tapping along their length with a hammer and wooden block that fits tightly between the stops. If the binding is severe, you may need to pry the stop off and nail it in a new position.

4. Lubricate the sash.
Once you get the window moving, scrape or chisel any built-up paint off the edges of the sash or between the stops. Lightly sand its jambs; then lubricate with a candle or with paraffin, paste wax, or bar soap.

EXPERTS' INSIGHT

OTHER DOUBLE-HUNG MECHANISMS

The spring lift shown on page 349 and the weight-and-pulley system shown on pages 350–351 are the most common mechanisms for double-hung windows. Another type uses a tension spring—a flat metal strap that attaches to a spring-loaded drum unit in the sash. Finding replacement drum units may be difficult. A friction sash is made of vinyl or aluminum; it grabs the sash tightly enough that it does not slide down when raised.

ADJUSTING A SPRING LIFT

*T*ube-type lifting devices house a spring-driven twist rod that helps lift the sash. To improve sash movement, you can adjust the spring devices as shown on this page. But before tampering with these, check to be sure the window has not been painted shut. If it has, follow the procedures on page 348. If the device doesn't seem to work at all, it is probably broken, and you'll need to replace it (see below).

> **YOU'LL NEED...**
> **TIME:** About 30 minutes per window.
> **SKILLS:** No special skills needed.
> **TOOLS:** Screwdriver or drill.

1. Unscrew the lift.
Grip the tube before you remove the screw, holding it in place, or the spring will unwind in a hurry. If the window sails up too easily, hold the screw and let the spring turn a couple of revolutions.

2. Rotate the lift.
If the window is hard to raise, tighten the spring by turning it clockwise. You may need to adjust the lifts on both sides.

REPLACING A SPRING LIFT

1. Remove the stop.
Using a utility knife, score the paint between the inside stop and the casing. Pry with a putty knife to remove the inside stop on one side of the sash. This should make enough room to remove the sash.

2. Pull out the sash.
Remove the screw that secures the tube, let the spring unwind, and then pull out the sash.

3. Replace the lift rod.
Remove and replace the twist rod/tube unit. Reinstall the sash and adjust the tube (see above).

REPLACING A SASH CORD

Each sash in an old double-hung window is connected to two weights that run through channels in each side of the window. A sash cord or chain is secured to the sash and runs through a pulley near the top of the jamb. Sometimes a window binds because the cord has come out of its groove in the side of the sash; if so, force it back into position. If a cord or chain has become detached from the sash, reattach it with a short screw. If the cord is broken, replace it. A cord will not last as long as a sash chain, which also looks better.

YOU'LL NEED...

TIME: 1 to 2 hours.
SKILLS: Basic carpentry skills.
TOOLS: Putty knife, utility knife, screwdriver or drill, and hammer.

1. Pry out the stop.
Usually you need to remove only one inside stop. Cut through the paint using a utility knife. Using a putty knife, pry carefully at several points to loosen the stop, and then remove the stop with a flat pry bar.

2. Lift out the sash.
Lift the sash and swing it clear from the frame. One or both cords may still be connected. Take care that a cord does not come loose and suddenly fly upward.

3. Detach the cord.
Hang on to the cord and pull it out of the sash; you may need to pry out a nail or unscrew a screw.
NOTE: *Be careful never to let go of the cord. Pull it out and slip a nail through the knot so that the cord cannot slip through the pulley.*

4. Open the access cover.
There will probably be an access cover at the base of the jamb; unscrew the fasteners that hold the cover in place. Gently pry it out to reveal the weights. If there is no access cover, you may have to pry off the jamb.

5. Feed in the sash cord.
Untie or cut the cord off of each weight and pull the weight out. Cut new cords or chains longer than they need to be. Feeding new sash cords or chains over pulleys calls for patience. Replace the cords or chains on both sides.

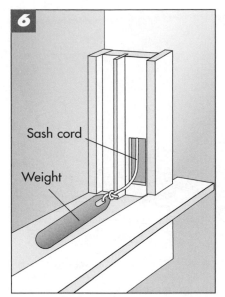

6. Attach the weight.

Once the new cord or chain is visible through the access hole, tie a knot in the other end so that it cannot slip through the pulley. Tie the cord or chain to the weight and tug to make sure the knot is secure. Slip the weight back in place.

7. Check the weight's position.

Weights should hang 3 inches above the channel bottoms when the lower sash is raised fully. Once you have determined the correct length, knot the other end of the cord or chain and fit it into the groove. Secure the cord or chain with a short screw—don't drive the screw into the windowpane.

8. Remove the upper sash.

To replace the cords on an upper sash, you have to remove the lower one, then one of the parting stops. Use the same techniques as for the lower sash.

9. Replace the stop.

When you replace stops, partially drive in longer nails, or drive in nails at different points. Raise and lower the sash to check the stop positioning; it should be fairly tight, yet allow for smooth operation.

EXPERTS' INSIGHT

REHABBING AN OLD DOUBLE-HUNG WINDOW?

An old window will probably never insulate as well as a newer window. The cavity that houses the weights (see page 310) cannot be filled with insulation, and the panes are single-glazed. So installing new windows may save money in the long run.

However if you have the time and energy, you can plug most of the leaks and make the window a smooth operator. Remove the sashes and sand their edges smooth. Repair the glazing and paint the glazing so that it is sealed with the glass (see pages 372–373). Caulk around all the casing and apron edges, both inside and outside.

If you install a friction sash channel, you can remove the pulleys and fill in the cavity with insulation. Adding combination storm/screen windows will add a great deal to the insulating ability of a window.

REPAIRING SLIDING WINDOWS

Tracks for sliding (or gliding) windows are notorious collectors of dust and grit, which make for rough opening and closing. Keep tracks clean with regular vacuuming and scrub them when grime starts to build up. Scrape any paint away. To improve performance, spray with a silicone lubricant. If a slider jams, binds, or jumps loose, something may be lodged in the track or the track may be bent. If all seems clear, lift out the sash and check its grooved edges. Clean and lubricate these, too, if needed.

YOU'LL NEED...

TIME: About 30 minutes per window.
SKILLS: Basic skills.
TOOLS: Hammer, screwdriver, and large pliers.

Remove a sash.
To remove a sliding sash, partially open the window, then lift it up and pull its lower edge toward you. The second sash may be fixed in place, or you may need to remove some hold-down hardware before it can be slid over and removed.

Straighten a track.
To straighten a bent track, cut a wood block to fit snugly in the channel and carefully tap the track against it. Or place a piece of metal on either side of the track and squeeze with a large pair of pliers.

EXPERTS' INSIGHT

HARDWARE REPAIRS FOR SLIDING WINDOWS

■ If a latch does not close readily, remove it and clean it with a brush and vacuum, then spray with silicone lubricant. Also check the strike, where the latch attaches, and clean away any obstructions. If the latch is broken, replace it.

■ To replace a roller or track, look for the manufacturer's name on the window's frame or the sash, and contact them by phone or on the web. A local hardware store may stock hardware for a window that's common in your area.

Adjust dogs.
"Catch-and-dog" window latches can get bent. Adjust them so that the dog's "hind leg" hits against the catch. Bigger windows roll on sets of nylon wheels called sheaves, which are self-lubricating and rarely need attention. If a sheave is mangled, remove the assembly and replace it.

FIXING AWNING WINDOWS

Awning windows are repaired much like casements (pages 354–355). If an arm is bent, place a piece of metal on either side and squeeze with a large pair of pliers. If you cannot straighten an arm, you may need to replace it.

Keep operators moving freely. A stiff arm assembly could pull screws loose or even force apart the sash joints. Clean off rust with steel wool and lubricate with graphite or paraffin wax; never use oil because it attracts dust.

YOU'LL NEED...
TIME: About 30 minutes per window.
SKILLS: Basic skills.
TOOLS: Hammer and screwdriver.

1. Unscrew the arm.
To remove an awning sash, open it as far as you can. Disconnect the operator's side or scissors arm, typically attached with two screws.

2. Disengage the sash.
Tilt the sash to a horizontal position. Pry the sliding hinges to the side to disengage the sash. To completely remove a sash, tap out the pins of the upper hinges or unscrew the hinges from the jamb or from the sash.

REPAIRING JALOUSIE WINDOWS

Jalousie window mechanisms depend on a series of gears and levers that may be concealed in the jambs. Keep a jalousie operating smoothly by lubricating all the parts regularly with graphite or silicone—never oil, which will attract dust.

Because they have so many moving parts, jalousies are relatively difficult to repair. Often you must dismantle the entire window to get at the vertical arms. If your unit jams, try freeing it with graphite or another non-oil lubricant.

YOU'LL NEED...
TIME: 30 minutes per window.
SKILLS: Basic skills.
TOOLS: Hammer and screwdriver.

Remove a slat.
Simple tab-like clips hold jalousie slats in place. To remove one, just bend open the tab, slide the clip back slightly, and slide out the pane. Replace the slat, then bend each clip holder back to its original shape.

Service a crank.
If a crank mechanism is stuck or is hard to operate, don't force it. Lubricate the crank shaft and pivot points, and then work the handle back and forth slowly. If the crank turns without opening the slats, purchase and install a replacement crank.

REPAIRING CASEMENT WINDOWS

Accumulations of paint, grease, or dirt cause most casement window difficulties. If your casement is malfunctioning, check all sash and frame edges. A few minutes with a wire brush or scraper may remove the debris that is causing the rub.

Examine the unit's mechanical components. Lubricant may be all you need. Use automobile grease or oil for parts that are encased in a housing (such as the crank operator). Where parts will be exposed to the elements and dust, use graphite, paste wax, or silicone lubricant to avoid attracting dust.

If an arm is bent, remove it and set it on a hard, flat surface. Place a piece of metal on top, and tap with a hammer to straighten the arm. Or use a large pair of pliers.

If a sash binds, partially close it and look for places where the window rubs against the sash. On a metal unit, scraping away excess paint may solve the problem.

Wood casements sometimes suffer the same problems that bedevil doors. Solve these problems by adapting the door-fitting and planing techniques illustrated on pages 360–361. Remove about ¹⁄₁₆ inch extra wood, then apply primer and paint.

YOU'LL NEED...

TIME: 20 to 30 minutes per window.
SKILLS: Basic skills.
TOOLS: Hammer, screwdriver, wire brush or scraper, pliers, lubricant, and perhaps a plane.

Clean the arm mechanism.
If the sash is difficult to close, try cleaning the sliding arm mechanism with a wire brush. Lubricate with graphite or silicone.

Service the sliding mechanism.
Sill-mounted sliding shoes trap dirt. Unscrew the channel, clean it and the sill, and then lubricate with paste wax.

Tighten latch screws.
Tighten any loose latch screws. If a screw won't tighten, tap slivers of wood into the screw holes and drive the screws again. If a handle won't pull its sash snug, shim under it or add weather stripping.

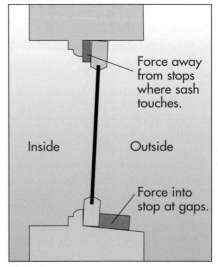

Unwarp.
If a wood sash has warped, counter-warp it with wood strips. Temporarily screw or nail the pieces so they warp the window in the opposite direction. Leave the strips in place for a couple of weeks.

Lubricate a crank.
To keep cranks turning freely, apply graphite or a light oil. With some cranks you may need to take off the handle first.

Dismantle an operator.
To dismantle an operator, disconnect the slide arm from the sash, then unscrew it from the frame.

Repack with lubricant.
If the gears are encrusted with old grease, soak the operator mechanism in a solvent, then repack it with a multipurpose lubricant or automobile grease.

INSULATION ABILITY OF WINDOW TREATMENTS

Treatment	Description	Summer Reflective Efficiency	Winter Insulating Efficiency
Venetian blinds	Multiple parallel slats	Effective when closed	Virtually none
Draperies	Tightly woven white fabric	Effective when closed	Fairly effective if tight-fitting
Shades	White shade cloth	Effective when closed	Virtually none
Double-glazing	Insulating glass or single-glazing plus storm window	Not very effective	Cuts heat loss by 50%
Triple- and Low-E glazing	Insulating glass plus storm or coated glass	Low-E is fairly reflective	Cuts heat loss by 70%
Thermal shades	Quilted, fiber-filled material sealed tightly to a window frame	Very effective	Cuts heat loss by 80%

REPAIRING WINDOW SHADES

A window shade (right) has a hollow roller with a coiled spring inside. Drawing down the shade puts tension on the spring; a ratchet and flat pin at one end hold this tension until you release it. A stationary pin at the other end turns freely in its bracket.

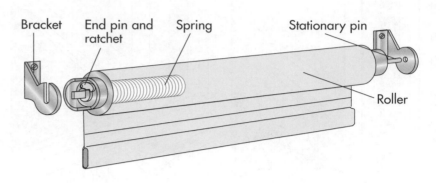

Bracket　　End pin and ratchet　　Spring　　Stationary pin

Roller

YOU'LL NEED...

TIME: 20 to 30 minutes per window.
SKILLS: Basic skills.
TOOLS: Framing square, scissors or utility knife, staple gun, and saw.

Shade material

Measure shade material.
If you take down an old shade and unroll it, you will see that its shade material has been stapled to the roller. Take off the old material. Then square off the edge of the new material. Carefully align this edge with the guideline on the roller before you drive in the new staples.

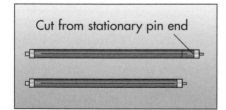

Cut from stationary pin end

Cut roller.
Remove the material, saw the roller to length with a fine-toothed saw, reinsert the stationary pin, cut the material to size, and replace it.

TROUBLESHOOTING WINDOW SHADES

Problem	Cause	Solution
Goes up with a bang	Too much tension on the spring	Take down the shade, unroll a few inches, and replace it in its bracket
Goes up too slowly	Not enough tension on the spring	Increase tension by rerolling
Will not catch	Bent or worn brackets; ratchet not holding	Align brackets; if ratchet is bad, replace roller
Binds	Not enough clearance from brackets	Bend brackets apart or shorten stationary pin
Falls	Excess clearance at brackets; broken spring	Relocate brackets; if spring is shot, replace roller

Width

Height

Inside mount

Width

Height

Outside mount

Measure for inside or outside mount.
For inside mounting, measure from jamb to jamb and subtract ⅛ inch for clearance. Measure for length and add 1½ inches. For outside

mounting, the width should be at least 1½ inches larger than the opening. The length should be 1½ inches longer than the span from the top of the upper trim to the sill.

REPAIRING VENETIAN BLINDS

*I*nside the head box of a venetian blind, a tilt tube supports a pair of tape ladders on which the blind's slats rest. To open or close the slats, pull one end of a tilt cord wrapped around the pulley of a worm gear. This gear rotates the tube and changes the pitch of the slats. A lift cord, strung over a series of pulleys and down through the slats to the base piece, raises and lowers the entire slat assembly.

When the tilting mechanism balks, look for cord threads or dirt in the worm gear. If the blind refuses to go up or down, the lift cord has either broken, frayed, or jammed. If so replace both cords and check the tape ladders as well.

YOU'LL NEED...

TIME: 2 hours to replace both cords and ladders.
SKILLS: Basic skills.
TOOLS: Screwdriver, utility knife, and staple gun.

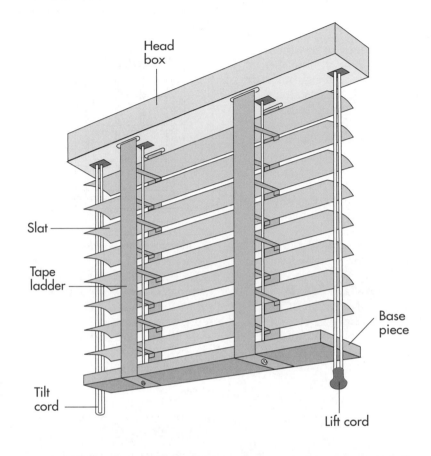

Head box

Slat

Tape ladder

Tilt cord

Base piece

Lift cord

Clip

Staple

Utility knife

1. Disassemble the blind.
Remove any clamps at the bottom of the base. On wood blinds the tapes are stapled. Snip off the lift cord at either side and remove by pulling as if raising the blind. Slide out the slats. In the head box, free the tapes by removing the clips holding the tapes to the tilt tube.

Tilt pulley

Tilt tube

Lift lock

Tilt cord

Lift cord

2. Thread lift cords.
Attach the new tapes to the tilt tube and the base piece, then extend the ladders and slide the slats into place. Thread the lift cords from the base piece on each side up, over the pulleys, and back down through the lift lock.

Clip

Worm gear

3. Thread tilt cord.
Note that the ladders' rungs are offset from each other. Weave the lift cord on alternate sides of the rungs. Snip any tassels from the old tilt cord, thread the new cord over the worm gear pulley, and replace the tassels.

INSTALLING INTERIOR STORM SASHES

Fitting a storm sash on the inner side of an existing window cuts heat loss in half without the expense of buying exterior storm windows. You can install kit sashes, as shown on these pages, or make your own from ⅛-inch acrylic held in place with wood picture-frame molding. Fasten acrylic to window casings with screws and then apply self-adhesive weather stripping around the edges so you can remove the pane easily.

If you're considering new exterior storm windows, turn to 378-379.

YOU'LL NEED...

TIME: 2 to 3 hours per window.
SKILLS: Basic skills.
TOOLS: Tape measure, framing square, utility knife, sanding block, and hacksaw.

1. Measure the window.
Measure to the outside of casings. Test-fit a piece of acrylic into the trim pieces (see below), then subtract enough to allow for the self-adhesive trim at the sides, top, and sill. Measure and mark a piece of acrylic with a knife at the beginning and end of each cut.

2. Trim the acrylic.
Lay the acrylic piece on a flat surface, protective film–side down. Hold a framing square or drywall square firmly in place and draw a utility knife along the straightedge several times. Place the score on a table edge and push down on both sides to snap the cut. Smooth rough edges with a sanding block.

3. Cut the sill.
When you measure for cutting the sill trim, be sure to allow for the strips at the sides. Hold the sill trim firmly in place and cut with a hacksaw. Cut slowly so you do not bend the trim. Snap the sill piece onto the bottom of the pane.

4. Apply self-adhesive trim.
Most side and top trims snap open and have adhesive backings. Cut them to fit using a hacksaw. Snap the pieces onto the perimeter of the pane. After assembly, lift the unit into place and check that it fits; you may need to recut a piece.

5. Use joiner strips for large windows.
Special joiner strips splice together more than one acrylic sheet for large windows or patio doors. Snap the flexible strips onto a sheet so the joiner strips will fit together as shown, then add the second sheet.

6. Install the sash.
Secure the sill trim. To attach the side and top pieces, remove the adhesive backing's protective paper and press only when you are sure the position is correct; if you reposition it, the adhesive will not be as strong. Make sure there are no air gaps.

7. Remove the pane for cleaning.
To remove the pane for cleaning or ventilation, snap open the side and top trim and lift out the acrylic.

EXPERTS' INSIGHT

WORKING WITH AND MAINTAINING ACRYLIC

Acrylic is in some ways easier to work with than glass. You can drill holes through it, and it's much easier to trim off a small amount.

However acrylic scratches easily. Don't remove the protective film until the pane is completely installed. Wash acrylic with mild liquid detergent and lots of water or a manufacturer-specified cleaner.

If an inside sash collects condensed water when the weather is cold, remove the pane and dry both the pane and the window.

USING WINDOW TREATMENTS IN COLD CLIMATES

On average, windows comprise only 10 percent of the wall area of a house. Yet they account for as much as 40 percent of a house's heat loss.

R-value measures resistance to heat flow. To determine your window's total R-value, add up the R-values of all your window's features using the chart at right.

A home energy audit—free from many gas and electric utility companies and many state energy agencies—shows you the savings and payback period for new items.

Effective window treatment involves more than simply hanging drapes. The temperature difference between indoors and outdoors creates a convection current between the glass and the insulation. This causes the cold air generated in the airspace to flow out at the bottom, reducing the R-value of the treatment. In addition moisture in the air condenses on

the cold glass. The condensate may run down onto the sill right away, or it may accumulate as frost to later melt and run down. Either way the condensate may damage the sill.

WINDOW TREATMENT R-VALUES

Treatment	R-Value
Single-glazed	0.9
Double-glazed (DG)	1.9
Low-E glass	1.3
Interior storm sash	1.8
Exterior storm/screen	1.8
Quilted shade	3.2

How condensation occurs.
The key to window insulation is a vapor-impervious construction and tight air seals at the sides and bottom. If a storm window—either interior or exterior—is not well sealed, the mix of cold and warm air will create vapor that collects on the windowpane.

UNDERSTANDING INTERIOR DOORS

Almost every modern wood panel door has a vertical-stile and horizontal-rail framework. This construction helps counteract the wood's tendency to shrink, swell, and warp with humidity changes. With a panel door (right), you can see that framing. Spaces between frame members are paneled with wood, louvered slats, or glass.

Smooth-surfaced "flush doors" hide their framing beneath two or three layers of veneer. Alternating the veneer directions minimizes warping. A solid-core flush door has a dense center of hardwood blocks or particleboard; a hollow-core door uses lighter material in the interior, such as ribbons of corrugated cardboard or rigid foam insulation.

For sliding and bifold doors, see pages 364–365.

Panel doors.
Made of milled pine components, panel doors are easy to plane and, if necessary, cut down to fit an opening. Cheaper types are made of molded hardboard.

Hollow-core doors.
Covered with oak, birch, or lauan-mahogany veneer, hollow-core doors are inexpensive. They are difficult to cut down, though, because there is only 2 to 3 inches of framing at the top and bottom.

FREEING A BINDING DOOR

When a hinged door sticks, don't be too quick to take it down to plane its edges. Many difficulties are better corrected by making minor adjustments with the door in place.

Most problems result from one or more of the following causes: loose hinge screws, paint that is too thick on the jamb and/or door edge, improperly aligned hinges, an improperly aligned strike plate, a frame that is out of square (usually because the house has settled), or warping of the door.

YOU'LL NEED...
TIME: 30 to 90 minutes, depending on whether you have to plane the door
SKILLS: No special skills needed.
TOOLS: Hammer, nail set, chisel, wedge, plane, and screwdriver.

Where's the rub?
If a door sticks or refuses to fit into its frame, open the door and pull up on the handle, then let go. If either hinge is loose, screws need to be tightened. Next close the door as far as it will go without forcing it, and carefully examine the perimeter. Look for an uneven gap along the hinge jamb; this means that the hinges need attention. If the door seems too big for its frame—or out of square with it—mark the tight spots, then sand or plane those spots.

1. Shim the door.

Loose hinge screws can cause sags. To tighten them, first wedge the door open under the latch edge. (Hinges usually come loose for a reason—often because the door binds when it is closed. After tightening the screws, take steps to make sure that the door does not bind.)

2. Plug the screw holes.

Remove the screws and plug their holes with glue-coated golf tees, wood splinters, or dowels. Drive new screws into each plug. If this does not work, try driving longer screws. Make sure the screws are driven straight, so their heads are flat; angled screw heads can cause the door to bind.

3. Shim out a hinge.

If the door binds on the hinge side, scrape and sand away any built-up paint on the edge of the door and the jamb. A hinge leaf should be flush with the surrounding surface. If either leaf is set in, remove the screws, insert a cardboard shim, and rescrew.

1. Plane the door top in place, if possible.

If the door binds, gently close the door and scribe a cut line at all points where binding occurs, using the jamb as a guide. Usually you won't have to remove the door from its hinges to plane the top or the latch side. First bevel any edges to prevent splintering. For instructions on planing, see pages 263–264.

2. Tap out the hinge pins.

To trim the bottom or an edge you can't reach with the door in place, remove the door. Shim the bottom of the door so it is stable. Use a nail set or screwdriver to hammer out the hinge pins, bottom first, then the top. If the hinge is rusty and the pin is stuck, try squirting with penetrating oil. If that doesn't work, you may need to remove the screws from one hinge leaf.

3. Plane the door.

Brace the door for planing. Avoid planing the hinge side, if possible. If you must do so, first remove the hinges. You may have to reset the hinges afterwards.

CORRECTING STRIKE PROBLEMS

When a door will not latch, or if it rattles when latched, examine the strike plate attached to the jamb. Minor adjustments often will solve the problem.

If the latch does not engage the strike plate, determine if the latch is too far from the strike. Scratches on the strike plate probably mean the latch is hitting the strike but missing the hole.

A door that does not fit snugly against its stop molding almost certainly will rattle. To silence it, move the strike plate or reposition the stop.

You'll Need...

TIME: About 30 minutes to adjust a strike plate.
SKILLS: Basic carpentry skills.
TOOLS: Screwdriver, file, drill, and chisel.

File and move the strike plate.
If the strike plate is off only ⅛ inch or so, remove the strike plate and enlarge its opening with a file. You may need to chisel away some wood when reinstalling. For bigger shifts, relocate the strike. You'll need to extend the mortise (see page 368).

Shim the strike.
If the strike is too far away to engage the latch, first check if the hinges need to be shimmed out (see page 361). If the hinges fit properly, shim out the strike using thick cardboard.

SILENCING SQUEAKY HINGES

If a hinge squeaks, it may be under extra pressure because the door is binding (see pages 360–361). Or the hinge may be rusty because of damp conditions. Cleaning and lubricating may solve the problem; but in the case of bad rust, you're better off replacing the hinge.

You might solve the problem by oiling with the pin in place. Spread a cloth on the floor and squirt some penetrating oil into the moving parts. Open and close the door to work the lubricant in.

You'll Need...

TIME: About 15 minutes per hinge.
SKILLS: Basic carpentry skills.
TOOLS: Hammer, nail set, drill, steel wool, and wire-brush pipe cleaner.

1. Clean the pins.
If oiling does not quiet a rusty hinge, shim the bottom of the door so it is stable. Remove the hinge pin. Clean the pin with steel wool. Poke out the pin hole with a wire-brush pipe cleaner.

2. Put graphite on moving parts.
Coat moving parts with graphite. When you replace the pin, don't drive it tight; leave space for prying it out again and adding more graphite in the future.

LUBRICATING BALKY LATCHES

Old latches have springs that may break. If lubricating a latch does not free it, remove the unit and take it to a locksmith, who may be able to repair it. Or consider buying and installing a replacement (see pages 368–369).

A latch that has been painted is in danger of binding. Remove all paint by carefully scraping with a chisel or by using a wire-brush attachment on a drill.

If you're going to use powdered graphite to lubricate the lock, place a newspaper under the area to protect carpeting.

YOU'LL NEED...

TIME: 10 to 15 minutes per latch.
SKILLS: Basic skills.
TOOLS: Screwdriver.

Apply graphite to latch.
Turn the handle to retract the latch bolt, then puff powdered graphite into the works. Turn the handle repeatedly to work the bolt back and forth, and apply more graphite if needed. If this does not solve the problem, you may need a new latch.

Apply graphite to thumb latch.
Lubricate a thumb-operated latch lever by puffing graphite powder into the lock body. Move the latch up and down to work in the graphite. Wipe away any excess.

DEALING WITH A WARPED DOOR

If a door rattles when closed, or if you have to press hard to get the latch to engage, the door may be warped. Close the door until it just touches the stop, then check to see if the door meets the stop all along its length (see page 360). If there is a gap at either end or in the middle, the simplest solution is to reposition the stop rather than trying to straighten the door.

If a door is badly warped yet valuable, try straightening it out: Remove the door, set it on pieces of wood, and weight it to counter-warp it. Give it at least a week to straighten.

YOU'LL NEED...

TIME: 2 hours to add a hinge; a week if you weight the door.
SKILLS: Basic carpentry skills.
TOOLS: Hammer, nail set, chisel, pry bar, and screwdriver.

1. Move the stop.
To reposition a stop, cut through the paint lines (if any) and gently pry the stop away. Close the door, and scribe a line on the jamb to indicate where the stop should be. Drill pilot holes and drive new finishing nails to reattach the stop.

2. Add a hinge.
If a door is warped along the hinge side, you may be able to straighten it by adding a hinge in the middle. Install the jamb side hinge and trace the door hinge. Remove the door and chisel the mortise (see page 366). Rehang and attach the hinge. With a helper, force the door straight and insert the pins.

REPAIRING BIFOLD DOORS

Bifold doors are commonly used for closets. Because they don't swing far outward, they save space in a bedroom.

Most bifold doors are light-weight, with light-duty hardware to match. Roughhousing kids can easily break slats or bend a hinge or a track. Straighten a bent track by placing a strip of wood inside and tapping with a hammer; or use a pair of pliers and two strips of metal.

YOU'LL NEED...

TIME: 15 to 30 minutes for most repairs, as long as you have the necessary hardware.
SKILLS: Basic carpentry skills.
TOOLS: Open-end wrench, screwdriver, and drill.

Anatomy of a bifold door.
A bifold door has two halves that are hinged together. One half of the door pivots on fixed pins that attach to holders with slots at the floor and the header jamb. The other half of the door slides along a header track—secured to the header jamb—as the center hinges open or close. The pin that runs in the header track does not support the door; it only guides it.

EXPERTS' INSIGHT

INSTALLING A NEW SET OF BIFOLDS

Installing a new bifold door is straightforward. A unit comes as a kit, with the doors hinged and the hardware supplied. Bifolds typically fit into 24-, 30-, 32-, and 36-inch openings. A typical closet has two bifolds in a 6-foot-wide opening. Flush, panel, and louvered doors are available. Painting can take a long time, especially if the bifold has louvers. Consider buying a prefinished door, or purchase a unit with good-looking wood so that you need only apply a clear finish. More expensive units are available with mirror panels, minimizing the surface area of wood to be finished.

Adjusting the hardware.
Ideally when a bifold door is closed, it should be aligned with the jamb on all three sides. However if the opening is out of square, you may need to compromise on one side. In a typical arrangement, the top assembly guide (above left) fits into a hole and can be adjusted out or in. At the bottom of the door you may find an adjustable pin-and-slot arrangement (above right); loosen the nut to slide the slot. On other models you simply pick the door up, move it over slightly, and set the bottom pin in a different part of the slot. Use an open-end wrench to make adjustments.

REPAIRING SLIDING DOORS

Sliding doors, also called bypass or gliding doors, come in pairs, and slide past each other to open or close. Though flush bypass doors are the most common, paneled and louvered models are also available.

Exterior glass patio doors roll on wheels along a bottom track. Adjust and maintain these as you would a sliding window (see page 352). Be aware, however, that these doors are quite heavy.

Interior bypass doors are usually easy to maintain. However if the door itself is warped, it should be replaced.

YOU'LL NEED...

TIME: About 15 to 20 minutes per door.
SKILLS: Basic skills.
TOOLS: Slot and phillips screwdrivers, and pliers.

How a bypass door works.
At the top of an interior bypass door, a roller hanger glides through a metal track. Rollers are typically nylon and need no lubrication. The track must be attached firmly to the header because it is the door's sole support. At the bottom of the door opening, a floor guide (see below) provides only guidance.

Removing a bypass door.
To remove a bypass door, lift it above the floor guide and tilt it out slightly. Then pick the door up and guide it out of the track. Be careful; some units are heavy.

Check for a key opening.
With some models you can free the door only when its wheels are at a key opening in the track.

Adjust wheel alignment.
Raise one side or the other by adjusting the roller hanger. In the type shown above, first slightly loosen the two screws. Then insert a screwdriver into the slot and pry the hanger up or down. Tighten the screws.

Fix or replace floor guides.
If a floor guide is bent, try bending it back into position with a pair of pliers. If it is broken, or if it is difficult to straighten, replace it.

INSTALLING A DOOR

Replacing a door in an existing jamb (the three pieces that form a doorway) can be challenging, especially if the jamb is out of square. (If you need to install a door with a new jamb, see pages 370–371.)

There should be a gap of ⅛ inch between the door and the jamb on all three sides, and a gap of about ⅜ inch between the door and the finished floor. Never cut more than ¾ inch from either end—this would weaken the door's rail.

Most doors are 80 inches tall but may be taller in older homes.

YOU'LL NEED...

TIME: 2 to 4 hours.
SKILLS: Good carpentry skills, including chiseling a mortise.
TOOLS: Hammer, plane, chisel, drill, screwdriver, center punch, and utility knife or butt marker.

1. Plane or cut the door.
Check the jamb for square. Have a helper hold the door in or against the jamb, and mark for any needed cutting or planing. If you only have to plane, work from the door edge toward the center of the door. (For how to cut the door, see page 367.)

2. Mark for hinges.
Set the door in the jamb and use shims to wedge it in place. Check that the gaps are consistent. Place the top hinge 6 inches from the top, and the bottom hinge about 9 inches from the floor. Use a pencil to mark for the bottom and top of each hinge.

3. Scribe marks for the hinges.
Hold the hinge in place as a template. Use a utility knife to make a light mark around the hinge, then deepen the cut. Or use a butt marker (see inset), which has chisel edges that will make indentations for a perfect cut. Hold it in place and pound on it with a hammer.

4. Chisel out the mortise.
Using a knife or a chisel, make a cut along the face of the door, as deep as the hinge is thick. Holding the chisel with the beveled edge down, make a series of cuts inside the mortise. Then holding the chisel flat-side down, knock out chips from the side.

5. Finish chiseling.
Cut away enough material so that, when installed, the hinge leaf sits flush with the surface of the door edge. To shave away a small amount of wood, try using the chisel like a knife, pushing without using a hammer.

6. Install the hinge leaf.

Install separate hinge leaves on the door and the jamb. Position a leaf in its mortise and mark for drilling with a center punch. Predrill all the holes. Screw the hinge leaves to the mortises.

Hinge pin

Hinge leaf

7. Hang the door.

Have a helper hold the door in place and slip the hinge leaves together. Insert the pins. Check that the door swings freely and closes completely against the stop without binding. To make minor adjustments, see pages 360–362; see pages 368–369 for how to install a latch.

TOOLS TO USE

A TOOL KIT FOR DOORS

If you have an older home, chances are good you will need to work on doors from time to time. Gather the right tools and keep them in good working order. In addition to the standard carpentry tools, consider these:

■ A power planer quickly (though messily) trims and smoothes; get one with a carbide blade for longevity.

■ A belt sander equipped with a coarse sanding belt works nearly as quickly as a power planer.

■ Buy a butt marker to match the size of your hinge. It makes it easy to cut a mortise that fits snugly and looks professional.

CUTTING A DOOR

*U*se a knife to score a line wherever you will be cutting across the grain of solid wood, or whenever you will cut a flush door's plywood surface. To avoid splintering the door face, make your cut below that line.

Newer solid-core doors are filled with a soft type of particleboard material—they have solid wood only for an inch or so around their perimeters. If you have to cut off more than an inch, the particleboard will be exposed; paint it with two coats of sealer.

YOU'LL NEED...

TIME: About 2 hours to cut down a hollow-core door.
SKILLS: Measuring, cutting a straight line, and smoothing.
TOOLS: Knife, circular saw, straightedge, chisel, and hammer.

Score just above cut line.

1. Cut the veneer, then the door.

Using a straightedge clamped in position, score the veneer about $1/16$ inch above where you want your cut. It will take several passes with your knife to do this. Move and clamp the straightedge in position for cutting with a circular saw (see page 233). Complete the cut.

GLUE Cap piece

Cavity

2. Insert a cap piece.

If you cut off more than an inch, the door will be hollow at the place you just cut. (You may need to clear out some cardboard honeycomb with a chisel). Cut a piece of softwood to the needed width and length. Apply wood glue to the upper and lower edges of the cavity, and tap the cap into position. Clamp firmly.

INSTALLING HANDLES AND LOCKS

Once the door has been hung so that it swings freely and closes snugly against the stop, the next step is to install the handle. An entry handle simply opens from either side; a privacy handle can be locked from one side. Purchase drill bits in sizes recommended by the manufacturer. (For instructions on installing other locks, see page 384.)

YOU'LL NEED...

TIME: About 45 minutes.
SKILLS: Measuring precisely, chiseling, drilling, and fastening with screws.
TOOLS: Drill with hole saw and bits (see lockset instructions), utility knife or butt marker, tape measure, center punch, awl, screwdriver, hammer, and chisel.

Awl

Template provided with lockset

1. Mark for lockset holes.

The handle set or dead bolt will come with a paper or cardboard template. Tape it or hold it against the door. If a strike already exists in the jamb, align the template with it so you won't have to cut a new mortise for the strike. With an awl or the point of a spade bit, mark for the two holes by piercing through the template.

Hole saw

2. Drill the large hole.

Use a hole saw to drill the larger hole through the face of the door first. To avoid splintering the veneer, drill just far enough that the pilot bit of the hole saw pokes through. Then drill from the other side.

Spade bit

3. Drill the bolt hole.

Use a spade bit to drill through the edge, taking care to hold the bit parallel to the surface of the door. Some types of locksets require that you continue drilling into the rear of the large hole approximately ½ inch.

4. Mortise the latch bolt.

Insert the bolt through the smaller hole. Temporarily screw it centered in the door, and mark for its mortise with a sharp pencil or a knife. Cut and chisel a mortise as you did for the hinges (page 366). Depending on the type of bolt, this mortise may be deeper near the center than at the edges.

Mortise

5. Install the handle.

Install the bolt by setting it in the mortise, drilling pilot holes, and driving the screws provided. Then install the lockset or handles according to the manufacturer's directions. Tighten all screws. Test the mechanisms from both sides of the door to make sure they operate smoothly; you may need to clean out or widen your holes.

6. Install the strike.

Mark the jamb for the correct location of the strike. The latch or bolt should be vertically centered in the strike opening. Horizontally, make sure the latch or bolt will enter the door while holding it fairly tight against the door stop. Mortise the jamb, drill pilot holes, and install the strike with the screws provided.

Assembling a dead bolt.

Install a dead bolt much as you would a handle. Mark for the position of the two holes and drill them. Insert the bolt and latch face, mark for the mortise, and cut it with a chisel.

Screw the latch face (above right) into the mortise. For

many lock types, you'll need to use a screwdriver to partially extend the bolt. Insert the lock tailpiece through the slot in the bolt. Slip on the interior turn bolt or lock until the two pieces sit flush against the door. Fasten the retaining screws and install the strike plate.

EXPERTS' INSIGHT

CHOOSING A DEAD BOLT

A high-quality dead bolt, properly installed, is usually the most secure lock for a door. For added security, purchase a unit with a metal strike enclosure, which extends deep into the door jamb.

A double-keyed dead bolt, which locks with a key on the inside as well as on the outside, offers the best security in situations where an intruder could reach through a window to the bolt. However it is not safe in case of fire—if you don't have the key handy, you could be trapped inside.

INSTALLING A PREHUNG DOOR

Building a custom door saves money, but takes time and expertise. Prehung units cost more, but you get everything you need—door, hinges, jamb, stop and casing moldings, and even a latch if you want it—all in one accurately made component.

See page 288 if you need to frame for the door. Before you buy a prehung unit, measure the thickness of the wall; plaster and drywall surfaces call for different jamb widths.

See page 288 if you need to frame for the door.

YOU'LL NEED...

TIME: About 2 hours.
SKILLS: Moderate carpentry skills.
TOOLS: Hammer, level, framing square, and saw.

Choosing a prehung door.
A prehung door comes already assembled, with the holes precut for the handle and the strike plate. The casing can be removed from either side of a prehung door. A standard jamb is 3⅝ inches wide to fit into a standard stud-and-drywall wall; in an older home, you may need a wider jamb.

1. Shim a prehung door.
Remove the casing on one side. Set the door into the opening, with the other casing (not visible above) flush against the wall. If necessary shim the hinge side to make it plumb. Check the other two jamb pieces for square by closing the door; the gap should be even all around.

2. Drive nails.
Open the door and shim it at the bottom so it is stable. Anchor the hinge jamb securely with 8d finishing nails that enter the framing. To hide nails, simply remove the stop, drive the nails, then replace the stop. Drive nails to attach the latch jamb, and check again for square.

INSTALLING A SPLIT-JAMB PREHUNG DOOR

With a split-jamb door, the side and top jambs consist of two tongue-and-groove halves that slide together to accommodate variations in wall thickness. This is particularly useful in an old home with plaster walls that may vary in thickness. The door is held in place mainly by finishing nails driven through the casings into the doorway framing.

This works fine for lightweight hollow-core doors. For heavier solid-wood panel doors and even heavier solid-core doors, however, nailing the casings alone is not enough. For these doors, specify solid jambs of a width to match wall thickness.

YOU'LL NEED...

TIME: 1 to 2 hours.
SKILLS: Moderate carpentry skills.
TOOLS: Hammer, level, nail set, screwdriver, and chisel.

Right/left hand.
A hinge "hand" refers to the side of the door that it is on. A right-hand hinge swings to the right as you push it open.

1. Test the fit.
Remove packing materials that hold the two jamb pieces together. Separate the jamb pieces, leaving the door closed inside the stop jambs. With a helper, insert the two pieces into the opening, and make sure they will fit.

2. Level and nail the casing.
Set aside the non-door part of the casing. With the door centered, drive an 8d finishing nail through the top outside edge of the casing into the stud. With a level held vertically against the inside edge of the side casing, shim the jamb at the hinge locations to plumb the casing.

3. Nail the jamb.
Drive 8d finishing nails in the hinge-side casing every 16 inches. Drive 6d finishing nails through the jamb—not the stop—and shims into a stud. Shim the latch-side jamb to make the gap between the door and jamb even, then nail with 8d finishing nails.

4. Add the second jamb.
Insert the second jamb so that the tongues fit into the grooves. Nail around the casings with 8d finishing nails every 16 inches.

REPLACING WINDOWPANES

Faced with a broken window, you have three options: Remove the sash and take it to a hardware store or glass shop for reglazing; buy a new pane that is cut to size, and install it yourself; or cut the glass yourself from standard-sized sheets kept on hand for such emergencies.

Dismantling a window (see page 346) is sometimes far more work than simply replacing the glass. Cutting glass isn't difficult, but you might break a pane or two before getting the knack. A hardware store will cut glass to the size you need.

YOU'LL NEED...

TIME: About 30 minutes a pane.
SKILLS: Basic skills.
TOOLS: Putty knife, scraper, caulking gun, and paintbrush.

---

1. Chip off the old glazing.
NOTE: *Wear heavy gloves and long clothing when handling broken glass.* Carefully pull out all the pieces of the old pane. Chipping off old glazing compound can be the hardest part of the job. Use a putty knife or old chisel, or soften old glazing with a soldering iron or heat gun.

2. Roughen the groove.
Scrape away the last of the old compound, then roughen the groove with a scraper so the new glazing compound will adhere properly. Be sure to remove all the old glazier's points, which may be tiny metal triangles instead of the push-type points shown in Step 6.

3. Measure the sash.
Sashes aren't always perfectly square, so measure at several points, then subtract ⅛ inch from each dimension to determine the glass size. Have the glass cut at a hardware store or glass shop, or cut it yourself.

4. Prime the groove and apply a bead of glazing.
Prime the groove with linseed oil, turpentine, or oil-based paint. Untreated wood will draw oil from the glazing compound, shortening its life. Before you insert the new pane, apply a ⅛-inch-thick bead of caulk or glazing compound. This helps seal and cushion the glass.

5. Press the pane into place.
Line up one edge of the pane in the sash, lower it into place, and press gently with your palm or fingertips to seal it into the glazing compound.

6. Add glazier's points.

Approximately every 12 inches around the perimeter, press a glazier's point (see inset) into the sash with a putty knife. Don't push too hard—you may crack the glass.

7. Apply glazing compound.

If the glazing compound is in a can, grab a hunk and roll it into a "snake." Alternatively, use glazing compound in a caulk tube. Apply a generous bead of glazing compound. Press it into place to make sure it sticks to both the glass and wood.

8. Bevel the compound.

Working in only one direction, firmly draw a putty knife all along the bead. If the compound sticks to the knife, wet the knife with turpentine. If small ridges appear, lightly run your finger in the opposite direction to smooth the compound.

9. Paint the compound.

Let the compound dry for a week before painting. Paint should overlap the glass about 1⁄16 inch for a tight seal.

Clips for a metal sash.

Spring clips substitute for glazier's points in steel sashes. Install as shown here. Metal windows needn't be primed before installing the glass.

Gasket for storm window.

In an aluminum storm window, a rubber gasket, forced into place with a putty knife, holds the glass. If the gasket is cracked or broken, replace it.

REPLACING SILLS AND SADDLES

Windowsills take a terrific beating from both rain and the sun. Alternate soaking and baking can make them veritable sponges.

The best preventive is a couple of coats of paint applied annually. If a sill is too far gone for that, consider repair options (see the "Experts' Insight" box below).

If the sill is heavily damaged, you may need to install a new sill. Door sills, called saddles or thresholds, also fail over time. Replace either by following the procedures illustrated here.

Determine if the sill or saddle fits under the jambs on either side, then measure, and buy a new piece of sill stock. The drawings at right show how to install a new piece of wood in either situation—but you might opt to replace a saddle with a preformed, predrilled metal or plastic unit.

If you can get the old sill out intact, use it as a template for marking the replacement. If not, measure exactly for a snug fit.

For more about how windows and doors are put together, see pages 346 and 360. To learn about weather-stripping-type thresholds, see page 376.

If the window has problems in addition to the sill, it's probably time to consider installing a replacement window.

YOU'LL NEED...

TIME: 1 to 2 hours per sill.
SKILLS: Basic carpentry skills.
TOOLS: Backsaw, chisel, hammer, nail set, flat pry bar, drill, and caulking gun.

1. Remove the windowsill.
Removing the sill will probably be the most difficult part of the job. You'll have to take off the apron, the stool, and stop molding to remove a sill.

Use a chisel or old screwdriver to probe for nails that may be holding

2. Saw the sill if needed.
If the sill is embedded on either side, saw out a section from the center. Use a handsaw (a backsaw is shown) or a reciprocating saw, taking care not to damage underlying wood. Remove the middle piece, then drive the end pieces inward and pry them out.

the piece in place.

If you can't get the nails out, saw out a section as shown below. You can also demolish it by splitting it along the grain with a hammer and chisel, then pulling out the splintered remains.

EXPERTS' INSIGHT

REPAIRING A SILL

Replacing a sill, though sometimes necessary, is a difficult and demanding task. Before you start removing pieces, consider the possibility of repair. New products make it possible to repair wood pieces that are heavily damaged.

If the wood is cracked and weak, apply liquid hardener, which strengthens the fibers.

If an area is rotted, use a hammer and chisel to carve away the rotted material. Mix and apply two-part epoxy wood filler. Once it dries, the filler can be planed, sanded, and painted like wood.

3. Tap the new sill into place.
Gently tap the new sill or saddle into place. Don't force it. If it resists, remove and sand the ends, beveling them slightly.

4. Nail the sill from underneath.
Using rust-resistant nails or deck screws, secure the windowsill from underneath. Countersink the fasteners, then caulk the holes and the ends of the sill.

Nail door saddles onto the framing sill.
Nail or screw a saddle at both ends and in the middle. Countersink fastener heads with a nail set and hide with putty. Caulk both ends of the saddle.

MAINTAINING SCREENING

Even rustproof screening materials (see page 377) require occasional attention. Check the caulking around the frames of combination units, and replace any worn-out gaskets. Vacuum dirt that collects on the screening. Clean oxidized aluminum with car polish.

Older wood-framed screens require careful monitoring and diligent maintenance. Repaint the frames as soon as the old paint starts to fail. Check each unit when you take it down and set aside those that need repair.

Consider how many windows you actually open up during the summer months. Leaving a storm window in place not only saves you some work, it also helps keep an air-conditioned room cool—as long as the window does not receive direct sunlight.

Clean screens.
Remove dust and debris by spraying a screen with a blast from a hose. Scrub metal screens with a stiff brush. Clean the frames as well as the screening.

Paint steel screens.
If older steel screening is heavily rusted, replace it. If the rust is only modest, apply paint that is made to go over rusty metal. A paint pad is the easiest method. Paint one side, let it dry, then paint the other side. To unclog holes, gently rub the back side with a dry pad.

REPAIRING SCREENS AND STORMS

The little parts on an aluminum storm/screen—the splining, gaskets, plastic pins, and sliding clips that hook to the storm's frame—are notoriously fragile. To find replacements, look for the manufacturer's name on the frame, or bring broken parts to a hardware store.

Wood storm or screen frames that have been painted too many times may need to be sanded or planed, then repainted. Installing weather stripping can make wood storms more energy-efficient. Position felt or rubber weather stripping on the window's frame or the frame of the storm to create a tight seal when the storm is attached. You may need to move the closing hardware in order to accommodate the thickness of the weather stripping.

Adjust or replace screen/storm door closers as soon as they begin to malfunction; doors that slam or flap in the breeze wear out quickly. A closer should shut the door slowly but completely. Replacement closers are inexpensive and easy to install.

YOU'LL NEED...
TIME: 10 minutes to 2 hours, depending on the damage.
SKILLS: Basic skills.
TOOLS: Needle-nose pliers, hammer, drill, shears, and screwdriver.

Repair a wooden frame.
Reinforce corner joints in a wooden frame using mending plates. Position a plate, drill pilot holes, and drive screws to fasten the plate. When possible install a plate on both sides; offset the plates so the screws don't run into each other.

Seal air leaks.
Air leaks around interior sashes or storms cause condensation to form on the sash that's not leaking. The solution is to caulk the air leak.

Maintain a closer.
Every autumn, lubricate door closers by wiping the shaft with oil. Check the adjustment for proper operation. Once a closer starts to fail, replace it.

Patch a screen.
Mend a small puncture with a dab of superglue. To patch a hole in a metal screen, cut a patch, unravel a few strands, fit the patch over the hole, and bend the strands toward the hole. Repairing fiberglass screening is difficult; you're better off replacing the entire screen.

REPLACING SCREENING

Install screening much as an artist stretches a canvas—fasten it at one end of the frame, pull the material taut, then secure it at the sides and the other end.

With wood frames, pry screen moldings loose with a putty knife. Work from the center to the ends, applying leverage near the nails. If molding breaks, replace it.

Standard aluminum screening is subject to staining; "charcoal" or "silver-gray" aluminum is easier to maintain. Fiberglass won't stain, but its filaments are thicker, which affects visibility.

YOU'LL NEED...

TIME: 30 minutes per screen.
SKILLS: Basic skills.
TOOLS: Putty knife, shears or scissors, utility knife, staple gun, saw, and spline roller.

1. Attach the screen at the top.
With shears, cut the screening slightly wider and at least 1 foot longer than the frame, then staple the top edge. Nail a strip of wood to the bench or floor, roll the screen over it, and nail another strip on top of the first.

2. Insert wedges and fasten screening.
Rip-cut two wedges and insert them between the cleats and frame on each side. Tap the wedges until the screening is tight. Staple the screening to the bottom edge, then the sides. Trim the excess and refit the screen moldings.

1. To replace screening in an aluminum frame, pry out the spline.
For aluminum frames, remove the old mesh by prying out the spline. You may need to buy new splining.

2. Cut new screening.
Square up the frame, lay new screening over it, and cut it the same size as the outside of the frame.

3. Push the screening into place and install the spline.
Bend the screening edges and force them into the channel with the convex wheel of the spline roller. Force the tubular spline into the channel with the concave wheel of the spline roller, tightening the screening.

INSTALLING NEW STORM/SCREEN WINDOWS

Door and window units for new construction arrive with doors or sashes already hung in their frames. Carpenters build "rough" openings, tip the units in place, and add trim.

Combination screen/storm doors and windows also arrive assembled. Because openings for these units are already finished, combinations usually are made-to-order. Installation may be included in the purchase price, but you can save 10 to 15 percent by installing units yourself.

Professional installers are usually paid by the piece, rather than by the hour. This can lead to shoddy installation. If you hire pros, make it clear that you will not write the check unless the windows are installed correctly.

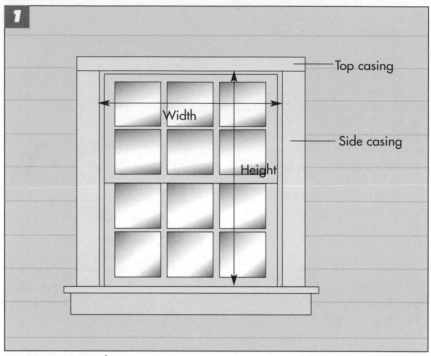

YOU'LL NEED...

TIME: 2 to 4 hours for a window.
SKILLS: Moderate carpentry skills.
TOOLS: Hammer, drill, screwdriver, and caulking gun.

1. Measure window.
A storm/screen unit has a flange that fits over the window casing. This allows some leeway, so the unit does not have to fit precisely. Check the casing for square, and take into account any out-of-squareness. Measure the width between the inside edges of the side casings, and measure the height between the top casing and the sill.

EXPERTS' INSIGHT

BUYING STORM/SCREEN WINDOWS

Combination windows and doors pay for themselves with energy savings, but beware of shoddy products. Poorly made or poorly fitted units can leak air, are difficult to operate, and eventually turn into eyesores.

■ It's worth the extra expense to buy units that are made of thicker-gauge aluminum with an anodized or powdered coating.

■ See that the pins and sliding clips are strong and that replacement parts are available. Consider buying some replacement parts up front; they may be difficult to find later.

■ Better units have warrantees against defects. Choose a company that has been around for a while; a fly-by-night outfit may not be there when you need a part or service.

■ Check the corners of the frames. Lapped joints are stronger and tighter than mitered joints. If you can see light through the joints, you can be sure that they'll admit air.

■ Combinations come in double- or triple-track designs. With double-track units, you must seasonally remove and replace the bottom sash (either storm or screen). Triple-track units have tracks for the top and bottom storm sashes and the screen sash, and are self-storing—you don't have to remove the storm or screen sash you are not using. The deeper the tracks are, the higher a unit's insulation value will be.

2. Trace the outline.

Place the combination unit on the sill; center it between the side casings. The units should be installed square, even if the opening is not square. To check for square, slide a sash nearly all the way up, and see that it aligns with the frame. Sashes should glide smoothly; any binding means the frame is not straight. Trace the outline of the unit with a pencil.

Pencil line

Caulk

3. Caulk the casing.

Scrape and clean away any debris that could inhibit a tight seal between the combination and the casing. Using a caulking gun, run a bead of latex/silicone caulk around the casings about 1 inch inside the pencil lines. Also run a bead along the sill.

4. Drive screws.

Align the frame with the pencil line, press the frame into the caulk, and drive several screws. Test that the sashes operate smoothly and make adjustments if needed. Drive a screw into every available hole. If screws are difficult to drive, or if you are within 2 inches of the end of a piece of casing, drill a pilot hole before driving the screw.

5. Caulk the outside.

Caulk around the outside of the frame where it meets the top and side casings. Also caulk the bottom where it meets the sill.

INSTALLING A STORM DOOR

Assuming your exterior door is a standard 80 inches tall and 3 feet wide or narrower, you can choose standard-size prehung storm doors.

A combination storm door features interchangeable glass panels for winter and screen panels for summer. Some have both upper and lower interchangeable panels. These maximize solar gain during the winter and allow ventilation during the summer. Others have solid lower panels, which are more practical if you have children and/or animals that constantly push against and damage the lower screen unit.

Don't be too frugal when it comes to doors that handle a lot of traffic. Only the highest-quality door will withstand children running in and out, and adults carrying grocery bags in both arms.

A storm/screen security door has an attractive grate and a sturdy lock, so you can leave the door open to summer breezes.

A combination door typically attaches to the brick molding. Measure the inside dimensions of the molding and purchase a door designed to fit.

YOU'LL NEED...

TIME: 2 hours.
SKILLS: Basic carpentry skills.
TOOLS: Hacksaw, drill, screwdriver or screwdriver bit, caulking gun, hammer, level, and tape measure.

1. Temporarily attach the drip cap.
Unpack all the parts and remove the storm and screen panels from the door. Position the drip cap in the center of the top brick molding with the fuzzy gasket pointing out. Drill pilot holes and attach the drip cap with two screws.

2. Cut the hinge flange.
Make sure you know which side of the hinge flange (also called a Z-bar) is up. Measure the opening height on the hinge side, from the bottom of the drip cap to the door sill. Set the hinge flange on a scrap of wood and cut it to the measured length, minus ⅛ inch.

3. Attach top of the hinge flange.
Apply a bead of caulk to the back of the hinge flange. Have a helper hold the door in position while you work. Align the hinge flange according to the manufacturer's directions. At the top screw hole, drill a pilot hole and drive a screw.

Hinge flange

Level

4. Plumb and attach the door.
Check that the hinge flange is plumb. If it is not, loosen the top screw to reposition the flange. Drill pilot holes and drive screws to attach the door.

5. Install the drip cap.

Remove the drip cap. Apply a bead of latex/silicone caulk to its back and reinstall it so that the gap between the top of the door and the cap is even. Drill pilot holes and drive the screws.

6. Install the latching flange.

Install the storm or screen panels in the door. Check that the door swings freely. Measure, cut, caulk, and install the latching flange (or Z-bar) so that the gap between the door and the flange is even.

7. Install the sweep.

Peel off any protective film from the bottom of the door and the sweep. Slide the rubber gasket onto the bottom of the sweep. Slip the sweep onto the bottom of the door. Slowly close the door and adjust the position of the sweep so it seals at the sill without binding. Drive screws to secure the sweep.

8. Install and adjust the latch.

Assemble and install the latch as instructed by the manufacturer. If the latch does not close easily and latch snugly, loosen the screws and adjust the latching pin.

9. Install the closer.

Install and adjust the pneumatic door closer. Hold the closer in place and drill holes in the door (some units will have predrilled holes). Fasten the closer to the door and mark for the bracket that attaches to the stop. Drill holes and fasten the bracket in place.

EXPERTS' INSIGHT

STORM/SCREEN DOOR OPTIONS

Those flimsy aluminum combination doors of yesteryear are still sold, but more substantial units are available. A door with a foam or wood core is difficult to dent. Scratch-resistant surfaces withstand the attentions of pets wanting to come in. Better doors have gaskets that seal storm sashes tight to keep out the cold. Many sweeps have rubber flanges at the bottom that seal just like a standard door threshold.

SECURING WINDOWS

Intruders usually enter homes through doors, say police. However you can't expect burglars to stand on tradition—especially if you have windows that they easily could force open and climb through without being noticed.

A large expanse of fixed glass is less of a problem than you may think. The clatter from smashing a picture window probably would call attention to a break-in. Most burglars are cautious about being caught, so they don't bother with homes that are secure, opting to move on to easier targets.

If the doors are locked, burglars will concentrate on smaller, operable windows. If the window can't be forced open, a burglar may stick tape to a pane, break it, and quietly pull away the pieces to gain access to the latch.

The solution is to lock your windows in both their closed and open positions. This way no one can reach inside and enlarge the opening. The drawings below and on the next page show a variety of ways to secure windows and sliding doors. Be sure, however, that whatever method you use doesn't block a potential fire exit.

Most homes have many windows. Securing every one can be costly and time-consuming, so start with all sliding glass doors and windows accessible from ground level. Analyze which upper-level windows could be reached from a balcony, garage or porch roof, or tree. Enterprising second-story burglars may bring along a ladder to get at the ones you think are inaccessible.

For an extra measure of protection, hire a security company to install sensing devices in your windows and doors. In a typical setup, when a window is broken, an alarm signal travels to the security company, triggering a call to the police.

Make sure all windows work properly. Sashes that wobble when you crank them, rattle in high winds, or have to be propped open offer only token resistance to break-ins. (For window repairs, see pages 349–355 and 372–373.)

> ### YOU'LL NEED...
> **TIME:** About 20 minutes per window.
> **SKILLS:** Basic carpentry skills.
> **TOOLS:** Drill and bits, screwdriver, pliers, and hammer.

The problem with a sash lock.
Ordinary sash locks offer little security because you can open most of them easily with a knife blade, as shown. A heavy-duty model that clicks shut offers more resistance.

Install a key lock.
Key locks can't be jimmied, even if the glass is broken. Most will also let you lock the window in a partly open position. You'll need to drill a hole in the upper sash for every position you want to be able to lock.

Ventilation position

Using nails as locks.
With the sash closed, drill a hole on each side, as shown above, through the bottom sash and most of the way into the top sash. Open the window halfway, and drill again. To secure the window in either position, insert two nails.

Check a casement window.
Many casement windows won't open enough to admit an adult. To check, open the window and measure from the inside edge of the sash to the jamb.

Remove an operator crank.
If a fully opened window will admit a person, open it partially so the opening is 10 inches or less. Then remove the operator crank and set it out of reach.

Install a chain lock.
Install a door-type chain lock to keep windows from opening. Fasten it down with the biggest screws possible.

Install a hasp or a stop.
A hasp on a basement window can be secured with a padlock. Use a keyless combination lock or keep the key somewhere that's handy, but not on the sill. If your windows don't have hasps, drive long screws into a stop on each side. Leave a few inches to open the window for ventilation.

Add a grill or grate.
Custom-made grills mortared into the foundation give basement windows a behind-bars look—but they provide peace of mind in a high-crime area. Scissors-type gates and hinged iron shutters can be padlocked from the inside, yet opened for escape in case of an emergency.

The problem with a sliding window.
Thieves like sliding windows (and sliding glass doors) because some can be jimmied easily from their tracks, even when the door locksets are in the locked position.

SECURING DOORS

The best way to secure a windowless door is with a dead-bolt lock (see page 369). Here are additional security measures you may choose to take.

Double-cylinder dead-bolt locks employ special one-way screws that you can turn in, but not out; otherwise an intruder could simply remove the assembly. Fittings with a double-cylinder lock generally include an extra set of conventional, slotted screws. Mount the lock and strike with these, make any adjustments, then withdraw the slotted screws and replace them with the tamperproof versions.

All surface-mounted hardware depends upon screws for holding power; if the screws that came with your lock don't penetrate at least halfway into the door, discard them and buy longer ones. For added strength, coat the screws with glue before driving them into pilot holes.

Mount any surface lock about 8 to 10 inches higher than the existing knob set so that you can see and operate it easily.

In addition to the devices shown here, a variety of sliding bolts and other locking devices are available in decorative finishes.

NOTE: *Whichever security measures you choose, be sure you install them such that family members can quickly exit the house in case of fire.*

YOU'LL NEED...

TIME: About 30 minutes.
SKILLS: Basic carpentry skills.
TOOLS: Screwdriver, pliers, drill, and hole saw or spade bit for the diameter hole specified for the lock.

Attach a chain lock.
For extra protection that's quick and simple, install a chain lock. Mount the hardware with screws that penetrate the door frame and the jamb studs.

Install a bar.
An accessory bar mounts to the door frame to jam the sliding door. It prevents an intruder from forcing the lock, but doesn't protect against jimmying the door up. Alternatively, cut a piece of wood to fit tightly in the bottom track and keep the sliding door from moving.

Top of patio door

Use a nail as a security pin.
Secure sliding glass patio doors by drilling holes through both the track and the sash frames. Slip nails into the holes to prevent the doors from opening.

Attach a toe lock.
Toe-operated locks are convenient and the least obtrusive. Mount the lock on the casing and drill a hole in the sash into which a locking rod enters.

ROOFING, SIDING, AND WEATHERIZATION

UNDERSTANDING ROOFS

A pitched roof sheds water much the same way a duck's feathers do. Courses of roofing material—most often some variation of the **shingle**—lie one atop the other and overlap, like a bird's feathers. Shingles on a roof are layered at least two deep, with exposed portions slightly smaller than half the total area of the shingle. At the top, a **ridge vent** or an extra layer of shingles covers the ridge.

Valleys, the places where two slopes meet, direct runoff into gutters, which in turn direct the water into downspouts. For additional protection against leakage, metal or composition flashings are placed under the shingles at the roof's most vulnerable points. Typically these include valleys, dormers, vents, and chimneys, or anywhere the roof's surface is penetrated.

Valleys are notorious problem areas; the flatter the roof, the greater the potential for leaks. Metal **valley flashing** must be wide enough and the pieces must overlap correctly. If no flashing is used, roofing must be woven together seamlessly—a job that's definitely for pros. A valley that does not have metal flashing is vulnerable to damage; avoid walking on it.

Any area with flashing—especially around a chimney—is liable to leak. **Chimney flashing** must be installed correctly and sealed tightly against the vertical surface that it abuts.

Vents, whether they are plumbing pipes or exhaust fans, usually come with integral flashing. Typically, the lower half of the flashing is exposed, and the upper half is covered with roofing.

Beneath the roofing material lies a house's most complex structure, framing (typically **gable** or **hip**). The framing ties together the wall structures and supports not only the weight of the shingles but also other loads, such as snow and ice in colder climates. **Rafters,** rising from the top plate of the wall to the **ridge board,** define the roof's pitch. **Collar ties** in the attic help keep the rafters from spreading; **headers** box in any openings.

Deck sheathing, usually plywood, goes on top of the rafters to give the structure rigidity. A layer of **roofing felt** seals the sheathing against moisture. Rafter ends are trimmed at the eaves with a **fascia board** (to which a **gutter** is fastened) and along the rake with **rake boards.** Once the trim is protected with drip cap, the shingles can go on.

UNDERSTANDING EXTERIOR WALLS

Regardless of your home's exterior skin (siding or brick), its skeleton probably looks like the one shown here. The **sill plate** rests on the masonry foundation. **Rim joists,** collectively called a box sill, rest on the outside perimeter of the sill plate. Floor joists (which also act as ceiling joists for the basement, if there is a basement) attach to the rim joists. In some cases a short framed wall rises from the **foundation,** and the joists rest on this wall. If your basement ceiling is open, periodically check the rim joists, the sill plate, and the **sill seal.**

Attend to any moisture immediately because rot here could cause structural damage. It is also here that termites and other wood-boring insects often enter the house.

Exterior wall framing is made of 2×4 or 2×6 lumber (2×6s are common in newer homes in cold climates because they accommodate thicker insulation). A **sole plate** rests on the joists. Vertical **studs** are usually spaced 16 inches on center (sometimes they are 24 inches on center). The **top plate** is usually doubled to ensure that it can support second-story joists or the roof.

Over a door or window, a header carries the load and must be as strong as the rest of the wall.

Insulation between the studs conserves heat (see pages 426–432 for more about insulation). Wood or composition board **sheathing** adds insulation and strength. Then a layer of **building wrap,** either asphalt-saturated building paper or plastic, seals the sheathing. It is essential that the building wrap be installed correctly so that moisture is sealed out rather than trapped inside the wall.

Outside, **siding** faces the elements and gives your home its visual character. Shown here is horizontal lap siding, named because the boards overlap each other. Other types of siding may be vertical or horizontal, but all overlap in some way in order to seal the exterior. Vinyl and aluminum siding often give the appearance of wood, but with differing maintenance requirements. Siding made of pressed board needs to be kept well protected or it will disintegrate quickly.

Regardless of its composition, siding deserves a careful semiannual inspection. Scan its surface systematically, using binoculars for closeups of high places if necessary. Look for cracks, splits, peeling paint, and evidence of rot or insect damage. Any breaks in your home's skin—no matter how small—will eventually admit water into wall cavities. If you neglect the repairs explained in this section (see pages 403–411), moisture could wreck insulation, framing, or even **interior wall surfaces.**

If a new paint job is imminent, see pages 542–555. To learn about basic wall-building techniques, turn to pages 284–292.

During your inspection, if you suspect that a wall may be infested with termites or other insects, read the information on pages 412–413 about identifying insects and what to do about them.

Top plate

Interior wall surface

Wall stud

Insulation

Sole plate

Subfloor

Rim joist

Sill plate

Sill seal

Siding

Building wrap

Sheathing

Foundation

PROTECTING YOUR ROOF

Note that the first five categories in this chart work well on the pitched roofs explained on page 386. But they will not protect a flat or only slightly sloping surface from standing water. Such surfaces require a watertight membrane system and often a contractor's help.

Asphalt shingles and roll roofing are the least expensive options; slate and clay tiles are the most expensive. Most do-it-yourselfers can apply asphalt shingle and wood shingles and shakes. Other types require advanced or pro skills.

ROOF MATERIAL COMPARISON

Material	Features	Maintenance	Life Span
Asphalt shingles	Most popular by far, these are made of roofing felt saturated with asphalt and coated with mineral granules; newer types have a fiberglass base for better weather- and fire-resistance	Little at first, but over the years, shingles curl, crack, and lose surface granules; most cement themselves down in the hot sun; repairs are fairly easy (see page 393)	15 to 30 years under temperate weather conditions; better-quality shingles carry 25-year guarantees
Wood shingles and shakes	Shingles have a uniform, machine-sawn appearance; shakes, a rustic, hand-split look; both have a poor fire rating unless specially treated; both are expensive	Unsealed types sometimes rot, warp, and split—and soon weather to a soft gray; like asphalt shingles, they are not difficult to repair or replace (see page 394)	20 years or more for shingles; up to 50 years for shakes if maintained properly
Slate or clay tiles	Both are heavy, expensive, and absolutely fireproof; tiles are more common in the Southwest, and slate in the East, where the quarries are located	An occasional cracked or chipped tile can be tricky to repair (see page 392); slate is somewhat easier to repair (see page 395)	75 years or more, provided repairs are made before underlayment is damaged
Roll roofing or selvage	Same material as asphalt shingles, but comes in the form of wide strips that are lapped horizontally across the roof's surface	Lightweight, single-layer installations fail frequently—but repairs are easy	5 to 15 years; ask if company will come back for patching
Metal roofing	Older types include terne—a tin/steel alloy—and copper; modern styles include corrugated or ribbed aluminum and galvanized-steel panels. Aluminum, steel, and terne often are painted	All must be flashed and fastened with the same type of metal or electrolytic action will cause deterioration; may need periodic painting.	35 years for aluminum and steel; copper and terne are even more durable
Built-up and "rubber" roofing	Used on flat or low-pitched roofs, fabricated on the job by laminating layers of felt with asphalt or coal tar, then topped with gravel; "rubber" or modified-bitumen roll roofing is installed by torching it down	Leaks due to a poor job are fairly common; fortunately, repairs are not very difficult	5 to 20 years; generally, the more layers, the longer life you can expect it to have; a rubber roof lasts 30 years or more

USING AN EXTENSION LADDER

For strength and rigidity, select a ladder with a duty rating of at least 250 pounds. It should extend 3 feet above the highest eaves on your house. Add another foot to this distance to make up for the propping angle. The extended height of a ladder is about 3 feet less than the total of its sections.

If you have never scaled an extension ladder, ask someone to steady it from below when you make your first few climbs. You will soon gain confidence.

CAUTION!
WATCH OUT FOR POWER LINES
Metal—and even wet wooden or fiberglass—ladders can conduct electricity. Be especially careful when moving or extending a ladder near power lines. In addition, phone and cable lines can be damaged if hit by a ladder.

Always stay clear of power lines, even if your ladder is made of a nonconductive material.

Never allow more than one person on a ladder at a time. Don't use a ladder on a windy day—not only is it hazardous for

Leg extension.
When the feet of a ladder must span uneven terrain, you can use a sturdy 2×4 to fashion an extension for one foot. Use at least two strong clamps to securely fasten the extension.

you to work in heavy winds, an unattended ladder can blow over, leaving you stranded.

Store ladders indoors, away from moisture and "second-story" burglars. Don't paint a wooden ladder; paint can hide defects.

Ladder brace.
The top of a ladder can easily damage a gutter or even siding. A brace improves a ladder's stability, protects siding and gutters, spans obstacles, and keeps the ladder away from the house.

1. Walk the ladder up.
To set up a ladder, place its feet firmly against the foundation. Do not extend it yet; wait until it's vertical. "Walk" the ladder up, hand over hand, keeping your arms straight. It will seem to get lighter as it rises.

2. Pull the rope.
To extend the ladder, brace a rail with your foot and pull the ladder carefully away from the house until you feel you can hold it securely; you may need help. Pull the rope to raise the top section. Go a little higher than you need, then let it slide back down. Make sure both locks catch.

3. Position the ladder.
Position the ladder so that the distance from the base to the wall is about one-fourth of its extended length. Make sure the ladder's feet dig a bit into the ground.

INSPECTING A ROOF

*T*o ensure a tight roof overhead, you should examine it every spring and fall. You don't have to haul out the extension ladder and risk life and limb crawling onto the roof. Just scan it from all sides through binoculars, paying special attention to the problem areas illustrated here.

If you do decide to climb up for a closer look, exercise caution. Also bear in mind that the sun does more damage than the wind and rain combined, so you may want to focus most of your effort on the sunny side of the house. Don't mount a roof on a hot, sunny day. Shingles (especially asphalt shingles) are easily damaged when hot.

If a number of shingles are broken, blistered, or balding and many have lost their luster, prepare for a reroofing job.

Clean the gutters.
Keep your hips between the rails, and don't overreach; erect ladders are easily tipped with little motion. For solutions to gutter problems, see pages 400–401.

Use a stabilizer.
For roof work, buy a pair of metal roofing jacks, which are held in place with nails driven under a shingle. Install two jacks and stretch a 2×4 between them. Or secure the ladder with ropes tied to a tree on the other side. Or hook a stabilizer over the ridge.

EXPERTS' INSIGHT

ICE DAMS

In an area with freezing weather, the attic must be kept cold in the winter. If not, snow can melt, flow down near the eaves, and then freeze. The resulting "ice dam" can work its way under shingles and flashing, seriously damaging the roof's sheathing and possibly the framing. If you see signs of ice dams, install attic insulation (pages 424–425). This will keep heat from escaping into the attic space.

Ridge shingle

Ridge shingle.
Ridge shingles often fail first. Look for cracks and wind damage. In the case of asphalt shingles, the mineral granules may be worn away. A leak here can show up anywhere inside.

Valley.
Valleys are another place where deterioration causes problems. Make sure any flashing is sound. Shingles should lie flat on top of the flashing. If leaks occur during windy rainstorms, the shingles that lie on the flashing may not be cut correctly; ask a pro.

Flashing.
Check other flashing too. It should be tight, rust-free, and sealed with pliable caulking or roofing cement. Installing a new vent like the one shown above is not difficult, but other types of flashing require a pro.

Missing shingle.
Loose, curled, or missing shingles leak moisture that weakens sheathing and harms walls and ceilings. If individual shingles have been damaged by a falling branch, replace them singly. If shingles show general wear and tear, it's time for a reroofing job.

Pinpoint leaks.
Water that gets through a leak in your roof will often follow a meandering, brooklike course. It can travel under sheathing, down a rafter, even along an electrical cable, before showing up as a drip or damp spot on a ceiling or wall.

You may be able to trace the trickle to its source from the attic. Look for water stains on framing and sheathing. Keep in mind that a leak will originate higher than the area where it first appeared. Even then the cause of the leak may be above the point of entry into the attic. Often the culprits are damaged flashing and damaged or mis-applied shingles.

On a sunny day, a leak may appear as a pinhole of light in the attic. If you find one, drive a nail up through it from the attic to mark the spot on the roof itself. Attach a string to guide water to a bucket until you can make the repair.

Granules in the gutter.
A large accumulation of granules in the gutter means your roof is losing its surface coating. Expect problems soon.

Flooding gutter.
Watch during a heavy rain to see if gutters are free-flowing. Flooding can work up under lower shingle courses.

SOLVING ROOF PROBLEMS

*I*f you are queasy about moving around on high places—especially if your roof is steeply pitched—hire a professional for even small jobs.

If you conquer your fears, however, you will find most repairs are relatively simple. Often the biggest challenges are hoisting up your tools and materials and getting around on the roof.

On gentle slopes wear shoes with rubber soles. Attack steep pitches by hooking or tying an extension ladder over the ridge of the roof. Or use ladder jacks and a length of 2×4 (see page 390). Do not step on gutters or rely on them for support.

With any type of roof, don't walk on it more than necessary. And don't go up at all during hot or cold weather extremes. Try to repair asphalt shingles on medium-warm days (40°–80°F); asphalt roofing turns brittle in cold weather and is too soft to handle when hot.

Wood shingles and shakes are not temperature-sensitive, but they are affected by humidity. Soaking them makes them much more pliable; dry shingles may split when you drive nails in them. Wet wood shingles can be slippery.

Only a few supplies are required for repair work. Roofing cement is available in cans, and you can apply it with a putty knife or a scrap of wood. Butyl caulk and "gutter caulk" are messy to work with, but worth the trouble because they adhere so well. For fastening use galvanized roofing nails that are long enough to penetrate all the way through the sheathing. If you have several layers of roofing, you may need nails as long as 2 inches. Wood shingles and slate tiles require shingle nails, which have thinner shanks. In your garage you may find shingles or roll goods left over from the installation; otherwise take a sample to buy materials of matching color.

Patch cracks, minor splits, and holes with roofing cement. Drive home popped nails and seal them or the shingles that cover them. Make sure that all shingles lie flat. If any are even slightly curled, fasten them down with dabs of cement. Don't be stingy with roofing cement or caulking around the flashing.

REPAIRING SPANISH TILE

*S*panish ceramic clay tiles weigh as much as 15 pounds each. And just to make it more difficult, they must be maneuvered on a fragile, slippery surface that may shift underfoot. For your own safety, hire a contractor who specializes in tile roofs for replacement and major repair jobs. If you do venture onto a tile roof, always spread your weight over at least two tiles.

Tiles can last 75 to 100 years if they are exposed only to the elements. However, tiles are brittle and become more so over time. A falling branch or a person walking on the roof can easily break an individual tile. If tiles are failing in several places, even though they have not been bumped, all the tiles probably need to be replaced.

Some clay tiles are rounded, while others are nearly flat. All types are made to interlock, so you probably cannot replace a broken tile with one of a different style.

You can seal small cracks and flashing with roofing cement, though the resulting patch will not be pleasant to look at. Bigger gaps, and especially cap tiles along the ridge, should be mortared by a professional contractor.

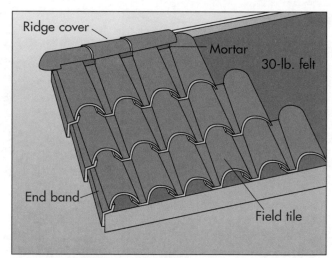

How Spanish tiles are installed.

The roof structure—both the rafters and the sheathing—must be extra-strong to accommodate a tile roof. In a typical installation, thick 30-pound roofing felt is first laid on the sheathing. The tiles themselves interlock and are nailed to the sheathing. Tiles at the ridge are cemented in place and sealed using mortar. Consider installing newer concrete tiles, which last even longer than ceramic tiles.

REPAIRING ASPHALT SHINGLES

Buy roofing cement in caulking tubes to seal minor cracks and holes and to glue down curled shingles. If you have a larger job, buy the roofing cement in larger containers—1-gallon or even 5-gallon buckets.

If the damage is extensive, replace the shingle. When working with asphalt shingles, wait for a warm day when the shingles will be flexible and easier to work with. Avoid ending up with exposed nails as much as possible. If you must leave an exposed nail, cover it well with roofing cement.

YOU'LL NEED...

TIME: About 30 minutes.
SKILLS: Basic roofing skills.
TOOLS: Hammer, pry bar, putty knife, utility knife, flat shovel, caulking gun.

1. Remove the nails.
Loosen the nails in the shingle above by slipping a flat shovel underneath. Lift the shingle above carefully, to avoid cracking it. Pull all four of the nails with a pry bar and slide the bad shingle out.

2. Cut a shingle and slip it in.
Remove 1 inch from the top edge of the new shingle by cutting the nongranular side with a knife. Bend the strip back and forth until it snaps. Slip the new shingle into place under the shingle above. Note the positions of the nails.

3. Drive nails.
If possible, lift the shingle above and drive nails close to the old nail holes. The nailhead should cover the old hole, but be far enough away that the nail bites into the sheathing. It may work to push the nail in place, slip a pry bar over the nailhead, and pound on the pry bar.

4. Cover heads with cement.
Coat the nailheads with roofing cement, then firmly press the upper course back into place. If necessary, seal the old holes as well. If the shingle curls up, weight it down temporarily.

Repair with flashing.
You also can back up a damaged shingle with a piece of metal flashing. Secure the flashing by setting it in a bed of roofing cement. Then cover the top of the metal with more cement and press the shingle into the cement.

REPAIRING WOOD SHINGLES

A new replacement shingle may differ in color from the surrounding shingles. In time it will weather and look the same.

Choose grade #1 shingles, made of heartwood, which resists insects and fungi. They will last far longer than less expensive shingles made from sapwood.

When replacing shingles, be sure to match the spacing between the existing shingles. Butting the replacement shingle against the old shingles may create a tight joint that traps moisture, which will encourage rot and decay.

YOU'LL NEED...

TIME: About 30 to 60 minutes per shingle.
SKILLS: Basic carpentry skills.
TOOLS: Hammer, chisel, pry bar, utility knife, saw, nail set, drill, caulking gun.

Nail a cracked shingle.
Mend splits by drilling pilot holes and driving shingle or siding nails, which have smaller heads than roofing nails. Seal the gap and the nailheads with roofing cement or butyl caulk (which can be purchased in a color to nearly match the shingles).

Back a hole with flashing.
If a knothole has opened, drive a sheet of aluminum flashing material under the shingle. Be sure that it extends several inches above the hole. If the spot is highly visible, paint the metal to resemble the shingles.

1. Flatten nails.
To remove a damaged shingle, split it along the grain with a chisel and pull the pieces out. The nails that held it in place will remain. Place the flat end of a pry bar over the old nailheads and strike with a hammer to drive the nailheads flush.

2. Tap in a new shingle.
Cut a new shingle to width so that there are appropriate gaps on both sides. With a block of wood and a hammer, drive the new shingle until it is flush with the row and the nailheads are covered.

3. Nail and seal.
Drive two shingle nails into the new shingle at 45 degrees, close to the butt of the shingle above. Use a nail set to drive nailheads flush; seal with caulk.

REPAIRING SLATE SHINGLES

Slate roofs last for decades if installed and maintained properly. In addition to a regular inspection a couple of times each year, inspect a slate roof after violent storms.

Because walking on a slate roof may damage the slate tiles, the easiest, safest method of inspection is to stand on the ground and use a pair of binoculars to look for signs of damage or missing tiles. **NOTE:** *Slate tiles can be extremely slippery, especially if they are damp or wet. Use care when working on a slate roof.*

YOU'LL NEED...

TIME: About 1 hour, depending on the extent of the damage.
SKILLS: Moderate carpentry skills.
TOOLS: Hacksaw or slate ripper, glass cutter, drill, hammer, speed square, nail set, tin snips.

1. Cut the concealed nails.
Slip a hacksaw blade under the broken slate, and cut the nails concealed under the course above. (If you live in an area where slate roofs are common, you may be able to buy a slate ripper. This handy tool quickly cuts through the hidden nails.)

2. Cut a slate tile.
Cut a slate tile so there is a gap on either side that matches the gaps in the rest of the roof. To cut slate, score both sides deeply with a glass cutter. Align the score over an edge and snap downward.

3. Drill pilot holes.
Equip a drill with a masonry bit that is slightly wider than the shank of the nails you will drive. Drill two holes about ¾ inch above the bottom edge of the course above, in the gaps, as shown.

4. Attach with nails.
Drive in galvanized shingle or siding nails, which have smaller heads than roofing nails, through the holes you just drilled. Drive the nails just flush using a nail set.

5. Slip in flashing.
Cut a piece of galvanized or copper flashing about 4 inches wide and 6 inches long. Slightly cup it to provide tension and slip it under the slate to cover the nails. (Or use a pre-cupped "bib" made for this purpose.)

REPAIRING AND REPLACING FLASHING

Think of flashing as a special-purpose shingle. Like a shingle, flashing overlaps and interweaves with other roofing materials to shed water.

Flashing is made of thin-gauge metal that is bent and formed to fit angled joints where two or more surfaces abut. Because these intersections are vulnerable to leakage, flashing deserves closer scrutiny than the rest of your roof.

Look for flashing that has pulled away from adjoining surfaces and for roofing cement or caulk that has dried and cracked. Even tiny holes can leak; when in doubt, apply new cement or caulk.

Rusted, cracked, or corroded flashing around chimneys, dormers, and plumbing vents will last for a few more years if you trowel on a coat of fibered asphalt-aluminum roof paint. If there is widespread deterioration or valley-flashing failure, call in a roofer or sheet-metal specialist to replace these sections entirely.

You can replace small flashing pieces as long as you buy precise duplicates and replace them in their exact original positions.

Take care that two types of metal do not come in contact with each other, or corrosion could result. For durability at a reasonable price, choose aluminum flashing. Vent flashing comes as a single molded piece of metal or plastic. Simply fit the piece over the pipe and cover with roofing on the uphill side.

YOU'LL NEED...

TIME: 4 to 6 hours.
SKILLS: Moderate carpentry skills.
TOOLS: Tin snips, putty knife, hammer, cold chisel, trowel, joint strike, caulking gun, ladder, rope.

Open- and closed-valley flashing.
Because it is visible, open-valley flashing is easy to inspect. Cement down any shingles that are even slightly curled or loose.

Closed-valley flashing hides beneath the roofing. In some cases shingles are so interlaced on top that it is impossible to check the flashing.

Drip cap.
Drip cap flashing keeps water from seeping under the frames over windows and doors. The drip cap should be several inches high so that water cannot work its way up and around it. Check drip caps periodically for damage.

Flashing for a dormer.
To reflash dormers buy pieces of flashing bent at 90 degrees. Using the old flashing as a guide, tuck the flashing under the siding on the dormer. Use valley flashing along the peak. For brick use step flashing capped with counter-flashing let into mortar joints, as shown on page 397.

Replace a vent.
Don't bother repairing faulty vent flashing. Just install a new neoprene and aluminum replacement. You'll need to replace only a few shingles (see pages 392–395).

FLASHING A CHIMNEY

Most chimneys have a two-part flashing system to ride out minor structural shifting. Step flashing and base flashing fit under shingles along the sides of the chimney and lie on top of the shingles below the chimney. Counterflashing is applied over the base and step flashing and serves as a cap to keep water out. Its top edge, bent into an L shape, is mortared into the chimney's mortar joints to hold it securely.

Replacing chimney flashing calls for time and patience. If you are unsure how the old flashing was installed, or if the old flashing leaked because it was not installed properly (rather than because of metal failure), call in a pro. Whenever possible buy flashing pieces already cut and bent to fit. If necessary, form sheet metal by clamping it between two pieces of wood and bending it.

1. Install the base flashing.
To avoid confusion, work by removing one or two pieces and replacing them; then move on to the next pieces. To replace base flashing, apply asphalt primer to the bricks and install the flashing to the front. It should overlap the roof shingles by 4 inches.

2. Add the step flashing.
To remove a piece of old step flashing, gently pry up a shingle and pry out the nail. Working from the bottom up, slip each piece of new flashing under a shingle, work roofing cement under the flashing, and drive a nail. Also use roofing cement to join the flashing pieces to each other.

3. Flash the cricket.
If there is a cricket on the up-roof side and it is rotted, build a replacement out of plywood. You may need to cut away some roofing to do so. Use roofing cement to embed the rear corner flashings and base flashing that covers the cricket. Nail the flashing to the deck only.

4. Set the counterflashing.
Set the counterflashing on the front and sides into raked-out mortar joints. Refill the joints with masonry caulk.

5. Flash the corners.
Make and install counterflashing suitable to the situation on the up-roof corners and side of the chimney. Install it with as few nails as possible; setting metal in a thick layer of roofing cement provides a firm installation. Where you must drive nails, cover the heads with roofing cement.

CLEANING AND REPAIRING A MASONRY CHIMNEY

Chimneys have two enemies: heat and water. The crackling fire you enjoy on winter evenings subjects masonry to temperature extremes that can chip out mortar, especially at the top where the flue penetrates the cap.

Most chimneys have a ceramic flue liner running up through the center. Concrete blocks surround the liner, and bricks cover the blocks. Other chimneys are all brick; a few use firebrick instead of a ceramic tile flue liner. Many also include a chimney cap to keep out rain, nesting birds, and downdrafts. Regardless of your chimney's construction, it pays to inspect it every fall. Examine every visible surface, including the attic. Look for cracks and deteriorated mortar.

Occasionally test for hot spots by feeling with your hand. These may indicate a broken flue—a definite fire hazard that a mason should fix before you use the fireplace again.

How often a fireplace flue needs cleaning depends on how much you use it and the type of wood you burn. Pine and other sappy species produce creosote, which cakes the flue and constricts the opening. The result: smoking and a possible chimney fire. Hire a chimney sweep to clean your chimney, or do the job yourself, as shown here. A faulty firebox design or downdrafts also cause smoking (pages 529–530 offer solutions to these problems).

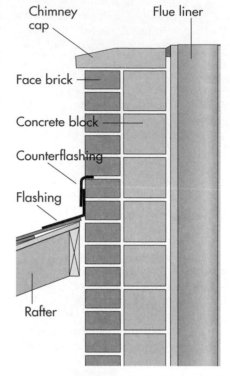

Chimney cap · Flue liner · Face brick · Concrete block · Counterflashing · Flashing · Rafter

YOU'LL NEED...

TIME: 2 to 8 hours.
SKILLS: Basic masonry skills.
TOOLS: Hammer, cold chisel, caulking gun, sweep tools.

1. Seal the fireplace.
Before brushing, open the damper and seal the fireplace opening with a wet sheet, canvas, or poly-ethylene sheeting. Be sure the opening is sealed very tightly and firmly. Measure the diameter and length of your chimney, and buy chimney brushes and extension handles to fit.

Round brush · Square brush · Extension handle

2. Brush the chimney.
From the top, insert the brush, moving it up and down to dislodge debris from the flue liner. Add an extension and repeat until you reach the damper at the bottom. Wait approximately a half hour for the dust to settle. Slowly remove the sheeting. Wet down the soot before you clean out the firebox. Vacuum around the damper before closing it.

3. Repoint and apply caulk.
Rain erodes mortar joints. Chip away loose material, then repoint as explained on pages 525–530. Apply a generous bead of masonry or butyl caulk around the flue for a flexible seal that rides out expansion and contraction. If the area is badly damaged with large, loose pieces, call in a pro.

PREVENTING ATTIC CONDENSATION

An attic that cannot breathe properly has problems. During hot weather, temperatures may reach 150°F, placing a lot of demand on your cooling system. And during cold spells, the temperature difference between the attic and the heated spaces below causes moisture condensation. This can lower the R-value of insulation, rot framing and sheathing, and shorten the life of your roof.

The solution to both problems is to provide adequate airflow through inlets at the eaves (or soffits), then up and out the roof via vents near or at the ridge.

How much ventilation your attic needs depends on whether the insulation includes a vapor barrier (see page 424). If it does, there should be 1 square foot of venting for every 300 square feet of attic floor space. If there is no vapor barrier, double this figure.

Vents do no good if they are clogged. Make sure that insulation does not lap over a soffit vent; you may have to section off the area with wood blocking. Also check that gable and ridge vents are free of caked-on dust.

Soffit and gable vents.
In an unfinished attic, you might get by with gable louver vents at both ends. The larger and higher the vents, the more effective they will be. A gable fan, controlled by a heat-sensitive switch, can keep your attic cool, reducing energy costs. Better yet, add eaves vents as well.

Soffit and roof vents.
Finished attics need both eaves vents and roof louvers. Inlets and outlets should be about equal in area. A ridge vent (see below) may run continuously along a ridge. If the roof is insulated, special channels may be needed to allow air to flow from the eaves up to the ridge vent.

Choosing vents.
There are ventilation components for almost any roof. Breathers are easy to install, but you need many of them. Soffit strip vents provide greater airflow. Up top, you can choose gable or roof-mounted louvers (shown above). A ridge vent is an unobtrusive answer, but a professional roofer must install it. Add design interest with a cupola. Penthouse louvers work well on big, flat roofs. Many of these projects are big jobs best left to a contractor.

REPAIRING AND MAINTAINING GUTTER SYSTEMS

Your roof's drainage system diverts thousands of gallons of water away from your house annually, so you can see why it merits a semiannual inspection.

Here's how the drainage system works: All gutters slope slightly toward their outlets. From there two elbows connect to the downspout; at the bottom a third elbow directs the spout outlet away from the wall.

Check gutters and downspouts every spring before heavy rains begin and late in the fall after leaves have fallen. Remove all debris logging the system, look for rust or corrosion, and be vigilant in looking for low spots where water may pool.

Standing water is the cause of most gutter problems, so check that gutters slope down toward their outlets. Pour or spray water into a gutter and watch what happens. Eliminate sags by lifting the gutter section slightly. Look for and repair loose hangers, or bend up the hanger with a pair of pliers. If this doesn't do the trick, install an additional hanger.

If you have widespread drainage problems, call gutter companies for prices on replacing the entire system. They can install seamless aluminum gutters with leaf protectors for virtually maintenance-free operation.

Clean a gutter.
Debris clogs up gutters and downspouts and holds moisture that causes rust, rot, and corrosion. Clear away debris by hand (wear gloves). Finish up by using a wire brush to scrape away caked-on debris.

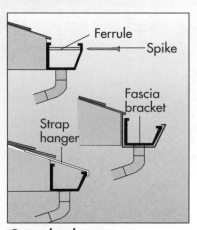

Gutter hardware.
There are three forms of gutter hangers: a spike and a ferrule driven through the gutter into rafter ends, a strap nailed to the roof sheathing, or a fascia bracket attached to the fascia. If a gutter sags, add a strap hanger.

Blast water from a hose.
Hose your gutters clean, beginning at the high end of each run—or in the middle of runs having spouts at both ends. Often you can blast out spout blockage with water pressure or a plumber's snake. Otherwise you may have to dismantle the downspouts.

Make minor repairs.
If the inside of a gutter is rusting, scrape and wire-brush it clean, then apply a thin coat of roofing cement. Seal any cracks or gaps at joints using gutter caulk. If sections of a downspout are coming loose, drill pilot holes and drive short sheetmetal screws.

Patch a gutter.
Patch a rusted-out gutter with metal flashing. Bend a piece of sheet metal so it can rest in the opening. Spread a layer of roofing cement and set the patch into the cement. Then coat the patch with more roofing cement.

Install a screen guard.
Screen guards keep out leaves. Buy guards made to fit your size of gutter. Slip the inner edge under the first course of shingles and bend the screen into place.

Add a wire-cage strainer.
Wire-cage strainers eliminate downspout clogging. However, you will still have to clear debris from around the cages.

Replace a downspout section.
Cut downspouts with a fine-tooth hacksaw. Mark a line around the circumference so the edges will be square. Use a file or sandpaper to remove any burrs.

Redirect water with a splash block.
Splash blocks must be pitched away from the foundation walls. Use gravel to raise and shim a splash block.

Or use an extension.
If water puddles near the house, or if your basement leaks during rainfalls, take steps to move the water at least 8 feet away from the house. A corrugated plastic extension stays in place; a perforated roll-up hose extends like a party noisemaker when the water comes down.

UNDERSTANDING BRICK WALLS

Most "brick" or "stone" houses built after World War II do not have solid masonry walls. Instead, builders faced conventional framing with a masonry veneer—combining the weather resistance of brick or stone with the superior insulating qualities of wood stud construction. An older home may have two thicknesses of brick instead of a wood frame.

Check the section view at right. Studs, not bricks, bear the load. A single tier of brick connects to the studs with short metal strips called ties. Between the brick and the sheathing is an airspace, which drains away moisture that might penetrate the brick surface. Weep holes near the bottom allow condensed moisture to drip away;

never block up a weep hole.

The foundation must support the heavy masonry skin as well as the framing system. If veneer is added to a wall, an inspector must make sure the foundation is strong enough to carry the load.

Although masonry-veneer walls are relatively impervious to weather and time, inspect them periodically. Pay particular attention to mortar joints that may need to be repointed (see pages 525–526). Solid masonry walls—usually used today only for garages, garden walls, and commercial structures—may consist of several tiers of brick or stone or of concrete blocks that have been veneered.

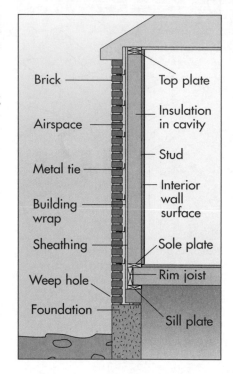

UNDERSTANDING STUCCO WALLS

Stucco walls usually begin with wood-stud framing, although stucco can be applied directly to masonry surfaces. Often, as the drawing at right shows, spacer strips are nailed to the sheathing, and metal lath resembling chicken wire is attached to the spacers. In some installations the spacer strips are omitted. In such a case, stucco—a cement-based plaster—is troweled onto the metal lath.

As with interior plasterwork, it takes two or three layers of stucco to build up a smooth surface. A scratch coat oozes through the lath for a good grip; the brown coat (which is omitted in some installations) smoothes out major irregularities in the surface. The finish coat completes the job.

As with concrete, you can trowel, scrape, stipple, and spatter stucco for textures ranging from glassy smooth to rugged rustic. Many textures reflect the

personality of a certain installer and may be difficult to reproduce; others are simple to mimic once you know which tools to use. You also can add coloring pigments to the finish coat of both cement and vinyl stucco for an exterior that will never need painting.

Properly applied, stucco lasts for decades with little attention. Watch, though, for cracks that may develop around windows, doors, and chimneys. If not sealed, these may admit moisture that could eventually rot framing. As with masonry-veneer walls, keep your eye on long, running cracks that might indicate settlement.

For information on patching cracks and holes, see pages 410–411. If you are planning to paint stucco, be sure to apply a coating formulated for use on stucco (see pages 534–535).

WHERE SEALING IS NEEDED

Different building materials swell and shrink at different rates. This results in cracks where siding meets masonry, where siding butts trim, and where flashing contacts roofing. Use caulk wherever unlike materials meet. The illustration below shows typical spots to check.

Caulking material falls into two categories—rubber-derived formulations, such as latex and butyl, and synthetic-based, high-performance materials. The type you select depends upon the job you want it to do.

Before buying, read the product data for preparation requirements, materials the caulk will adhere to, and paintability. The chart below compares the common sealants.

Chimney cap
Chimney flashing
Skylight
Vent
Around windows
Electrical fixtures
Joints where different materials meet
Plumbing and electrical penetrations
Siding and trim joints

CHOOSING SEALANTS

Type	Characteristics	Cost
Latex	Inexpensive and easy to work with; liable to shrink and crack in time	Inexpensive
Latex/silicone or latex/acrylic	Good general-purpose, fast-drying sealant; remains flexible for years; ideal for filling small cracks and joints; paintable	Moderate
"Tub and tile" caulk	Highly adhesive and waterproof; good for wet areas, such as tubs and showers	Moderate
Butyl or "gutter"	Excellent exterior caulk for gutter seams, flashings, storm windows, and large joints; paintable	Moderate
Silicone	The most durable caulk; remains flexible, but many types do not stick well; water-based products perform better and are paintable	Most expensive
Foam	Quickly fills wide cracks and openings; remains flexible; paintable, but impossible to smooth out; "non-expanding" type is easier to control	Moderate

REPAIRING WOOD SIDING AND SHINGLES

Damaged siding permits moisture to enter exterior walls, where it can rot the sheathing and even the framing. It needs quick attention.

Keep exterior walls well covered with quality paint (see pages 546–557). Make repairs as soon as you spot damage. Pack small cracks, splits, and open seams with latex/silicone or butyl caulk.

You may be able to repair splits and holes using epoxy wood filler (see page 408). If not, you'll have to replace the damaged board or shingle. If more than a few boards or shingles are failing, consider re-siding the entire wall.

1. Loosen the board.
To remove a length of siding, cut through the paint along its bottom edge. Work a chisel under its lower edge, then switch to a flat pry bar. To keep from damaging the surrounding siding, pry by pulling away from the house rather than pushing toward it.

2. Pry it away.
Each course of lapped siding is held in place by nails driven through the course above it. First deal with the lower nails. If the nails begin to come out with the board, jam the nail with a pry bar and tap the board down. This may cause the heads to pop out, making them easy to pry away. The same can be done for the nails in the course above.

YOU'LL NEED...

TIME: 1 to 3 hours for one course.
SKILLS: Moderate carpentry skills.
TOOLS: Chisel, hammer, pry bar, close-work hacksaw, square, putty knife, utility knife, plane, backsaw, drill, caulking gun.

3. Cut nails that won't pop out.
If the nails aren't cooperating, or if they are not accessible from the surface, slip a hacksaw blade underneath the siding and cut them. A close-work hacksaw works well for this. Be careful not to scrape the siding beneath the damage.

4. Prepare to cut out the damaged area.
To cut a piece to length, tap wedges under the course above and use a square to mark the cut lines. Cut first with a utility knife to diminish splintering.

5. Saw the siding.

Use a backsaw or fine-toothed handsaw to cut the face of the siding. Use short strokes, holding the top of the blade to keep it from buckling. As you finish each cut, be careful not to cut siding below the damaged area.

6. Split away the damage.

Split the damaged area along the grain and remove a piece at a time. Carefully pry away all remnants under the board above. Pry away or pound down all nails. Check that the replacement piece can slide all the way up into position.

7. Seal the building wrap.

If you puncture the building paper underneath, seal it with roofing cement. Or cut a piece of roofing felt (tar paper) slightly larger than the opening and shoehorn it in. Fasten any loose paper with roofing nails or staples.

8. Slip in the patch.

Cut the replacement for a snug fit, then slide it under the board above, tap it into place, and remove the wedges. Avoid too tight a fit, however. Use a block plane to skim off one edge if you have to force the patch.

9. Drill pilot holes.

Wherever you will drive a nail less than 3 inches from the end or edge of a board, drill a pilot hole first to prevent splitting the board.

10. Nail, and caulk the seams.

Finally nail the new board at the top and bottom. Use siding nails, which have thin shanks. Fill nail holes and the vertical seams with caulk, then prime and paint.

REPLACING A SECTION OF ALUMINUM SIDING

Most aluminum siding is shaped like beveled wood siding and installed horizontally, as shown here. The less common vertical aluminum siding interlocks in much the same way, so repairs are essentially the same.

Because siding pieces are very long, it usually is easier to patch a damaged spot rather than replace the whole piece. The patch fits over the existing siding, so the cut does not have to be precise. A repair like this will result in joints that look nearly the same as other joints.

YOU'LL NEED...

TIME: An hour to cut and replace a section.
SKILLS: Basic cutting skills.
TOOLS: Square, utility knife, perhaps a circular saw, tin snips, flat pry bar, pliers, caulking gun.

1. Cut out the damaged section.
Using a square as a guide, cut a rectangle around the damaged area. It will take several passes with a utility knife to cut through the siding; you may need to change blades partway through.

2. Finish the cut.
You may find it easier to finish the cut using a pair of tin snips. A circular saw with the blade installed backwards makes cutting easy, but take care not to damage nearby pieces. Pull the cutout away and unsnap it from the wall.

3. Cut the patch.
Cut a patch of matching siding at least 3 inches wider than the cut-out area. Cut off its nailing strip along the top. Test to see that the piece will fit. Its top should slip at least ¼ inch up under the piece above, and its bottom should be able to snap into place.

4. Apply caulk.
Clean the area of all residue. Use a caulking gun to apply clear silicone sealant to the perimeter of the hole.

5. Lock the patch in place.
Slip the patch into place and slide it up until it locks in place. Press the sides flat and wipe away any squeezed-out caulk.

REPLACING ALUMINUM END CAPS

Corners of a house often get bumped, so it's common to see aluminum end caps that are dented. Replacing them is not difficult.

The original installer may have left some end caps in your garage or basement. If not, bring an old end cap to your supply source to find an exact replacement.

Chances are that the old siding has faded, so you may not be able to get an exact color match. If so, paint the pieces to match the siding before installing them.

You'll Need...

TIME: About an hour to replace six or seven end caps.
SKILLS: Basic cutting, fastening, and caulking skills.
TOOLS: Hacksaw, hammer, flat pry bar, drill, blind pop riveter.

1. Cut damaged caps.
In some cases broken or dented corner caps will pull out easily. However, you may need to pry out the siding above to get at the nails. If you cannot pull out the nails without damaging the siding, cut through them with a hacksaw. If you can't get to the nails, cut through the corner piece itself.

2. Remove nails.
Remove the damaged corner caps, then take out the remaining nails with a flat pry bar. Use a scrap of wood to prevent denting the siding as you pry.

3. Nail new end caps.
Starting at the bottom, slide each replacement cap under the bottom lip of the course above, and slide it up until it snaps into place. Taking care not to dent the siding, attach each cap with one or two nails or screws. You may need to angle the fastener in order to hit solid wood.

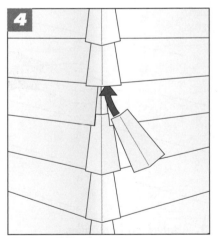

4. Install the last piece.
Cut the nailing strip off of the top replacement cap so it can slip under the course above by about ¼ inch. Test to see that it fits snugly and can snap into place at the bottom. Apply silicone caulk to the back side of the cap, slide the cap into place, and wipe away any excess caulk.

Attach a replacement post.
If you have to replace a dented corner post (a problem common to aluminum and vinyl siding), cut through the sides with a knife; it will take several passes. Cut the flange off a replacement piece and test to see that it fits. Apply clear silicone caulk to the flanges and attach using screws or blind pop rivets.

REPAIRING DENTED ALUMINUM SIDING

This technique is more time-consuming than patching with a replacement piece (page 406), but it's useful if you have a hard time finding siding to match.

Automobile-body filler is available at an auto parts store. It comes as a two-part epoxy; add a bit of hardener and mix with a small scrap of plastic or wood. It quickly hardens to the point where it can be planed or sanded. An hour or two later, it can be painted.

YOU'LL NEED...

TIME: Several hours, including time for the material to harden.
SKILLS: Basic patching skills, spraying paint.
TOOLS: Lock-joint pliers, drill, wide putty knife, sanding block, spray paint can, painting tools.

TOOLS TO USE

BODY REPAIR TOOLS

If you have a number of dents to patch, invest in some tools that will enable you to quickly make and smooth the patches.
■ Self-tapping screws with large heads can be quickly driven into the soft aluminum and pulled out.
■ A pull-style paint scraper (with removable blades) makes it easy to scrape away excess body filler when it is partially hardened.
■ To grind down the patch after it has fully hardened, use a vibrating or random-orbit power sander.

1. Drill a series of holes.
Equip a drill with a ⅛-inch bit, and drill several holes in the middle of the dented area. One or two of these will be pilot holes for the pull-out screw (Step 2), and the others will help the body filler to grab tightly onto the siding.

2. Pull out the dent.
Drive a No. 8 screw slightly into the deepest point of the dent. Grab the screw head with lock-joint pliers, and pull the dent partway out. Do not pull the siding out beyond the surrounding surface. If the dent is large, repeat this process with other screws in other locations.

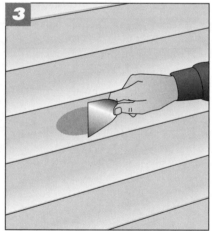

3. Apply auto-body filler.
Sand the dented area until it is bare of paint. Mix and apply two-part auto-body filler using a wide putty knife or the plastic scraper that comes with the filler. Smooth the patch so it is slightly higher than the surrounding siding. Once it has started to harden, scrape it down further.

Foam painting pad

4. Finish the patch.
Sand the area with 120-grit paper until it is smooth and level with the surrounding surface. Spray on metal primer, then apply color-matched paint suited for aluminum siding.

REPLACING A VINYL SIDING STRIP

*I*n some cases you can repair a section of vinyl by slipping a patch over the damaged area, in much the same way as shown for aluminum siding on page 406. However, many types of vinyl siding do not allow you to slip the top edge of the patch securely under the course above. Fortunately vinyl bends without denting, so you can pry out the top course far enough to remove existing nails and fasten the top of the repair piece.

YOU'LL NEED...

TIME: An hour for most repairs.
SKILLS: Basic carpentry skills.
TOOLS: Zip tool (made especially for vinyl siding), pry bar, utility knife, square hammer.

EXPERTS' INSIGHT

PAINTING VINYL SIDING

Vinyl siding is advertised as eliminating the need for painting. But some types (especially older and less expensive vinyl siding) may fade significantly in the sun. If you prepare carefully, you can apply paint to vinyl. First rough the vinyl with a hand or power sander and 60-grit sandpaper. Then apply a coat of alcohol-based primer, followed by exterior paint.

1. Pry out the damaged strip.
Unless you want to replace the entire strip, use a utility knife to cut it in place (see page 406). To remove a strip, insert a Zip tool under the lower lip, pull down, and slide the tool to the left or right. Also pull out the bottom of the course above.

2. Install the new strip.
Carefully pry the upper course back, and use blocks to hold it away from the house so you can get at the nails. Remove the nails and the damaged piece. Fasten the new strip by nailing through the centers of the nail slots. Do not drive the nails tightly.

3. Finish the patch.
Relock the new strip by pulling down and sliding the Zip tool while pressing in along the bottom edge.

Patch

Patching vinyl siding.
To fix a tear, you needn't replace the piece. Cut a piece of plastic slightly larger than the damaged area. On the back side of the siding, apply PVC pipe primer, then cement. Press the patch into the cement and hold it for a few seconds.

REPAIRING STUCCO WALLS

Small cracks in stucco can be filled with butyl or silicone/latex caulk and then painted. But if there are many cracks or if a section is coming loose, you must chip away the old material down to the lath or masonry underneath, then build up a new surface in two or three layers. Problem areas larger than 8 feet square usually require restuccoing of the entire wall. This is a major job that you may want to leave to a professional.

Make repairs during mild weather when there's no danger of freezing. Plan on the project taking at least three days. Wait at least six weeks before painting, then prime and apply paint recommended for concrete and stucco.

Colored stucco is difficult to match. Experiment with pigments, keeping in mind that colors will fade as much as 70 percent by the time the stucco dries. Never let the coloring pigment exceed 3 percent of the batch's total volume.

Blending the patch's final surface with the surrounding area can be difficult. Consult with a pro to find out (or guess at) the technique and tool used by the original installer.

YOU'LL NEED...

TIME: 3 working days for a large patch, extended over 10 to 12 days to cover drying time.
SKILLS: Moderate to advanced masonry skills; knowledge of the special technique used by the original stucco contractor.
TOOLS: Cold chisel, pry bar, hammer, stapler, trowel, hawk, improvised rake, spray hose, metal straightedge.

1. Prepare the area.
Chip away loose stucco using a cold chisel, pry bar, and hammer. You may need to use wire cutters or tin snips to cut the metal lath. Staple new roofing felt and metal lath onto the sheathing. Make sure the surrounding stucco is firmly attached to the wall; if not, chip away some more.

3. Scarify.
When the stucco begins to firm up, scratch it with a scarifying tool, or an improvised rake made by driving nails through a piece of wood every inch. The scratches should be about ⅛ inch deep.

2. Trowel the first coat.
Mix a batch of stucco base coat, following directions on the bag. Place a dollop of stucco on a hawk or a piece of plywood, and push the stucco into the metal lath using a straight trowel. Apply the first coat to a depth of about ¼ inch below the surrounding surfaces. Smooth the area.

TOOLS TO USE

FINISHING STUCCO
Stuccoers use a variety of tools to achieve the final surface. If you are unsure how to mimic the surrounding area, spread stucco on a plywood scrap and practice using these methods:

■ Dab at the stucco with your palm or a trowel and pull straight back to achieve peaks. Perhaps "knock down" the peaks by lightly passing over the surface with a trowel.

■ Produce a basically smooth surface. Dip a whisk broom in a bucket of stucco and dash it at the wall to produce hills. Perhaps knock them down.

■ Make a swirled surface by brushing with a whisk broom using wavy or arcing strokes.

4. Cure the base coat slowly.

The more slowly the stucco cures (dries out), the stronger it will be. Mist the scratch coat with a fine spray as often as necessary to keep it damp for two days. In windy or sunny weather, repeat several times a day. If the air is dry, tape a piece of plastic over the patch while it cures.

5. Add the brown coat.

Some installations omit this step and go straight to the finish coat (Step 7). Mix a batch of stucco for the second or "brown" coat. Apply this coat to within about ⅛ inch of the surface, and level it off with a metal straightedge or a large trowel.

6. Float the surface.

"Float" the brown coat by working it with a trowel until bleed water comes to the surface. (See page 675 for more about floating.) Avoid overworking; stop once the water has appeared.

7. Texture the finish coat.

Mist the brown coat for two days and wait a week. While you are waiting, practice applying finish stucco to a scrap of plywood until you can achieve a texture that blends in with the rest of the wall. Moisten the brown coat and mix a batch of finish stucco. Smooth on the finish coat. Texture it within a half hour.

DEALING WITH WOOD-BORING INSECTS

Wood-eating insects fall into two groups—subterranean (those that eat wood but nest underground) and nonsubterranean (those that live in the wood itself).

Watch for subterranean insects in early spring and fall. This is when the reproductive members of termite colonies sprout wings, take off on mating flights, discard the wings, and establish nesting places. If you find a pile of wings, suspect a colony nearby.

Nonsubterranean wood-boring insects, including powder-post beetles and carpenter ants, as well as several termite species, remain above ground. Sometimes you can spot their entrance holes in the wood's surface; a pile of sawdust pellets is another telltale sign.

If you suspect termites, call a licensed pest exterminator. Don't panic—although these pests can demolish a house, it would take years to do so.

Exterminators surround the house with what amounts to an underground moat of insecticide, usually by injecting chemicals into the soil with special equipment. Isolated from the earth, worker termites in the house soon die of thirst; the remainder of the colony starves or moves on.

Nonsubterranean termites confine their activities to limited areas, such as the inside of a porch column, a window, or a door frame. If the wood has not been weakened structurally, the extermination process will consist of boring holes into the wood and injecting a liquid or powdered chemical. If the damage is more extensive, the wood member must be cut away and replaced with new treated lumber.

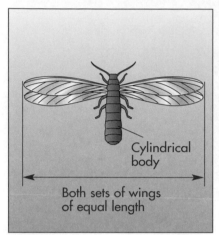

Termites.
Termites resemble ants but have cylindrical bodies and are light gray in color. During the mating season, workers have two pairs of equal-sized wings; otherwise they are wingless. Most termites live in the ground outside the house and make daily forays into the house to retrieve wood fibers.

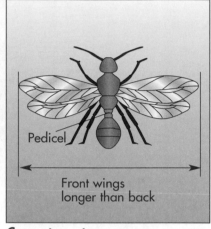

Carpenter ants.
Winged carpenter ants have a very thin waist called a pedicel, and the back pair of wings is shorter than the front. Carpenter ants make their homes in moist wood. If you take steps to keep out moisture, they will die off.

Termite damage.
Subterranean termites form tunnels in the direction of the wood grain, sometimes leaving nothing but a shell. By the time the damage is visible, the board is typically too far gone to save.

Carpenter ant damage.
Nonsubterranean insects burrow across the grain. Occasionally their tunnels break through the surface. This type of damage often becomes evident in time to save the board.

How they get in.

Most termites live in the forest, where they have an abundant supply of food in the form of dead and fallen trees. Unfortunately they don't distinguish between wood in its natural state and wood that has been through a sawmill. To discourage termites from picnicking in your home, clear away any firewood or construction debris near your house. Because they can gain access through even tiny holes, you will probably not be able to fence them out. Call in an exterminator if they have already invaded your home.

Apply insecticide in a crawlspace.

Many homes in termite-infested areas are built on crawlspace foundations. Termiticide should be applied around the bases of all rigid structures that are between the soil and the sill or floor framing. These structures include masonry walls, masonry piers, and plumbing pipes. As a second line of defense, foundation walls and piers should be capped with sheetmetal termite shields. Know the effective life of your shields and replace them before your house is reinfested.

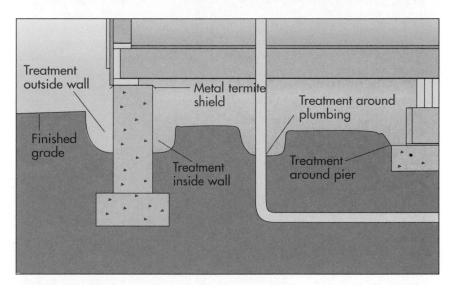

Treating a basement.

Professionals treat full-basement foundations as if they were boats floating in a sea of termites. The soil outside the wall is treated all the way to the footing, and termiticide is applied to the entire soil surface before the basement floor slab is poured. If the foundation wall consists of hollow masonry blocks, the wall is capped with solid concrete and a sheet-metal shield. If termites are found after the home is built, holes are typically drilled and filled with termiticide all around the foundation.

UNDERSTANDING WEATHERIZATION AND VENTILATION

Chapter 11 (pages 433–456) deals with heating and cooling equipment, the biggest energy consumers in most homes. The rest of this chapter describes their silent partners—the weather stripping, insulation, and ventilation systems that help you make the most of that precious energy.

These three components work to control the heat that your home loses in the winter and gains in the summer. Weather stripping seals outside walls, windows, and doors, keeping outside air out and inside air in. Insulation retards heat transfer through solid surfaces. Ventilation exhausts excess heat, as well as stale air and humidity. Older homes often suffer

from too little weather stripping and insulation, while some newer homes lack sufficient ventilation.

Chances are your home could stand some upgrading on all of these counts (see the drawing below for points you should check). Start with weather stripping. It's the easiest and least expensive component to deal with. You need a tight seal at all doors, windows, and anything else that opens. Caulk, a form of weather stripping, fills gaps between immovable elements where air could penetrate. For caulking basics, see page 403. Window putty, also called glazing compound, seals joints between glass and wood (see pages 372–373).

Once your home is snugly weather-stripped, you can assess the effectiveness of its insulation. You need the most insulation up top, either above your topmost ceilings or between the rafters. Next in line are the exterior walls. If your home sits atop a crawl-space or unheated basement, there should be insulation around ducts and pipes, as well as under the first-level floor or around the space's perimeter.

After you've tightened up your home's weather stripping and insulation, take a fresh look at its ventilation. Roof, soffit, and gable vents let an attic breathe (see page 399). Vent fans do the same for other areas (see pages 113–115).

A house that's efficiently tight, yet able to breathe.
In an energy-efficient home, insulation—either fiberglass batts or blown-in—completely fills the spaces between wall studs and ceiling joists of the top floor. Caulk seals exterior door and window moldings tightly against the siding. Flexible weather stripping makes a tight seal when a window or door is closed. Attic vents allow moisture to exit the house.

IDENTIFYING HIDDEN AIR LEAKS

You would never think of leaving a window open in the winter—unless someone else was paying the heating bill. Yet the total of all the little cracks and holes in the floors, walls, and ceilings of an average older home is often equivalent to an area of 2 square feet.

House doctors—technicians who specialize in finding and sealing such cracks—call these "hidden" heat leaks, because we never seem to see them.

The illustration at right points out the leaks that you can uncover if you give your house a good once-over. The chart below shows the square-inch area of these leaks, both before and after treatment. After you've pinpointed the problem areas, use the techniques on pages 416–423 to plug these leaks.

SIZING UP TYPICAL RESIDENTIAL AIR LEAKS

Leak	Square Inches
Ceiling	
1 Dropped/100 square feet	
no vapor barrier	78
with vapor barrier	8
2 Chimney, framing gap	12
gap weather-stripped	1
3 Whole-house fan, closed	8
covered with tight box	0.6
4 Lighting fixture, recessed	4
surface-mount	0.3
5 Pipe or duct, uncaulked	1
caulked at ceiling	0.2
Interior Wall	
6 Electrical outlet or switch	0.2
with cover gasket	0.03
Exterior Wall	
7 Sill on masonry:	
uncaulked	65
caulked	13
8 Band or box sill:	
uncaulked	65
caulked	13

Leak	Square Inches
Exterior Wall, continued	
9 Floor/wall joint:	
uncaulked	27
baseboard caulked	7
10 Electric outlet or switch	0.2
with cover gasket	0.05
Doors	
11 Attic fold-down	17
weather-stripped	8
12 Entrance	8
weather-stripped	6
with magnetic seal	4
13 Attic hatch	6
weather-stripped	3
Door and Window Frames	
14 Brick wall:	
uncaulked frame	2
caulked	0.4
15 Wood wall:	
uncaulked frame	0.6
caulked	0.1

Leak	Square Inches
Vents	
16 Range, damper open	9
damper closed	2
17 Dryer, damper open	4
damper closed	1
Fireplace	
18 Damper open	54
average damper	
closed	9
clean, tight damper	5
with stove insert	2
Heating System	
19 Ducts	
in unheated space	56
caulked and taped	28
20 Furnace with flame-	
retention head	
burner	12
add stack damper	9

APPLYING CAULK

If you have never used caulk, start in an inconspicuous area until you can hone your skills. Some types stick more readily to fingers and tools than to the surfaces that they're sealing. It takes a tube or two to learn how hard to squeeze and how fast to move the nozzle for a smooth, unbroken bead.

For most jobs you can use an inexpensive caulk gun. Its squeeze handle pushes a plunger against the bottom of a caulk tube, forcing caulk through the nozzle. See page 481 to choose the right type of caulk for the job.

Before applying caulk, first scrape out the old, cracked caulk and flaked paint. Be sure the surfaces are dry. Even high-quality caulk may crack or come loose in time, so if the gap to be caulked is wider than 1/8 inch, consider covering the area with molding or use foam sealant.

Pre-fill wide gaps.
Pack 3/4-inch or wider gaps with closed-cell foam backer strips, then complete the seal by caulking. For a big job, save money by buying a full-barrel gun and loading it with compound sold in bulk.

Use foam sealant.
Alternatively, apply foam sealant. Purchase the "non-expanding" type, which actually does expand some. Shake the can, hold it upside down, insert the tip into the opening, and squeeze.

1. Load a caulking gun.
To load a caulking gun, invert its plunger handle and pull the plunger all the way back. Some guns have a tab that you push before you can pull the plunger back. Insert the caulk tube, then push the plunger forward until it stops.

2. Cut the nozzle.
Snip off the nozzle's tip. The closer the cut is to the tip, the narrower the bead will be. With some tubes, you need to puncture the inside seal with a wire or a long nail.

3. Caulk an inside corner.
Between perpendicular surfaces, bisect the angle with the gun's nozzle to make a smooth concave bead. Hold the gun at a 45-degree angle and pull it toward you in a smooth, steady stroke, maintaining an even pressure on the trigger. You should not apply caulk at temperatures below 50°F.

Masking tape

4. Finish the line.

At the end of a stroke, lift the tip with a twist to catch caulk oozing from the nozzle, then quickly release the plunger. Remove any excess from the nozzle.

5. Smooth...

Smooth the bead of caulk using a moist fingertip or a moist, tightly wadded rag. Try to smooth it in one stroke, applying even pressure. This takes some practice.

...or, tape and caulk.

For a nearly perfect line, first press masking tape on each side of the joint. Caulk, wipe with your finger, and pull away the tape.

Caulk a flat surface.

Between flat surfaces, straddle the joint with the nozzle and pack it so that the caulk bulges out slightly.

Store used tubes.

Save partial tubes by sealing them with a nail or screw. Or invert the cut-off tip of the nozzle and stuff it into the opening.

Using squeeze tubes.

Toothpaste-style tubes are handy for tub and sink caulking and for minor touch-up jobs. Snip the tube's tip with a utility knife and squeeze. If you replace the tip's cap, you can likely reuse the tube several times.

PLUGGING AIR LEAKS

Usually you can feel any heat leaks that are caused by inadequate weather stripping or caulking. On a cool, windy day, systematically pass your hand around the perimeter of a door, window, or any openable part of your home. Do you feel a draft? If so you've located an air gap that needs to be sealed. Continue searching and you may find others.

Note that some types of heat loss, such as radiation through single-pane windows, seem to produce a draft but actually don't. If you have doubts about whether you've found a leak or the effects of radiation, hold a sheet of plastic food wrap over the opening. If the plastic moves, there's an air leak around the opening and you need weather stripping or caulk.

Seal a floor/wall joint.
Prior to installing finish flooring and baseboard, staple polyethylene sheeting over non-hardening sealant to close the joint between a floor and a wall.

Seal cable entrances.
Seal service-entrance cable penetrations with moldable non-hardening duct-sealing compound. Alternatively, use foam sealant.

Seal canopies.
Use silicone caulk (which resists hardening even when it gets hot) to seal fixture canopies up against the ceiling. This is necessary only on a ceiling directly below an attic.

Fill around a vent pipe.
In the attic, seal around vent pipes. First lay a generous bead of latex/silicone caulk. Cut a piece of plastic 4 or 5 inches wide and embed its bottom in the caulk as you wrap it around the pipe. Secure the top of the plastic with duct tape.

Use duct tape for ducts.
Believe it or not, duct tape has an official function—to seal ducts. Purchase professional-quality duct tape, which will last far longer than the cheaper variety. Clean and dry the area before application. Press the duct tape into place carefully so there are no folds and few wrinkles.

Caulk the ceiling drywall.
Up in the attic, you may need to push aside insulation to see the ceiling's drywall or plaster. Close the joint between the drywall and the wall's top plate with latex/silicone caulk.

Caulk vent fans.
Working from the attic above, seal a bathroom vent with silicone caulk. Where the fan's ductwork exits the house, check that the louvers are working smoothly so the opening shuts when the fan is not operating.

Fill around large pipes.
Another solution for large pipe gaps is foam weather stripping. Find a type of foam that just fills the gap, without too much cramming. Complete the seal and give it a finished look by installing a pipe flange; fill the back of the flange with latex/silicone caulk.

Caulk around electrical cable.
Seal all electrical penetrations with butyl, silicone, or latex/silicone caulk.

Caulk around pipes.
Smaller gaps around pipes can be filled with either silicone or latex/silicone caulk.

Cover an attic opening.
If an interior wall opens to the attic, cut pieces of 1× lumber or plywood to fit snugly. Caulk the pieces in place over the openings.

Caulk a house sill.
Although the weight of the house rests on it, a sill can leak air. Seal the wood sill/masonry foundation joint with long-lasting butyl, silicone, or latex/silicone caulk.

Use foam for large gaps.
Large gaps around pipes can be filled with foam sealant. To add further protection, cover the sealant with plastic, using staples and duct tape.

Seal moldings.
If there is a baseboard on an exterior wall, seal it with latex/silicone caulk. Smooth the caulk with a wet finger, then paint.

WEATHER-STRIPPING WINDOWS WITH SPRING METAL

Although not as easy to install as other types of weather stripping, bronze or aluminum spring metal makes the best seal, especially where the sash slides against the frame. Designed to fit inside window channels or frames, its out-of-harm's-way location helps it survive years of openings and closings. Plus, it is all but invisible. Press-in-place plastic V-strip seals just as well but is likely to pull away after repeated slidings of the sash.

Spring metal comes in kit form—with enough strips and nails to treat a typical window. Or you can buy it by the running foot in coil form. Get the type with predrilled holes.

This page show how to fit spring metal around double-hung and casement sashes, but you can easily adapt these techniques to suit other window types (see page 347). To provide a tight seal, be sure the metal compresses when the window shuts.

Many older double-hung windows have the top sash painted or even nailed shut. This seals it tightly but may make it difficult to clean the window. You may choose to loosen the top sash and install spring metal weather stripping.

Spring metal cuts easily with tin snips. Unroll it carefully to avoid kinking.

YOU'LL NEED...

TIME: 30 to 60 minutes per double-hung window.
SKILLS: Basic carpentry skills.
TOOLS: Screwdriver, utility knife, tin snips, hammer.

Sash channels.
Before cutting and fitting the new weather stripping, fully open the sash. For double-hung windows, fit strips to completely fill the sash when it is fully closed. Nail the strips with the open side facing the exterior. Drive all the nails, then pry the leaves apart to obtain a tight seal.

Bottom of lower sash.
Fasten a strip to the underside of the lower sash bottom rail. If the upper sash is not fixed in place, do the same to the top rail of the upper sash.

Where the sashes meet.
Where the sashes meet when closed, nail a strip to the bottom rail of the upper sash with the open side facing down. You may need to flatten the strip in order to make it fit.

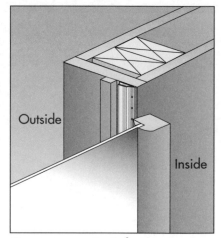

On a casement window.
On casement windows, nail strips to the frame. Install strips spring-side-in so sashes open freely.

WEATHER-STRIPPING WINDOWS WITH GASKETS

Rolled vinyl, foam, and other gasket-type weather stripping products work well for two surfaces that meet, rather than slide against, each other. When the window closes, they compress to seal air leaks. Some types are attached to metal strips. Bulbous types provide better seals. Stretch the gasket material slightly as you attach it and make sure there are no gaps at the corners. Some types are nailed or screwed in place, while others are self-adhesive.

Exterior installation provides a tighter seal and is less noticeable. Work carefully if you are on an upper floor (see page 389).

(see page 389)

YOU'LL NEED...

TIME: 30 minutes per window.
SKILLS: None required.
TOOLS: Scissors or utility knife, hammer.

Top and bottom sashes.
Seal the top and bottom sashes by attaching a strip to the outside of the upper sash top rail and the outside of the lower sash bottom rail. Make sure that the weather stripping seals completely at all points—but not so tightly as to make it difficult to close the sash.

Between the sashes.
Create a tight seal between two sashes by attaching a strip to the bottom of the upper sash. The strip should completely cover the gap, yet allow the window to close fully.

On a casement window.
On casement windows, attach strips to the sash or to the casing and the sill, whichever provides a tighter squeeze.

Foam for a double-hung window.
For double-hung windows, use foam only on the top and bottom of the sashes, or attach it to the frame at the top and bottom. Foam can't handle friction.

Foam for a casement window.
On metal casement or awning windows, stick press-in-place foam tape onto the frame. You will probably need to use the thinnest material available. Apply the foam to all four sides of the opening.

WEATHER-STRIPPING DOORS

Doors leak twice as much air as windows and are used more often, so it's worth checking your doors' weather stripping.

Close the door and look—first from the outside, then from the inside—for gaps in the weather stripping. When the wind is blowing, hold a sheet of plastic food wrap near the door on the inside to detect leaks. Check for crimped, flattened, or missing weather stripping at the top and sides. You might be able to adjust spring metal by prying lightly on the spring section. Other types probably will have to be replaced.

Feel along the threshold. Air infiltration means you need one of the bottom-of-the-door devices shown on page 423. And how's the door itself? Warping, an out-of-square frame, or deteriorated caulk around the edges give air a chance to make an end-run around even the tightest weather stripping. (See pages 360–363 for repairing doors.) Examine storm doors too. The felt gasket around the frame and the sweep or gasket at the bottom of the door may need replacement.

Check any interior doors that open to an attic, garage, basement, or other unheated space. Builders often don't bother to seal these big heat-losers at all. Worse yet, some contractors cut costs by installing hollow-core doors that have little insulation value. If that's the case at your house, your best bet would be to invest in the far greater thermal efficiency of a solid- or foam-core door.

YOU'LL NEED...
TIME: 30 minutes per door.
SKILLS: Basic skills.
TOOLS: Scissors, utility knife, tin snips, hacksaw, hammer.

Foam tape.
Foam tape installs easily but does not always do the trick. If the door closes tightly, the foam may tear off or prevent the door from latching. Use it when there is a gap between the door and the stop. Cut strips to length, peel off the backing, and press the foam in place on the inside of the stops.

Metal-and-vinyl strips.
This material is effective and durable, and can be used in conjunction with spring metal. Close the door. Cut pieces to fit using tin snips or a hacksaw. Press each piece so it just touches the door. Drive the screws provided into the center of each slot so you can adjust the position if needed.

Spring metal.
Cut spring metal carefully to fit, using tin snips. Nail each strip to the jamb inside the stop, with the open end facing the exterior. On the latch side, notch-cut the piece to fit tightly around the strike plate.

Between double doors.
If you have an older set of double (French) doors, apply foam tape to the inside of the half-round molding. If the molding is damaged, replace it. Alternatively, use insulated molding like the type shown above. Nail the molding to the face of the door that's usually the closed door.

SEALING UNDERNEATH DOORS

A door's bottom edge poses two weather-stripping problems. First the threshold has to withstand lots of traffic. Second any seal attached to the door must clear carpeting or other uneven floor spots within the arc that the door traverses.

The devices shown here solve these difficulties with varying degrees of effectiveness. If your door has a badly worn threshold, consider replacing it with a metal or wood threshold that has a replaceable gasket.

You'll Need...

TIME: 45 minutes to replace a threshold, 20 minutes to install a door sweep.
SKILLS: Basic carpentry skills.
TOOLS: Drill, screwdriver, tin snips, hammer, hacksaw, handsaw.

Door sweep.
This is the easiest solution, as long as the threshold is above the level of the carpeting or flooring. Close the door. Cut the sweep carefully to fit using tin snips or a hacksaw. Position the sweep so its gasket just touches the threshold. Drive screws into the centers of the slots so you can adjust the sweep up or down as needed.

Door shoe.
A shoe makes a durable seal and has a drip cap that sheds water away from the door. If there is not enough clearance under the door, you will have to remove the door and cut or plane its bottom (see pages 366–367).

Threshold with gasket.
A bulb threshold works like a door shoe (above right). It provides an excellent seal, but the door bottom must be cut accurately. Bevel the door bottom as shown, so it seals tighter as it closes. Replace the rubber bulb periodically.

Drip cap.
If water seeps under your door and into the house, nail a drip cap to its outside face.

Storm door sweep.
Don't forget storm doors. You can buy replacement rubber or plastic sweeps for these that install on the outside. You may need to drill pilot holes through the metal door before driving screws.

INSULATING AN ATTIC FLOOR

A poorly insulated attic sends heat right through the roof in cold weather and serves as a solar collector on hot, sunny days. The solution is to insulate the attic floor. If the space will be used only for storage, insulate the floor as shown on this page. If the space is finished or you intend to finish it later, insulate the ceiling and walls as shown on page 425.

First look for leaks that might damage insulation, and make sure you have adequate ventilation (see page 399). You may choose to cut summer heat buildup with an attic fan or whole-house fan (see pages 112–115).

If your attic has a floor, you have two options: pull up sections and work the insulation under, or hire a contractor to blow in loose-fill through holes bored into the floor. If the attic lacks a floor, bring up planks or plywood panels to set atop the joists. This will allow you to move around without stepping through the ceiling.

If there already is a vapor barrier, use unfaced materials so moisture doesn't get trapped between the two barriers. Be sure not to cover recessed light fixtures or exhaust fans; doing so could cause a fire. Instead, install baffles that keep the insulation about 3 inches away on all sides. **NOTE:** *Some insulating materials, such as fiberglass and mineral wool, are harmful to lungs and skin. Be sure to wear a painter's mask, gloves, and long sleeves.*

Allow for ventilation.
When placing batts or blankets, take care not to jam them against the roof; leave space at the eaves for airflow.

Cut pieces to fit tightly.
To cut a blanket or batt, place it on a piece of plywood with the facing side up. Use a piece of 2×4 as a guide and to compress the insulation. Cut with a utility knife. When you encounter bridging or other obstacles, cut for a snug fit.

You'll Need...
Time: 4 to 6 hours for an attic.
Skills: Basic skills for batts and blankets; intermediate skills for blowing in loose-fill insulation.
Tools: Utility knife, staple gun, rented blower for loose-fill.

Experts' Insight

Vapor Barriers
When warm air meets a cold surface, condensation results, producing moisture that can damage insulation as well as a house's structure. A properly installed vapor barrier—which may be the paper, foil, or plastic facing of the insulation or a sheet of plastic—keeps moisture from collecting.

In most areas, the vapor barrier should be placed on the side of the insulation that faces inside. In the Southeast, however, the vapor barrier should face the outside. Check with your building department if you are not sure.

Loose-fill insulation.
For loose-fill, nail baffles at the eaves. Or buy special plastic baffles that will fit between joists and ensure airflow. Insulation should cover the wall top plate but not obstruct airflow. Pour some insulation between joists, then level it with a board. Be sure you don't leave low spots or voids.

INSULATING A FINISHED ATTIC

*I*n a finished attic, the space above collar ties, coupled with gable louvers at the ends (see page 399), gets rid of winter condensation as well as summer heat. If you don't have collar ties, install them.

If your attic already is finished, you'll have to cut holes in the knee walls and the ceiling to gain access to insulate these areas. For patching walls and ceilings, see pages 560–567.

Install collar ties.
Add collar ties if your attic has none. Use 2×4s for spans of 6 feet or less; use 2×6s or larger for longer spans. Plan the height, and use a chalk line to mark the locations on the joists. Cut the ties to fit, then nail or screw them to the rafters. You may also choose to install knee walls (see below).

Staple blankets.
Staple insulation blankets to the collar ties, with the vapor barrier side facing correctly (see page 424). Continue down the roof and the knee wall to the floor.

Add to existing insulation.
If you're adding to existing insulation, cut away its stapled flange and push it to the back of the cavity. Slash the old vapor barrier. Place the new insulation over the old. Staple flanges to the rafters, with the vapor barrier facing correctly. Lap the insulation joints (as shown above) as you go.

Fill the knee-wall space.
In a finished attic, make openings to get at spaces above collar ties and behind knee and end walls. Lay loose-fill or blanket material between joists in the knee-wall space. Use a broom handle to push into "unreachable" spots.

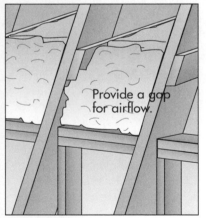

Fill the ceiling.
Don't insulate between the roof rafters in the knee-wall space. Place material between the wall studs, with the vapor barrier facing correctly. Pour loose-fill material between the rafters in the sloping part of the ceiling. Finish off with batts in the attic above the collar ties.

INSULATING A CRAWLSPACE

After attics, unheated crawlspaces are the next vital places to insulate. You have two options: drape batts or blankets around the perimeter walls, or suspend material between floor joists.

Draping the walls creates a sealed air chamber, which gains further insulation value. With some houses, however, you have no choice but to insulate between the floor joists.

Wrapping a crawlspace is a dirty but straightforward task—as long as you have enough space to move around. You'll need unfaced batts or blankets, 6-mil polyethylene sheeting to cover the ground, 1×2s and nails, and rocks or bricks. Wear goggles, gloves, knee pads, and protective clothing.

Close off unnecessary openings, but don't seal vents permanently; a crawlspace needs these for "breathing" in hot, muggy weather. A crawlspace must have at least two vents, located at opposite corners, that can be opened in the summer. A crawlspace that can't breathe turns into a giant moisture chamber in hot, humid weather.

WARNING: *If you live in an extremely cold region, such as Alaska, the Northern Plains, or northern Maine, don't use the technique explained on this page; it could cause frost heaving that might damage your foundation. Check with local contractors or your building code department for techniques used in your area.*

YOU'LL NEED...

TIME: 4 to 8 hours, depending on accessibility of the crawlspace.
SKILLS: Basic skills.
TOOLS: Utility knife, hammer, saw, drill, safety goggles.

1. Insulate between joists.
For walls perpendicular to joists, place insulation against the rim joist. Cut pieces oversize so they fit snugly. Next unroll enough insulation to overlap the sill plate and cascade down, covering the earth at the wall's base. Secure the insulation by nailing or screwing on a 1×2.

2. Insulate along the rim joists.
Where a wall is parallel to the joists, let the material drape over the rim joist, down the wall, and over 2 feet of the ground. Secure the insulation with a 1×2.

3. Add a vapor barrier.
After insulating the walls, roll up the batts and lay a polyethylene vapor barrier on the floor. Lap the joints by 6 inches. Attach the vapor barrier to the foundation with duct tape. Also tape the joints between the strips. Make sure you don't puncture the plastic.

4. Weight the insulation.
Weight the polyethylene and insulation with rocks or bricks. Don't use wood—it could rot or attract termites.

INSULATING A FLOOR

*F*loors built over crawlspaces, enclosed porches, or other unheated areas need insulation too. If the joists are covered underneath, your best bet is to have a contractor blow in loose-fill insulation (see pages 430–431). If you have open joists, install batts, blankets, or rigid planks, using one of the methods shown here.

Rigid insulation planks can be easily and quickly attached to the underside of joists if no obstacles, such as pipes or ducting, get in the way. However they don't provide as great an R-value. It's usually worthwhile to cut blankets or batts to fit around obstacles.

Unless you're simply adding another layer to existing insulation, get faced material and install it with the vapor barrier side facing the heated area. Foil facing works well here because it reflects heat back into living areas. Pay special attention to achieving good coverage at joists and headers around the floor's edges.

Cold slab floors present a special problem because you can't get material under them where it would do the most good. It may help to hire a contractor to wrap the outside of your foundation. Keep in mind you'll probably end up with a higher R-value by insulating the floor itself. To do this, glue down wood sleepers (see page 334), place rigid insulation planks between the sleepers, then lay new subflooring and finish flooring.

YOU'LL NEED...

TIME: 6 to 8 hours, depending on the number of obstacles, such as pipes, that you have to go around.
SKILLS: Basic skills.
TOOLS: Utility knife, straightedge, tin snips, stapler, hammer, saw.

Fold to seal the joist.
Start each insulation strip by folding it so that the insulation covers the rim joist. You can staple chicken wire to the joists to support the batts.

Seal around obstacles.
If you encounter a pipe or other obstacle, cut one or two slits in the insulation at the opening. Slip the insulation in place, then cut the insulation to fit snugly around the obstacle. Seal the slits with duct tape.

Support the insulation.
Or you can support the insulation with friction-fit rods that slip between the joists. Leave some airspace between the insulation and the floor.

Rigid foam.
To install rigid planks, apply adhesive to the bottoms of the joists and press the lightweight foam strips in place.

INSULATING DUCTWORK AND PIPES

As much as 20 percent of your heating and cooling energy can escape via ducts. If you insulate the ducts that run through your attic, garage, and other unheated areas, you can prevent most of this loss.

Purchase 2-inch-thick duct blankets or standard insulation, which cuts heat loss by about one-third more than 1-inch material. You'll also need several rolls of duct tape to seal all duct joints before you insulate. If your ducts don't have dampers to balance airflow, consider adding some prior to insulating.

YOU'LL NEED...

TIME: 2 to 4 hours, depending on access to the ducts or pipes.
SKILLS: Basic skills.
TOOLS: Utility knife or hacksaw.

EXPERTS' INSIGHT

INSULATING A PARTIALLY FINISHED ROOM

In a partially finished space, you may be depending on radiated heat from the ducts to keep things warm. In this situation, you would be better off to insulate the walls and forget about the ducts.

If the area receives only occasional use, consider installing a couple of basement registers and insulating the ducts and floor above.

Insulate around ducts.
For ducts that run between joists, cut blankets to fit and staple them to the floor, as shown. Install the insulation with the vapor barrier facing out. Avoid compressing the insulation—the fluffier it is, the better it works. Seal any joints with duct tape.

Seal the end.
Take special care to seal the end of a duct. Extend the wrapped insulation several inches beyond the end of the duct. Cut an insert with a flap, as shown above, so the insulation fits snugly into the opening and the flaps extend several inches in all directions. Fold and tape the flap as you would a package.

Wrap rectangular ducts.
For other ducts, wrap insulation around all sides, and seal the joints with tape. Install with the vapor barrier facing out and avoid compressing the insulation. Take the time to cut carefully around obstacles so the insulation seals tightly without compressing.

Insulate hot-water pipes.
Foam pipe insulation comes in various lengths. A lengthwise slit lets you fit the sleeve on the pipe. Cut pieces to length using a utility knife. Wrapping hot-water pipes saves energy costs. You can wrap cold-water pipes, too, to reduce condensation and prevent water damage to structures. At elbows, cut the pieces at 45 degrees for a mitered joint.

INSULATING BASEMENT WALLS

Basement walls are made of solid masonry, which readily transfers heat and cold from the outside. This makes adding insulation a standard part of a typical basement renovation. If your winters are mild, you can get by with an R-value of 7; in colder areas, aim for at least R-11.

To achieve these R-values with batts or blankets, frame out 2×3 or 2×4 stud walls over the masonry walls (see pages 284–290). Then staple the insulation between the studs of your new built-out walls. Cover the wall surface with drywall or paneling.

Rigid foam insulation planks allow you keep a new wall's thickness to a minimum by furring out the walls with 1× lumber (see pages 291–292).

Solve moisture problems before you begin. Seepage or leaks render insulating materials useless—even if your basement leaks or floods only once every 10 years. Don't worry about mild condensation; insulation and a vapor barrier will eliminate this.

Wall spaces above ground level are more in need of insulation, so pay particular attention there. You may choose to replace a window with glass block.

As with crawlspace walls, these insulating techniques could cause frost-heave problems in extremely cold regions. Check your local building codes for approved insulation procedures.

1. Staple insulation to studs.
If you choose fiberglass batt or blanket insulation, frame up new stud walls. Staple insulation between the studs. Don't skimp on the staples: Drive one every 10 or 12 inches.

2. Insulate the sill.
Above the sill, fit in small pieces of insulation. Allow the pieces to drape over the top of the stud wall for complete coverage. Secure the insulation with tape, staples, or wood strips (see page 426).

Mastic

1. To install rigid foam, make a grid and glue pieces to the wall.
For rigid foam insulation, attach a grid of 1×2s or 1×3s to the basement wall. Use construction adhesive to cement the planks to the walls between the furring strips. Measure as you go to ensure tight fits. Cover the framing and insulation with drywall.

Vapor barrier to inside   Joist

1×3

2. Insulate the sill.
Cut pieces of batts or blankets to fit snugly in the spaces over the top of the sill. Have the vapor barrier face inside.

INSULATING EXISTING EXTERIOR WALLS

An older wood-frame home may lack insulation in some or all of its exterior walls. The solution is to have a pro blow in insulation. This is a tedious and expensive process, but usually pays off in the long run. (However, adding insulation to a home with double-brick construction is seldom cost-effective.) Unless you choose liquid foam, you'll need a vapor barrier to protect the new insulation from condensation (see box, below right).

YOU'LL NEED...

TIME: Several days for an entire house.
SKILLS: Advanced insulation skills (often a job for a professional contractor).
TOOLS: Drill, tape measure, wall-refinishing tools, and specialized tools for blowing insulation into wall cavities.

1. Check the wall cavity.
Determine whether the wall cavities run unimpeded from the attic to the basement by dropping down a weighted string. If they do, you can pour in loose-fill insulation from the attic.

2. Identify the framing members.
Most wall cavities have headers, sills, and blocking, so you can remove exterior siding and bore a series of holes to gain access. To insulate an entire wall, all the framing members must be identified, and a hole must be drilled into every cavity.

EXPERTS' INSIGHT

IMPROVING EXISTING INSULATION

Existing insulation in an older home may have compressed to the point where it does little good. If the walls still feel cold after weather-stripping and sealing your home (pages 414–423), it may make economic sense to upgrade their R-value. Get several written bids that specify the R-values as well as the amounts of material needed. A properly insulated 2×4 wall should have a value of at least R-10.

Wall with no vapor barrier

Wall with vapor barrier

Provide a vapor barrier.
Without a vapor barrier, all insulation, except foam, will quickly turn into a soggy mess.

Unfortunately, it isn't feasible to get a continuous waterproof membrane into a finished wall. However, you can seal the wall's interior surface for the same effect. Caulk any cracks you find at the floor and ceiling and around doors or windows (see pages 416–417). Then apply at least two coats of waterproof oil- or alkyd-base paint, or use a paint especially formulated for this purpose.

3. Remove siding and drill holes.

If the siding is horizontal, remove strips at the top, under windows, and possibly at the 4-foot level, just under fire blocking. After peeling back the building paper, use a hole saw to bore holes into each cavity.

If the house has shingle siding, individual shingles can be easily removed and replaced. With other types of siding, it is common to drill holes with a hole saw and fill them later with the circular plug that was cut out by the hole saw.

4. Probe the wall.

Probe with a steel tape or a plumb bob to see if there are obstructions that might create uninsulated pockets. For a complete job, this probing should be done in every wall cavity.

5. Blow in insulation.

First blow material into the cavity to the level of the inlet hole, then flip the nozzle up to fill the space above.

6. Plug the holes.

After filling each cavity, insert a snap-in plug to seal the hole. Then apply building wrap or paper over the sheathing.

7. Replace the siding.

Finally replace siding materials. Use the same installation techniques described for siding repairs on pages 404–411.

INSULATING OUTSIDE FOUNDATION WALLS

Surprisingly the average basement accounts for 20 percent of a home's heat loss.

The best location for foundation insulation is along the outside of a masonry wall, where it can protect the masonry from damaging frost. The mass of the masonry acts to moderate the temperature swings of the outdoor air. The insulation keeps the wall warmer in summer, reducing condensation and basement humidity.

YOU'LL NEED...

TIME: 2 days for an entire house.
SKILLS: Basic excavating and carpentry skills.
TOOLS: Shovel, wire brush, hammer, pry bar, utility knife, square, wide putty knife, paintbrush, roller.

1. Remove siding and excavate.
Remove several bottom courses of siding (see pages 482 and 496). Save the siding for reinstallation. Excavate a trench around the foundation 2 feet below the sill and 2 feet wide. Place the excavated soil onto sheets of polyethylene.

2. Attach polystyrene insulation.
Fasten 1-inch-thick sheets of foam insulation to the foundation, using fender washers and masonry nails. Install L-shaped aluminum window flashing against the building sheathing and over the top edge of the foam.

3. Tape the joints.
Scratch the surface of the foam with a wire brush to give the protective coating a "tooth" to adhere to. Apply self-adhesive fiberglass drywall tape to all the joints and corners.

4. Stucco the surface.
Brush on fiberglass-reinforced latex coating or surface bonding cement. Cover an area from the flashing to several inches below the final ground level.

5. Lay sloping insulation.
Lay horizontal 2×8-foot sheets of foam so they slope away from the foundation at the rate of 1 inch per foot minimum. Replace the soil and grade the area so it slopes away from the building. Replace the bottom courses of siding. Plant grass seed or lay sod.

HEATING AND COOLING

GETTING TO KNOW YOUR HVAC SYSTEM

How's the climate in your home? Whether you feel too hot, too cold, or just right depends on the temperature and humidity of the air around you. Your home's air circulation system—whether it be forced-air, piped, or radiant—adds or removes heat. It may also control the humidity level by adding or removing moisture.

This chapter shows how heating and cooling systems work, how you can maintain and improve their efficiency, and what your choices are in new equipment. It also offers tips about what you can do to lower your expenses for gas, oil, or electricity.

As a homeowner, you should have a basic understanding of your system. Leafing through this chapter will help; however, because system technology varies, there is no substitute for consulting a pro.

These two pages identify and explain the three most common HVAC (heating, venting, and air-conditioning) systems. You may also have a heat pump (pages 444–445) or central air-conditioning (pages 452–453). Your heating plant may be a furnace (which heats air) or a boiler (which produces hot water or steam). Either is usually fired by gas or oil, but wood is also still used; see pages 440–451.

Though heating and cooling components vary enormously, all take advantage of heat's inherent tendency to move from a warmer object or space to a cooler one. This means you can couple a heat source, such as a burner, electric resistance element, or heat pump, with a heating plant, usually a furnace or boiler, to send heated air, water, or steam via a distribution network to a home's various rooms. After the medium gives off its heat, it then recirculates to the heating plant. A control unit, almost always a thermostat, maintains a preset temperature by switching the heating plant on and off.

FORCED-AIR SYSTEM

Ducted systems circulate air from a furnace to registers in each room via a network of ducts. Modern forced-air versions have a blower that pushes treated air through supply ducts and pulls it back through return ducts.

An older home may have a less-efficient gravity system, which works the same way but without a blower. Warm air rises from the furnace to the rooms, and cool air falls through the returns. Supply and return registers may be on the floors or in the walls.

Blower-driven forced-air heating systems have two advantages over steam and radiant systems: They can be easily adapted to centrally cool a home, and the system can be easily adapted to humidify the home.

Troubleshooting and maintenance tips for air furnace systems can be found on pages 436–439.

How the air moves.
In a typical forced-air system, a furnace, usually fired by gas or oil, heats the air inside. A blower, powered by an electric motor, sends air out of the furnace and into the main duct, called the plenum. Smaller supply ducts tap into the plenum and carry warm air to individual rooms via supply registers, which usually can be controlled by simple levers. A separate system of return ducts carries cool air back to the furnace.

Hot-Water or Steam Heat

In a piped system, water or steam distributes the heat. The heating plant, called a boiler, sends hot water or steam through supply lines to radiators in each room of the house.

In a hot-water system, warm water circulates up to the radiators, often (but not always) helped by a circulating pump. Cooler water flows back to the boiler via return lines. Heat rises and falls slowly, so the radiators maintain fairly even temperatures.

Most steam systems have only one pipe running to each radiator. Because steam rises, no circulation pump is needed. Steam radiators are usually either very hot or completely cold.

If your home has hot-water or steam heat, check pages 446–451 for more detailed information.

How the water circulates.
A hot-water system is "closed," meaning that the same water keeps circulating through the pipes, often without being changed for years. A steam boiler must have water added regularly, because steam dissipates into the rooms during heating.

Radiant Heat

Radiant heating warms the floor or ceiling in a room, silently providing even heat. Some systems use electrical cables; others circulate hot water through small-diameter tubing.

In most areas, electric radiant heat is expensive, and usually used only for added-on powder rooms and other small spaces.

Older hot-water radiant heat often consists of copper pipes run through concrete floors. This type tends to corrode and often needs to be completely replaced after a number of decades. Newer tubing is made of extremely durable polystyrene and can be attached under a wood floor or run under ceramic tiles.

If you have radiant heat, do not bore holes or break into the floor unless you are certain where the lines run.

Maintaining radiant heat.
In a radiant system, pipes or tubes usually run through or under the floor, so the heating takes up no wall or floor space in a room. The heat is wonderfully even and gentle; many people love the feel of a warm floor in the winter.

Radiant heat is easiest to install in the ceiling, but because this is less efficient, it should be done only in areas with mild winters.

Because the tubing or cables are buried, fixable problems are either at the electrical circuit panel or at the connections to the boiler.

Maintaining a Forced-Air System

A forced-air heating/cooling system completely recirculates the air in your home as many as three times every hour—a big job. Fortunately most components of a forced-air system are easy to take care of—once you know what they are and where they're located.

Begin by noting which registers supply treated hot air and which ones return cold air to the furnace (see anatomy drawing on page 434). Most rooms have at least one hot-air supply register. Supply registers usually have adjustable dampers that let you modulate the airflow or shut it off entirely.

Cold-air return registers typically are larger and less numerous. Many homes have only one per floor, located in a hallway or other central spot. Returns never have dampers, because shutting one off would partially suffocate the system.

Make sure registers aren't blocked by furniture, draperies, or carpeting. Supply registers must have unobstructed space above. You may choose to equip some registers with plastic diverters that channel air horizontally for more even heating distribution. Return registers must be open to air currents from all directions.

To trace the entire duct network, take a trip to your crawlspace or basement. The drawing below shows how ducts eventually connect to the furnace and how air moves within it.

While the blower is operating, feel the joints of all accessible ducts. Any leaks will decrease your system's efficiency. Seal joints using professional-quality duct tape, which remains durable even when exposed to heat. If a joint is widely parted, drill pilot holes and drive sheetmetal screws before taping.

In an older home, the ducts may be clogged with debris, or may contain mold or mildew that disperses into the air when the blower operates. Have a heating pro check for these possibilities.

Keeping Air Moving

Sizes and shapes may differ, but all forced-air furnaces work essentially like the one illustrated at right.

Return air passes through an air filter into a blower compartment. The blower then pushes air into a second compartment, where it's warmed by a heat source. This source might be electrical heating elements (see page 439), a gas- or oil-fired heat exchanger (see pages 440, 442), or a heat pump (see page 444). If you have central air-conditioning, a cooling coil in the supply duct above the heat source extracts heat from the moving air during hot months (see pages 452–453).

The heated or cooled air then moves into a plenum from which the supply ducts radiate to carry air to the various rooms.

Air enters this particular furnace at the bottom and exits at the top. Known as an upflow type, it's best suited to basement installations. Other types send the heated air downward or to the side.

Refrigerant lines

Plenum

Conditioned air

Return air duct

Heat source

Air filter

Cooling coil

Blower

REPLACING A FILTER

Blowing air from a furnace stirs up dust and perhaps pollen. A high-quality filter catches nearly all of these particles.

A neglected filter chokes airflow and makes the unit work harder, thus wasting energy. A severely clogged filter can cause a furnace to overheat and shut down.

Some filters can be cleaned, while others must be replaced. Inexpensive filters trap only larger particles. To keep your air even cleaner, purchase the highest-quality filter available for your furnace. Some types trap some mold and bacteria as well.

To effectively remove pollen, mold, and bacteria as well as nearly all dust, have a contractor install an electrostatic filter, which is typically attached near the plenum.

1. Open the door.
Most blower doors lift or swing open. On counterflow models, the door will be at the top of the furnace. Purchase an exact replacement filter made for your furnace make and model.

2. Replace the filter.
Many filters slide out. Look for dirt on or around the blower, too. Vacuum, if necessary. A hammock-type filter wraps around the base of the blower; it is also easy to replace.

OILING AND ADJUSTING BLOWERS

Make blower maintenance part of your seasonal tune-up schedule—and check out the unit whenever air seems to be moving faster or slower than usual.

Some blowers have direct-drive motors; others operate with an adjustable V-belt-and-pulley setup (shown at right). You needn't adjust the direct-drive type, but the V-belt type may need oil; check the manufacturer's instructions.

With either model, look for lubrication ports on the motor and on the blower pulley on belt-drive units, as shown at right. Lubricate at the beginning of each heating and cooling season.

An adjustable motor pulley lets you change the speed of a belt-drive model by loosening a setscrew and adjusting the distance between pulley faces.

Oil the ports.
If a motor has oil ports, they'll be at each end of the shaft. Also, check for lubrication points on the blower fan. With an oil can, squirt a few drops of SAE-10 nondetergent oil into these ports.

Adjust the belt.
Adjust the belt so it's loose without slipping; it should depress about 1 inch. Keep mounting bolts tight. Check the belt for fraying, cracks, and signs of wear. Keep a spare belt on hand.

BALANCING AN AIR SYSTEM

*I*f some rooms in your home are consistently too hot or cold, a simple balancing project may solve the problem. A forced-air system can be balanced by reducing the airflow to a room that is too warm. Warm air can then reach colder areas, typically those farthest from the furnace.

Partially closing registers in a hot room will cool the room off, but won't redirect the air. Instead, adjust dampers in the ductwork. Dampers are controlled by a handle or a locknut arrangement. You may find one at the point where each duct takes off from the furnace plenum. If your system lacks dampers, consider installing them.

Wait for a cold day to begin the procedure. If only one or two rooms have airflow problems, you might be tempted to adjust only one or two dampers. However you'll get better results by tuning the entire system.

1. Open the dampers.
To open a damper, loosen the locknut and turn the handle parallel to the duct. To identify which ducts serve each room, close them one at a time to determine which room isn't getting air. Label the dampers.

Open the registers in all the rooms, and open all the dampers in the ducts.

2. Tape thermometers in rooms.
Synchronize several thermometers by laying them together for 30 minutes and then noting any differences. Tape a thermometer on a wall in each room, 3 feet above the floor but not above a supply register.

Summer and winter settings.
If you have central cooling, you may have to rebalance the ducts every summer and winter. Mark seasonal settings on the ducts.

3. Adjust dampers.
Adjust dampers to the rooms, starting with the one where your home's thermostat is located.

4. Recheck the temperatures.
Note any increase in air delivery to other rooms. Recheck the temperatures and continue adjusting dampers until you achieve the balance you desire.

MAINTAINING AN ELECTRIC RESISTANCE FURNACE

To envision an electric-resistance furnace, think of a giant toaster with a fan blowing through it. As air pushed by the blower moves through the heating elements, it picks up warmth, then continues into the plenum and ducts to registers in each room.

Because no combustion occurs in an electric furnace, it doesn't require the flue or heat exchanger needed for gas and oil furnaces. Therefore maintenance is almost nil. Operating costs, however, usually run substantially higher for electric units.

Check the anatomy drawing at right. An air-circulation switch, often on the house thermostat but sometimes on the furnace, lets you run the blower continuously. Underneath, accessible through a removable cover, there may be fuses or breakers for each of the heating elements. A transformer steps up amperage to the high levels needed for heating. Relays turn the elements on or off according to signals from the thermostat.

The chart below lists the few things that can go wrong with electric-resistance furnaces and what you can do about them. Always shut off the furnace's main circuit breaker before removing the control or access panels. You'll find the breaker located next to the furnace or in your home's main service panel. Don't attempt to work on the heat elements—that's a job for a professional.

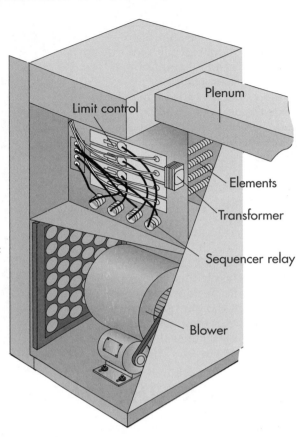

Limit control
Plenum
Elements
Transformer
Sequencer relay
Blower

TROUBLESHOOTING AN ELECTRIC FURNACE

Problem	Causes	Solutions
No heat	Furnace switch or main breaker open; thermostat set too low	Check the switch, the fuse or breakers, and the thermostat. If the blower runs but there's no heat, check the fuse or breaker block.
Cycles on and off too often	Clogged filter or failing blower, causing unit to overheat	Replace the filter. Oil and adjust the blower (see page 437).
Not enough heat	Improper thermostat setting; defective heating element; clogged filter or duct	Check the thermostat, then the fuse or breaker; replace a blown fuse or flip on the breaker. If the fuse blows or the breaker trips when you turn on the power, call a professional. Replace the filter.

Heater unit
Duct
Coil
Control

Heat pump.
If your home has a heat pump, it may have resistance-type duct heaters, like the one shown here. These mini-furnaces automatically pitch in when the temperature drops below what a heat pump can handle by itself. See pages 444–445 for more about heat pumps.

UNDERSTANDING A GAS FURNACE

Burners in a gas furnace are simple, but the controls needed to automatically turn the burners on and off and to provide safety are more complex.

A set of tubes called a manifold feeds the burners a mixture of gas and air, which is ignited by the pilot. The blower pushes air through the heat exchanger and up to the plenum. Flue gases exit past the exchanger up the flue and chimney.

For safety, a combination valve is connected to the pilot. If the pilot goes out, the valve shuts off the gas. A second safety—the limit switch in the plenum—turns off the gas if the plenum gets too hot; it also stops the blower when the temperature in the plenum drops to a certain level after the burners have shut down.

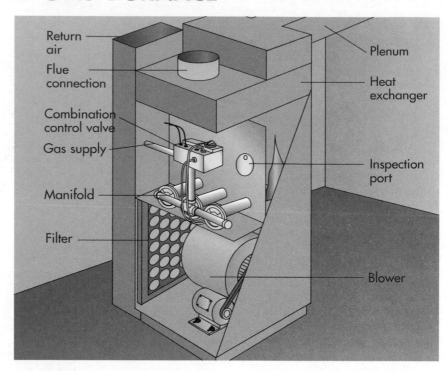

CHECKING THE FLUE AND CHIMNEY

Flues can develop leaks, releasing highly lethal carbon monoxide into your home's air. The same can happen if the chimney becomes partially clogged with debris or animal nests.

These dangers warrant an annual checkup. Inspect all the points illustrated at far right, paying special attention to the pipe between the furnace flue and the chimney. For more about chimneys and flues, see page 468.

For no charge, the gas company will probably inspect your flue and test for carbon monoxide. If they find a problem, they may shut off your furnace. Ask for an exact description of the problem, as well as the steps you should take to make your flue safe. If the problem cannot be solved by a simple step like sealing joints in the flue, call in a professional.

Test the draft.
Hold a candle to the opening in the top access panel with the furnace running. A flue leak will blow out the flame.

Possible sources of leaks.
Any of these problems may cause a carbon monoxide leak. If you suspect a damaged flue pipe, replace the pipe. An improperly installed flue pipe can also be the culprit. The flue must be the correct size; the slope and number of bends of the pipe are also factors.

LIGHTING A PILOT, REPLACING A THERMOCOUPLE

Some gas furnaces, boilers, and water heaters ignite with an electrical spark system. Most, however, depend on a gas pilot light for firing. When the unit fails to operate, it's usually because the pilot has gone out; you may need to replace the thermocouple or make adjustments.

To relight a pilot, follow the steps on the instruction plate attached to the furnace. With most, you'll find a gas cock with three settings—off, pilot, and on. Turn the cock to "off," wait a few minutes for residual gas to clear, then switch to the "pilot" setting. Hold a long lighted match or stick to the pilot, depress a reset button, and hold it down for a minute.

If the pilot stays lit, turn the cock to "on" and the burners will fire. If the pilot goes out again after you release the reset, repeat the entire procedure, holding the reset down a little longer.

If you can't get the pilot lighted after two or three tries, most likely you'll need to replace the thermocouple, a copper tube with a bulbous end that gets heated by the pilot flame.

To replace a thermocouple, shut off the gas inlet valve and remove the access cover so you can see the burners. Disconnect the thermocouple from the control by unscrewing a hold-down nut. At the other end, it may be held in place with a nut or it may simply pull out. Purchase two replacements of the same length (so you can have one on hand for the next replacement). When you install the replacement, take care not to kink the tube and make sure the bulbous end is touched by the pilot flame.

A weak or wavering pilot flame also may shut everything down. The flame should be blue, with the tip barely flecked by yellow. If the pilot flame doesn't fit this description, make sure that it isn't being buffeted by a draft. Then try cleaning out the opening of the pilot tube with a needle or nail.

TROUBLESHOOTING A GAS FURNACE

Problem	Causes	Solutions
No heat	Thermostat too low; switch, fuse, or circuit breaker open; gas shut off; pilot out	Check thermostat, switch, and fuse or breaker. Relight pilot.
Cycles too often	Usually a clogged filter or a blower problem	Replace filter. Oil and adjust blower.
Not enough heat	A clogged filter; burners may need cleaning	Replace filter. Have burners cleaned by a professional.
Blower runs constantly	Fan switch set for continuous circulation; limit control out of adjustment	Reset fan switch on furnace or adjust limit control (page 439).
Furnace squeaks or rumbles	Squealing: blower belt slipping or bearings need lubrication Rumbling with burners off: misadjusted pilot Rumbling with burners on: dirty burners	Oil blower and adjust belt (page 437). Adjust pilot (see above). Have burners cleaned by a professional.

UNDERSTANDING AN OIL FURNACE

Compared to gas and electric furnaces, an oil-fired forced-air heating plant has more components. It has the same filter-and-blower unit common to the other furnace types, but the heat producer in an oil furnace—its burner—includes a second motor/blower setup. This one combines oil with air, ignites the mixture with an electric spark, then blasts a torchlike flame into a fireproof compartment just below the heat exchanger.

Examine the drawing at right. The combustion air blower pulls in air through an adjustable shutter, mixes it with oil in an air tube, sets it afire with a pair of electrodes, and then forces it through a nozzle into the combustion chamber. A transformer steps up voltage to the electrodes. In some models, a primary safety control keeps an electric eye on the flame; if it fails to light, the safety shuts down the burner. Other types do the same job with a heat sensor in the flue pipe.

The motor on the combustion air blower also drives an oil pump. This pulls oil through lines from the fuel-oil tank. An automotive-type filter strains the fuel.

Despite this complexity, modern oil burners are reliable. They do, however, require annual tune-ups, which, if neglected, will add to your fuel-oil bills. The box at right lists the jobs that generally need to be completed before each heating season.

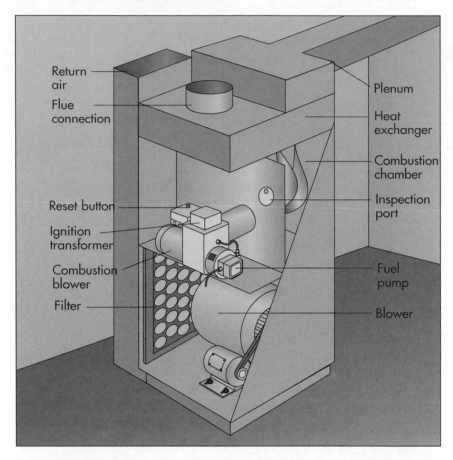

Return air

Flue connection

Reset button

Ignition transformer

Combustion blower

Filter

Plenum

Heat exchanger

Combustion chamber

Inspection port

Fuel pump

Blower

EXPERTS' INSIGHT

REGULAR MAINTENANCE FOR AN OIL BURNER

■ Clean or change the oil filter in the fuel line at least once a year. Some oil filters have a replaceable cartridge; basket types must be washed with kerosene. With either, make sure to install a new gasket when you reassemble the filter.

■ If your unit has a pump strainer, you should clean it annually. Soak it in kerosene and replace the gasket.

■ Clean the fan blades monthly with a long-handled brush.

■ Lubricate the burner motor every month or two, unless it's permanently lubricated (in which case you won't find lubrication ports, or the instruction plate will so indicate). Most require light oil. Look for instructions on the housing.

■ Check all flue connections annually (see page 440).

■ Get a professional tune-up at the start of the heating season. Insist that the service technician take instrument readings for combustion efficiency, smoke density, and draft. The technician also should check the firing system, clean the ignition electrodes, and clean or replace the combustion nozzle.

CHECKING SAFETY CONTROLS

If an oil burner shuts down, reset the safety switch and try again. If the burner kicks off again, shut off all power—the burner motor and ignition may be protected by separate fuses or breakers.

If your burner has an electric-eye primary safety, look for an access cover that lets you get to its photocell. Wipe the photocell with a clean rag or tissue to remove soot. Reassemble it, turn on the burner, and see if the furnace fires.

The second type of safety—a stack switch—mounts on the flue. Remove the screw holding the unit to the stack, slide it out, and wipe off the sensor.

Don't continually try to restart a balky oil burner. Unburned oil could accumulate in the combustion chamber and "flash back." If the furnace won't fire after three attempts, call for professional service.

Disconnect switches.
There may be one burner disconnect switch on the side of the furnace and another outside the furnace room. Switch them off before attempting any repairs.

Reset the safety switch.
If the primary safety or stack switch shuts off, wait 5 minutes, then press the reset lever or button. Combustion air blowers usually are protected by an overload device. Restart by pressing the reset button.

TROUBLESHOOTING BEFORE CALLING FOR SERVICE

Problem	Causes	Solutions
Burner doesn't run	Thermostat setting is too low; main switch, a circuit breaker, or fuse is open; motor may be overheated	Set the thermostat 5°F higher than usual. Check switches, breakers, and fuses. Oil motor. Press reset.
Burner runs but won't fire	Oil or spark is not getting to the unit; safeties are sooty	Make sure oil valves are open and there's oil in the tank—don't trust the gauge: dip a rod into it. Clean safeties.
Burner cycles too often	Clogged blower filter or other blower problems; improperly set limit control	Replace filter. Oil and adjust blower (see page 437). Check and adjust limit control.
Burner smokes or squeals	Combustion air blower motor needs oiling	Shut off the unit, let it cool, and fill the oil cups; check them again after the motor has run for an hour or so.
Chimney smokes	A cold flue causes this when the burner first fires; but if smoking persists, it's a sign of incomplete combustion, which means the unit is wasting fuel.	Call for service and request the instrument tests listed in the box on page 442. Don't attempt to adjust a burner yourself.

Understanding a Heat Pump

Of all heating components, a heat pump is the most complex. It is best understood as a reversible air-conditioner. Like an air-conditioner, it can lower indoor temperatures by removing heat from the air and expelling it outside; it's also capable of extracting heat from outside air and pumping it indoors.

To do its job, a heat pump—like all refrigeration devices—takes advantage of liquid's tendency to absorb heat as it expands and turns into a gas, giving off heat as it's compressed into a liquid (see anatomy diagrams at right).

A split-system heat pump (shown at right in the heating mode) uses two units, one outdoors and one indoors. In the outdoor unit, a fan moves air through a coil that absorbs heat. A compressor then superheats the vapor and sends it through refrigerant lines to a second coil in the furnace. There a blower pushes return air through the coil, warming the air and forcing it into the ducts. Meanwhile refrigerant travels back to the outdoor unit to begin another full cycle through the pump.

An automatic reversing valve reverses these flows. It has to be automatic because when outside air temperatures approach the freezing mark, heat pumps tend to freeze up. When this happens, a sensor activates the reversing valve and the unit defrosts itself.

In some heat pumps, the compressor, fan, coils, reversing valve, and blower are enclosed in a single outdoor cabinet, as shown at right. Only the system's main supply and return ducts penetrate exterior walls; there is no separate furnace.

Anatomy of a Heat Pump

COOLING MODE

Heat dissipated outdoors — Liquid → — Cool air distributed indoors

Outdoor coil — Hot gas — Warm gas — Indoor coil

HEATING MODE

Heat drawn from cool outdoor air — ← Liquid — Warm air distributed indoors

Outdoor coil — Warm gas — Hot gas — Indoor coil

Split-System Heat Pump

Outdoor unit — Reversing valve — Compressor
Fan
Coil
← Liquid
Vapor →
Air supply
Coil
Blower

Single-Unit Heat Pump

Reversing valve — Blower — Optional heating element
Coil — Supply →
Fan — ← Return
Accumulator
Compressor

OPERATING A HEAT PUMP

Heat pumps work well down to temperatures of about 15°F. If temps go below that, most units require a backup heating source, usually electric-resistance elements installed in the furnace, the ducts, or the pump cabinet. These units also take over for the pump while it's defrosting.

When a heat pump's defrost cycle runs continuously—or not at all—the backup system takes over, a shift you might not notice until your electric bill arrives. That's why it pays to familiarize yourself with what happens during a normal defrost cycle.

When the temperature hovers around freezing, frost forms on the outdoor coil. When this occurs, the reversing valve should activate to melt the ice. You may hear gurgling or even see steam rising from the outdoor unit.

Heavy ice accumulation means the unit isn't defrosting. No ice, or defrost cycles that last longer than 15 minutes, indicate that the pump is stuck in cooling mode.

For either condition, check the outdoor coil. Leaves, snow, or other matter may be cutting off airflow through the coil. Clear the obstruction and the system should return to normal operation.

If it doesn't return to normal and the coil remains coated with ice, the reversing switch may be stuck. Try freeing it by switching your house thermostat to the cooling mode. If the ice remains on the coil after an hour, flip the system selector switch to the "emergency heat" setting and call a heating contractor for service.

If all electrical power has been off for more than an hour at temperatures lower than 50°F, because of either a power outage or a tripped circuit breaker, do not attempt to restart a heat pump for at least 6 hours after the power has been restored. Instead, turn the system selector switch to "emergency heat," wait 6 hours, then return to the normal heat setting; turning the system switch to "off" doesn't shut off the heater. This time-delay gives the heating element in the compressor's oil crankcase time to warm up the system's lubricant and prevent valve damage.

The chart below identifies the most common maladies of heat pumps and what to do about them. As with other heating units, it's good to have a heat pump serviced annually.

TROUBLESHOOTING A HEAT PUMP SYSTEM

Problem	Causes	Solution
Pump does not run	No power to the unit or the thermostat is not calling for heat	Check the thermostat setting, the electrical disconnect switch, and the fuses or breakers in the circuit panel. Most pumps have a "reset" switch in the outdoor cabinet.
Short cycles	An obstruction blocking the outdoor coil; malfunctioning blower unit; clogged filter	Clear the outdoor coil (see above). Check the filter and blower unit (see page 437).
Long or frequent defrost cycles	A blocked outdoor coil could cause defrosting that lasts longer than 15 minutes or that occurs more than twice an hour.	See text above for symptoms and what to do.
Uneven heating	Heat pumps deliver a cooler flow of air than you may be used to. Also, indoor temperatures normally will drop 2° to 3°F when the outside temperature reaches the system's balance point differential. This is the point at which the backup heating kicks in.	Minimize airflow discomfort by carefully balancing the duct system (see page 438). To offset the balance point differential, you may have to raise the thermostat setting in colder weather.

MAINTAINING PIPED SYSTEMS

In many hot-water heating systems, the water temperature reaches 240°F, far above the 212°F needed to produce steam. Yet because the water travels slowly through pipes and loses heat along the way, hot-water radiators are less hot than steam radiators when the heat is on.

The main difference between the two is that hot-water systems are sealed, and contain only carefully controlled amounts of air in the radiation units, piping, and boiler. Steam systems, on the other hand, are open-ended and must "breathe."

This explains why you can often hear hissing radiators and banging pipes with a steam system. The steam has to push the air ahead of it up the riser (vertical) pipes and out the vents on each radiator.

Conversely, hot water has little air to impede its progress and circulates smoothly through the system, generally with nothing more than a few muffled thumps to let you know it's operating. You may also hear a circulating pump come on from time to time.

A hot-water system may have heavy radiators or more-compact convectors. However, because steam heat is so hot, it always uses heavy cast-iron radiators.

Steam boilers require regular monitoring because they must be continually filled to the proper level. Hot-water boilers call for less maintenance.

Steam system.
Most steam-heat piping systems employ a one-pipe distribution network like the one at left. A single pipe serves as both supply and return for each radiator. Steam rises from the boiler to the radiators, gives off its heat, and condenses to water. Then the condensate drops back down the same pipe to a return main. This feeds the boiler with water to be boiled for the next steam cycle. Some steam radiators have a second pipe for the returning condensed water.

Hot-water system.
Most hot-water systems use the two-pipe network shown at left. Water flows through radiation units and returns through separate pipes. An expansion tank serves as a cushion, allowing water pressure to increase and circulate more readily. Unlike steam radiators, hot-water units can be partially closed down to regulate the amount of water flowing through them, and therefore the heat.

In a "series loop" system (not shown), water flows from one radiation unit to the next in a chain; there are no mains. Turning off one radiator stops the flow of water to the other units.

TROUBLESHOOTING RADIATORS

Steam and water radiation units—old-fashioned upright radiators or newer upright or baseboard convectors—are simply pipes that dissipate heat. Their maintenance consists of making sure water or steam can flow through the pipes.

If a steam unit doesn't heat well, check its air vent. Liquids and gases can't get into a pipe that's full of air. See that it slopes toward the pipe (toward the return pipe in a two-pipe system); trapped water will keep it from heating up.

Steam radiators are difficult to regulate. Turning a valve to an in-between position won't modulate the heat; it just causes the unit to bang. What you need is an adjustable air vent, available from some plumbing suppliers. Decreasing the size of the vent's aperture slows the rate at which steam enters the radiator.

Hot-water radiators—especially the ones farthest from the boiler—should be bled every fall. You can adjust for heat simply by turning the inlet valve.

Stopping leaks.
If an inlet valve leaks, try tightening its packing nut. Then try tightening the nuts on either side of the valve. If that doesn't work, drain the system if you have hot water, or turn off the heat if you have steam. Disassemble and repack it as you would a faucet (page 130). Or replace the valve.

Bleed a hot-water unit.
If the upper portion of a hot-water radiator does not warm up, bleed it. Hold a rag or a small cup under the bleeder valve, and open it using a screwdriver, pliers, or a special key. Air or spluttering water will probably come out. When only water squirts out, close the valve.

Air vents for steam units.
If a radiator warms only slightly, but evenly, water may be trapped inside. Poke the airhole with a wire to clear it or replace the vent.

Slope and position.
Make sure a radiator is pitched toward the return pipe. In addition, remove obstructions like draperies or furniture. Radiators depend on air circulating freely around them. Use only radiator covers designed to aid circulation.

Maintaining a Steam Boiler

A steam boiler works like a giant tea kettle. A gas or oil burner heats water to the boiling point, sending steam to radiators.

Some boilers have an automatic feed, usually combined with the low-water cutoff, that supplies fresh "makeup" water when needed. With others, you must manually open and close an ordinary valve. Preventive maintenance includes checking controls monthly and occasionally flushing the boiler (see page 450).

To prolong boiler life and maximize efficiency, schedule an annual checkup in the spring just before you shut down the heating system. Rust thrives when the unit is idle. Ask about chemically treating the boiler water to reduce its oxygen content to prevent rusting.

If a gas pilot light won't stay lit, see page 441 for relighting it and replacing a thermocouple.

How it works.
Modern-day boilers are complex. The water doesn't simply rest inside a big kettle—that would take hours to heat up. Rather, water circulates around the heat source through a series of passages or tubes. Boilers also require controls to monitor and regulate their operation. These include a pressure gauge and regulator that shuts down the heat source when steam reaches a preset level, a pressure-relief valve that releases steam if the regulator fails, and a low-water cutoff that shuts down the system if the water level gets too low.

Water level.
Check the glass water-level gauge every 10 to 14 days during the heating season. If you have an automatic feed, inspect it monthly. Check when the boiler cycle is not firing. If the level is low, open the supply valve (not shown) until you reach the correct level.

Relief valve.
This is a safety device that protects against overheating. Test it once a year. With the boiler running, lift the lever for less than a second. It should release steam, then reseat tightly when you let go. If not, have it replaced.

Blow-off valve.
Open the blow-off valve (also called the low-water cutoff) once a month during heating season—more often if your water has lots of sediment. Turn down the thermostat, open the valve, and allow water to run until it's clear of sediment and debris. Be careful because the water will be hot.

TROUBLESHOOTING A STEAM BOILER

If a boiler goes cold, check to be sure its main switch hasn't been inadvertently turned off, then look for a blown fuse or tripped circuit breaker at the electrical circuit panel. Also try raising the thermostat setting and see that the thermostat is working.

If the boiler's burner unit is getting power, check the gauge glass to see if the boiler has enough water. When the water level drops below a certain point, the low-water cutoff turns off the burner or the electric heating elements; otherwise heat would "cook" the tank.

You can easily add water to a boiler—but first examine the return lines for leakage. Most steam systems gradually lose water through evaporation, but a big

return leak will trip the low-water cutoff after just a couple of heating cycles. (Because supply lines carry only steam under relatively low pressure, they rarely develop leaks.)

If you have a leak in a supply or return, call a plumber, not a heating contractor. One of the techniques on page 128 might allow you to run the system until help arrives.

When you do add water to a boiler, be certain that you don't overfill it. Steam systems depend on an airspace above the water line, called a chest, where steam builds up a head. If you flood the chest, water could back up the return lines or trip the relief valve—both messy situations.

If your boiler has an automatic water-feeding device, you won't notice any problems with the water level; the automatic feed will make up any shortage with each heating cycle. This means that a leak could go unnoticed for quite some time. Also constantly introducing fresh, cold water to the system will add to fuel and water bills. This is why you should shut off the feed every so often—most systems have valves or bypass piping for that purpose—and keep an eye on the water level for a few days.

Remember to flush the automatic feed at the intervals recommended by the manufacturer. A feed that gets stuck open could flood the boiler.

TROUBLESHOOTING BEFORE CALLING FOR SERVICE

Problem	Causes	Solutions
No heat	No power to the unit; no water; burner problems	Check the thermostat, switches, fuses or breakers, and the water level. Boiler burners differ little from those on furnaces (see pages 440–443).
Poor heat	Rust and scale in a boiler, constricting passages and reducing efficiency; buildup on heating surfaces of soot from combustion	Flush the boiler (see page 450). Cleaning the heating surfaces is a job for a professional.
Chronically low water level	Leaking return lines or, more serious, a leak within the boiler itself	For return-line leaks, see the main text above. Boiler leaks require major repairs or may mean you need to buy a new unit.
Clouded gauge glass	Usually the boiler needs flushing, but sometimes the glass itself needs cleaning	Flush boiler (see page 450). To clean gauge glass, turn off boiler, close valves, loosen nuts above and below glass, lift up the glass, pull it out, and clean it with a bottle brush.
Noisy pipes	Probably water trapped in return lines or in the return main	Check the pitch of all returns—they must slope back toward the boiler. Adjust the slant, if necessary, with new pipe hangers.

MAINTAINING A HOT-WATER BOILER

Hot-water controls typically include a combination gauge, often called an altitude gauge, that lets you keep an eye on both water temperature and pressure. It also lets you know when the boiler needs water or is malfunctioning. With some systems, a pressure-reducing valve takes care of the water problem automatically.

Hot-water systems depend on an expansion tank that must be properly charged with air to prevent the water from boiling. With newer installations you'll find this tank hung from the ceiling near the boiler, as in the drawing at right. In older homes it may be located in the attic.

Newer expansion tanks include a purge valve that simultaneously releases water and lets in air. Older versions have a gauge glass, like the one on a steam boiler.

If your system is a forced-water (hydronic) system, look for one or more motor-driven pumps—called circulators—on return lines near the boiler. Some circulator motors are lubricated permanently and do not need maintenance. Others require a few drops of light oil annually. Read the instruction plate attached to the motor, however, because overboiling also causes problems.

Systems that have more than one circulator may be zoned to independently control the temperatures in different areas of your house. Zoned systems have low-voltage, motor-driven zone valves on the supply lines. Each valve obeys orders from its own thermostat. These require no regular maintenance, but they can fail occasionally (see the chart on page 451).

If the pilot light won't stay lit, see page 441 for relighting it and for replacing a thermocouple.

EXPERTS' INSIGHT

FLUSHING THE SYSTEM

Flush a steam boiler if the water in the gauge glass is rusty and flushing through the blow-off valve doesn't clear it. Flush a hot-water boiler if you need to work on a radiator or a pipe.

To do this, shut off the power and automatic feed, if you have one. Open vents or bleeder valves in the highest radiators. Attach hoses to the boiler drain and the return drain, open them, and let the water run out. Shut the drains, refill the boiler, and drain it again. Repeat the process until the water in the gauge is clear. For a hot-water system, you'll need to bleed all the radiators.

Combination gauge.
A combination gauge on the boiler has three indicators. The moving pointer shows actual pressure; the fixed pointer, the minimum pressure. If the moving pointer drops below the minimum, the system needs water. The lower temperature gauge shows water temperature. Maximum boiler water temperature is set by moving a pointer along the sliding scale of an aquastat (shown above right). Don't tamper with an aquastat setting.

Pressure-reducing valve.
This safety device automatically maintains the correct water pressure. To be sure it's doing its job, check the combination gauge and call for repairs, if necessary. If there's no pressure-reducing valve, you can manually feed the boiler by opening the feed water valve and closing it again when pressure reaches 12 pounds per square inch (psi). High water consumption means there's a leak in the supply or return piping or in the boiler itself.

TROUBLESHOOTING A HOT-WATER BOILER

Despite their complexity, hot-water boilers provide trouble-free service for years. When a problem does develop, it is usually with the expansion tank or a circulator, not the boiler itself.

Get to know your boiler and all the controls and valves. Especially in an older home, these may be complicated. If necessary call in a heating expert to explain it, and label all the valves.

Water spurting from a pressure-relief valve means that there's not enough air in the tank. The tank has filled with water, which expands as it heats up and trips the safety. Check this by touching the tank when the system is

heating. Normally the bottom half will feel hotter than the top; if the top seems hot also, it means the tank has filled with water and must be bled.

With most tanks, you'll need to first let the system cool. Then attach a hose to the tank's purge valve and run off two or three buckets of water. The valve lets in air at the same time. An older tank might have an ordinary valve rather than the purge type. With these, first close a second valve in the line between the tank and boiler, and then completely drain the tank.

After bleeding the tank, return all valves to their normal settings

and start the boiler. Let it run for about an hour, then check the system's pressure on the combination gauge.

When a circulator fails, its motor may continue to run. This happens because the motor and pump are connected by a spring-loaded coupling designed to break if the pump jams. However, the system will not heat properly. Usually the broken coupling makes a racket. A leaking circulator means the pump seal must be replaced. Call a service technician for all repairs to a circulator.

TROUBLESHOOTING BEFORE CALLING FOR SERVICE

Problem	Causes	Solutions
No heat	No power to the boiler; low water level; burner problems	Raise the thermostat. Check the switches, fuses, circuit breakers, and water level. Troubleshoot the burner's safety controls.
Poor heat	A sudden change usually means too much or too little water; a gradual change results from deposits in the boiler or on the heat exchanger	Check the combination gauge, then the expansion tank. If the problem developed slowly, try flushing the boiler, then call a professional for a tune-up.
Leaks	The circulator; pressure-relief valve; piping; or, more rarely, boiler tank	Is water coming from the pressure-reducing valve, underside of a circulator, or supply or return pipes? Water may travel quite a distance from a leak, but always in a downward direction. Consider repairing pipes yourself (see pages 128–129), or call a plumber for service.
Only some radiators heat up	Suspect trapped air, especially in units far from the boiler. If an entire zone is cold, the problem lies with a zone valve or its circulator.	Bleed air from the cool units. Check the circulator. If a zone valve is stuck, you'll feel heat in the pipe up to the valve but not beyond.
Clanging pipes	A sudden racket usually means a circulator has gone bad. Chronic banging noises may be the result of improperly pitched return lines.	Check the circulator. For banging, use a level to check the slope of all return lines (see page 447).

MAINTAINING A CENTRAL AIR-CONDITIONER

You've probably noticed that degree for degree, cooling consumes far more energy than heating. Why?

The answer lies in the nature of the cooling process. The cooling unit must absorb heat from the air—a big task in itself. It also has to reduce humidity to a more comfortable level. It does this by overchilling the air, then pushing controlled amounts of warm, humid air through the cooling coil, causing moisture to form on the coil. This moisture is carried away through a condensate drain.

What's more, cool air weighs more than warm air, so, unlike heat, it doesn't tend to rise of its own accord. The result: First you pay dearly to lower the temperature and humidity of the air, then you need additional energy to move the air around.

Any inefficiency in a room air-conditioner or a central system just compounds the already heavy electrical load that it pulls. To minimize this energy draw, keep your home's cooling equipment in top operating order. These pages show you how.

Begin by familiarizing yourself with the two main components of a cooling system. One of these is the condensing unit, in which refrigerant is condensed into a liquid. You'll always find this component located outdoors, where it can release heat (and most of the system's noise) to the outdoor air.

The condensing unit sends the now-cool refrigerant to an evaporator coil inside the house. Here, a blower moves air through the coil to cool and dehumidify it. If your home has a central system hooked to a forced-air heating system, the evaporator coil is located in the furnace plenum, as illustrated below and on page 524. In this case, the conditioned air is moved into the house by the furnace blower.

Room air-conditioning units house all their parts in a single, two-compartment cabinet (see page 454). Heat pumps, which are essentially two-way air-conditioners, have additional components (see pages 444–445).

If you have an older home with piped or radiant heating, some new techniques allow installers to add central air by snaking small-diameter ducts through walls and ceilings. The resulting system is a little noisy but cools effectively.

How it works.

To trace the circuits of heat and cold through a whole-house air-conditioning system, study the drawing at right. Outdoors a compressor and condenser coil "make cold" by pressurizing refrigerant gas, which loses heat as it turns into a liquid. The coil, a network of tubing and fins, transfers the heat to the outdoor air pulled through it by a fan. Cool refrigerant flows through tubing to the evaporator coil, where the refrigerant absorbs heat from air pushed through it by the furnace blower. Cool, dry air then moves into the plenum. Meanwhile water that condensed from the air in the plenum runs down a condensate drain. Finally the refrigerant, a hot gas once again, returns through another line to the condensing unit.

Condenser coil

Fan

Compressor

Plenum

Refrigerant lines

Evaporator coil

Condensate drain

Blower

TROUBLESHOOTING A CENTRAL AIR-CONDITIONER

It's cost-effective to schedule a tune-up at the start of every cooling season. For example, some of the refrigerant may have leaked out, which can gradually diminish your system's efficiency. When anything goes wrong with a central air-conditioner, call a service contractor.

You can forestall repairs by following these maintenance procedures once a month during the cooling season. The condenser coils resemble an automobile radiator, with loops of tubing laced through a honeycomb of aluminum fins. Leaves, debris, or even a heavy accumulation of household dust on these fins chokes off the airflow upon which cooling systems depend.

When you clean the fins, treat them gingerly; they bend easily. Sharp tools may puncture the relatively soft copper tubing.

Don't neglect your furnace blower unit, either. Moving cool, heavy air strains the belts and bearings. To learn about keeping blowers working, see page 437.

Clean regularly.
Keep the condensing unit clear so air can flow freely. First shut off power and turn up the thermostat. Remove the grille and any housing, and brush away leaves and dust. Cover the fan and electrical parts with plastic to keep them dry. Hose the coils and fins clean. Keep shrubs pruned back.

Check the drain.
During humid weather, check the condensate drain to be sure that it's carrying off excess moisture. If water puddles under the coils, the drain line is probably clogged. If it is clogged, disconnect the line and flush it with a hose. Then pour in a little household bleach, and reattach the line.

Change the filter.
A clogged filter can shut down a unit. Change filters several times per season. Never run a system without a filter.

TROUBLESHOOTING BEFORE CALLING FOR SERVICE

Problem	Causes	Solutions
System not running	Incorrect thermostat setting; no power to the unit	Be sure the room temperature is above the thermostat setting. Check circuit breakers and main power switch.
System runs but doesn't cool	May need refrigerant; airflow problems	Check for a clogged filter or malfunctioning blower. Look for blockages at the condensing unit. Low refrigerant must be recharged (replenished) by a professional.
System cycles too often	May indicate airflow problems; defective thermostat	Check the condensing unit's airflow, then the filter and blower. Check the thermostat.
Uneven cooling	If some rooms are too cool and others too warm, the duct system needs balancing.	To balance an air system, see page 438. If the house doesn't cool sufficiently, the unit may be undersized.

MAINTAINING A ROOM AIR-CONDITIONER

Most room air-conditioners are permanently lubricated. Routine upkeep consists only of keeping filters and coils clean.

When a unit refuses to run, make sure its filter is clean and that the power cord is plugged in. Check the main service panel for a blown fuse or tripped circuit breaker. Wait 5 minutes before you restart a room air-conditioner after it turns off, so that built-up heat can dissipate first.

If the unit cycles on or off too often or otherwise runs erratically, suspect thermostat problems. Often this means that the thermostat sensor has been knocked out of position. The sensor should be near the coil, but not touching it. Adjust it by carefully bending the wire.

If you hear a gurgling noise, or if water drips from the front panel, shut off the power and check with a level to make sure the cabinet's outer section slopes toward its condensate drain.

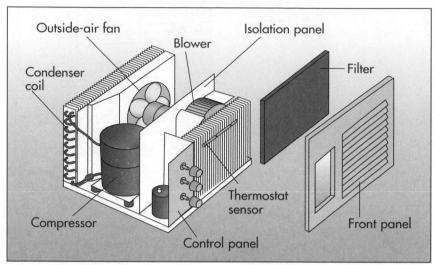

How it works.

A window-installed room air-conditioner has all the same components of a central system, but it's scaled down to fit into a two-section enclosure.

The unit's smaller inside cell includes a blower, evaporator coil, and thermostat sensor that reads the temperature of air coming into the evaporator coil. The thermostat is located behind the control panel. A removable front panel covers everything and often holds the filter as well.

An isolation panel separates the components that are inside and those that are outside the window. The panel may have a shutter you adjust from the control panel to bring in outside air.

In the outside portion of the unit, a fan moves air through a condenser coil, where the refrigerant is liquefied and sent to the evaporator coil.

Clean or replace the filter.

Turn off the unit and remove or tilt back the cover to get at the filter. Some types of filters need to be vacuumed; others should be washed or replaced. Clean or change the filter every two to three weeks during the cooling season.

Check the condenser coil.

Every month, check the condenser coil and the intake vents for obstructions, such as leaves or dirt. Hose out this part of the unit every spring.

Check the drain outlet.

Also check the condensate drain outlet. If it's plugged up or the unit is not properly pitched away from the house, condensation can't run out.

USING AN EVAPORATIVE COOLER

*I*n many areas summer heat is associated with high humidity. The usual solution is a refrigerant-charged air-conditioner that wrings both heat and humidity from the air—at a high cost in electricity.

Some regions suffer from too-low humidity. In these areas, humidity can be traded for cooling through the simple phenomenon of evaporative cooling, and at much lower cost.

Nature's equivalent to a man-made evaporative cooler is a thunderstorm on a hot day. We all have felt the dramatic drop in temperature that occurs after the rain stops. The cooling is due not to the rain itself but to water evaporation after the storm is over.

An evaporative cooler consists of a water reservoir, a water-soaked fibrous pad, and a blower that pulls air through the wet pad.

The blower draws in hot, dry air from outside and discharges the cooled air into the house. Leaving a window open in the room to be cooled allows the cooled air to flow through the room on its way outside.

Depending on the size required, evaporative coolers can be installed on the roof, on the ground, in a wall, or in a window.

When the water evaporates from the cooling pad, any mineral content in the water is left behind on the pad. These mineral deposits build up rapidly in regions that have hard water. Check the pads once each month. Some pads can be demineralized by soaking them in a commercial lime remover; others must be replaced.

EXPERTS' INSIGHT

WHAT'S THE RIGHT SIZE?

Evaporative coolers are sized by cubic feet of air they move per minute (cfm). Here's how to find the size unit you need.

Compute the volume of your home's conditioned space in cubic feet; for example, 8×24×40 feet equals 7,680 cubic feet. In the chart at right, find the location nearest you and the recommended minutes per air change. For example, Phoenix, AZ—2 minutes. Divide volume by minutes to find cooler cfm; for example: 7,680 cubic feet ÷ 2 minutes equals 3,840 cfm unit. For an uninsulated home, multiply by 2; highly insulated, divide by 2.

RECOMMENDED MINUTES PER AIR CHANGE

State, City	Temp. Drop (°F)	Minutes per Air Change
AL, Birmingham	18	NR
AZ, Phoenix	30	2
AR, Little Rock	18	NR
CA, Los Angeles	18	2
CO, Denver	27	4
GA, Atlanta	16	NR
ID, Boise	25	4
KS, Topeka	20	3
MT, Great Falls	25	NR
NE, North Platte	22	3
NV, Las Vegas	34	3
NM, Albuquerque	28	3
ND, Bismarck	22	3
OK, Tulsa	22	1.3
SD, Rapid City	23	3
TX, Dallas	22	2
UT, Salt Lake City	28	4
WY, Casper	27	4

NR = not recommended due to high ambient air humidity.

Installing a Programmable Thermostat

Programming a heating and cooling system often results in a sizable reduction in energy bills. Generally the greater the spread in degrees between the "home" and "away" (or day and night) settings—called the setback—the more energy savings you'll realize. The exception is the water heater. Water heats slowly and may require an hour or more to raise the temperature back up again.

Timed thermostats include a 24-hour clock. You select the beginning and ending times for the setback period, then forget about it. Another type uses a photocell to switch from one setting to another at dusk and dawn.

Keep the thermostat away from drafts or heat sources such as lamps, and locate it well away from any heat ducts.

Adjusting the setback may require experimentation. Begin by trying a setting 10°F lower or higher than your normal heating and cooling levels. If the house cools down or warms up too much, decrease the setback to 8°F Also adjust the timings on the setback cycle to accommodate your schedule.

If your home has a heat pump, consult your heating contractor before buying a timed thermostat. Using a programmable thermostat with a heat pump may actually add to your utility bills.

You'll Need...

Time: 10 to 20 minutes.
Skills: Basic skills.
Tools: Level, screwdriver, wire stripper.

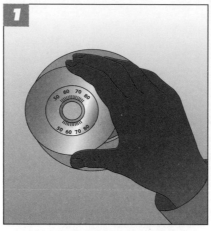

1. Detach the old thermostat.
Shut off the furnace or boiler and the electricity. Remove the cover plate and the dial, unscrew the mounting screws, and pull out the thermostat. Wrap the wires around a pencil so they can't fall back into the wall. Label the wires and sketch a diagram as to which terminals they were connected to.

2. Level and mount the plate.
Thread the wires through the access hole in the new unit's mounting plate, and make sure that the unit can press flush against the wall. Check for level and drive mounting screws. If the screws encounter only drywall, install plastic anchors.

3. Connect the wires.
Hook the wires to the appropriate terminals, using your labels as guides; wires generally are color-coded. After the wires are connected, gently push any excess wire back into the wall.

4. Attach the cover and operate.
Attach the cover to the back plate. Turn on the electricity and the furnace; then program the unit. Fine-tune settings over a period of a few weeks.

TILING

PLANNING YOUR TILING PROJECT

Good architectural design often goes unnoticed. A well-proportioned house or intelligently laid-out kitchen simply has a natural rightness about it. In the same way, instead of shouting for attention, a well-designed tile installation should just fit in. When a surfacing material jumps out at you, the design probably has failed.

The age of your house, the decorating style you seek to capture, and your budget all affect the design you choose. Books, magazines, and tile brochures are probably the best sources of ideas. However be sure the types and patterns of tile that you find attractive suit your space.

Proportion tile to room size.
As a general rule, tile size should be proportional to the size of the room. That is, small tiles generally work best in small rooms and large tiles look better in large rooms. Larger tiles seem less large when used on horizontal surfaces. Use larger tiles on lower surfaces; wall tiles or countertop tiles that are bigger than the floor tiles tend to make a room top-heavy.

Plan for comfort as well as style.
Radiant heating systems in which heated water passes through tubing embedded in or under the floor surface are becoming increasingly popular. Tile is a great choice for the finish surface on a radiant floor. Because the tubing usually is embedded in concrete, the concrete pad can be used as an ideal setting bed for tile. Also tile is a highly conductive material that transmits heat quickly and efficiently. If you are tiling a new addition or need to improve heating in a room, consider incorporating a radiant heating system into the design.

EXPERTS' INSIGHT

DESIGNING WITH COLOR

With so many stunning tile colors readily available, it's tempting to wield a broad brush and let the color fly. But because today's fashionable color is often tomorrow's eyesore, white and almond tend to be the tones of choice for most homeowners. These light neutral tones help brighten up rooms and can coexist with almost any other colors as your decorating schemes change. But many people think too much white or off-white is monotonous. Accent and border colors often cancel out this impression. In rooms with plenty of windows, consider using darker tiles to offset the ambient lighting.

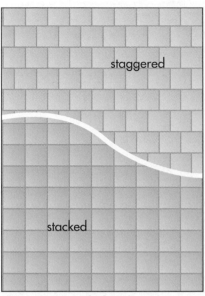

Stagger or stack the tile.
Area tiles usually are installed in a grid pattern or a staggered pattern. A stacked pattern is the easiest to install, and the clean straight lines appeal to many people. Although they require careful alignment, staggered joints have a pleasingly retro look.

Make the most of one color.
Using only one color of tile does not have to result in a plain-looking installation. Use tiles of different sizes to add a level of contrast. Consider different grout colors and grout joint sizes. Or, use tiles with only small variations in color.

Consider herringbone.
Plain rectangular tiles gain a new dimension when installed in a herringbone pattern. As a variation, wrap a small square tile with rectangular tiles.

Mix shapes with colors.
Manufacturers offer tiles purposely sized to allow for mixing different shapes into a coherent whole. You can add further interest with this approach by using two or more colors as well.

Define your space.
Borders help define the perimeters of a tile installation and can add a whole new level of interest to the surface. Here, variously colored and sized tiles create a border surrounding a field of tiles installed diagonally.

SELECTING THE RIGHT TILE FOR THE JOB

Although simplicity is part of the universal appeal of ceramic tile (it is essentially a thin a slab of baked clay), don't assume that just any tile will suit your project. You'll have to consider several factors as you select the right tile for the job: The material from which the tile is made (ceramic tile is made from clay; some tiles do not use clay at all but are actually slabs of stone milled into regular shapes), the degree of firing, the type of glaze, and the shape of the tile.

If you are planning several tiling projects for your home, you may want to contact one of the associations created by tile manufacturers, designers, retailers, and installation contractors. These groups have developed standards and acceptable practices relating to tile and tile installations.

The American National Standards Institute (ANSI) has prepared a list of minimal standards that are followed by all professionals in the industry. The Tile Council of America (TCA) publishes the inexpensive annual *Handbook for Ceramic Tile Installation,* which sets forth the ANSI standards. Contact the TCA at P.O. Box 1787, Clemson, SC 29633 or at www.tileusa.com/ publication_main.htm.

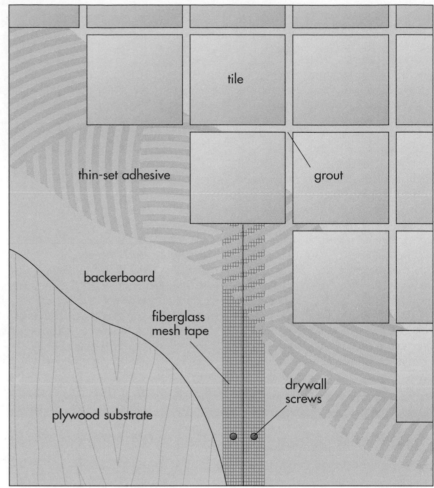

Plan out a typical installation.
Installing tile is a bit like making a sandwich: You proceed one layer at a time. The substrate, often plywood, is the layer in direct contact with the framing (studs for a wall installation or joists for a floor installation). Backerboard serves as the setting bed for the tiles themselves. Tiles form the outer layer. Adhesive is used to bond each layer.

TILE INSTALLATION CHECKLIST

The ANSI standards cover proper materials and installations for just about any type of tile job you can imagine. Use this simple checklist as a design and shopping guide.

Type of Tile
☐ glazed wall tile
☐ glazed floor tile
☐ ceramic mosaic tile
☐ paver or quarry tile
☐ natural stone

Location of Installation
☐ always dry or limited water exposure
☐ frequently wet
☐ interior
☐ exterior
☐ subject to freezing

Special Requirements
☐ fire resistant
☐ stain resistant
☐ crack resistant
☐ color
☐ heavy use

WATER ABSORPTION

Clay absorbs water, and water can cause cracks in tiles and create damage beneath the surface. Ceramic tiles that have been kiln-dried longer and at higher temperatures absorb less water, but they also cost more. So it makes sense to choose tiles precisely rated for the protection you need.

Tile Rating	Best Uses
Nonvitreous	This tile typically is used for decorative purposes only. It is intended for use indoors, in dry locations, such as a fireplace surround or a decorative frieze in a dining room
Semivitreous	This type of tile is used indoors in dry to occasionally wet locations, such as a kitchen wall or behind a serving area in a dining room.
Vitreous	This multipurpose tile is used indoors or outdoors or in wet or dry locations for anything from bathroom floors or walls to a patio surface.
Impervious	Such tile generally is used only in hospitals, restaurants, and other commercial locations where the ability to thoroughly clean is important.

Choose a glaze.
A glaze is a protective and decorative coating, often colored, that is fired onto the surface of tiles. Glazes can be glossy, matte, or textured. Glazing is not related directly to the water-absorption categories listed above. Although glazing does keep moisture from penetrating the top surface, the unglazed sides and bottoms of the tile don't have the same protection.

Choose different sizes and shapes.
Square tiles are the most common and the easiest to install. But rectangles, hexagons, and other shapes are readily available. An easy and inexpensive way to add interest to a tile installation is to mix shapes, sizes, and colors; tile retailers and home centers offer a wide range of options.

Select the type of ceramic tile.
Modern ceramic tile is made from refined clay, usually mixed with additives and water. It then is hardened in a kiln. Several different types of tile are created through that process. Quarry tiles are unglazed and vitreous tiles, usually ½ inch thick and used for flooring. Pavers are ⅜-inch-thick vitreous floor tiles and are available glazed or unglazed.

Consider stone tile.
Use natural stone tile on floors, walls, and countertops. Marble, granite, flagstone, and slate are widely available; other types of stone may be available in your area. Dimensioned (or gauged) stone is cut to a uniform size and thickness and can be installed much like ceramic tile. Hand-split (or cleft) stone tiles vary in size and thickness.

EXPERTS' INSIGHT

OTHER TILING CHOICES

Cement-bodied tiles are made with a concrete mix that is extruded or cast, then cured to form a strong, dense tile. They usually are stained to look like pavers, quarry tile, stone, or brick. Often you can buy them with a factory-applied sealer. Brick-veneer tile is made like ceramic tile, but with a coarser body that simulates brick. Terrazzo is manufactured with small pieces of granite or marble set in mortar, then polished. Precast terrazzo tiles are available for floors and walls.

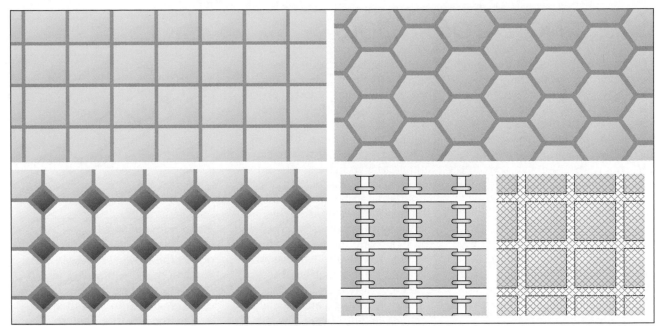

Use mosaic tile.
Mosaic tiles are 1- or 2-inch squares or similarly sized hexagons or pentagons mounted together as a larger unit. Most commercially available mosaics are vitreous and freeze-thaw stable and can be used on most tiling projects. Mosaic tiles are sold almost exclusively mounted on sheets or joined with adhesive strips. Back-mounted mosaic tiles are much easier to install than individual tiles. They can be mounted with standard thin-set adhesive and grout.

MEASUREMENTS

NOMINAL VS. ACTUAL SIZE

Most do-it-yourselfers learn quickly that when buying lumber, a 2×4 doesn't measure 2 inches by 4 inches. The tile trade has a similar discrepancy. Individual ceramic tiles are often sold with dimensional names that describe their installed size, that is, the size of the tile plus a standard grout joint. Thus, 6×6-inch tiles measure $\frac{1}{8}$ inch shorter in each direction. The actual size will be $5\frac{7}{8} \times 5\frac{7}{8}$ inches. Only when installed with a $\frac{1}{8}$-inch grout joint will the installed size of the tile be about 6×6. Always check the actual size of the tiles before you buy them.

Determine the right trim tiles.
In general, tiles are divided into field tiles, which are flat, and trim tiles, which are shaped irregularly to turn corners or define the edges of an installation. There are dozens of trim-tile profiles, and the names of each can be confusing. When choosing tiles, be sure to check the availability of these specialty tiles and select a style with trim tiles suitable for your project.

SELECTING LAYOUT TOOLS

Layout involves little more than measuring and marking. The tools required are inexpensive hand tools. You probably own most, if not all, of them already.

For making scale drawings, **graph paper** is often the best material to use. You can buy graph paper with various sizes of grids; ¼ inch is the most common. Measure the area to be tiled and sketch it so each ¼-inch grid represents 1 linear foot. The only accessories you will need are a **ruler, pencil,** and **eraser.** Graph paper also comes in handy when sketching tile designs; just let each grid represent a tile.

An **architect's rule** can be used in place of graph paper. An architect's rule has three sides, with different scales marked along each edge. It allows you to quickly convert measured distances to scale, or to count the grids on graph paper. The trick is to choose a scale that will fit on the paper.

A **combination square** or a framing square can be used for measuring short distances and precisely marking square corners. You can get by with one or the other, but chances are that you will use both of them if they are available. A framing square can double as a straightedge to aid in layout and tile installation. Or use short, straight boards called layout sticks, shown at *right.*

A **tape measure** is indispensible for laying out and marking tiles for cutting. You also must have an accurate 2- or 4-foot **level** to check horizontal and vertical surfaces for plumb and to mark accurate layout lines.

An inexpensive **plumb bob** is necessary for finding plumb, and a **chalk line** allows you to quickly mark layout lines. Most chalk lines will perform double duty as plumb bobs. So that you'll be able to clearly see your mark, buy yellow chalk for dark tile and blue chalk for light-colored tile.

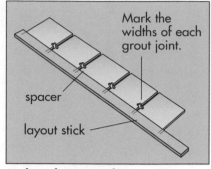

Make a layout stick.
When tiling large, flat surfaces, one of the handiest tools is one you can make yourself. A layout stick is just a homemade ruler that allows you to lay out an installation without having to measure and mark for each tile location. Line up a row of tiles on a flat surface, with spacers between. Set a straight piece of pine alongside the tiles. Start at one end of the stick and mark the width of the grout joint between each tile. You will need a new layout stick if you change tiles or grout widths on a new installation.

CHOOSING CUTTING TOOLS

One of the goals of setting tile is to lay out the job in a way that minimizes the need to cut tile. But at the very least you will need to cut tiles for corners and around fixtures.

Tile-cutting tools range from the slow and tedious to the fast and furious. Deciding on which tools you need is largely a matter of the size of your project and the number of cuts required.

A **snap cutter** is similar to a handheld glass cutter except that it is mounted on a guide bar. Various models operate differently, but all follow a basic two-step approach. First the tile is set in the cutter and scored along the snap line. Then the handle is pressed down to snap the tile along the line.

Tile nippers resemble pliers, but they are equipped with carbide-tipped edges. They are indispensable for making small notches and curves in tile. They can also be used for breaking off pieces of tile that have been scored with a snap cutter. Nippers usually leave a rough edge. Use a **rubbing stone** to smooth sharp edges. A **rod saw** is a strip of tungsten carbide that fits into a standard **hacksaw** body. It's a slow but handy way to cut tight curves. Another faster option for making small cuts is a power **diamond-tipped cutter.**

A **wet saw** is a power tool that quickly makes smooth, straight cuts in tile and other masonry. Wet saws are equipped with a pump that sprays water to cool the blade and remove chips. They are messy, but not particularly dangerous or difficult to use. If fact you might enjoy watching just how easily the blade cuts its way through a piece of tile, marble, or granite.

For drilling holes, use a **carbide-tipped hole saw** mounted on an **electric** or a **cordless power drill.**

CAUTION!
DON'T BUY WHEN YOU CAN RENT
New home improvement projects offer the perfect excuse to add new tools to your collection. However, some tiling tools are so specialized that you won't use them again until your next tiling job. Too many tools can quickly destroy your project budget. Tool-rental stores offer a variety of tools, many specifically chosen for do-it-yourselfers needing special tools for a short period of time. For tiling projects, it's especially smart to rent power tools, such as a wet saw or a diamond-tipped cutter. Also, check with your tile supplier. Often the store will lend customers tools at no charge if the tiles were purchased there.

---

hacksaw
rod saw blade
extension cord
hole saw
heavy-duty electric drill
nippers
cordless power drill
snap cutter
wet saw
rubbing stone
diamond-tipped cutter

SELECTING INSTALLATION TOOLS

For mixing thin-set mortar and grout, you need a sturdy bucket. An empty, clean **drywall-compound bucket** will suffice for relatively small jobs, but a **mortar-mixing box** is better for larger jobs. A **mortar mixer** is a great time saver for mixing two or more gallons of thin-set mortar or grout. The mixer is mounted, like a drill bit, on an electric drill.

Notched trowels have two smooth sides for spreading adhesive and two notched sides for combing the adhesive to the right depth. Check the tile and adhesive manufacturers' recommendations for the proper notch size.

You'll need a **beating block** to press the tiles evenly into the adhesive. Use a piece of 2× lumber covered with terrycloth or buy a rubber-faced model. With Mexican pavers and other irregular tiles, use a **rubber mallet** instead.

A canvas **drop cloth** readily absorbs moisture and has enough heft to protect surfaces from dropped tiles. Use **masking tape** to cover plumbing fixtures.

¼ " notched trowel

mixing box

⅛ " notched trowel

mortar mixer

THIN-SET MORTAR

mortar

beating block

rubber mallet

drop cloth

masking tape

CHOOSING GROUTING TOOLS

Many of the tools used for applying thin-set mortar also can be used for spreading grout. A **grouting float** is a rubber-backed trowel used for pressing the grout into the joints. It also removes excess grout from the tiling surface, although a **squeegee** may be more thorough. A **mason's trowel** is handy for finishing grout joints, although you also can use a **putty knife** or the handle of an **old toothbrush**. A **margin trowel** is used to mix small batches and for scooping adhesive or grout onto the setting surface. A **grout bag** is useful when you need to force grout into joints that can't be reached easily with a grout float.

Good-quality **sponges** are best for cleaning grout off the tile surface. Look for sponges made especially for tiling work. Use **cheesecloth** to remove the haze left on the tile after the grout has set for a while. For applying caulk and sealant around edges, you will need a **caulking gun.**

sponges

mason's trowel

margin trowel

grout bag

grouting float

cheesecloth

squeegee

putty knife

caulking gun

old toothbrush

USING TILE SPACERS

The space between tiles serves two important functions: It provides room for the grout essential to any tile job, and it allows for some creativity in your design. You can change the look of a finished tile installation significantly by changing the width of the grout joint or by altering the color of the grout.

Tile spacers are small pieces of plastic used to ensure consistent width of the grout joints. They come in a variety of sizes and shapes to match different types of tile and tile installations. Many types of ceramic tile today are self-spacing, that is, they have small lugs along their sides that ensure proper spacing. If you use self-spacing tiles, you need not use tile spacers unless you prefer a wider grout joint than the lugs allow.

Purchase manufactured spacers.
Buy plastic tile spacers from your tile supplier. They are available in sizes from $\frac{1}{16}$ inch to $\frac{1}{2}$ inch. X-shaped spacers are the most common. They are placed at each corner. Though less common, plain spacers often are preferred for spacing and holding wall tiles firmly in place.

CAUTION!
REMOVE SPACERS
Spacers should be left in place until the adhesive has set enough to prevent the tiles from slipping out of alignment. They should then be removed—even if the package they came in says otherwise. If spacers are left in place, they prevent grout from completely filling the joints and can result in a weak installation. If the spacers are difficult to remove, use needle-nose pliers to form a hook from a length of clothes hanger wire. Then use the hook to pry out the spacers.

Make your own spacers.
Plastic spacers are one of the least expensive materials used for tile installation. But for a small job or in a pinch, you may use an alternative. Look for objects that have a consistent size, such as wooden matchsticks, toothpicks, or nails. Nylon cord can be used over a long run. Remember to remove the spacers before grouting.

SELECTING ADHESIVES

*T*he setting adhesive bonds the bottom of the tile with the setting bed. Recent improvements in setting adhesives make it easy for do-it-yourselfers to set tile with professional results. Although adhesives fall into the broad categories of organic mastic and thin-set mortar, in reality there are many types of products and manufacturers. The first step in choosing an adhesive is to determine what kind of installation you are doing (wet or dry? indoor or outdoor? floor or wall?) and to what substrate the tile will be applied.

Organic mastics are popular because they require no mixing. However, they are not suitable for areas exposed to heat or for exterior installations. Thin-set mortars usually are mixed by the installer. A variety of thin-set additives are available to create an adhesive best suited to specific installations. The chart below offers general guidelines.

Buy ready-mixed organic mastic.
Organic mastic is a premixed adhesive that is easy to use. It is especially popular for use on walls because tiles will not slip when set in place.

Mix your own thin-set mortar.
Thin-set mortar requires more work than does organic mastic, but offers superior bonding strength and flexibility.

CHOOSING THIN-SET MORTARS	
Type	**Description and Uses**
Water-mixed mortar	Also referred to as *dry-set mortar,* this is a blend of Portland cement, sand, and additives. Mix with water.
Latex- and acrylic-mixed mortar	Also referred to as *latex mortar,* this mortar is similar to water-mixed mortar, but has latex or acrylic added to it. The additives improve adhesion and reduce water absorption; they may be premixed with the mortar in dry form or added as a liquid by the installer. It's an excellent choice for wet and dry installations.
Epoxy mortar	This is a mixture of sand, cement, and liquid resins and hardeners. It's costly, but effective with any setting material and is good choice when the substrate is incompatible with other adhesives.
Medium-bed mortar	This adhesive remains stronger than regular thin-set mortar when applied in layers of more than 1/4 inch. It's useful with tiles that do not have uniform backs, such as handmade tiles.

Choosing Setting Beds

A tile installation is only as good as the surface to which it is applied. Investing in adequate materials for the setting bed is as important as buying the right tile for your project. Tiled floors, in particular, require an extremely stiff setting bed; any imperfection in the subfloor can crack tiles and ruin your project.

You may be able to set the tile over an existing subfloor or wall surface, or you may want to add a layer or two of setting material to ensure a stiff and durable installation. The introduction of cement-based and gypsum-based backerboard has dramatically simplified tile installations without compromising strength and durability. Previously tile was applied over thick beds of mortar, almost exclusively by trained professionals. The process was time consuming and required skill and experience.

EXPERTS' INSIGHT

MORTAR-BED INSTALLATIONS

Modern thin-set mortars are typically applied in a layer only ⅛ to ¼ inch thick; that's how they get their name. Traditional (mudset) tile installations use thick mortar as the setting bed. Mortar, with wire-mesh reinforcement, is poured over tar paper to a thickness of 1 to 2 inches. Then the tiles are set on the mortar before it cures. Mortar-bed installations are strong and particularly useful on shower floors.

moisture-resistant drywall

cement-based backerboard

gypsum-based backerboard

concrete slab

drywall

plywood

Choose a setting bed.

Backerboard often is called cement board, although some products contain no cement. Sold in varying thicknesses and sizes, backerboard is easy to install and provides a ready-made surface for setting tile. Cement-based backerboard has a mesh coat and is cut using a carbide-tipped scoring tool.

Gypsum-based backerboard can be cut with a utility knife.

Concrete slabs (old or newly poured) are ideal setting beds for tile floors. With suitable adhesives, tile can be installed over plywood. A double layer of drywall (regular or moisture-resistant) is a suitable setting bed only in dry areas.

SELECTING GROUT

Grout is a mortar used to fill the joints between tiles. It stiffens the tile installation and helps prevent moisture from penetrating the joint. Grout usually is sold with all of the dry ingredients mixed together; the installer adds the liquid. It also is available in caulking-gun tubes with all of the wet and dry ingredients already mixed and ready for application.

Grout not only seal joints, it plays an important role in the overall design. The width and color of the grout joint can radically alter the finished look of a tile installation. Choose a grout color to complement, match, or contrast with the tile. Increase or decrease the joint size to provide the most appropriate balance for that size room.

CHOOSING GROUT

Type	Description and Uses
Plain grout	Also referred to as unsanded grout, this is a mixture of Portland cement and additives chosen to achieve specific characteristics. It is used for grout joints of $\frac{1}{16}$ inch or less. It's also recommended for absorptive tile and marble.
Sanded grout	This is similar to plain grout but has sand added. It is used for grout joints greater than $\frac{1}{16}$ inch. The ratio between sand and cement varies, depending on the size of the joint.
Epoxy grout	This grout contains epoxy resin and hardener. It's used when chemical and stain resistance are required or where high temperatures are likely.
Colored grout	Offered in premixed packages in a wide assortment of colors and formulations, you can usually find a colored grout to match any need and fill any typical grout joint. Natural grout can be used if you prefer the look of cement.
Mortar	This is similar to sanded grout, but is used for joints between brick pavers, slate, or other masonry materials.
Premixed grout	Some grouts are available premixed and ready to use out of the container. Choices are smaller, and the cost is high, but it may be a good choice for small jobs.

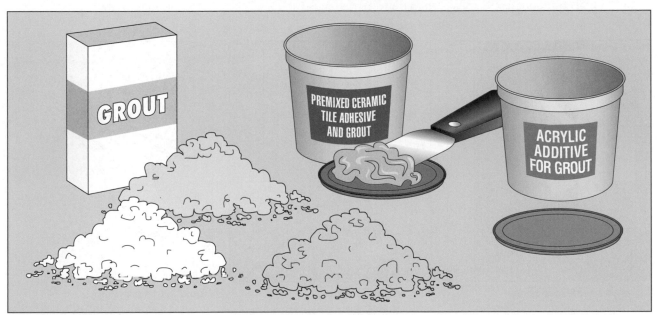

Know your grout.
Grout and tile are the two visible materials on a tiled surface. A good tile installation requires a good grouting job. Use the best ingredients, mix them right, and apply the grout so it completely fills the joints between tiles. Although tile is completely inflexible, you can achieve some flexibility in the grout joints by adding latex or acrylic additives to the grout. Additives also can increase water and stain resistance. When grout joints begin to fail, they should be repaired immediately or water damage could occur behind the tile.

SELECTING MEMBRANES

In addition to backerboard or other setting bed materials (page 470), some installations call for use of a membrane. The two types are waterproofing membranes and isolation membranes.

Waterproofing membranes are used to prevent moisture from penetrating through the surface (usually the grout joint). If water will often sit on your floor tiles, or if your wall tiles will be in a room that often becomes very humid, moisture can seep through grout or unglazed tiles and cause serious damage to the substrate and even the structural wood. A sealer (page 473) may solve the problem for wall tiles, but floor tiles that will get soaked need a membrane.

Tar paper (that is, felt paper saturated with tar) has long been the standard waterproofing membrane. Polyethylene sheeting is another inexpensive option. The most effective waterproofing membrane is chlorinated

polyethylene (CPE), a strong and thick sheet that is joined to the substrate with adhesive. Liquid membranes are applied with trowel or brush.

The function of an isolation membrane is to protect the tiled surface from damage due to

movement in the underlying surface. Use one when you tile over an existing floor that shows signs of movement from seasonal changes or settling of the house. Chlorinated polyethylene sheets are often used as isolation membranes.

Tar paper waterproofing.
Tar paper is an inexpensive and easy-to-install membrane. It is sold in rolls of varying widths and lengths and can be stapled or nailed to studs or drywall.

CPE waterproofing.
Chlorinated polyethylene is a durable and flexible product that offers the best water resistance of any available membrane. It is particularly effective on floors that will be wet on a regular basis.

Liquid waterproofing.
Single-component liquid membranes are spread on the setting bed. Once cured, they form a reasonably waterproof layer. Multicomponent membranes require liquid and fabric installed in layers.

CHOOSING CAULK AND SEALERS

*T*iles may last centuries, but a tile installation has no chance of reaching such a ripe age unless it is maintained regularly. Some components of the installation need to be replaced or renewed every few years. *Caulk* refers to a variety of flexible products used to fill joints that should not be grouted for one reason or another. *Sealers* are protective coatings applied over the entire tiled surface or all the grout lines; they prevent staining and protect tile and grout from water infiltration.

The best choice for a long-lasting, mildew-free joint in high-moisture installations is silicone caulk. Latex caulk is not suitable for tile jobs. Use siliconized acrylic caulk in areas exposed to only minimal moisture. Tub-and-tile caulk contains a mildewcide, but it is not always effective.

Where to caulk.
Use caulk instead of grout in expansion joints (see box below), between dissimilar materials, and around penetrations in the tiled surface such as between tiles and a

sink. Like grout, caulk is available in sanded and plain formulations, and in colors that match the grout. Caulk tubes used with a caulk gun are the easiest to use. Buy a squeeze tube for small jobs.

TILE AND GROUT SEALERS

Sealers are used on unglazed tile and stone products. They are also applied to grout. *Penetrating sealers* are intended to be absorbed beneath the surface of the tile and grout. They reduce the absorbency of the surface without necessarily adding a sheen. *Coating sealers* are formulated to remain on the surface, where they generally add a glossy or semiglossy sheen. Use a *grout sealer* on a wall with glazed tile. It will keep your grout watertight and make it easier to clean. Usually, you must wait two weeks after tile installation before applying grout sealer.

EXPERTS' INSIGHT

EXPANSION JOINTS

■ Tile and grout generally don't expand and contract with seasonal and temperature changes, but the materials beneath and around them may. Expansion joints are safety features that anticipate that movement and prevent the tile and grout from being damaged by it. On most installations, expansion joints are intended to look like grout joints, but they are filled with a flexible material such as silicone caulk.

■ Use expansion joints around the perimeters of all tile installations, especially where the tile edges meet a different material. Use them where floors meet walls, countertops meet backsplashes, and where tile meets wood or another material. Any runs of tile on a floor that exceed 24 feet must be interrupted with an expansion joint.

■ The most typical method of creating an expansion gap is to leave a ¼-inch joint between the tile and the adjoining surface, then fill the joint with caulk. The setting bed should also be designed with expansion joints.

ASSESSING SUBSTRATES

*T*he *substrate* of a floor or wall includes the setting bed (page 470) and any other layers beneath the tile surface. Even if tile adheres firmly to its setting bed, it won't last long if that setting bed isn't part of a completely sound and sturdy substrate.

The structural needs of your substrate may change when you add a new type of surface. For example, if you are planning to install ceramic tile on a floor that currently is covered with resilient sheet flooring, you will be adding a lot of weight to the underlying framing. If you doubt that the joists and subfloor are strong enough, consult a professional.

A quick way to tell if a floor is firm enough to handle ceramic tile: Jump on it. If it feels springy, there's a good chance that your tiles or grout lines will crack in time. Add a layer of plywood or backerboard to strengthen it, or consult a professional.

Walls should be firm to the touch. New tiles will not add significant strength.

SUBSTRATE RECOMMENDATIONS

Substrate	Preparation
Exposed joists	▪ Verify that the framing will support the new floor. ▪ Install ¾-inch CDX plywood. ▪ Install backerboard or underlayment-grade plywood.
Concrete slab	▪ Repair cracks or low spots in the concrete. ▪ Ensure that the slab is flat, clean, and dry. ▪ Roughen the surface to improve adhesion.
Finished floor	▪ Verify that the framing will support the new floor. ▪ If necessary, remove the finish flooring. ▪ Install backerboard or underlayment-grade plywood over suitable subfloor, or over the old finish flooring.
Wall paneling	▪ Remove thin sheet paneling. ▪ Install backerboard, plywood, or drywall.
Drywall	▪ Scrape away any loose paint and roughen the surface with sandpaper. ▪ Clean the surface or apply deglosser. ▪ Add a second layer of drywall for added strength.
Masonry or plaster walls	▪ Repair cracks and level indentations. ▪ Ensure that the surface is sound, not soft and crumbling or springy when pressed. ▪ Clean the surface or apply deglosser.

Wood Floor Substrate

floor joist · plywood · adhesive · waterproofing membrane (as needed) · backerboard · fiberglass tape · setting adhesive

Concrete Substrate

coarse sand · plastic sheeting · 6" mesh · concrete · setting adhesive

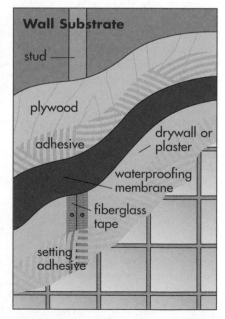

Wall Substrate

stud · plywood · adhesive · drywall or plaster · waterproofing membrane · fiberglass tape · setting adhesive

CALCULATING MATERIALS

Before you go shopping for tile and setting materials, determine how much of each material you need. Fortunately that doesn't mean that you have to count every last tile you intend to install. Tiling materials are usually sold by the square foot, so for most jobs, all you have to do is measure the surface to be tiled, then take that number to the store with you.

Buy more tile than you plan to use. Expect to break a few tiles, and to need a few more than anticipated. It's handy to have a few extra tiles should you need any replacements someday. So get an extra 5 to 10 percent more than your estimate.

Where to Buy

Tile and setting materials are widely available. Small lumber yards and hardware stores may carry a limited selection, while home centers and tile outlets offer a much wider choice. It pays to shop around, because prices and selection can vary significantly. Of course you should shop for a good price, but also look for a retailer who is knowledgeable and willing to answer questions. A little good advice might save you plenty of time and money. Be sure to ask about the store's policy on returns. In the event that you buy considerably more than you need, you should be able to return unopened boxes and packages for a refund.

Metrics

Tiles are manufactured and sold all over the world. So the tiles you choose may have been manufactured to a metric size, which was then rounded off to inches. So, for example, you may have a "13-inch" Italian tile that actually measures $13^3/_{16}$ inches.

Multiply width times length to find the square footage.

Determine square footage.
If you are tiling a single rectangular surface, simply measure the width and the length (in feet), and multiply the two numbers to determine the square footage. For multiple surfaces, calculate each one separately, then add the results. When a door or a window interferes, include it in your initial calculation, then find the square footage of the obstruction and subtract it from the overall total.

If you will be installing large, expensive tiles, make a drawing of your space, with exact dimensions, and bring it to your dealer, who can help you to determine the most economical layout.

ESTIMATING GROUT AND ADHESIVES

The amount of grout you need depends on the size of the tiles and on the width and depth of the grout joint. Packages of grout often include tables for estimating the amount needed. This chart gives you a rough idea of how many square feet can be covered with one pound of grout. The figures should be treated only as estimates, but they do show how much the coverage changes depending on tile size.

Tile Size	Joint Width	Coverage per Pound of Grout
2"×2"×$^1/_4$"	$^1/_{16}$"	24 square feet
$4^1/_4$"×$4^1/_4$"×$^5/_{16}$"	$^1/_{16}$"	16 square feet
$4^1/_4$"×$4^1/_4$"×$^5/_{16}$"	$^1/_8$"	8 square feet
6"×6"×$^1/_4$"	$^1/_{16}$"	28 square feet
6"×6"×$^1/_4$"	$^1/_8$"	14 square feet
12"×12"×$^3/_8$"	$^1/_{16}$"	37 square feet

When applied with the trowel notch size recommended by the manufacturer, one gallon of adhesive will cover 30 to 50 square feet of wall and 20 to 40 square feet of floor.

PREPARING THE SITE

When tiling floors or installing wall tiles down to the floor line, remove baseboard trim. If the baseboard is trimmed with shoe molding (a thin rounded strip attached to the floor), you probably need only remove the shoe, leaving the baseboard in place, in order to tile the floor. If you plan to reuse the trim, take care not to damage it as you remove it. Insert a thin pry bar or stiff putty knife to lift the shoe or pull the baseboard from the wall. Gradually work your way along the molding until it comes off. Write numbers on the backs of the pieces to help you remember where they go. Remove as many obstacles as possible so you will not have to make many precise tile cuts. When preparing to tile a floor, set a tile on the floor and use it as a guide for cutting the bottoms of casing molding.

If you are tiling a bathroom, remember that removing and replacing a toilet is easier than tiling around it, and will lead to a much cleaner-looking job. (Be sure to stuff a rag in the soil pipe to prevent sewer gas from backing up

Remove door if installing floor tile.

Cover doors and vents with plastic sheeting.

Remove base shoe to install floor tile.

Remove toilet, plug soil pipe.

Trim the bottom of casing so the tile can slip under.

into the bathroom.) You may want to remove the vanity as well as doors. (You may also need to trim the doors after the tile is installed.)

When preparing to tile walls, remove electrical outlet covers (the outlet box may have to be adjusted before replacing the covers), and fixtures. Sinks and appliances may have to be

removed, depending on your installation. Because the tiles add thickness to the wall, it is usually best to leave window and door casings in place. Keep dust and odors from spreading throughout the house by taping plastic sheeting over doorways. Cover vents with plastic as well.

PREPARING SURFACES TO BE TILED

Floors
■ Remove the original flooring, if it is not firmly stuck to the subfloor, if it is uneven, or if the thinset mortar will not adhere to it.
■ Make sure that the subfloor is at least 1⅛ inch thick and composed of suitable materials (usually a combination of plywood, backerboard, or concrete).
■ If a plywood floor seems loose in spots, drive nails or screws through it into floor joists.
■ Fill low spots in the subfloor, then smooth the surface and clean it thoroughly.

Walls
■ Remove wallpaper, thin paneling, or anything else that flexes when you press it.
■ When tiling over new drywall, don't bother taping the joints but do seal the surface with a thin coat of adhesive applied with the flat side of a trowel.
■ Scrape away loose paint.
■ Lightly sand glossy surfaces to remove the sheen.
■ Patch holes and cracks, and sand smooth.
■ Thoroughly clean the wall and allow it to dry.

Countertops
■ Remove sink or faucets, and other obstacles.
■ Remove old tile if it exists.
■ To tile over a square-edged laminated countertop that is sound, give it a thorough sanding and remove the backsplash.
■ If you have a post-form countertop with curved edges, remove it and install a new substrate of plywood and backerboard.
■ Make sure the substrate is thick enough for trim pieces and that the trim won't prevent drawers from opening.

LAYING OUT THE JOB

*T*ile looks best when it is set in a straight line and at least appears to be square and level with adjacent surfaces. Laying out the installation is the most important step for ensuring such an outcome. Tile is an unforgiving material, and floors and walls are rarely as square and level as you might think—or hope. One of the secrets to a successful layout, therefore, is learning how to fudge the installation so the fudging isn't apparent. The other secret is to plan for as few cut tiles as possible. Adjust the layout to minimize cuts and hide those cut tiles along less conspicuous walls and under baseboard trim. Don't be surprised if your house exceeds some of the tolerances recommended here. Tile setters have had to deal with such irregularities for centuries, and cures are plentiful.

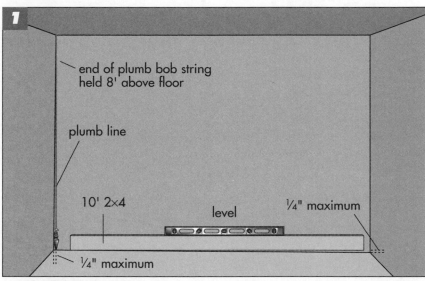

end of plumb bob string held 8' above floor

plumb line

10' 2×4

level

¼" maximum

¼" maximum

1. Check for tolerances.
Check tiling surfaces for square, level, and plumb using the techniques shown below. If a surface is out of alignment in excess of the amounts shown above, the best solution is to change the surfaces—for instance, fur out a wall, or shim up a subfloor. If this is not feasible, make the unevenness less visible by avoiding narrow tile pieces at the corner. You might be able to split the difference, making two edges slightly out of line instead of having one edge that is way off.

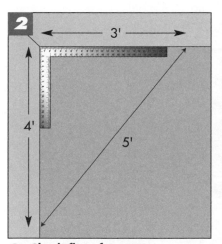

3'

4'

5'

2. Check floor for square.
For small rooms, check the squareness of the floor by setting a framing square at inside and outside corners. For larger rooms, use the 3-4-5 method: Measure along one wall exactly three feet from the corner, and along the other wall four feet. If the distance between those points is exactly five feet, the floor is square.

high point of floor

3. Check floor for level.
Use a 2- or 4-foot level to check along each wall. To check for level over a longer span, place the level on the edge of a straight 6- or 8-foot board. If the floor is only slightly out of level, and you are not planning to run tile up the wall, this should not affect your installation.

Bubble indicates level.

4. Check walls for plumb.
Place a level vertically on the wall at various spots, or use a plumb bob. Set the level horizontally on the wall to see how flat it is (you can also stretch a string tightly along the wall). A wavy wall, even if it is plumb, should be corrected before tiling.

EXPERTS' INSIGHT

PLANNING FOR FOCAL POINTS

When you walk into a room for the first time, chances are there is something there that catches your eye immediately. As you stand in the room, other areas may become more noticeable. It might be another doorway, a fireplace, a window, counters, or appliance groupings. Plan your layout so that the installation looks best in these focal areas. For example, cut tiles placed around a sink should all be of equal size. If your floor is out of square so that you must have a line of cut tiles that grow progressively smaller, plan so it will be behind a couch or in an area that is not a focal point. Use perpendicular lines and full tiles at focal points.

chalkline

framing square

5. Establish reference lines.
Accurate reference lines are critical to the success of a tile installation. Trace around a piece of plywood with two factory edges, or chalk two lines that are perfectly perpendicular. You will place the first tile at the intersection; this tile establishes the alignment and position of the rest of the tiles. (For instructions on your specific tiling project and more information on how to plot reference lines see pages 503 and 509.)

Start installation with three full tiles at the corner.

chalkline

Laying out an L-shaped room.
Often, the outside corner of an L-shaped room will be a focal point, so start there. Here's the simplest way to lay it out: From the corner, extend two straight lines along the floor to the opposing wall. Plan to set three full tiles at the corner, then extend the layout. This will not work, however, if the outside corner is seriously out of square. Also if this method results in very small pieces along a wall, it may be best to modify it.

6

Money $ Saver

USING TILE SCRAPS
By making adjustments in your layout, you can save some money. That's because you can plan ahead to use as many of your tile cutoffs as possible. As explained below, avoid using tiles that are less than half size. There are times when you won't have a choice, however, especially if you are tiling an oddly shaped room or an irregular surface. In those cases, try to use tiles that have already been cut rather than wasting full ones. Tile scraps can also be used for mosaic installations.

6. Do a dry run.
With reference lines drawn, you can measure from the lines to the walls and calculate how the tiles will be arranged. However, the safest method is to set tiles in place along the reference lines.

For this dry run, don't use any adhesive, but be sure to space the tiles properly. Take your time, and find out how each edge will look. Don't hesitate to change the entire layout if it will make for a more attractive appearance.

CAUTION!
AVOID THIN TILES
One of the golden rules of tile setting is to use as many full tiles as possible. Another rule is to avoid using tiles that have been cut in size by more than half. Sometimes those rules are easier to remember than to follow. Then follow the most important rule: Avoid using very thin tiles. Not only are they unattractive, but they also may not adhere properly. When your layout reveals the need for one row of very thin tiles, make an adjustment. Plan to cut tiles along two rows rather than one; that way they won't be so thin.

Hiding cut tiles.
One big advantage of a careful and thorough layout is that you can plan where cut tiles will go. A simple rule of thumb is to place cut tiles in the least visible areas. On a floor installation, for example, one wall may be largely covered with furniture.

If you place cut tiles under or behind the furniture, they are not likely to be seen. On other installations, you may prefer to adjust the layout so that it has evenly sized cut tiles along the opposite edges.

CUTTING WITH A CIRCULAR SAW

Whether crosscutting 2×4s, ripping plywood, or cutting tiles or bricks with a masonry blade, you'll do the job better if you follow a few basic rules for using a circular saw.

Whenever you cut, allow the saw to reach full operating speed, then slowly push the blade into the wood. Some carpenters look at the blade as they cut; others rely on the gunsight notch. Choose the method that suits you best. Avoid making slight turns as you cut. Instead, find the right path, and push the saw through the material smoothly. It will take some practice before you can do this consistently. This is a powerful tool with sharp teeth, so take care; it demands your respect. Support the material to avoid having the saw bind and possibly kick back at you. Don't wear looose sleeves or position your face near the blade.

Support the material properly.
A well-supported board results in clean, safe cuts. If the scrap piece is short, support the board on the nonscrap side. If the scrap is long, it could bind the blade or splinter as it falls away at the end of the cut, so support it in four places.

Square the blade.
Turn the saw upside-down, hold a square against the blade, and adjust it. (Be sure to position the square between the teeth.) Cut some scrap pieces and check to make sure the saw cuts squarely through the thickness of the board.

TOOLS TO USE

CIRCULAR SAW AND BLADES

■ Choose a circular saw that is comfortable. It should have some heft, but should not be so heavy that it is difficult to maneuver. You should be able to see the blade and gunsight notch easily. Check for ease of depth and angle adjustments.

■ If you buy only one blade for cutting lumber and plywood, chose a carbide-tipped combination blade that has at least 24 teeth. It works well for rough work and makes cuts clean enough for most finish work. For more specialized uses, buy a plywood blade, a finishing blade, or a masonry blade.

Align the blade with the cut line.
Once you have drawn an accurate cutoff line and have properly supported the board, position the saw blade on the scrap side of the line. The teeth on most blades are offset in an alternating pattern. When preparing to cut, look at a tooth that points toward the cutoff line.

Make a plunge cut.
Use a plunge cut, also called a pocket cut, to make a hole or slit in the middle of a board or sheet. Set the blade to the correct depth. Retract the safety guard and tilt the saw forward, setting the front of the baseplate on the stock. Start the saw and lower it slowly into the cut line until the base rests on the stock. Complete the cut.

DRILLING

An electric drill enables you not only to drill a hole of about any size with ease, but also to drive screws into wood or metal, buff and grind, and even mix mortar or paint.

Experts keep two drills on hand—one for drilling pilot holes and the other for driving screws. That way, they don't waste time changing bits. A drill with a keyless chuck speeds up a bit change, although you may find bits slip during heavy-duty tasks.

In addition to the bits shown at right, purchase a magnetic sleeve that holds inexpensive screwdriver bits. This simple tool will make driving screws nearly as easy as pounding nails.

EXPERTS' INSIGHT

CHOOSING A DRILL

■ Avoid buying a cheap drill with a ¼-inch chuck. It will not have the power you need and will soon burn out. A good drill will be variable-speed and reversing (VSR), will have a ⅜-inch chuck, and will pull at least 3 amps. One tipoff to a better-quality tool is the cord. Look for a long cord that flexes more like rubber than plastic.

■ Choose a heavy-duty, ½-inch drill if you will be using it to mix mortar. A smaller drill can burn out quickly while churning this thick substance.

■ A cordless drill can make your work go more easily, but only if it is powerful enough to do most things that a corded drill can do.

■ A hammer drill is useful if you need to drill a number of holes in concrete.

Choose the right bit.
Use standard twist or spade bits for boring through wood. A carbide-tipped masonry bit drills through concrete or brick. Use a carbide-tipped hole saw for larger holes. A ceramic tile bit will make a hole in tile without cracking it.

Drill through ceramic tile.
Wall tiles are usually soft, but floor tiles can be very tough. Nick the surface of the tile just enough so the bit will not wander as you drill. Keep the bit and the hole lubricated with a few drops of oil. Use a masonry bit or ceramic tile bit like the one shown above.

Use a hole saw.
Cutting a hole in the middle of a tile is easy to do with a carbide-tipped hole saw. Measure to the center of the hole (you will need to make two measurements), and place the tile on a flat surface that you don't mind damaging. Nick the center point to keep the starter bit from wandering. Keep the drill perpendicular in both directions as you drill, and don't press too hard.

Drill into masonry and concrete.
Use a masonry bit when drilling masonry surfaces. Usually brick is easy to drill into and concrete is more difficult. Check the bit often to make sure it's not overheating. Stop if you see smoke. Spraying the bit with window cleaner as you work keeps the bit cool, and the foaming action brings debris up and out of the hole.

CUTTING BACKERBOARD

Backerboard usually has to be cut to size before it can be installed. You may also have to drill holes in the board so that it will slide into place. If you have ever installed drywall, you will find the score-and-snap method to be very familiar. There are several types of backerboard on the market, and new materials are introduced from time to time. Be sure to follow the manufacturer's instructions if they vary from the process described here. You can cut backerboard with power tools, but it will be messier, not any faster, and may damage your blade or motor.

YOU'LL NEED

SKILLS: Measuring, cutting.
TIME: Each cut requires no more than 5 to 10 minutes.
TOOLS: Drywall square or straightedge, utility knife or scoring tool, and rubbing stone.

1. Score the board.
For cement-based board, measure carefully and mark cut off lines on both sides of the backerboard. Align a straight edge with the line on one side. Pull the scoring tool along the straight edge; make as many passes as are necessary to break through the mesh on the surface. Place the straight edge on the other side and repeat the process. The mesh must be completely severed on each side. (A faster but somewhat riskier method: Proceed as you would for drywall, cutting one side, snapping the cut edge over, then cutting the other side.)

2. Snap.
Place the backerboard on a flat surface. Press down with your hand on one side of the cut line. With the other hand, lift up just enough to snap the board along the scored edges. Some types of backerboard may break easier if you elevate the board on one side of scoring line, then press down.

3. Smooth edges.
Be careful when handling the cut board. Some types of backerboard may leave a sharp edge along the cut line. The best way to smooth the edge is to use a rubbing stone.

TOOLS TO USE

A HOLE SAW

Cement-based backerboard is often used under tiled surfaces in wet areas. That means you may have to fit it over plumbing protrusions in the wall, countertop, or floor. Most holes can be drilled quickly and effectively using a power drill equipped with a carbide-tip hole saw. The hole saw should be available where you buy your tile or at any large home center. Another method is to mark and score a circle on both sides of the board, then tap through with a hammer.

INSTALLING BACKERBOARD

If it has been cut correctly, backerboard is fairly easy to install. Each type is installed with screws or nails, then the seams are joined with fiberglass tape and mortar. If you are planning to tile in a wet area, remember to take proper waterproofing steps. Cement-based backerboard itself is not damaged by moisture, but it is not waterproof. Water can permeate the board and the underlying framing, causing serious damage. For best results, install a waterproofing membrane behind the backerboard (page 472). Use the type of fasteners recommended by the manufacturer. Roofing nails work, but corrosion-resistant screws offer superior holding power. Edges of backerboard must by supported by studs or joists, or glued with construction adhesive to a sound wall surface.

1. Attach to walls.
Attach backerboard directly to bare studs or over an existing layer of drywall. In either case, make sure the drywall screws or nails are long enough to penetrate the framing at least ¾ inch.

2. Attach to floors.
Coat the clean subfloor with adhesive applied with a notched trowel. Set the boards so that all joints fall over floor joists. Press the board into the adhesive before fastening with screws.

3. Finish the joints.
With all boards fastened, apply adhesive-backed fiberglass-mesh tape to the joints. Holding a trowel nearly flat, spread adhesive over the tape, pressing it into the mesh. Feather the edges of the adhesive for a smooth finish. Make sure there are no high spots; shallow low spots are not a problem.

MIXING THIN-SET MORTAR

With the setting bed in place—cleaned, and marked for the layout—it is time to prepare the adhesive. For tiling walls, you will probably use an adhesive that does not have to be mixed. For tiling floors, you can use premixed thin-set or floor tile adhesive, but the thin-set mortar that you mix yourself will be the strongest (see page 469).

Mixing will be easier if all the ingredients are at room temperature; buy the powder and any additives in advance and store them overnight in a heated part of the house. Mixing can get sloppy, especially if you are using a power mixer. Place the bucket in the middle of the area to be tiled, or on top of a drop cloth.

Use a heavy-duty, ½-inch drill for power mixing, as a smaller drill may burn out. Keep a second bucket on hand, about half full of water, for cleaning your mixer.

Mixing by hand.
Mix small batches of thin-set mortar (less than two gallons) by hand. Use a trowel or a stiff piece of wood, and make sure you scrape the bottom of the bucket as you stir.

Using a mortar mixer.
Mix larger batches with a mortar mixer mounted on a powerful drill. Clamp the bucket with your feet to keep it from spinning. Set the mixer in and start mixing with short bursts of power to keep the mixture from spilling.

EXPERTS' INSIGHT

HOW MUCH TO MIX?

Like other cement-based adhesives, thin-set mortar begins to cure almost as quickly as it is mixed. If you mix too much at once, it may be unusable when you reach the bottom of the bucket. On the other hand, it is a waste of time to mix batches that are too small. Professional tile setters mix enough adhesive to last them somewhere between 30 and 60 minutes. However, if you are working in a room with dry air, you may need to mix less mortar. Experiment with progressively larger batches.

Proper consistency.
It takes some practice and experience to know when the mortar has just the right amount of ingredients. The mix is too loose if it runs off the mixing tool. Add more dry ingredients and mix some more. Lift the mixer again.

The mortar is ready when it falls off, but no longer runs off, the mixing tool. If the mortar starts drying out before you've used it up, discard the batch and mix a new one. Adding more liquid at that point will.make the mortar less adherent.

SPREADING THIN-SET MORTAR

After mixing the mortar, let it rest for 10 minutes before applying. Scoop a small amount onto the setting surface and comb it with a notched trowel. If the ridges hold their shape and do not flatten out, the batch is ready to spread. Begin spreading mortar at the intersection of your reference lines. Take care not to cover up the lines. Work in small areas. If you've never tiled before, spread only enough to cover 2 or 3 square feet. As you gain experience, you can expand the size of the working area. Packages of thin-set mortar refer to the *open time*—the amount of time you have to set tiles on combed adhesive. Use a margin trowel (see page 467) to scoop adhesive onto the bottom of your notched trowel, or drop dollops of mortar onto the floor and then spread them out. Give the thin-set mortar a quick stir from time to time.

Hold at 30° angle.

1. Apply the thin-set mortar.
Hold the smooth edge of the trowel at a 30-degree angle to the surface. Press adhesive firmly onto the surface. Use sweeping strokes to spread to a consistent depth. Don't cover reference lines.

Hold at 45° to 75° angle.

2. Comb the thinset mortar.
Turn the trowel to the notched edge. Hold the trowel at a 45- to 75-degree angle to form the proper depth of ridge. Comb over the entire surface to produce equally sized ridges.

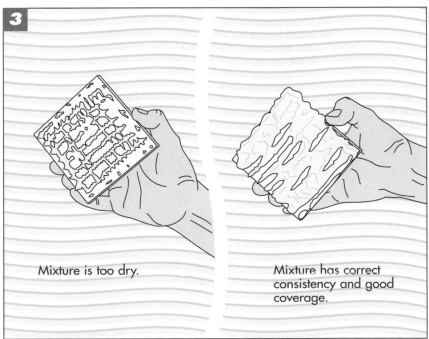

Mixture is too dry.

Mixture has correct consistency and good coverage.

3. Check the coverage.
After spreading and combing a small amount of the mortar, press a tile in place. Twist it a bit so that it is set in the adhesive, then pry it up and look at the bottom. About 75 percent of the surface should be covered. If too little adhesive has stuck to the tile bottom, the mixture is probably too dry.

CAUTION!
WORKING WITH EPOXY ADHESIVE

Epoxy-based adhesives are expensive and tricky to use. Fortunately, they are usually not needed for residential tile jobs. But if you have a setting bed that is incompatible with other adhesives, or are installing tile in an area likely to receive extreme heat, epoxies may be necessary. Read all instructions carefully. Wear a charcoal-filter mask, work in a well-ventilated area, and avoid skin contact with the mixed solution. Mix epoxy adhesive by hand and carefully follow the manufacturer's instructions about the proportion of wet and dry ingredients.

CUTTING TILE

adjustable fence

1. To use a snap cutter, mark and position the tile.

Mark a cut line on the tile with a pencil or felt-tipped pen. Place a tile in the cutter, glazed side up, aligning the cut line with the cutting wheel. Set and lock the fence on the cutter to hold the tile in place.

2. Score the tile.

Hold the tile in place with one hand and the handle with the other. Set the cutting wheel on the top of the tile. Pull or push (depending on your model) the handle while maintaining steady pressure on the tile. Try to score the tile evenly on the first pass.

3. Snap the tile.

When the tile has been scored, press back on the handle just enough to snap the tile along the score line. If the tile will not break, the score line was probably incomplete or not deep enough.

Tube leads to a bucket of water.

Use a wet saw.

Wear safety glasses and hearing protection. See that the blade is in good condition and that the water bucket is full. Place the tile on the sliding table and lock the fence to hold the tile in place. Turn the saw on, and make sure water is running onto the blade. Press down on the tile as you slide it through, taking care to keep your fingers out of the way. When the water runs out, refill the bucket; do not cut with the saw for even a few seconds unless water is running onto the blade.

CAUTION!
BEWARE OF EDGES

One of the advantages of a wet saw is that it makes very smooth cuts. When using a snap cutter or tile nippers, however, the resulting edges can be razor sharp. After cutting the tile, immediately smooth those edges. Grasp the tile on an uncut edge. Move a rubbing stone back and forth over the cut side, smoothing and rounding over the edge as you go. If you do not have a rubbing stone, you can achieve the same result with carbide-grit sandpaper. Use a sanding block, or wrap the sandpaper around a block of wood.

TRIMMING TILE

Use tile nippers for a curved cut...

For cuts that are not straight, use a rod saw (see below right) or tile nippers. (Most floor tiles cannot be cut with a rod saw, so you will need to use nippers.) Practice on scrap pieces of tile to get the hang of it. Hold the nippers roughly parallel to the cut line, and bite away small chunks.

...for a notch...

If the notch will have square corners, use a snap cutter to score at least some of the lines; this will make it a bit easier to nibble precisely up to the lines. Nibbling a notch requires patience. Bite away only a little at a time or you may break the whole piece.

...or for a sliver.

Nippers are also useful for very narrow straight cuts when you do not have a wet saw. Use the snap cutter or a glass cutter to score the glaze on the tile. Place the jaws close to, and parallel with, the score line. Take a series of bites along the cut line.

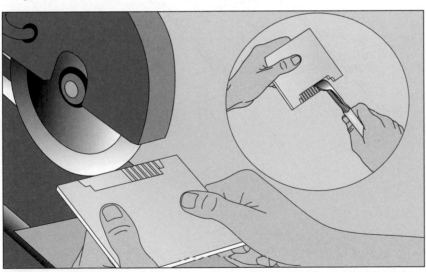

Make irregular cuts.

Use a wet saw to make irregular cuts that would take a long time to accomplish with nippers. To make a series of closely spaced, parallel cuts with the wet saw, hold the tile in your hands. Rest your hands on the sliding table as you move the tile into the blade. By holding the tile at the correct angle, you can produce a series of cuts that all end at the cut line. Break off the tile pieces with your fingers or nippers, then clean up the cut edge with a rubbing stone.

TOOLS TO USE

THE ROD SAW

A rod saw (shown on page 465) is a cylindrical hacksaw blade made of tungsten carbide. If you are on a tight budget or do not have very many odd-shaped cuts to make, this tool can be a handy accessory. Set the rod saw snugly in the hacksaw body, firmly support the tile, and cut using a sawing motion. With a rod saw you can cut fairly quickly through wall tiles, but it will be rough going—and perhaps impossible—with floor tiles. A rod saw is useful for cutting tight curves.

SETTING TILE

When the adhesive has been combed to the right thickness, immediately begin setting tiles. The most important tile is the first one you set; make sure that it is aligned perfectly with your layout so that the rest of the tiles will fall into place nicely. You will be rewarded at this stage for having spent all that time on the layout. Your reference lines will help to guide you through the entire process; take care not to cover them over with adhesive.

Work in sections small enough to set the tiles before the adhesive begins to dry out. Start by spreading adhesive in a 2- to 3-square-foot area; set the tiles and remove excess adhesive before moving on to the next section. With practice, you can work in larger sections. If the adhesive has begun to skin over, do not set tiles in it. Rather, scoop up and discard the adhesive and apply a fresh layer.

Whenever possible, set all full tiles first, then set the cut tiles. But also avoid kneeling on top of just-set tiles in order to lay the cut ones. On a large job, you might want to set all of the full tiles one day, then handle the cut tiles the next day.

Take care not to tile yourself into a corner. Set tiles so that you can leave the room without walking on them. Don't disturb floor tiles until the adhesive has cured—preferably overnight.

YOU'LL NEED

TIME: About one hour for every 3 to 5 square feet of field tiles; small, complex installations take two to three times as long.
SKILLS: Setting tiles into the adhesive and cutting tiles to fit.
TOOLS: Beating block and hammer, putty knife or trowel, sponge, and tile cutter.

1. Begin at the corner.
With the adhesive spread, place the first tile at the intersection of the reference lines. Press and twist it slightly into place, aligning the tile with both lines. Do not slide the tile through the adhesive.

2. Follow the layout.
Place another tile next to the first. Use spacers unless the tiles are self-spacing. Press and twist the tile to ensure that it is fully embedded in the adhesive. Accurate placement of the first few tiles is critical.

3. Fill in the field.
Continue setting tiles along the layout lines in the section. Then set the tiles in the field, working out from the corner. Insert spacers as shown. (Spacers can also be laid flat at the intersection of the grout lines, but must be removed before grouting.) If the tiles are self-spacing, keep an eye on the gaps between tiles to make sure that they remain uniform. Avoid sliding the tiles once they have been set in the adhesive. Check the backs of the tiles from time to time to see that they are adhering properly.

carpet-wrapped beating block

Remove excess adhesive.

4. Use a beating block.

After setting tiles in one section, use a beating block (see page 466 for tips on making a beating block) to ensure a level surface and full adhesion. Place the beating block so that it spans several tiles, and give it a few light taps with a hammer. Make sure each tile gets tapped this way.

5. Clean the joint.

Immediately after setting tiles in each section, remove excess adhesive before it starts to dry. Clean the tile with a damp sponge, and use a putty knife, utility knife, or margin trowel to remove excess from between tiles.

marker tile

thickness of 2 grout joints

tile to be cut

6. Cut tiles last.

When all of the full tiles have been set in the field, begin setting cut tiles around the perimeter. Because walls are rarely square, it is usually best to cut one tile at a time. The safest method is to measure each tile "in place." Set the tile to be cut directly on top of the adjacent tile. Then set another full tile on top, two grout joints away from the wall. Use the top tile to mark the cut line.

7. Back-buttering tiles.

When you are unable to use a trowel to apply the adhesive on the setting surface, *back-butter* individual tiles: Use a notched trowel or a putty knife, depending on the size of the tile, and spread adhesive on the back. Use enough adhesive so that the tile will be level with other tiles.

SETTING MOSAIC TILE

Historically tile mosaic has been an elaborate decorative technique using small pieces of tile, stone, and shells set one by one to produce unique patterns. Today mosaic tiles are almost always sold in sheets, with small tiles held together by a mesh or paper backing or with small adhesive dots. These sheets make installation much quicker than setting tiles individually. You can find mosaic tiles in a variety of patterns, glazed and unglazed. Glass mosaic tiles are available in 1-inch squares. Mosaic tiles are particularly suitable for use on floors, but are also popular for walls and countertops.

EXPERTS' INSIGHT

ARRANGING PATTERNS

Sheets of mosaic tiles are sometimes composed of randomly arranged tiles in a variety of colors. This randomness looks best when it has a balance to it; colors should be scattered around the surface, not clumped together. You can control the balance somewhat by planning the arrangement of the tile sheets. Before you start spreading adhesive and setting the tiles, take time to study the patterns on individual sheets. You may find that some sheets look better than others when placed next to each other. Some mosaic sheets are set according to a pattern. In that case, install the tiles so that you continue, rather than disrupt, the pattern.

Set mosaic tiles.
Back-mounted mosaic tiles should be set in thin-set adhesive. Because various backing materials perform differently, check with the supplier for any special instructions. Take care to ensure that each individual tile on a sheet is fully embedded in the adhesive. Move a beating block (see page 466) slowly across the whole sheet, lightly tapping it as you go.

Cut little pieces with a snap cutter.

Cut mosaics.
One advantage of small mosaic tiles is that you can often manage an installation without having to cut individual tiles. Use a utility knife to cut strips of tiles away from the sheet. If you do need to fill in spaces with small, cut tiles, remove the tiles from the backing and cut them with a snap cutter or nippers. Back-butter the tiles with adhesive before setting.

WORKING WITH IRREGULARLY SHAPED TILE

Handmade paver tiles lend a pleasing informality to a room. Mexican tiles, *saltillos,* are one common choice; they have the added benefit of being very inexpensive. Handmade tiles will not be uniformly shaped; they can vary widely in shape, thickness, size, and color from tile to tile. Choose the tiles by inspecting each one and discarding those with severe blemishes.

Irregularly shaped tiles present several installation challenges. Not only are sizes unpredictable, but some of them may be significantly warped. Tiles of different thicknesses can create a tripping hazard if not installed with care. Because the backs are often not flat, back-butter each tile with adhesive. Handmade tiles cannot be cut easily with a snap cutter; a wet saw is much more effective. Some types require application of a sealer before grouting.

Floor layout for irregular pavers.
When the tiles are not of predictably uniform size, layout becomes less precise. Rather than using plastic spacers, break the layout into a grid. For tiles that are approximately 12 inches square, use chalk lines to make 3-foot squares; each square will hold nine tiles. Dry-fit the tiles first, adjusting the spaces between them by sight. Then set the tiles one square at a time.

1. Set the tile.
Comb on thin-set mortar (page 485). For tiles with irregular backs, apply adhesive on the backs as well to ensure an adequate bond. To make sure you can compensate for warped tiles and varying thicknesses, use a trowel with ½-inch notches to spread the adhesive.

2. Tap with a mallet.
With uniform, machine-made pavers, you can use a beating block as described on page 489. With handmade pavers, however, tap on each tile individually. Use a soft mallet, not a hammer. You can set a rag on the paver to protect the surface further.

3. Clean the tiles.
Remove mortar that oozes up between the tiles. Take care to keep mortar off the surface of the tiles. Before grouting, clean the tiles with a sponge and water. Apply sealer to unsealed tiles before grouting.

WORKING WITH STONE TILE

Stone tiles are made from stone that is quarried all over the world. Many types are available, and they vary widely in color and price. Polished stone has a shiny, almost glazelike finish that looks best on walls and interior floors. Honed stone has a smooth, matte finish that does not show wear as much as does polished stone. If properly sealed, honed tiles can be used in wet areas where polished stone would be too slippery. Flamed stone has a rough finish that is most useful on heavily traveled floors. Most stone is brittle, so the the substrate must be strong— at a minimum, backerboard over 3/4-inch plywood. Because stone is heavy, be sure your floor joists are strong enough to hold it. Check with an engineer or architect if you are not sure. Cut stone tile with a wet saw, and use a blade suitable for the type of stone you are cutting.

TYPES OF STONE

Type	Description	Pros	Cons
Marble	A limestone that has been changed deep beneath the earth's surface into a hard composition of crystals. Characterized by varied patterns and colors of veins.	Elegant appearance, used in many of the world's most famous buildings; beautiful and long-lasting.	Veins add to appeal, but weaken the marble. Dark-colored marble can fade in sunlight. Easily scratched and stained.
Granite	Quartz-based stone with a tough, glossy appearance. Colors range from light to dark, with varying patterns and graining.	Harder than marble; resists scratching. Easy to care for; resists acids. Excellent choice for kitchen countertops. Generally very dense and capable of withstanding freeze-thaw cycles.	Quarried all over the world, with varying characteristics from each region. Softer granites can sometimes show wear.
Slate	A rough-surfaced tile that is split, rather than sliced, from quarried stone. Available in slabs or as cut tiles, usually 12 inches square. Gauged slate is ground smooth on the bottom, while ungauged (or cleft) slate is rough on both sides.	Widely available and reasonably priced.	Somewhat brittle, with less range of colors than other stones. Dark slate may fade in sunlight. Irregular surface can produce undesirable flooring. Ungauged slate needs to be set in a thick mortar bed.

Materials to Use with Stone Tile

Be sure to get the right materials for setting, grouting, and sealing your stone tiles.

■ Latex-modified thin-set mortar works for most installations, but epoxy thin-set may be needed. Do not use organic mastics. Marble is somewhat transparent, so use white thin-set rather than gray.

■ With ceramic tile, a contrasting grout color is often used as part of the design. With stone tile, and especially with marble and granite, the objective is usually to minimize or eliminate the visual impact of the grout joints, so the surface resembles a solid whole. Choose a grout color that closely matches the stone. Use unsanded grout with marble and slate tiles, and epoxy adhesive as grout with closely spaced granite tiles.

■ Clear sealers can improve the appearance of stone tile and protect it from dirt, water, and stains. Use a low-sheen penetrating sealer on a floor; glossy sealers work well with other surfaces. Choose a sealer recommended for your type of stone. Test on a scrap tile to make sure it won't discolor your tiles. Granite usually needs no sealer.

EXPERTS' INSIGHT

SHOPPING FOR STONE

Often the most attractive stones are the weakest because of their deep veins. Stone tiles are often sorted according to their background color, but variations within the sorted colors can be substantial. Look through each box of tiles before you buy. Get extras so you can return tiles that are unsatisfactory. Buy only from a knowledgeable and reputable dealer.

SETTING GRANITE AND MARBLE TILE

Granite and marble are usually quarried and then manufactured to uniform sizes and thicknesses. Standard tiles are 12 inches square and ⅜-inch thick with one side polished smooth. To minimize chipping, the exposed edges of granite and marble tiles are beveled. In fact, the edges are usually so smooth and straight that the grout joint between tiles can be very thin; sometimes the tiles are installed without any grout joints at all. Do a complete dry run before applying adhesive and laying tiles.

YOU'LL NEED

TIME: About a day for a 12-foot-long countertop.
SKILLS: Cutting and setting tiles and carefully aligning tiles.
TOOLS: Wet saw or grinder with a diamond blade.

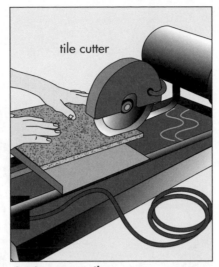

Cutting stone tiles.
Use a wet saw. Natural stone sometimes breaks along existing fissure lines when you try to cut it. If this becomes a problem, cut the tile through only two-thirds of its thickness, then flip it over and finish the cut from the other side.

TOOLS TO USE

STONE CUTTER

The best tool for making neat rectangular cutouts is a small stone cutter equipped with a diamond blade. Rent or borrow one from the tile dealer or a rental store. (Tile setters often mount a diamond blade on an electric grinder.) After cutting in each direction, knock the cutout free and use tile nippers and a rubbing stone to clean up the corners.

Set in silicone caulk.
It may not look professional, but many tile setters use this technique. After you have done a complete dry run and know exactly where each tile will go. Lift up one or two tiles at a time and make squiggles of clear silicone caulk on the substrate. Set the tiles in it quickly but carefully.

Seal it first.
Manufacturers recommend that some types of stone tiles be set with an expensive epoxy mortar. An alternative technique is to coat the back of the tiles with nonpourous epoxy. Once the coating has dried, the tiles can be set with regular thin-set mortar.

Finish the edge.
You can buy special edging tiles for some types of stone. Or install narrow strips on the edge, and set the tiles on top of them, to produce the illusion of a massive slab. Have the exposed edges polished by the dealer, or polish them with a rubbing stone, and perhaps brush on several coats of clear lacquer.

GROUTING TILE

Grout is a thin mortar mixture that is used to fill the joints between tiles. It protects tile edges from nicks and cracks, and it helps keep water from working its way below the tile surface. The size and color of the grout joint can be as important to the finished appearance of a floor as the tile itself. So it pays to choose and apply the grout carefully. (See page 471 for more on grout selection.) Do not apply grout until the adhesive has set, which normally takes up to 24 hours. If you are tiling more than one surface, such as a bathroom floor and walls, set the tiles on all the surfaces before you begin grouting. Then grout the walls before the floor. For stronger and less permeable grout, mix the powder with latex additive rather than water.

YOU'LL NEED

TIME: Several hours for a typical bathroom floor.
SKILLS: Mixing and spreading grout, shaping grout joints, and careful cleanup.
TOOLS: Bucket, trowel or mortar mixer; awl; rubber gloves; grout float; sponge; and joint shaper.

CAUTION!
USING COLORED GROUT
If you are using colored grout, mix a small test batch. Let it dry so you can see the finished color. Also spread some of the grout on a scrap tile to see if it stains the tile surface. When adding color additive to grout, mix it in before adding the liquid. And make note of the exact quantities of ingredients used so that you can mix consistent colors from one batch to the next.

1. Mix by hand...
Measure the liquid and pour it into the bucket. Add the dry ingredients a little at a time. Stir cautiously with a clean trowel or piece of wood. Add more dry ingredients as needed.

...or use a mortar mixer.
For preparing large amounts, use a mortar mixer attached to an electric drill. Set the blade in the mixture, then mix at a slow speed. Don't lift the blade out until it has stopped turning.

2. Remove spacers, clean joints.
Before you begin spreading grout, remove all of the spacers between tiles. An awl or some other thin tool will make removal easier. Also remove any adhesive that was squeezed into the joints between tiles. A razor blade or grout saw will speed this process. Vacuum the joints and put masking tape over all expansion joints, which will be caulked later.

3. Apply the grout.

For a floor, dump enough grout on the tiles to cover about 3 square feet. For a wall, scoop a good-sized dollop up with the float. Hold the grout float at about a 35-degree angle, and spread the grout diagonally across the tiles. Press the grout firmly and completely into the joints. Make two or three passes, working in a different direction for each pass.

Tilt the float up so it is nearly perpendicular to the surface, and wipe away excess grout. Move diagonally to the joints, to avoid digging into them with the float.

4. Wipe away the excess.

When you have finished grouting one area, use a dampened sponge to wipe the tiles. Use a circular motion. If the grout is hard to wipe from the tiles, don't wait so long next time. Take care that the joints are consistent in depth. Rinse the sponge often.

TOOLS TO USE

A Grout Bag

A grout (or mortar) bag looks a bit like a pastry bag used for decorating cakes. It is useful for grouting joints that can't be reached with a trowel, or for particularly porous tiles that soak up grout quicker than you can clean it off the surface. Use a tip on the grout bag no wider than the width of the joint. Fill the bag with grout, then place the tip in the joint. Move the bag as you squeeze grout into the joint. Grout the full length of joints rather than grouting around each tile. Let the grout harden a little, then shape the joints (see page 602). Once the grout has set for 30 minutes or more, sweep the joints with a broom or stiff brush to remove the excess.

EXPERTS' INSIGHT

WATCH THE GAPS

Don't forget about the expansion joints. These joints at corners and edges must be filled with expandable caulk, which allows the surfaces to expand and contract without cracking or damaging the tiles. Use masking tape to keep grout out of the expansion joints. Some grout will still seep under the tape and into the joint. So when you have finished grouting, remove the tape and clean out the grout. Or wait for it to dry, and cut it out with a grout saw or utility knife. Let the joint dry completely, and vacuum before caulking.

5. Shape the joints.

After wiping the tiles, clean and shape the joints. Pull a barely dampened sponge along grout lines, removing high spots as you go. Some people like thick grout lines that are nearly flush with the surface of the tile, while others prefer grout lines that recede. The important thing is that they be consistent. Buy an adjustable grout shaper, or use a toothbrush handle or a wood dowel. The shaper should be a bit wider than the joint.

6. Fill the gaps.

If you notice a gap or inadvertently pull grout out from a joint, fill it right away with grout. Wearing rubber gloves, press a small amount into the void, filling it completely. Then shape the joint and remove any excess grout.

7. Remove the grout film.

Once you have cleaned the tile surfaces of grout and shaped the joints, let the grout set up for another 15 or 20 minutes. With your sponge and a bucket of clean water, and wearing a rubber glove, start the final cleaning of the tiles. Timing is critical: The grout should be dry enough to not be affected by the sponge, yet haze on the tile surface should be not so dry that it is difficult to remove. Rinse the sponge and wring it out. Pass the sponge slowly over a line of tiles. Flip the sponge over and make another straight run. Rinse the sponge and continue. With proper timing and careful execution, this process should remove nearly all of the grout residue from the tile surface. After another 15 minutes, polish the tiles with a dry piece of cheesecloth or a clean rag.

CAULKING AND SEALING

Caulk fills expansion joints around the perimeter of a tiled surface. Its flexibility allows adjacent surfaces to expand and contract without damaging tile; and it won't crack, as grout would. Many fine tile jobs have been marred by ugly caulking, so take the time to do it right. (See page 473 for information on choosing caulk.) Practice on scrap pieces until you feel you've got the knack. Place the tube in the gun, cut the tip, and puncture the seal with a long nail. Some people like to cut the tip at a severe angle, while others like to cut it nearly straight across. Have a damp rag handy, soaked with water or mineral spirits, depending on the type of caulk you are using.

YOU'LL NEED

TIME: Less than an hour for most projects.
SKILLS: Applying and smoothing caulk, and using a paint roller.
TOOLS: Caulk gun, paint roller and tray or paintbrush, and rag.

EXPERTS' INSIGHT

GROUT SEALERS

You can significantly improve the durability of grout joints by sealing them. Wait until the grout has fully cured—a week or two—before applying grout sealer. Use a disposable foam-rubber paintbrush, which allows you to cover the grout without getting sealer on the tile. Allow the first coat to dry, then apply a second. Renew the grout sealer from time to time.

Apply and smooth caulk.
Position the tip of the tube on the surface to be caulked, and get yourself into a comfortable position. Squeeze the trigger carefully until caulk begins to flow. Continue squeezing as you pull the gun along. Either leave the bead of caulk as it is, or use a wet finger or damp rag to smooth it. Strive for a consistent-looking line.

Seal the tile.
Some tiles must be sealed when they are installed; others must have a sealer reapplied every few years. Check with the tile manufacturer for specific instructions. If you are installing unsealed tiles, you may have to apply the sealer before grouting. Renew the sealer as needed. A foam-rubber paint roller works well for most types of tile sealer.

TILING FLOORS

Unless your home was seriously underbuilt, your floors are strong enough so that you can install carpeting or another type of resilient flooring with confidence. But ceramic tile has much more demanding requirements. The weight of the tiles is not usually the problem; deflection is. If a ceramic tile floor flexes, grout and even tiles can crack. If you have any doubts about the strength of the floor, ask a contractor to inspect it before you begin tiling.

Sometimes a bouncy floor can be firmed up by driving screws through the subflooring and into joists. Or, you may have to add another subfloor layer, or even beef up the joists. However, if you build up the floor so much that the new tile surface will be a half inch or more higher than an adjacent floor surface, it will look and feel awkward. That's why in some situations it is simply not practical to lay a ceramic tile floor.

Anatomy of a floor.
Floor joist strength is determined by the size of the joist, the length of the joist's span between supports, and the amount of space between joists. If your joists have spaces larger than 16 inches between them, for instance, then you will need an extra strong subfloor. Plywood is the best subfloor material, but many older homes have strong subfloors made with planks of 1× lumber.

Backerboard
Older installations set tiles on a thick bed of mortar. Backerboard is an excellent modern day substitute. Use as thick a board as possible, installed over a plywood subfloor. See pages 482–483 for cutting and installation help.

Plywood
Although plywood is somewhat soft and flexible, it also has great strength. When two sheets are laminated together, the result is a very firm surface.

Concrete
Concrete is the best subsurface and works well for straightening out-of-level floors. Do not use curing or acceleration chemicals if you pour a concrete floor. An older concrete surface must be sound; tiling will not strengthen it.

Preparing a wood floor for tile.
If you will be tiling directly over plywood, it is best to install two layers of ⅝-inch-minimum plywood, rather than one thick sheet. Use exterior-grade plywood for the top layer. The edges should always fall over a joist, but stagger the sheets so that the joints do not fall directly over each other. Coat the bottom sheet with construction adhesive before setting the top sheet in place. Leave a gap of ⅛ inch or more around all edges of the top sheets, including at the joints. Fasten the plywood with screws or ring-shank nails. If an existing plywood subfloor is strong enough, sand the surface thoroughly, then vacuum. Talk to your tile dealer about the best adhesive to use.

If the existing floor is composed of 1× or 2× planking in good condition, drive screws into joists wherever it seems at all loose, and perhaps install a layer of plywood over it. If it has cracks and does not feel strong, remove the planking and install plywood.

Preparing a concrete floor for tile.
Concrete is a great base for tile, as long as it is structurally sound and flat. Some slabs may actually be too smooth, and should be scruffed up a bit by grinding with an abrasive wheel. Do not install tile over concrete that was treated with a curing or acceleration chemical when it was poured. These additives will prevent adhesive from bonding properly. If you are uncertain about whether or not such additives were used, try to locate the builder of the house or the concrete contractor. They may have a record. You can also test the slab yourself by sprinkling water on it. If the water isn't absorbed, the concrete was probably treated. Apply a latex bonding agent or add a subfloor.

Install plywood.
For the top layer of plywood, leave ⅛-inch gaps between the sheets. Fasten with screws or ring-shank nails in a 6-inch grid in the field, and every 4 inches at the joints and around the perimeter.

Beef up a wood floor.
Strengthen a weak subfloor by installing wood or metal cross bridging between joists. Close small gaps between joists and the existing subfloor with shims, or drive screws from above.

Fill in low spots.
Clean out low spots in a concrete slab and fill with thinset mortar. Use a trowel or straightedge to level the surface.

Dealing with cracks.
Cover small cracks in concrete with an isolation membrane (see page 472). Cracks that result in uneven surfaces indicate underlying structural problems; do not tile over such a surface.

EXPERTS' INSIGHT

REPLACING BASEBOARD

■ As long as you're tiling your floor, you may want to update your baseboards as well. New tile may well emphasize your old baseboard's imperfections.

■ Old vinyl cove base can get pretty ratty-looking. Install new cove base after the tile job is done. Make sure that the new material is as wide as the original stuff or you will have an ugly line on the wall. Apply with cove base adhesive or latex silicone caulk.

■ The base shoe gets banged up in time, too, so go ahead and replace it as well. Use stain or paint on it, then cut it with a miter box and fasten it with finishing nails.

Remove the baseboard.

Before tiling a floor, remove the baseboard from the surrounding walls. If the joint between the baseboard and wall is sealed with paint, score it with a utility knife first. Pull vinyl cove base away with a putty knife. If it resists removal, try heating the vinyl with a hair dryer to loosen the adhesive. Use a pry bar to remove wood baseboard. Protect the wall with a thin piece of wood. If your baseboard has a *shoe*—a small rounded molding at the bottom—remove that piece.

Trim casing and doors.

It is usually not a good idea to remove door casings. But cutting tile to fit around casing is difficult, and usually leads to a sloppy-looking job. So trim the bottom of the casing, and fit the tiles beneath it. With the subfloor installed, place a tile up against the casing. Lay a handsaw on the tile as you cut through the casing.

To make sure a door will swing freely after the tiles are installed, place tiles on the floor nearby. If not, use the tiles and a pencil to scribe a cut line at the door's bottom. Allow for a gap of at least ¼ inch. Remove the door by popping out the hinge pins. Place masking tape along the bottom of the most visible side of the door, and mark a cut line. Cut through the tape using a circular saw with a clamped straightedge as a guide.

Check floors for level.
Use a carpenter's level and a straight board to check the floor for level and to find any spots that are not flat. If the entire floor is out of level with the wall, it can still be tiled. If you plan to extend tile up the wall, however, you should consider leveling the floor or using tapered baseboard to make the transition attractive.

Level a floor.
Small bumps in the floor must be dealt with before you begin tiling. If the wood subfloor comes up in places, try driving screws through the flooring and into a joist to level it out. You may be able to take out small high spots with a belt sander.

To straighten out dips and low areas, or to level out an entire floor, use a self-leveling floor patch. These are made by manufacturers of tile adhesive.

Place barriers where necessary to keep the compound where it belongs. Mix the dry ingredients with water, then pour it on the floor. The mixture will level itself out to a certain degree, but use a long flat trowel to help things along. The compound should be cured and ready for tiling within a few hours. Most self-leveling compounds are intended to function at depths no greater than 1 inch. If the work seems intimidating, talk to a contractor about preparing a level subfloor for you.

TILING A KITCHEN FLOOR

*T*iling a kitchen floor can be a major disruption to any household. This project may affect access to food, meal preparation, and upset traffic patterns through the kitchen. Some preparation can be done well in advance of the tiling; some cabinets can be removed, new subflooring applied, and doors removed. For the tiling itself, set aside a long weekend so that the kitchen can be back in operation as quickly as possible.

YOU'LL NEED

TIME: 3–4 days to prepare, lay out, and tile an average-size kitchen.
SKILLS: Disconnecting and removing appliances, removing base cabinets, preparing a subfloor, and tiling the floor.
TOOLS: Screwdriver, hammer, pry bar, and putty knife.

TOOLS TO USE

KNEE PADS

Tiling floors is hard on your knees. In addition to the stress of kneeling much of the time, your knees are vulnerable to injury from tools and pieces of material left around the work area. That's why contractors who spend a lot of time working at floor level consider knee pads essential. For occasional use on wood or tile floors, non-marring foam, rubber, or rubber-capped pads are a good choice. (You'll find these useful for gardening as well.) For heavy-duty protection, but less comfort, buy the skateboarder-type knee pads that have a hard nylon shield on the front.

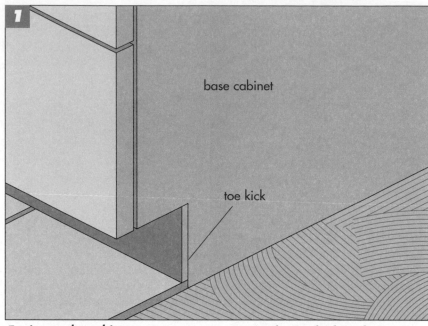

1. Assess the cabinets.
As a general rule, there is no need to install tile where it will be covered by cabinet bases or other permanent fixtures. Instead, use a thin pry bar and stiff putty knife to remove the toe kick and any molding along the floor. Set tile up to the cabinet. After all the tile is installed and grouted, trim the upper edge of toe kick to fit and reinstall it and the molding

2. Remove cabinets where needed.
Sometimes cabinets must be removed to take out the old flooring or to replace the subfloor. Remove fasteners holding the countertop in place, and the screws that join cabinets to each other and to the wall. In addition, remove overlapping pieces of toe kick and other molding.

3. Consider the appliances.

One of the issues you will have to address is whether or not to tile beneath appliances. Think of how your kitchen floor would look if your home were empty and up for sale. Untiled spaces where appliances usually sit would be unattractive to potential buyers.

Freestanding appliances, such as refrigerators, ranges, and dishwashers, should be removed from the kitchen to install tile underneath the appliance location. It is also best to tile beneath built-in appliances, although the work can be trickier. Often, when you tile beneath a built-in dishwasher,

for example, you raise the floor level such that the dishwasher will no longer fit under the countertop. You can raise or notch out the countertop a bit to accommodate the appliance. Adjustments may also have to be made in the plumbing connections.

4. Lay out the job.

At the center of the floor, mark perpendicular reference lines with a pencil or chalk line. (In odd-shape rooms you may want to center the layout on the most visible section of the floor rather than in the center of the room.) Check to make

sure that the lines are square (see pages 477–479). Using appropriate spacers if needed with your tile, dry set tiles along the reference lines to check the layout. Adjust the layout to minimize the number of cut tiles and to avoid creating any extremely small pieces.

5. Set the tiles.

Begin at the intersecting reference lines and spread thin-set mortar over a small area. Do not cover the lines. Set properly spaced tiles. Use a beating block (see page 466) after setting each section of tiles. Check alignment as you go.

TILING A BATHROOM FLOOR

*T*ile is a great material for bathroom floors: tough, attractive, and easy to clean. Many bathrooms have tile on every surface; plan ahead if you want to resurface your walls, countertops, or tub and shower areas. One of the great joys of tiling a bathroom is the chance to experiment with bold colors and unusual designs.

A typical bathroom floor does not require a waterproof installation, although you should choose tiles and setting materials that are suitable for a surface that will get wet from time to time.

EXPERTS' INSIGHT

REMOVING SINKS

If you have a pedestal or wall-mounted sink with legs sink, remove it before you start to tile. Shut off the water supply and disconnect the supply lines. Remove the trap with a pipe wrench. Unbolt and remove the top of a pedestal sink, then unbolt and remove the pedestal. (One-piece pedestal sinks are bolted to the floor and wall.) Remove the legs of a wall-mounted sink and pull the sink up and off of the mounting bracket. You may also want to remove a vanity, depending on its position.

1. Assess the toilet.
When tiling over a finished bathroom floor, the toilet can be left in place. But you will have to cut tiles to fit all around the base, which will probably leave you with an unprofessional-looking job. It is easier in the long run to remove the toilet and tile up to the closet flange. With fewer cut tiles, the job will look better and pose fewer maintenance problems.

2. Remove the toilet.
Shut off the water supply and disconnect the supply line. Flush the toilet, then sponge the remaining water from the tank. Pry off the decorative caps, then unscrew the flange nuts. If the nut is rusted tight, cut through it with a hacksaw; the easiest way is to cut down, as shown, and then unscrew it. With a helper, lift the toilet off the flange, and carry it to another room. Stuff a rag in the closet flange (make sure it's large enough so it won't fall down the hole) to contain sewer gases, and scrape off any wax, putty, or caulk.

3. Lay out the job.

Small, rectangular bathroom floors are relatively easy to lay out. Arrange grout joints so that they are parallel to the most visible straight edges in the room, such as along counters and tubs. Hide cut tiles in less exposed spots. In such a small area, it is worth your while to check the layout by dry-setting all of the tiles before you begin the installation. See pages 477–479.

4. Set the tiles.

Set full tiles as close as possible to the closet flange. Use nippers to cut tiles to fit around the flange. You don't have to worry about precision here, since the toilet will cover the area.

wax ring

horn

closet flange

5. Reset the toilet.

After the tile has been grouted, reset the toilet. Install new bolts in the flange; they may need to be longer than the old ones to compensate for the height of the tiles. Clean the horn of the bowl and install a new wax ring. If the flange is well below the tile surface, you may need a second wax ring to seal the gap. Set the toilet over the bolts, then tighten the nuts.

EXPERTS' INSIGHT

TILING OVER TILE

■ When remodeling a bathroom, you may want to replace an old tiled floor with new tiling. Removing the old tile can be a major headache, and it may not be necessary. Instead, you can use the existing floor as a setting bed for the new tile.

■ First, make certain that there are no structural problems with the floor—if the grout is significantly cracked and tiles are loose, it could signal underlying problems that need to be addressed before proceeding. Talk to your tile dealer about the best products and techniques to use over a tiled floor. Normally, the old tiles will need to be sanded heavily, to rough up the glazed surface. You may also need to fill in old grout joints if they aren't level with the tile surface.

■ Keep in mind that the new tile will add to the height of your bathroom floor. Place tiles on top of your existing floor to find out whether this new height will make it awkward to move from the hall into the bathroom. Usually, a threshold will smooth the transition.

TILING AN ENTRYWAY

Most professional tilesetters agree that the best substrate for tile is an old-fashioned mortar bed. But laying it smooth is a job for the pros. Backerboard has made it easier for do-it-yourselfers to install their own tile. There are times, though, when backerboard won't work. This is often the case when you cannot afford to raise the height of the finish floor too much. Entryways frequently pose this dilemma, because the floor connects with several rooms and often a stairway as well. In those situations, a modified mortar-bed installation is best.

YOU'LL NEED

TIME: 2–4 days, depending on the size of the entryway and the amount of preparation needed. Allow time for cement to cure. **SKILLS:** Troweling cement to a consistent thickness; preparing a subfloor; and tiling a floor. **TOOLS:** Steel trowel, stapler, utility knife, and paint roller.

EXPERTS' INSIGHT

BRINGING THE OUTDOORS IN

Often the best types of tile to use for an entryway are those that are commonly used on exterior applications, such as unglazed pavers, (machine- or handmade), slate, and half brick. If you also plan to tile an adjacent patio, porch, or other entrance to the house, use matching tiles inside and out to unify the spaces. Be sure the tiles you choose won't become slippery when wet.

Measure felt paper, cut with a utility knife 2–4 inches longer than needed. Roll it loosely, then unroll in position.

1. Prepare floor.
Stabilize any spongy areas of the floor using drywall screws twice as long as the thickness of your flooring. If necessary, add plywood so your subfloor totals at least 1⅛-inch in thickness. Install 15-pound felt roofing paper overlapping the edges 2 to 3 inches, and staple the paper to the subfloor every 6 to 8 inches. After stapling, trim the edges with a utility knife so the felt doesn't ride up any adjacent molding or stairs.

metal lath

stapler

2. Attach metal lath.
Staple galvanized metal lath (mesh) over the felt paper. Available at masonry-supply stores and large home centers in 2-foot-wide strips, the lath can be cut with tin snips. Butt the pieces together; don't overlap them.

3. Spread the mortar.

Prepare a cement mixture of half portland cement and half fine (builders) sand. The fine sand should not contain stones that would make the surface bumpy.

Spread cement with a steel trowel to a depth of ¼ inch, smoothing all ridges. Avoid smearing mortar on stair riser or adjacent molding.

4. Smooth the surface.

Let the mortar cure over night. Then carefully go over the cement with a trowel to scrape away any high spots. Sweep it to remove any loose material.

5. Lay out and set tiles.

An entryway can be difficult to lay out because different parts of the floor are visible from different directions. Choose the most public point of view and plan your layout around it. Dry fit the tiles to ensure there won't be any slivers of tile.

6. Grout and seal.

If the tiles were not sealed when you bought them, apply the sealer recommended by the tile maker before grouting. After the tiles are grouted (see pages 494–496), wait about a week before applying a liquid top coat, which should be renewed once or twice a year.

CHOOSING SEALERS AND FINISHES

Grout lines, unglazed tile, and unpolished natural stone are vulnerable to stains, dirt, grease, and mildew. For protection of porous surfaces apply a sealer or finish (the terms are interchangeable). Product types vary according to porosity of the material being covered and the degree of sheen you want. All require that the surface is clean, dry, and free of any other coatings or wax before application. Typically sealers and finishes can be applied in one coat but for very porous surfaces like brick, two coats are needed. Confirm that the sealer or finish you choose is rated for outdoor use; some are rated for indoor use only. Use a small paint brush when sealing the grout alone; apply it with a roller when sealing tile and grout.

TILING WALLS

Walls often are not very flat. Flexible drywall can be installed over bowed and twisted studs; once it is covered with paint or wallpaper, most people will never notice. But if you try to install tile on an irregular wall, the underlying problem will be magnified. It is very difficult to correct carpentry errors with tile. So check the walls carefully—and make necessary corrections—before you begin tiling.

YOU'LL NEED

TIME: About one hour per 5 square feet to set and grout tile, plus time for wall preparation.
SKILLS: Checking walls for straightness and squareness, preparing a substrate, installing tile, and grouting.
TOOLS: Level, straightedge, and tiling and grouting tools.

1. Assess the walls.
Use a carpenter's level to check walls for plumb. Set a long level or straightedge against the wall at various points to determine if the wall is flat. An out-of-plumb wall can be tiled, but it may affect the appearance of adjoining surfaces. If the wall is not reasonably flat, repair it first.

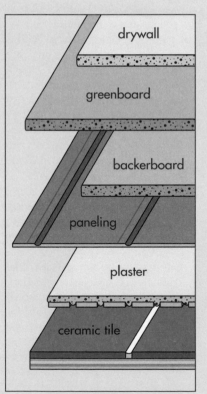

WALL SUBSTRATES

Tile can be installed over most existing wall surfaces as long as the wall is flat and in sound condition.

Drywall: The most common wall surface, and a good substrate for tile in dry locations. Can also be used in moderately wet areas if you brush on liquid waterproofing before tiling. Repair holes or cracks with patching compound. Remove wall paper and loose paint. Lightly sand painted surfaces. Perhaps add a second layer of drywall for added strength or to cover damaged areas.

Moisture-resistant drywall: Commonly known as greenboard or blueboard, it is similar to standard drywall, but is water-resistant—-though not waterproof. It can be used in fairly wet areas, but should receive the same waterproofing installation as regular drywall.

Backerboard: An ideal substrate for tile, especially as part of a waterproof installation on shower walls or bathtub surrounds. When installing backerboard over an existing wall surface, use corrosion-resistant nails or screws that are long enough to penetrate the wall studs.

Wall paneling: Most sheet paneling is too thin and fragile to be used as a substrate for tile. Remove the paneling and cover the wall with backerboard or drywall before tiling.

Plaster: Install tile over plaster that is hard, flat, and in good condition. If the plaster crumbles when you poke it with a knife, it is too weak and should be replaced with backerboard or drywall. Repair cracks and indentations.

Ceramic tile: You can tile directly over a previously tiled surface as long as it is in good condition. Remove loose or broken tile and fill the cavity with mortar. Aggressively sand the surface to remove the glaze.

In each case,
a = b.

All vertical lines
should be plumb.

2. Establish a center line and lay out.

On a large wall, it is usually best to start the layout with a vertical line somewhere near the middle. If a single obstruction, such as a wall or a window, is reasonably centered in the room, then draw a line through its center. With two obstructions, make your center line at the middle of the distance between their inside edges. If you have a single offset obstruction, divide the unobstructed portion of the wall in half.

Then add a horizontal line to divide the wall into four quadrants. Add reference lines to separate the field tiles from any trim tiles. Use a carpenter's level to establish vertical and horizontal reference lines.

On a wall that is less than 8 feet wide, you may want to make sure that the cut tiles on either side are close to the same size. The only way to ensure this is to make a complete dry run of one horizontal course.

EXPERTS' INSIGHT

EXTENDING ELECTRICAL BOXES

When tiling around electrical outlets and switches, remove the cover plates and set tile right up to the cutout in the wall. This may mean that you will have to move the electrical box forward, so that it will be flush with the finished tile surface. Extension rings are available at electrical supply outlets; mount them on the existing boxes. Before you begin tiling, make sure that you can find extension rings in the size you need, or talk to an electrician about other options.

Use a level to draw a vertical and a horizontal line.

masking tape

3. Hold the tiles.

Gravity works against you when installing wall tiles. Wall tile adhesive usually is sticky enough to prevent tiles from falling off, and most wall tiles are self-spaced so they will not slide down. In a more difficult installation, you may have to use spacers to keep the tiles from slipping, and masking tape to hold them on the wall. On each column of tiles, affix tape that is taut and well-adhered to the wall tile while the adhesive cures.

TILING A WINDOW RECESS

A tiled window recess won't rot, will prevent and resist water stains, and won't get scratched by cats seeking a sunny refuge. Plain terra cotta tiles are an attractive choice; decorative, hand-painted tiles can add a splash of color. If the surrounding wall is tiled, incorporate the window recess into the larger project. Use bullnose tiles or special windowsill tiles to round the edges. It is usually best to tile the recess after the wall, so that the recess tiles can overlap the wall tile. In a tub surround with a window, cut down on maintenance problems by replacing sashes with glass block and then tiling the recess.

YOU'LL NEED

TIME: Less than a day of labor, but allow a day for the adhesive to cure before grouting.
SKILLS: Careful removal of molding and setting wall tile.
TOOLS: Flat pry bar, and tiling and grouting tools.

EXPERTS' INSIGHT

TILE AS TRIM

Tile is most often used to cover fairly broad areas; it makes for a wall that is low in maintenance as well as attractive. Sometimes, however, tile can make a stunning impact when it is used for small accents. One excellent example: Wood casing trim around doors and windows serves to hide an unattractive gap between materials. Tile can perform that function just as well, and with a good deal more pizzazz, especially if you choose decorative trim tiles.

1. Remove molding and sill.
Remove the window casing, then pry off the sill. You may need to cut the sill to get it out. Now examine the jamb and decide how far inward toward the window the tile will extend. If the window has stop molding, decide whether to leave it in place or remove it. You can tile directly on top of the jamb or install backerboard first.

2. Prepare the wall.
Stuff the gap with fiberglass insulation if none exists; take care on an old window not to hinder the movement of the weights that are attached by ropes to the sashes. If you will be tiling the wall, apply fiberglass mesh joint tape, and fill in with joint compound. Allow to dry, apply a second coat, and sand smooth. If you will be painting the wall, carefully install metal outside corner bead, apply joint compound, and sand. Sand the jamb as well.

3. Support top pieces.

Install any wall tiles flush to the jamb so you will have a consistent grout line at the corners (see *right*). Make a support system using three boards to hold the ceiling tiles in place. Allow them to set before continuing.

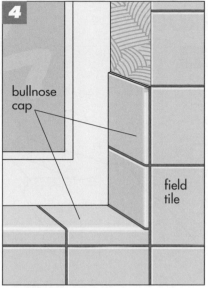

4. Set the tiles.

Set tiles in adhesive and grout the same as for a standard wall installation. Use bullnose caps for a tiled wall (as shown) or for a painted wall. Or, use one of the other options pictured *below*.

5. Caulk the window.

Take special care to completely caulk the joint between the tile and the window; you don't want all your work to be destroyed in a few years by water damage.

Other corner options.

The arrangement shown in the steps above, with bullnose caps used on the recessed surfaces, is the most common. You may prefer to use bullnose on the

wall (*above, left*). Or use corner edging tiles similar to V-cap tiles used on countertops, but without the raised lip (*center*); install the edging pieces before tiling the recess. For a decorative touch,

apply a border trim around the recess (*above, right*). Install bullnose pieces in the recess so they cap the border trim, or butt field tiles up to the border pieces if they have a finished edge.

TILING A TUB SURROUND

*I*n a tub that also contains a shower, plan to install tile from the top of the tub to about 6 inches above the shower head. If the tub doesn't have a shower, tile at least one foot above the tub (more if you anticipate a lot of splashing). If you want to tile the ceiling as well, use a fast-setting adhesive; it will hold the tiles in place without support. (Install ceiling tile so that it doesn't have to line up with the wall tiles—say, diagonally—because getting it to fit will be very difficult. If an end wall continues out past the tub, continue the tiles at least one full vertical row beyond the tub, and run it down to the floor. Use bullnose cap tiles for the edges.

Set the tile on a backerboard substrate (see pages 482–483 for information on backerboard). The backerboard itself should be installed over a waterproofing membrane of 15-lb. felt paper or 4-mil polyethylene. Overlay the edges of the membrane and seal the seams of the backerboard with fiberglass mesh tape bedded in adhesive.

If you have a window with wood casing and jambs, consider tearing it out or cutting back the casing and tiling the recess (pages 510–511). You can eliminate the problems of a wood window altogether by installing glass block.

YOU'LL NEED

TIME: A day to prepare the substrate, most of a day to tile, and a few hours to grout.
SKILLS: Cutting and installing backerboard, patching walls, cutting and installing tile.
TOOLS: Drill, hole saw, scraping tool, wall patching tools, level, a straight board, notched trowel, snap cutter, nibbler, hacksaw with rod saw, grouting float.

1. Remove the hardware.
You don't want to cut tiles to fit precisely around hardware. Pry the shower-arm escutcheon away from the wall, and perhaps remove the shower arm as well. Remove the tub spout; most can be unscrewed by sticking the handle of a screwdriver or hammer in the spout and turning counterclockwise. Remove the faucet handles and escutcheons.

2. Prepare and lay out.
The walls must be solid, and at least close to plumb and square (see page 477). If necessary, remove the existing substrate and install a waterproofing membrane and backerboard. Be sure that the new surface is flush with any adjoining surface.

Establish a vertical reference line by laying the tiles in a row on the tub and making sure you will either have the same size tile on each end, or that you will not have any very narrow pieces. If the end walls are out of square with the rear wall, factor in how the pieces will change size as you move upward. Measuring from the low point of the tub if it is not level, establish a horizontal reference line and tack a very straight batten board along its length.

3. Cut the tile.

Use a snap cutter for the straight cuts. Hold the tile in place and mark it for cutting. Align it on the cutter, score the surface by pushing down while sliding the cutter once across the tile, then push down on the handle. For a series of cuts of the same size, use the adjustable guide. Smooth the ragged cut edges with a rubbing stone or file.

4. Set the tile.

Apply adhesive with a notched trowel, taking care not to cover your layout lines. Set the tiles, giving each a little twist and pushing to make sure it sticks. Start with the row sitting on the batten. Most wall tiles are self-spacing. Once you have several rows installed, remove the batten and install the bottom row.

5. Cut tile around pipes.

Cuts around pipes usually do not have to be precise because the opening is covered with an escutcheon. Use a nibbler to eat away at a curved cut, or a hacksaw equipped with a rod-saw blade. To cut a hole, use a tile-cutting hole saw. Or, set the tile on a piece of scrap wood, drill a series of closely spaced holes with a masonry bit, and tap out the hole.

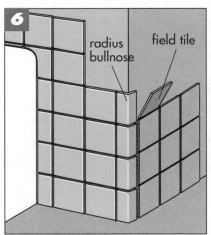

6. Install end and corner tiles.

Cut the curved piece at the corner of the tub with a hacksaw fitted with a rod-saw blade; it may take several attempts to get it just right. Use radius bullnose tiles everywhere there is an exposed edge. (Do not use a field tile edged with grout—it will look very sloppy.)

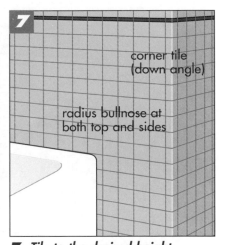

7. Tile to the desired height.

When you reach your top row, wipe away excess adhesive from the wall as you install bullnose caps. Use outside corner pieces ("down angles"), which have two cap edges, at all outside corners.

8. *Attach ceramic accessories.*
Apply adhesive and use masking tape to hold soap dishes and other accessories in place until they are set. Take the tape off after a day or two and apply grout, but wait a week or so before using.

grouting float

toothbrush handle

9. *Grout, caulk, and seal.*
Mix the grout with latex additive, and push it into the joints with a grouting float held nearly flat. Tip the float up and wipe away the excess. Carefully wipe the surface to produce consistent grout lines. Use a toothbrush handle or other tool to shape the joints. Caulk the corners and edges. Wipe and dry-buff the haze.

10. *Reattach the hardware.*
Reattach the plumbing hardware. If you need to install a shower arm, use a thin tool handle to tighten it. If the new tile has caused valves or nipples to be recessed too far and you can't install a faucet or spout, visit a plumbing supplier and pick up suitable extensions. Once the grout has cured, apply sealer.

TILING AN ACCESS PANEL

magnetic cabinet-door catches

Plumbing access panels are usually located in an adjoining room, but yours might be in the bathroom. The panel may have been installed when the bathroom was built, or it might have been built out of necessity when a plumber needed to gain access to the pipes and valves supplying the tub. Don't just tile over the panel;

a plumber may need to get in there again someday. The easiest solution is to cover the panel with a piece of plastic, well-painted plywood, or a plastic access panel made for the purpose (available at home centers).

Or, make a tiled access panel. Cut a piece of plywood sized to hold full tiles. Install tiles on it so they

will align with the surrounding tiles, and trim the edges with painted wood molding; drive screws through the molding to hold the panel in place. Or skip the molding, and attach with magnetic cabinet door catches, as shown *above*.

MASONRY

GETTING TO KNOW YOUR STRUCTURES

Garage floors.

To withstand the weight of cars and small trucks, a garage floor slab should be at least 4 inches thick. It should be strengthened with reinforcing wire mesh and be poured on top of at least 4 inches of solidly tamped gravel or sand.

A footing running around the perimeter of the slab adds extra support for the garage walls. It can be shallow if there is no significant frost danger in your area or if local building codes permit a "floating" slab—one that can rise or fall an inch or so with frost heave. Otherwise, the footing should extend below the frost line. Anchor bolts in the footing allow you to firmly attach the bottom plate of the wall framing.

To handle condensation, blown-in rain or snow, and moisture from vehicles, the slab should slope toward the floor drain or garage door at a rate of ¼ inch per foot.

Footings.

Before building a masonry wall, you must pour a solid footing or the wall will crack. (The exception is a dry stone wall, which has no mortar joints.) How extensive the footing should be depends on how much weight it must carry. For a low garden wall you need only a small pad. A tall masonry or concrete wall, however, requires a substantial footing that extends below the frost line.

To support posts for a deck, gazebo, or similar project, you need to set post footings below the frost line in areas with frost or your structure will move up and down with the changing seasons. Simply dig holes and pour in the concrete footings. Or, insert cylindrical concrete tube forms into the holes before pouring the concrete.

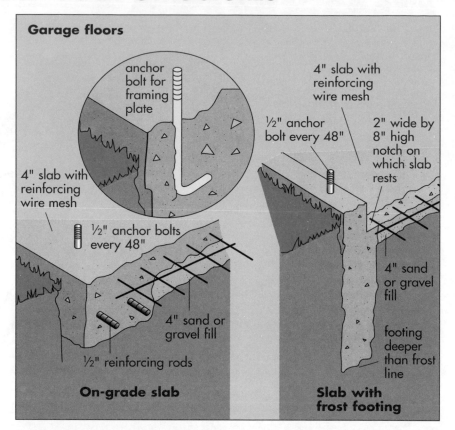

Garage floors

anchor bolt for framing plate

4" slab with reinforcing wire mesh

½" anchor bolt every 48"

2" wide by 8" high notch on which slab rests

4" slab with reinforcing wire mesh

½" anchor bolts every 48"

4" sand or gravel fill

4" sand or gravel fill

½" reinforcing rods

footing deeper than frost line

On-grade slab

Slab with frost footing

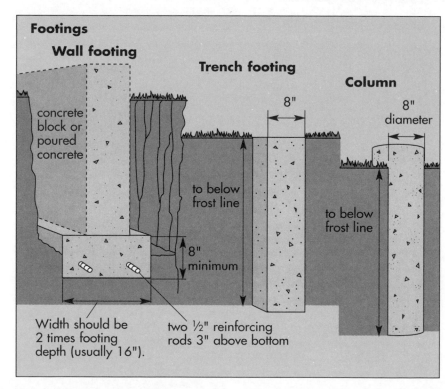

Footings

Wall footing

Trench footing

Column

concrete block or poured concrete

8"

8" diameter

to below frost line

to below frost line

8" minimum

Width should be 2 times footing depth (usually 16").

two ½" reinforcing rods 3" above bottom

SELECTING MASONRY AND CONCRETE TOOLS

Successful masonry and concrete work requires special techniques. Having the correct tool is essential if you want to end up with straight mortar lines and smooth surfaces. Compared with carpentry tools, masonry tools are not expensive, so don't hesitate to buy top-quality tools. Cheap tools can make the job more difficult and lead to shoddy-looking work that you'll have to live with a long time. If your budget is tight, consider renting professional-quality tools rather than buying something from the bargain bin.

A **circular saw, framing square, tape measure, chalk line, line level,** and **4-foot level** are general-purpose tools you'll need. For mixing and transporting masonry materials and concrete, get a sturdy contractor-quality **wheelbarrow** with a capacity of at least 3 cubic feet. Make sure the tire is an air-filled type. A **mortar box** is handy for mixing a lot of material, and a **mortar hoe** allows you to mix materials more easily than a garden hoe or a shovel.

To prepare the site and move concrete and mortar ingredients you'll need a **round-point shovel** for general digging, a **square-blade shovel** for moving sand and wet concrete, and a **spade** for squaring up a slab excavation or a footing trench.

Use a **tamper** to prepare soil for masonry surfaces. The beginning steps in finishing concrete require a **darby**, a **wood float**, and a **bull float**. For final finishing, use a magnesium or steel **finishing trowel** (usually it's best to have both). An **edger** is necessary to round off and strengthen edges of slabs. Make control joints with a **jointer** while the material is still wet. Or, cut joints after concrete is set using a circular saw equipped with a **masonry blade**.

Cutting bricks, blocks, or stones will be much easier if you have a bricklayer's hammer, a brick set or **masonry chisel**, and a 2-pound **baby sledgehammer**.

When building concrete or masonry walls, you'll need **line blocks, line clips, mason's line**, a modular **spacing rule**, and a **plumb bob** (a chalk line can be used in place of a plumb bob).

For placing mortar, use a well-balanced pointed **brick trowel**. Use a **pointing trowel**, $\frac{3}{8}$**-inch back filler**, or a **sled jointer** to tuckpoint, or force, mortar into joints being repaired. Finish the joints with a **joint strike**; these are available in different shapes and help you strike (finish) mortar joints between bricks, blocks, or stones. A good stiff **hand brush** is necessary for finishing the job, along with a variety of stiff brushes for cleanup.

If you finish the concrete with a nonskid surface, have handy a stiff-bristled push broom. To cure concrete, you need a garden hose with an adjustable nozzle or an oscillating lawn sprinkler.

masonry blade

edger

jointer

steel finishing trowel

circular saw

magnesium finishing trowel

line clip

line blocks

tape measure

plumb bob

modular spacing rule

4-foot level

framing square

chalk line

line level

mason's line

hand brush

sled jointer

⅜" back filler

wood
float

pointing trowel

brick trowel

bull
float

joint strike

darby

tamper

wheelbarrow

brick
set

square-blade
shovel

baby
sledgehammer

spade

round-
point shovel

bricklayer's
hammer

mortar box

masonry chisel

mortar hoe

FIGURING CONCRETE NEEDS

With the help of a simple calculator, you can determine accurately how much concrete you need. Suppliers measure and sell concrete by the yard, which means cubic yard (3×3×3 feet or 27 cubic feet).

Measure the project accurately, especially the depth of slabs and any variations in the excavation. A large slab that is only ½ inch thicker than you think it is will need a lot more concrete than your calculation. Double-check the figures with a concrete supplier—you both have an interest in getting the measurement right.

landing: 32" (2.66')×4'×4'
= 42.56 cubic feet

step #3: 24" (2')×10" (.83')×4'
= 6.64 cubic feet

step #2: 16" (1.33')×10" (.83')×4'
= 4.41 cubic feet

step #1: 8" (.66')×10" (.83')×4'
= 2.19 cubic feet

footing: 40" (3.33')×10" (.83')×48" (4')
= 11.05 cubic feet

> **CAUTION!**
> Don't underestimate. Nothing is worse than finding out that you are just a few cubic feet short of having enough concrete. Aim at having a little too much concrete; adding more after the first batch has set will weaken the final product.

Calculate for steps and footings.
To estimate concrete needs, divide odd-shaped jobs into easy-to-figure sections. Add the results to get total volume. In this example, the steps have 8-inch (.66-foot) risers and 10-inch (.83-foot) treads, and the landing is 4×4 feet. (To get the measurement in feet, divide inches by 12.) Use this formula: Length × width × depth equals volume. The sum of the volumes of this footing, landing, and steps is about 67 cubic feet. Assuming you'll fill the forms about two-thirds full of rubble (see page 670), you need about 22 cubic feet of concrete. If you add in a 10-percent cushion, you get around 25 cubic feet. Divide that by 27 (the cubic feet in a cubic yard), and your estimate is a bit less than 1 cubic yard.

To find the area of a cylindrical pier, square the radius and multiply by 3.14, then multiply

Calculate for a slab.
To estimate concrete for a rectangular slab, multiply width times length times depth. In the slab shown, this is 10×12×.33 feet = 39.6, which rounds up to 40 cubic feet. Add 10 percent for a cushion and divide by 27, and you find that you need 1⅔ cubic yards. For a circular slab, determine the area in square feet by squaring the radius of the circle (half the diameter) and multiplying by 3.14. Then multiply by the depth of the slab to determine the volume in cubic feet. Divide by 27 and add 10 percent for excavation variation.

CONCRETE ESTIMATOR

Slab Thickness	Concrete required in yards or cubic feet by surface area of job in square feet				
	20	50	100	200	500
4 inches	.2	.6	1.2	2.5	6.2
	(6.7)	(16.7)	(33.3)	(66.7)	(166.7)
6 inches	.4	.9	1.9	3.7	9.3
	(10)	(25)	(50)	(100)	(250)
8 inches	.5	1.3	2.5	5.9	12.5
	(13.3)	(33.3)	(66.6)	(133.3)	(333.3)

One yard of concrete equals 27 cubic feet.

BUYING CONCRETE

You can buy concrete three different ways. For small jobs, such as setting a few fence posts, buy bags of premixed concrete that you simply mix with water. Premix comes in bags weighing up to 80 pounds that contain cement, sand, and aggregate mixed together. Each sack contains enough mixture to make from ⅓ to ⅔ cubic foot.

For jobs that require half a cubic yard or more of concrete, it's best to order ready-mix concrete delivered in a concrete truck. This is not only much easier than mixing your own, but you will be assured of a reliable mix.

If you have a large job that requires you to work in small stages, it makes sense to buy cement, sand, and aggregate and mix your own concrete. In a mortar box or a machine mixer, combine 10 shovelfuls of Portland cement, 22 shovelfuls of sand, and 30 shovelfuls of aggregate for each cubic foot of concrete. Making small batches allows you to place and finish one section at a time.

The ideal temperature for working concrete is 70 degrees. Warmer or colder temperatures hasten or retard the rate of setting and curing. Avoid severe cold because freezing can ruin concrete.

Money $ Saver

ON-SITE MIXING TRUCKS
Standard concrete trucks carry concrete that has been mixed at the company's site; thus, the supplier will be reluctant to sell less than a yard of concrete. A new innovation is a delivery truck that mixes the concrete right at the site. Usually, this is more economical for smaller amounts of concrete.

CONCRETE MIXING PROPORTIONS

Coarse Aggregate
Use ¾- to 1-inch gravel
50–60 percent*

Sand
40–50 percent

+

Cement
Use five, 94-pound bags of Portland cement for concrete strong enough to withstand 3,000 pounds per square inch (PSI) or six bags to withstand 3,500 psi***

= 1½ tons**

= 1 cubic yard of concrete

* The more aggregate, the stronger the mix.

** These ingredients can be purchased separately or together in a mixture commonly known as con-mix.

*** For projects requiring extra lateral strength, such as a driveway.

1. To mix your own concrete, layer the ingredients and combine.
Shovel the gravel, sand, and cement in the order shown to achieve a consistent mix in the shortest time. This way, it is less likely that the finer ingredients will settle to the bottom. Mix together the dry ingredients with a mortar hoe before adding water.

2. Mix in the water.
Add small amounts of water to the dry mix, and stir it thoroughly with a mortar hoe. Eventually, the mixture will take on the consistency of mud. When it turns a uniform shiny gray color, the mixture is close to the correct consistency; test it using the procedure in Step 3.

distinct groove

Mixture is correct.

indistinct groove

Add water.

groove caved in

Add sand, gravel, and cement.

3. Test the consistency or slump.
Smack the top of the concrete with the back of your shovel to make a smooth surface. Chop it to create a groove about 2 inches deep. If the surface stays smooth and the groove maintains its shape, you have the right mixture. If the groove is indistinct, add water. If the groove caves in, add more dry ingredients.

PATCHING HOLES IN CONCRETE

*F*or spalled (flaking) surfaces or for hairline cracks and small broken areas, use the patch materials discussed in the chart on page 522. If your concrete surface is badly settled and cracked, however, remove the damaged section and pour new concrete. Concrete patches rarely blend in, so if you are concerned with appearance, you may want to replace entire sections regardless of the extent of the damage.

YOU'LL NEED

TIME: 1 to 2 hours for several small patches; a full day to remove and repour a section.
SKILLS: Chiseling, mixing concrete, finishing concrete.
TOOLS: Cold chisel, baby sledge, brush, finishing trowel, mixing trough or wheelbarrow.

EXPERTS' INSIGHT

CHECK OUT CRACKING

■ Spalling or cracking in an old slab may be caused by freezing and thawing cycles or by settling of the ground under the slab.
■ If a slab is less than three years old and it's spalling, the concrete probably was mixed incorrectly. More flaking likely will occur in the future. Serious cracks also can result from a weak mix, the failure to install reinforcing metal where it should have been, or unstable ground beneath the slab. Your best bet is to tear up the concrete and begin again.

1. To repair a spalled area, "key" the hole with a chisel.
All around the damaged area, hold a cold chisel at an angle and pound with a baby sledgehammer to remove the top ½ to 1 inch of the concrete surface. "Key" the hole by undercutting the edges so the bottom of the hole is larger than the top. This keying effect helps lock the new patching material into the old concrete, making a permanent bond.

2. Clean and dampen the hole.
Brush out dust and small particles. If any of the area surrounding the hole appears loose, remove it as well. Wet the hole with water, but don't leave any standing water. You may want to apply a latex bonding agent to the area to ensure that the new material adheres to the old surface.

3. Pour and finish the patch.
Mix the patching compound and pour it in. Tamp it firmly in place to make sure all areas are firmly in contact and there are no air bubbles in the material. To allow for shrinkage, mound the patching compound slightly higher than the surrounding surface. Finish with a steel trowel.

CONCRETE PATCH SELECTOR

Type	Uses	Description and Mixing Instructions
Latex, vinyl, and epoxy patch	Use for general-purpose repair jobs, such as filling hairline cracks, repairing small breaks and patches, and tuckpointing small areas. Latex and epoxy are best for patio surfaces.	Sold in powdered form with or without a liquid binder. Mix with the appropriate binder, usually a sticky white liquid, to a whipped-cream consistency. Mixing any product with a latex reinforcer makes it stronger, as will adding extra Portland cement to concrete.
Hydraulic cement	Use to plug water leaks in masonry walls and floor surfaces. This fast-drying formulation allows you to make the repair even while the water is leaking in.	Available in powdered form. Mix a small amount with water or a commercial binder, then work quickly.
Dry, premixed concrete	Use wherever you need to replace whole sections of concrete.	Mix with water. The thicker the consistency, the faster it sets up.

TOOLS TO USE

RENT AN ELECTRIC HAMMER

If you're faced with demolishing a 2- or 3-inch-thick concrete slab, try breaking it up with a sledgehammer. If the slab is thick or if the going gets rough, how-ever, don't take the chance of straining your back.

Call a rental center for an electric hammer that will help you break up the slab without much back-breaking strain. (You won't need a pneumatic jackhammer unless you have an extra-large job.) Wear safety goggles and gloves to protect your eyes and hands from flying concrete fragments.

1. *For a larger section, remove damaged concrete.*

Score the bottom of the control joints (grooves) that separate the damaged section from adjacent ones. Use a brick set or cold chisel and a baby sledge to chisel a line of white marks along the control joints. This will produce a row of hairline cracks that prevent random cracking beyond the expansion joint as you work.

Break out pieces by hammering at the same spot with an 8- or 10-inch maul until the concrete fractures. Using a sledgehammer, break it into pieces small enough to lift without straining your back. Use pieces of rubble, as shown in the inset, to break large pieces apart. Carefully chip away final areas along the control joints. Then clear away the waste.

2. *Form and pour a new slab.*

Chop out any roots; they may have been the cause of your problem to begin with. Build forms and expansion material, as shown above. Spread sand or crushed rock to fill in low spots in the subgrade. Tamp the whole area firmly. Lay in reinforcing wire mesh to within 2 inches of the form's edges. Position the mesh midway, vertically, in the slab by laying it on pieces of small debris or rubble. Pour concrete mix in the form and finish it. Duplicate the finish texture and color of the existing concrete as closely as possible.

REPAIRING BASEMENT LEAKS

Basement leaks not only make life miserable, but they can weaken the foundation of your home. Basement walls should seal out a moderate amount of water, but few will withstand a great deal of water pressure. If the wall leaks only during heavy rains, you may be able to solve the problem by adding extensions to your gutter downspouts to direct rainwater away from the basement walls. You may find that your yard slopes in a way that causes rainwater to flow toward your home. If so, some corrective landscaping may be needed to solve your problem.

YOU'LL NEED

TIME: Several hours for most small patching jobs; several days or more if you need to seal the outside of the wall.
SKILLS: No special skills needed.
TOOLS: Stiff brush, cold chisel, baby sledgehammer.

1. For slow seepage or damp walls, brush on interior sealer.
Clean away dirt, grease, and dust from the wall. If you are using a cement-based sealing product, wet the wall thoroughly with a fine mist from a garden hose. Mix the liquid and powder components of the sealer thoroughly and apply with a stiff brush.

2. Fill any cracks.
As you brush, be sure to fill in all the pores in the wall. Go over cracks several times to fill them. If a crack is too large to fill in with sealer, use hydraulic cement (see below). With some sealers, you must keep the sealant wet for several days to ensure bonding. Apply a second coat if necessary.

1. To plug leaking holes or cracks, widen and "key" the spot.
Enlarge the hole or crack with a cold chisel and hammer. Undercut it to make a "key," so the plug won't come loose. Make the hole at least ½ inch deep. Whisk out fragments of concrete.

2. Mix the cement.
In a bucket, add water to the dry hydraulic cement mix until it has a puttylike consistency. Then work it by hand. For a hole, roll it into the shape of a plug. Roll a long snake shape for a crack.

3. Apply the cement.
Squeeze the material into the opening. Keep pushing and pushing to make sure it fills every tiny crevice. Any water leaking through the wall at the time of the repair should stop running. Hold the cement in place for several minutes to allow the patch to set.

SOLVING BASEMENT WATER PROBLEMS

Problem	Symptoms/Tests	Causes	Solution
Condensation	Damp walls, dripping pipes, rusty hardware, mildew. To identify condensation, tape a mirror in the dampest spot and wait 24 hours. If it's foggy or beaded with water, suspect condensation.	Excess humidity in the air, usually from an internal source, such as a basement shower, washing machine, unvented dryer, or from a significant difference between the wall temperature and inside air temperature.	Install a dehumidifier, improve ventilation, and seal interior walls.
Seepage	Dampness on a section of a wall or floor, most often on a wall near floor level. As with condensation, tape a mirror to the wall. If moisture condenses behind it, seepage is the culprit.	Surface water is forcing its way through pores in the foundation or an expansion joint. The source may be poor drainage or a leaky window well.	Improve exterior drainage. If problem is minor, an interior sealer may work. If not, waterproof the outside of the foundation.
Leaks	Localized wetness that seems to be oozing or even trickling from a wall or floor. It usually appears during heavy rain. Test by running a hose outside near the leak. Pay particular attention to mortar joints between blocks.	Cracks that may result from normal settling or improperly poured concrete. (If you see a cracklike line running horizontally around your basement wall, it may be that the builders poured part of the wall and allowed it to harden before pouring the rest.) Faulty roof drainage or a grade that slopes toward the wall exacerbates the problem.	Improve exterior drainage. You may be able to plug several holes. For widespread leakage, waterproof the entire foundation and install drain tile.
Subterranean water	A thin, barely noticeable film of water on the basement floor is often the first sign. Test by laying down plastic sheeting for two days. Penetrating moisture will dampen the concrete underneath.	Usually a spring or a high water table forces water up from below under high pressure, turning your basement into a well. This may happen only during rainy periods.	Install a sump pump. Drainage tile around the perimeter of the foundation may help, but only if it drains to a low spot or a storm sewer.

1. To seal a wall from the outside, excavate to the trouble area.
If the problem is fairly high up on the foundation wall, you may be able to do the digging yourself. Otherwise, hire an excavating contractor to backhoe a trench wide enough for you to work in. Remove the dirt close to the wall by hand. Brush the wall clean.

2. Apply sealer.
You can hire contractors who specialize in this type of coating. To do it yourself, wash the wall clean, allow it to dry, and apply two coats of tarlike bituminous sealer. Or, backplaster the wall with two coats of mortar and apply the sealer.

3. Install perforated drainpipe and a polyethylene barrier.
Dig a trench along the footing and install a sloping, perforated drainpipe embedded in gravel. Stick heavy-gauge polyethylene sheeting to the wall sealer. Drape it over the footing, but not the gravel drain. Overlap all seams at least 6 inches.

PATCHING CRACKS AND TUCKPOINTING

*E*ven well-built masonry walls require occasional repairs. Mortar joints that are exposed to the weather typically need to be tuckpointed every 30 years or so.

Cracking, the most common masonry malady, results from uneven settling of footings or from expansion and contraction due to temperature changes. Expansion cracks usually occur with uniform width and often follow joints between bricks or blocks. Settling cracks taper along a mostly vertical path, are widest at the top, and end as hairline cracks near the bottom of the wall.

Horizontal cracking may appear in basement walls made of concrete blocks. Usually the cause is pressure from backfill soil and water pushing in from the outside. If the wall bulges noticeably, you have a serious problem. You may need to dig out the backfill and re-lay the blocks—a job most suited to a professional contractor.

The same procedures are used to repair a cracked mortar line and for tuckpointing. For a long-lasting tuckpointing job, chisel or grind out all the joints. If your grout lines generally are worn and cracking, you need to tuckpoint the entire area or the problem will worsen rapidly.

Tuckpointing is painstaking, slow work. It can be done from a ladder, but you'll find the work easier, and you'll do a better job, if you set up scaffolding.

YOU'LL NEED

TIME: 2 hours to tuckpoint 25 square feet of wall.
SKILLS: Working with mortar.
TOOLS: Joint strike or sled jointer, pointing trowel, ⅜-inch back filler, cold chisel, baby sledgehammer, stiff brush, whisk broom.

1. Chisel out the joints...
With a baby sledge and a cold chisel, remove mortar from joints to a depth of ⅜ to 1 inch. It is possible to tuckpoint without chiseling out old mortar, but the tuckpointing will not last as long. Because chips will fly as you work, wear safety goggles and heavy gloves.

or use a grinder.
If you need to work on a large area, rent or purchase a 4-inch grinder to efficiently remove old mortar. Whichever method you use, if the joint crumbles easily all the way through the wall, tear down the whole section and re-lay the bricks with new mortar. Tuckpointing by itself will not add strength to weak masonry joints.

2. Scrape and brush out debris.
Use the point of a cold chisel or the tip of a pointed trowel to scrape away patches of mortar that remain after chiseling or grinding. Briskly sweep away debris with a stiff whisk broom. Mix the mortar using 1 part Portland cement to 2 parts masonry sand and enough water to form a puttylike consistency.

EXPERTS' INSIGHT

WAIT FOR WALL MOVEMENT TO STOP

■ To repair wall cracks caused by settling, you must wait until the movement stops before patching or tuckpointing. This may be as long as a year after the first signs of cracking appear.

■ To determine if settling still is occurring, bridge the crack with a piece of duct tape and check it occasionally for twists, tears, or pulling loose.

3. Place the mortar.

Load an upside-down trowel with mortar and hold it against the wall. With a ⅜-inch back filler, force the mortar into the joints. Fill the head (vertical) joints first, then the bed (horizontal) joints. It will take practice before you can tuckpoint without dropping mortar or smearing bricks.

4. Strike the joints.

Use a damp sponge to wipe away excess mortar while it is still wet. Brush the joints to remove mortar crumbs. Correct timing is essential for striking the joints. The mortar should be stiff, but not hard. Choose the appearance of your joint from those shown *below*.

5. Restrike and brush.

To ensure that your joints are watertight, strike them a second time, making sure they seal tightly against the bricks. Let the mortar set up somewhat, then brush away crumbs with a stiff brush. Scrub mortar stains off the wall within 24 hours.

CHOOSING A MORTAR JOINT

Struck joint

Make a struck joint with the edge of a pointed trowel, angling the joint from top to bottom. This is an attractive joint, but will collect water on the lower edge.

V-joint

Use a V-shaped strike or a bent piece of metal to make a V-joint. Strike it quickly after the bricks are laid or the mortar will bunch up. This joint sheds water well.

Flush joint

Cut the excess mortar from the face of bricks as you lay them. Every two courses, check to see if joints are tight.

Concave joint

This is the most common brick joint. Strike it using a piece of pipe or a jointer made for this purpose. It sheds water well and is the easiest to make watertight.

Weathered joint

Use a pointed trowel, as with a struck joint, but hold it in the opposite way, angling from bottom to top. It's difficult to make this joint look consistent.

Raked joint

A raked joint looks great, but it is the weakest and the least water-resistant joint. To strike it, use a trimmed piece of wood or

REPLACING BRICKS AND BLOCKS

A few damaged or deteriorated bricks don't spell doom for a wall. They can be replaced with relative ease. Begin by examining your wall carefully. If the damaged bricks or concrete blocks are directly over or under a door or window, there is a chance the wall could sag if you remove several bricks or blocks at once. To avoid collapsing a section of wall, replace one brick at a time, rather than removing several at once. Call in a professional mason if you

YOU'LL NEED

TIME: About 1 hour to replace a brick or a concrete block.
SKILLS: Careful chiseling, mixing mortar, pointing mortar lines.
TOOLS: Baby sledgehammer, cold chisel, drill with masonry bit, pointed trowel, pointing tool.

1. Chip out the old brick.
Use a baby sledgehammer and cold chisel to chip away the old mortar and brick. Drill a series of holes with a masonry bit to make it easy to break the brick apart, remove the pieces, and ensure that you do not damage surrounding bricks. Brush away debris and dampen all surfaces of the cavity.

2. Slide the new brick in.
Lay a ½- to 1-inch-deep bed of mortar on the bottom of the cavity. Butter the top and ends of the new brick. Slip the brick in without compressing the bed of mortar. Or, use an upside-down trowel to help slide the brick in (see Step 2 *below*). Adjust the brick so all the joints are even. Strike the joints to match the rest of the wall.

baby sledgehammer

1. To replace a block face, remove the old block face.
Unless the entire concrete block is fractured, remove only the damaged face and leave the rest of it. Use a baby sledge and a cold chisel. It may help to bore a series of holes in the block using a drill with a masonry bit.

Rest block on trowel.

2. Set a new block face in place.
Use a circular saw with a masonry blade to notch the webbing of a new block. Then use a chisel to release one face of the block. Dry-fit the new block face to make sure it is flush with the wall surface. Lay a bed of mortar and butter the block face on three sides. Slip the block in using a pointed trowel.

wood wedges

3. Hold in place with wedges.
The new block face will not stay in place as easily as a new brick, so use wedges to hold it firmly in the correct position. Once the mortar stiffens, remove the wedges, fill in the holes left by the wedges, and strike the joints.

REMOVING EFFLORESCENCE AND STAINS

Efflorescence is a white powder that results when mineral salts in mortar are dissolved by water. These deposits usually disappear after a few years. If you want to get rid of them now or if you have other stains or problems, try the techniques listed in the chart below. As a general rule, try common household cleaners first; use acid only if necessary. Do not use acid on limestone or marble.

CAUTION: *Always pour acid slowly into water; never poor water into acid.*

YOU'LL NEED

Time: 1 to 2 hours to scrub away most stains.
Skills: Basic skills.
Tools: Protective eyewear, gloves, heavy clothing, stiff brush, water bucket.

REMOVING STAINS FROM BRICK WALLS AND PATIOS

Type of Stain	Remedy
Efflorescence	Try water and a brush and wait a few days. If something stronger is needed, scrub the wall with a solution of 1 part muriatic acid to 15 parts clean water. Rinse with water when finished.
Mortar smears	Remove with a muriatic acid solution as strong as 1 part acid to 10 parts water if your bricks are dark; 1-to-15 solution for lighter bricks. Let stand for 10 to 15 minutes, then rinse thoroughly.
Mildew	Scrub gently with a solution of 1 part bleach to 3 parts water, with a little laundry detergent or trisodium phosphate mixed in. Let stand for 15 minutes, then rinse.
Hardened paint	Scrape off as much as possible with a putty knife. Scrub with a metal-bristled brush and cold water. If this doesn't work, try a commercial paint remover, but test it on a small spot first to make sure it does not stain the brick.
Graffiti	Purchase a spray-paint remover and follow directions.
Iron rust	Try scrubbing with household bleach; let it stand for 15 minutes, then rinse. If that doesn't work, scrub with a solution of 1 pound oxalic acid to 1 gallon of water. Let stand for 5 minutes, then rinse thoroughly. Test on a small area first to make sure it will not stain the brick.

REPAIRING CHIMNEYS

A chimney is susceptible to a number of problems, ranging from the buildup of flammable deposits in the flue to damaged and leaking masonry. Serious damage requires repair by a professional mason. Homeowners willing to get up on the roof can handle basic inspection, repairs, and minor improvements. This section shows the basic steps for inspecting your chimney to keep it in safe working order and some improvements to make future maintenance procedures simple.

YOU'LL NEED

TIME: 1 to 2 hours to make a yearly inspection; several hours to clean out a chimney.
SKILLS: For most jobs, no special skills are needed.
TOOLS: Rope, tuckpointing tools, mason's trowel.

CAUTION!
AN OUNCE OF PREVENTION
■ If your fireplace chimney becomes caked with flammable deposits, you could have a flue fire. This is extremely dangerous; the heat is intense, and the fire is difficult to put out. A flue fire can possibly even lead to a house fire. So be sure your chimney is clean before you light a fire.
■ If your fireplace has not been used for a while, have it examined by a professional who specializes in chimneys.
■ Your chimney often is connected to the framing of your house. The weight of a damaged chimney can lead to serious structural problems. If you suspect severe damage, call in a professional.

Understand chimney anatomy.
The **firebox** has splayed sides that serve to pull air across the **hearth** to the base of the fire. The sloping upper rear wall of the firebox deflects heat back into the room. At the top of the firebox, the **throat** pulls smoke up into the flue. A **damper** there allows you to control the draft and close the flue when the fireplace is not in use.

Higher up the chimney, a **smoke shelf** stops cold air from coming down the flue and diverts it back up the **flue**. Without the smoke shelf, cold air from the outside would drop down and push smoke into the living area.

Many fireplaces have an **ash door**, plus an ash pit and a clean-out door, allowing you to remove your ashes from the outside of the house. Some ash pits have an air vent to create a better draft.

Inspect your upper chimney.
The part of your chimney that is exposed to weather is the most likely to fail. Inspect it thoroughly for crumbling bricks and mortar. (Your chimney may not look quite like the drawing above; it may be all brick, for instance.) Replace broken bricks and tuckpoint them if necessary (see pages 525–527). Make sure the chimney cap overhangs the brick. Check for loose or missing flashing.

Make a new chimney cap.
Chimney caps often are constructed incorrectly so they don't protect the bricks from water damage. Shown here is a design for a cap you can pour in place. Hold the form in place with a few masonry nails and remove it after the concrete has set. When finishing the concrete, be sure to slope it away from the flue so water can run off easily.

1. *To clean a fireplace chimney, seal off the inside opening.*
Cleaning produces a great deal of hard-to-vacuum soot, so make sure it cannot enter your home. Firmly tape a wet sheet or a piece of heavy polyethylene sheeting to the opening. Check that there are no cracks for soot to seep through.

2. *Make a "brush."*
You can rent or buy a regular chimney brush with extensions for reaching down your chimney. Or, make a cleaning tool out of a piece of canvas and a rope. Wrap chains or pieces of broken bricks in the canvas, tie a rope to it, and lower it into the flue.

3. *Sweep the flue.*
Move your "brush" vigorously up and down in the flue, slowly moving downward as you work. Lower the brush all the way down to the damper, pull it up, and repeat the process until you no longer hear caked deposits being dislodged from the flue.

EXPERTS' INSIGHT

AN ANNUAL CHECKUP
Every year, make a quick inspection of your chimney. Look at the following:
■ See if any tree branches are within 10 feet of the chimney. Trim off the branches if they are; they can cause draw problems and create fire hazards.
■ Check to see that the damper and its controls work smoothly. Use a flashlight to see if it opens and closes completely.
■ Check the draw. When you light a fire, the smoke should rise easily and not flow into your living area.
■ Clean out ashes that have accumulated in the ash pit.
■ On the roof and in the attic, check the chimney bricks and repair any damaged areas.

Install a screen cap.
Here is an easy way to keep birds and squirrels out of your chimney, and protect the inside from water damage. Measure the outside dimensions of your flue and purchase a screen cap to fit it. Installation is simple—place it on top of the flue and tighten the hold-down screws.

Money $ Saver

GAS FIRED UNITS
■ If your old chimney is not safe for wood-burning fires, before you install a gas unit make sure it poses no structural dangers. Make any needed repairs to ensure it will not collapse and will not compromise the framing.
■ If you want to have a fire in your fireplace without replacing the entire chimney, consider installing a gas-fired unit. This needs little or no venting, so it does not matter if your chimney draws poorly. Though it's not a wood-burning fireplace, it does have advantages: You don't have to haul and store logs, it's easy to start, and many slide-in models have heat-circulating systems that efficiently heat your home.

REPAIRING CONCRETE STEPS

Once a crack develops in concrete, water seeps in and causes further damage, especially in regions that have freezing temperatures. Fix small cracks and chips in your stairs right away or you may have to replace the whole stairway. If your steps are made partially of brick, see pages 525–527 for brick repairs.

Buy patching concrete or concrete sand mix and add extra Portland cement. Mix in only enough water to make the material doughlike. If the chipped-out area is large, drive masonry screws partially into the damaged area to help anchor the patch in place.

YOU'LL NEED

TIME: 2 hours for most repairs.
SKILLS: No special skills needed.
TOOLS: Hammer and cold chisel, pointed trowel.

Replace chips with epoxy cement.
If a piece or two has broken out in such a way that it will fit back in place, you can glue it back on. Clean both pieces and make sure they are dry. Mix epoxy cement, apply it to the chipped-out spot, and brace the chip in place with a brick and a piece of wood.

EXPERTS' INSIGHT

WHERE THE STEPS MEET THE HOUSE

If you have a crack where your concrete steps butt against the house, any patch you make probably will crack again within a year or two. The steps and the house rest on different foundations, so they shift and settle in different directions. If you don't seal the crack, the problem will get worse. Here's how to seal out moisture and debris.
■ If the crack is small, seal it with silicone, butyl rubber, or siliconized acrylic caulk.
■ If the crack is large, insert expansion joint material into it for the best seal, or use oakum.

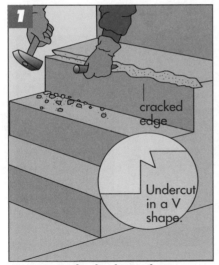

1. To mend a broken edge, chip out the edge.
If an edge is broken or cracked, remove all loose material so no cracks remain. With a hammer and cold chisel, cut the edge back to make a V-shaped groove (see inset). Clean the area thoroughly and moisten it.

2. Make a form and fill.
Use bricks to hold a board against the riser to act as a form for the concrete. Mix the patch material and pack it into the groove. Smooth the top of the patch. As the material begins to set up, remove the form and smooth the edges of the patch.

3. Cure the patch slowly.
To ensure that the patch will stick, make sure it cures slowly. Cover the repair with polyethylene sheeting and hold it in place with scraps of lumber. Keep the patched area damp for about a week by spraying it with water.

REPAIRING RAILINGS

Here's a common and pesky problem: The metal railing on a concrete stairway comes loose, either at its base where it connects to the step or at the top where it connects to the house.

Often the problem is rusty metal. If only screws are rusty, you can replace them. If the bottom of the railing itself is rusted away, it may be time for a new railing.

Just as often, the screws or anchors were not large enough for the job and have come loose and cracked the concrete. To make these repairs, you can use epoxy putty, anchoring cement, masonry screws, or masonry anchors.

YOU'LL NEED

TIME: 2 hours for most repairs.
SKILLS: No special skills needed.
TOOLS: Hammer and cold chisel, drill with masonry bit, trowel.

1. To re-install a bolt on a stair, chip away a hole.
Remove loose material. Enlarge the hole, if necessary, so it will be deep enough for the new bolt and so the epoxy putty or anchoring cement has plenty of area to grab onto. "Key" the hole by making it larger at the bottom than at the top; this provides a greater area for the patch to stick to.

2. Install bolt and cement.
Hold the bolt in position and fill the hole with epoxy putty or anchoring cement. Make sure the bolt sticks up at the correct height, is plumb, and is in the correct position. Tamp the epoxy putty or cement firmly and meld it with the concrete surface.

Anchor the top of the rail.
At the point where the rail meets the house, you need some serious fastening power. Small screws with plastic anchors will not do the trick.

If the concrete has broken away, you will need to set bolts

in cement or epoxy putty. Or, fill the old hole and use a masonry screw or anchor. Masonry screws can be driven directly into pilot holes. Simply drill the hole and drive in the screw.

You also can use masonry anchors, also called lag shields. Drill the correct-size hole (in

some cases you can simply enlarge the old hole) and tap the anchor in until it is flush with the wall surface. Then hold the bracket in position and drive the screw in place.

SURFACE FINISHING

CHOOSING EXTERIOR PAINT

House paints made to cover siding and exterior trim tend to be more durable and more expensive than interior paint. That's because exterior paints contain additional resins and other ingredients that make them last longer and resist moisture. Also many have a larger amount of pigmenting, which gives them a deeper, more vivid color.

Like interior paint, exterior paint comes in two basic varieties: water-thinned (latex) and solvent-thinned (oil- or alkyd-based). Those with oil and alkyd bases dry slowly, making them susceptible during application to being marred by insects and sudden rainstorms. Once they set up, they develop a hard surface that is resistant to water. However, unless the surface is very well prepared, they are prone to flaking.

Properly applied, modern latex exterior paint (though not porch and deck paint) is more durable than solvent-based paint. Latex paints are easier to work with, dry quickly, and have a porous, "breathing" quality that makes

them less likely to flake. They will likely peel, however, if applied over an improperly prepared oil- or alkyd-based finish.

Chalking-type latex paints shed dirt by gradually eroding with each rainfall. Usually you can see the "chalk" on foundation walls, shrubbery, and your coat sleeve if you brush against a painted surface. Newer formulations achieve durability without this chalking feature.

Latex paints tend to show brush marks, while solvent-based paints "level" to a more even surface. If a surface will be often handled or walked on (as is the case with a porch), solvent-based paint provides a more durable surface.

Do not use latex paint over a surface covered with solvent-based paint, unless you first apply a primer or thoroughly sand the surface. To find out which type of paint is present, remove a flake or chip and see whether it is flexible. Latex paint will bend slightly before cracking; a flake of solvent-based paint will snap readily. If you bring in a chip, a paint dealer

can tell you for sure. If you're not certain what type of paint was used before, it's safest to apply a solvent-thinned paint.

Most people prefer a flat, eggshell, or satin finish for large exterior expanses. Reserve semigloss and gloss for areas subject to hard use or for trim.

What about one-coat house paints? If you plan to match or approximate the present color, any paint will cover in one coat. However, products sold with a one-coat guarantee are thicker, with more resins and pigments. Most guarantees specify that the paint must be applied over sound existing surfaces or primed new wood. You will pay more for a one-coat paint, but the extra money spent might pay off handsomely, especially in terms of time saved.

The chart on the opposite page will help you sort through the often-confusing array of products found in paint stores. As a general rule, the more expensive the paint, the more durable it will be.

ESTIMATING PAINT NEEDS

How much paint you need depends upon the type and condition of the surfaces that you'll be covering, the method of application, and the paint itself. Conditions vary considerably, so read the manufacturer's coverage figures, then buy a little more than you need.

If your home has narrow lap siding, add another 10 percent to your estimate. For textured materials, such as shingles or shakes, add 20 percent. Masonry and stucco—both porous surfaces that soak up lots of paint—can take up to 50 percent more.

To compute surface area, measure from the foundation to the eaves and multiply by the distance around the house. For each gable end, measure the distance from eaves to the peak, measure the width of the wall, and multiply the two. Then divide the result by two.

If you buy paint of a standard color, most stores will let you return unopened cans. Check with your retailer about return policies for custom-mixed paint.

COMPARING EXTERIOR PAINTS

Type	Characteristics/Uses	Application
Vinyl latex	Easy cleanup, durability, and fast drying make latex the choice for amateurs. It can be applied over damp surfaces. Latex is naturally mildew-proof but is incompatible with a previous solvent-based finish.	Don't thin latex. Apply with one stroke of the brush or roller; if you work it out too far, you'll get thin spots.
Acrylic latex	The highest-quality latex paints contain 100 percent acrylic resins; vinyl resins are not as durable. It dries faster than most and will cover just about any building material, including masonry and properly primed metal.	Application technique is about the same as vinyl latex paint.
Alkyd	Alkyd, the most common type of solvent-thinned paint, has most of the same properties as oil-based types, but dries more rapidly; good over old oil- or alkyd-based coatings; excellent hiding power.	Thicker consistency makes alkyd more tiring to apply, but it levels smoother than latex.
Oil	Slow drying times (12 to 48 hours), strong odors, and messy cleanup make oil a less popular choice for amateurs, though some pros swear by its durability.	Drying time makes marring by bugs and rain real perils.
Primers	Use a recommended primer to seal new wood or metal, to kill stains, or prior to applying latex paint over existing solvent-based paint. Alcohol-based primer is the most effective, but solvent and latex types also work.	Priming usually is easier than finishing, but porous surfaces can soak up a lot of primer.
Stains	Solvent- or latex-type stains provide transparent, semi-transparent, or opaque finishes for natural wood siding and trim; some include preservatives or offer a weathered look.	Brush, roll, or spray on almost any way you prefer.
Porch and deck	Alkyd and polyurethane types are the most durable because they produce a hard, washable surface. Some types are formulated for concrete floors. Surface preparation varies; colors are limited.	With most types, you just pour the paint on the floor, then work it outward with a long-handled roller or applicator.
Metal	Solvent- or water-thinned types include rust-resisting priming ingredients so you needn't worry about small bare spots. All-bare metal should be primed separately. Rusty-metal primer seals a rusty spot.	Brush, roll, or spray on for a broad range of finish effects.
Marine	Formulated especially for boats, marine paint provides a super-durable finish on wood and some metal trim. It's expensive, so it's generally inappropriate for large areas.	A gooey consistency makes it difficult to apply.
Masonry	This category includes latex, epoxy, Portland cement, rubber, and alkyd. Some serve as their own primers. Seal masonry with clear silicone. For basement waterproofing techniques, see page 532.	Latex is easy to apply; other types can be a lot of work.

Choosing Interior Paint

Many people consider interior painting an easy chore requiring no particular skill. As a result, they may plunge in unprepared and produce a botched job that haunts them for years. While it is true that almost any handy person can learn to paint well, it takes practice and attention to detail to produce smooth walls with evenly distributed color. This section will help you learn the correct way to paint or wallpaper a room, seal wood grain, and apply special finishing treatments.

Start by choosing the right paint. A well-informed salesperson can answer your questions, as long as you give the necessary information—the type and color of paint that's on the wall, the condition of the wall, and what sort of wear you expect the wall to endure. If a salesperson is not helpful, go to a different store.

A close reading of the paint can will tell you a few key things. The chart on the opposite page compares paints you're most likely to use.

Whichever type you choose, it's wise to spend more for high-quality paint. Cheaper paint may not cover in one coat, may be more likely to peel in time, and could fade, especially in direct sunlight. Given the amount of time you will spend preparing and painting your walls, it even makes sense to throw out a can of paint if you are displeased with the color.

The most common choice for interior painting is latex. High-quality latex paints are nearly as durable as solvent-thinned products. Latex cleans up with water, has less of an odor than solvent-thinned paint, is environmentally friendly, and dries to the touch quickly, so you can usually put furniture back in the room in an hour or so. However, dried latex paint takes weeks to completely cure. Handle it with care during that time because it can be easily stained or damaged.

If latex paint is applied over solvent-thinned paint, it will likely peel off in time—a disastrous result that will require hours of tedious scraping to remedy. If you suspect that the existing paint may not be latex, take a chip to a salesperson for testing. A latex paint chip will bend a bit before breaking; a solvent-based chip will be more brittle. If you have solvent-thinned paint on the wall, either cover it with a new coat of solvent-thinned paint or apply primer first (see box below).

Solvent-thinned paints, usually alkyd-based, require a solvent, such as mineral spirits (paint thinner), for cleanup. Spend more for odorless thinner; smelly products are unpleasant to breathe. Solvent-based paints generally are more durable than water-thinned paints.

Interior paints come in different sheens. From dullest to shiniest, the most common designations are: ceiling paint, flat, eggshell, satin (or low-luster), semigloss, and high-gloss. The glossier a finish, the harder and more durable it will be—and the more imperfections it will show.

Flat paint is generally considered "washable" but not "scrubbable." Eggshell or satin finishes have a low sheen but can be scrubbed occasionally. Semi- and high-gloss paints are popular for woodwork, kitchens, baths, and other areas that endure hard wear or in which there is high humidity. Again, higher-quality paint is more washable than cheap paint, no matter what the sheen.

Colors are notoriously tricky to choose. They react to each other and cast reflections that may change the appearance of everything in a room. Colors vary under different lighting, and large areas might become far more intense than you imagine when you are looking at small paint-sample chips. Consider buying a quart of the hue that catches your eye and trying it out on a sizable area before you invest in several gallons of paint that may not be returnable.

Experts' Insight

To Prime or Not to Prime

If the wall to be painted is in sound condition, if the new color is close to the existing color, and if you are sure the new paint will stick, then no primer is needed. However, you will need primer for the following conditions:

■ Stains—either localized or spread throughout the room because of smoke—may bleed through repeated coats of paint. The solution is to apply a stain-killing primer. For small spots, you can use a spray-on primer.

■ If the existing paint is solvent-thinned and you want to apply latex paint, apply an appropriate primer first. Solvent-thinned or alcohol-based primers work best.

■ If a wall has been patched, or if new drywall needs to be covered, apply latex primer first.

■ If your paint will not easily cover the existing color, purchase primer and have it tinted to approximate the paint color.

COMPARING INTERIOR PAINTS

Paint	Uses	Features/Characteristics	Thinner/Primer
Latex	The choice for most interior paint jobs; don't use it over unprimed wood, metal, or wallpaper.	Glosses vary from flat to high. It adheres to all but slick surfaces. Latex usually dries fast enough to apply two coats in one day. It is less durable than alkyd-base paints.	Latex is easy to clean up with water and soap. Prepare raw surfaces with a latex or alkyd primer.
Alkyd	Use alkyd for a rough surface or super hiding power. Don't apply over unprimed drywall—it will roughen the surface.	Dries somewhat more slowly than latex and has a slightly stronger odor. Alkyd might be banned in some areas.	For thinning and cleanup, use solvents. Coat unfinished surfaces with alkyd primer.
Oil	Natural-resin oil paints have all but disappeared.	Oil dries slowly, gives off flammable fumes, and doesn't stand up as well as alkyds.	Thin and clean up with mineral spirits, low-odor thinner, or turpentine.
Oil-based primer	Good all-purpose primer	Oil-based primer dries slowly and gives off fumes.	Thin and clean up with mineral spirits.
Latex primer	Prepares patched areas and new drywall	Inexpensive, dries quickly	Easy to clean up with water and soap
Alcohol-based primer	Best primer for most purposes	Kills almost any stain and gives tooth to slick surfaces	Thin and clean up with denatured alcohol.
One-coat	Use it only if surface is sealed, is of a similar color, and doesn't have a lot of patchwork that needs to be covered.	One-coats are ordinary latex or alkyd paints with additional pigment to increase hiding power and are therefore more expensive.	Thinning lessens paint's ability to hide flaws. Clean up with water or solvent, depending on whether latex or alkyd.
Texture paint	Designed to cover up imperfections and give the look of stucco-finish plaster	Some premixed; with others, you must stir in "sand." Application is moderately difficult; paint a section at a time, and keep the desired effect consistent.	Thinning defeats the purpose; stirring can be arduous. Check label for compatible primers.
Acoustic	Coats acoustic tiles without affecting their sound-deadening qualities	Apply acoustic paint by spraying or use a special roller. Color choice is limited.	Thin and clean up with water; no primer is necessary.
Metal	Use over primed or bare metal surfaces; "rusty-metal primer" can be applied over rust.	Self-primers are designed to adhere to bare surfaces. Preparation depends on the type and condition of metal (see pages 554–555).	Some are thinned with water, others need solvent or mineral spirits. Primer depends on the metal being covered.

CHOOSING BRUSHES

Selecting the right brush for a paint job isn't difficult. Except for foam types, all brushes fall into one of two categories: natural-bristle brushes and synthetic-bristle brushes. Natural-bristle brushes are made with animal hairs and formerly were considered the finest type available. However, some of today's synthetic varieties perform just as well.

If you're using an oil-based paint, choose a natural-bristle or a quality synthetic-bristle brush. Never use a natural-bristle brush with water-thinned finishes. The bristles will become mop-like, resulting in a streaked finish. Many paintbrush manufacturers label the brush package or handle with the type of finish for which the brush is designed.

Disposable brushes come in a wide range of widths and sizes and are suitable for many painting projects. Because they are

inexpensive, they can be tossed when the job's done, saving considerable cleanup time. However, painting with a disposable brush may mean you have to apply two coats of paint, where a high-quality brush would cover with one coat. Also a cheaper brush may shed some bristle hairs, which are tedious to remove.

Should you spend extra for a quality brush, or are the inexpensive ones the better buy? If you're willing to take the time to clean your brush after using it, buy better quality. It will serve you well for years. However, if you paint only occasionally and don't like cleaning up, a less-expensive brush is the wiser investment.

To test a brush for quality, spread the bristles and inspect their tips. Quality natural-bristle brushes will have little "flags," like split ends, on the bristle ends. The more the better. On better-quality

synthetic brushes, you'll see fuzzy-looking tips.

Check the brush's ferrule, the aluminum or stainless-steel band near the handle. It should be wrapped tightly and neatly around the brush and solidly secured to the handle.

Among your first buys should be a 4-inch wall brush, a 2-inch trim brush, and a 2-inch sash-trim brush. Later you might want to add a 6-inch wall brush for masonry paint jobs and a round brush for delicate work. A brush spinner speeds cleanup jobs.

The four handle styles shown below serve different functions. A beaver-tail handle lets you grip a wider brush in the palm of your hand; pencil and flat handles allow greater fingertip control; the kaiser handle also offers good control, plus a grip that's comfortable to your hand.

6" Wall Sash Round Foam Foam Beaver-tail Flat Kaiser

4" Wall Sash-trim Brush spinner Pencil

BRUSH STYLES   **HANDLE STYLES**

USING AND CARING FOR BRUSHES

Your brush will be a pleasure to use as long as you pay attention to proper loading, cleaning, and storing recommendations.

Before you use a new paintbrush for the first time, spin it by the handle between your hands, then slap it against the edge of a table to remove loose bristles. Work the bristles against a rough surface, such as a concrete wall, to soften the ends. To condition a natural-bristle brush, soak it 24 hours in linseed oil.

When you start painting, you may find more loose bristles and stray ones that stick out from the sides of the ferrule. Pick out loose bristles. Remove stray bristles by using a putty knife to force them against the ferrule so you can snap them off.

Loading the brush.
Dip the brush into the paint to only one-third the length of its bristles. If you go deeper, you'll waste paint and create a mess. Squeeze the excess paint from the bristles by scraping them lightly against the side of the container as you remove the brush.

How to hold it.
Hold small brushes between your thumb and your index finger. For larger brushes, use a palm grip or lay your fingers on the ferrule. Some people prefer to hold a large brush with three or four fingers on the ferrule.

Temporary storage.
If your work is interrupted for an hour or less, leave the brush in the paint. Position it so the paint covers the bristle tips only. For longer interruptions, wrap the brush in foil or plastic. If you'll use the brush within a day or two, immerse it in solvent or water, as shown above. Drill a hole in the handle for hanging.

Cleaning.
To clean a brush, work out the remaining paint by firmly stroking the brush back and forth on newspaper. Work until the brush is dry. Before storing a brush for an extended period, remove all the paint you can with the appropriate thinner. Work the bristles, as shown.

Shaping and storing.
Wash the brush in soap and water, shape the bristles, and let them dry. Then wrap the brush in the cardboard cover it was sold in. Or wrap it with several layers of paper toweling. The bristles should be held in shape but not squeezed.

CHOOSING ROLLERS AND PADS

Most people find it efficient to paint trim and edges (such as where the ceiling meets the wall or where the wall meets the trim) with a brush, and then paint the large expanses of walls and ceilings using a roller. But don't hesitate to try different tools and techniques.

Rollers range in width from 4 to 18 inches. They have a plastic or wooden handle (often machined to accept an extension handle) and a metal frame on which the roller cover is inserted.

Spend more for a professional-quality roller frame that rolls smoothly. A cheaper model may make it difficult to load the roller cover. Buy an extension handle that allows you to easily reach the ceiling—it will save you plenty of time and energy. Some extension handles are adjustable for length.

Trim rollers reach into small and hard-to-get-at areas. Once you get the knack of using a trim roller, they're as easy to control as trim brushes. Trim rollers come in varying widths and configurations. The 3-inch-wide version gets into areas too tight for a full-size roller. Cone-shaped types are used for inside corners, around door and window casings, and almost any point where two surfaces intersect. Doughnut-style rollers paint moldings and other fine work.

A high-quality roller cover (also called a roller sleeve) has a lint-free pile that is uniform in texture and securely fastened. Cheaper covers tend to apply paint unevenly or shed fibers onto the wall. Buy a cover made for the type of paint you will apply.

Mohair covers are designed for gloss finishes and varnishes; they produce a smooth finish because the nap is short and tightly woven. Dynel, acetate, and polyurethane foam covers can be used with all paints. Use a lamb's-wool roller cover for solvent-thinned paint.

Choose a cover with a thick nap—say, $3/4$-inch—for rough surfaces and to achieve one-coat coverage. A thick nap will produce a slight pebbly stipple. Use a short-nap cover, either $3/8$- or $1/4$-inch, to produce a smoother surface. If you're using water-thinned paint, buy a cover with a plastic sleeve. For solvent-thinned paint, use a cardboard sleeve.

Pad painters are also handy. The pads may be a carpetlike material or plastic foam inserted in a plastic mop-like applicator or a paint-brush handle. Although excellent for applying paint to almost any surface, they really earn their keep when you have to paint shakes, fencing, screening, and shutters.

A paint tray, either metal or plastic, completes the system. If you'll be working on a stepladder, buy a paint tray that has ladder hooks to keep the tray secure. To save on cleanup time, purchase plastic tray inserts, which you throw away once the painting is done. With these, the paint never touches your tray.

Roller cover

Roller frame

Doughnut-style roller

Trim roller

Extension handle

Cone-shaped roller

Paint tray

Pad painter

USING A ROLLER

Anyone who has ever painted with rollers or pads will vouch for the ease with which these lay down paint.

However, an even application does not come automatically. Keep your eyes peeled for skid marks on the painted surface. Rollers tend to slide as they move, causing small tracks in the finish, which will show when the finish has dried.

Most surfaces are irregular to some extent. To achieve the best coverage when using a roller or pad, lay on the paint from several different directions. In this way, you won't miss shallow depressions, such as joints between drywall panels. After applying paint to an area, go over it again with light vertical passes, taking care to even out thick spots.

Cover the floor and any furniture with a heavy drop cloth. Even when used carefully, rollers do scatter paint speckles.

Loading a roller.
Fill the well of the tray, but not the slanted portion. Push the roller into the paint, pull it back a bit, then repeat until paint covers the entire roller. Even out the paint on the slanted part of the tray.

Rolling a wall.
For the best coverage, apply the paint in two or more directions. Minimize dripping by starting the roller on the upstroke. Don't work a roller too quickly, especially when the roller cover is loaded with paint: You'll splatter, which wastes paint and makes a mess.

Rolling woodwork.
Rollers work well on wide, flat woodwork, such as raised-panel doors. Paint the recesses first, then finish the flush surfaces. If you do not like the pebbly stipple that the roller produces, run a brush over the paint immediately after using the roller.

Cleaning solvent-thinned paint.
To clean a roller cover, work out all the excess paint you can on newspaper. Turn to fresh pages as needed. With solvent-thinned paint, pour solvent into the tray and work the roller back and forth. Repeat until the solvent remains clear.

Cleaning latex paint.
Wash out water-based paints in a sink. Let water run over the roller until it is clear. Squeezing the roller speeds things. Wring the cover dry by squeezing it between your hands. Wrap clean, dry roller covers in aluminum foil or plastic bags. Clean pad painters as you would roller covers.

Using a Power Roller

If you have ever painted a room with a roller, you know that most of your time is spent loading just the right amount of paint onto the roller. After about every 50 to 100 square feet, you have to pour more paint into the paint tray.

Power paint rollers and pads eliminate both of these steps and more than double your speed. The power equipment will pump from a 1-gallon can or a 5-gallon can.

Before purchasing a power roller, see that it will be reasonably easy to clean; most are designed for latex paint and water cleanup. Choose a model with few parts to disassemble.

Before painting, practice on a large scrap of cardboard. Turn on the paint control for a few seconds at a time until you get a sense of how much on-time is required. Rollers generally require on-times of about 5 seconds; pads require 1 to 2 seconds.

1. *Prepare the can.*
After opening the paint container and stirring the paint, put the special cover on the paint can. Set the can into the base of the paint pumping unit and then lock it securely in place. Insert the suction tube into the hole in the cover. Push it to the bottom, then raise it ½ inch.

2. *Assemble the tube and roller.*
Hook up the parts according to the manufacturer's directions. Especially if the parts are all plastic, take care not to cross-thread when screwing the pieces together. Some types have a long handle that fills with paint and makes it easy to reach the ceiling.

3. *Apply paint.*
Turn the flow on and off with the switch on the handle. Don't overload the roller or it will leak and spatter.

4. *Clean the parts.*
When you're finished painting, run the roller or pad dry, remove the arm, and purge the paint from the hose, letting it run into the paint can.

5. *Clean the roller.*
Attach the paint hose to a faucet adapter—if there is one—and run water through the roller until it is clean. Squeeze the excess water from the roller and stand it on end to dry. Clean the seals on the roller arm.

USING A STEPLADDER

*T*o avoid breaking into a cold sweat every time you get above the third rung of a stepladder, select a ladder you can trust, then learn a few safety habits.

Aluminum ladders are lightweight and easy to transport, but they tend to flex, making them unstable. Wooden ladders are more stable when new, but they become wobbly after repeated use. Fiberglass stepladders are the most reliable.

A label on the ladder provides its strength rating. Type III household-grade ladders are rated at 200 pounds; Type II commercial-grade, 225 pounds; and Type I industrial-grade, 250 pounds. Each type has been tested at 4 times these loads. For security and durability, buy at least a Type II ladder.

Lengths range from 2 to 16 feet; 6-footers are suitable for most indoor needs.

If you follow these simple safety rules, you needn't worry about stepladder accidents.

■ If possible, lean a stepladder against a wall. Make sure that the legs rest solidly on the floor.

■ When you open the ladder, double-check that you've opened it fully and that you've locked the bucket tray and braces in position.

■ Work from a ladder that is tall enough for the job. Don't climb higher than one step below the top, and never stand on the bucket tray.

■ Never paint a wooden ladder. Paint hides defects in the wood, preventing you from discovering possible problems.

■ Never climb a stepladder that has loose or broken rungs or a split or broken side rail.

■ Rather than leaning way over to the side to reach a spot, take a few seconds to move the ladder.

Testing for stability.
Open the ladder and test it by lifting one side and pulling it toward you. Keep the braces fully open and locked. If a ladder feels wobbly, throw it out and buy a new one.

Making a scaffold.
Two stepladders and a 2×12 make a convenient scaffold. If you don't have two stepladders, you can use a sawhorse to support one end of a scaffold plank.

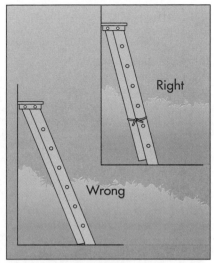

Leaning a stepladder.
Prop a stepladder against a wall at a fairly steep angle so that the back legs don't catch on the floor. To make sure that the back legs do not destabilize the ladder, tie the legs shut.

Working on stairs.
In a high stairwell, use an extension ladder, a sawhorse, and a plank. To protect the wall, pad the ladder rails.

IDENTIFYING AND SOLVING PAINT PROBLEMS

Perennial paint and surface problems (see page 847) will pop right through a new paint job. If your house suffers from any of these, get to the root of the problem and correct the condition. Only then is it time to scrape the surface, prime, and proceed with painting the final coat.

Most paint problems are the result of moisture attacking from underneath the paint. New energy-efficient construction methods can contribute to these problems by sealing a house so tight that it cannot breathe. The solution is adequate ventilation; see page 414. This is particularly true in moist areas like the kitchen, bathroom, and laundry. Ducted ventilation fans provide the best way to remove excess moisture vapor. Good vapor barriers on inside walls also help control moisture problems (see page 424).

Control moisture.
Lessen the effects of moisture by installing ducted ventilation fans (see pages 112–115). If you don't have fans, opening a window helps. If exterior walls don't have a vapor barrier, painting the interior wall with nonpermeable paint will prevent vapor penetration.

Eaves and soffit problems.
Poor ventilation in the attic may cause soffits to peel. Before you repaint, correct this by adding soffit vents (see page 399). Leaky gutters drip water onto eaves and then onto the house siding, so maintain or replace gutters (see pages 400–401).

Cut back foliage.
Leaves hold moisture after a rain. Trim trees and shrubs often, especially those along the house's foundation.

Maintain caulking.
Remove old, cracked caulking material with a putty knife, then apply new caulk (see page 403).

Window glazing.
Replace any loose and missing glazing compound on windows. Let the glazing dry for a week before you paint it.

REMEDIES FOR COMMON PAINT PROBLEMS

Problem		Causes	Remedy
Peeling		Moisture from inside or prolonged contact with rain or other moisture; finish coat applied over wet surface	Improve ventilation by installing siding, gable, or soffit vents.
Alligatoring		Usually a finish coat applied over a wet primer, or too much oil in the thinner	Sand and scrape down to bare wood, apply primer, and let dry thoroughly.
Checking		Shrinking and swelling of the building material over a period of time	Remove paint to bare wood, prime the area, and let dry.
Blistering		Finish coat applied over surfaces that are not completely dry	Remove paint to bare wood, prime the area, and let dry.
Bleeding		Sap and pitch working out of the wood	Apply stain-killing sealer to all knots and pitch pockets to prepare the surface for a coat of finish.
Nail stains		Using nails that are not rust-resistant	Sand the surface and seal with alcohol-based primer, then repaint.
Mildew		Usually a combination of moisture, high humidity, and inadequate ventilation	Scrub off the mildew with a bleach solution, let the wood dry thoroughly, then paint with mildew-resistant paint.
Chalking		Formulation of paint used	Before painting, wash thoroughly; some older paints are made to chalk (see page 534).

REMOVING OLD EXTERIOR PAINT

Many of the problems described on the preceding pages require you to strip down the defective areas to bare wood and prime them before painting. Unfortunately, there's no easy way to do this tedious job. A variety of stripping techniques are shown on these pages. Often it takes a combination of techniques to tackle a job. Experiment to find the mix that works best.

If paint is peeling from very large areas, get advice from a local painter. Preparation of old wood can be tricky, and sometimes homeowners spend tons of time stripping and repainting, only to have the new paint peel. If possible, strip and paint a small area and wait a year to see how well the paint sticks.

Old paint comes off most readily when it's dry. Start in the worst spot, work a scraper underneath, and lift off as much of the old finish as you can. You'll have better luck chipping from the edges of bad spots, rather than trying to wear through an unbroken surface.

Once you master a pull scraper, it's possible to get down to bare wood with a single stroke. Hold the blade at an angle and apply firm pressure as you drag it along. When a blade stops cutting well, either change it or sharpen it as you would a knife or chisel (see page 239).

When you reach tight-sticking paint, feather the edges by sanding. Then spot-prime all bare areas, slightly overlapping the sound paint.

Remove paint from metal surfaces with a wire brush attachment on an electric drill. Don't worry about baring the metal; just remove rust, as well as the loose or caked paint, then prime it (see pages 554–555).

Chemical paint strippers should be your last alternative. Although effective, you risk dripping the remover on sound paint, creating more problems.

If you have large areas of masonry to strip, consider hiring a professional contractor to sand-blast them. Make it clear that the contractor will clean away all dust and sand when finished.

> ### YOU'LL NEED...
> **TIME:** Several days for an entire house.
> **SKILLS:** Basic skills.
> **TOOLS:** Putty knife, scraper, pull scraper, electric paint softener, wire brush, drill with wire brush attachment, propane torch or heat gun, and power sander.

Removing loose paint with a putty knife.
Remove what paint you can by scraping with a putty knife. Scrape in at least two directions at all spots to make sure you're getting all the loose stuff. Then go over the area with a wire brush. This combination works well for small areas or places where the paint is very loose.

Using a sharp pull scraper.
Most jobs call for harder work. Purchase a pull scraper with multiple replacement blades. Experiment to find which angle works best; you want to remove the paint without digging into the wood. Press down hard as you scrape; it sometimes helps to push on the tool with one hand while you pull with the other hand.

Removing paint with a power sander.
Power-sand large areas with an orbital sander equipped with fairly rough sandpaper—60- or 80-grit. Change the paper once it stops being effective. If you are skillful, you may want to try a belt sander, which removes paint more quickly. Be careful: It is easy to dig into the wood when using a belt sander.

Using an electric paint softener.
For heavy paint deposits, use an electric paint softener. Hold the tool on the paint until it starts to bubble or wrinkle, then scrape off the paint. A paint-removing heat gun, shaped much like a blow dryer for hair, works similarly.

Using chemical paint removers.
Chemical paint removers are best for heavy paint deposits on small areas. Follow the manufacturer's directions to the letter.

Using a propane torch to soften paint.
A propane torch with a spreader tip "cooks" paint fast so you can scrape it off. Be careful not to start a fire, and have an extinguisher handy. The resulting surface may be slightly charred in places. Be sure to seal it with a high-quality primer before painting or the paint may peel from the charred areas.

PREPARING EXTERIOR SURFACES

*I*f your siding and trim is in good shape, you can happily sidestep the most maddening part of an exterior paint job—removing chipped or peeling paint (see pages 546–547). But don't get out your paint clothes and brushes quite yet.

Go around the house and take off all screens, storm windows, and hardware that can be removed. Inspect the exterior and replace damaged siding materials (see pages 404–408). Use a nail set to drive protruding nails below the surface.

Give your house a bath. You'll need a garden hose and a car-wash brush attachment, a scrub brush or sponge for stubborn dirt, and a mixture of water and trisodium phosphate (TSP) to remove dirt and reduce the gloss of existing oil- or alkyd-based paints.

Remove loose and cracked glazing from the windows and reglaze them (see pages 372–373). Glazing should dry a week before painting. Also caulk all cracks and gaps in the siding; around porch columns; and under, over, and around windows and doors (see page 403).

If you're using an oil- or alkyd-based paint, wait at least a week after the bath before you paint the house. You can paint with latex the next day. When the siding is dry, spot-prime all bare areas. Don't miss exposed metal surfaces on gutters, downspouts, and windows.

YOU'LL NEED...

TIME: 5 to 6 hours to thoroughly wash and rinse a house.
SKILLS: Basic skills.
TOOLS: Whisk broom, hose, scrub brushes, car-wash brush, hammer, nail set, screwdriver, and a caulking gun.

Clean the siding.
Wash the house from the top down, using a mixture of trisodium phosphate (TSP) and water. Rinse well. Let dry one day for latex or one week for oil paint. For mildewed areas, scrub with household bleach and water or a commercial cleaner. Repaint with mildewcide paint.

Make needed repairs.
Set popped nails and spot-prime them. Also caulk cracks, replace damaged siding, and prime bare metal spots.

Brush away dust.
With a whisk broom or a paintbrush, flick off the dust you missed with the hose. Keep this brush handy as you paint, to clear away other debris.

Remove obstacles.
Take off fixtures or cover them the day you paint. Remember to take down other accessories, such as house numbers and the mailbox. To speed up the job, remove, clean, and paint screens, storm windows, shutters, and other detachable components separately.

PREPARING AND PLANNING TO PAINT

*B*egin exterior painting when the sun has dried off the prepared surfaces. Follow the sun so you're working in the shade; this gives the paint a chance to cure slowly and adhere better.

Work from the top to the bottom of the house to avoid the mess caused by spilled or splattered paint. For a one-story house, do the siding first, then go back and paint the windows, doors, railings, steps, and so forth. If you're painting a two-story structure, do the trim as you go to avoid leaning your ladder against fresh paint.

Always paint above the top of the ladder. Don't try to paint under it, or you'll have ladder tracks where the rails touched the siding.

Protect nearby foliage.
A little paint spattered on grass will disappear with the next mowing, but it will remain on mulch and taller plants. Protect shrubs, flowers, patios, and walks with drop cloths. Use rope and canvas or old sheets to tie tall bushes back out of the way.

Safely set up ladders.
Set ladders on sure footing—never a plastic drop cloth. If the ground is uneven, dig a small hole for one of the legs, or place a wide board under a leg, positioned so that the ladder does not wobble. Use a ladder brace for stability and to hold the ladder away from the side wall for more painting room.

Bucket hook

Hang the paint with a bucket hook.
To keep the paint bucket from spilling, hang it from a ladder rung with a bucket hook, which you can buy or make from heavy-gauge wire.

5'

Work close to the ladder.
For safety's sake, don't stretch more than an arm's length on either side of the ladder—it's just not worth the risk. Move the ladder instead.

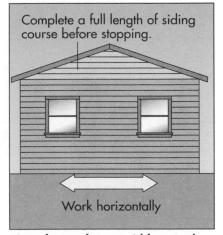

Complete a full length of siding course before stopping.

Work horizontally

Time the work to avoid lap marks.
Plan the work so that sundown does not catch you in the middle of several courses of siding. Otherwise you will get lap marks.

PAINTING SIDING

Horizontal or vertical siding can be covered quickly, especially if it has a smooth surface. It is usually most efficient to paint siding first, then trim.

If you're applying primer, follow the same procedures as for the finish paint. You may notice lap marks with the primer as it sinks into the wood or other material to seal it. These won't show after you've applied the finish coat.

Remove lighting fixtures and turn off electricity so you can safely paint behind and below them. Let the paint dry before replacing the fixtures.

YOU'LL NEED...

TIME: 4 to 6 days for a small house.
SKILLS: Basic painting skills.
TOOLS: Brushes, ladder, screwdriver, and drop cloths.

Hit the siding bottoms.
Start by painting the underside of a horizontal siding course. If you do the faces first, you'll be touching up continually. Coat the undersides of three or four courses, using plenty of paint so the wood seals properly. Level out the paint with the tip of the paintbrush.

Stab into corners.
When painting next to a casing, paint the corner first, then the underside of the siding. Stab the bristles up into the corner.

Flow the paint.
Apply plenty of paint to the surface of the course and don't worry about lap marks yet. Just cover and seal the surface thoroughly. Fill in the face of the siding courses, flowing the paint onto the surface with fairly short horizontal strokes. You needn't exert much pressure on the brush.

Level the paint.
When the surface is covered with paint, level and smooth it with a horizontal stroke. Make sure tiny cracks are filled. Don't try to save money by brushing the paint thin; even it out on the surface, using fairly long brushstrokes.

Take care at the edges.
Tip the bristles downward as you cut in along the bottom of the last course of siding. This keeps paint off the foundation.

FINISHING SHINGLES AND SHAKES

Because shingles and shakes are porous, painting or staining them can take longer than you think, and it may use up more paint than is commonly estimated.

If the wood is new, you can give it a natural look simply by sealing it with a clear sealer. Because there is no pigment in the sealer, you can slop it onto the wood without worrying about lap marks.

Semitransparent and solid stains (see pages 534–535) require more care because they contain a pigment that must be smoothed to prevent lap marks. Also, because the pigment in stain settles fairly quickly, you'll need to give the liquid a few good stirs with a paint paddle every so often to keep the finish color consistent.

If you're planning to paint new shingles, test the paint on several that have dark brown stains. If the stains bleed through, apply a stain-killing primer first.

Both paint and stain will dry quickly. Always work into a wet edge and finish out a course of siding before you leave for any length of time.

Keep the ferrule and handle of your brush wiped clean; that can be difficult if you're working with stain. Follow the leveling-out technique described on page 550. If you can, rent a power paint sprayer (see page 558). After spraying, touch up with a brush. If you use a roller or pad painter, use covers with medium to long nap length.

1. Flow the paint.
Do the underside of shingles first, as you would with lap siding. Brush out any runs down the striations. Apply paints and stains in the direction of the grain or striations. Check the area often for missed spots.

2. Erase drips.
Check frequently for drips and runs. Smooth them out with a fairly dry brush while the finish is still tacky.

Using pads and rollers
Pad applicators make finishing shingles and shakes easier. Most are designed for edges as well as faces.

Corner rollers work well for undersides. Use a medium- or long-nap roller or a wide brush for the faces.

YOU'LL NEED...
TIME: 4 to 6 days for a small house.
SKILLS: Basic painting skills.
TOOLS: Brushes, ladder, drop cloths, screwdriver, power sprayer, corner roller, and pad applicator.

PAINTING TRIM

If someone gives you the choice of painting the siding on a house or the trim, choose the siding. Although it doesn't consume much paint, trimming out a house takes an inordinate amount of time. Using the same paint color for the trim as the siding helps some, but the job is tedious, nonetheless.

Before you get out your sash brush and begin work, study the illustrations on this page for some of the situations you'll encounter.

YOU'LL NEED...

TIME: 45 minutes to an hour for a window.
SKILLS: Intermediate painting skills.
TOOLS: Sash brush, screwdriver, masking tape.

Seal the joints between trim and siding.
Paint a tight seal between the trim and siding material, especially over the tops of doors and windows. This seal is best made by slightly overlapping the siding paint (see page 550). That allows you to cut a clean line between the trim and the siding.

Paint a window.
Paint the outside of windows in the order indicated above, starting with the muntins and then working outward.

EXPERTS' INSIGHT

USING MASKING TAPE

Applying masking tape can make for clean paint lines at joints between two different surfaces. However, because slight flaws in exterior painting will not be as noticeable as they would be in interior painting, most house painters do not use it. After a few hours of practice, you can learn to cut a clean line using a brush alone. You may, however, choose to use masking tape on windowpanes and to cover hardware.

Protect windowsills.
Windowsills take a beating from the elements. If they're weather-worn, give them several coats of paint. Stop applying coats only after the paint has stopped soaking into the wood.

Paint a door.
Mask or remove the knob set and other hardware before painting doors. Paint the door in the order shown above.

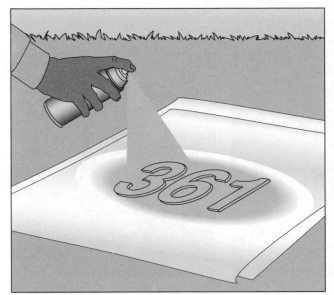

Spray hardware.
To save time and create a professional appearance, remove hardware that is to be painted or covered with clear finish, and position it on a sheet of newspaper. Spray-paint it using a can. Keep the nozzle moving at all times and use light applications to prevent buildup and drips (see page 559).

Use a pad for screening.
Paint or varnish screening first, then the frame. Use a special applicator pad to paint the screening—it is designed to apply paint without filling in the screen. (Spray-painting is another option for painting screening; see page 557.)

Avoid paint runs.
It takes concentration and a methodical approach to erase all paint drips and runs. Every few minutes, when your brush is fairly dry, look back at your work and brush away imperfections using light, even strokes. When painting a downspout, be sure to paint parallel to the flutes. If you don't, you risk messy drips and sags.

Finish with the railings.
Do ornamental metal and wood last. Prepare the surfaces properly and use the correct primer (see pages 554–555). It's difficult to paint small intersecting members (like those of a railing) without creating drips. If possible, use spray paint for these.

PREPARING AND PRIMING METAL

All metals oxidize if they're not properly coated, and paint can't adhere to the oxide coating. To stop the oxidation process, strip away grease, dirt, and rust, then apply a primer that is chemically formulated to neutralize oxidation. This primer also provides a surface to which the finish coat can adhere.

Primer made for automobile bodies is usually a good choice, but consult with your paint dealer to make sure. You also can buy special metal paints that combine the primer with a finish coating. Use these over surfaces that are in at least fairly good condition. Aluminized paint includes aluminum dust as a pigment and also works as a combination primer-finish on metals not exposed to severe weathering.

The finish paint must protect against weather and abrasion. Once the surface has been adequately primed, you can use almost any paint—exterior-grade for outdoors, indoor types for inside jobs. However, don't apply a lacquer over anything but a lacquer-based finish paint or primer.

Even polished decorative metals, such as brass, copper, and bronze, need protection if you want them to keep their shine. Buff tarnished hardware items with fine steel wool, metal polish, or a felt wheel and abrasive compound, then coat them with clear lacquer or polyurethane.

YOU'LL NEED...

TIME: 4 to 6 hours to prep and paint a metal railing.
SKILLS: Basic painting skills.
TOOLS: Paintbrushes, wire brush, drill with wire-brush attachment, sandpaper, and steel wool.

Remove paint.
Paint remover works better on metal than on wood. Use it to take off multiple layers.

Feather edges of well-stuck paint.
Use a loose piece of sandpaper or a hand sanding block to feather the edges of the remaining sound paint. Otherwise, the repaired area will show through. Finally, wash or brush any paint flakes and dust away from the work area.

Wash and wire-brush surface.
Wash the surface with a commercial degreaser, then wire-brush away any rust or peeling paint. A brush wheel attachment on a power drill makes short work of this task.

EXPERTS' INSIGHT

RUSTY-METAL PRIMER

Standard metal primer works only when all the rust has first been removed and the surface is completely dry. Rusty-metal primer, on the other hand, can be applied directly on top of rust. It will not smooth the bumpy surface of the rust, but it will stop the rust from spreading and will provide "tooth" for the finish paint to adhere to.

Prepare gutters and downspouts.
Clean and paint the inside of metal gutters first. Gutters and downspouts (shown) often need only spot-sanding and priming.

Apply primer or sander.
Treat sound paint with liquid sander. This product produces a "tooth" to which the new paint can adhere. Alternatively, sand the old paint thoroughly or apply alcohol-based primer.

Sand the primer.
Lightly sand primed surfaces with very fine sandpaper or steel wool. Don't sand through the primer.

PAINTING METAL

S pray, brush, or roll paint onto metal finishes. Whichever application you choose, bear in mind that several thin coats will hold up better than one or two thick layers. Let each coat dry before applying the next. Brushed or rolled-on paint should dry at least overnight (36 hours is better) before you apply another coat.

A good job calls for patience and good lighting so you can correct problems before the paint dries. Work the paint in one direction and move from dry to wet areas. Don't lap brushstrokes by painting over a dry edge. Smooth corners, too, so they don't dry with accumulations of paint.

Apply the paint.
Flow the paint on with smooth, even strokes. After a few minutes, check the freshly painted areas for drips, runs, and sags. When you're painting a complicated piece such as a radiator or chair, be sure to look from several different angles so you can spot places you missed.

Seal gutters.
To make galvanized gutters really last, paint the inside surfaces with an asphalt-based paint. Besides protecting the metal, it seals tiny leaks. After using the appropriate metal primer, the top coat of paint can be almost any outdoor type. (Aluminum or plastic gutters never need to be painted.)

YOU'LL NEED...
TIME: This will depend on the size of the object, but allow plenty of time for repeated coats with drying time in between.
SKILLS: Basic painting skills.
TOOLS: Brushes and drop cloths.

PAINTING MASONRY

Several types of paint will adhere to masonry. A paint dealer will carry paints designed for many types of surfaces and situations. Because they dry to a very hard finish, epoxy paints are probably the best all-around choice for floors, walls that are washed frequently, and exterior applications. Portland cement paint is another good choice; it works well on all walls except those previously painted with another type of finish. Latex paint, probably the easiest to apply, also adheres to foundation walls. Check with your paint dealer for other types suitable for specific applications.

Before painting a masonry surface—especially basement walls and floors—be sure to correct any existing moisture problems (see pages 523–524). If you don't, no paint will adhere. Also, remove peeling paint with a wire brush, and make necessary masonry repairs (see pages 525–528).

To finish the prep work, degrease the surface using detergent and water. Then etch the surface with a mixture of 1 part muriatic acid to 3 parts water. This removes and neutralizes alkaline material in the mortar joints. (Be sure to wear rubber gloves and a long-sleeved shirt to protect your skin from the acid.) Finally, rinse the surface with clear water.

After the surface has dried thoroughly, apply the finish with a wide short-bristled brush or a roller cover with a long nap.

Painting a floor.
Apply a degreasing solution to an oily garage or basement floor. Some products spray on; others require a scrub brush. Use a roller with an extension handle to paint a floor—to prevent backache from bending over. Paint one section at a time.

Fill in a pitted surface.
Smooth a rough-textured wall (but not a floor) with a 1:1 Portland cement and tile-grout mix, scrubbing it into depressions. To smooth a light texture, use an abrasive tool.

Apply the paint.
Apply paint with an old or cheap stiff-bristle brush. You'll have to push hard on the brush and even scrub it into very porous surfaces. If you want a rough texture, use a long-nap roller to apply the finish.

Painting stairs.
To paint steps that are used daily, paint the risers and every other tread. When the finish is dry on those, paint the treads you skipped.

YOU'LL NEED...

TIME: 6 to 8 hours to paint a basement.
SKILLS: Basic painting skills.
TOOLS: Scrub brush, paintbrush, roller with an extension handle.

SPRAY-PAINTING

Spray-painting is by far the fastest means of applying paint, stain, or other finishes. When done carefully, spraying yields professional-looking results that are hard to match with a brush or roller.

Spray-painting does have its drawbacks. It consumes much more finish than painting with a brush or roller. It's also messy. Overspray makes spraying impractical in many situations, such as in finished rooms or outside where a neighbor's car or house will be affected. Some communities even prohibit outdoor spraying.

You'll need plenty of ventilation if you spray-paint inside. Open nearby windows and, if there's an exhaust fan close by, turn it on. Always wear a painter's mask to keep from inhaling airborne paint particles, and wear a hat and protective clothing. Painting outside is less hazardous in terms of ventilation, but wear your mask nonetheless.

Here are some spray-painting pointers to keep in mind:

■ Prepare all surfaces the same way you would if you were to paint them with a brush or roller.

■ Tightly cover anything you don't want painted. For smaller areas, use newspaper and masking tape; for large areas, use drop cloths sealed at the edges with masking tape.

■ When spraying solvent-thinned paint indoors, make sure there is no open flame in the workshop area—the evaporating solvent is extremely flammable.

■ Never spray outdoors on a windy day. The air must be fairly calm or you won't get a nice finish—and you risk overspraying your neighbor's car. Even on calm days, make sure no valuable items are nearby.

■ Paint mixtures must be specially prepared for a spray gun. If the paint is too thick, it will clog the gun. If it's too thin, the paint will run on the surface. Even with the right mixture, have a brush handy to catch runs and drips.

■ When painting fencing with a spray gun, have a helper hold a wide piece of cardboard behind the fence to catch the overspray.

■ Don't spray gutters, corner trim, or siding material that joins the foundation of your home unless you have the roof, corner, or foundation covered properly.

■ Don't spray-paint windows; instead, use a sash brush. The same rule applies for other trim—doors, basement sashes, and storm windows. However, a spray gun is excellent for painting screens.

Setting up a spray booth.
If you can't take your work outside, set up a paint booth inside. For small projects, your booth can be as simple as newspaper pages taped together and positioned behind and below the item to be sprayed. Use a cardboard panel as a shield to absorb overspray.

If you're painting a large piece or have a lot of spraying to do, fabricate a booth from 4-mil polyethylene plastic film and fasten it to the walls and floor in a corner of your workshop, basement, or garage.

How large a booth you need depends on the scale of the project being painted, of course. Be sure to give yourself plenty of

working room. Overspray carries a surprising distance, and cleaning it off masonry is a chore you want to avoid.

Keep the top of the booth open to allow paint fumes to escape. For safety reasons and skin protection, wear a spray mask, hat, rubber gloves, and long sleeves.

USING A SPRAY GUN

The first rule of spray-painting is to keep the equipment clean. If you don't, you'll spend most of your time dealing with equipment malfunctions and cleaning up spatters and runs. You'll also end up with a shoddy-looking job.

Also crucial is the thickness of paint being sprayed. If it's too thin, it will not cover and will drip and run. If it's too thick, it will clog your equipment and produce a finish that looks spattered. For the best results, read the container label and follow the paint and sprayer manufacturers' advice.

Your spray technique also deserves consideration. When you spray, keep a stiff wrist and hold the spray gun nozzle 8 to 10 inches away from the surface, parallel to the ground. And don't start spraying from a still position. Begin your movement, then pull the trigger and start spraying.

Fan the spray on the surface, using several light coats instead of one heavy coat. The paint will be thick at the center and feathered out at the edges. So, as you paint, overlap your spray pattern by about one third so the thickness of the paint will be uniform.

On gutters, point the gun away from the roof. Along foundations, paint the bottom two courses of siding with a brush, or mask off the foundation to at least a foot below the last siding course.

Strain the paint.
Before putting paint into the gun's reservoir, run the paint through a strainer to rid the mixture of impurities that may clog the gun.

Test the machine.
Experiment on scrap material to gauge the proper distance between the gun and the surface. Also, you can adjust most guns for different spray patterns.

Apply the paint.
Hold the gun perpendicular to the surface—don't swing it in an arc. Keep your wrist stiff to deter this temptation. For lap siding, angle the gun to spray the undersides. Apply a thin coating, and then let overspray fill it in.

Overlap the strokes.
Lap successive strokes by about one-third of the spray width to achieve even paint coverage.

YOU'LL NEED...

TIME: 6 hours to paint the exterior of a small house.
SKILLS: Intermediate painting skills and basic mechanical skills.
TOOLS: Spray gun, filter for paint, brushes, drop cloths.

USING A SPRAY CAN

Painting with spray cans is expensive, but the time you save compensates for the added expense. This is especially true when dealing with hard-to-paint items, such as wicker furniture, radiators, and small cabinets.

First shake the can. When you hear the rattle of the metal ball that mixes the paint, shake the can for another minute or so.

To prevent the nozzle from clogging, after each use invert the can and depress the button until only propellant comes out. Then wipe the nozzle clean. If the nozzle clogs, often you can open it by using a needle to puncture the paint seal over the spray hole. If this doesn't work, buy a low-cost replacement nozzle.

NOTE: *Aerosol paint is flammable, so don't spray-paint near flames.*

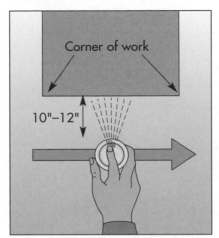

Apply with even strokes.
Hold the can 10 to 12 inches from the surface. Apply smooth, even strokes, moving the can parallel to the surface, rather than just pointing it in different directions. Don't try to cover the surface completely in the first stroke, or the thick paint may sag or drip. Apply several thin coats instead.

Lap the strokes.
Overlap the strokes by about one-third. After you've made several passes, stop and check to make sure the surface is covered.

Painting lattice.
On openwork like lattice, tilt the can at an angle to minimize the paint flowing through the openings. Crisscross your spray patterns to catch all the edges.

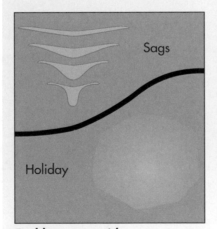

Problems to avoid.
Sags and runs are caused by too much paint. Wipe away the excess, then spot-spray with short bursts to blend in the touch-up.

Holidays occur when there's not enough paint on the surface. Spot-in these areas, as you would a sag or run.

Fogging is the dull, pebbled effect produced when the spray can is held too far away. Spot-spray these areas as well.

Orange-peeling results from too thick a covering of paint or from too much air pressure. Wipe and spot-paint these areas.

REPAIRING DRYWALL

Drywall—also known as plasterboard and by trade names such as Sheetrock®—consists of big sheets of pressed gypsum faced with heavy paper on both sides. After the sheets have been nailed, screwed, or glued to studs, the joints are covered with a perforated paper or fiberglass mesh tape. Joints are then filled and smoothed over with joint compound, often referred to as mud, to create a smooth surface.

Drywall repairs are easy once you get the knack of working with the material, especially the joint compound. See pages 293–298 for more about working with drywall.

YOU'LL NEED...

TIME: 10 to 20 minutes, depending on the size of the repair.
SKILLS: Basic skills.
TOOLS: Drywall taping knives, sanding block, sponge, putty knife, paintbrush, hammer, drill.

Filling a small hole.
For very small holes, apply joint compound to the void with a putty knife. Allow the compound to dry. If it shrinks, you may need to apply a second coat. To smooth the patch, either sand it or wipe it gently with a damp sponge.

EXPERTS' INSIGHT

JOINT COMPOUND

Ready-mixed joint compound comes in buckets; just scoop it out and apply it. Ready-mix is easy to sand, but it dries slowly and is not strong.

Dry-mix joint compound comes in bags of powder that you mix with water. Bags are typically labeled 90, 45, or 20; the compound will harden (though not dry) in roughly that many minutes. Regular dry-mix is stronger than ready-mix; "easy-sand" dry-mix is not.

Use ready-mix for small repairs. For substantial patches, or to speed up the drying time, apply one coat of dry-mix and use ready-mix for the top coats.

1. To fill a dent, apply joint compound.
Brush away any loose material. Use a taping blade to first pack the dent with joint compound and then to level it off. If the patch shrinks after drying, apply a second and perhaps a third coat.

2. Smooth the compound.
Sand the surface very lightly—or smooth it by wiping with a damp sponge.

3. Prime and paint.
Joint compound must be primed before you paint. Just about any type of primer, including latex, will do the job. Some paints are self-priming.

1. To repair loose tape, remove the tape.

If drywall tape is peeling, pull it gently off; you may need to pry it up with a putty knife first. Use a sharp knife to make a clean break at the point where the tape becomes firmly embedded. If the tape has a bubble, cut around the area with a utility knife, and pry out the damaged tape.

4" taping knife

2. Install new tape.

Wipe away any dust and debris. Cut a piece of fiberglass mesh tape to roughly fit; it's all right if it is a bit short at either end. Press the tape into place. Apply joint compound over the tape and use gentle strokes of a 4-inch taping knife to cover the tape.

6" taping knife

3. Cover with joint compound.

If you are applying ready-mix, or "easy-sand" compound, mound the compound up a bit. If you re-apply regular dry-mix compound, level it with the knife. Let it dry, then apply one and perhaps two more coats, feathering the edges. The patch should look and feel even with the surrounding wall. Sand, prime, and paint.

Stud

1. If nails have popped out, secure them with new fasteners.

If a nail is very loose, it may have missed the stud entirely; pull it out and drive a nail or screws into the stud. If it feels pretty firm, it either wasn't driven all the way or it barely caught the stud. Drive new ringshank nails or drywall screws just above and below the popped nail.

2. Set the fasteners.

If using nails, "dimple" the nails below the surface by tapping with a hammer. Take care not to break the paper. Drive screws slightly below the surface. Run a taping knife over the area to make sure that the fastener heads are recessed. Fill the dimples or screw holes with joint compound.

4" taping knife

3. Cover with joint compound.

After the compound has dried, apply a second and perhaps third coat, until the hole is filled to the same level as the surrounding wall. Sand, prime, and paint.

PATCHING HOLES IN DRYWALL

*U*sually the space between studs is 14½ inches. If a hole or damaged area is fairly large, cut out a section that spans from stud to stud so the patch can be solidly attached to nailers fastened to the studs, as shown on page 563. Smaller holes can be patched without attaching to framing, but they will not be as strong.

Most drywall is ½ inch thick, but some walls have ⅜- or ⅝-inch-thick drywall. Purchase patching drywall to match your existing material.

If a wall is damaged due to a doorknob that knocks against it, install a stop at the bottom of the door to prevent further damage.

YOU'LL NEED...

TIME: 30 minutes of actual work, plus drying time.
SKILLS: Basic skills.
TOOLS: Taping knives, keyhole saw or drywall saw, hammer, drill, utility knife, sanding block or sponge, paintbrush.

EXPERTS' INSIGHT

OTHER PATCHING MATERIALS

Special drywall patching kits save time and hassle. Some kits use a screen that adheres to the front of the drywall; just apply joint compound over the screen. Other kits have clips that clasp a patch firmly to the surrounding drywall. You cut the patch, clip it, apply mesh tape, and cover with joint compound.

1. To repair a small hole, prepare the backing.
Cut a piece of pegboard that is slightly larger than the damaged area, but small enough to slip through the hole. Or use a piece of wood through which you have drilled two holes.

2. Insert the backing.
Tie a wire to the pegboard, smear joint compound on the inside perimeter of the pegboard, and slip the patch into the wall. When you pull back on the wire, the patch should cling to the back of the wall.

3. Tighten.
Tie the wire on the patch to a pencil or small stick, and twist it tight. After the patch dries, cut the wire off and use a taping knife to fill the recess with joint compound. (See page 560 for how to choose joint compound.)

4. Fill and patch.
Allow the joint compound to dry. Apply two or three more coats, until the patch looks and feels level with the surrounding wall. Sand smooth or use a damp sponge to level the repair. Prime and paint.

1. For a medium-size hole, cut out a rectangle.

For holes up to 8 inches wide, mark a rectangle and cut it with a keyhole saw or a drywall saw.

Face paper Backing

2. Cut the patch.

Cut a drywall rectangle 2 inches larger than the hole on all sides. Turn the patch upside down and carefully use a utility knife to remove the 2-inch perimeter, but leave the face paper intact. Test to see that the patch fits comfortably into the hole.

3. Prepare for the patch.

Use a taping knife to spread a medium-thick bed of joint compound around the perimeter of the damaged area.

4. Install the patch.

Insert the patch and smooth the face paper against the wall all around. (The face paper takes the place of drywall tape.) Blend the patch with the surrounding surface by feathering the edges with coats of joint compound. Sand or smooth with a damp sponge, then prime and paint.

2×2 nailer

To repair a large area, frame the sides.

For larger holes, cut a rectangle that spans from stud to stud. Cut 2×2 nailers slightly longer than the opening's height. Position the nailers as shown, and attach them by driving nails or screws.

Mesh tape

Patch and tape.

Nail or screw the drywall patch into place. Apply fiberglass mesh tape to the perimeter, then cover it with three coats of joint compound. Allow each coat to dry and feather the edges to blend the patch with the wall. Sand it smooth or wipe it with a damp sponge. Prime and paint.

REPAIRING CRACKED PLASTER

*E*xamine plaster walls and ceilings before patching to make sure that repairs will last. Press hard with your hand on the surface all around any cracks. Here's what you may find:

■ If the plaster is solid and there are only a few hairline cracks, fill them with caulk or an aerosol crack sealer.

■ If the plaster is solid but there is a web of hairline cracks, the plaster itself is failing, perhaps because it was mixed incorrectly when installed. Usually the problem is cosmetic only, but could return after painting. Aerosol crack sealer may help, as may painting with latex semigloss paint, which remains flexible. Otherwise, either hire a plasterer or cover the surface with drywall.

■ If the area feels spongy, the plaster and perhaps the lath has come loose from the wall. Either remove all loose material and patch, or hire a plasterer. In extreme cases, or in the case of a loose ceiling, consider applying new drywall over the surface and taping it.

■ If a crack widens over time, the house is settling or you have a structural problem. You'll have to update repairs every so often. Seal the crack with flexible caulk.

The repairs shown here and on the next three pages are homeowner-friendly. For a new plaster surface that is rock-hard, you'll need to hire a plasterer.

YOU'LL NEED...

TIME: 1 hour of work, but allow for 2 overnight periods of drying.
SKILLS: Basic skills.
TOOLS: Hammer, chisel or old screwdriver, putty knife, taping knife, old toothbrush, sanding block, and a sponge.

1. Enlarge the crack.
Widen a medium-size crack to at least ¼ inch with a chisel or old screwdriver, and blow out any loose plaster. Press on the area of the wall surrounding the crack. If any part is spongy, chip away the plaster until you come to solid material, then patch as shown on pages 566–567.

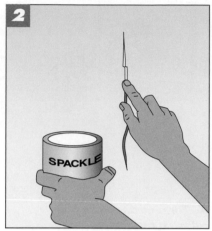

2. Fill with caulk or spackle.
Apply vinyl spackling compound, which retains some flexibility. Work it into the crack, and let it mound up a little. When it has dried, sand or sponge it smooth. Alternatively, fill the crack with latex/silicone caulk, which is more flexible but also more difficult to level with the surrounding wall.

3. Seal the patch.
Seal patches with primer before painting or the patch may "bleed" through and change the color of the paint.

EXPERTS' INSIGHT

PLASTER PATCHING MATERIALS

■ Dry-mix joint compound is strong, making it a good choice for wide cracks and holes.

■ Vinyl surfacing compound is soft and flexible. Use it for narrow cracks or holes.

■ Patching plaster or gauging plaster creates a genuine plaster surface, but it takes time to learn how to apply it correctly.

■ Latex/silicone caulk stays flexible and so can accommodate shifting cracks.

■ Aerosol crack seal is ideal for small cracks. Spray it just before priming.

1. For a wide crack, use a chisel to "key" it.

Undercut wide cracks, making them broader at the bottom than the surface to lock in the filler material (see inset). Sometimes you can do this by scraping with a chisel or screwdriver; some people prefer to use an old-fashioned "church-key" type of can opener.

2. Remove loose material.

Clean the debris and crumbly material out of the crack with an old toothbrush or a wire brush. It helps to vacuum out the hole.

3. Wet the area.

Use a small brush to wet the crack before patching.

For a patch that is less likely to crack, apply fiberglass mesh tape over the crack. This will make the repaired area bulge a bit, so you will need to feather the compound out on each side (see page 567).

4. Force compound into the crack.

Pack joint compound, surfacing compound, or patching plaster into the crack with a putty knife or a wide-blade taping knife. First force the material into the crack, and then level it off.

5. Apply additional coats.

Let the compound harden, then level off the repair with a second and perhaps a third application. If you are using soft compound, mound the patch up a bit because it's easy to sand or sponge it down.

6. Smooth and seal.

Allow the patch to dry thoroughly, then either sand it smooth or rub it with a damp sponge. If you have not embedded mesh tape in the patch, spray the area with aerosol crack sealer. Seal it with primer, then paint it.

REPAIRING HOLES IN PLASTER

Before you attack a big hole or bulge, find out what caused the plaster to fail. See page 866 for some tips. If the wall is water-stained or damp, solve the leak or plumbing problem and wait a month or two to make sure the area will stay dry.

In most cases, a hole in plaster is just the tip of the iceberg; the surrounding surface is likely loose and weak. Always cut back to sound plaster; you won't get a solid bond with crumbling edges. If most or all of a wall is loose and weak, consider removing all the plaster and installing drywall over the lath. You could also cover the plaster with drywall, but that will necessitate modifying your moldings to accommodate the thicker wall. See pages 293–298 for hanging and taping drywall. Usually you can remove the plaster only and leave the wood or metal lath in place. If the lath is rotted or badly rusted, replace it.

You may be able to fill a medium-size hole with dry-mix joint compound only, but make a stiff mix of the compound to ward off sags. Patching plaster is less likely to sag.

Once you have chipped away the loose plaster, carefully measure its thickness, which can vary considerably from area to area even on a single wall. The patching drywall may be thinner, but should not be thicker than the plaster. Usually, either 3/8- or 1/2-inch drywall will work.

YOU'LL NEED...

TIME: An hour of work and a day of drying time.
SKILLS: Basic skills.
TOOLS: Hammer, drill, masonry chisel or old screwdriver, utility knife, taping knife, sanding block, sponge, painting tools.

1. Remove all loose plaster.
Dig back with a masonry chisel, flat pry bar, or old screwdriver until you encounter solid plaster. Brush out any remaining debris.

2. "Key" the opening.
Though not as important as with cracks, undercutting the edges makes a stronger repair. Scrape with a utility knife, chisel, screwdriver, or "church-key" type of can opener.

Drywall patch

3. Cut and screw a drywall patch.
If there is wood lath behind the hole, cut a piece of drywall—the same thickness or thinner than the plaster—to roughly fit in the hole. Make sure it does not stick out past the plaster. Attach it to the lath with 1 1/4-inch drywall screws driven into the lath.

4. Fill the perimeter.
Blend a stiff batch of dry-mix joint compound, and use a taping knife to press it into the spaces between the patch and the wall. Then smooth the surface.

5. Add mesh tape.
While the compound is wet, cut pieces of fiberglass mesh tape and embed them in the compound. This will bond the compound with the surrounding wall and protect against cracks.

6. Smooth over the mesh.
Apply more joint compound and spread it over the mesh. The idea is to cover the mesh, but not build up the compound too thick. After it has dried, apply two more coats of ready-mix compound or surfacing compound.

7. Sand and finish.
Once the compound has dried, sand it smooth or rub lightly with a damp sponge to level the area. Apply primer and paint.

REPAIRING PANELING

If you scratch or mar paneling, you usually can make a cosmetic repair in a few minutes with paste wax or a crayonlike touch-up stick. Don't try to spot-sand and refinish your prefinished paneling; you risk doing more harm than good.

If a panel has suffered serious damage, you'll have to replace it entirely. Finding a match may be your biggest challenge.

If your paneling was glued directly to drywall, you may have to replace the drywall before reinstalling the paneling. If electrical wiring runs in the wall you're working on, shut off the power to the circuit before doing any cutting, sawing, or nailing.

YOU'LL NEED...
TIME: An hour of work per panel.
SKILLS: Basic skills.
TOOLS: Hammer, pry bar, pliers, taping knives, chisel, caulking gun, and nail set.

1. Remove the damaged panel.
Identify and mark the edges of the damaged panel. Pry off the baseboard and top molding by inserting a taping or putty knife, then a pry bar. Pull out the nails with pliers, then pull the panel off. Start at the bottom, where there's usually no adhesive. Pull out nails as they pop. Finish prying the panel away, working from the bottom to the top. Use a wood block to protect adjacent panels.

2. Install the new panel.
Remove all old adhesive with a scraper or chisel. Apply panel adhesive to studs with a caulking gun. Nail the panel loosely at the top and wedge it out, as shown, until the adhesive gets tacky. Press the panel into place, then use a wood block to tap it against the studs, as shown. Nail the edges with color-matched brads.

PREPARING INTERIOR SURFACES FOR PAINT

Paint works wonders for a room's appearance, but it can't perform miracles. Paint will not heal cracked walls, smooth rough textures, or fill any but the tiniest nail holes. In fact, paint applied to a wall that is not well prepared may peel, causing you major headaches later.

After you've cleared the room, but before you've opened the first paint can, give every surface careful scrutiny. Start with the walls, checking for cracks, runs, or ridges in the old paint. All of these can be treated easily with a scraper and sandpaper; then use a primer for bare spots. Use a paint remover to strip cracked or gloppy paint from woodwork. If the old paint is peeling, suspect moisture or poor preparation. Both problems require removing the old

paint and priming the surface. Of course, any moisture leaks should be immediately corrected at the source.

Mend superficial plaster or drywall blemishes with surfacing or joint compound. Bigger repairs (see pages 560–567) require more time, not only for patching, but also for curing and priming. (On textured walls, you may have trouble blending the patched area completely with its surroundings.)

You can paint over clean, sound wallpaper, but in most cases you're better off stripping it (see page 577). If you decide to paint over wallpaper, paint a small test spot in an inconspicuous area and wait a few days. If the pattern bleeds through, apply stain-killing primer. If the paper begins to peel, strip all of the wallpaper.

After you've made repairs, give the ceiling, walls, and woodwork a thorough bath with household detergent, and rinse well. Prime exposed spots with a compatible primer. At this point, you've completed at least 50 percent of your painting project.

Use heavy-duty drop cloths that will stay in place to protect floors and rugs. If you step on a drip, you will likely track paint around the room, so cover a broad area.

YOU'LL NEED...

TIME: 2 to 4 hours per room.
SKILLS: Basic skills.
TOOLS: Portable light, screwdriver, putty knife, sandpaper, sponge or mop.

1. Clear and protect the room.
If practical, remove all furniture from the room. You may choose to group heavy items in the middle and protect them with drop cloths. Cover the floor carefully. Ideally, you should tape down a layer of heavy cardboard or plastic, and cover that with a heavy-duty drop cloth.

2. Provide lighting.
Set up strong lights so you can see what you're painting. Provide general lighting. Also, aim other lights at angles to highlight minor imperfections. If there is a ceiling light, disconnect it and let it hang (see page 570). Cover the globe to protect against spatters. Alternatively, disconnect the light entirely and replace it with a simple work light.

3. Remove coverplates.

It always saves time to remove obstacles rather than paint around them. Even if you plan to paint switch and receptacle plates, remove them and paint them separately.

4. Patch holes and cracks.

Regardless of the size, fill every hole and crack with vinyl surfacing compound. Allow it to dry, then sand it smooth. Prime all patches before painting.

5. Ensure the paint will stick.

Sand rough spots smooth, and sand any runs from previous paint jobs. To ensure that the new paint will stick, you have three options: (1) Sand all the walls and trim using 80- or 100-grit sandpaper on a drywall-type sanding pole; (2) apply liquid sander, which removes the sheen from glossy and semigloss paints; (3) paint the room with primer. If you will apply latex paint over existing solvent-thinned paint, perform at least two of these operations.

6. Clean the surfaces.

Wash the ceiling and walls with a sponge or mop, paying special attention to the tops of baseboards and moldings. Any dust will cling to your brush or roller and mar the paint job.

PAINTING CEILINGS

To succeed at painting a room, start at the top and work your way down. In other words, the ceiling comes first.

Unless the surface is brand new, you usually can get by with one coat of paint on a ceiling. Even stubborn stains will disappear if you spot-prime them first.

If you're planning a one-coat application, let the paint lap onto the walls. If you will apply two coats to the ceiling, cut in (trim up to the ceiling/wall line) with a trim brush. Otherwise, the paint will build up on the wall and leave a ridge.

Paint across the ceiling at the room's narrow dimension, especially if you're using a fast-drying paint. Otherwise, the paint may lose its wet edge.

A roller frame with an extension handle greatly speeds up the job, although you still need a trim brush to cut in the ceiling paint where it meets the walls. A doughnut-style roller makes quick work of painting the corner between a wall and the ceiling.

Rollers emit a fine spray of paint that settles over the room like dust. Cover furniture in the room, as well as the floor, carpeting, and woodwork. Canvas drop cloths work best because they absorb spills and are easy to walk on, but plastic drop cloths or newspapers will do the job too.

Buy ceiling paint—it is flatter than flat wall paint and hides imperfections very well. It is not scrubbable, but ceilings are not prone to handprints and smudges.

YOU'LL NEED...

TIME: 3 to 4 hours.
SKILLS: Basic painting skills.
TOOLS: Drop cloths, brushes, ladder, and a roller with an extension handle.

1. Protect lights.
Usually you can remove a light fixture's canopy. Remove the canopy's mounting screws and allow the fixture to hang down, as long as it is not a heavy chandelier. (See page 98 for how to dismantle fixtures.) Wrap the fixture in plastic, or cover the finish parts with masking tape.

2. Paint the corners.
Start a ceiling job by cutting in a strip along the walls, as shown. If you'll be applying only one coat, lap the paint onto the wall as well.

3. Roll and cross-roll.
Start rolling the paint with a series of diagonal swaths. Don't worry about spreading the paint evenly; just get it on the ceiling. Then even out the paint and fill in any open areas by cross-rolling.

4. Level the paint.
Continue working, spreading the paint from dry areas into the wet paint. Rollers slip on smooth surfaces, so check for skips. After you've finished a section, check to see whether you've created thick lap marks. If so, even them out by going over them lightly with a fairly dry roller.

PAINTING WALLS

Once the walls have been patched, perhaps primed, and cleaned thoroughly, the ceiling has been painted, and all of the switch and receptacle plates have been removed, you're ready to paint walls. Do all the edging first. This includes cutting in the ceiling and around moldings and trims. Once these details are done, it's payback time: You can paint the big, flat surfaces quickly.

A neat job requires concentration and a methodical approach. Take care to keep the edges wet to prevent lap marks. Keep the roller from slipping to the side and causing skid marks. Avoid the temptation to make a roller load last too long, or you will end up with places that are not fully covered.

When painting with semigloss or high-gloss finish, make the final brush strokes away from light sources, including windows. This way, the tiny ridges that a brush leaves won't be as noticeable.

Always give paint a brisk stirring before starting, even if the paint was just shaken at the store. As you work, stir the paint occasionally. Keep an eye on the paint in the roller tray. As long as you're filling the roller, the paint will remain properly blended. If you leave the tray for an hour or so, cover it with plastic wrap. When you're ready to get back to work, stir the paint lightly with a paint paddle. When left untouched, paint skins over.

YOU'LL NEED...
TIME: 5 to 6 hours for a 14×16-foot room.
SKILLS: Basic painting skills.
TOOLS: Drop cloths, ladder, brushes, specialty paint applicators for painting around trim, roller, extension handle.

1. Brush the corners.
Begin painting walls by cutting in the corners and around all of the woodwork. With practice, you can cut neat lines without the use of masking tape. If you will paint the trim later, lap the wall paint onto the trim slightly. Paint about 3 inches out from the edges.

2. Apply paint.
For large surfaces, load the roller and apply the paint in a large "M" shape. Start the roller going up, then pull it down.

3. Even out the paint.
Level and fill in the M shapes by cross-rolling. You can work horizontally, as shown, or vertically. By working the paint this way, you get an even paint surface. Watch for roller skids.

4. Paint in planned sections.
Determine how much area a loaded roller can fully cover. Do not attempt to "stretch" the paint, or you will probably need to apply another coat. (You can see the coverage clearly only after the paint has dried.) Plan to work in sections that are similar in size.

PAINTING WOODWORK

Painting woodwork is hard work. Next to prepping, it's the most time-consuming painting job. If you master the tricks shown here, however, you'll minimize the tedium and speed your progress.

If at all possible, learn to paint freehand. With practice, anyone with a fairly steady hand and good brushes can master freehand techniques and save a tremendous amount of time compared to applying masking tape.

A coat of paint will probably emphasize rather than cover imperfections. Before you begin painting, patch holes with wood filler. Let the material dry overnight, then apply primer.

If you'll be using the same paint on the woodwork as on the walls, paint the woodwork as you come to it. Generally, however, you should use a higher gloss on woodwork. If you do, or if the woodwork will be another color, paint the walls first.

Windows and raised-panel doors are the toughest assignments because of the amount of cutting in and the fact that you can't use full brush strokes. If you can't paint freehand, cover the glass with masking tape or use a painter's shield. Some people find it efficient to paint windows somewhat sloppily and then scrape the excess afterwards. Use a razor blade scraping tool to clean off smeared paint.

Painting a sash window.
Paint double-hung windows in the sequence shown, starting with the muntins, then working outward. Move the sashes several times while the paint is drying to make sure the sashes do not dry shut.

Casement window sequence.
Use the same sequence shown at left for casement windows. Keep the window slightly open until the paint is dry.

Mask window panes ...
Painter's masking tape protects windowpanes from paint. Peel off the tape immediately after you finish painting; if you wait until the paint is fully dry, you could crack it as you remove the tape.

... or use a shield.
A painter's shield keeps paint off the glass, too. Keep a damp cloth handy to frequently clean the shield's edge as you work around the muntins.

YOU'LL NEED...

TIME: 1 to 2 hours for a standard window.
SKILLS: Moderate painting skills.
TOOLS: Sash brush, masking tape, painter's shield, putty knife, and a drop cloth.

Panel door sequence.

Start painting panel doors at the molding edges. Then fill in the panels, the hinge stile, the rails, and the latch stile. To apply a gloss finish, use a cross-brush method: Apply paint on the door horizontally, then make vertical finishing strokes. Always finish a door once you've started it. If you don't, the lap marks may show.

Roll flush doors.

Flush doors are easier and quicker to paint. Either a brush or a roller will give good results. If you use a roller, be sure to roll the entire surface, because any brush marks will look very different.

Painting baseboards.

Paint the top edge of a baseboard first. Next cut in along the floor, and then fill in between. Painter's masking tape helps if you don't have a steady hand.

Clean as you go.

Have on hand a rag dampened with water or mineral spirits, depending on the type of paint. Clean up overlapping paint smudges as soon as they occur. If you don't, the paint will set up and be much tougher to remove.

Keep the floor clean.

A cloth wrapped around a putty knife works well to clean up paint drippings on hardwood and resilient flooring along baseboards.

Seal a stain.

If a woodwork stain bleeds through the paint, spray or brush on a stain-killing primer, let dry, then repaint.

PAINTING CABINETS

This is an inexpensive way to make a dramatic improvement in the appearance of a kitchen. It requires painstaking, methodical work, but it is well worth the effort.

Purchase paint made especially for cabinets. Alkyd paint generally outperforms latex, but many types of latex paint are durable and washable. For two weeks after application, handle latex painted cabinets carefully and certainly do not scrub them.

While you're at it, you may choose to install new shelf paper on shelves and drawer bottoms.

YOU'LL NEED...
TIME: 2 days to paint cabinets in a medium-size kitchen.
SKILLS: Basic painting skills.
TOOLS: Screwdriver, putty knife, drop cloth, and a trim brush.

Remove doors and drawers.
Before painting cabinets, dismantle them as much as possible. Unscrew and remove all hinges and knobs or pulls. Lay a drop cloth or newspapers on the floor; you may need to use an adjacent room as well. Stand the drawers upright, or prop them so no edge touches the drop cloth.

Paint the drawer faces and doors with a roller or a brush. Aim to make the roller stipple or brush strokes consistent for all the drawers and doors.

Place doors on small scraps of wood. Paint the insides first, wait a day, then flip and paint the outsides. Paint the edges of doors first, then the faces. Check all around each piece to make sure there are no drips or sags.

Work from inside to outside.
Begin painting cabinets at their least accessible points and work outward. Do the inside edges first, then move toward outer surfaces. You may be able to use a roller for the faces, as long as you can roll all the surfaces; any brush strokes will be noticeable.

Prop a piece to paint both sides.
To paint both sides and the edges of a shelf in one session, drive in four small nails to serve as legs. Paint the underside, then the top.

Strip the hardware.
Clean previously painted cabinet, door, or window hardware by soaking it overnight in paint stripper. Rinse with mineral spirits. Buff the surfaces lightly with steel wool. Alternatively, buy and install new hardware.

CLEANING UP AFTER PAINTING

*E*ven if you've thoroughly covered and masked the surfaces you don't want to paint, there will likely be splatters to clean. For water-thinned finishes, use dishwashing detergent in warm water with a soft cloth to remove stray paint. If the paint is solvent-thinned, use thinner on a soft cloth. Where thinner has been applied, follow up with water and household detergent.

If you happen to scuff freshly painted walls or woodwork, don't attempt to wash the scuff mark until the paint has had time to cure—at least 30 days.

Store paint in a cool, dry place. If you don't use the paint within a two-year period, dispose of it properly (see page 19).

Take canvas and plastic drop cloths outdoors and thoroughly shake them. You can wash a canvas drop cloth in the washing machine.

Clean drips quickly.
Wipe away splatters with soap and water or the solvent used to thin the paint. It's best to catch these splatters as you work, rather than hours or days later.

Pull away masking tape.
Remove masking tape as soon as you have completed a line, while the paint is still wet. Otherwise the paint will tear and you'll end up with a ragged and crumbling edge.

Scrape up dried paint.
Use a razor-blade scraper to chip off big paint droplets that have already set. A putty knife will work, too. Acetone or latex paint remover will clean away dried latex paint; use paint stripper sparingly to remove dried solvent-thinned paint.

Razor-blade window panes.
Use a razor-blade scraper to trim around windowpanes. Try not to break the seal between the glass and the paint.

Reseal paint cans.
If more than a quart of material remains, seal it in the original paint can. Tap the lid with a hammer and block of wood to shut it tightly. Store paint cans upside down to prevent a skin from forming. If you end up with less than a quart, pour the paint into a glass jar that seals tightly. The paint will keep better in this small container.

CHOOSING WALLPAPER

Wallpapering a room—once a messy, tricky task best left to professionals—is now almost as easy as painting. Improved wall coverings deserve part of the credit; they don't rip, shrink, or wrinkle as easily as older papers.

New slower-acting adhesives help, too, by giving you more time to hang the materials correctly.

On the following pages, every step of the job is covered—from removing old wallpaper to the advanced techniques needed for

doing ceiling work. Because prepasted and vinyl coverings are easiest for beginners, there are sections devoted to hanging these time and effort savers (see pages 586 and 587).

SELECTING WALLCOVERINGS

Type	Use	Application Tips	Cost
Solid paper	The least-expensive type of wall covering. Can be damaged if scrubbed, so use only in a low-traffic areas.	Difficult to strip. Hang with wheat-based paste. Work carefully because this material is easy to tear. Butt edges and roll seams; clean immediately, using a damp (not wet) sponge.	Low
Vinyl-coated paper	Most any situation, except where there's high humidity. More durable than solid paper.	Paste and hang one strip at a time; roll the seams and immediately clean the adhesive from each seam.	Wide range
Paper-backed vinyl	Excellent for high-traffic or high-humidity areas	May be stripped. Hand-printed vinyls must be trimmed. Use plenty of adhesive; do not stretch as you hang. If the seams curl, paste them down with vinyl-to-vinyl adhesive; remove excess adhesive immediately.	Wide range
Cloth-backed vinyl	Excellent for high-traffic and high-humidity areas.	May be stripped. Stiff and difficult to shape to wall or ceiling surfaces. If the paper is lightweight, use a wheat-paste adhesive; if heavy, use a vinyl adhesive.	High
Wet-look vinyl	Kitchens, bathrooms, laundry areas, and mudrooms	You may need to apply a lining paper first; surface imperfections will show.	Medium
Flocked	Avoid in high-traffic or difficult-to-clean areas.	Keep adhesive off the face; if adhesive does get on the face, remove it immediately with clear water and blot, don't rub. If flocking mats, gently go over it with a suede brush.	High
Foil	Kitchens, bathrooms, and laundry areas, because it is easy to clean	Consider hiring a pro; this is difficult to hang. Don't crease paper as you paste and hang it. Be careful around electrical switches and outlets.	High
Burlap/ grass cloth	Anywhere except in hard-use areas where there's lots of grease, dampness, and dirt	Lining paper required. Butt edges and roll seams. Mix vinyl adhesive with ½ pint less water than instructed; apply two coats of adhesive with a mohair paint roller cover.	High
Hand-screened paper	To achieve a stylish effect	Because it is expensive and often made of paper that is easily torn, consider hiring a professional.	Very high

REMOVING OLD WALLPAPER

Unless you're working with a strippable-type paper, stripping old paper is a messy, time-consuming task. Before you decide to take on the job, ask yourself if you really need to take the old paper off before applying the new. If the old wallpaper is on the wall nice and tight, leave it there. You can eradicate a small blemish by cutting away the damaged section and piecing-in a patch to level the surface. Bubbles can be slit, reglued, and flattened.

If the old paper is loose or in bad shape, you have no choice but to remove it.

YOU'LL NEED...

TIME: 6 to 8 hours for a room.
SKILLS: Basic skills.
TOOLS: Taping knife, scoring tool, sponge, spray bottle, scraper, and a wallpaper steamer.

Scrape and peel loose paper.
Some heavier wall coverings—especially vinyl types—can be peeled off in strips. Loosen an edge with a taping knife and pull it down or up. A wallpaper scraper with a replaceable blade is the best tool, though a paint scraper can work. Slip it under the paper with one hand and peel with the other.

Use a scoring tool.
If the paper won't peel off in one continuous strip, make slits just deep enough to cut the paper. A wallpaper scoring tool (shown) does this quickly. Use it like a computer mouse to make a random pattern of curved cuts.

Scrub with wallpaper remover.
After scoring the paper, soak the slits with a liquid wallpaper remover. If the wall covering has a light vinyl coating, it may help to sand the coating first. Scrape off the old paper.

Use a sprayer.
If the wall is plaster, soak the paper thoroughly with mist from a plant sprayer or a pump sprayer. When wet enough, use a scraper to remove the paper. Avoid soaking drywall, which can be damaged by excess moisture.

Use a wallpaper steamer.
A wallpaper steamer works well for removing lots of paper. It has a small boiler that furnishes steam to a plate that you hold against the wall. Especially if you're dealing with nonstrippable wallpaper, you can remove more old paper in an hour with a steamer than you previously could in a day of soaking and hard work.

PREPARING WALLS FOR PAPERING

For sheer dramatic impact, few interior wall treatments rival wallpaper. For a clean-looking job, take the time to prepare the walls meticulously. Most coverings will show rather than hide every nick, hole, and ridge.

You're in luck if the wall you want to paper is painted and in good repair. If the paint is glossy, simply dull the gloss with an abrasive so the adhesive will stick properly. Wash down the area with a strong household detergent, let it dry, and then hang the paper.

If the paint is peeling from the surface, remove it with a scraper, wash down the walls, then seal the surface with a sealer or wallpaper sizing. For walls with a sand or textured finish, first scrape and lightly sand the surface, then cover it with lining paper.

Lining paper is a plain, light-weight wallpaper with no pattern. You apply it with presized wheat paste, butting the edges and rolling the seams. The edges do not need to be butted tightly. A liner can solve minor but not major wall problems.

Nicked, cracked, and crumbling walls or ceilings call for corrective action. See pages 560–567 for ways to repair drywall and plaster.

YOU'LL NEED...
TIME: 4 hours for a small room.
SKILLS: Basic painting skills are similar to the skills needed to prepare and size walls.
TOOLS: Sandpaper, straightedge, utility knife, brush, roller with an extension handle, and a screwdriver.

Patch a damaged area.
If the old paper is loose in just a few spots and you plan to paper over it, temporarily tape a piece of wallpaper over the damaged area. Use a straightedge and utility knife to double-cut a rectangle; slice through both the patch and the old paper. This will produce a patch that fits precisely.

Adhere loose paper.
Lightly sand any seam overlaps. If you don't, the seams will show through the new wallpaper. Remove grease and dirt by washing the entire surface. Glue down curled edges with wallpaper adhesive. Vinyl-to-vinyl adhesive is the strongest; coat both the paper and the wall surface.

Remove coverplates.
Remove all hardware and turn off electrical circuits before you hang paper. If you don't, your trimming task will be more difficult—and dangerous.

Apply sizing.
Use sizing to seal new walls or those covered with wallpaper. The sizing keeps the porous surfaces from absorbing the adhesive. Consult with your wall covering dealer if you are unsure whether you need sizing.

HANGING WALLPAPER

One key to a visually successful papering job is finding the point in the room where a pattern mismatch will not be noticed. You can count on a mismatch, because the last strip you put up will have to be trimmed lengthwise to butt up against the first strip.

One such point is adjacent to a door or window frame. This gives only a few inches of discord above or below the opening. The ideal location is often above the entry door into a room, because the mismatch is hidden behind you as you enter the room. Other spots are an inconspicuous corner or a location that will be covered by draperies or furniture.

The first strip is very important because it "locks in position" all the strips that follow. Unless the first one is plumb, all the other strips will be out of alignment, and the error will compound itself as you apply each successive strip to the walls.

Because wallpapering is a messy job, take special pains to "work clean." Wash your hands often. Use clean water and a sponge to wipe away paste after hanging each strip of paper. Keep the pasting table free of adhesive, and clean your tools if they have paste on them.

If you're using prepasted paper, disregard Step 3 and simply soak the strip in your water trough (see page 586).

YOU'LL NEED...
TIME: 10 hours for a small room.
SKILLS: Good wallpapering skills can be learned with a few hours of practice.
TOOLS: Tools are listed in the Experts' Insight box, above.

EXPERTS' INSIGHT

FIGURING WALLCOVERING NEEDS

■ First determine how much material you need. Measure the height of each wall, then measure the distance around the room, including door and window openings. Multiply these two figures, and you'll have the area of the wall surface. You may need extra to match patterns (see page 581). A wallpaper dealer will translate these figures into the number of rolls needed.

■ After selecting the type of wallpaper (see page 576), ask the salesperson to recommend the right adhesive and the quantity you need. Foils, paper-backed burlap, vinyls, backed flocks, hand prints, murals, and borders require vinyl adhesive. Prepasted wallpaper requires no adhesive, just a shallow trough wide enough to soak each rolled-up strip before you hang it.

■ Standard tools include a paint roller and tray (if you don't use a paste brush), a utility knife with plenty of sharp blades, a tape measure, an 8-foot straightedge, a plumb bob, a chalk line, long-bladed scissors, a stepladder, drop cloths, a wall scraper, and sponges. You'll need a pasting table unless you're using prepasted paper. Rent one or use two card tables or sawhorses covered with a sheet of hardboard.

■ Special tools include a paste brush, a water tray for prepasted paper, a seam roller, and a smoothing brush.

■ Once you have the paper, go around the room and lightly mark lines where the seams will go. This will help you plan the location of the mismatch.

1. Chalk a reference line.
Hang a chalk line from a tacked nail near the top of the wall to near the bottom. Snap the line, and double-check with a level to see that it is plumb.

2. Uncurl the paper.
Uncurl the paper by unrolling it against the edge of a table. Cut the first strip several inches longer than needed.

3. Apply paste.

You'll need a worktable large enough to accommodate at least one full-length wallpaper strip, plus one booked strip (see Step 4). A simple sheet of plywood on a set of sawhorses or a worktable works well. Keep the table clean; wipe up spilled paste immediately.

Consult with your dealer and read the manufacturer's instructions for the best type of adhesive. Premixed paste is the easiest to use and is worth the extra cost. Wheat-based adhesive is strong enough for most coverings. Clay-based adhesive is stronger but difficult to work with. Apply the paste to half of the strip, leaving an inch at the end to grasp. Fold it over and paste the other half.

4. "Book" the paper.

"Book" the pasted paper by folding it over twice. Let the pasted paper rest in this fashion for a few minutes, or according to the manufacturer's directions. Resting time is critical; it allows the covering to absorb the adhesive.

5. Apply at the top.

Unfold the top half of the pasted paper. Align the paper with the plumb chalk line you snapped, and overlap the paper slightly onto the ceiling. Check that the side of the paper aligns precisely with the plumb line; make any adjustments sooner rather than later.

6. Remove bubbles.

Smooth the paper onto the surface with the wall brush or a clean sponge. Work from the center to the edges of the paper to remove all air bubbles. Continue to check the plumb line, because brushing may cause the covering to slide.

7. Apply the lower half.

Reach behind the strip and unfold the bottom half. Slip it into place against the plumb mark. You can pull and reposition it as needed.

8. Finish applying the first strip.
Smooth the lower section of paper. With a level, check for plumb. If the strip is not plumb, start again. Smooth with vertical strokes.

Straight pattern

Drop pattern

Measuring and cutting strips to match a pattern
Each strip must not only span from ceiling to baseboard with a few inches to spare; it must be long enough to do so while matching the pattern of the strip it butts against. Place the strip to be cut next to the one it will butt against in order to measure.

A paper with a vertical pattern does not need to be matched. A pattern with a straight horizontal design is easy to match. If the pattern has diagonal lines, you may need to waste a good deal of material. With a drop pattern, the design element of one strip is repeated lower than the strip it abuts. The larger the pattern, or the "repeat," the more material is likely to be wasted.

9. Trim the edges.
Tap the paper into the corners with the brush. Gently press the paper into the corner at the ceiling and against the top of the base molding. Using a utility knife, cut it carefully to avoid tearing. Be sure to use a very sharp blade, and change blades often to ensure a razor-sharp edge. A metal straightedge can help.

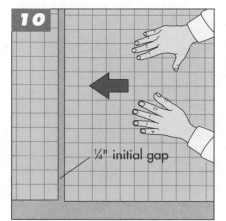

¼" initial gap

10. Butt the next strip.
Cut the next strip following the guidelines presented above. Double-check that it will span from ceiling to floor while matching the pattern of its neighbor. Butt seams by aligning the new strip about ¼ inch from the adjoining one. Slide it over so that the edges buckle slightly. Smooth the new strip as in Step 8.

11. Roll the seams.
About 15 minutes after you've hung each strip, roll the seams with a seam roller to ensure good adhesion. Do not roll flocked papers. If a seam refuses to lie flat, apply vinyl-to-vinyl adhesive and re-roll the seam.

PAPERING AROUND CORNERS

Consider yourself lucky if you find a corner in an older house that's plumb. To negotiate problem corners, you'll need to master "double-cutting."

As you hang adjacent strips, overlap them by at least ½ inch, making sure the pattern matches. With a straightedge as a guide, use a razor-sharp utility knife to cut through both layers of paper. Make the cut while the paste on the paper is still soft.

Carefully pull both selvages—the scrap pieces—from the surface, as shown in the box below. With a smoothing brush, smooth the seam created when you removed the selvages.

At either an inside or outside corner, be sure you firmly tap the paper against the surface with the brush. After you've finished the corner, stick a series of thin straight pins near the edge of the corner—not in it—to "clamp" the paper until the adhesive dries. Arrange the pins in such a way in the pattern that holes won't show once the pins have been removed.

1. Measure for the corner strip.
Measure the distance from the corner to the near edge of the last strip of paper you applied, both top and bottom. Add 1 inch to the measurements.

2. Hang and trim the corner strip.
Cut, paste, and hang this strip so it butts the previous strip. Tap it firmly into the corner. Cut slits at the top and bottom corners as shown. Trim the strip at the top and bottom.

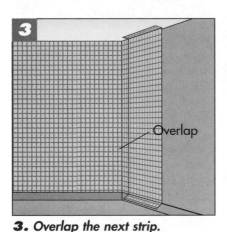

3. Overlap the next strip.
Snap a new plumb line on the wall, allowing for at least a 1-inch overlap, or more if the pattern necessitates it, on top of the previous strip. Hang the next strip with its edge on the plumb line. Tap the paper into the corner.

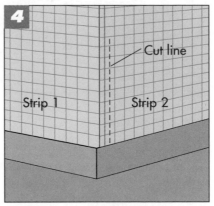

4. Wrap an outside corner.
On outside corners, wrap the paper approximately 1 inch around the corner. Apply the next strip, overlapping it, and double-cut with a utility knife.

Make a double-cut seam.
Double-cut through both thicknesses of wallpaper. Peel off the waste from the outer paper. Slightly lift the edge of that strip, and peel out the waste edge from the inner strip. Smooth both strips, then roll the seam.

PAPERING AROUND OPENINGS

One of the more demanding tasks in a wallpapering project is cutting around moldings and openings. Mistakes here will be embarrassingly noticeable. So take the time necessary to achieve straight lines and tight fits.

Always work with a knife that has a sharp blade to avoid pulling or tearing the covering. Before making your cuts around casings, be sure that the covering is snug against it. Otherwise, you may find to your dismay that the line you've cut falls short of covering the wall. If you don't feel comfortable making the cuts freehand, slip a metal straightedge into the joint and then make the cut using it as a guide.

YOU'LL NEED...

TIME: 30 minutes per opening.
SKILLS: Intermediate skills.
TOOLS: Smoothing brush, utility knife or razor blade, paste brush, straightedge, seam roller.

EXPERTS' INSIGHT

REPAIRING TORN PAPER

If you do make a mistake and tear the paper, deal with the problem immediately. If you cannot repair the tear to your satisfaction, remove and replace the entire strip of wallpaper.

To repair a tear, lift the two sides, apply extra adhesive, and press the sides back in place. Wipe the surface clean of excess adhesive. If you need extra holding power, apply vinyl-to-vinyl adhesive.

Cutting around casings.
Let the strip adjoining the opening overlap the casings. Begin to smooth the covering, but don't come too close to the casing or you may tear the covering. Once the strip is correctly aligned and the paper is partially smoothed, make a cut at the corner of the casing to allow you to smooth the covering all the way up to the casing. Use a taping blade or a straightedge to create a crease at the point where the casing meets the wall. Cut the crease along the side of the casing with a sharp utility knife.

Cutting the top of casings.
At the top of the casing, crease the paper and cut it where the molding joins the wall. Then smooth the edge of the wallpaper. If the casing is thick, a minor cutting mistake here might not be noticeable.

At a wall opening.

When you encounter a recess or an entryway without a door, first hang the covering on the interior walls of the opening. Allow at least 1 inch of overhang along the sides and the top. Make diagonal slits at the two corners, and wrap the paper around the outside corners. Paper the outside wall, letting the pieces "go wild" for a couple of inches before trimming.

Around cabinetry.

Trim along the top of fireplace mantels or bookcases before you do the sides. This allows you to wrap the paper around the sides and make truer cuts.

Improvise for complicated cuts.

To fit around tricky corners and moldings, you will need to cut slits so the paper will lie flat. Use plenty of adhesive.

Around an outlet or switch.

Shut off the electricity to circuits before you work around switches and outlets. Apply paper right over the outlet or switch, then trim away the overlap. Make sure the opening is small enough that the coverplate will conceal it but large enough that no paper protrudes into the electrical box. If you make a mistake, an oversize coverplate may hide it.

PAPERING OVER A COVERPLATE

To add a professional touch to your wallpapering job, paper over the switch and receptacle cover plates.

Some fanatics paint the switch toggles and receptacles with matching background paint. Before you go that far, however, consider the possibility that anyone with failing eyesight might not be able to find the camouflaged switch or outlet.

YOU'LL NEED...

TIME: About 15 minutes per coverplate.
SKILLS: Basic wallpapering skills.
TOOLS: Pin, pencil, masking tape, brush, scissors, and a utility knife.

1. Cut a rectangle.
Install the coverplate where it will go. Cut a rectangular section of matching wallpaper, line it up over the coverplate so the pattern matches, and temporarily tape it to the wall.

2. Mark the corners.
Gently feel the outline of the coverplate under the paper and prick a tiny hole at each corner of the plate, using a straight pin.

3. Trace the outline.
Remove both the paper and the coverplate. Lay the paper face-down on a worktable, and place the coverplate face-up on top. Line up the plate corners with the pin holes and trace the outline on the back side of the paper.

4. Trim the cover.
Cut the paper so there is a ½-inch border around the outline of the coverplate. Trim the corners at 45-degree angles down to the outline.

5. Glue the cover.
Brush vinyl-to-vinyl adhesive primer onto the front of the plate. Allow it to dry, then apply vinyl-to-vinyl adhesive over the primer. Place the plate face-down on the paper and press firmly. Smooth out any bubbles. Line up the corners and fold the edges of the paper around the plate.

6. Secure with tape.
Tape the edges of the paper to the back side of the plate with masking tape. Let the adhesive dry before proceeding further.

7. Cut the opening.
Using a sharp utility knife, carefully cut out the openings in the plate. If the cut paper edges are loose, apply more adhesive under the paper.

8. Fasten the plate.
Punch through the paper with an awl or nail at the locations of the coverplate screw holes. Fasten the plate with the coverplate screws.

HANGING PREPASTED WALLCOVERINGS

Prepasted wallcoverings are the no-fuss, little-muss way to a beautifully papered room. There are some secrets to success, however, including wall preparation, adhesive soaking time, and careful attention to smoothing and trimming.

Soaking time is critical. Be sure to follow the manufacturer's directions to the letter so that the tackiness of the adhesive will be just right.

Occasionally, depending on the porosity of the wall surface, there won't be enough adhesive on the covering to hold it to the wall. If this occurs, mix a small amount of the proper adhesive for the paper (or use premixed adhesive) and apply it to the edges and ends of the strips after the strips have been cut to length and soaked. Or apply the adhesive directly to the wall.

YOU'LL NEED...
TIME: 10 to 15 minutes per strip.
SKILLS: Basic wallpapering skills.
TOOLS: Water trough plus other wallpapering tools listed earlier.

Roll the paper.
Cut the strips to length. Loosely reroll the paper with the pattern side in. This will permit the water to activate the paste.

Soak the paper.
Fill the trough with enough water to cover the roll. Submerge the paper in the water, weighting it with a rod.

Unroll and apply.
After soaking, remove the paper by letting it unroll gradually as you make your way up the ladder. Smooth, roll, and trim the paper.

HANGING VINYL WALLCOVERING

Vinyl wallcovering is heavier than most standard coverings. You can buy it in wide widths, which reduces the number of seams to fit and roll. Also, the material usually is easy to strip from a wall or ceiling surface.

The heavy vinyls have another important advantage. The strips hide defects in a drywall or plaster wall that is in poor condition.

You can use regular wallpaper adhesive to apply lightweight vinyl papers, but special vinyl adhesive is best. Because vinyl won't stick to itself without special adhesive, all seams that are not butted should be double-cut (see page 582).

If you apply untrimmed vinyl with butted seams, be sure the adhesive is soft on both the strips. Lap the seams about 1 inch. Make a freehand cut through both layers of paper, pull loose the selvages, and smooth the seam. If lapping is necessary, be sure to use vinyl-to-vinyl adhesive at the joint. Apply the adhesive just as you would regular wallpaper paste.

1. Apply adhesive.
Cut the first strip several inches longer than the height of the wall. Cut the subsequent strips so they match the pattern (see page 581). Spread the vinyl adhesive that the manufacturer has recommended, using a mohair paint roller. Fold and book the strip as you would a standard covering (see page 580). With pure vinyl wall covering, there is no need to wait for the adhesive to soak in.

Mohair paint roller

YOU'LL NEED...
TIME: 10 to 15 minutes per strip.
SKILLS: Basic wallpapering skills.
TOOLS: Paint roller, utility knife, wood straightedge, seam roller, vinyl wallpaper paste, vinyl-to-vinyl adhesive, razor blade.

2. Smooth the strips.
Apply strips following the instructions on pages 579–586. Smoothing vinyl is more demanding work than smoothing other types of coverings. Use a wood straightedge (shown). Don't use a steel straightedge unless its edges have been rounded.

3. Eliminate any bubbles.
After 20 minutes, hold a bright light against the wall to check for bubbles. Puncture each bubble with a razor, and roll the covering flat using a seam roller or a wood straightedge. If you spot a bubble after the adhesive has dried, use a syringe to squirt adhesive into the space behind the bubble.